D1559424

THE FATHERS
OF THE CHURCH

A NEW TRANSLATION

VOLUME 133

THE FATHERS
OF THE CHURCH

A NEW TRANSLATION

RUFINUS OF AQUILEIA

HISTORY OF THE CHURCH

Translated by

PHILIP R. AMIDON, SJ

Creighton University

THE CATHOLIC UNIVERSITY OF AMERICA PRESS

Washington, D.C.

Copyright © 2016
THE CATHOLIC UNIVERSITY OF AMERICA PRESS
All rights reserved
Printed in the United States of America

The paper used in this publication meets the minimum
requirements of the American National Standards for Information
Science—Permanence of Paper for Printed Library Materials,
ANSI Z39.48 – 1984.
∞

Church History of Rufinus of Aquileia, Books 10 and 11 Translated
with notes by Philip R. Amidon, S.J. (1997) extracts (c.27,000w)
from pp. vii–xii & 3–112
By Permission of Oxford University Press
© 1997 by Philip Amidon

Library of Congress Cataloging-in-Publication Data
Names: Eusebius, of Caesarea, Bishop of Caesarea,
approximately 260–approximately 340, author. | Rufinus,
of Aquileia, 345–410. | Amidon,
Philip R., writer of added commentary, translator.
Title: History of the church / Rufinus of Aquileia ; translated
by Philip R.Amidon, SJ, Creighton University.
Other titles: Ecclesiastical history. English
Description: Washington, D.C. : The Catholic University of
America Press, [2016] | Series: The Fathers of the church,
a new translation ; volume 133 | Translated into English from
Rufinus's Latin translation; originally written in Greek. |
Includes bibliographical references and indexes.
Identifiers: LCCN 2016022644 | ISBN 9780813229027
(cloth : alk. paper)
Subjects: LCSH: Church history—Primitive and early church,
ca. 30–600.
Classification: LCC BR160.E5 E5 2016 | DDC 270.1—dc23
LC record available at https://lccn.loc.gov/2016022644

CONTENTS

ABBREVIATIONS

AAAd	*Antichità altoadriatiche*
ANRW	*Aufstieg und Niedergang der römischen Welt*
Antiq.	Josephus, *Antiquitates Iudaicae*
Athan., *Dokument*	*Athanasius Werke 3.1: Dokumente zur Geschichte des arianischen Streites,* ed. Christoph Brennecke, Uta Heil, et al. Berlin: De Gruyter, 2007
Baldini	A. Baldini, "Problemi della tradizione sulla 'distruzione' del Serapeo di Alessandria," *Rivista storica dell'antichità* 15 (1985): 97–152
Barnes	T. D. Barnes, *Athanasius and Constantius.* Cambridge, MA: Harvard University Press, 1993
Bellum	Josephus, *Bellum Iudaicum*
CAH	*The Cambridge Ancient History,* London: Cambridge University Press, 1970
CCL	Corpus Christianorum, Series Latina
CSEL	Corpus Scriptorum Ecclesiasticorum Latinorum
C.Th.	*Codex Theodosianus*
Cassian, *Coll.*	John Cassian, *Collationes*
DEC	*Decrees of the Ecumenical Councils,* ed. N. P. Tanner. London: Sheed and Ward, 1990
DHGE	*Dictionnaire d'histoire et de géographie ecclésiastiques*
DMP	*De mortibus persecutorum*
Elliott	J. K. Elliott, *The Apocryphal New Testament.* Oxford: Clarendon, 1993

EOMIA	Ecclesiae Occidentalis Monumenta Iuris Antiquissima, ed. C. H. Turner. Oxford: Clarendon, 1899–1939
Epiphanius, *Pan.*	Epiphanius, *Panarion*
Eusebius, *HE*	Eusebius, *Church History*
Eusebius, *Vit. Const.*	Eusebius, *Life of Constantine*
FIRA	*Fontes iuris romani anteiustiniani,* ed. Riccobono, Baviera, et al. Florence: 1940–43
GCS	Die griechischen christlichen Schriftsteller
Hefele-Leclercq	C. J. Hefele and H. Leclercq, *Histoire des conciles d'après les documents originaux.* Paris: Letouzey, 1907–52
HM	*Historia monachorum*
JECS	*Journal of Early Christian Studies*
Jones	A. H. M. Jones, *The Later Roman Empire.* Oxford: Clarendon, 1964
JRS	*Journal of Roman Studies*
JTS	*Journal of Theological Studies*
Kelly, *Popes*	J. N. D. Kelly, *Oxford Dictionary of the Popes.* Oxford: Clarendon, 1986
LXX	Septuagint
Paschoud	François Paschoud, *Zosime. Histoire nouvelle.* Paris: Les Belles Lettres, 1971–89
PG	Patrologia Graeca (Migne)
Philostorgius	Philostorgius, *Church History*
PL	Patrologia Latina (Migne)
PLRE	*Prosopography of the Later Roman Empire,* ed. Jones, Martindale, and Morris. Cambridge: University Press, 1971–92
PW	Pauly-Wissowa, *Realencyclopädie der klassischen Altertumswissenschaft*
RAC	*Reallexikon für Antike und Christentum*
Schürer	Emil Schürer, *The History of the Jewish People in the Age of Jesus Christ,* revised by Geza Vermes, Fergus Millar, and Martin Goodman. Edinburgh, T. & T. Clark, 1973–87

Schwartz	Eduard Schwartz, *Gesammelte Schriften.* Berlin: De Gruyter, 1938–63
Schwartz/Mommsen	Eduard Schwartz and Theodor Mommsen, eds., *Eusebius Werke 2. Die Kirchengeschichte.* Berlin: Akademie Verlag, 1999
SHA	*Scriptores historiae augustae*
Socrates	Socrates, *Church History*
Sozomen	Sozomen, *Church History*
Thelamon, *PC*	Françoise Thelamon, *Païens et chrétiens au IVe siècle.* Paris: Études augustiniennes, 1981
Theodoret, *HE*	Theodoret, *Church History*
TU	Texte und Untersuchungen
ZAC	*Zeitschrift für antikes Christentum*
Zecchini	Giuseppe Zecchini, "Barbari e romani in Rufino di Concordia," *AAAd* 31.2 (1987): 29–60
ZKG	*Zeitschrift für Kirchengeschichte*
ZNW	*Zeitschrift für die neutestamentliche Wissenschaft und die Kunde des Urchristentums*

BIBLIOGRAPHY

General

Ayres, Lewis. *Nicaea and its Legacy: An Approach to Fourth-Century Trinitarian Theology.* Oxford: Clarendon, 2004.

Baldini, Antonio. "Problemi della tradizione sulla 'distruzione' del Serapeo di Alessandria." *Rivista storica dell'antichità* 15 (1985): 97–152.

Bardy, Gustave. *Eusèbe de Césarée. Histoire ecclésiastique.* Paris: Cerf, 1952–60.

Barnes, Michel R., and Daniel H. Williams, eds. *Arianism after Arius.* Edinburgh: T. and T. Clark, 1993.

Barnes, Timothy D. *Athanasius and Constantius.* Cambridge, MA: Harvard University Press, 1993.

Bonneau, Danielle. *La crue du Nil.* Paris: Klincksieck, 1964.

Brennecke, H. C. *Hilarius von Poitiers und die Bischofsopposition gegen Konstantius II.* Berlin: De Gruyter, 1984.

———. *Studien zur Geschichte der Homöer.* Tübingen: Mohr Siebeck, 1988.

Budischovsky, M.-C. "La diffusion des cultes égyptiens d'Aquilée à travers les pays alpins." *AAAd* 9 (1976): 202–27.

———. "Les cultes orientaux à Aquilée et leur diffusion en Instrie et en Vénétie." *AAAd* 12 (1977): 99–123.

Cassola, F. "Aquileia e l'Oriente mediterraneo." *AAAd* 12 (1977): 67–97.

Cavallera, Ferdinand. *Le schisme d'Antioche (IVe –Ve siècle).* Paris: Picard, 1905.

Dattrino, Lorenzo. *Rufino. Storia della chiesa.* Rome: Città Nuova Editrice, 1986.

Dolzani, C. "Presenze di origine egiziana nell'ambiente aquileiese e nell'alto adriatico." *AAAd* 12 (1977): 125–34.

Duval, Yves-Marie. "Sur quelques sources latines de l'*Histoire de l'Église* de Rufin d'Aquilée." *Cassiodorus* 3 (1997): 131–51.

Elze, Martin. *Tatian und seine Theologie.* Göttingen: Vandenhoeck und Ruprecht, 1960.

Gallay, Paul. *La vie de saint Grégoire de Nazianze.* Paris: Vitte, 1943.

Guignard, Christophe. *La lettre de Julius Africanus à Aristide sur la généalogie du Christ. TU* 167. Berlin and Boston: De Gruyter, 2011.

Hammond, C. P. "The Last Ten Years of Rufinus' Life and the Date of His Move South from Aquileia." *JTS* NS 28 (1977): 372–429.

Heil, Gunther. *De vita Gregorii Thaumaturgi,* in *Gregorii Nysseni Sermones.* Pars II. Edited by Friedhelm Mann, 3–57. *Gregorii Nysseni Opera* 10.1. Leiden: Brill, 1990.

Karmann, Thomas R. *Meletius von Antiochien: Studien zur Geschichte des trinitäts-theologischen Streits in den Jahren 360–364 n. Chr. (Regensburger Studien zur Theologie,* 68). Frankfurt am Main: Lang, 2009.

Kelly, J. N. D. *Early Christian Creeds.* London: Longman, 1972.

Kopecek, Thomas A. *A History of Neo-Arianism.* Cambridge, MA: Philadelphia Patristic Foundation, 1979.

Lenski, Noel. *Failure of Empire: Valens and the Roman State in the Fourth Century A.D.* Berkeley: University of California Press, 2002.

Maier, Gerhard. *Die Johannesoffenbarung und die Kirche.* Tübingen: Mohr Siebeck, 1981.

McGiffert, Arthur C. "The Church History of Eusebius." In *The Nicene and Post-Nicene Fathers,* Second Series, 1. Edited by Philip Schaff and Henry Wace, 1–403. Grand Rapids: Eerdmans, 1976.

Millar, Fergus. "Paul of Samosata, Zenobia, and Aurelian: The Church, Local Culture, and Political Allegiance in Third-Century Syria." *JRS* 61 (1971): 1–17.

Morlet, S., and L. Perrone, eds. *Eusèbe de Césarée. Histoire ecclésiastique. Commentaire, Tome I.* Paris: Cerf, 2012.

Murphy, F. X. *Rufinus of Aquileia (345–411): His Life and Works.* Washington, DC: The Catholic University of America Press, 1945.

Parvis, Sara. *Marcellus of Ancyra and the Lost Years of the Arian Controversy, 325–345.* Oxford: Clarendon, 2006.

Paschoud, François. *Zosime. Histoire nouvelle.* Paris: Les Belles Lettres, 1971–89.

Schürer, Emil. *The History of the Jewish People in the Age of Jesus Christ.* Revised by Geza Vermes, Fergus Millar, and Martin Goodman. Edinburgh: T. & T. Clark, 1973–87.

Schwartz, Eduard. *Gesammelte Schriften.* Berlin: De Gruyter, 1938–63.

Schwartz, Eduard, and Theodor Mommsen, eds. *Eusebius Werke 2. Die Kirchengeschichte.* Berlin: Akademie Verlag, 1999.

Simonetti, Manlio. *La crisi ariana nel IV secolo. Studia Ephemeridis "Augustinianum"* 11. Rome: Institutum Patristicum "Augustinianum," 1975.

———. *Rufino di Concordia. Storia della chiesa. Corpus Scriptorum Ecclesiae Aquileiensis* V/2. Rome: Città Nuova Editrice, 2000.

Spoerl, Kelley M. "The Schism at Antioch since Cavallera." In *Arianism after Arius.* Edited by M. R. Barnes and D. H. Williams, 101–26. Edinburgh: T. and T. Clark, 1993.

Tabbernee, William. *Fake Prophecy and Polluted Sacraments: Ecclesiastical and Imperial Reactions to Montanism.* Leiden: Brill, 2007.

Thelamon, Françoise. *Païens et chrétiens au IVe siècle.* Paris: Études augustiniennes, 1981.

———. "Rufin historien de son temps." *AAAd* 31.1 (1987): 41–59.

———. "'Apôtres et prophètes de notre temps.'" *AAAd* 39 (1992): 171–98.

Williams, Rowan. *Arius: Heresy and Tradition.* Second Edition. London: SCM, 2001.

Zecchini, Giuseppe. "Barbari e romani in Rufino di Concordia," *AAAd* 31.2 (1987): 29–60.

Works on Rufinus's Translations

Bammel, Caroline H. "Rufinus' Translation of Origen's Commentary on Romans and the Pelagian Controversy." *AAAd* 39 (1992): 131–49.

Brooks, E. C. "The Translation Techniques of Rufinus of Aquileia (343–411)." *Studia Patristica* 17 (1982): 357–64.

Chin, Catherine M. "Rufinus of Aquileia and Alexandrian Afterlives: Translation as Origenism." *JECS* 18 (2010): 617–47.

Christensen, Torben. *Rufinus of Aquileia and the Historia Ecclesiastica, Lib. VIII–IX, of Eusebius.* Copenhagen: The Royal Danish Academy of Sciences and Letters, 1989.

Crouzel, Henri. "Rufino traduttore del 'Peri Archon' di Origene." *AAAd* 31.1 (1987): 29–39.

Humphries, Mark. "Rufinus's Eusebius: Translation, Continuation, and Edition in the Latin *Ecclesiastical History*." *JECS* 16 (2008): 143–64.

Marti, H. "Rufinus' Translation of St. Basil's Sermon on Fasting." *Studia Patristica* 16.2 (1985): 418–22.

Moreschini, Claudio. "Rufino traduttore di Gregorio Nazianzeno." *AAAd* 31 (1987): 227–85.

Oulton, J. E. L. "Rufinus's Translation of the Church History of Eusebius." *JTS* 30 (1929): 150–74.

Pace, Nicola. *Ricerche sulla traduzione di Rufino del "De principiis" di Origene.* Florence: La Nuova Italia, 1990.

Silvas, Anna M. *The Asketikon of St Basil the Great,* 102–29. Oxford: Clarendon, 2005.

Simonetti, Manlio. "L'attività letteraria di Rufino negli anni della controversia origeniana." *AAAd* 39 (1992): 89–107.

Wagner, M. M. *Rufinus the Translator.* Washington, DC: The Catholic University of America Press, 1945.

Winkelmann, Friedhelm. "Einige Bemerkungen zu den Aussagen des Rufinus von Aquileia und des Hieronymus über ihre Übersetzungstheorie und -methode." In *Kyriakon. Festschrift Johannes Quasten.* Edited by P. Granfield and J. Jungmann, 532–47. Münster: Aschendorff, 1970.

INTRODUCTION

INTRODUCTION

I. Life and Works of Rufinus

What is known of the life of Tyrannius (or Turranius) Rufinus is well set out in F. X. Murphy's authoritative biography.[1] He was born around 345 in Iulia Concordia (west of Aquileia). His parents were noble and wealthy, to judge from his education, which he completed in Rome. While a student there he became fast friends with Jerome.

Athanasius had popularized monasticism in the West during his long exile there, a year of which was spent in Aquileia around the time of Rufinus's birth. By 370 there was an ascetic community in Aquileia that Rufinus joined upon his return from Rome. He was baptized in 369 or 370. His enthusiasm for the monastic life inspired him, as it did other Western Christians, to visit its birthplace, and he made his way to Egypt at the end of 372 or early in 373.

It was about the same time, in November of 372, that Antonia Melania, a widow of the highest nobility who had likewise taken up the ascetic life, sailed from Rome to the East. She arrived in Alexandria about the same time as Rufinus (although there is no reason to suppose they traveled together), just in time to witness the outbreak of the "Arian" persecution that followed Athanasius's death (in May of 373). She decided to follow a group of exiles from the persecution to Diocaesarea in Palestine, from where she went on to Jerusalem in 375.

1. *Rufinus of Aquileia (345–411): His Life and Works* (Washington, DC: The Catholic University of America Press, 1945). See also C. P. Hammond's indispensable article, "The Last Ten Years of Rufinus' Life and the Date of His Move South from Aquileia," *JTS*, NS 28 (1977): 372–429, and G. Fedalto, "Rufino di Concordia. Elementi di una biografia," *AAAd* 39 (1992): 19–44.

Rufinus meanwhile stayed in Egypt to continue his studies for six years under Didymus the Blind and others; it was Didymus who introduced him to Origen's works. He spent 378(?) visiting the other homeland of monasticism, in Palestine and Syria, and then returned to Alexandria for a final two years of study with Didymus.

Melania meanwhile had founded a monastery in Jerusalem where Rufinus joined her perhaps in 380. It was a double monastery, for women and men, the first such Latin foundation in the Holy Land, and it included a guest house for pilgrims. Rufinus, in his part of the monastery, directed the copying of books (including the Latin classics, for which there would have been some demand in the new Latin colonies of the Near East). He must have been ordained presbyter about this time.

Jerome arrived in 385 to tour the Near East, and in 386 his friend Paula began work on a double monastery in Bethlehem after the example of Melania and Rufinus. His relationship with Rufinus, however, cooled for a number of reasons,[2] until it was finally disrupted by the outbreak of the Origenist controversy. Both of them had admired Origen greatly, but Epiphanius of Salamis's attempt (in 393) to get John of Jerusalem to condemn Origen as the forerunner of Arius drew different responses from them. Rufinus followed John in refusing to do so, while Jerome agreed to the condemnation. The two of them, together with their monks, were divided over the issue, which dragged on for years. Jerome and Rufinus were finally reconciled in 397, the year Rufinus returned to Italy, taking his books with him.

He found, when he arrived in Rome, that rumor of the Origenist quarrel had far outrun him. It was not long before he was asked to translate Pamphilus's *Vindication of Origen.* To it he added his own *The Falsification of Origen's Works,* in which he asserted that the heterodox views found in Origen's books were the falsifications and interpolations of his enemies.

He spent the fall of 397 and spring of 398 at the monastery of Pinetum, near Terracina, where he translated Basil's *Rules*

---

2. See J. N. D. Kelly, *Jerome* (New York: Harper and Row, 1975), 196.

for Abbot Ursacius. It was also in 398 that at the instance of the noble scholar Macarius he undertook his fateful translation of Origen's *First Principles*. In his preface he repeated his view that the text had been corrupted by Origen's enemies, and he explained that he had therefore altered or replaced statements of doubtful orthodoxy with other, sounder ones taken from Origen's other works. He also said that in doing so he was simply following Jerome's lead, both in translating Origen into Latin and in suppressing suspect passages in him (he did not mention him by name but alluded to him so clearly that the reference was unmistakable). Word of his project got around Rome, and the anti-Origenist party denounced him and complained to Jerome.

His translation of the letter to St. James the Apostle attributed to Clement of Rome may perhaps be dated to around this time, but by the second half of 398 Rufinus had had enough of the Origenist controversy; he left Rome for the more peaceful atmosphere of Aquileia after writing Jerome an apparently amicable letter explaining his move. Jerome, meanwhile, stung by his friend's public reminder of his own earlier infatuation with Origen, made a literal translation of the *First Principles* and sent it to Rome, together with an angry open letter to his friends there in which he practically accused Rufinus's translation of fostering heresy. He also wrote a private letter to Rufinus explaining the apologetic purpose of the open letter; he evidently hoped to avoid a public break. But Jerome's friends in Rome withheld the letter from Rufinus and drummed up a campaign against him throughout Italy.

Once settled in Aquileia, Rufinus continued producing translations: of Basil's homilies and Gregory's discourses, the *Sentences of Sextus,* Adamantius's *De recta in Deum fide,* the *Commentary on the Apostles' Creed,* and Origen on Joshua, Judges, and Psalms 36–38.

Pope Siricius died in November of 399 and was succeeded by Anastasius, who proved more sympathetic to Rufinus's anti-Origenist foes. Theophilus of Alexandria now took the field against Origen, presiding over a council that condemned him in 400. The emperor confirmed its sentence and proscribed Origen's works; Theophilus communicated this in a letter to

Anastasius. The pope in turn confirmed the council's sentence and communicated his decision to Simplician of Milan, inviting him and his colleagues in northern Italy to add their own confirmation. But Simplician died that year, so Anastasius wrote to his successor Venerius repeating his invitation. Rufinus, by now feeling himself under increasing pressure, composed his *Apology to Anastasius.* Anastasius made no direct answer, but to John of Jerusalem, who had expressed concern about his old friend, he replied condemning Origen but adding that he wished to know nothing about Rufinus, neither where he was nor what he was about.

Rufinus, worried and resentful at having received no reply to his letter to Jerome (as he thought), replied to Jerome's criticisms in 401 with his *Apology against Jerome.* In it he defended himself against the imputation of heresy and furnished massive evidence of Jerome's own earlier devotion not only to Origen's exegesis but to his speculative theology as well. It was the final break; Jerome replied the same year with his ferocious *Apology against Rufinus,* and although the latter, after one final private letter, discontinued the public argument thereafter, Jerome pursued him with vitriolic pen even beyond the grave, much to Augustine's dismay.

It was in November of this year that Alaric and his Goths marched into Italy and in 402 laid siege to Milan. With his city under threat, Chromatius of Aquileia asked Rufinus to translate Eusebius of Caesarea's *Church History,* the reading of which he thought might divert his people's attention from their danger. Eusebius's work had, since its publication in 325, acquired an extensive and well-deserved reputation for its learned and edifying survey of Christian history from its beginning to the end of the pagan persecutions. Rufinus agreed to Chromatius's request and in 402 or 403 published a free translation of the original, together with his own continuation of it to carry it forward to the year 395 (the date of Theodosius's death).

By then the Gothic threat had receded, and Rufinus may well have left Aquileia for Rome at this time; he was almost certainly there by the middle of 406 and probably earlier. The atmosphere there had become more congenial to him since the

return of his powerful patroness Melania in 400, the succession
of Innocent I in 402 following the death of Anastasius, and the
new antipathy many people felt for the anti-Origenist party due
to the exile of John Chrysostom, the most celebrated victim of
Theophilus's campaign against the Origenist monks. It cannot
be proved beyond all objection that he left Aquileia before 407,
but the circumstantial evidence is strong.[3] The years 403–406,
at any rate, saw him back at work on translations of Origen: his
commentaries on Genesis, Exodus, and Leviticus, and the Letter to the Romans. He also translated the *History of the Monks
in Egypt,* perhaps as a contribution to the campaign in favor
of John Chrysostom, and the pseudo-Clementine *Recognitions.*
Pelagius, also in Rome at this time, was put into fateful contact
with Origen through his translations. He laid Origen/Rufinus
under heavy tribute in forming his own doctrine on free will
and grace, being influenced in particular by the Commentary
on Romans.

The Elder Melania left Italy to return to the Holy Land in
406 or early 407. Rufinus also thought of returning there, but
for some reason he put it off, and in 408 he was forced to join
the great caravan of his fellow Romans fleeing to Sicily before a
new invasion of Goths. There, from across the strait, he watched
Rhegium go up in flames under Alaric's assault, and there he
died in 410 or 411, still at work translating (Origen on Song of
Songs, 1 Samuel, Numbers, and perhaps Deuteronomy).[4]

II. The *History of the Church*

Modifications to the Original

The preface with which Rufinus introduces his work shows
that he did intend to give his readers and listeners the history
of Eusebius, in however modified a fashion.[5] Those acquainted

3. See Hammond (note 1 above).

4. Not all of Rufinus's works are noted here, and the dates of composition
of many of them must remain conjectural. For a complete list, see Hammond,
428–29.

5. For Rufinus's intention to fashion one integrated history in his trans-

with the original will recognize in his translation much that is familiar: the view of the Christian faith as a phenomenon reaching back to the beginning of the human race, the rhythm of persecution and respite that characterizes the history of the church, the power of God manifest in the vulnerability of the faithful, and the continuity of faith and order guaranteed by apostolic succession and illustrated by the innovative method of the citation of sources.[6]

They will also recognize the firm editorial hand that Rufinus applies to the original, adding to it, deleting from it, and sometimes rewriting it. He aims for a narrative that will be more coherent to his readers and listeners, and display more clearly the unity of the church in faith and order, than would be true (he evidently thinks) of one that cleaved more closely to the text of the original. Some of his alterations are simply matters of style. Rufinus excises repetitions, rearranges passages for a smoother flow of narrative, and simplifies tortuous constructions.

Other alterations are more substantial. Rufinus occasionally adds material or corrects Eusebius on factual matters of greater or less importance. Of greater moment, however, are those which flow from his different notion of the way in which historiography may or may not assist the Christian faithful. Eusebius tells of a church united in doctrine and practice throughout its generations in the variety of its circumstances. Rufinus tries to accentuate the unity by muffling any hint of alteration in faith and order throughout the Christian centuries among those in communion with reputable bishops. For him the one faith of Christianity is that declared by the Council of Nicaea of 325, whose creed and canons are the final documents he cites in

---

lation and continuation of Eusebius, see the indispensable study by Mark Humphries, "Rufinus's Eusebius: Translation, Continuation, and Edition in the Latin *Ecclesiastical History*," *JECS* 16 (2008): 143–64. On Rufinus's theology of translation, see Catherine M. Chin, "Rufinus of Aquileia and Alexandrian Afterlives: Translation as Origenism," *JECS* 18 (2010): 617–47.

6. Arnaldo Momigliano, *The Classical Foundations of Modern Historiography* (Berkeley: University of California Press, 1990), 138–42, has noted how the church historians' citation of sources, unprecedented in ancient historiography, serves their central purpose of displaying the essential unity of the Christian people, its particular identity, and its variety and diversity.

his history. Their crowning place at the beginning of his continuation suggests their sufficiency as the constitution of the church. All passages of even the mildest subordinationist flavor in the original version of Eusebius's history are overwritten with a broad pro-Nicene nib. He "updates" the canon of scripture to conform to the usage of his own time.[7] And reputable bishops simply do not change their minds about points of doctrine; Dionysius of Alexandria's comment in the original about his doctrinal concessions during his discussions with sectarians (7.24.6–8) is censored by Rufinus.

Bishops, it has often been noted, are important in Eusebius's history, but he allows even those of repute to fall out on occasion. Rufinus does not. He damps the note of conflict between Cyprian and Stephen of Rome over rebaptism (7.2–3; 7.5.3). In the original of 7.32.8–12, two illustrious future bishops of Laodicea, Anatolius and Eusebius, find themselves in opposite camps during a siege of Alexandria; Rufinus won't have this, and simply eliminates Eusebius from the story when he "translates" it. In his continuation in 10.2, the emperor opens the Council of Nicaea by solemnly burning to ashes the complaints against each other that the bishops have submitted to him, and in 10.18 the confessor bishops abandon the council that had met to try Athanasius.

Bishops he does not consider praiseworthy are treated otherwise. Irenaeus's stance against Victor of Rome suffices to tarnish the latter's reputation for Rufinus, who actually sharpens the tone of criticism of him by the bishops of Gaul (5.24.10–11). And sectarian or heretical bishops he treats as severely as does Eusebius, as we see with Paul of Samosata.

If in Rufinus the doctrine of the church is portrayed as unaltered, so are its practices. In 1.11.5 he rewrites the citation from Josephus about the meaning of the baptism administered by John the Baptist in order to make it resemble the Christian rite. In 2.17.9 he rewrites the citation from Philo in order (one may suppose) to project back into the author's time the description of the monastic houses of his own.

7. Cf. J. E. L. Oulton, "Rufinus's Translation of the Church History of Eusebius," *JTS* 29 (1930): 153–58.

The relation of Christianity to the Roman empire also becomes, in Rufinus's translation, that of his own time: it is, as the Theodosian legislation declared it, the official religion of the state. The empire, which, Eusebius says, was in its beginnings at the time when the Word became flesh, becomes in Rufinus a state whose growth was brought about by that very Word (1.2.23). He excises Melito of Sardis's reference to other religions besides Christianity that have prayed for the emperors and been protected by them (4.26.7–8). And Constantine under his pen becomes the ruler who orders all Roman subjects to worship the Christian God (9.9.12).

Many of Rufinus's alterations to Eusebius, then, spring from his desire to reduce the variety in doctrine and practice in Christianity; church unity for him seems to require uniformity in usage. Catherine Chin has noticed how Rufinus intended to contribute to the development of a library of Latin Christian literature;[8] we may hazard the guess that he thought the readers of church history in his part of the world would be better reassured of the authenticity of their faith by his simplified portrait of its history than by the more complex original in Eusebius.

There are two other tendencies in Rufinus that may perhaps be attributed to the same motive. Part of Eusebius's account of Christian identity is formulated in contradistinction to that of the Jews, whose calamities Eusebius portrays as divine punishment for their hostility to Christ and his disciples. The theme becomes more pronounced in Rufinus. Where Josephus (quoted accurately by Eusebius) speaks of the whole Jewish people perishing through the madness of the insurgents in Jerusalem, Rufinus adds "deservedly" (3.6.16; see also 3.1.1). He also sanctions with a divine decree the imperial law excluding the Jews from Jerusalem (4.6.3). He increases their punishment: the Roman commander who in the original is ordered to clear the Jews from Mesopotamia is in Rufinus told to annihilate them (4.2.5). When in Eusebius they are besieged, in Rufinus they are destroyed (4.5.2). One gets the disquieting impression that

---

8. Chin (see note 5 above), 618.

for Rufinus the identity of the church is bound up with the disappearance of the Jewish people.

The other tendency is his evident desire to clarify the restricted authority of women to receive and communicate the Christian faith. In 4.23.13 the suitable intellectual nourishment offered to Chrysophora by Dionysius of Corinth becomes in Rufinus the nourishment "suited to her gender and capacity." In 5.1.41–42 he will not allow the martyr Blandina to put on Christ or represent him to others, and suppresses the references thereto in the original. And in 10.11 he repeatedly restricts the authority of the captive woman, whose miraculous powers initiate the conversion of Georgia, to expound Christian doctrine and practice. The holiness and courage of women, however, especially in enduring martyrdom, remains undimmed in Rufinus's text; he does not stint his translation of their heroic fidelity in suffering. And the title he gives the empress Helena in 10.8 of "servant of the servants of Christ" suggests high sanctity. It may be, then, that his determination to portray a church unaltered in time is again showing itself.

Three of the longer insertions in fact that Rufinus makes into Eusebius follow the latter's inclination to celebrate holy persons. He expands the notice about the martyrs in 8.9.7–8. He takes pains to claim for orthodoxy the "Arian" hero Lucian of Antioch by having him defend the faith in edifying terms in 9.6.3. He validates the sentence of the council that condemned Paul of Samosata by recounting the miracles of one of its leading members, Gregory Thaumaturgus (following 7.28.2).[9]

Rufinus's great addition to Eusebius is of course his continuation in the last two books, which carry the story forward from 325 to 395, the year of the death of Theodosius I. He intended them to form one history with the books of Eusebius that go before. The last two books have sometimes been published in translation separately in modern times, under titles that give the impression that they are an independent work,[10] a proce-

9. The material he substitutes about Constantine for the original in 9.9 is, by contrast, part of his re-presentation of the emperor in view of a smoother transition into the opening pages of his continuation.

10. Cf. Lorenzo Dattrino, *Rufino. Storia della chiesa* (Rome: Città Nuova

dure that may perhaps be justified in that it makes more readily available some useful and influential material. But it keeps one from glimpsing the intention, the extent, and the potential influence of his achievement.

His continuation in the last two books is clearly marked by the pattern of Eusebius's original. It begins, as does Eusebius, with episcopal succession. Both then proceed to an exposition of the Christian faith, Rufinus by quoting the Creed of Nicaea. This is followed in both by a demonstration of how Christianity has existed outside the Roman empire, Eusebius by showing how it existed in ages and realms beyond it, back to the beginning of the human race (1.4), and Rufinus by telling of its appearance in Georgia and Ethiopia. And both conclude with the overthrow of pagan political power within the empire.

Sources for the Continuation

Eusebius, with his innovative citation of sources and his reference to his own *Chronicle,* lets us know a great deal about the derivation of his material. Rufinus does not do the same for his own continuation. He occasionally mentions living witnesses he consulted (for example, in 10.10, 10.11, and 10.37), but the only documents he cites explicitly are those of the Council of Nicaea (10.6). He himself says in his preface to the work as a whole that he relied "on what has come down to us from those before us, and ... on what we remembered," and in the preface to the continuation, "[the material that] we either found in the writings of those before us or we remembered." Scholars in the last century, however, noted the existence of Greek texts paralleling much of Rufinus's continuation in Gelasius of Cyzicus's *Syntagma* (fifth century) and in the *Chronicle* of George the Monk (ninth century), and began a long and continuing debate about their relationship to Rufinus: were they translations from his Latin, or were they, conversely, survivors of a

Editrice, 1986); Philip R. Amidon, *The Church History of Rufinus of Aquileia* (New York: Oxford University Press, 1997); Manlio Simonetti, *Tyrannii Rufini. Scripta Varia. Storia della chiesa,* in Corpus Scriptorum Ecclesiae Aquileiensis V/2 (Rome: Città Nuova Editrice, 2000).

long-vanished continuation of Eusebius's history by Gelasius of Caesarea, which Rufinus had translated without attribution? The debate, which has almost cleanly divided German- and French-language scholarship, has been conducted passionately at times, since it seems to involve the question of Rufinus's honor as well as of his method. Following its tortuous course (during which the "Gelasian" history lost a good deal of the ground first claimed for it) can prove tedious, but those who wish may find its initial stages reviewed in my earlier translation of Rufinus of 1997.[11]

The debate entered a new stage more recently with two contributions: that of Y.-M. Duval,[12] which sets out the Latin sources, especially Jerome's *Chronicle*, from which Rufinus drew directly, and that of Peter van Nuffelen,[13] which reviews the ancient references to the historian known as "Gelasius of Caesarea" and relocates his work to a time between 439 and 475. The debate is not yet over for all that; it has not yet included the evidence of Philostorgius, whose history, completed between 425 and 433, shows signs both of its author's intention to combat the kind of pro-Nicene historiography represented by Rufinus, and of his ignorance of Latin. Whichever history he was attacking was available to him in Greek before he started writing his own.

Rufinus's translations have always provoked controversy, his *Church History* no less so than the others. One may well come away from his *Church History* with mixed feelings. His remarkable ability as both translator and censor has resulted in a work that betrays almost no evidence (apart from his brief remark in the closing paragraph of the preface) of the considerable alterations he introduced into the original. The alterations evidently proceeded from his conviction that the unity of the Christian people could not be displayed to the faithful of his own time and place without subduing the rich variety of the circumstanc-

11. Pp. xiii–xvi; see Amidon reference in note 10 above.
12. "Sur quelques sources latines de l'*Histoire de l'Église* de Rufin d'Aquilée," *Cassiodorus* 3 (1997): 131–51.
13. "Gélase de Césarée, un compilateur du cinquième siècle," *Byzantinische Zeitschrift* 95 (2002): 621–39.

es in which the history of the church unfolded in the Eusebian narrative. Doctrines and practices remain unaltered from the outset, quarrels among reputable church leaders vanish, the Jews are eliminated, and the authority of women is checked. He might have argued that he was true to Eusebius's announced intention in 1.1.5 to compose something of benefit to others. His preface suggests that he intended to offer his readers the nourishment suited to their needs. Whether or not his sometimes disquieting alterations to Eusebius's recipe produced the desired fare may remain in dispute.

However Rufinus's methods of translation and composition are assessed, the importance of his history is vast. It was an instant and lasting success; Augustine is only one of the Western Christians who relied on it for a portrayal of the first centuries of Christian history when the dwindling knowledge of Greek in their part of the church made Eusebius's original inaccessible. It was only in the sixteenth century that new Latin and German translations of that history appeared. In the meantime, the Rufinian history became so closely identified with the original that even its continuation was sometimes ascribed to Eusebius too. It was, in the West, the one available history of the early church, offering to Latin historiography its critically important innovation in the citation of sources.

Notes on the Translation

Rufinus regularly translates ἱερεύς as *sacerdos* and ἀρχιερεύς as *pontifex;* I have rendered them "priest" and "high priest" respectively. Πρεσβύτερος he transliterates as *presbyter;* I have retained the transliteration (reserving "elder" for the translation of *senior*). Readers should be aware, though, that bishops (*episkopoi/ episcopi*) were very often called "priests" ("priesthood" in this history usually means "episcopate" when the Christian church is referred to). But bishops (*episkopoi*) could also be called *presbyteroi;* Eusebius himself uses *episkopos* and *presbyteros* of the same man in 3.23.7–8, and Rufinus follows suit. The entry under πρεσβύτερος in Lampe's *Patristic Greek Lexicon* reveals the breadth of usage the word had in the Greek-speaking church (where it was sometimes used simply in the original sense of "elder," whether a member of the clergy or not). The context will usually show what is meant when it is used of the Christian clergy (as for instance in 7.30.2).

I have used the equals sign (=) as a shorthand way of matching passages in Rufinus with those in the original that they supposedly translate. The sign is not meant to suggest that there is a close or accurate rendition in each case.

References to Psalms employ the Septuagint numbering.

This is the first English translation of Rufinus's history as a whole. I have revised my earlier translation of the continuation,[14] correcting what seemed advisable and updating the notes. It is impossible to acknowledge all those on whose scholarship it depends, but particular mention must be made of Theodor Mommsen's critical edition of the text translated,[15] of Arthur C. McGiffert's translation of Eusebius's *Church History*,[16] unequaled for its style, accuracy, and indispensable notes, and, for Rufinus's continuation, of Françoise Thelamon's equally indispensable study.[17]

14. See note 10 above.

15. *Eusebius Werke* II/1–3: *Die Kirchengeschichte,* ed. Eduard Schwartz and Theodor Mommsen (Berlin: Akademie Verlag, 1999).

16. In The Nicene and Post-Nicene Fathers, II/1 (Grand Rapids: Eerdmans, 1976).

17. *Païens et chrétiens au IVe siècle* (Paris: Études augustiniennes, 1981).

HISTORY OF THE CHURCH

PREFACE OF RUFINUS

Translating the *Church History* of Eusebius[1]

T IS THE BUSINESS of skillful physicians, they say, to provide some sort of medicine or potion when they see that cities or regions are threatened by epidemics, so that people may be protected by it from the death that threatens them. This is the sort of medical art which you have practiced, my reverend father Chromatius,[2] at this time when the Goths have burst through the barriers into Italy with Alaric at their head, and a lethal plague is spreading far and wide, to the ruin of fields, herds, and men: you have sought some remedy to protect from cruel death the people God has entrusted to you, a remedy by which ailing spirits may be diverted from the thought of impending evil and give their attention to something better. Thus you have charged me to translate into Latin the church history which that most learned man Eusebius of Caesarea composed in Greek, that the attention of those who hear it may be occupied and they may for a while come to forget present evils while their interest is directed to the affairs of the past.

1. Despite the short prologue before his Book 10, reminding the readers that what follows is his own continuation of Eusebius's history, the title given here, *Church History*, may lull the unwary into ascribing to Eusebius himself the contents of Books 10 and 11 as well. Thus Gregory of Tours in *Hist. Franc.* 9.15 will credit Eusebius with the story of Arius's death in 10.14. (The subtitle on this page, "Translating the *Church History* of Eusebius," has been added by the translator and the editor of this volume.)

2. Bishop of Aquileia ca. 388–407 and Rufinus's patron. The usefulness of history as a diversion from present evils was commonplace: cf. Polybius, 1.1.2, and Livy, *Praef.* 5. The scripture reference below is to Mt 14.15–21; Mk 6.35–44; Lk 9.12–17; Jn 6.5–14.

At first I wanted to beg off the work as being unequal to it and as having lost fluency in Latin after so many years, but then it occurred to me that what you had ordered me to do was not unrelated to apostolic tradition. On the occasion when the crowds of those listening to him were hungry in the desert, the Lord said to the apostles, "You give them something to eat." Philip, one of the apostles, realizing that the signs of divine power are clearer when they are accomplished by those who are least, did not bring out the loaves stored in the apostles' bag; he said rather that there was a small boy there who had five loaves and two fish, adding apologetically in this regard, "But what are these among so many?" so that the divine power might be even more evident where the resources were hopelessly slim. Now I know that you stand in this very tradition, and it occurred to me that you might have followed Philip's example, when you saw that the crowds needed to be fed, and chosen a small boy who would not only produce the five loaves doubled, as he had received them, but would also, in fulfillment of the gospel mystery, add the two little fish caught by his own effort. I have therefore proceeded to carry out your order as well as I could, certain that our shortcomings would be excused on account of the authority of the one who issued it.

Now it should be noted that since the tenth book of this work in Greek has very little history in it, all the rest of it being taken up with bishops' panegyrics which add nothing to our knowledge of the facts, we have omitted what seemed superfluous and joined what history there was in it to the ninth book, which we have made the conclusion of Eusebius's account. The tenth and eleventh books we composed based partly on what has come down from those before us, and partly on what we remembered, adding them like two little fish to the aforesaid loaves. If you approve and bless them, I am certain that they will satisfy the crowds. Now the entire work treats the affairs of the church from the Savior's Ascension and after, while the two short books go from the time of Constantine after the persecution to the death of the emperor Theodosius.

BOOK ONE

1. That he is himself[1] God and Lord and creator of everything and administrator of all things, according to what is written in the law and the prophets

2. On the time of Christ's birth according to the flesh

3. On Judas the Galilean and Theudas

4. On Herod, that he came to the kingship from foreign stock

5. That in Herod's time the succession of kings was interrupted, according to Daniel's prophecy

6. On the difference between the genealogies composed by Matthew and Luke, and what Africanus says about them

7. On the slaughter of the infants in Bethlehem, and the presence of the Magi

8. On the torments that Herod himself underwent, who ordered the infants to be killed

9. On the cruelty of Herod, which he practiced at the time of his death

10. On the reign of Archelaus after Herod

11. That the Acts produced by the Jews are false is proved by a comparison of the times, even from Josephus's testimony

12. That there were four high priests from the high priest Annas to Caiaphas, and they held the high priesthood each for one year during the years when Christ finished his preaching

13. Josephus's testimony about John the Baptist, and that he declares him to have been a just man, and that it was the Jews who ended up paying the penalty for his murder

14. Josephus's testimony about Christ

15. Narrative about King Abgar

---

1. A reference to "the Savior" in the last sentence of the preface.

21

16. The letter of Abgar to the Lord, and of the Lord to him, and the material which was translated from Syriac as a result

1.1.1. What I propose to describe are the successions of the holy apostles, and the times which have passed from that of our Savior to our own; what was done during them which affected the situation of the church; who the men of distinction were who governed the churches in the most renowned locations, or who during each of these times imparted the word of God admirably by what they wrote or taught; who it was also that, in proposing new doctrines against religion and falling into the depths of error by their love of controversy, acknowledged that they were authors and teachers of false knowledge: how many they were and when, 2. these folk who like fell wolves maimed Christ's flock far and wide; those evils which ravaged the Jewish people in recompense for the plots they hatched against the Savior; in which ways, how often, and in which times the doctrine of Christ and the divine word was attacked by the gentiles; how many there were who fought for the truth of God's word, during these storms, even to the suffering of tortures and shedding of blood; the martyrdoms undergone in our own times, and the singular and most merciful relief accorded by our Lord and Savior during them to each person in turn. This being my aim, I can only take as my starting point the actual presence of our Lord and Savior Jesus Christ in his body.

3. I beg for mercy, however, aware as I am that what we are attempting in this work is beyond our abilities, that we may fully and faithfully relate the deeds that were done and dare to be the first to set out upon the rough path of this journey, one taken by almost no one of us. And although I am sure that God will be our guide and that we will have the support of our Lord and Savior, we can nonetheless see no footprints of people who went before and upon whom we could rely, apart from occasional notices and documents which have reached us from various people concerning the historical events of the period of each. They serve as torches[2] kindled from afar for us who find

---

2. Polybius, 10.43–47, describes the method of torch signals for sending messages in code.

ourselves in darkness, as it were, and we are counseled by their voices, as though from a lofty look-out post, whither we should bend our steps and direct the way of our discourse, that it may be free of error.

4. We have tried, therefore, to select from what they have said in various places whatever we thought suitable to the work in hand, plucking the flowers of the learned from the fields of thought, as it were, and binding them into the bouquet of historical narrative. In this I considered that it would be a highly welcome thing to gather together and arrange in due order the successions of at least the most prominent of our Savior's apostles, even if not of all of them, which have been handed on to whichever churches are more distinguished.

5. The task I have taken on seems all the more necessary as I find that, as I said above, no writer, of those belonging to the church at least, has given attention to this topic. In doing this I also hope that this labor of ours proves of great benefit to the scholarly in its presentation of history. 6. Although I already touched on many of these same matters briefly and summarily in the annals, in that book, that is, the book that we wrote with an account of the years,[3] in the present book we have tried to tell more fully of the several events.

7. My account will therefore begin, as we promised, with Christ the Lord himself. 8. Now since we aim to write the history of the Christians, it seems to follow that we should first explain a bit further how this race of people began, or what meaning the name itself has after which this nation or people is called.[4] [1.2.1]. Since, then, the manner of Christ's being is

---

3. Eusebius refers to his *Chronici canones*, which survives in revised form in an Armenian translation and (in part) in Jerome's *Chronicon*. Cf. Osvalda Andrei, "*Canons chronologiques* et *Histoire ecclésiastique*," in *Eusèbe de Césarée. Histoire ecclésiastique*, Commentaire I, ed. S. Morlet and L. Perrone (Paris: Cerf, 2012), 33–82.

4. Eusebius in 1.2–4 explains the antiquity of the Christian name and people through its origin in Christ, the originator, with the Father, of all creation. On the literary character of this section, see Sebastien Morlet, "L'introduction de *l'Histoire ecclésiastique* d'Eusèbe de Césarée (I, 2–4): Étude génétique, littéraire et rhétorique," *Revue des études augustiniennes et patristiques* 52/1 (2006): 57–95.

twofold, the divine nature together with the human one being fully present in him,[5] let us consider the divine substance in him as the head, and the human one, which he assumed for our salvation, the feet; only thus will our tale take its course more perfectly if it begins with the head, with, that is, an account of his divinity; by this means both the antiquity and the nobility of the Christians, that people whose name is thought to be so novel, may be shown.

2. No words will be equal to expounding and disclosing Christ's origin and the actual nature of his substance, if in fact the divine utterance declares of him, "Who will tell of his generation?" And elsewhere as well we find the following heavenly words used of him: "For no one knows the Son except the Father, and no one knows the Father except the Son."[6] Only the Father who begot him is said to know the Son, therefore. And it cannot be doubted that the one who has reserved the knowledge of the Son to the Father alone has excluded others from a conceptual scrutiny.[7]

3. In these books, therefore, which are believed to have been composed by the divine Spirit, he is proclaimed always to have been the eternal light even before the beginning of the world, and is also said to have subsisted as the substantial wisdom and living Word in the beginning in the Father's presence, and as God the Word.[8] Who then could encompass in speech him who is described as having been always, before all visible and invisible creation,[9] and as having been already in the beginning, born from the Father himself, and as having existed with the Father eternally? Who will put into words him who is lord and leader of all of the heavenly, immortal, and divine powers,

5. *Christus duplici ex modo constat et divina in eo pariter atque humana natura plenitudinem tenet* = Διττοῦ δὲ ὄντος τοῦ κατ' αὐτὸν τρόπου. For meaning of equals sign, see p. 15 above.

6. Is 53.8; Mt 11.27; Lk 10.22. Rufinus departs from Eusebius often in 1.2.2–16 in additions and subtractions.

7. *et sine dubio exclusit ceteros a discutienda notitia, qui ad unum solum patrem filii scientiam revocavit:* Rufinus adds. *Discutere* is here equivalent to ἐρευνᾶν. Athanasius warns against this kind of investigation of the Son's relationship to the Father: ἐρευνῶν τὰ ἀνερεύνητα (*Ep. ad Serapionem* 3.4.3).

8. Prv 8.23; Jn 1.1–9.　　　　9. Col 1.15–16.

prince of the heavenly host, angel of great counsel,[10] and executor of the Father's will, who is known to have created and originated with the Father all that is as his true and only-begotten Son, lord and king and ruler of all that is created, governing all things with the Father's power and might? It is possible only if we are molded by the secret and mystical language of the divine books to an understanding of the fullness that is his. John, in sum, filled with God's spirit as he is, says, "In the beginning was the Word, and the Word was in God's presence, and the Word was God. It was in the beginning in God's presence. Everything was made through it and without it was made nothing."[11]

4. Moses as well, the greatest and earliest of the prophets, declared the same thing many centuries before, when under heavenly inspiration and filled with God, he revealed the origin of the world and the beginnings of things: he states in mystical and sacred language that it is the Father with the Son who is the originator of all things.[12] What he says is, "And God said, 'Let us make man in our image and likeness.'"[13] David too, himself the oldest of the prophets, even if later than Moses, says, "By the word of the Lord the heavens were established, and by the breath of his mouth all their power." 5. And there is another utterance of his which says the same: "He spoke and they were made; he commanded and they were created."[14] With these words it is clear that he has represented the person of the Father who commands and of the Son who works.

6. Since therefore, in these and a great many other passages scattered throughout the divine books, he declares the Son to be the creator of everything with the Father,[15] it remains for us to touch as briefly as possible upon the activities which he carried out in providing for the human race after the origination of the world. 7. For it can be shown that he presented him-

---

10. Jos 5.14; Is 9.5 (LXX).   11. Jn 1.1–3.

12. ... *conditorem omnium patrem cum filio ... designat.* What Eusebius says is that the Father handed over to Christ, the divine Word, the making of what is inferior (τῶν ὑποβεβηκότων).

13. Gn 1.26.

14. Ps 32.6, 9. Psalm numbering is from LXX, here and elsewhere.

15. *creator omnium cum patre filius* (not in Eusebius).

self even earlier to many men endowed with piety, and taught them[16] what could be seen to concern divine worship. But he is described as having made himself known more clearly and intimately, as far as it was right for God to do so with human beings, to Abraham and his family, and is said to have acted as an instructor and counselor to his kin. It is written in fact in the divine utterances that God appeared to Abraham as an ordinary human being while he was sitting by the oak of Mamre. But he rose when he saw the human being and adored him as God and venerated him as Lord. The very words which he used prove that he was not unaware of the divine presence, for he said, "Sovereign Lord, who judge the whole earth, will you not do justice?"[17]

8. All of which words are to be understood as directed not to the Father, but to the Son, as indicated by the way in which the dispensation in the flesh was later accomplished more fully. And the same prophet David says of God, "He sent his word and healed them and freed them from their corruptions."[18]

9. And the divine words testify even more clearly about him through Moses, that he is himself Lord with the Lord, when he says, "The Lord rained fire and brimstone on Sodom and Gomorrah from the Lord."[19] The same scripture indicates that he, the same one, was God when he appeared to Jacob, since he says to Jacob, "Your name will no longer be Jacob; your name will be Israel, because you have proved strong with God." And shortly after, it says, "And Jacob called that place 'Sight of God,' saying, 'I have seen God face to face, and my soul has been saved.'"[20] 10. It is not right to think such things of any of the angels or the heavenly powers. For the divine words speak of none of them as Lord or God if they are ever bidden by a heavenly command to approach mortals.

16. *multis quidem et antea pietate praeditis viris adstitisse et docuisse* ... What Eusebius says is that the divine Word "never tired of behaving piously toward the Father."

17. Gn 18.1–2, 25.   18. Ps 106.20.

19. Gn 19.24. Rufinus's *dominus [est] ipse cum domino* translates "Moses speaks of him most clearly as a second Lord after the Father" (δεύτερον μετὰ τὸν πατέρα κύριον).

20. Gn 32.28, 30.

11/12. He also, when he presented himself to Moses's successor Joshua, and Joshua asked him who he was, indicated this in the clearest possible way when he said, "I am the captain of the powers of the Lord." And when his servant upon hearing this adored him, as was fitting, he said to him, "Untie the thong of your shoe; for the place in which you are standing is holy ground."[21] 13. What is to be considered here is the similarity of what is commanded, because this person was none other than the one who had said to Moses from the burning bush, "Do not come near; loose the shoes from your feet; for the place in which you are standing is holy ground." And he added, "I am the God of your fathers, the God of Abraham and the God of Isaac and the God of Jacob."[22]

14. It is evident, then, from all of this, that the Son has been designated Word of God and God and Lord and creator of all things with the Father.[23] But now let us also see how he himself shows that he exists substantially as God's wisdom in the divine utterances given through Solomon, when he speaks of the selfsame wisdom in the following mystical terms: "I, wisdom, had my dwelling; I called upon counsel, knowledge, and understanding; it is through me that kings rule and through me that the powerful write justice; the mighty are magnified through me, and through me rulers obtain land." 15. And later he adds, "The Lord created me the beginning of his ways in his work; before the ages he established me, in the beginning before he made the earth, before the springs of water issued forth; before the mountains were established, and before all the hills he produced me. When he was making ready the sky, I was with him, and when he was fixing fast the springs under the sky, I was with him arranging them. I was the one in whom he daily delighted. I rejoiced before him, however, all the time that he rejoiced in the world completed."[24]

21. Jos 5.14, 15.
22. Ex 3.5–6.
23. *verbum dei et deus et dominus et creator omnium cum patre filius designatus est.* Eusebius: God's Word and Wisdom "served (ὑπηρετησαμένη) God the Father of all in the fashioning of all created things."
24. Prv 8.12, 15, 16, 22–25, 27, 28, 30, 31.

16. From all of this it is evident that the wisdom begotten from the Father himself has been from the beginning, or rather even before every beginning that can be called such.

17. Let us now see why it is that he did not previously make himself known to everyone everywhere, as he has done now, and why his faith and knowledge did not reach all. A world still uncultured and lacking all knowledge could not yet receive the full teaching of Christ's wisdom. 18. At the very beginning, in fact, when the first humans to be created still lived in happiness, they fell into this mortal life subject to frailty when by their negligence they ruined what God had committed to them, and exchanged the delights of paradise for the dwelling of this earth, which is damned by the divine curse.[25] And now those who sprang from such parents and spread out over the earth 19. wandered about rather like wild beasts without cities to foster companionship, customs to enjoin rectitude, and laws to encourage right living. And as for arts, crafts, schools, and anything to do with philosophy, the very name was unknown to them; they roamed as wild savages through wildernesses without settlements. And if through the benevolence of their creator any seeds of good germinated in them naturally, they left them untended and inchoate, resorting rather to the evil practices toward which the human race is so strongly inclined. The result was that sometimes they were depraved by the foul crimes they committed against each other, and sometimes were even killed by each other, their savagery proceeding to the point where they even devoured each other. 20. This is the origin of those battles of gods and giants which have bequeathed to the world the fables of wickedness, until the divine retribution brought upon that foul arrogance the Flood at one time, and the devastation of the fiery rain at another, curbing the enormity of the crimes with a diversity of punishments.

21. Since, however, its creator resolved that the human race, infected by the sickness and contamination of malice, should

25. The following account of the gradual progress of humankind from savagery to civilization is part of a widespread and deeply-rooted tradition; cf. W. K. C. Guthrie, *A History of Greek Philosophy*, III (Cambridge University Press, 1969), 60–63. It may go back to the fifth-century BCE Xenophanes.

be cured rather than destroyed, he himself, God the Word
and the Father's Wisdom, who was in the beginning in God's
presence, took pity then on those minds darkened by depravity
and obfuscated by the darkness of blindness, and would send
at times deputations of angels and ministering powers, and at
other times would come himself with indescribable gracious-
ness, and, if he found anywhere some rare person who was
mindful of God and justice, would strive to reform the human
race and recall it from darkness by divine revelations, salutary
counsels, and that instruction which befits God. This he did
in human likeness only, in which alone can human beings be
taught anything, and instructed and helped, 22. until gradually he converted an entire nation, called the Hebrews, to his
religion and worship. And since they were still untaught and
infected by the contamination of their former life, he also impressed upon them, through the prophet Moses, the figures
and foreshadowing of the divine worship by means of certain
mystical Sabbaths, the bodily circumcision whose higher meaning is found in the spirit, and other such legal enactments as
elements of a more sacred education to come at some future
time.

23. Now since this law shone out upon this world as a sort
of first gleam of light, and filled the sea and the lands far and
wide with its fragrance, the lawmakers and philosophers who
were of sound intelligence in various parts of the earth, when
they caught a whiff of it, began gradually to impart and in-
still into their audiences precepts enjoining self-restraint and
propriety, and redolent of morality and justice, and to recall
the wild and savage manners of humankind to decent and
moral customs. Sometimes they taught men to come together
in friendship and to submit to pacts of concord, and at other
times people learned to help each other and to have things for
common use, until the human mind became willing to adopt
more sensible habits and to accept the companionship of people with each other;[26] the purpose was that with such habitu-

26. "Sometimes they taught ... people with each other": Rufinus adds, perhaps echoing Lucretius, 5.1019–25.

al practices as their preparation, people might be rendered equipped and ready for divine teachings as well, and able to take in the knowledge of God, the father of all. It was then that once again the very teacher of all virtues, who is himself the speech, reason, word, and wisdom of God, the very one who with the Father in the beginning had created humankind, he himself, I say, took to himself the substance of human nature as well, put on the likeness of the form of a slave in no way differing from that which we are,[27] and, during the time when he himself had brought it about that the Roman empire had advanced to greater splendor and extent,[28] entered this world by being born in the same way as we are, but without any evident progenitor; and having done so, he did and bore those things which the prophets had foretold of him. For men divinely inspired sang in sacred language of a human being who would at the same time be God and who would arrive in this world to be the teacher to all the nations of the devotion and worship to be offered to the Father; they also sang of the way he would die when he left this life, how he would return from the dead to the living in an unheard-of manner, and after that would go to heaven, from where he had come down, and would go back unto God.

24. Although very many prophets clearly indicated these things, I will refer to what one of them, Daniel, disclosed, citing him to the extent that necessity may allow. He speaks thus of him: "I looked, and behold, seats had been placed, and the Ancient of Days sat, and his clothing was like white snow, and the hair of his head like pure wool: his throne was a flame of fire, his wheels burning fire. A river of fire was running before him. The hearing began, and the books were opened." 25. And later: "I looked, and behold, one like a Son of Man came with the clouds of heaven and came even unto the Ancient of Days, and was presented before him, and there was given to him supremacy, honor, and rule, and all peoples, tribes, and tongues

27. Phil 2.7.
28. ... *tempore, quo Romani imperii regnum nobilius latiusque consurgere ipse praestiterat* = ἀρχομένης τῆς Ῥωμαίων βασιλείας ("when the Roman empire was beginning").

will serve him. His power is eternal power, which will not pass away, and his kingdom will not be destroyed."[29]

26. It is quite evident that all of this is said of none other than Our Savior, who was God the Word in the beginning in God's presence. For he is called Son of Man because he was born in the flesh in the latest times. 27. Those who wish to know more about this may consult what is maintained about these matters in the places where we have set them out.

1.3.1. It is now time to see how this name of Christ, about which we have spoken, was once depicted by the prophets as well. 2. Moses was himself the first of these; when he wanted to show the depths of awe and mystery contained in Christ's name, and had been ordered to describe in the law the figures and images of the heavenly mysteries as he had been shown them on the mountain,[30] and had handed on the ceremony of ordaining the high priest insofar as a mortal might teach this, he gave the name of "Christ," by the mystery of spiritual anointing, to him who, he decreed, should surpass all human beings in honor and worthiness.[31] His purpose was that those instructed by the law might thereby learn that what is to be held in honor and reverence above all human beings is called "Christ."

3. Not only that, but Moses, seeing far in advance through God's spirit who it was that was to succeed him, and knowing beforehand that the one who would receive the rule after him would be the minister of a higher mystery, 4. called him Jesus who had formerly been called Auses by his parents;[32] for he knew that in the mystery of this word lay the king of a greater glory than mortal nature admits. 5. The name thus bears a double significance, expressing as it does the tokens on the one hand of the high priesthood and on the other of the royal state. And Jesus Christ, inasmuch as he is king and high priest, is named correspondingly, so that the people, when spiritual-

29. Dn 7.9–10, 13–14.
30. Cf. Ex 25.40.
31. Lv 4.5, 16 speaks of the "anointed priest"; "anointed" in the LXX is *christos*.
32. Nm 13.16: Moses changes the name of Hoshea (LXX [H]ause), son of Nun, to Joshua (LXX Jesus).

ly instructed through the foregoing mysteries, might acknowledge that he lacked nothing pertaining either to sanctity or to
authority.

6. Thus the prophets, under the guidance of the divine spirit, foresaw both the impiety of the Jews and the salvation of the
gentiles in him. Something of the sort was foretold by one of
them, called Jeremiah, when he said, "The spirit of our face,
Christ the Lord, has been caught in our corruptions; of him
we said: We will live in his shadow among the nations."[33] David
as well, that splendid seer, speaks of him as follows: "Why have
the nations raged and the peoples laid vain plans? The kings
of the earth arose, and the princes came together against the
Lord and against his Christ." And shortly after he speaks in the
person of Christ himself: "The Lord said to me: you are my son;
this day I have begotten you. Ask of me and I will give you the
nations as your inheritance, and the ends of the earth as your
possession."[34]

7. But it was not only the high priests among the Hebrews
who were consecrated with the oil of anointing; the kings as
well were themselves called "Christs," even if only symbolically,
since they were allotted the royal scepter when at the divine
bidding they were smeared by the prophets with some consecrated ointment. By this means the image and likeness of the
heavenly king was preserved in them too.[35]

8. In the order of prophets as well we find many consecrated in like manner with the oil of anointing who devoted themselves to communicating God's messages, the future having
been made known to them. From all of this it is evident that
the Son of God and the Word and Wisdom of the Father, because he is true king of all the ages and because he is true high
priest of the future and because he is true prophet, the one
who inspires and fills the prophets, was therefore truly called
Christ, the figure and likeness of whose name had preceded

33. Lam 4.20. Rufinus changes "their corruptions" in LXX and Eusebius
to "our."

34. Ps 2.1–2, 7–8.

35. Rufinus condenses Eusebius's 3.8–12 in his 3.8; 3.13 follows. He transfers to his 3.17/18 Eusebius's remark about the name "Christians" in 3.10.

him in the high priests, prophets, and kings whom we listed above. Now because, as we said, they were called Christs for the short space of this life, they were indeed consecrated by being anointed for the preservation of the one image of the true Christ, but even though this was done by means of some mystical confection, it was still of the oil belonging to the matter and liquid which is found among us. But this true Christ, who came from heaven and for whom all that had gone before was done, did not make use of the ointments obtained from human resources, 13. but was made Christ in a new and unique way when instilled and anointed with the Father's spirit. It was as the seer Isaiah had foretold of him many centuries earlier when, speaking in the person of Christ himself, he said, "The spirit of the Lord is upon me, because of which he has anointed me; he has sent me to evangelize the poor, to proclaim release to the captives and sight to the blind."[36]

14. Nor was it Isaiah alone who foretold this in divine utterances; David when likewise inspired testifies about Christ, saying to Christ himself, "Your throne, O God, is for age upon age; the rod of equity is the rod of your kingdom. You have loved justice and hated iniquity, because of which God, your God, has anointed you with the oil of gladness above your fellows."[37] With these words he does clearly indicate first that he is God, but then he mentions secondly the royal scepter in him with the words "rod of equity." 15. And after that he shows how he was made Christ when he says that God was anointed by God not with common oil, but with the oil of gladness, and not like his fellows, those, that is, who preceded him in his likeness, but above his fellows. Now in the sacred books the "oil of gladness" has the spiritual meaning of "Holy Spirit."

16. Concerning his high priesthood as well, this same David elsewhere speaks as follows in obscure language, declaring of the Son as though in the person of the Father, "From the womb before the morning star I begot you. The Lord has sworn and he will not repent: you are a priest forever according to the or-

36. Is 61.1; Lk 4.18.
37. Ps 44.7–8.

der of Melchizedek."[38] 17/18. This Melchizedek is said in the sacred books to have been priest of God most high, but not one who was anointed with ordinary oil, or who received the priesthood in succession to his ancestors, as was the custom among the Hebrews. And therefore Christ is spoken of as the priest to come according to his own order, Christ who is consecrated not with liquid oil but by the power of the heavenly Spirit. It is for that reason, finally, that while there were many Christs among the Hebrews who were anointed with oil solemnly consecrated for this purpose, and while, whether they were kings or prophets or even high priests, they were appointed in this way, none of them was able to give a name derived from this word to a nation or to his disciples or followers, and to call his disciples "Christians," except for this one alone who is the true Christ, anointed not with human oil but by the Father's Spirit. He it is who has caused the peoples of his followers and the entire nation throughout the whole world which belongs to his name, to be called by the enduring name of "Christians," derived from the word referring to the true Christ. If therefore you ask about Christ's ancestry and want to know from whom is the one from whom are all things, listen to the divine words spoken through that most splendid seer David in the person of the highest Father himself, as we cited them a little earlier: "From the womb before the morning star I begot you."[39] And although the term "womb" seems hardly suitable for one who is rightly believed incorporeal, yet what is meant, according to the rules of figurative and spiritual language, is that the Father did not produce the Son from outside and from another source. On the contrary, he did so from himself and, if it may be said, from inside himself, that he that has been born might be just what he that begot him is, and might not be viewed as taken in from outside by adoption, but, as the term "womb" implies, might be described, with all due respect to his incorporeality, as brought

38. Ps 109.3–4. In the following section (3.17/18) Rufinus revises and expands Eusebius; the latter's statement that Christ was "invested with being (οὐσιωμένον) by God before the world was built" (Eusebius 3.18) becomes: the Son was "brought forth from within [the Father] (*intrinsecus editus*)."

39. Ps 109.3.

forth from within in a truly natural way. And the words "before the morning star" mean before the beginning of the world and of all creation.

19. The distinction which is made between the true Christ and those symbolic ones who went before is, to be sure, an obvious proof of this, because those earlier Christs were known to hardly anyone apart from their own nation, while not only the name, but the authority and sovereignty as well of this, the true Christ, has spread through all the nations and over the whole earth, that name which is consecrated not only by knowledge of the word representing it, but also by worship of his divinity and reverence for his sanctity. For in every land Christ Jesus is worshiped and adored as Word and Wisdom of the Father, and as God and Lord, as the divine utterance proclaims of him: "that in Jesus' name every knee should bend, of those in heaven and those on earth and those below, and every tongue acknowledge that Christ is Lord in the glory of God the Father."[40] Hence not only his authority and sovereignty, but a devotion and love so great for him have ripened in the minds of those who believe, that they do not hesitate to lay down their lives for his name and bend their necks to the persecutors' swords, if only the holy faith and reverence that they have for his name may be safeguarded.

1.4.1. The remarks hitherto have been a necessary preface to the narrative of events which we have decided to prosecute; through them the name of Christ Jesus, Our Lord and Savior, may be shown to be no sort of novel term, or one derived from his birth in the flesh, but one which arises from God himself. But since the Christian people seem to have a name newly coined, and its religious observances appear to have arisen recently, let us demonstrate the antiquity which this very novelty embodies.[41]

5. I believe that the Hebrew race is considered the oldest of almost all the nations, no one seeming to think otherwise, because, among other things, that nation has a rather secret

40. Phil 2.10–11.

41. Rufinus omits 4.2 and 4.4, which he may have thought repetitious, and puts 4.3 after 4.10, where it fits better.

worship and religious observance contained in its divine books; they include notices of many men endowed with the virtues of justice and piety, some of whom lived before the Flood and some after the Flood. Among them is found an account of Noah, his sons, and his whole family, which extends down to Abraham, who we know is the ancestor of the Hebrew nation.

6. If someone were then to claim that all of those listed in chronological order from Abraham back to the first human being were Christians, in fact and in religion even if not in name, I would not disagree. 7. For since the name "Christian" means someone who, in believing in Christ, holds fast to faith, piety, and justice through his teaching, cleaves earnestly to divine wisdom, and pursues virtue wholeheartedly; if, I say, this is what the word "Christian" means, and if it designates the followers of the true religion, well then, what Christians now profess to be is what these holy men were, about whom we have just spoken. 8. For neither did they practice bodily circumcision or observance of the Sabbath, just as we do not, or any religious rules about diet or the other things which were handed down through Moses to be kept by later generations in a rather figurative and spiritual sense. Since, then, these men we have just mentioned were religious without all these practices, but followed the faith of the Christ whom we ourselves now follow and who, as we earlier proved, appeared often to them, taught them, and counseled them about the things which pertain to faith and piety, there can be no doubt that that people which followed the same God as originator of and guide to life, and which kept to a similar religious practice, began and originated with them.

9. This religion was, in sum, anticipated and foreshadowed in them to such a degree, that they may not be considered foreign to it even in their name, the only respect in which they appear to differ: the divine utterances testify that they too even then were called not only Christians, but Christs. For we hear the following said of them in the person of God to the foreign nations: "Do not touch my Christs, and do no harm to my prophets."[42]

42. Ps 104.15.

10. Since these things were said of Abraham or of those who adhered at this time to the worship of God, it is quite obvious, and clearer than light itself, that what is meant is that in these folk, and before them, the Christian people already existed then, and carried out fully that practice of piety and religion, which we know has now been shared with all peoples and communicated to all the nations through the advent of Christ in the flesh. By this means the treasure of wisdom and piety, which was kept as it were within a narrow room for some few worshipers, could enrich the whole world by the outpouring of faith and religion, and what had previously been provided to individuals severally could now suddenly be lavished upon whole races, peoples, and nations together.

3. One of the most remarkable of the prophets, seeing in advance by divine inspiration that this was to happen, was overcome by wonder, and, utterly bewildered in his amazement, cried out, "Who ever heard the like? Who ever spoke such words? Has the earth given birth in one day? Has a nation been born all at once?" And again in another place he affirms of these same folk, that the divine word foretold that a nation was to be brought to birth all together, when he says, "A new name, however, will be given to those who will serve me, a name which will be blessed over the lands."[43] Now which name that is so new has been given to the nations other than the Christian one? But by "new name" the passage means one recently extended, not recently invented. And truly, that this was to be so, and that this blessing of name and faith was to be bestowed on all nations, was something about which the divine utterances were by no means silent. 11. For of Abraham himself, while he was still uncircumcised, the divine word says, "Abraham believed God, and this was reckoned to him as justice, and he was called the friend of God."[44]

12. He is said therefore to have believed him who, as we explained earlier, appeared to him frequently and taught him the things pertaining to piety and religion, Christ that is, upon

43. Is 66.8; 65.16.
44. Gn 15.6; 2 Chr 20.7; Is 41.8; Jas 2.23.

whom, as has often been proved, all that has taken place or is to take place depends. It is from him as well that Abraham received the following replies: "And in you all the tribes on earth will be blessed." And again: "I will make of you a nation great and numerous, and in you will all the nations on earth be blessed."[45] 13. This obviously means that that form of worship and that grace of faith which were then granted to Abraham and those few others who were distinguished for their faith and piety at that time, were later to be bestowed through divine grace as a blessing on all nations through every land. For it is certain that, just as he was justified when he believed him who appeared to him, and kept the precepts of the true God in his faith and works after rejecting and disdaining the superstitions of his ancestors, and for this reason heard it said to him, "In you will be blessed all the tribes and all the nations on earth," 14. so also Christians likewise do the same in faith and works, in order that, once they have renounced the error of their ancestors' superstition, they may follow the God whom Abraham followed, and be justified from a faith like his, just as Abraham was justified.

15. What is there, then, that forbids us to ascribe one and the same practice of religion to those in whom there is found one and the same form of faith and works? The religion of the Christians is not, then, novel or foreign or of recent origin, but, if it is right to speak the truth openly, is the first one of all, co-eval with the very origin and birth of the world, and with Christ himself as its God, its teacher, and its founder, received its aspect and form right from the beginning. This should suffice concerning these matters.

1.5.1. Having then prefaced our history with that which due order required should precede it, it remains for us to proceed to what is like the beginning of our journey: the presence in the body of our Lord and Savior, and the things which happened thereafter; we call in prayer upon God himself, the almighty Father of the Word, and upon him as well who is our subject, Jesus Christ, our Lord and Savior, the heavenly Word of God, to be the helper and author of our narrative.

45. Gn 12.3; 18.18.

2. It was, then, in the forty-second year of the reign of Caesar Augustus, but the twenty-eighth year since the subjugation of Egypt and the death of Antony and Cleopatra, the latter of whom was the last of the Ptolemies in Egypt when their kingdom fell, that our Lord and Savior Jesus Christ was born in Bethlehem,[46] a town in Judea, during the first census enrollment while Cyrinus was governor of Syria; this was in accordance with all that had been prophesied of him.[47] 3. This census taken in the time of Cyrinus is also mentioned by Josephus, the famous historian of the Hebrews, joining to this narrative that of the sect of the Galileans, which arose at this same time and about which our author Luke speaks as follows in the Acts of the Apostles: "After him Judas the Galilean arose in the days of the census enrollment, and drew the people off after him. But he himself perished, and all those who believed in him were scattered."[48] 4. Josephus, whom we just mentioned, speaks of this same matter in his history, in the eighteenth book of the *Antiquities,* as follows:

"Cyrinus[49] was one of the men with a seat in the Roman senate who rose to the rank of consul through the several magistracies, and was in other respects as well worthy of esteem; he came with a few men to Syria, having been sent by Caesar to administer justice to the nations and at the same time to be the assessor of inheritances."

5. And a little later he says, "Judas, a Gaulanite, a man from the city of Gamala, associated with himself some Pharisee named Zadok and did his best to incite the people, claiming that the census registration would simply mean the imposition of the

46. In 43 BCE Octavian was declared consul (Julius Caesar had been assassinated in 44) and the triumvirate of Antony, Octavian, and Lepidus was established. In 31 BCE Antony was defeated at the Battle of Actium, and the following year Antony and Cleopatra committed suicide.

47. Cf. Mi 5.2. "Cyrinus" is an example of Rufinus's carelessness in transcribing names from (or back from) the Greek, Κυρίνιος (Κυρήνιος in Lk 2.2) being the usual transcription of "Quirinius."

48. Acts 5.37.

49. P. Sulpicius Quirinus, consul in 12 BCE and afterwards perhaps proconsul of Asia, conducted, as governor of Syria, a census of Judea, which had come under direct Roman administration in 6 CE.

most open form of slavery, and at the same time he exhorted his nation not to lose its freedom."[50]

6. He also writes about the same thing in the second book of *The Jewish War:* "At this time a man from Galilee named Judas compelled the peoples to move toward secession, urging them that it would be the worst thing for them if they agreed to pay taxes to the Romans and accepted a mortal lord after God."[51]

Thus far Josephus.

1.6.1. It was at this same time that Herod obtained the kingship over the Jewish people,[52] the first person of foreign stock to do so; in him was fulfilled the prophecy made earlier by Moses that "a ruler would not fail from Judah, nor a leader from his thighs, until the one should come for whom it had been reserved."[53] Moses also declared of him that the nations would await him. 2. For this prediction remained unfulfilled as long as they were governed by rulers from their own nation, and those, beginning with Moses himself, who made the prediction, lasted until the emperor Augustus. It was then, as I just said, that Herod received from the Romans the government of the Jews as the first man of foreign stock to do so. Herod, according to what Josephus says at least, was Idumaean on his father's side, and Arab on his mother's.[54] Africanus, though, who is himself considered a first-rate historian, says,

50. *Antiquities* 18.4. See Emil Schürer, *The History of the Jewish People in the Age of Jesus Christ,* revised by Geza Vermes and Fergus Millar (Edinburgh: T. & T. Clark, 1973–87), 1.381–82. This initial revolt against direct taxation by the Romans met with little success at first, but was the impetus to the eventual formation of the Zealot party.

51. *Bellum* 2.118. The attribution to Rufinus of the ancient Latin translation of the *Bellum Iudaicum* (cf. Cassiodorus, *Institutiones* 1.17.1) has not withstood critical scrutiny. Cf. Giuliana Ussani, "Studi preparatorii ad una edizione della traduzione latina in sette libri del *Bellum Iudaicum,*" *Bollettino del Comitato per la preparazione della edizione nazionale dei classici greci e latini,* n.s. I (1945): 85–102. For a summary of the issue, see Tommaso Leoni, "Translations and Adaptations of Josephus's Writings in Antiquity and the Middle Ages," *Ostraka* 16/2 (2007): 481–85.

52. Almost half a century earlier, in fact, Herod having been named King of Judea by the Roman Senate in 40 BCE.

53. Gn 49.10. *usque quo veniret cui repositum est* = ἕως ἂν ἔλθῃ ᾧ ἀπόκειται. LXX: "until there comes what is reserved for him" (ἕως ἂν ἔλθῃ τὰ ἀποκείμενα αὐτῷ).

54. *Antiquities* 14.8–9, 403; *Bellum* 1.123, 181.

"Those who have investigated the matter carefully say that one Antipater was the father of Herod of Ascalon; he himself was the son of a Herod who was the sacristan of a temple of Apollo. 3. This Antipater was captured by Idumaean robbers when quite young and remained with the brigands because his father could not ransom his son due to his family's poverty. The boy was in fact brought up in the life and manners of the robbers, and later became the close friend of one Hyrcanus, a Jewish high priest; from him was begotten the Herod who lived in the Savior's time."[55]

4. So says Africanus. Since, then, the government of the Jews had fallen to the lot of someone of foreign stock, the expectation of the nations foretold by the prophets was also clearly at hand, seeing that the line of their rulers and kings, which had started with Moses himself, had failed. 5. For before they had been led off into the Babylonian captivity, Saul had first reigned over them, and then David. For before the kings they had been ruled by judges, the heads of this people after Moses and his successor Joshua. 6. Even after their return from Babylon they did not lack a government founded on the highest principles. For the business of state was conducted by the high priests, until the Roman officer Pompey came to Jerusalem, attacked it with a Roman force and captured it, and defiled all the holy and most sacred parts of the temple, not refraining even from intruding into the very sanctuary.[56] Aristobulus, moreover, who at that time exercised both the royal and high priestly powers in succession from his grandfather, he sent bound to Rome with his children, leaving the high priesthood to his brother Hyrcanus. And he made the whole Jewish nation tributary to the Roman government from then on.[57]

55. On Africanus, (c. 180–c. 250), cf. Martin Walraff et al., eds., *Iulius Africanus. Chronographiae: The Extant Fragments* (Berlin and New York: De Gruyter, 2007). The excerpt is F87a. On Herod's ancestry, cf. Schürer, 1.234 n.3.

56. Pompey's capture of Jerusalem is in Josephus, *Antiq.* 14.57–76; Cicero, *Pro Flacco* 67; Tacitus, *Hist.* 5.9; Dio Cassius, 27.16.4. When the last Hasmonean ruler, Alexandra, died in 67 BCE, her sons Hyrcanus II and Aristobulus II disputed the succession, the latter winning a temporary victory. But Pompey, who was engaged in subjugating the Near East, favored his brother and laid siege to the Temple Mount in Jerusalem, where his supporters were entrenched. A massacre followed the breaching of its walls late in 63. Schürer, 1.233–40.

57. Josephus, *Antiq.* 14.79; *Bellum* 1.153, 157. On the grant of the high

7. But when Hyrcanus, the last person upon whom the high priesthood of the Jews devolved, was captured by the Parthians, Herod became the first foreigner, as I said earlier, to obtain the governance of the Jewish nation through a measure passed by the senate when Augustus was emperor.[58] 8. It was in the time of Augustus that, with the Savior's advent now at hand, the salvation and calling of the gentiles, which had been awaited in accordance with what the prophets had foretold, also took place. From this time on, at all events, with the interruption of the succession of leaders and rulers who had descended from Judah's thighs, the line of the priesthood, which had run unswervingly from grandfathers and great-grandfathers, was also, and in consequence, suddenly disrupted.

9. Josephus is the best witness to this as well; he says that after the kingdom of the Jews was granted to Herod by the Romans, he no longer appointed high priests according to their birth, but gave the priesthood to any commoner. He reports that his successor Archelaus did likewise in appointing priests; after him, he says, the Romans regained the governance of the Jews. 10. Josephus relates that Herod even kept the sacred robe of the supreme high priest locked away under his seal, and never allowed the high priests its use or its power. His successor Archelaus did the same, and the Romans after them continued this customary injustice against the high priesthood.[59]

11. These statements may serve us as proof of the prophecy which was fulfilled by the advent of our Lord and Savior. Not only that, but it is also clear that the number of the weeks

priesthood to the Hasmoneans as hereditary, see Schürer, 1.193–94; 1 Mc 14.35–47.

58. The Parthians took advantage of Roman political divisions to overrun the Near East in 40 BCE and take prisoner Hyrcanus, whom Caesar had confirmed as high priest and named ethnarch in 47. Josephus, *Bellum* 1.256–60, 273; *Antiq.* 14.348, 351, 353, 379, 387; 20.248.

Herod fled to Rome and, in recognition of his steadfast support in its struggle with Parthia, was named King of Judea by the senate in the same year (with Octavian's consent, although the latter was not declared Augustus until 27 BCE).

59. On the appointment of the high priests and the custody of their robe, see Josephus, *Antiq.* 15.22; 15.403–9; 18.90–95; 20.12; 20.247–49.

in the prophet Daniel was completed, which, it was indicated, would last until Christ the ruler. We have explained this elsewhere.[60] The same prophet indicates that after the completion of these weeks, the anointing was to be abolished which the Jews safeguarded as something most sacred. This is most clearly shown to be fulfilled in that very time when our Lord Jesus Christ came. These remarks of ours, then, are offered as essential to establishing the truth concerning the times.

1.7.1. Now the genealogy of Christ having been handed down to us differently by the evangelists Matthew and Luke,[61] there are a great number of people who think that they contradict each other. In this matter, since many even of the faithful out of ignorance of the truth resort to certain arguments which they form from their own opinions, let us present the account concerning this matter as well which has come down to us. Africanus, whom we mentioned earlier, wrote to one Aristides about the agreement of the gospels and about the genealogies which are recorded differently by Matthew and Luke, and he proved that the opinions of others are far from the truth, while he himself presented the results of his research in the following words:[62]

2. "Among the people of Israel, the names in their genealogies are listed sometimes in the sequence provided by nature, and sometimes in that of law. Natural sequence is considered to be that resulting from the actual relationship in seed and blood, while that which is of law refers to a son begotten by another man who is substituted under the name of a brother who died without children.[63] For since they had not yet received the hope of resurrection, it was by this means that they produced a sort of image of the resurrection, lest the defect of sterility wipe out a family name. 3. Since, then, their genealogies were

60. Eusebius comments on Dn 9.24–27 in *Demonstratio evangelica* 8.2.55–129 and *Eclogae propheticae* 153.12–165.

61. Mt 1.1–17; Lk 3.23–38.

62. Text, translation, and commentary: Christophe Guignard, *La lettre de Julius Africanus à Aristide sur la généalogie du Christ* (*TU* 167; Berlin and Boston: De Gruyter, 2011). Rufinus's translation is noticed on pp. 24–25.

63. Cf. Dt 25.5–6.

kept in this way, so that some were reckoned as sons by natural generation, while others by the provision of the law from substitution were considered sons of other men than had begotten them, each of the evangelists has one of these two ways of arranging the sequence: one of them lists it according to those who begot, and the other according to those who, as it were, begot. 4. And thus it is that neither gospel lies, since one follows the order of nature, and the other that of law. For the family descending from Solomon and that from Nathan were connected with each other both by legal substitutions, which happened in the case of those who died without children, and by second marriages as well, by which one and the same man, the offspring of one set of parents, was viewed as the son of yet others. The result is that both of the genealogical descriptions going down to Joseph contain family lines that are completely real; their arrangements, however different, have been thoroughly researched.

5. "To make this clearer, let us list the sequences themselves in the genealogies. The genealogy from David through Solomon, which Matthew recounts, puts Matthan, who is said to have begotten Joseph's father Jacob, in third place from the end. Luke nonetheless, when he constructs the genealogy through Nathan, from David, puts Malchi in that same third place. He speaks of 'Joseph, who was of Heli, who was of Malchi.' 6. It is then incumbent upon us to show how it is that Joseph is said by Matthew to have as father Jacob, who is descended through Solomon, while according to Luke it was Heli, who is descended through Nathan, so that these men, Jacob and Heli, who were two brothers having one of them Matthan and the other Melchi as fathers from different families, appear to be the very ones who were Joseph's ancestors.

7/8. "This is the way of it: Matthan and Melchi begot each a son at different times from the same wife, Estha, because Matthan, whose descent was through Solomon, was the first to take her as wife; he died, leaving one son, Jacob. Since the law does not forbid a widow to marry another man, Melchi, whose family was descended through Nathan, took Matthan's relict as wife after his death, since he was of the same tribe, but not from the same family. From her he too got a son named Heli, and thus it came about that Jacob and Heli were brothers from the same womb, their fathers being from different families. 9. One of them, Jacob, took the wife of his brother Heli, in accordance with the law, when he died without children, and begot Joseph. Joseph was his son by the nature of procreation, and it is written accordingly: 'Jacob begot Joseph.' According to the precept of the law, however, he was Heli's son; it was his wife whom Jacob had taken, because he was his brother, in order to raise up seed for his brother.

10. "And thus the genealogies are found to be valid and intact: both the one propounded by Matthew when he says, 'Jacob begot Joseph,' and the one which Luke advances with a suitable observation when he says that 'he was regarded as the son of Joseph, who was of Jacob.' It is intimated by the same distinction that the latter will be regarded as the son of Heli, who was of Melchi, because the evangelist indicated thereby this succession according to the law, which is based upon a kind of adoption in connection with the deceased rather than a real act of generation,[64] and he did so quite aptly by his observation. This was lest he in any way suggest that anyone begot offspring in this kind of genealogy, and for this reason he made a proper distinction in going up rather than down, to arrive at Adam and at God himself.

11. "This account has not been improvised by us or thought up without any sources of authentication; our Savior's own relatives have handed it down, whether from a desire to show the quality of their parentage or to tell of what really took place. They added that when the Idumaean robbers attacked the city of Ascalon and took captive Antipater, the son of one Herod, a sacristan, along with the rest of the plunder they seized from the temple of Apollo, which was attached to the city wall, it later happened that Antipater became friends with the high priest Hyrcanus. 12. And he proved himself so useful in every way that when Hyrcanus died, it was his realm that, thanks to

---

64. ... *quae velut adoptione quadam erga defunctos constat magis quam germinis veritate* ... : not in Eusebius.

his ambition, he received from the Romans for his son Herod as the kingdom of the Jewish nation.[65]

"Now these matters are related in the other histories of the pagans as well.[66] 13. But the men just mentioned recorded this matter in particular: that at this time all of the genealogies of the Hebrews were kept in the more secret archives of the temple; they also contained the ancestries of anyone of foreign stock, such as Achior of the Ammonites[67] and Ruth of the Moabites, and others as well from Egypt who are said to have commingled with the Israelites. Now Herod, when he was sovereign, realized that if such information about families remained in existence, it would result in grievous vilification of him, and so, roused by the awareness of his humble parentage, he ordered all the books to be burned which contained family records, reckoning that he could pass for well-born if no one could insist from the volumes of records that he was a newcomer to the Israelite nation, only lately arrived.[68] 14. Now there were then a few zealous and diligent men who kept partial transcriptions of this sort of books at home, or who knew their genealogies by heart, especially those who remembered the high birth from which they were descended. Among them were the *desposynoi*, whom we mentioned a little earlier: those who were known as the Lord's or the Master's folk on account of their relationship with the family of Christ. They were also Nazarenes from the village of Cochaba of the Jews[69] who would go around through the whole

65. Cf. 1.6.3. Antipater was named procurator of Judea by Caesar in 47 BCE in return for his support in Caesar's war with King Ptolemy in Egypt. Antipater in turn appointed his young son Herod governor of Galilee, but was then poisoned to death in 43 BCE, Judea subsequently falling to the Parthians as mentioned in note 58 above. Cf. Schürer, 1.270–80.

66. On the non-Jewish sources, cf. Schürer, 1.63–68.

67. Achior: Jdt 5.5–6.21; 14.5–10.

68. The story of the burning of the genealogies is implicitly contradicted by Josephus, who says that he found his genealogy in the public records (*Vita* 6). Cf. also *C. Apion.* 1.30–36.

69. ... *qui et Nazaraei fuerunt ex vico Cocchaba Iudaeorum* = [δεσπόσυνοι καλούμενοι] ἀπό τε Ναζάρων καὶ Κωχαβα κώμων Ἰουδαϊκῶν ("from the Jewish villages of Nazareth and Cochaba"). Epiphanius repeatedly associates the Nazarenes with Cochaba (*Panarion* 29.7.7; 30.2.8–9, 18.1; 40.1.5). The *desposynoi* are the Lord's relatives mentioned in 1.7.11 (from *despotēs*, "master").

region informing others of the genealogy just mentioned, partly from memory and partly also from the Books of Days,[70] as far as was possible. 15. These having been thoroughly examined by us with the fullest possible care, the truth of the gospels is completely manifested thereby."[71]

16/17. Such do we learn from Africanus. The genealogy having been traced down to Joseph in this way, there can be no further doubt that Mary was of the same clan and the same tribe, if in fact the law of Moses forbids marriages between persons of different tribes; it bids an unmarried woman to be joined to someone of the same people and the same family, lest confusion arise about inheritance from mixed marriage, and property be transferred unlawfully from one tribe to another.[72] And that should suffice for this matter.

1.8.1. Christ therefore having been born in Bethlehem of Judea, in fulfillment of the prophecy, in the time of the Herod mentioned earlier, some men from the people of the Magi arrived from the East and asked Herod where the recently-born king of the Jews was, insisting that they had seen his star in the east, that it had led them on their way, and that this was the reason for their making such great haste to adore and venerate the recently-born king. When he heard this, he was utterly terrified, fearing that his sovereignty was in peril. Summoning the teachers of the law, therefore, he asked them where they expected Christ to be born. And since the place of his birth was indicated by the utterances of Micah to be Bethlehem, the king issued a single decree ordering all the unweaned boys from two years and under to be slain, not only in Bethlehem, but in its entire neighborhood as well, according to the time which he had discovered from the Magi, seeking if possible to kill Jesus

---

70. *dierum* [*libri*] = [βίβλος] τῶν ἡμερῶν. On the difficulty of identifying the title, see Guignard (note 62 above), 447–49. Rufinus's translation of the title may suggest that he tried to reconcile it with the Hebrew title of the Books of Chronicles.

71. "... completely manifested thereby." What Eusebius says is: "Whether this be so or not, it is hard to imagine a clearer account ..."

Rufinus omits the additional genealogical note on Joseph in Eusebius 1.7.16, probably because he considered it redundant.

72. Nm 36.

together with those of his age. 2. But the boy forestalled the king's plot when he was taken away to Egypt, his parents having been warned in advance of the king's malice by an angel. Such are we told by the sacred words of the gospel as well.[73]

3. But it will be worth our while to see how Herod was repaid for his cruelty to Christ and his coevals. There came upon him at once, without delay, that divine retribution which not only inflicted immediate death, but also showed the agonies with which he was to be tormented after he died. 4. The tale of the prosperity in which his realm had flourished until that time would be long indeed: a prosperity darkened by the disasters befalling his house. Were I to recount the disgrace of his marriage, the deaths of his children, of whom he himself was the murderer, and the calamities befalling his sister and all of his other relatives, the pages would seem to belong rather to tragedy than to history. Those who want to know more may consult Josephus.[74]

5. Since, then, divine retribution hurried him off to his death for the sacrilege which he had committed against the Savior and the crime which he had carried out against his coevals, I do not think it improper if we use Josephus's own words to explain the end to which it brought him. The passage is from the seventeenth book of his *Antiquities*.[75]

"His illness pressed more heavily upon Herod each day as it inflicted upon him the punishment for the crime he had previously committed. 6. On the outside he was scorched by a slow-burning fire on the surface of his body, while within him a great conflagration was concealed. He had a constant and insatiable desire for food, nor could the ravening jaws of his appetite ever be satisfied, his innards being set about with ulcers; he was also tormented by the severest possible intestinal pains. 7. A thin, sallow fluid meandered around his swollen feet, having spread with the swelling even from his lower members right to his private parts; his very genitals festered in decay, swarming with worms; his breathing was also indescribably heavy, and his

---

73. Mt 2.
74. Cf. Schürer, 1.302–4, 320–29.
75. *Antiq.* 17.168–70.

tumescence disgusting and abominable. And the stench was made worse by all of these sufferings, whether it came from the decay of his members or his gasping for air. Thus exhausted by his torments in every member, his strength was not equal to bearing them. 8. Those therefore skilled in interpretation said that this God-sent punishment was being exacted from the sovereign on account of his many cruel and irreligious deeds."

Such is the account given in the history just mentioned by the man to whom we referred a little earlier. 9. And in the second book[76] this same historian writes of him as well in a similar way, saying,

"Afterwards indeed the disease claimed him for its own, invading his whole body with various infections. A prolonged fever troubled him on the one hand, and an unbearable itching spread over the whole surface of his body on the other; he was afflicted by quite frequent pains in his intestines; a swelling from dropsy afflicted his feet, extending right to his private parts; his gangrenous genitals bristled with the swarm of worms bred by their decay; and his labored breathing and rapid panting were forced from the severe convulsions of his innards, so that the soothsayers said that these were not illnesses of the body but the punishments of divine retribution. 10. Although he was attacked by so many even fatal diseases, he still held on to the hope that he might survive, and took thought for remedies and cures. He crossed the Jordan, accordingly, and availed himself of the hot waters at Callirhoe, which are said to be beneficial even to those who drink them. 11. The doctors, though, decided that his whole body should be warmed with hot oil. And when he was set down in this preparation, all of his members so utterly collapsed that his very eyes were loosed from their sockets. He was carried back to Jericho and, warned by the lamentation of his servants, he began to lose hope. He then ordered the soldiers to be given fifty drachmas apiece, but he bestowed the greatest amount of money on the officers and his friends.

12. "He himself, however, by now quite mad, was driven to a horrible crime in which he threatened death itself, so to speak.

76. *Bellum* 1.656–60.

He ordered all the men of high birth and of the first rank to be
gathered to himself from each of the villages and strongholds
throughout Judea, and to be shut up in the place called the
hippodrome. 13. Then summoning his sister Salome and her
husband Alexas, he said, 'I know that the Jews will rejoice at
my death, but I will be able to have mourners and a respectable funeral from the abundance of the grief-stricken, if you
are willing to follow my orders. As soon as I breathe my last, kill
all of these men of high birth from all of Judea whom I have ordered kept under guard—the soldiers are ready for this—that
all Judea, and every house in it, may grieve at my death, however unwillingly."[77]

14. And a little further on Josephus says, "Once again,
strained by hunger and racked by coughs, he sensed from the
severity of his pains that the end of his life was at hand, and so,
taking an apple, he asked for a knife, since it was his habit to
eat fruit after he had himself peeled and sliced it. Then looking around to make sure there was no one to prevent him, he
raised his right hand and prepared to stab himself."[78]

15. The same writer goes on to say that shortly before he
breathed his last, he gave unholy orders that a third son of his
should be murdered after the two whom he had already killed,
and that his flight from his final day should be marked not
only by his agonizing bodily pains, but also by the abomination of a murder of this sort.[79] 16. Such was Herod's end: the
fitting punishment imposed on him for the crime he had committed against the children in Bethlehem and for his designs
against our Lord and Savior. As for his succession, the gospel
tells us that after Joseph, prompted by an angel, took the boy
and his mother from Egypt and returned to the land of Judea,
"He heard," says the evangelist, "that Archelaus was reigning
in place of his father Herod, and so he feared to go there; but
prompted by his dreams, he went off to the region of Galilee."[80]

77. Salome did not execute the order: *Antiq.* 17.193.

78. *Bellum* 1.662. His cousin Achiab seized his hand and stopped him.

79. *Antiq.* 17.187, 191. The third son was Antipater; the other two were Alexander and Aristobulus. Cf. Schürer, 1.321–26.

80. Mt 2.22.

1.9.1. The historian mentioned earlier agrees in what he writes with this true gospel account, carefully following these matters out: that by the bequest of his father Herod, supported by Caesar Augustus, Archelaus succeeded to the kingdom of the Jews; that he fell from power after ten years; and that Philip and his younger brother Herod, together with Lysanias, governed the kingdom of Judea when it had been divided into tetrarchies.[81]

2. The same historian says in his eighteenth book that in the twelfth year of Tiberius Caesar, who had succeeded Augustus as sovereign after the latter had ruled for fifty-seven years, Pontius Pilate became procurator of Judea and held that post for ten years in succession, almost until Tiberius's death. 3. All of this reveals the shamelessly counterfeit nature of the Acts, so recently concocted, which are mustered against Christ the Lord, and in which the dates mentioned are the first evidence of their falsity. 4. For these false Acts place the time of the outrage committed against the Savior in the fourth consulship of Tiberius, the consulship which fell in the seventh year of his reign. But it can be clearly shown that at that time Pilate had not yet even been sent to Judea as its procurator; such is the testimony of that most excellent historian Josephus, who quite plainly indicates that Pilate became procurator of Judea in the twelfth year of Tiberius Caesar.[82] 1.10.1. The evangelist agrees in this with the historian when he says that it was "in the fifteenth year of Tiberius Caesar,"[83] which was the fourth year of Pilate's procuratorship, when also Herod, Lysias, and Philip were tetrarchs of Judea, that our Lord and Savior Jesus Christ was thirty years old and when he came to John to be baptized. For this was when he began the proclamation of the gospel.

2. Sacred scripture says that the entire period of his teaching was spent under the high priests Annas and Caiaphas;[84] he

81. Josephus's references are in Schürer, 1.330–57.
82. Cf. *Antiq.* 18.32–35, 88–89. Pilate's term of office is usually dated 26/27–37. Discussion: *Anchor Bible Dictionary*, 5.396–97. On the spurious fourth-century *Acts of Pilate*, see 9.5.1, and Elliott, *Apocryphal New Testament*, 164.
83. Lk 3.1.
84. Lk 3.2; Jn 11.49, 51; 18.13.

began to teach at the beginning of the high priesthood of Annas, and continued on to the beginning of Caiaphas's, making scarcely four years in all. 3. The precepts of the law, moreover, yielding now during that time to violence and corruption, the high-priestly honor was of course given to no one in consideration of his life or birth; the Roman authorities bestowed the high priesthood now on some, now on others, so that they now succeeded each other yearly.[85] 4. Josephus finally records that after Annas there were four who held the high-priestly office in succession until the time of Caiaphas. He says,

"Valerius Gratus drove Annas from the priesthood and appointed Ishmael, son of Baffi, high priest. Shortly afterwards, though, he deposed him and replaced him in the high priesthood with Eleazar, the son of the high priest Annanias. 5. One year later, however, he expelled him from office as well, handing over the high priesthood to one Symon, son of Canifi; he too did not last in office more than one year, and was succeeded by Joseph, also called Caiaphas."[86]

6. And thus the entire time when our Lord and Savior is said to have taught on earth is confined within a space of four years, within which those four successions of the high priesthood are recorded which Josephus mentions, each scarcely lasting a year. The gospel, therefore, agrees with what Josephus writes when it states that Caiaphas was high priest in the year when the Savior suffered. 7. Shortly after he began his preaching, then, our Lord and Savior chose twelve of the disciples from among all of them, and, giving them precedence over his other followers, called them "apostles," according to the special privilege of this choice; "apostle" means "sent." He also chose seventy others after them, whom he sent two by two in advance to each of the places and cities to which he himself was to go.[87]

1.11.1. Now a short time later John the Baptist was executed by Herod's son, Herod; the gospels also tell of this. Josephus in his writings indeed agrees with what they say too: he also mentions Herodias by name, saying that she was removed by

85. Cf. Schürer, 2.227–36.
86. *Antiq.* 18.34–35. "Baffi" is "Phabi" in Josephus, and "Canifi" is "Camith."
87. Mt 10.1–4; Mk 3.14–19; Lk 6.13–16; 10.1.

force from her husband Philip, [Herod's] brother who was still alive, and joined by Herod in an incestuous marriage to himself after he had rejected his own lawful wife.[88] He says that Herodias was the daughter of Aretas, the king of Arabia, and also reports that it was on her account that John the Baptist was killed by [Herod]. 2. He says that war broke out between Aretas and Herod to avenge his daughter's disgrace. Herod's army was wiped out in this war, he says, adding that all of this befell him because of his crime in murdering John.

3. Josephus says as well that John was an exceedingly just man, beyond anyone else, as the gospels confirm, and was beheaded by Herod because of Herodias; it was also because of her that he was driven from his realm and banished to Vienne, a city in Gaul.[89] 4. The following is what he writes in his own words in the eighteenth book of the *Antiquities:*[90]

"It seemed to some of the Jews, however, that Herod's army perished because the divine retribution was stirred against him, and quite justly, to exact satisfaction for John, called 'the Baptist,' 5. an exceptionally good man whom Herod had punished. He had been teaching the Jews to attend to virtue, to practice justice toward each other and piety toward God, and to join together through baptism. For baptism would be acceptable in this way: if it were used not only to wash away sins, but were also practiced for bodily purity and for the justice and purification of the soul,[91] and were considered a sort of seal and faithful guardian of all the virtues together. 6. As he was im-

88. Mt 14.1–12; Mk 6.17–29; Josephus, *Antiq.* 18.109–15. "Removed by force" (*violenter abstractae*): Eusebius says simply that Herod took her away, Josephus that she accepted his proposal of marriage while he was lodging with her husband and her.

89. He was actually banished to Lyons (*Antiq.* 18.252, correcting *Bellum* 2.183).

90. *Antiq.* 18.116–19.

91. ... *baptismum acceptabile fore, si non solum ad abluenda peccata sumatur, verum et ad castimoniam corporis* ... Rufinus here alters the original; Josephus (quoted exactly by Eusebius, as usual) says, "Baptism would be acceptable to [God] if it were not used to win pardon for any sins, but to consecrate the body, the soul having already been purified by just behavior" (*Antiq.* 18.117). This is an example of Rufinus's tendency to conceal any evidence of change in doctrine or discipline in the Christian faith.

parting such precepts to them and immense crowds were gathering to hear him, Herod feared that the people, moved by his teaching, might defect from their king, for he saw that the populace was ready to obey his precepts and counsel in everything. He therefore thought it better to forestall the man by killing him before there was any sign of rebellion, than to experience regret when it was too late, after the disruptions had occurred. Simply from Herod's suspicion, then, John was taken bound to the stronghold of Machaerus and there beheaded."

7. Such are his words about John. Josephus also writes as follows in the same books of his histories about the Savior Lord:

"During these same times there was a wise man, Jesus, if indeed it is right to call him a man. For he was a worker of marvelous deeds and a teacher of those people who are glad to hear the truth. He joined to himself many both of the Jews and of the gentiles. He was [the] Christ. 8. When Pilate ordered that he be crucified, because of the charge brought against him by the leading men of our people, those who had loved him from the beginning did not abandon him. For he appeared to them alive again on the third day, just as the divinely-inspired prophets had foretold: this and countless other miracles that would happen concerning him. The name 'Christian' and the people who derive their name from him, have lasted to the present day."[92]

9. Since, then, the historian of the Hebrews has himself long ago included in his books these matters concerning both John the Baptist and our Lord and Savior—which cannot be denied—there is no means left for these shameless, treacherous folk to avoid being convicted, upon the clearest evidence, of having devised falsely the Acts which they afterwards fabricated. But let that suffice concerning this.

1.12.1. Now the names of the apostles of our Lord and Savior which are recorded are plain to all from the gospels themselves.[93] The names of the seventy disciples, however, we have nowhere found written; one of them, though, is said to be Barnabas, who is also mentioned in the Acts of the Apostles. Paul mentions him as well in his writings. They say, finally, that

92. *Antiq.* 18.63–64.
93. Mt 10.2–4; Mk 3.14–19; Lk 6.13–16.

he is the one who wrote to the Corinthians with Sosthenes and Paul.[94] 2. Now Clement in the fourth book of the *Dispositions*[95] mentions Cephas, of whom Paul says, "But when Cephas came to Antioch, I stood up to him,"[96] and he says that he was one of the seventy disciples and had the same name as the apostle Peter. 3. He also says that Matthias, who was added to the number of the apostles in place of Judas, was one of them, as was the one appointed with him for the drawing of lots.[97] They say that Thaddaeus was another of them;[98] I think it necessary also to tell the story about him which has come down to us. 4. For you will find that the Savior had more than seventy disciples if you observe what Paul shows when he says that after the Resurrection the Lord appeared first to Cephas, then to those eleven, and after them to more than five hundred brothers together, of whom he says that some had fallen asleep, while most were still alive at the time he was writing. 5. He says that afterwards he also appeared to James, who was one of those called the brothers of the Savior. Then after that, as though there were other apostles besides these twelve but resembling them, just as he was, Paul goes on and says, "Afterwards he appeared to all the apostles, but last of all he was also seen by me."[99] That should suffice concerning this.

1.13.1. Now the story about Thaddaeus which we promised runs like this. The divinity of our Lord and Savior Jesus Christ was being talked of in every place because of his miracles; the power he showed in his healings and cures drew countless people, both those nearby and foreigners from afar, especially those who suffered from some disease. 2. Now there was a king named Abgar who was an outstanding ruler of a people beyond the Euphrates, but was himself under the sway of a bodily illness which

94. Acts 4.36; 13.1, etc; Gal 2.1, 13; 1 Cor 1.1.

95. *Dispositiones* = Ὑποτυπώσεις. Eusebius says it was in the fifth book of the *Hypotypōseis;* it is *Fragment* 4 in Otto Stählin, ed., *Clemens Alexandrinus* 3 (GCS 17, 1970), p. 196.

96. Gal 2.11. "Peter" and "Cephas" are distinguished in *Epistula apostolorum* 2.

97. Acts 1.15–26.

98. Mt 10.3; Mk 3.18. Eusebius records here the tradition that listed Thaddaeus's namesake among the seventy disciples.

99. 1 Cor 15.5–8.

defied human skill. When he heard of Jesus's name and of his miraculous powers, he begged him in a letter he sent by someone that he might be released from the bonds of the long illness which oppressed him. 3. The Lord, however, put off working his bodily cure for the time, but he was granted the favor of a letter in answer from the Savior, in which it was at the same time promised him that his desire would soon be fulfilled. 4. Then finally, after the Lord's Resurrection and Ascension into heaven, the apostle Thomas, prompted by God, sent out Thaddaeus, one of the seventy disciples, as an evangelist and preacher of God's word to the city of Edessa; he was at the same time to fulfill what had been promised by the Lord. 5. This is what we found written down in the public records of the city of Edessa, in which the Abgar just mentioned was king, on the pages which in olden times preserved the deeds of King Abgar. As proof of what we say, we subjoin a translation of the very letters from Syriac.[100]

Letter Written to Jesus by King Abgar, Toparch, and Brought to Jerusalem by the Courier Ananias

6. "Abgar, toparch, son of Uchamas,[101] to Jesus the good savior, who has appeared in the region of Jerusalem, greetings! I have heard of you and the cures that you perform: that they

---

100. Abgar V ("Abgar the Black") was king of Edessa, 4 BCE–7 CE, and 13–50 CE. On the document that follows, see Sebastian Brock, "Eusebius and Syriac Christianity," in *Eusebius, Christianity and Judaism*, ed. H. W. Attridge and G. Hata (Detroit, MI: Wayne State University Press, 1992), 212–34. It is paralleled by the Syriac *Teaching of Addai*, whose author "evidently had access to the Syriac original underlying Eusebius's Greek" (Brock, 213). The documents are printed side by side in Brock, 215–21. For a reconsideration of the framework of the account, see Ilaria Ramelli, "Abgar Ukkama e Abgar il Grande alla luce di recenti apporti storiografici," *Aevum* 78/1 (2004): 103–8, and Christian Marek, "Jesus und Abgar. Das Rätsel vom Beginn einer Legende," in *Geschichten und ihre Geschichte*, ed. Therese Fuhrer *et al.* (Basel: Schwabe Verlag, 2004), 269–310. Marek finds the prevailing skepticism concerning the legend somewhat doctrinaire.

101. *Abgarus Uchamae filius* = Ἀβγαρος Οὔχαμα, the second word being actually a transcription of the Syriac for "black." Rufinus seems to have taken the epithet for a patronymic, and thus introduced a new character into western literature.

are accomplished by you without medicaments or herbs, and that with a simple word you make the blind see and the lame walk, that you cleanse lepers and expel demons and unclean spirits, and cure and heal those suffering from chronic illnesses; and that you even revive the dead. 7. After hearing all of these things about you I decided that they meant one of two things: either that you are God and came down from heaven to do these things, or that you are God's son who do these things. 8. In writing to you I would ask you, therefore, that you would deign to undertake the journey to the place where I am and cure the sickness from which I have suffered for so long. For I have also learned that the Jews are grumbling about you and attempting to plot against you. 9. My city, however, small though it is, is respectable, and should suffice for both of us."

Jesus's Reply in Answer to the Toparch Abgar, Brought by the Courier Ananias

10. "Blessed are you who have believed in me, even though you have not seen me. For it is written of me that those who see me will not believe in me, and those who do not themselves see me will believe and live. Concerning what you write to me, however, asking that I come to you, it behooves me to fulfill here everything for which I was sent, and after I have fulfilled it to return to him by whom I was sent. When therefore I have been taken up, I will send you one of my disciples to cure your illness and bestow life upon you and those with you."

11. Attached to the letters was the following as well in Syriac: "Now after Jesus was taken up, Judas, also called Thomas, sent him the apostle Thaddaeus, one of the seventy. When he came, he stayed with Tobias, son of Tobias. When Abgar heard about him, and was told that the apostle of Jesus had come, just as he had written him, 12. and when Thaddaeus began to cure every infirmity and disease with God's power, so that everyone was amazed, Abgar, thinking over the wonders which he was performing, remembered that he would be the one about whom Jesus had written to him, saying, 'When I have been taken up, I will send you one of my disciples to heal your illness.'

13. And calling to his presence Tobias, with whom he was staying, he said to him, 'I have heard that some powerful man has come and is staying in your house; bring him to me.' And when Tobias returned to Thaddaeus, he told him, 'The toparch Abgar has called me to him and told me to bring you to him to cure him.' Thaddaeus said, 'I will come, for it is especially on his account that I have been sent.'

14. "On the following morning, then, Tobias took Thaddaeus to Abgar. And as soon as he went in, Abgar, who had his nobles with him, saw something of divine brightness on the face of the apostle Thaddaeus. When Abgar saw it, he worshiped Thaddaeus, to the amazement of everyone who was attending the king, for they had seen nothing of it; it had been shown to Abgar alone. 15. He began to speak to Thaddaeus: 'You are truly a disciple of Jesus, the Son of God, who told me, "I will send you one of my disciples to cure you and bestow life upon you."' Thaddaeus replied, 'Because you have been wonderful in your belief in him who sent me, I have therefore been sent to you. If you persevere in faith and belief in him, all the desires of your heart will be granted you.' 16. Abgar said to him, 'So utterly have I believed in him, that if only my army were large enough, and if the Roman authorities did not prevent me, I would wish even to butcher the Jews who crucified him.' Thaddaeus replied, 'Our Lord fulfilled his Father's will, and when he had fulfilled it he was taken up again to the Father.' 17. Abgar said to him, 'And I know and believe in him and in his Father.' Thaddaeus replied, 'For that reason I place my hand upon you in his name.' And when he had done so, he was at once freed completely from the illness which had afflicted him.

18. "Abgar was amazed to find that what he had heard about Jesus by word of mouth had been fulfilled by his disciple Thaddaeus in fact and in effect: he had cured him without medicaments and herbs. And he was not alone; when one Abdus, son of Abdas, who suffered from gout, prostrated himself before him, he healed him by laying hands on him, and also healed many other citizens of that city who were afflicted by various ailments. And so while performing great and marvelous works, he preached God's word.

19. "After this, Abgar said to Thaddaeus, 'You are doing these things with God's power, and we are all amazed when we see them. I ask you now: tell me about Jesus's advent, how it happened, and about his power by which he did the things of which I have heard.' 20. Thaddaeus replied, 'I will not speak just now, but since I have been sent to preach the word, gather to me all of your citizens tomorrow, and I will preach before them and sow the word of life in them: how Jesus's advent took place and why, and for what reason he was sent from the Father; the excellent qualities of his deeds and the mysteries about which he spoke in this world and the power by which he performed them. I will also speak of the freshness of his preaching, and of how, being so small and lowly, he thus humbled himself, and, setting aside his majesty, he made little of his godhead, so much so that he was even crucified, descended into hell, broke apart the barrier which from ages past no one had broken, and raised the dead; alone he descended, but he ascended with a great multitude to his Father.'

21. "Abgar therefore ordered all the city-folk to come together at an early hour to hear Thaddaeus's preaching. And afterwards he ordered him to be given gold and silver, but he did not accept it, saying, 'If we have abandoned what is ours, how can we accept what is another's?' 22. These things took place in the 340th year."[102]

It will be useful, I think, to include in this place in our books this material, which we have translated word for word from the Syriac.

---

102. The 340th year of the Edessene calendar is probably 29 CE. Cf. Brock (note 100 above), 231.

BOOK TWO

23. The suffering of James, who was called the Lord's brother

24. That Annianus was ordained the first bishop of the church of Alexandria after Mark

25. The persecution of Nero, under whom Paul and Peter were adorned by their devout profession

26. That the Jews were afflicted by countless evils and finally rose up in arms against the Romans

Preface.1. In the preceding chapter we touched as briefly as possible upon whatever it seemed good to note at the beginning of a church history, concerning either the Savior's divinity or the ancient character of our religion and the antiquity of its teaching, remarking as well that Christianity, however new it may seem, has been handed down from of old; we also included the Advent of our Lord and Savior himself, so recently fulfilled, and completed by his sufferings, and the choosing of the apostles. 2. Let us now see what followed after his Ascension; part of it will be what we teach from the witness of the sacred scriptures, and part of it what we prove from what we have reliably established outside of them in records devised for the memory of posterity.

2.1.1. The first person, then, to be appointed by lot to the apostleship in place of Judas, the betrayer, was Matthias, who was one of the Lord's disciples, as was shown earlier. Seven deacons were also ordained by prayer and the imposition of the apostles' hands, to be of service to the widows. Among them was Stephen, who was also the first after the Lord to be stoned right after his ordination by those who had killed the Lord too; and for this reason he was granted his name, "Stephen," by Christ.[1]

2. Then afterwards the histories also speak of James, who was called the Lord's brother inasmuch as he was the son of Joseph, who was considered the father of Christ because the virgin Mary had in fact been betrothed to him; and before she was united with him she was found to be with child from the Holy Spirit, as the gospels attest.[2] This James, surnamed Justus

1. Cf. 1.12.3; Acts 1.15–26; 6.1–6, 8–60. *Stephanos* means "crown."
2. Mt 1.18.

by those of old on account of his virtues and excellence of life, was the first, the histories say, to receive the chair of the church in Jerusalem; 3. so says Clement in the sixth book of the *Dispositions:*

"After the Savior was taken up, Peter and James and John, although they had been given precedence by him over almost everyone else, did not claim for themselves the glory of supremacy, but appointed James, surnamed Justus, bishop of the apostles."[3]

4. The same author adds the following about him in the seventh book of the same work:

"After the Resurrection, the Lord handed on all knowledge to James, surnamed Justus, and to John and Peter, and they to the other apostles. Those apostles handed it on to those seventy disciples, of whom one was Barnabas. 5. We know that there were two Jameses: one was this one named Justus, who was thrown down from the pinnacle of the temple, struck with a fuller's club, and handed over to death, while the other was the one who was beheaded by Herod."[4]

Paul too mentions this James Justus when he writes, "I saw none other of the apostles except James, the Lord's brother."[5] 6. It was also at this time that Thaddaeus, whom we mentioned earlier, 7. was sent at the Lord's bidding to King Abgar and not only released him from his bodily illness, but also joined the whole city of Edessa to Christ the Lord with a faith so strong that to this very day that city is dedicated to Christ with a particular devotion, since it merited to receive something written by the Lord and Savior himself.

8.[6] Meanwhile the first persecution against God's church, which took place in Jerusalem at the time of the first martyr, Stephen, scattered all the disciples, except for the twelve, through all of Judea and Samaria; or rather, as the sacred scrip-

---

3. *apostolorum episcopum* = ἐπίσκοπον τῶν Ἱεροσολύμων ("bishop of Jerusalem"). On James's being called "Justus," see 2.23.4. On Clement's *Dispositions,* see Book 1, note 95. This fragment is 10. On James's appointment by Christ and the apostles, see 7.19.

4. James and the fuller's club: 2.23. James and Herod: Acts 12.2. *Dispositions* (*Hypotypōseis*) *Fr.* 13.

5. Gal 1.19.

6. The background to 2.1.8–11 is in Acts 8.1–13.

ture shows, it disseminated them. A number of them went to Phoenicia, and as far as Cyprus and Antioch; they did not yet venture to entrust the mystery of faith to the gentiles, but proclaimed it to the Jews.

9. Paul meanwhile was ravaging the church, entering houses and dragging men and women off to prison. 10. But Philip, one of the seven ordained deacons with Stephen, went down to Samaria filled with the Lord's power, and was the first to proclaim God's word to the Samaritan people. The divine grace in him worked to such effect that he confounded even Simon Magus with his preaching; the latter was so famous at the time among the Samaritans, that he was thought to be the great power of God. 11. But when he saw the signs and miracles worked by Philip through the power of divine grace, he yielded in his astonishment and fear and pretended to believe in Christ, going so far as to accept baptism.

12. What is really astounding is that even today the same procedure is followed by those who have received from him a sort of inherited simulation belonging to this impurest of sects, and who, trained as they are in the craft of their founder, enter the church by some deception, steal its bath, and defile what is holy to us as with the contagion of some disease. For their poisonous speech crawls among the flocks like a canker, the secret bites of their words infecting the careless with a deadly virus, until the shepherd's attentiveness searches out and brings to light their malignant secrets, just as he himself, when caught by Simon Peter's diligence, paid the penalty he deserved.[7]

13. Now as the proclamation of the divine word was progressing day by day, there arrived from the territory of Ethiopia, through God's providence, an official of the queen of that nation—for it is the custom of that people even now to be ruled by women—whose purpose it was to discharge his vows in Jerusalem. Philip, prompted by the Holy Spirit, handed on to him, as the first of all the gentiles, the mystery of faith and the sacrament of baptism, and consecrated him to God as a sort of firstfruits of all the nations.[8] It is thought that upon his return to his

7. Acts 8.9–24. More about Simon in 2.13–14.
8. Acts 8.26–39.

homeland, he preached to the native peoples the knowledge of the supreme God and the salvific foreknowledge of our Lord, as it had been handed on to him. In this the events themselves fulfilled through him the prophecy which runs: 14. "Ethiopia will be the first with its hands to God."[9] While this was going on, Paul, the chosen vessel, not from human beings or through a human being, but through the revelation of Jesus Christ and God the Father, who raised him from the dead, was called to the apostleship by a heavenly voice coming down to him.[10]

2.2.1. In the meantime, the happy news of the Resurrection and miracles of our Lord Jesus Christ, and of his Ascension to heaven, had now spread through every place, and this blessed rumor had reached every ear, and since it was the Roman custom of old that the governors of the provinces should report to the sovereign or the senate anything new that happened in the provinces of which they had charge, lest they seem unaware of anything that was taking place, Pilate reported to the emperor Tiberius the Resurrection from the dead of our Lord and Savior Jesus Christ, and the rest of his miracles, 2. adding that, since he had risen after his death, he was now believed by a great many to be God.[11] Tiberius reported what he had learned to the senate. The senate, though, is said to have disregarded it, inasmuch as the news had not been reported to it first, but popular opinion had usurped its own authority. For there was a law established of old that no one might be considered a god by the Romans who had not been confirmed by the decree and pronouncement of the senate. The real reason why this happened, however, was lest the divine power be thought to stand in need of human support.

3. The senate, then, withheld its approval, according to what we have just said, but Tiberius held to his judgment that nothing should be done in opposition to the teaching of Christ. 4. Tertullian, a man supremely knowledgeable about Roman laws and customs and quite famous among our writers, reports this

9. Ps 67.32 (LXX).
10. Gal 1.1; Acts 9.3–6; 22.6–10; 26.12–18.
11. Tertullian mentions Pilate's report to Tiberius in *Apologeticum* 21.24; cf. also Elliott, 205–8.

matter in the following way in his *Apology*, which he wrote for our faith against the gentiles:

5. "To review briefly the origin of laws of this sort, there was a decree of old that no god should be deified by an emperor, unless he had been approved by the senate. Marcus Aemilius knows this about his god Alburnus. And this supports our argument, because among you divinity is granted according to human judgment, and if a god does not please a human being, he will not be a god, so it is humans who will have to be propitious to gods. 6. Tiberius, then, in whose time the name 'Christian' entered into the world, received from Palestine in Syria the report which disclosed the reality of this divinity and passed it on to the senate with the prior verdict of his own favorable endorsement; the senate, because it had not itself approved it, rejected it. Caesar held to his judgment, threatening to punish those who accused Christians." So says Tertullian.[12]

It was assuredly divine providence that pushed this into Caesar's mind, so that the gospel message might speed to every place without hindrance, in the very beginning at least.

2.3.1. Hence it came about that it suddenly lit up the whole earth with the brightness of celestial light, like radiance issuing from heaven or a ray bursting from the sun, that the prophecy might be fulfilled which runs, "Their sound has gone out into all the earth"—that of the evangelists and apostles, that is— "and to the ends of the earth their words."[13] 2. From this time on, great crowds of people in every city and village gathered to the churches like grain to the threshing-floor at harvest-time. Those among them who were held fast by the fetters of unhealthy superstition handed on to them by their ancestors, once they had been freed as though from tyrannical domination by the teaching of Christ together with the miracles they saw happening, and had received the knowledge of the true God, came

---

12. Rufinus here simply copies out Tertullian, *Apologeticum* 5.1–2, rather than translating him back into Latin. It is uncertain who Marcus Aemilius and Alburnus were (the same incident is mentioned by Tertullian in *Ad nationes* 1.10.14). The senate's regulation of deification is treated by Th. Mommsen, *Römisches Staatsrecht* 3.1049–51.

13. Ps 18.5 (LXX).

to the one true God and Lord, and their Creator, acknowledging him sincerely and ruing their former error.

3. When therefore the divine condescension was being poured out more generously now upon all peoples everywhere, even the gentiles, Cornelius, in Caesarea in Palestine, an enormous city, was the first of them to be brought with his whole house to faith in Christ under Peter's ministry.[14] From then on a great number of other gentiles in Antioch came to believe, drawn by the preaching of those who, as we said earlier, had been disseminated through every place by the violence unleashed against Stephen. It was through them that there was gathered in Antioch a most vibrant church, in which there were also a great many men of the prophetic order, among them Barnabas and Paul. With all of them living equally in God's grace and unanimity, it was there that the disciples were first called Christians, the word taken as though from an ever-flowing spring. 4. It was at this time that Agabus, one of the prophets there, forewarned in divine utterance that a severe famine was coming. Paul and Barnabas were sent to Jerusalem with alms collected from the brothers to assist the saints.

2.4.1. Tiberius meanwhile reached the end of his life after reigning for about twenty-two years. Gaius succeeded him as sovereign and immediately handed over the government of the Jews to Agrippa, together with the tetrarchies of Philip and Lysanias; shortly afterwards he gave him Herod's as well. Herod himself, who had brought about John's murder and taken part in the Lord's passion, he sentenced to perpetual banishment after he had been tortured in many different ways, as Josephus writes in the passages we cited earlier.[15]

---

14. Acts 10. For the rest of 2.3.3–4, see Acts 11.19–30. "As we said earlier" in the next sentence refers to 2.1.8.

15. "Cited earlier": cf. 1.11.3. Tiberius reigned from August 29, 14, to March 16, 37, and was succeeded by Gaius Caligula, who in 39 banished Herod Antipas to Lyons on various charges, and handed over his tetrarchy to his accuser, Agrippa I, one of Herod the Great's grandsons. Cf. Josephus, *Bellum* 2.181–83; *Antiq.* 18.224–55; Schürer, 1.340–53. Eusebius says nothing about Herod being tortured, only that he was punished by perpetual exile "on account of his many offenses (πλείστων ἕνεκα ... αἰτιῶν)." This becomes *multis excruciatum modis* in Rufinus, who may have read αἰκιῶν.

2. It was at this time that Philo flourished, the most distinguished of writers, who was considered the first among the first not only in our disciplines but in those of the pagans as well. While Hebrew in ancestry, he was more famous and renowned in Alexandria than any of the other men of fame and renown. 3. And his talent and achievement in the study of the divine laws and ancestral traditions will be evident to all from the writings he has left us. It would be difficult to indicate adequately his knowledge of literature, or of philosophy, and particularly his ability in the study of Plato and Pythagoras, where he outdid all of his contemporaries and almost all of those who preceded him.

2.5.1. He was the one who told in five books all of the evils that befell the Jews in Gaius's time.[16] He also mentions Gaius's insanity, saying that he became so arrogant that he wanted to be called a god. And in those same books, where he tells of the calamities of the Jews, he also describes his own embassy which he undertook to the city of Rome for his fellow tribesmen, the Jews, and how, when he pleaded the case for his ancestral laws in Gaius's presence, he returned home with nothing but mockery; he almost met his death, in fact. 2. Josephus also mentions these matters in the eighteenth book of his *Antiquities*,[17] where he writes,

"And when in fact strife broke out in Alexandria between the Jews and the pagans, 3. three representatives from each party were sent to Gaius; one of the representatives of the pa-

16. On the relationship of these five books to Philo's surviving *In Flaccum* and *De legatione ad Gaium*, see F. H. Colson, *Philo* X (Loeb, 1971), xvi–xxvi. On the frequent difficulty of matching the traditional titles to Philo's surviving works, see *The Cambridge Companion to Philo,* ed. Adam Kamesar (Cambridge, 2009), 32–64.

17. *Antiq.* 18.257–60. The emperor Caligula's desire to be worshiped soon became notorious, and the refusal of the Jews to do so gave the Alexandrians an excuse to vent their chronic hostility against them. They were abetted in this by the governor of Egypt, A. Avillius Flaccus, and the arrival of Agrippa I in Alexandria in August of 38 was greeted with outrageous demonstrations and demands that statues of the emperor should be set up in the Jewish synagogues. This and the other anti-Jewish measures that followed led to the dispatch to the emperor, in 40, of two delegations from Alexandria, of the Jews and of the pagans, the former headed by Philo. Cf. Schürer, 1.388–98.

gan party was someone named Apion. While he had a great many things with which to charge the Jews, his chief accusation was that they did not pay honor to Caesar, as was the custom with everyone subject to Roman authority. They erected, he said, neither altars nor temples to Gaius, nor anything else of the sort in which divine honors were paid to him by the provincials. They were the only ones who neither decreed statues to him nor took the oath sworn in his name. 4. When Apion had brought up these and more serious matters by which he thought he might rouse Gaius, Philo, a man of the highest ability, knowledgeable about philosophy, brother of Alexander the Alabarch, and head of the Jewish embassy, swept the charges powerfully aside. 5. But Gaius rebuffed him and ordered him to leave his presence at once while in his fury he mulled over what sort of evil he might bring upon them. When Philo went out bearing the insult, he said to the Jews gathered around him: 'We must be of good cheer if Gaius is angry with us, since divine assistance must needs be present where that which is human has failed.'"

6. Thus far Josephus. Philo himself in the very book which he wrote about his embassy relates in detail everything which he did. I will mention only those things which will show the readers clearly the divine retribution which they suffered for the crimes they dared to commit against Christ. 7. He tells first of all how in Tiberius's time, Seianus in the city of Rome, who was in high standing with the emperor, did his best to wipe out their entire nation, while in Judea Pilate, under whom the crime was committed against the Savior, upset them completely when he tried to violate the temple, which at that time remained still intact in Jerusalem.[18]

2.6.1. After Tiberius's death his successor Gaius too, he says,

18. L. Aelius Seianus acquired immense power under Tiberius, especially after the latter retired from Rome in 26. He expected his own images to be worshiped (Dio Cassius 58.4.4; 58.11.2; Suetonius, *Tiberius* 48.2). The Jewish refusal to do so made him anxious to wipe out their whole nation (*Flaccus* 1; *Legatio* 159–161). The reference to Pilate's violation of the temple concerns his appropriation of the temple treasures to build an aqueduct to Jerusalem (cf. Schürer, 1.385).

while he treated a great many others harshly, was most bitterly cruel to the Jewish people, as may easily be learned from what the same writer says:

2. "Gaius's character was deeply perverted, as he showed to all people, but especially to the Jewish nation. It was with a particular savagery that he ordered that, beginning in Alexandria, their places which they have consecrated for divine worship should be seized and desecrated in violation of the religion and custom of the people by being filled with his statues, standards, and images. The temple in the holy city as well, which alone had remained untouched by this wholesale sacrilegious contagion and since ancestral times had continued on as a refuge, he dared to transform into a temple bearing his own name, so that it would be called the 'Sanctuary of the God Gaius, the New Zeus most Noble.'"[19]

3. And our author continues in the second book of his work *On the Virtues* with the countless other calamities, surpassing anything bewailed in tragedy, that were inflicted on the Jews in Alexandria under Gaius. And what Josephus writes about Pilate's time agrees with this when in the second book of *The Jewish War* he mourns over the evils which befell the whole people for their crimes against the Savior. 4. Listen to what he says:

"Pilate, the procurator sent by Tiberius to Judea, ordered Caesar's images to be brought covered into Jerusalem by night and set up. When day broke, this threw the Jewish people into great confusion, amazed and upset as they were at this new sight. For they supposed from this that their laws and all their ancestral customs were now being scorned and despised, since it had been unlawful for their forebears to have anything of the sort within the walls of that city."[20]

---

19. *Legatio* 346. Gaius's identification of himself with Jupiter and his command that sacrifice be offered to him: Dio Cassius 59.44; 59.26.5, 8; 59.28.3–7; Suetonius, *Gaius* 22; 57; Josephus, *Antiq.* 19.4. His plan to erect his statue in the temple in Jerusalem: *Antiq.* 18.261–309 (he desisted at Agrippa's request: 289–300). Also *Bellum* 2.184–204; Schürer, 1.394–96. Eusebius's citations of Philo in 2.5.7 and 2.6.2 are studied by Sabrina Inowlocki, "Philo's *Legatio ad Gaium* in Eusebius of Caesarea's Works," *Studia Philonica* 16 (2004): 30–49.

20. Cf. Philo, *Legatio* 299–305 (*De virtutibus* is an alternate title); Josephus, *Bellum* 2.169; *Antiq.* 18.55–59; Schürer, 1.380–81.

5. But this was of course the swift retribution punishing them for their irreligious declaration when, as the gospel reports, the whole people shouted together, "We have no king but Caesar!"[21] 6. Then the same writer mentions another form of retaliation inflicted on them when he says,

"After this they were once again upset when they saw the sacred funds, which are called *korbanas* in their native language, transferred unlawfully to profane expenditure for a public aqueduct stretching to a length of three hundred stadia; the people were infuriated at this. 7. And when Pilate came to Jerusalem, they dared to approach him and weary him with their clamor. He had foreseen that there would be a riot, so he had mixed his soldiers in with the crowd of commoners, their weapons concealed, having ordered them to use clubs, not swords, on the rioters. And when the time came and the signal was given from the dais, they began to be struck and knocked down, and a lot of them perished from the injuries they got from being beaten, but even more of them from being trampled on by the crowds of their fellows when they turned to headlong flight. The rest scattered and, frightened by the deaths of their fellows, buried their grief under silence."[22]

8. The same writer explains that many additional catastrophes befell them in Jerusalem while they kept plotting rebellion, showing that after the time of the sacrilege they committed, neither the mania for rebellion nor wars nor deaths ever departed from them, until at last, in Vespasian's time, the final, lethal evil of the siege closed round them. To this did the divine retribution sentence the Jews for the crime they had committed.

2.7. As for Pilate, who fulfilled the office of an evil judge against the Savior, he was tormented by such and so many catastrophic evils in this same time of Gaius, that he is said to have transfixed himself with his own hand and to have thrown away his wicked life with violence, nor could the agent of such an enormity escape unpunished, as we find in the histories of the

21. Jn 19.15.
22. *Bellum* 2.175–77. Parallel: *Antiq.* 18.60–62. On the temple treasures, cf. Schürer, 2.279–81. On the incident, Schürer, 1.385.

pagans, those, that is, who record the Olympiads and compose the chronicles for the memory of posterity.[23]

2.8.1. Now when Gaius had reigned for not even four years, he was succeeded as emperor by Claudius, under whom a severe famine took hold of the whole earth. Our prophets, however, had long before foretold that it would happen: the Acts of the Apostles relates that a prophet named Agabus announced that there would be a widespread famine under the emperor Claudius. 2. Luke, who tells this of Agabus, adds that each person sent as great a donation as he could through the brothers Paul and Barnabas, who were in Antioch, to the holy ones living in Jerusalem. And he goes on,

2.9.1. "Now at that time," meaning obviously the time when the famine took place under Claudius, "King Herod put forth his hands to strike certain members of the church, and he killed James, the brother of John, with the sword."[24] 2. Clement of Alexandria in the seventh book of his *Dispositions* tells a story about this James, which came to him from the tradition of his predecessors and which is worth recording:

"Because the one who had delivered him," James that is, "to the judge for martyrdom was moved to acknowledge that he too was a Christian, both were taken together to be tortured. 3. And while they were on the way, he asked James to pardon him. He thought for a moment, and then said, 'Peace be with you,' and kissed him. And so both were beheaded together."

4. But then, he says,[25] as the holy scripture relates, when Herod saw that the murder of James was welcome to the Jews, he went further and put Peter in prison, planning doubtless to punish him as well. [Which he would have done] if divine assistance had not arrived in the person of an angel who came to him at night, miraculously released him from his fetters, and

23. No such record is found in the extant pagan histories; on Christian legends of his suicide, cf. Schürer, 1.387n144.

24. Acts 11.27–12.2. Also on the famine: Dio Cassius 60.11.1–5; Tacitus, *Annals* 12.43. Gaius reigned from March 16, 37, to January 24, 41.

25. The phrase "he says" (*inquit*) is not in Eusebius, and is Rufinus's way of marking the following passage (from Acts 12.3–11) as included in *Hypotypōseis*, Fr. 14.

bade him go forth free to the ministry of preaching. This then is what happened with Peter.

2.10.1. The king's crime committed against the apostles allowed of no delay in requital, however; the right hand of God brought retribution at once, as the story contained in the Acts of the Apostles teaches us:

"When Herod had come down to Caesarea and had sat down before the dais on the appointed day dressed in a splendid royal robe, and was addressing the people from on high, and when the people shouted to him, 'God, not man, is speaking!' an angel of God struck him at once because he had not given the glory to God, and swarming with worms he expired."[26]

2. Now it is marvelous to see how closely the sacred scriptures agree with the historian of that nation. For Josephus, recording the same event in the nineteenth book of the *Antiquities*,[27] reports it in the following words:

3. "He had completed the third year of his rule over all of Judea, when it happened that he came to Caesarea, which had formerly been called Pyrgos Stratonis. He was putting on performances for the citizens there in honor of Caesar, it being a festal day dedicated to Caesar's welfare, it seems, and the men from the whole province who were high in rank and office had gathered, when, on the second day of the performances, 4. arrayed in a shining robe marvelously woven of gold and silver, he made his way to the theater at the beginning of the day. There, when the first rays of the sun smote the silver robe full on, the brilliance of the glittering metal flooded the spectators with a redoubled light in the reflected radiance, so that the terror of the sight dazzled the onlookers, and the presumptuousness of the craftsman worked a deception thereby that was beyond what is natural to humankind.[28] 5. The crowd broke immediately into shouts of flattery which resounded with esteem but redounded to his doom, and from every side he was acclaimed by the audience as a god, the people begging him to be pro-

---

26. Acts 12.19, 21–23.

27. *Antiq.* 19.343–51. The "third year" referred to below is 44.

28. ... *ut ... per hoc plus aliquid de eo, quam humanae naturae est, artifex adrogantia mentiretur ...* : Rufinus adds.

pitious with the words, 'Heretofore we feared you as a man; henceforth we acknowledge that you are above humankind.' 6. The king, however, neither checked the unlawful acclamation nor shuddered at the impiety of the improper flattery, until looking around a little later he saw an angel[29] looming over his head, and perceived at once that he whom he had known as the provider of good was now the agent of his doom. 7. And behold, he was seized at once by a torment of incredible stomach pain and respiration, and looking around at his friends, he said,

"'Behold me, this god of yours; see how I am being pushed and driven from life immediately, because the divine power is of course proving false the statements just made about me, and I whom you were just now calling immortal am even now being snatched away in haste to death. But the sentence which God has passed must be accepted. For we have lived a life not to be scorned, and the age which we have attained is thought blessed.'

"When he had said this, he was attacked by the pain more severely and was at once carried back to the palace. 8. When it was reported that he was near death, an enormous crowd of every age and sex came together and, prostrate upon haircloth according to ancestral custom, begged almighty God to preserve the king, while the entire royal house resounded with groans and lamentation. The king himself meanwhile was reclining on a lofty balcony, and when he looked down and saw everyone lying prostrate and weeping, he could not refrain from tears himself. 9. And after being tormented for five days successively by stomach pains, he departed from life in agony in his fifty-fourth year, the seventh of his reign. For he had reigned for four years under Gaius Caesar when he had Philip's tetrarchy for three years, adding Herod's to it in the fourth year, and completing the three remaining years under Claudius Caesar."

10. I am amazed that Josephus agrees here so completely with sacred scripture, as he does in so many other instances.

---

29. Eusebius replaces Josephus's owl with an angel (in accordance with Acts 12.23).

As far as his sole difference goes, concerning the king's name, the time, the events, and the topic show that it was the same king, so that it may be that, as we have found to be true of many other Jewish names, he too had two names, one of which Luke used, and the other Josephus.[30]

2.11.1. Now Luke in Acts also presents Gamaliel speaking as follows at the time when the apostles were being discussed in a meeting of the Jews: "One Theudas arose who claimed to be a magician; he was destroyed, and all who followed him were dispersed." Let us then see what Josephus writes about him as well in the same book.[31]

2. "When Fadus was procurator of Judea, some imposter, a magician named Theudas, persuaded a multitude of the people to take what they owned, leave the cities, and settle on the banks of the Jordan River. He also said he was a prophet and could part the waters of the river with a word of command and give his followers an easy crossing of the river. 3. He deceived many by saying so. But Fadus did not indulge his madness for long, but sent a troop of cavalry which charged down upon them unexpectedly, killing a great number of them and taking many others alive; the severed head of Theudas himself it sent to Jerusalem."

After this the same writer mentions the famine which occurred under Claudius. His words:

2.12.1. "At this time a widespread famine besieged even Judea, during which Queen Helena, as she was named, purchased grain at great expense from Egypt, brought it to Jerusalem, and distributed it to the needy."[32]

2. Nothing could agree more closely than do these words with what is found in the Acts of the Apostles: "The disciples

30. He was Herod Agrippa I (in contrast to Herod Antipas in 2.10.9 just above); cf. Schürer, 1.442n1.

31. Acts 5.36; *Antiq.* 20.97–98. Cuspius Fadus was procurator 44(?)–46. Schürer, 1.455–56.

32. *Antiq.* 20.101. Helena was the mother of King Izates of Adiabene, both of them converts to Judaism. Her story is in *Antiq.* 20.17–96. She happened to be visiting Jerusalem at the time of the famine and brought grain for it: 20.51–53. Schürer, 3.163–65.

who were in Antioch sent a donation to the holy ones in Judea, each contributing what he could; it was brought by Barnabas and Paul and distributed by the elders."[33] 3. This Helena mentioned by the historian has an imposing tomb still to be seen before the gates of Jerusalem, although she is said to have ruled Adiabene.

2.13.1. Meanwhile, since the faith of our Lord and Savior Jesus Christ was growing in the minds of all, and his religion was daily increasing, the enemy of human welfare by no means remained quiet, but came first to the greatest of cities, the head of all of them, and to it summoned Simon, about whom we spoke earlier.[34] Seconding his nefarious arts with his own greater resources, he clapped most of the citizens of that city into the fetters of his error. 2. Justin, the man who excels among writers and who was born not long after the time of the apostles, describes these matters; I will set out what pertains to him in the proper place.[35] He relates these things in the following way in the *Apology* which he wrote on behalf of our faith to the emperor Antoninus:

3. "And after the Ascension of the Lord into heaven, the demons stirred up some men who called themselves gods and whom we drove away. Lastly someone named Simon, a Samaritan from a village called Gitta, was raised up in Claudius Caesar's time by magical arts and demonic assistance in your city, which rules over all; most people having been deceived by his illusions, he was pronounced a god and was granted the honor of a statue among you as a god; it was placed on the Tiber River between two bridges and bore the inscription written in Latin: 'To the Holy God Simon.' 4. Almost all the Samaritans and quite a few from other peoples worshiped and acknowledged him as the highest god. They have also deified with him, as a sort of first mind, one Selene, his companion in error and deception; she was formerly in a brothel in Tyre, a city in Phoenicia."[36]

---

33. Acts 11.29–30.   34. Cf. 2.1.10–12.

35. 4.11.8–4.12; 4.16–18.

36. *Apol.* 1.26.1–3. Claudius reigned 41–54. The testimony about Simon given by Justin (100–165) is the earliest after the New Testament, Justin's own Samaritan origins lending it weight. He is wrong, though, about the inscrip-

5. Thus far Justin. Irenaeus agrees with him in what he writes in the first book of *Against the Heresies*,[37] in which he fully relates both who Simon himself was, and how impure his works and teaching were. It is too much to include here, since those who wish to know about these things in detail may learn thoroughly from Irenaeus's own books about him and about the other founders of the various sects and about their poisonous doctrines. 6. Simon, then, we are told, was the source of the whole perversion and the origin of every heresy. From his time down to the present, his followers, while feigning to betake themselves to the purest philosophy, that of the Christians, which they see admired by all for its integrity of life and holiness of manners, have again been fastened in the fetters of the idolatrous superstition which they appeared to abandon, worshiping and venerating the picture and image of Simon and of that Selene who we said was his companion in misdeed and disgrace. To them they offer the fragrance of incense; to them they offer sacrifices and impure libations.

7. But they commit acts even more depraved and detestable than these. For they say that some of their customs are so indescribable that, when one first hears of them, one loses one's senses, and, as though stunned by their force, remains dazed and even driven mad. That being so, they say that it is impossible either to write them down or to communicate them by word of mouth. Those who hear this are so awed that they believe it to be so. And the things are furthermore of the sort which for their sheer impurity and obscenity will be abhorrent and detestable to chaste and decent ears. 8. Whatever one could imagine that is disgraceful and impure would not, it is said, be as impure as they. The devotees of this filthiest of sects affirm that they keep this business a secret hidden away among them-

tion on the statue on the Tiber island, which he gives as SIMONI DEO SANC-TO; it actually reads SEMONI SANCO DEO FIDIO (*CIL* 6.567), Semo Sancus being an old Latin god of obscure credentials.

In 13.4 and 6 Rufinus, with the Syriac translator, reads "Selene" instead of the "Helena" in Justin and Eusebius; this variant is also found in the Pseudo-Clementine *Recognitions* 2.8.1 and 2.9.1.

37. 1.23.1–4.

selves, in this way abominably duping unhappy women who are burdened with sins, as the apostle says.[38]

2.14.1. This Simon, then, was the father and originator at this time of such evils, he whom the devil raised up from among his attendants and compelled to go to the greatest of cities, Rome, that he might offer resistance there to those mightiest of athletes, the apostles of our Lord and Savior Jesus Christ, who had been sent by him in his place for just this purpose. 2. But the divine power and grace never abandons its own, especially in the battle that is the greatest; it quenches with all swiftness the fire that has been kindled by the evil one, and destroys every height that exalts itself against the knowledge of God.[39] 3. That was why neither Simon nor anyone else who clashed with the apostles then could prevail, because the light of truth and the brightness of the divine word, which had recently shone forth for the salvation of humankind, were dispersing the darkness of this entire falsehood and driving the mists of ignorance from human minds. 4. In the end, the aforesaid magician suffered blindness at once in his disturbed mind when, smitten by the brilliance of the true light, he, being the one who had previously been convicted by the apostle Peter in Judea for the misdeeds he had committed,[40] fled across the sea and made his way from the east to the west, hoping to find refuge only in flight.

5. He therefore entered the city of Rome, and, assisted by the demonic power that stood by him and clung to him—they call it a *paredros*—made in a short time such progress in evil that he was even granted by the Roman citizens the honor of an image as though he were a god.[41] 6. But the fabricated divinity did not maintain the deception for long. For in this same time of Claudius, divine providence in its kindness brought forthwith to the city of Rome that most estimable of all the

38. 2 Tm 3.6. Since, according to 2.13.6, Simon was the originator of all heresies, the practices here referred to may be those attributed to the "Gnostics" in Epiphanius, *Pan.* 26.

39. 2 Cor 10.5.

40. Acts 8.18–24.

41. On *paredros,* cf. Eusebius, 4.7.9; on the image, cf. 2.13.3.

apostles, Peter, the greatest in the magnificence of his faith and the first in rank among the first, that he might contend against the common bane of the human race, since he was a leader and commander of the divine forces with the knowledge to wage God's battles and lead his soldiers. He came from the east like a heavenly merchant bringing the wares of the divine light to those prepared to buy them, and with the word of the salvific message was the first in the city of Rome to open the door of the heavenly kingdom with the keys of his gospel.

2.15.1. When therefore the bright light of God's word appeared for the city of Rome, Simon's darkness was extinguished with its originator.[42]

Now the message of truth and light proclaimed by Peter illuminated everyone's mind with its agreeable words, so that those who heard him each day could never get enough. So they were not satisfied with just listening, but all of them begged his disciple Mark to write down what he was preaching, that they might have a permanent record of it and be able to continue reflecting on his words at home and away. Nor did they stop begging him until they got what they wanted. This was why the gospel called "According to Mark" came to be written. 2. Peter, when he discovered through the Holy Spirit that his spiritual property had been filched from him, was delighted by the faith they had shown thereby, and, considering their devotion, he confirmed what had been done and handed on the writing to the churches to be read permanently. Clement in the sixth book of the *Dispositions* relates that this was so done, and the bishop of Hierapolis, Papias, supports him; the latter adds that Peter, in his first letter, which he writes from the city of Rome, and in which he calls Rome "Babylon" figuratively, mentions Mark when he says, "the chosen one in Babylon greets you, as does Mark my son."[43]

42. For Peter's debates with Simon, see *Clementine Recognitions* 1.72–3.49; *Clementine Homilies* 2.35; 3.29–30; 3.38–43; 3.58; 16–19. Simon's departure for Rome and Peter's decision to follow him are in *Recognitions* 3.63–65; their combat in Rome with wonders and words are in *Acts of Peter* 4–32; Simon's defeat is in *Apostolic Constitutions* 6.9.

43. 1 Pt 5.13. There is more on Papias in 3.3.9. On Peter and Mark cf. 3.39.15; 6.14.5–7.

2.16.1 They say that this Mark was the first to travel to Egypt and there preach the gospel which he had written, and that he was the first to establish the church in Alexandria. 2. It is also said that when he began, such a multitude of men and women believed and were brought together by the example of his sobriety and continence, that the very customs of those who had come to believe through him, and their frugal and modest dinners, were described in the books of that most learned man Philo, 2.17.1. who, we are told, came to Rome in the time of the emperor Claudius, saw the apostle Peter, and clung to his discourses as he preached the word of God. This seems quite likely, since we know that the writing of which we spoke was composed afterwards. It is quite clear that it includes all the customs of the church which were then handed down and are still observed by us.

2. He also describes clearly the lives of the ascetics, those, that is, who are now in the churches and monastic houses.[44] Hence he quite plainly shows that he not only knew our manner of life but embraced it, since he praised to the skies the apostolic men of his time, the believers who were for the most part, as far as we can tell, from the Hebrew people, since we know that those of the Israelites who became believers in the apostles' time adhered still to Jewish customs and the observances of the law. 3. When describing this matter in the treatise which he entitled *The Contemplative Life or Suppliants,* he accordingly adds nothing on his own or from an extraneous source, but says first of all that the men are called "worshipers," and the women with them likewise. The name comes from the fact either that they cultivated the coarse and untaught souls of those who gathered to them, or that they persevered in the worship of God with a pure and unblemished conscience.[45]

44. *eorum dumtaxat qui nunc in ecclesiis vel monasteriis degunt:* Rufinus adds.

45. Eusebius cites Philo, *De vita contemplativa* 2, who explains that the group called *therapeutai/therapeutrides* receive their name from the spiritual remedy provided from their way of life, or from their worship. Rufinus translates their name as *cultores/cultrices,* which shares with the Greek original the notion of "worship," but not that of "healing," and so he modifies the exegesis to give it a more appropriately agricultural tone.

Eusebius and Rufinus assume that Philo is describing an actual group of ascetics; in modern times it has been suggested that he intended a figurative

4. Whether he himself gave the name to those first [believers], deriving it from how they behaved, or whether those who lived according to the gospel were really called such in the beginning before the name "Christian" had spread to every place, does not matter, as long as the name is validated by the reality of those to whom it belongs.

5. He says then first of all that those who adopt this way of life give up all their property and yield their possessions to those concerned.[46] Then he says that they all firmly reject the cares of life, leave the city, and dwell in gardens and tiny plots of land, shunning associations with different ends in view and comrades who live differently, knowing that such things are an obstacle to those who choose to enter upon the hard road to virtue. Such was the rule of life said to have been followed by those first believers, spurred as they were by the ardor of their faith, 6. as we clearly read in the Acts of the Apostles; they sold their possessions and lands and placed the proceeds at the feet of the apostles, and they were shared out to each according to need, so that no one among them was needy.[47] 7. Since therefore he writes that those in Alexandria who believed acted like those in Jerusalem who had believed before, one can be sure that the same behavior and the same customs indicate beyond any doubt the same religious faith. To sum up, he begins the book we mentioned as follows:[48]

---

account of the ideal Jewish life or a utopian portrayal: cf., e.g., Troels Engberg-Pedersen, "Philo's *De vita contemplativa* as a Philosopher's Dream," *Journal for the Study of Judaism* 30 (1999): 40–64, and Mary Ann Beavis, "Philo's Therapeutai: Philosopher's Dream or Utopian Construction?" *Journal for the Study of the Pseudepigrapha and Related Literature* 14 (2004): 30–42.

46. ... *bonis suis quibus interest* [*cedunt*] = ἐξίστασθαι τοῖς προσήκουσι τῶν ὑπαρχόντων. The Greek *can* bear Rufinus's translation, but προσήκοντες can also mean "kin," and this is what the original in Philo, 13, clearly says: they yielded their property to their relatives. Eusebius may have chosen the equivocal word in his paraphrase of Philo in order to obscure the original (without precisely falsifying it), since he wants to enlist him as a witness to the lifestyle of the primitive Christian community. Cf. Sabrina Inowlocki, "Eusebius of Caesarea's *Interpretatio Christiana* of Philo's *De vita contemplativa*," *Harvard Theological Review* 97 (2004): 305–28.

47. Acts 4.32–35.

48. "begins the book": Eusebius says, "continues as follows." There follows Philo, 21–22.

"This race of people is found in many parts of the earth, for it behooved all of Greece and every barbarian land to share in this perfect good. There are more of them in Egypt, however, in each of its districts, but especially around Alexandria. 8. For all the best people from every place hasten there like colonists to the soil of their fertile homeland. There is a region suited to asceticism rather than agriculture which is above a lake called Mareia and which lies along some low hills rising gently and easily; it promotes both security and moderation in climate."

9. After this he describes their dwellings, the kind and location of those of each person, and then says the following of the churches as well which they have:

"There is in each place a house devoted to prayer, which is called a *semneion* or monastic house [*monasterium*]. *Semneion* in our language can have the meaning of an assembly-place of honorable folk; into it they withdraw," he says, "and perform the mysteries belonging to an upright, chaste life. They bring nothing there at all that has to do with food or drink or the other bodily necessities, but only the books of the law and the scrolls of the prophets, as well as hymns to God and other like things, by being trained in which by study and practice they may be strengthened by their unceasing efforts for the perfect and blessed life."[49]

And further on he says,

10. "From dawn until evening all their time is spent in the studies by which they are introduced to the divine way of life through the sacred writings, adapting their ancestral laws to an allegorical interpretation. The reason is that they believe that the things written in the letter of the law are forms and images of some deep, divine mystery hidden within. 11. They also have some dialogues and expositions of those men of old who were the founders of their sect and who, it is plain, handed down to them the rule about allegorical and figurative interpretation in a

49. Philo, 25. Eusebius copies Philo accurately; Rufinus modifies the original to bring it into conformity with the monastic life of his own time. What it actually says is, "In each house [οἰκίᾳ] there is a sacred room [οἴκημα ἱερόν] which is called a sanctuary [σεμνεῖον] and secluded chamber [μοναστήριον], in which they perform in seclusion [μονούμενοι] the mysteries of the ascetic life [σεμνοῦ βίου]."

great many of their writings; they follow their practices together with their customs as the leaders and originators of their way."[50]

12. It is clear that our author was speaking of the gospels and the writings of the apostles, which teach how the law and the prophets are to be understood spiritually. 13. Shortly thereafter he goes on to say that they compose new psalms; he writes as follows: "They therefore not only interpret the hymns of old perceptively, but themselves compose new ones for God, setting them to every sort of meter and melody in a pleasant and quite becoming arrangement."[51]

14. He lists many other things in this book which are practiced by our people in church or in the monastic houses. But we must hasten on to mention those among them which are specifically characteristic of the church, 15. and from which it should be plain to all that what is written pertains to the church. He says,

16. "They first establish continence in the soul as a foundation, and then go on to build the other virtues upon that. None of them takes food or drink before sunset, since they connect daylight with spiritual studies, and the concerns of the body with night. 17. Some of them even partake of food only after three days, those, that is, whom a more voracious appetite for study drives on. And those finally who are at home in wisdom's lecture-hall and in the deeper understanding of the sacred books are never satisfied as they feast as at rich banquets; the longer they gaze the hotter they burn, so that not even on the fourth day or the fifth, but only on the sixth do they finally allow their bodies the food that they need rather than want."[52]

Can there be any doubt that Philo is describing here our way of life? 18. If anyone remains unsure of this, we will cite yet another passage of his which even the stoutest unbeliever will admit fits absolutely no one except those of our faith. He says,

19. "There are women as well with the men of whom we are speaking. Most of them are virgins of great age who preserve the integrity of their chaste bodies not out of necessity, but devotion, since they yearn to consecrate themselves not only in

50. Philo, 28–29.   51. Philo, 29.
52. Philo, 34–35.

mind but also in body to the pursuit of wisdom. They consider it improper that a vessel made ready to take in wisdom should be surrendered to lust, and that mortal offspring should be born from those from whom that sacred and immortal intercourse with the divine word is sought which results in a posterity in no wise subject to the corruption of mortality."[53]

20. And if this still seems inadequate, listen to what he writes further on:

"In their treatment of the sacred books they prefer the allegorical interpretation, since the entire law seems to those men like a living being whose body is the letter itself and whose soul is what is indicated by the letter: the spiritual and invisible meaning which is hidden in the letter and which they contemplate, gazing at it as through a mirror from the loftier and more distinguished vantage-point to which their masters have raised them, and from which they produce some marvelous varieties of interpretation even from the words themselves."[54]

21. There is no need to add to this what he says about their assemblies, and that the men and the women gather separately in the same places, and that they keep the vigils just as is our custom, and especially on those days when the solemnity of the Lord's Passion is celebrated and when it is our custom to spend the night in fasting and to listen to the holy readings. 22. Our author describes all of this as happening in the same order and sequence as is the case with us. He adds that one of the assembly stands up in the middle and sings a psalm with a dignified cadence; that the whole assembly responds to him when he has sung one verse; and that they recline on the ground on those days, as it is said was the custom of old, and no one, as he says, has even a drop of wine, nor meat of any kind, but only water as drink and bread with salt or hyssop as food.[55]

23. He goes on to describe how the priests and ministers perform their offices, and which seat is occupied by the episcopal supremacy, which is above all.[56] If anyone wishes to know more

---

53. Philo, 68.   54. Philo, 78.

55. Philo, 32–33 (men and women separate in assembly); 83–87 (vigil); 80 (singing and response); 73 (diet).

56. Philo does not mention "priests"; he does mention "elders" (*presbyteroi:*

about any of these matters, we have shown from which source may be drawn those passages 24. in which our author has interwoven the beginnings of the organization of the church and the origin of the apostolic and evangelical tradition.

2.18.1. Our author Philo is most expressive in his language, most profound in his thought, most judicious in his interpretation and understanding of holy scripture, resourceful in ordering his speech, and even more so in uttering it. He himself has left us in fact many examples of his divine giftedness. He has first of all written books on Genesis in sequential order,[57] which he called *Allegorical Commentary on the Sacred Law.* He then composed others containing questions about various subjects at random, in which he sets out and solves the matters needing investigation; he calls them *Questions and Answers about Genesis and Exodus.* 2. There are other books of his as well, which bear the title *Propositions*[58] and which are about husbandry and about drunkenness, two books on each. There are also very many other books of his which are still to be found, such as *The Things for Which the Mind Should Beseech God, The Confusion of Tongues, Nature and Discovery,*[59] *The Assembly Required for the Sake of Instruction, Who Is the Heir of What Is Divine,* and *The Division Between Equals and Unequals.* He also writes about three virtues that Moses described along with others.

3. He writes further about those whose names have been changed in the scripture, and why they were changed; in these works he says that he also wrote a first and second book on [the?] testaments. 4. He has still another book about captivity,[60]

---

67), "attendants" (*diakonous:* 75), and the "president," who expounds the sacred scriptures (*proedros,* if the textual restoration in 75 may be trusted).

57. The difficulty of matching Philo's original works to the titles listed in 2.18 (see note 16) is only increased by Rufinus's translation. The situation suggests that what are presented as titles may sometimes be rather descriptions of contents.

58. *Propositionum:* Rufinus seems to have taken Eusebius's προβλημάτων τινων as a title.

59. *De natura et inventione* = Περὶ φυγῆς καὶ εὑρέσεως ("Flight and Discovery"). Rufinus must have read φύσεως.

60. *De captivitate* = Περὶ ἀποικίας, traditionally titled *De migratione Abraham.* Rufinus seems to have understood ἀποικία as equivalent to ἀποικεσία.

and about the life of that wise man who achieved perfection with respect to complete justice and natural laws. He also wrote about the giants, about the immutability of what is divine, the *Life of Moses,* and five books about dreams coming from God. Almost all of these concern Genesis. 5. He wrote as well five books of problems and solutions in Exodus, one about the tabernacle and about the ten words of the law, something about the matters which are presented in the guise of the decalogue, and about the animals which are designated for the sacrifices, and what kinds of sacrifices there are, and the rewards for those who are good and the curses for those who are evil which are set out in the law.

6. He also has some single volumes on providence, a book in defense of the Jews which concerns civic life, one to Alexander, who claimed that dumb animals had reason, and one which argues that everyone who sins is a slave. He has further something about everyone being free who is devoted to doing what is good, and one about the contemplative life or *Suppliants,* 7. the very one which also concerns the apostolic men and whose contents we described earlier. Another of his works gives interpretations of the Hebrew names in the law and the prophets.

8. He went to Rome in the time of the emperor Gaius,[61] and when he had written at great length about Gaius's impiety and impurity, giving it the ironic title of *The Virtues,* and had read it to the senate, he attracted so much admiration that his writings were judged worthy of inclusion in the libraries.

9. It was at this time that while the apostle Paul was going round from Jerusalem as far as Illyricum preaching the word of the Lord, the emperor Claudius drove the Jews from the city. Then Aquila and Priscilla, expelled with the rest of the Jews, came to Asia and there joined the apostle, who was then laying the first foundations of the church there, as we learn from the Acts of the Apostles.[62]

2.19.1. It was while Claudius was still in power that on the very feast of Passover there was an uprising that caused so great

---

61. Cf. 2.5.1.
62. Rom 15.19; Acts 18.2–3, 18–19, 23.

an upheaval among the Jews and devastation in Jerusalem, that those Jews alone who were killed by being overwhelmed by the crowds in the temple entrances numbered thirty thousand, and their festival was turned into mourning.[63] Josephus relates as well the very many additional evils inflicted upon the Jews, writing as follows: 2. "Claudius appointed Agrippa, the son of Agrippa, king of the Jews, and sent Felix as procurator of the whole province, as well as of Samaria, Galilee, and the region called 'Beyond the Jordan.'"[64]

2.20.1. And shortly thereafter he adds: 2. "There broke out a violent uprising of the high priests against the priests and the leaders of the people of Jerusalem, each of whom collected gangs of reckless youths who enjoyed revolution, and so they made themselves leaders each of his own faction. When they clashed with each other, they started the assault with abusive language and then proceeded to pelt each other with rocks; there was no one to restrain them, but everything was done as though in a city without a governor. 3. The high priests there-fore behaved with such arrogance that they sent their slaves to the threshing-floors and seized the tithes which were owed to the priests. And it happened that many of the lesser priests whose food supplies had been plundered died of starvation, so far had the violence of the revolt overturned all justice and right."[65]

4. A little later he adds, "It happened often enough that even in the center of the city they killed each other when they met, 5. especially on feast days when assassins mingling with the crowds wandered about with concealed daggers so as to kill at close quarters anyone marked out by them. And such was their cunning that when the one whom they had struck down with a secret blow collapsed, the assassins themselves pretended to

63. The riot was caused by a Roman soldier in a temple portico exposing himself indecently to the crowds (Josephus, *Bellum* 2.227; *Antiq.* 20.105–12).

64. Cf. *Bellum* 2.247. Despite Rufinus's *inquit* (which has no equivalent in Eusebius), this is not a direct quotation. On Felix, procurator c. 52–60? see Schürer, 1.460–65. On Agrippa II, Schürer, 1.471–83.

65. *Antiq.* 20.180–81; cf. Schürer, 1.464–65. "Lesser priests" (*minoribus sacerdotibus*) translates τοὺς ἀπορουμένους τῶν ἱερέων: "the priests who were destitute." On the meaning of "high priests," see Schürer, 2.227–36.

be indignant at those who would perpetrate such things in the center of the city, and in this way their crimes remained hidden. 6. It was Jonathan the high priest who was killed by them first, and after him a great many were murdered, so that by now the fear of death weighed more heavily than the deaths themselves, with everyone expecting to be killed at any moment as though permanently placed in the line of battle."[66]

2.21.1. And after this, following some other matter, he adds, "But worse than all of this devastation was the damage caused the Jews by an Egyptian false prophet; when he came to Judea, this man, a magician, persuaded others with his magical arts that he was a prophet, lost no time in gathering together upwards of thirty thousand men, and, leading them through the wilderness, came with them to the mountain called Olivet. He was ready to invade Jerusalem from there, to seize the city by force, and at the same time to subject the Roman garrison and people to his own usurpation, relying throughout on his supporters whom he had brought with him. 2. But Felix anticipated his attempt, heading out to meet him with an armed force. The rest of the people backed him as well, and when the engagement took place, the Egyptian was put to flight with a few others, while of the rest some were slain and others captured, and the reckless enterprise was suppressed."[67]

3. So says Josephus in the second book of his *History*. But it is worthwhile comparing what he writes about the Egyptian with what is set down in the Acts of the Apostles, where it was in Felix's time that the tribune who was in Jerusalem said to Paul, against whom the Jewish riot had broken out, "Are you not that Egyptian who, previous to these days, stirred up the people and led four thousand men of the assassins into the wilderness?"[68] But that should suffice concerning Felix.

2.19.2. Claudius, meanwhile, having completed his reign as Roman emperor after thirteen years and eight months, Nero

66. *Bellum* 2.254–56; *Antiq.* 20.160–66. The assassins' victims were those who collaborated with the Romans. The procurator Felix, however, was happy enough to use them against Jonathan; cf. Schürer, 1.463.

67. *Bellum* 2.261–63; Schürer, 1.464.

68. Acts 21.38.

succeeded him to power.[69] 2.22.1. It was he who sent Festus to Judea to succeed Felix, and it was before Festus that Paul was tried and sent in fetters to Rome. Aristarchus accompanied him, so that he calls him his fellow captive in his letters, and Luke as well; the latter recorded his deeds and those of the other apostles, but Paul's especially, about whom he also indicated in conclusion that he spent two years in the city of Rome preaching the word of God with no one hindering him.[70]

2. We are also assured that he represented and defended himself before Nero, and went forth once more to the task of preaching, returning afterwards to the same city, where he underwent martyrdom. It was then that, while in fetters, he wrote the second letter to Timothy, in which he refers both to his first defense and to his present suffering. 3. Let us look at his testimonies to each in turn. "In my first defense," Paul says, "no one supported me, but everyone deserted me. May they not be blamed! For the Lord stood by me and strengthened me, that through me the preaching might be completed and all the gentiles might hear it, and I was freed from the lion's mouth."[71]

4. He shows quite clearly hereby that first he was freed from the lion's mouth that he might complete the preaching he had begun, Nero being referred to as a lion because of his cruelty. Then he goes on in what follows to say, "The Lord freed me from the lion's mouth," for he foresaw in spirit his consummation, for which reason he also said, "and I was freed from the lion's mouth," 5. and further, "The Lord will free me from every evil work and keep me safe for his heavenly kingdom." He hereby showed that he was to be crowned with martyrdom forthwith. He writes about this more clearly in the same letter when he says, "I am already being offered up, and the time of my withdrawal is at hand."[72]

---

69. January 24, 41, to October 13, 54. Rufinus has transferred to here this chronological note from Eusebius, 2.19.2.

70. Paul before Festus: Acts 25–26. Aristarchus: Acts 19.29; 20.4; 27.2; Col 4.10; Phlm 24. Paul in Rome: Acts 28.30–31.

71. 2 Tm 4.16–17.

72. 2 Tm 4.18; 4.6. Rufinus omits 2.22.6, a note about when Luke probably wrote Acts.

7. Our reason for saying this is to show that Paul's martyrdom did not take place at the time Luke is speaking of when he concludes his narrative of what Paul did in Rome. 8. For it is possible that Nero was milder at the beginning and did not receive Paul's defense of our doctrine with scorn; perhaps it was only with the passage of time that his insane savagery toward the apostles grew along with his other evils.

2.23.1. The Jews, then, after Paul had been sent on by Festus to Caesar, to whom he had appealed, saw the plots they had hatched against him foiled, and so they turned their monstrous villainy against James, the Lord's brother, to whom the apostles had entrusted the episcopal seat in Jerusalem; they attacked him as follows. 2. They brought him forward and demanded that he deny his faith in Christ before all the people. But he, contrary to all of their expectations, spoke out quite clearly, and far more loudly than they wished, and professed with total assurance before the whole people, that our Savior and Lord Jesus Christ was God's Son. They could not bear to hear such an impressive and freely-given testimony from the man, especially since everyone considered him wholly just, on account of his religious and impeccably austere life, and so they proceeded to kill him, taking advantage of the governor's death, which had occurred then. For Festus had died at that time in Judea, and the province was without a governor and ruler.

3. How James died has already been shown by us in the passage quoted from Clement, where he tells of how he was hurled from the pinnacle of the temple and struck with a fuller's club.[73] Hegesippus, however, who lived right after the first generation of the apostles, gives a more reliable account of him in the following words in the fifth book of his *Memoirs:*[74]

4. "James, the Lord's brother, received the church with the

73. On James, see 2.1.3–5. Festus died in 62. The high priest Ananus ("Ananias" in Rufinus) took advantage of the ensuing chaos in Jerusalem to order the death of his opponents (more on this in 2.23.20–24). James was killed during this time. Cf. Schürer, 1.468.

74. Most of the remnants of the five books of *Memoirs* (*Hypomnēmata*) of the second-century anti-gnostic writer Hegesippus are in Eusebius; cf. N. Hyldahl, "Hegesipps Hypomnemata," *Studia Theologica* 14 (1960): 70–113.

apostles; he was called 'the Just' by everyone, and lived from the time of the Lord himself until our own.[75] Many men are called 'James,' but he was holy from his mother's womb. 5. He drank neither wine nor liquor, nor did he eat animal flesh; iron did not go up upon his head, nor was he anointed with oil, nor did he make use of the baths. 6. He alone might enter the holy of holies, for he did not wear wool, but linen. He would go into the temple alone and kneel there, praying for forgiveness for the people, so that his knees grew calloused like a camel's from praying, since he was always kneeling and never ceasing from prayer. 7. On account of his unbelievable austerity and perfect righteousness he was, therefore, called 'Justus' and 'Oblias,' which means 'bulwark of the people' and 'righteousness,' as the prophets said of him.[76]

8. "Some persons, then, from the seven sects among the people, about whom we wrote earlier, asked him which was the door of Jesus.[77] He replied that he was the Savior. 9. Some people on account of this believed that Jesus was the Christ. But those sects of which we spoke earlier believed neither that he had risen nor that he was to come to repay everyone according to the deeds of each. Those who did believe did so because of James. 10. Since many even of the ruling class were among those who believed, the Jews, the scribes, and the Pharisees were upset, saying, 'It will next be the whole people that believes in Jesus, that he is the Christ.' They met together with

75. Eusebius: "he was called 'just' by everyone, from the Lord's time until ours."

76. This description of James seems to follow that of the priests in the renewed temple in Ezek 44.15–21. This suggests that Hegesippus is drawing upon an earlier figurative portrayal of James in the eschatological Messianic temple, transforming it into a literal description of him as in the Herodian temple of his day. See Richard Bauckham's illuminating chapter, "For What Offence Was James Put to Death?" in *James the Just and Christian Origins, Supplements to Novum Testamentum* 48 (Leiden: Brill, 1999), ed. Bruce B. Chilton and Craig A. Evans, 199–232. If "Oblias" derives from *gvūl* ("boundary"), there may be a play on *gamal* ("camel"): Bauckham, 206–9. James is then portrayed as the bulwark whose prayers staved off the Roman assault until he was put to death.

77. "about whom we wrote earlier": actually found in 4.22.7. For "the door of Jesus" cf. Ps 117.20, and Bauckham, 209–10.

James, therefore, and said to him, 'We beg you to restrain the people, because they are wrong in thinking that Jesus is the Christ. We therefore beseech you to speak to all who come together on the day of Passover and persuade them of this about Jesus. For we all submit to you, and both we and the people testify of you that you are righteous and are no respecter of persons. 11. Speak to the people, then, and persuade them not to err, since we all obey you. Climb up therefore to the height on the pinnacle of the temple, that you may be seen by everyone from a lofty place and what you say may be heard by all, since on the Passover days a crowd gathers not only of Jews but of gentiles as well.'

12. "The scribes and Pharisees just mentioned, then, placed James on the temple pinnacle and shouted at him, 'O most righteous of men, to whom we must all submit, the people have gone astray after Jesus, who was crucified, so declare to us which the door of Jesus is!' 13. James in answer cried out to them at the top of his voice, 'Why are you asking me about the Son of Man? Behold, he is sitting in heaven at the right of the highest power, and is himself to come on the clouds of heaven!' 14. James's answer and testimony were enough for many of the people, and they were glad to hear what James declared, and so they began to glorify God and say, 'Hosanna to the Son of David!'

15. "Then the scribes and Pharisees began to say to each other, 'We have done wrong to provide Jesus with such testimony, but let us go up and fling him down, that the others may be terrified and not believe him.' At the same time they cried out with a loud voice, 'Oh, oh, even Justus has gone astray!' And they fulfilled the scripture found in Isaiah which says, 'Let us do away with the just man, for he is of no use to us; for which reason they shall eat the fruit of their works.'[78] 16. They went up, therefore, flung him down, and said to each other, 'Let us stone James the Just.' And they began to pelt him with stones, because when thrown down not only had he not been able to die; he had turned and, kneeling down, was saying, 'I ask you, Lord God the Father, to forgive them this sin, for they do not know what they are doing.' 17. And while they were heaping

78. Is 3.10 (LXX).

stones upon him from above as he was thus praying, one of the priests of the sons of Rechab, son of Rachabin, the ones about whom the prophet Jeremiah bore witness,[79] cried out, 'Stop this, please! What are you doing? This righteous man whom you are stoning is praying for you!' 18. And one of them, a fuller, snatching up the club they use to squeeze things out, struck him on the head; such was the martyrdom he achieved, and he was buried in the same place near the temple. He is the one who became a witness to Jews and gentiles of the truth that Jesus is the Christ. And it was not long afterwards that Vespasian began his assault."

19. Hegesippus thus relates more extensively, but in agreement with Clement, that James was considered to be so wonderful and so highly regarded by all in his observance of complete righteousness, that those of good sense even among the Jews believed that the reason for the assault in Jerusalem which immediately followed was the criminal violence which they had practiced upon him. 20. Josephus also shows clearly that he is of this mind when he says, "All of these things happened to the Jews to requite them for James the Just, the brother of Jesus, who is called the Christ, the man whom everyone acknowledged to be most righteous and pious, and whom the Jews killed."[80] 21. The same author also reports his death in the twentieth book of the *Antiquities* as follows:[81]

"Caesar sent Albinus to be prefect of Judea when he learned of Festus's death. The younger Ananias, however, who we said earlier had received the high priesthood, was reckless and haughty in demeanor, and sided with the Sadducees, who seem crueler than the rest of the Jews in passing judgment, as we showed earlier. 22. He thought that Festus's death had given

79. "Jewish exegesis understood the promise to the Rechabites in Jer 35.19 ... to mean that the Rechabites would be priests" (Bauckham, 213). Their abstention from wine and fidelity to God made their association with James quite natural. Rufinus follows Eusebius in transforming the Hebrew plural ('Ραχαβείμ: "Rechabites") into a proper name.

80. Not found in the surviving texts of Josephus, but Origen, *Contra Celsum* 1.47, also cites the passage as from him.

81. *Antiq.* 20.197, 199–203. Albinus was procurator 62–64. Cf. Schürer, 1.468–70. Josephus's earlier remarks on the Sadducees are in *Antiq.* 13.294.

him the chance to show his own haughtiness, and so he convened a court of judges and brought forward James, the brother of Jesus, who is called the Christ, and a great many others, whom he charged with breaking the law and handed over to be stoned. 23. This was a crime which was deeply resented by all of the city-folk who were more moderate and careful of justice and the law. They sent a delegation to Caesar secretly, begging him to write to Ananias to keep him from doing such things, since even earlier he had done wrong in performing such misdeeds. Some of them even went to meet Albinus as he was on his way to them from Alexandria and informed him that Ananias had had no right to convene a court of judges without consulting him. 24. Upset by what they said, he wrote in anger to Ananias, threatening to remove from him his judicial power,[82] which he was misusing, since even King Agrippa had deprived him of this honor after he had enjoyed it for only three months, and had appointed Jesus, son of Dammaeus, in his place."

Such are his words about James as well, to whom is ascribed the letter which is the first among those called "Catholic." 25. It is to be observed, however, that a number of people do not accept it, nor is it often mentioned by those of old, as is true also of the one ascribed to Jude, which is itself one of the seven. But we know that these letters too have been accepted by almost all the churches.

2.24. In the first year of Nero's reign, then, Annianus received the see of the church in Alexandria after Mark the evangelist.

2.25.1. Now as Nero's power grew, and after the many wicked and impure misdeeds which he devised, he went so far as to offend the Divinity itself. A long tale it would make, and one unsuited to our work, to relate his villainy and disgracefulness, especially when many have written of it fully. 2. Those who wish to learn about his discreditable life and the crimes with which

---

82. *comminatus ablaturum se ab eo iudicandi potestatem* = λήψεσθαι παρ᾽ αὐτοῦ δίκας ἀπειλῶν ("threatening to punish him"): a rare misreading by Rufinus of a Greek idiom. What the original says is that Agrippa deprived him of the high priesthood for what he had done. "Ananias" is "Ananus" in Josephus/ Eusebius. Cf. note 73 above.

it was freighted may do so from their books.[83] They will find in them that his life of crime reached the point where he did not spare even his relatives and household, but committed murder and incest against his mother, his brothers, his wives, and all those related to him by blood. 3. The only thing lacking to all of this was that he should be the first of the Roman emperors to turn the weapons of impiety against God himself. 4. As that noblest of writers, Tertullian, reports:

"Search your records, and you will find as well that Nero was the first to rampage with the imperial sword against this religion at the very moment when it was arising in Rome. What an honor for us to have such a herald of our condemnation! For those who know him realize that the only things he condemned were those which were exceptionally good. Domitian tried to live up to Nero's cruelty, but being human, he soon abandoned the attempt, even restoring those he had banished. Such have always been our persecutors: unjust, irreligious, and disgraceful; you yourselves regularly condemn them and restore those whom they condemned."[84]

So says Tertullian.

5. Nero, then, having declared himself openly the enemy of divinity and religion, sought first the deaths of the apostles as the leaders and standard-bearers in God's people. He condemned Paul to be beheaded in the city of Rome itself, and Peter to be crucified. I consider it needless to seek for testimony to them from an extraneous source, when their magnificent tombs bear witness even today to what took place. 6. Gaius, a writer of old, writes about them nonetheless; with Zephyrinus, the bishop of Rome, he records the following about the places of the apostles while arguing against a Cataphrygian named Proculus:[85]

83. Suetonius, *Nero* 26–38; Tacitus, *Annals* 13.15–20, 25, 45–47; 14.1–6, 56–65; 15.35–74; 16 *passim;* Dio Cassius 61.4–9; 62 *passim.*

84. *Apologeticum* 5.3–4. Rufinus copies out Tertullian's original directly (Eusebius translates only *Apol.* 5.3). He is quoted again in 3.20.7, less exactly.

85. "Proclus" is the usual spelling. Eusebius says that Gaius lived during Zephyrinus's time (198–217), not that the latter too wrote anything about the apostles. Proclus, as a Montanist, accepted as literally true the prophecy about the earthly kingdom of Christ to come (Rv 20.4–6), a prophecy that was sometimes understood to mean a restoration of pre-resurrection physical life. Gaius represented a group that reacted against this interpretation by re-

7. "I am in a position to show you the monuments of the apostles. If you go by the highway that leads to the Vatican,[86] or by the Ostian Way, you will find the monuments set up by which the Roman church is guarded as they stand on either side."

8. And that they both suffered at the same time is stated by Dionysius, the bishop of Corinth, when he was situated in the city[87] and set out his views in writing; he says, "But you, having as you do the admonition given you by Peter and Paul, have joined together the planting of the churches of Rome and Corinth. For both arrived together, taught in our church in Corinth, taught together throughout Italy and in this city, and were also crowned with martyrdom likewise at one and the same time." We relate this so that the account considered by everyone to be true may receive further confirmation.

2.26.1. Josephus, for his part, when he writes of the number of disasters which overtook the Jewish people, and of how their devastation was perpetuated, adds the following: "To the countless ills which had befallen the Jews, Florus, who was then procurator of Judea, added the following: he flogged men of high rank and in that most sacred of cities, Jerusalem, crucified them; this was at the time when revolutionary currents were upsetting Jewish affairs, in the twelfth year of Nero's reign."[88]

---

jecting the Book of Revelation outright, and with it the Gospel of John (since both were believed to be by the same author). Cf. Gerhard Maier, *Die Johannesoffenbarung und die Kirche* (Tübingen: Mohr Siebeck, 1981), 69–85. Cf. also 3.28.1–2; 3.31.4; 6.20.3.

In 3.28.1–2, Gaius will ascribe the doctrine of Christ's earthly kingdom to the Gnostic Cerinthus. In the present passage he recalls the two apostles who bore witness against it (as the Montanists understood it, at least): Peter, through Mk 12.25 (see 2.15), and Paul (1 Cor 15.35–57).

86. *si enim procedas via regali quae ad Vaticanum ducit ...* = ἐὰν γὰρ θελήσῃς ἀπελθεῖν ἐπὶ τὸν Βασικανόν ... Frédéric Tailliez, "Notes conjointes sur un passage fameux d'Eusèbe," *Orientalia Christiana Periodica* 9 (1943): 431–36, wonders if *via regali* suggests that Rufinus read Βασικανόν as βασιλικὴν ὁδόν.

On the nature and location of the monuments, see H. Chadwick, "St. Peter and St. Paul in Rome: The Problem of the *Memoria Apostolorum ad Catacumbas,*" *JTS* NS 8 (1957): 31–52.

87. *in urbe positus:* in Rome, that is. Rufinus takes Ῥωμαίοις ὁμιλῶν as "consorting with the Romans" rather than merely communicating with them.

88. Not an exact quotation; cf. *Antiq.* 20.252–57; *Bellum* 2.277–79; 2.301–24. Gessius Florus was procurator 64–66. Cf. Schürer, 1.470, 485–86.

2. He says that throughout Syria the most horrifying savagery was practiced upon those of the Jews who revolted, so that even those who were staying in the different cities among the gentiles were reckoned among the enemy. One could see the cities filled with unburied bodies, the old lying dead with the children, the corpses of women stripped bare and thrown out into the open with no respect for their gender, and the whole province brimming with evils uncounted. Far worse than this dreadful and shocking sight, however, was the brooding fear and anxiety over the evils yet to come, a threat which loomed larger every day. So says Josephus in so many words.[89] This will do for the present concerning the Jews.

89. *Bellum* 2.462, 465.

BOOK THREE

28. Cerinthus, the head of a deviant religion
29. Nicolaus and his followers
30. Those apostles who did not disdain marital rights

3.1.1. The Jews, then, were being devastated by the calamities they deserved.[1] As for the holy apostles of our Lord and Savior, and the other disciples, they made their way through each of the provinces of the earth. Thomas, we are told, was allotted Parthia; Matthew, Ethiopia; Bartholomew, Nearer India; Andrew, Scythia; and John, Asia, whence he stayed in Ephesus and died there. 2. Peter, we find, went around preaching in Pontus, Galatia, Bithynia, Cappadocia, and the other provinces at least that bordered on the Jews, and finally stayed in Rome, where he was crucified upside down; that is what he himself begged for, lest he seem to be equal to the Lord. 3. And what shall I say of Paul? He completed the proclamation of the gospel of Christ from Jerusalem even to Illyricum, and at the last suffered martyrdom under Nero. Origen sets these matters out in this order in the third book of his commentary on Genesis.[2]

3.3.1. Now the apostle Peter has left very few records of his preaching. There is one letter of his about which no one entertains any doubts. For many are unsure about the second [letter], although most accept that it too is to be read. 2. The writing, however, which is called the "Acts of Peter," and the gospel which bears his name,[3] and also his so-called "Preaching" or "Revelation," are not included among the canonical scriptures at all, and indeed none of the ancient writers uses their testimonies. 3. As our history unfolds, however, and as we mention the church writers, we will also in consequence, as suits the several passages, explain the books of scripture which are to be held authoritative, and which books are not to be followed.

1. *Igitur Iudaei debitis cladibus perurgebantur* = Τὰ μὲν δὴ κατὰ Ἰουδαίους ἐν τούτοις ἦν ("Such indeed was the situation of the Jews"): an example of Rufinus's tendency to accentuate the divine punishment of the Jews. Cf. also 3.6.16; 4.2.5; 4.5.2; 4.6.3.
2. On Paul preaching the gospel as far as Illyricum, cf. Rom 15.19. The citation from Origen is preserved only here. Rufinus omits 3.2 (about Linus as bishop of Rome after the martyrdom of Peter and Paul).
3. Gospel of Peter: 3.25.6; 6.12.

4. Peter's first letter, at any rate, was accepted by all of those of old, as we said.

5. There are also clearly fourteen letters of Paul which are regarded as authoritative, even though I realize that the Latins are unsure about the letter written to the Hebrews.[4] In due time, however, we will explain what each of the writers of old thought about it. 6. The writing of Hermas, which is called "The Shepherd" and the name of whose author Paul mentions in his letters,[5] is not accepted by most, but has been judged necessary by others on account of those who are undergoing their first instructions in the faith. Hence it is read in a number of churches, and many of the writers of old have used its testimonies. 7. Such may be said for the present in a preliminary way about the reliability of the sacred books; we will proceed shortly to support it by the confirmation of those of old as well.

3.4.1. That Paul, however, went round preaching the gospel to the gentiles from Jerusalem as far as Illyricum, may be shown from what he himself says and from what Luke writes in Acts. 2. Peter too indicates in which provinces he also preached Christ to those from the circumcision; he does so in his own words in that letter which beyond all doubt is his, and in which he writes to those who are in the dispersion, meaning certainly the Hebrews. For they are called "dispersed" because driven from their own habitations and situated in the dispersion, as he says, of Pontus, Galatia, Cappadocia, Asia, and Bithynia.[6] 3. Those of them found to be constant in faith and zealous for God's word were even entrusted with the governance of the churches founded by the apostles; it is not easy to list their names in full. From the apostle Paul's words, however, we can gather that there were very many; 4. he calls them sometimes "helpers," sometimes "fellow-soldiers," sometimes "fellow-prisoners" and fellow-workers in the gospel and companions. Luke as well in the Acts of the Apostles mentions a great many of his associates and sharers in his preaching; 5. he speaks for instance of Timothy and Titus, one of whom was appointed by him bishop in Ephesus, while the

---

4. Hebrews and the Latin Christians: cf. 6.20.3.
5. Rom 16.14.
6. 1 Pt 1.1.

other was charged by him to organize the churches on Crete.[7]
6. Luke's own family was from Antioch; by training he was a
physician, but was a companion of Paul and was an associate of
the other apostles and closely connected with them. He, then,
in keeping with the medicine which he had received from the
company or tradition of the apostles, composed for us two books
of remedies for the healing of souls rather than bodies: a gospel, which he introduces with the words "as those have handed
on to us who from the beginning saw for themselves and were
ministers of God's word, and whom I have followed from the beginning,"[8] and the Acts of the Apostles, about which he was acquainted no longer from what he had heard, but from what he
had viewed with his own eyes.

7. And they say that he wrote his gospel from what Paul said,
and that that was the one which the apostle used to call his gospel when he said "according to my gospel."[9] He was like Mark,
who wrote what had been preached by Peter. 8. Of Paul's companions there is also mention of Crescens, who went to Gaul,
while Linus and Clement were heads of the church in Rome. 9.
Paul himself testifies that they were his companions and helpers. 10. It is also known that Dionysius the Areopagite in Athens, whom Luke describes as the first one who believed when
Paul preached, was among his companions and received the
see of Athens.[10] 11. But let us return for the present to the narrative of our history.

3.5.1. After Nero, then, who was sovereign of Rome for thirteen years, Galba and Otho ruled for a year and six months,
leaving upon their deaths the reins of government to Vespasian.[11] He was at the time engaged in the war he was waging

7. Timothy is mentioned several times in Acts; Titus never. Titus 1.5 speaks
of the appointment of elders on Crete. Timothy's ordination by Paul as bishop
of Ephesus is in *Apostolic Constitutions* 7.46 and Nicephorus, *HE* 3.11, and his
station is suggested by both Letters to Timothy, especially perhaps 1 Tm 5.22.

8. Lk 1.1–3.

9. Rom 2.16; 16.25; 2 Tm 2.8.

10. Crescens: 2 Tm 4.10. Linus: 2 Tm 4.21. Clement: Phil 4.3. Dionysius:
Acts 17.34; Dionysius of Corinth mentions his ordination to Athens (cf.
4.23.3).

11. Nero died on June 9, 68. Galba succeeded him until January 15, 69,

against the Jews when he was chosen emperor by the very army with which he was attacking Judea. Setting out at once for Rome, he charged his son Titus to prosecute the war and the siege of Jerusalem. 2. And it was then that, after the Ascension of our Lord and Savior, divine punishment was exacted from the Jews for the crime committed against him, for their persecution of the apostles and the murder of Stephen, and also for the decapitation of the apostle James,[12] as well as the crime done against James, the Lord's brother, who was called Justus, in addition to all the others committed against those whom because of their faith in Christ they had beset with plots, deceits, and every sort of wicked trickery. As for the apostles, who had been driven away by them earlier and scattered everywhere, as we said previously, they went on their way in the power of Christ, who had bidden them, "Go and baptize all nations in my name."[13] 3. The church which had been gathered in Jerusalem, however, was commanded in a revelation from God to move out and go over to a town named Pella across the Jordan, so that once the holy and righteous men had been removed from the city, heaven might have an opportunity to bring retribution upon both the sacrilegious city and its irreligious people by utterly destroying their native place.

4. Those, then, who wish to know more about the extent of the evils by which the entire nation was punished, about how the land of Judea itself was devastated by war, famine, fire, and slaughter, about the many thousands of its peoples, fathers along with their wives and little ones, who were butchered be-

---

and Otho until April 20, 69. Vespasian was proclaimed emperor in Alexandria on July 1, 69.

12. On James, Acts 12.1–2. Rufinus makes explicit Eusebius's implication that the siege was divine punishment. The governor of Syria, Cestius Gallus, had been unable to suppress the revolt that had broken out in Jerusalem in the spring of 66 in reaction to the iniquities of the procurator Florus (see Book 2, note 88), and at the end of the year Nero had entrusted the situation to the experienced Vespasian. He occupied Galilee and was preparing to lay siege to Jerusalem when he received news of Nero's death on June 9, 68. He then suspended military operations and went to Alexandria for a year to secure his position, leaving his son Titus to prosecute the siege. On the war, see Schürer, 1.484–513.

13. Cf. Mt 28.19.

yond number and without distinction, about the different cities
which were besieged, the extent of the destruction of the magnificent city of Jerusalem itself in all its renown and the piles
of corpses which had met various deaths, about the manner in
which the battles had been waged in each instance, and how it
came about that, as the prophets had foretold, the abomination of desolation was erected in the very temple of highest renown, which was once God's, and how at last all was destroyed
by fire and devoured by flames—those seeking to know more
about this may read Josephus's history again. 5. We for our part
will borrow from it only what suffices for the work in hand. In it
he relates that on the feast day of Passover, people from all over
Judea had come together in Jerusalem as though assembled by
some lethal power; he says they numbered three million, the
just judgment of God having chosen this as the time of retribution,[14] 6. so that those who with their bloody hands and sacrilegious voices had outraged their savior and healer, the Christ of
the Lord, during the Passover days, might receive during those
same days the fatal stroke of the punishment they deserved
when their whole multitude was shut up as in a single prison.

7. I will pass over the tale of what was dealt them by sword-
stroke and the other instruments of war, and will relate only,
through the words of the historian mentioned above, the dire
famine that laid them low, so that the readers may realize how
great a crime it is to act with arrogance against Christ, and how
great the punishment meted out for it. 3.6.1. Let us therefore
open the fifth book of Josephus's history, which reveals the
whole of their grievous tragedy.

"For the wealthy, however, to stay was the same as to perish.[15]
For if they stayed in the city, they would on account of their
property be charged with the crime of planning to desert, and
would be killed. Now the pressure of the famine heightened

14. What Josephus actually says (in *Bellum* 6.425) is that a census of Jerusalem taken at Passover in Nero's time counted 2,700,000 present during the
feast. The city actually fell to the Romans in September of 70.

15. This passage is from *Bellum* 5.424–38. "To stay" means in Jerusalem; to
try to escape the city to flee to the Romans was dangerous, as the insurgents
would kill anyone they caught trying (the Romans would let most of them go
where they wanted).

the partisans' insolence, and their hunger and their boldness increased together. 2. Nowhere was there wheat available for the public at all, but the looters burst into houses and searched them, and if they found any, they punished the owners for the deception they had practiced, while if they did not find any, they tortured them all the same for having hidden it more cunningly and carefully. The proof that they had food they drew from the very fact that they were still alive, their bodies evidently still surviving, since they would certainly have already perished if they had had no food hidden away somewhere. Those of course whom they saw wasting away they were kind enough to leave alone, thinking it needless to kill people whom famine would soon take off.

3. "Many there were, however, who secretly bartered all their property for one measure of wheat, if they were wealthy, or for barley, if they were not, and, shutting themselves up in the inmost recesses of their houses, ate the grain without even baking it into bread, while others, to the extent that necessity or fear allowed, baked it. 4. No one waited for a table to be laid, but snatched their food half-burned from the fire as though it had been stolen, and devoured it. And the wretched food was itself the occasion for a miserable sight, with all the stronger folk seizing whatever was found and leaving the weaker with nothing but tears and grief. 5. And even though hunger surpasses every other hardship, there is yet nothing which it so overthrows and destroys like the sense of shame. Whatever is worthy of respect in a time of security is spurned under its pressure. Thus wives snatched food even from their husbands' hands, children from their parents', and, what is still more grievous, mothers from the hands and mouths of their little ones. And while their darling children wasted away in their arms and before their very eyes, no one hesitated to remove even the tiniest bits of nourishment from between their very teeth. 6. Not even those consuming the smallest particles of the most wretched food escaped notice; the looters were on the spot at once, and as soon as they saw anyone's doors closed, took it as a sign that those inside were eating; smashing open the doors, they rushed inside and, if there was anything still unswallowed, got it back

by forcing it from the people's very jaws, so to speak. 7. The elderly were beaten if they tried to claim any food. Women, their hair disheveled, were dragged off while trying to conceal whatever they might have been holding. No respect was shown for the white hair of the elderly, no pity for the children; children clinging to the tiniest bit of bread were dashed to the ground, shaken off from the very crusts onto which they had been hanging. And their savagery was kindled even more fiercely against those who forestalled their robbery by the food they succeeded in consuming; they devised horrible tortures for the wretches 8. by stopping up their digestive tracts. With others they drove sharpened stakes through their genitals—I shudder to tell what was done—in order to force the wretches to confess to even one loaf or a spoonful of flour. 9. For the torturers themselves were not suffering from hunger—it would in a way be more tolerable if it seemed they had done these things when forced by starvation—they acted so either because they wanted to lay food by for later, or because their cruelty grew stronger with exercise. 10. And those who managed to steal through the enemy pickets to gather herbs and sneak back they pounced upon and grabbed what they had brought as they were congratulating themselves upon having escaped from the enemy. They might beg all they liked and call upon God's name, fearful as it once was to them, asking that they might be allowed at least part of what they had sought out at the risk of death; they got nothing at all. They might in fact consider it a favor that they were allowed to depart with their lives if they were caught."

11. And somewhat later he continues:[16] "For the Jews all hope of being saved was blocked when exit from the city was, and the growing hardship of hunger laid waste homes together with families and the people, so that in the inner rooms the corpses of women and children lay strewn about, while in the streets lay the bodies of the unfortunate elderly, worn away by famine rather than age. 12. As for the youths and those of maturer age, they roamed the lanes and alleys like phantoms, collapsing wherever starvation overtook their steps. To bury one's

16. *Bellum* 5.512–19. Compare Tacitus, *Fragmenta Historiarum* 1 (=Sulpicius Severus, *Chron.* 2.30.3).

relatives, however, was impossible, given the great number of the dead and one's lack of strength, to say nothing of the uncertainty of one's own survival. For some there were who gave up the ghost over those whom they were burying, and many as well who breathed their last while following funeral processions before they had arrived at the grave. 13. But neither mourning nor grief was displayed as usual for those who had died; all of this was now reserved for the famine. Nor had the dryness resulting from starvation left anyone any moisture for tears. Deep silence beset the city, and a night full of death covered everything.

"The only thing worse than all of these evils was the energy of the looters, 14. who saw nothing wrong even with plundering graves and stripping the corpses. It was not so much that they were searching for loot as increasing their guilt by their mockery and testing the edge of their swords by chopping up corpses. Sometimes as well they tried [the sharpness of] the points on a number of those still breathing. When those who were half dead saw this, they would stretch out their hands to beg them to grant them too the favor of their crime, that they might be released more quickly from the torture of famine. But they with a new twist to their cruelty refused when asked to grant the death which they were inflicting so willingly; meanwhile those who were dying turned their eyes to the temple with groans, not grieving that they themselves were dying, but that the looters were being left alive and unpunished. 15. They at first had ordered the dead to be buried at public expense because the stench was unbearable. But when the number of those dying began to overwhelm all the available public funds, they threw the corpses from the wall. And when Titus, going round, saw the ramparts full of the corpses of the dead and their native earth moistened with the putrefaction of human bodies, he raised his hands to heaven with a loud groan and called God to witness that this was not his doing."

16. And somewhat later he continues further:[17] "I will not hesitate to express what I feel: it is my opinion that, even if the Roman attack on its irreligious folk had been suspended briefly,

17. *Bellum* 5.566.

the city would have been punished by the earth's splitting open or by a flood of water, or by the fires and thunderbolts of Sodom hurled down from heaven, since it had produced this present generation of men, which was far more wicked and depraved than those who suffered those things, a generation on whose account the whole people deservedly perished likewise."[18]

17. In the sixth book as well he writes as follows on the same topic:[19] "The multitude of those throughout the city who were starving to death was countless, nor can their misery be described. In whatever house any kind of food was found battles broke out at once, those dear to each other, including parents and children, killing each other, while each fought to snatch the food not only from the others' hands but even from their very jaws. 18. There was no respect even for the dead; even they, while breathing their last, were searched by the looters, lest any food remain in their bosoms. Others, gasping from hunger, staggered hither and yon like rabid dogs, and, as though driven by madness, broke into the same houses two or three times in a short space of time. 19. Necessity changed everything into food, even such things as not even dumb animals would eat. At the end they did not refrain even from leather or belts or their very shoes. They pulled down the hangings from the doorways[20] and chewed on them. Many ate stalks of old hay. They gathered refuse from wherever they could and sold the smallest amounts for four drachmas.

20. "But what need is there to explain in this way the severity of the famine, when there was an outrage committed there which has never been heard of among the Greeks or any of the barbarians, horrible indeed to relate and hardly to be believed. I would gladly indeed have kept silent about the enormity, lest I be suspected of telling fables, if I did not have many men within memory who were witnesses of the crime committed. Nor

---

18. *pro quibus omnis gens pariter mereretur extingui* = τῇ γοῦν τούτων ἀπονοίᾳ πᾶς ὁ λαὸς συναπώλετο ("through their madness the whole people perished with them").

19. *Bellum* 6.193–213.

20. *portarum ... indumenta* = τὰ δέρματα τῶν θυρεῶν ("the hides on their shields"). Rufinus seems to have read θυρῶν.

do I think that I would be doing my country any favor, were I to suppress the account of those evils which it endured. 21. There was a woman who came from the folk who dwelt beyond the Jordan River and whose name was Mary, daughter of Eleazar, from the village of Bethezob,²¹ which means "House of Hyssop." Well known for her family and wealth, she was in Jerusalem with the rest of the multitude which had gathered there, and endured the siege with all the others. 22. The property remaining to her, which she had brought into the city, was not only seized by the plunderers, but the henchmen belonging to the looters broke in at intervals to snatch whatever was left of her considerable resources, by which she eked out her daily existence. The woman was so enraged at this that her fury wore her out to the point where she would at times try with her curses and insults to provoke the looters to murder her. But since no one would kill her out of annoyance or pity, 23. and whatever food she had chanced to obtain had been obtained for others, and she no longer had the means of getting more anywhere, while severe hunger attacked her very innards and vitals and starvation was now driving her mad, she gave her ear to those worst of counselors, hunger and anger, and prepared to assail the very laws of nature. She had a small child she was nursing; she placed him before her and said, 24. 'O my child, unlucky as your mother is, you are unluckier still! Amid this war, famine, and looting, for what can I preserve you? Even if we hoped to survive, the yoke of Roman slavery looms over us. But as it is, that slavery has been forestalled by famine, while the looters are a more dreadful threat than either of the other dangers. Come then, my child, be food for your mother, fury for the looters, and a tale for the ages, the only one that has been lacking to the catastrophes of the Jews.'

25. "And with these words she killed her boy, put him over the fire, roasted him, ate half of him, covered the rest of him, and set him aside. The looters burst in as soon as they smelled the burnt flesh, and threatened to kill her if she did not show them immediately where the food was which they could tell she

---

21. Rufinus has corrected Eusebius's Βαθεζώρ.

had prepared. She replied, 'I have in fact saved the best part
for you.' And she uncovered at once the parts of the baby which
were left. 26. An immense horror gripped them immediately
and, savage at heart though they were, they stood frozen, unable to utter a sound. She, however, her face grim, spoke now
more grimly even than the looters themselves: 'This is my son,
my offspring, and my crime. Eat, for I myself have been the first
to eat what I bore. Do not be holier than its mother or milder
than a woman. For if religious scruples overcome you and you
abhor my food, I who have already feasted upon such as this
will feast upon it again.' 27. They thereupon departed trembling and terrified, they who, from all that she had, had left the
wretched mother only this food. The whole city was immediately filled with the news of this outrage, each person imagining
the crime that had been committed and shrinking from it as
though he himself had done it. 28. And all of those pressed
hard by the famine hastened the more quickly to their deaths,
calling those blessed who had perished before being defiled by
hearing of such wickedness."

Such is Josephus's account, and such the punishment, then,
inflicted upon the Jews for the crimes they committed against
the Christ of God. 3.7.1. But it is worth including in this history
the words of the Lord with which the Savior himself foretold
that such things were to happen: "Woe to those," he says, "who
are with child and giving suck or feeding at the breast in those
days. Pray, though, that your flight may not be in the winter
or on the Sabbath, for then the affliction will be so great that
there has not been the like from the beginning of the world
nor will ever be."[22] 2. Now the historian mentioned above, adding together all of those slain by starvation or the sword, puts
the number at 1,100,000, while stating that the rest, the robbers, assassins, and looters, killed each other off after the city
was destroyed.[23] But those youths who were selected because

22. Mt 24.19–21.

23. 1,100,000: *Bellum* 6.420. "Killed each other": what Eusebius says is that
they were killed when they informed on each other after the city's capture,
which is quite close to Josephus's own wording in 6.417; they were executed by
Titus's lieutenant, Fronto.

they were tall and handsome were, he says, reserved for the triumph, while the others who were above seventeen years of age were sent off in fetters to Egypt to work in the mines or were scattered throughout the other provinces, some destined for the gladiatorial games and others for the beasts. Those who were found to be under seventeen years of age were ordered to be sold into slavery throughout the various provinces; there were up to 90,000 of them.[24]

3. All of this took place in the second year of Vespasian's reign according to what Our Lord and Savior Jesus Christ himself had foretold, since the events that were to take place he already saw as present at the time, when, as the gospels affirm, he wept over the city when he saw it, and spoke the words as though in its hearing: 4. "If only you had known this day what is for your peace; but now it is hidden from your eyes, for days will come upon you, and your enemies will surround you with a rampart and go around you and hem you about on every side, and flatten you and your children in you to the ground." 5. And he spoke further as though about the people: "There will be great affliction on earth and wrath for this people, and they will fall by the sword and will be led captive to all the gentiles, and Jerusalem will be trampled by the gentiles until the times of the gentiles are completed." And further: "When you see Jerusalem surrounded by an army, know then that her desolation is at hand."[25] 6. Anyone, now, who compares the words of Our Lord and Savior with what the historian says about the war that took place and the destruction of the city, and sees the wondrous power of the divine foreknowledge, must acknowledge the divinity of the one who foretold this. 7. This came indeed upon the Jewish people as just retribution after the Savior's passion, because the entire people cried out that the author of life should be taken away from them. 8. There is, even so, nothing to keep us from adding some things which may show how God's mercy and clemency were offered to them, however

24. 90,000: *Bellum* 6.420 gives 97,000 as the total number of the prisoners captured during the entire war. It does not give the number of the youths sold. On what happened to them, see 6.417–18.

25. Lk 19.42–44; 21.23–24; 21.20.

ungrateful they were. What I mean is that for forty successive years after the commission of the crime, the punishment was put off. During them, all of the apostles, especially James, who was called the Lord's brother and had been appointed bishop in Jerusalem,[26] reminded the people unceasingly of the act of impiety they had committed and the monstrous outrage, so that they might perchance repent of what they had done and, it might be, weep for their crime and quench the avenging flames of punishment with their overflowing tears. 9. For by his patience God was showing them that he sought their repentance, "because God does not want the death of the sinner so much as that he be converted and live."[27] The divine majesty, though, strove still to soften the hardness of their minds by signs and wonders given from heaven, and by displaying to them rather than bringing down upon them his terrors and his dread right hand. What the historian who was mentioned earlier asserts concerning this will suffice here as in other matters.

3.8.1. Let us then read again what he says about this in the sixth book of his history.[28]

"The unhappy people," he says, "were persuaded by thoroughly wicked men and imposters who prophesied falsehood, not to believe the evident signs and indications of the divine wrath and indignation, which clearly foretold the coming destruction of the city and the people. As though they had been blasted and driven mad, and had neither eyes nor soul in themselves, they scorned all of heaven's messages. 2. A brightly shining star, that is, which was quite like a sword, loomed over the city, and besides that a comet was seen for a whole year burning with lethal flames. And even before the time of the destruction and the war, when the people were gathering for the Feast of Unleavened Bread on the eighth of the month of Xanthikos, which is April, such a bright light shone around the altar and temple at the ninth hour of the night, that everyone thought that it was broad daylight, and so it remained for half an hour. That seemed propitious to the ignorant and inexperienced, but the ominous nature of the portent did not escape those learned in the law and any of the reputa-

26. James, bishop: 2.1.3.   27. Ezek 18.23; 33.11.
28. Josephus, *Bellum* 6.288–304.

ble teachers. 3. During the very feast as well, a young cow was brought up to the place of sacrifice and standing by the altars gave birth to a lamb while being handled by the ministers. 4. The doors of the interior of the temple as well, which looked to the east, were clad in solid bronze, were of such an immense weight that they could scarcely be shut with twenty men pushing them with all their might, and were also held fast by iron bars and locks along with bolts sunk deep, appeared suddenly opened of their own accord in the sixth hour of the night.

5. "That is not all: some days after the feast, on the twenty-first of the month of Artemisios, which we call May, an uncanny sight appeared, which is almost unbelievable and the report of which would be thought false if the witness of the eyes had not been confirmed by the catastrophe which followed. For what was seen throughout the region near sunset were chariots with their horses borne through the air, troops of armed men mixed in the clouds, and the cities surrounded by unexpected armies. 6. On another feast, furthermore, the one which is called Pentecost, the priests who had gone into the temple at night to perform their offices, as usual, first were aware of some movement and noises, and then heard sudden voices saying, 'Let us depart from here.'[29] And there is something even more terrible. 7. Four years before the war, on the Feast of Booths, while the city still enjoyed peace and prosperity, someone named Jesus, the son of Ananias, a rustic commoner, began shouting, 'A voice from the east! A voice from the west! A voice from the four winds! A voice upon Jerusalem and upon the temple! A voice upon bridegrooms and brides! A voice upon the people!' He went about through all the streets crying this aloud day and night without stopping, 8. until some of the leading men among the people, annoyed at such an ominous presage, seized the man and beat him soundly. But he said nothing on his own behalf, nor did he even entreat those surrounding him, but continued to shout the same words with unflagging obstinacy. 9. Then the magistrates, realizing that the man was being moved by supernatural impulse, as indeed

---

29. *migremus hinc.* Rufinus seems to have read μεταβαίνωμεν rather than μεταβαίνομεν ("We depart"). See the apparatus *ad loc.* in Schwartz's edition. On the heavenly signs, compare Tacitus, *Hist.* 5.13.

he was, took him to the Roman judge, who had him scourged to the bone. But he responded with neither entreaties nor tears, but at almost every blow uttered the same message lamentably, in grief-stricken tones, adding, 'Woe! Woe to Jerusalem!'"

10. The same historian goes on to tell of something even more marvelous, namely that an oracle was found in some sacred writings which declared that a man would come forth at that time from their region who would rule the whole world. 11. The historian imagines that the oracle's prediction refers to Vespasian.[30] But Vespasian reigned only over those people who, it seemed, were subject to the Roman empire; hence the oracle's words are more fairly applied to Christ, to whom the Father said, "Ask me, and I will give you the nations for your inheritance and the ends of the earth for your possession." And it was through his apostles at that time that his "sound went forth into all the earth, and their words to the ends of the earth."[31]

3.9.1. It is, to be sure, worthwhile noting after this who this Josephus was, and where he came from and of what stock, since he has furnished us so much material and information about the events of history. He himself explains it as follows:

"I, Josephus, son of Matthias, a priest from Jerusalem, myself fought against the Romans at the start of the war, and was forced likewise to take part in the later battles."[32] 2. We know therefore that this man was considered most distinguished not only among the Jews, his own countrymen, but also among the Romans, so that his writings merited even a statue in Rome, and his books were included in its library. 3. For he composed his ancient history in twenty books, while his history of the Jewish war with the Romans runs to seven volumes. He asserts that he published it not only in Greek, but also in his native language, Hebrew,[33] for his countrymen, and he is worthy of belief beyond anyone else. 4. There are two other volumes as well by him on the ancientness of the Jews, in which he refutes Apion, a grammarian, who had written against the Jews in those times, and which are directed against some others who had attacked the customs and practices

30. *Bellum* 6.312–13. Tacitus, *Hist.* 5.13 likewise.
31. Ps 2.8; 18.5.   32. *Bellum* 1.3.
33. *Bellum* 1.3; *C. Apion.* 1.50.

of the Jewish people. 5. In the first of these two books he gives the following account of which writings are considered authoritative among the Hebrews according to ancestral tradition:[34]

3.10.1. "Nor do we have countless books, then, which disagree with each other, but only twenty-two books; they contain the sequence of all of the times, and are rightly believed to have been divinely inspired. 2. Five of them are Moses's; they contain the laws of life and the ancestry of the human race down to Moses himself, and cover a span of a little less than three thousand years. 3. The events of history from Moses's death down to Artaxerxes, who ruled over the Persians after Xerxes, have been recorded by the several prophets of those times in thirteen books. The remaining four books hand on to mortals hymns to God and precepts and admonitions about life. 4. From Artaxerxes down to our own time, however, while everything has been written, the writings are not considered as reliable as the first, since there did not exist in the same way a continuous and proven succession of prophets. 5. The facts themselves show, therefore, the respect we have for our scriptures. For even with all the centuries that have intervened, no one has ever dared to add, remove, or change anything; there is somehow in every one of our people this innate, inborn faith to believe that these are God's decrees, to cleave to them constantly, and for them, if necessary, to lay down our lives willingly."

6. It seems useful, I think, to include this passage of the historian as well. And there is yet another book of his, quite skillfully written, *It is Reason that Holds Sway in Us.*[35] Some have given the title "Maccabees" to this short work, because it contains the struggles and contests for religion in which the Maccabean brothers exerted themselves. 7. Our author also says, at the end of the twentieth book of the *Antiquities*,[36] that he intended to compose four books about God, and about his substance and laws, according to the Jewish faith and religion, and about why some things are allowed them and some not. He adds that there

---

34. *C. Apion.* 1.38–42. On the Old Testament canon see 4.26.14; 6.25.1–2.

35. *Quod animus sit qui imperium teneat in nobis* = Περὶ αὐτοκράτορος λογισμοῦ, a shortening of the traditional title of 4 Maccabees.

36. *Antiq.* 20.268.

were some other minor works composed by him. 8. And at the end of this twentieth book of the *Antiquities* he accuses one Justus from Tiberias, who attempted to undertake the same sort of work that he himself executed, of writing falsehood; he says,[37]

9. "But I have not imitated you in what I wrote. I offered my books to the emperors themselves just after the events had taken place, since I knew that I had kept to the truth throughout. Nor did I fail to win their approval. 10. I presented them as well to quite a few others, many of whom had themselves taken part in the battles, such as King Agrippa and a number of his relatives. 11. The emperor Titus in fact was so convinced that it was through these books that news of the events should reach all people, that he wrote an official order, with his own hand, that they should be read by everyone. As for King Agrippa, he testified to the accuracy of our work in sixty-two letters, two of which I have included."

That will suffice concerning these matters.

3.11. Let us now resume our narrative. After the martyrdom of James and the destruction of the city which followed hard upon it, it is said that the apostles and the other disciples of the Lord who were left at that time gathered together from every place along with those who were called relatives of the Lord according to the flesh—for there were quite a few of those too who were still left at that time—and took counsel together about who was worthy to succeed James. Everyone unanimously decided that Symeon, son of Cleopas, who is mentioned in the gospels, should receive the bishop's chair. He was said to have been the Savior's cousin according to the flesh, since Hegesippus affirms that Cleopas was Joseph's brother.[38]

3.12. At this time Vespasian, after the destruction of Jerusalem, ordered a search for any men of David's family who might be left, they being of royal ancestry. This was another occasion for a very grievous persecution to be unleashed upon the Jews.

3.13. Vespasian, after the tenth year of his reign, was suc-

---

37. *Vita* 361–64. Justus is not in fact mentioned in the *Antiquities*, but the *Vita* is found in manuscripts after the other work and might therefore have been viewed as a postscript to it.

38. "Cleopas" is "Clopas" in Eusebius. Cf. 4.22.4.

ceeded as ruler by his son Titus.[39] In the second year of the latter's reign, Linus, they say, after completing twelve years in the priesthood, handed on to Anencletus the episcopacy of the city of Rome. But Titus, after passing not more than two years and as many months as sovereign of Rome, left the government of the state to his brother Domitian.[40] 3.14. In the fourth year of Domitian, then, Annianus passed away in Alexandria after serving in the priesthood for twenty-two years. He was succeeded by Abilius. 3.15. In Rome Anencletus, after twelve years as bishop, handed on the chair of the priesthood to Clement, whom the apostle Paul describes as his assistant when he writes to the Philippians, "With Clement and my other assistants, whose names are in the book of life."[41]

3.16. Clement's letter written to the Corinthians is preserved; it is quite excellent and truly wonderful. He wrote it as representing the Roman church when dissension had arisen among the Corinthians. We know that it has been read to the people in many churches both in former times and in our own. As for the disturbance which arose among the Corinthians and the dissension among the people, Hegesippus, a most reliable witness, divulges it in speaking thus:[42]

3.17. "Domitian practiced great cruelty toward many, butchering a great number of distinguished and excellent men in Rome with no right or reason to do so, banishing countless others and seizing their property, and, finally, succeeding Nero in his battle against God and in his irreligious ways. For he was the second one, following him, to launch a persecution against ours, since his father, Vespasian, certainly did not wrong ours at all."[43]

3.18.1. It was at this time that the apostle and evangelist John

39. June 24, 79.   40. December 13, 81.
41. Phil 4.3.

42. *de seditione ... Hegesippus indicat hoc modo dicens ...* : Rufinus mistranslates here. Eusebius actually says, "And that there was indeed dissension among the Corinthians in his time is reliably testified to by Hegesippus." 3.17 is not, then, a citation from Hegesippus, whose remarks about this situation are not in fact known.

43. On Domitian's cruelty, executions, and exiles: Suetonius, *Domitian* 10–11; Dio Cassius 67.3.3–4; Eutropius 7.23.2; Aurelius Victor 11.2; Jerome, *Chron.* 94–95.

is said to have been banished to the island of Patmos on account of his preaching of the divine word and witness to the truth.[44] 2. Irenaeus in fact, when writing about the number of the name of the Antichrist, which is contained in Revelation, which is said to be John's, records the following about John in the fifth book *Against Heresies*:[45]

3. "Had it been necessary to make a clearer explanation concerning that name at this time, by whom might it have more fittingly been disclosed than by him who saw the revelation itself? For it has not been long since it occurred; it was almost in our own time, at the end of Domitian's reign."

4. Now the teachings of our faith increased so much in renown at this time, that even a number of writers not belonging to our religion included in their histories both the persecution of that time and the martyrdoms. Based on their careful investigation of the period, they state that in the fifteenth year of the emperor Domitian, Flavia Domitilla, the daughter of the sister of Flavius Clemens, then a former consul, was banished along with many others to the island of Pontia by the emperor for her witness to Christ.[46]

3.19. An old tradition has it that when Domitian ordered all of those to be executed who were descended from David's family and the royal line, some people were denounced to him in person as descendants of Jude, who is said to have been the Savior's brother according to the flesh; the hostility to which they were subjected came both from their descent from David's family and their relation to Christ himself. Hegesippus puts the matter clearly as follows:[47]

3.20.1. "Some of the relatives of our Lord according to the

44. Rv 1.9.

45. Rv 13.18; Irenaeus, *Adv. haer.* 5.30.3.

46. "then a former consul" (*unius tunc ex consulibus viri*): Eusebius says that he was actually a consul at the time. Suetonius, *Domitian* 15.1, says that the emperor put him to death "almost before the end of his consulship (*tantum non in ipso eius consulatu*)." Dio Cassius, 67.14.1–2, says that both Flavius Clemens and Flavia Domitilla were accused of atheism, the latter being banished to the island of Pandateria. Cf. also the Acts of Nereus and Achilleus and Jerome, *Ep.* 108.7.1 and *Chron.* 96.

47. Hegesippus: cf. 2.23.3. Jude related to Jesus: Mk 6.3.

flesh were still alive, grandsons of that Jude who was called the
Lord's brother according to the flesh; some people denounced
them as descendants from David's stock. Someone named Revocatus,⁴⁸ who had been sent for this, brought them to Domitian Caesar, who himself dreaded the coming of Christ, as
Herod had originally. 2. When asked by Domitian if they were
of David's family, they admitted it. Then he asked them how
much they owned and how much property they had. They replied that both of them possessed not more than nine thousand denarii, of which half belonged to each. Nor did they have
it in money, but in land valuation; they had thirty-nine *iugera*,
which they worked with their own hands, from which they were
fed, and on which they paid taxes. 3. At the same time, as proof
of their daily farm work, they held out their hands, which were
rough and calloused from their labor. 4. When asked about
Christ, about what sort of kingdom he had, who he was, and
from where and when he would come, they answered that the
kingdom assigned him was not of this world nor of this earth,
but that a heavenly kingdom was being prepared for him by
the work of angels at the completion of the age, when he would
come in glory to judge concerning the living and the dead, and
would render to each person according to the deeds and merits
of each. 5. At this Domitian, since he had not found anything
wrong that they had done, and had nothing but contempt for
their lowliness, bade them go free. He also issued decrees rescinding the persecution he had ordered loosed against the
churches. 6. Dismissed by him, they became church leaders in
the time now of peace, whether that was because of what they
deserved by their martyrdom,⁴⁹ or because of the privilege of
their high kinship, and they lived until Trajan's time."

7. Thus we find in Hegesippus. Tertullian speaks likewise
about Domitian, as follows: "Domitian once tried something
similar to live up to Nero's cruelty, but being human he quickly
desisted, so that he even recalled those he had sent into exile."⁵⁰

48. Revocatus = ὁ ῐουκᾱτος (from *evocatus*, here meaning "guard").
49. Eusebius: "because of their testimony" (ὡς ἂν δὴ μάρτυρας).
50. *Apologeticum* 5.4. Unlike 2.25.4, this is not an exact citation (the Greek text in the two places is different).

8. After Domitian had reigned for fifteen years, Nerva received the sovereignty. Under him all the honors conferred on Domitian were revoked. And all of those who had been banished by him were ordered recalled by senate decree, and their property restored. Those who have written the histories of those times testify to each of these matters.[51] 9. The writers of our own history assert that it was then, therefore, that the apostle John also returned to Ephesus, as to his own school,[52] after he was released from the island.

3.21. Nerva having died after a year, more or less,[53] Trajan succeeded to power. In his first year as sovereign, Abilius died in Alexandria after thirteen years in the priesthood. Cerdo succeeded him in the priesthood. In Rome during this time Clement also held office as bishop, the third after Paul and Peter. 3.22. In Antioch Evodius was the first, and Ignatius the second. In Jerusalem as well Symeon governed the church during that time, the second to do so, following James, the brother of the Lord.

3.23.1. During all of this, that man himself whom the Lord Jesus loved, the one who was both apostle and evangelist, John, was still alive and living in Asia, and governing the churches there after returning from the island following Domitian's death, as we said. 2. I will prove that this is so from two trustworthy witnesses. Irenaeus and Clement of Alexandria support the truth of this, 3. Irenaeus writing as follows in the second book *Against the Heresies:*[54] "And all the presbyters are witnesses who saw John, the Lord's disciple, in Asia, and know that John handed on these things; he remained with them until Trajan's time."

4. The same writer testifies to the same matter once again in the third book of the same work: "The church which is in Ephesus was founded by Paul but built by John, who remained

51. Suetonius, *Domitian* 23.1; Dio Cassius 68.1.1–2.1. Domitian reigned from September 14, 81, to September 18, 96.

52. *Ephesum quasi ad scholam propriam redisse* = τὴν ἐπὶ τῆς Ἐφέσου διατριβὴν ἀπειληφέναι. διατριβή can mean "school," but in this context the words mean "resumed his residence in Ephesus."

53. September 18, 96, to January 27, 98.

54. 2.22.5.

in it until Trajan's time. You have here a trustworthy witness with evidence concerning the apostle's time."[55] 5. Listen also to what is said by Clement, whose testimony we promised as well; he too has composed a narrative which is absolutely essential and which we believe will be of use to our readers if we include it. He writes as follows:[56]

"Listen to a tale that is not a tale, but a report about the apostle John passed on to the memories of all. When he returned to Ephesus from the island of Patmos after the tyrant's death, he was asked to enlighten the neighboring provinces as well, whether by founding churches in places where there were none, or, where they existed, by furnishing them with priests and ministers according to what the Holy Spirit would show him about each person. 7. When therefore he had come to one city not far away and had given satisfaction as usual to all the church people, he saw one youth who was robust and handsome, and exceedingly keen of mind as well. He caught the eye of the bishop, who had just been ordained, and said, 'I entrust this youth to you with all earnestness, with Christ and the whole church as my witnesses.' The bishop received him, promising to give him all of his attention, as he had been bidden. He repeated his request over and over, however, entrusting the youth to him with great earnestness, and afterwards returned to Ephesus.

8. "The presbyter took the lad who had been entrusted to him into his home, and reared, cherished, and cared for him, and finally granted him the grace of baptism. Afterwards, relying on the grace with which he had been fortified, he began to treat the youth a little less strictly. 9. He for his part, having gained his freedom while still immature, was at once taught to love vice and to enter upon the path of a corrupt life by his peers, who were fond of idleness and ease. First he was taken in by being enticed by their feasts, then they made him a partner and companion in their nightly thefts, and after that they

---

55. Eusebius/Irenaeus 3.3.4 does not say that John built the church, but just that he stayed in it. He also makes clear that it is the church that is the witness, and to the apostolic tradition.

56. Clement of Alexandria, *Quis dives salvetur* 42.1–15. The city in question below is Smyrna (*Paschal Chronicle* P 251 D).

drew him on to even greater misdeeds. 10. Since meanwhile
the youth was gradually being formed and taught to commit
crimes, and was of passionate temper, like a powerful and undisciplined horse that tears fearsomely at its bit as it abandons
the straight path, he despised his guardian and hurtled down
headlong, 11. evils succeeding evils so rapidly that he finally
despaired of the salvation granted him by God. Petty crimes
he now disdained; he undertook any that were more serious,
giving himself completely to depravity, and suffering no one
to outdo him in misconduct. In the end he made his followers
the very ones who had earlier been his teachers in crime, and
formed them into a gang of robbers, of which he was himself
the leader and savage chief, practicing with them every form
of cruelty.

"Now when time had passed and it seemed useful to do so,
12. John was again invited to that city, and when he had seen to
the other matters for which he had come, he said, 'Now, bishop, produce the deposit which Christ and I clearly entrusted
to you with the church which you govern as witness.' 13. He
was at a loss, at first thinking that some money which he had
not received was being demanded of him. But then he reflected
that John could neither practice deception nor request what he
had not given, and he continued speechless. John, seeing him
at a loss, said, 'What I am requesting from you is that youth and
your brother's soul.' The old man sighed deeply and broke into
tears. 'He is dead,' he said. 'How did he die?' asked the other.
'He died to God,' he said, 'because he turned out as badly as
possible, completely disgraceful, and in the end turned even
to robbery. And now he has taken over some mountain with a
large band of robbers.'

14. "When he heard this, the apostle immediately rent the
garment he was wearing and struck his head with loud groans.
'A fine guardian of your brother's soul I left you!' he said. 'But
now get me a horse and a guide!' 15. And when he reached
the place, he was seized by the robbers keeping watch. But he
tried neither to escape nor to avoid them at all; he only shouted, 'Bring me your chief; this is why I have come!' 16. He, when
he had armed himself and come, recognized the apostle John

from a distance, was struck with shame, and turned to flee. He spurred his horse after him at once and pursued him, heedless of his age, shouting, 17. 'Why are you fleeing your father, my son? Why are you fleeing an old man without weapons? Pity me, do not fear me; you still have hope for life. I will myself take responsibility for you before Christ. I will certainly suffer death willingly for you, as the Lord suffered it for us, and I will give my life for your life. Just stop and believe me, because Christ has sent me.' 18. When he heard this he stopped, looked down to the ground, and then threw away his weapons. Then he began to tremble, wept bitterly, and fell at the knees of the old man who came up to him, making restitution as best he could with his groans and lamentations, and was baptized again in the copious fonts of his own tears, concealing only his right hand. 19. The apostle for his part swore that he would win forgiveness for him from the Savior, at the same time falling at his knees and kissing fervently the right hand which had wrought the butchery with which his conscience tormented him, since it had now been cleansed by his penance. Bringing him back to the church, he poured out prayers for him unceasingly, underwent repeated fasts with him, and begged for him the forgiveness from God which he had promised him. He also calmed his frantic, terrified mind by various words of consolation like so many enchantments. Nor did he leave him until he was thoroughly reformed, whereupon he proceeded to put him in charge of the church,[57] furnishing thereby magnificent examples of true penance and outstanding evidence of the new rebirth, and displaying in him tokens and trophies of the resurrection made visible."

3.24.1. This passage from Clement is inserted here in our book not only for its historical value, but also because of its ben-

---

57. [*nec prius abstitit*], *quam eum . . . etiam ecclesiae praeficeret* = πρὶν αὐτὸν ἐπιστῆσαι τῇ ἐκκλησίᾳ. The Greek can mean simply that the man was brought in or presented to the church, but it can also readily bear Rufinus's translation of it. His fondness for the dramatic is well displayed here: the aged apostle presenting the robber chief to the church as its new bishop (perhaps with some soothing words about proven abilities in leadership and fund-raising?). It will be seen again in the last two books.

efit to our readers. Let us now explain, along with these other matters, what it was that this apostle wrote which is considered authoritative. 2. There is first the gospel under his name, which has resounded throughout the whole earth. Now the reason why it was placed by those of old after the other three gospels, is as follows. 3. The venerable apostles of Christ, truly worthy of God as they were, were renowned in every way for purity of life and virtues of mind, and as such did not place great store by elegance of language, since their souls were adorned with divine virtues. At the same time, trusting as they did in the grace of the signs granted them by our Lord Jesus Christ, they found the entirety of the preaching about the Lord not in the persuasive language of human speech, but in the demonstration of the Spirit[58] and in the power by which, through the wonders they achieved and the trust in their words that they won, they passed on the knowledge of the kingdom of heaven to the whole earth. They thus thought it of little worth to write many books, 4. since what was claimed by this sort of preaching required the support of the divine power, not the logic of human speech. Paul, then, who stands out among all the other apostles for the culture of his language and power of his thought, has not left more than the brief corpus of his letters, he who certainly held within himself enormous mysteries beyond count, seeing as he was snatched up even to the third heaven, where he viewed what was taking place; brought as well into that very paradise befitting God, he heard there ineffable words and received whatever teaching is found there as a student in that school for the time, whether he was in the body or out of it.[59]

5. The other disciples as well of our Lord and Savior, not only those who were of those twelve but others in addition who were nonetheless of the school of our Lord and Savior, have left some message, divinely inspired as they were, and they wanted it kept short and completely succinct. 6. Of these disciples of Our Lord, then, only Matthew and John are said to have applied themselves to writing, and were in a way compelled thereto. Matthew at first preached to the Hebrews, but then as he

58. 1 Cor 2.4.
59. 2 Cor 12.2–4.

made ready to go over to the gentiles, he composed a writing in his native language, and, summarizing what he had preached, he left it as a record to those from whom he was going forth to preach to the gentiles.[60] 7. After him the gospel writings of Luke and Mark were published for the reasons we mentioned earlier. As for John, they say that he preached the gospel without setting down anything in writing almost to the end of his life.[61] But when these three gospels came to his attention, it is related that while he acknowledged the accuracy and truth of what they said, he saw that certain things were missing from them, especially those which concerned what the Lord did at the outset of his preaching. 8. It is indisputable, that is, that in these three gospels the only things to be found are those which happened in the year when John the Baptist was imprisoned and executed. 9. You may in short observe that right at the beginning of his narrative, Matthew, after he tells of his forty-day fast and temptation, goes on immediately to say, "But hearing that John had been handed over, he left Judea and went to Galilee."

10. Mark speaks likewise: "After John had been handed over, Jesus went to Galilee." And Luke as well, before he begins reporting anything about what Jesus did, says, "Herod added to all the evils he had done and shut John up in prison."[62] 11. Since, therefore, these matters had evidently been omitted by them, the apostle John is said to have been asked to compose an account of what the Savior did before John was handed over, the matters which they had skipped. He says therefore in his gospel, "This Jesus did as the first of the signs." And he announces elsewhere as well, "For John had not yet been put in prison."[63] 12. It is clear from this that he is writing of what Jesus did before John was handed over. 13. Those therefore who consider this carefully will find that it is clear that the gospels do not disagree with each other, but that the events of which John writes belong to a time other than those of which the oth-

60. Matthew's Hebrew gospel: 3.27.4; 3.39.16; 5.8.2; 5.10.3; 6.25.4.
61. Luke, Mark, and John: 2.15.1; 3.4.6–7; 6.14.7.
62. Mt 4.12; Mk 1.14; Lk 3.19–20.
63. Jn 2.11; 3.24.

ers speak. Since, then, both Matthew and Luke had told of the Savior's birth according to the flesh, John does not speak of this; he begins with the doctrine about him as God and with his divinity. This was the topic which, we may be sure, had been reserved for him by the Holy Spirit as for someone exceptional. 14. Let this suffice concerning John's gospel, and what has already been said about Mark's gospel will do as well.[64]

15. As for Luke, he states at the beginning of his gospel the reason why he wrote it: that many others had rashly presumed to relate matters of which his own acquaintance was more accurate.[65] Wishing therefore to detach us from the others' accounts, he guaranteed the truth of what he himself wrote, confident as he was that he had followed the teaching of Paul and the other apostles who had handed on to him what they themselves had seen from the outset, and that this was what he was handing on to us through his own gospel. 16. These few remarks of ours about Luke will suffice as well. In due time, however, we will show more suitably and fully how all these matters stand by including what the authors of old have left in writing about them.

17. Letters of John have also survived, the first of which was never held to be doubtful either by those of old or those following them. Opinion about the other two, however, and about the Book of Revelation, continues to waver even now; 18. even those of old held them to be doubtful, as I said and as we will show by their own words in their proper place.[66]

3.25.1. Since, then, we have reached this point, let us list the complete canon of the New Testament,[67] and first of all let us yoke the heavenly chariot of all of the gospels with its team of four, to which the Acts of the Apostles should be joined. 2. After these should be added Paul's letters; the first letter of John should follow those; and the first of Peter's likewise. These are the writings which have never been held in any doubt at all. 3. Next come the writings which a number of people have considered doubtful: the Revelation of John, concerning which we will give the opinions of each of the people of old in their prop-

64. See 2.15.
66. Cf. 4.18.8; 4.24; 5.8; 6.25; 7.25.
65. Lk 1.1–4.
67. Cf. also 3.31.6.

er places; the letter of James, and also of Jude; the second letter
of Peter and the second and third of John, whether these may
be shown to be of the evangelist himself or of someone else of
the same name. 4. After these works come the writing which
is called the Acts of Paul, the short work known as the Shepherd's, and the Revelation of Peter, all of which are considered
extremely doubtful. A letter of Barnabas and the Teaching of
the Apostles, as it is called,[68] are also in circulation. 5. Some
people also join with these works the gospel which is called
"According to the Hebrews" and which is especially popular
among those Hebrews who appear to accept Christ; but it is opposed in the church.[69]

6. It was, however, incumbent upon us to list all these works,
that there might be no doubt about which of them have been
considered authoritative since olden times, and which have
aroused some persistent opposition or simply hesitation, even
though they have been accepted by most of the churches. It
should be noted, however, that those works which are ascribed
by the sectarians to the apostles, such as the ones which are
called the gospels of Peter,[70] Thomas, Matthias, and the rest of
the apostles, as well as the Acts of Andrew and John and the
other apostles, are nowhere mentioned or recorded in any of
the writings of those of old, those at least who succeeded the
apostles. 7. Their very style may be seen to be quite different
from that to which the church is used. And the thought itself,
and everything else they contain, disagree markedly with the
apostolic faith, which shows that they are forgeries produced
by sectarian perversity. Hence they are not to be ranked even
among the works which we said are considered doubtful, but
are to be rejected as completely foreign and as inconsistent
with the rule of piety.

68. *Doctrina quae dicitur apostolorum* = τῶν ἀποστόλων αἱ λεγόμεναι Διδαχαί.
Probably *The Didache*: cf. Kurt Niederwimmer, *Die Didache* (Göttingen: Vandenhoeck and Ruprecht, 1989), 15–18.

69. *sed in ecclesia contradicitur:* added by Rufinus. Gospel According to the
Hebrews: 3.39.17. On Rufinus's "updating" of the canon, see J. E. L. Oulton,
"Rufinus's Translation of the Church History of Eusebius," *JTS* 30 (1929):
156–58.

70. Gospel of Peter: 3.3.2; 6.12.

3.26.1. Now let us continue with our history. Simon the magician was succeeded by Menander, a weapon of the devil not inferior to the former, and himself a Samaritan; in the art of magic he alone proved to be not just equal to his master but even superior to his impiety. Puffed up by his greater marvels, he said that he was himself the savior sent from the heavenly and invisible aeons[71] for the salvation of humankind, 2. and claimed that no one could defeat the angels of the aeon[72] who had not first been properly trained by him in the art of magic, and, having been made immortal and eternal through the baptism given by him, become everlasting in this life. All of this may quite easily be learned from Irenaeus's books, for those who wish. 3. Justin as well, in the writings in which he mentions Simon, writes as follows about him too:[73]

"We know that one Menander, a Samaritan from the village of Capparattaea and a disciple of Simon, was spurred by demonic impulse to come to Antioch, where he deceived a great many by his magic art; he was even able to persuade his followers that they would not die. Some of them still profess these things."

This is truly a deception of the devil, that magicians should adopt the name of Christians in order thereby to besmirch the holy and venerable mystery of our religion, even though they mock and despise the teachings of the church about the immortality of the soul and the resurrection of the dead. But those who relied on such teachers were completely deprived of the hope of salvation and life.

3.27.1. There were others as well whom the same demon deceived in another way, even though he could not separate them from the love of Christ: they were the Ebionites, which means "the poor."[74] 2. For they really are poor, and lacking in the

---

71. *de caelestibus et invisibilibus saeculis destinatum.*

72. *angelos saeculi vincere* = αὐτῶν τῶν κοσμοποιῶν ἀγγέλων περιγενήσεσθαι ("defeat the world-creating angels"). On Menander, see Epiphanius, *Pan.* 22, and Barbara Aland, *Was ist Gnosis: Studien zum frühen Christentum, zu Marcion und zur kaiserzeitlichen Philosophie* (Tübingen: Mohr Siebeck, 2009), 77–80.

73. *Apol.* 1.26.4.

74. "Ebion" is Hebrew for "poor." On this Judeo-Christian sect, see H.-J. Schoeps, *DHGE* 14.1314–19. On the Gospel According to the Hebrews below, cf. 3.24.6; 3.39.16; 5.8.2; 5.10.3; 6.25.4.

knowledge of the glory of Christ, because they think he is only a human being, one who became a just man through progress in life and virtue and was begotten in the usual way from man and woman. They also think that the law is to be observed, and that faith in Christ alone is not enough for salvation. 3. Some of them, however, shun the impious assertion that he was born of man and woman, and acknowledge that it was from the Holy Spirit and the Virgin Mary, but they do not profess that he was always God and the Word and Wisdom of God. They also retain the corporal observance of the law. 4. They reject all of the Apostle's letters without distinction, however, and call him an apostate from the law. They use some one gospel which is called "According to the Hebrews," regarding all the rest as of no account. 5. They observe the Sabbath with the Jews according to the law, and Sunday as a holy day with us for the Lord's Resurrection. 6. Hence they are fittingly called Ebionites in accordance with the poverty of their understanding.

3.28.1. We are told that during this same time there arose the leader of another sect, Cerinthus. Gaius, whom we mentioned earlier, writes as follows of him in the dialogue contained in his arguments:[75]

2. "Cerinthus, moreover, proposes to us the following fantasies by way of certain revelations which it seems he thought were composed by a great apostle and revealed to him by angels. He says that after the resurrection there will be an earthly kingdom of Christ in Jerusalem, and human beings will consort with each other in the flesh once again subject to concupiscence. He also indicates, against the authority of scripture, that there will be a period of some thousand years during which, among many other perversions, there will be wedding feasts, or so he says to deceive those who are addicted to lust."

3. Dionysius too, when he treats of the Revelation of John[76] and discusses certain matters according to what has been handed down to the church from of old, mentions this man as follows:

75. Gaius: 2.25.6–7; 6.20.3. Cerinthus: 4.14.6; Epiphanius, *Pan.* 28. Compare 3.28.2–5 with 7.25.1–3.
76. Rufinus omits here "in the second book of *The Promises.*"

4. "Cerinthus, the founder of the Cerinthian sect, desired to lend to his inventions the lustre of high authority, in accordance with the perverse ideas of this writing, for his heresy was to declare that the kingdom of Christ to come would be earthly. 5. And since he was addicted to eating, gluttony, and lust, he decided that the future held what his own lust dictated to him. He announced that the urges of the stomach and of what is beneath the stomach would be satisfied by food, drink, and marriage. And that he might seem to have something to say more hallowed in tone, he spoke of festivals of the law to be celebrated again, and fleshly victims to be slaughtered once more."

6. As for Irenaeus, he also divulged the more secret aspects of this sect in the first book of his work; those who wish to know more may consult it.[77]

3.29.1. There was another sect as well, called the Nicolaitans, which lasted a very short while and which is also mentioned in the Revelation of John. They boast of having as their founder Nicolaus, one of those made deacons by the apostles with Stephen.[78] Clement of Alexandria in the third book of the *Stromata* writes as follows of him:

2. "He had a wife of exceptional beauty. And after the Ascension of our Lord and Savior, when he was scolded by the apostles for wrongful jealousy, he brought his wife forward and said that anyone might have her who wanted. They thought that the result of this would be that anyone would misuse his flesh in what he enjoyed, according to what Nicolaus had done and said. And in holding to what had been said and done in simplicity and innocence, those who under his name have acquired for themselves a sect for their own lust now practice indiscriminate and unlawful sexual intercourse without any shame. 3. But I have learned that Nicolaus had no relations with any woman at all except for the one he married. And as for his children, the daughters persevered in chaste virginity right to the end of their old age, while his son himself preserved the sanctity of his uncorrupted body. This being so, it is clear that when he brought his wife out in front of the apostles because he was sus-

77. Irenaeus, *Adv. haer.* 1.26.1.
78. Rv 2.6, 15; Acts 6.1–6; Clement, *Stromata* 3.25.6–26.3.

pected of jealousy, he did so from contempt of the vice of lust: he wanted thereby to show that he had refrained from what he had been thought to seek immoderately, teaching in this way that carnal pleasure is to be contemned and not sought out. His reason was, I think, that he did not want to serve two masters, lust and God, as the Savior taught.[79] 4. And they say that Matthias as well taught likewise that one must fight against the flesh and yield not an inch to its pleasure and lust, but nourish the soul on the provender of wisdom and help it always to grow with the food of knowledge."

This will suffice concerning those sects which strayed from the truth during the times mentioned and soon died out.

3.30.1. This Clement whom we have cited has the following things to say, among others, when he writes against those who scorn marriage: "Do they perhaps condemn even the apostles? For Peter and Philip had wives, and also gave their daughters in marriage to men. Nor does it bother Paul to mention and greet his consort in one of his letters; he says that he does not take her around with him so that he may more easily preach the gospel."[80]

2. Now since we have mentioned Clement, it will not be out of place to quote another remarkable narrative of his, which he includes in the seventh book of the same work: "They say that when blessed Peter saw his wife being led off to her suffering, he rejoiced at the grace of her election and return to her own home, called out after her as she was being led away, and addressed her by her own name: 'Remember the Lord, my wife!' Such were the marriages of the saints, such the perfect affection of the blessed."[81]

3.31.1. Since, then, we have already told of the deaths of Peter and Paul in what went before, 2. and have spoken in part of the time when John departed from this life,[82] it may now be fitting to speak of his resting place, relying on what Polycrates,

79. Mt 6.24; Lk 16.13.
80. *Stromata* 3.52.4–53.1. Peter: Mt 8.14; 1 Cor 9.5. Philip's daughters: Acts 21.9. Paul: 1 Cor 9.12; Phil 4.3.
81. *Stromata* 7.63.2–64.1.
82. Peter and Paul: 2.25.5–8. John: 3.23.1–4.

bishop of Ephesus, says. Polycrates in writing to Victor, bishop of Rome, mentions both him and Philip the apostle along with his daughters, as we have already quoted earlier:[83]

3. "Great luminaries have fallen asleep in the regions of Asia; the Lord will awaken them on the last day, that of his Advent, when he will come in glory and search out all his holy ones. I speak in fact of Philip, who was one of the apostles and who fell asleep in Hierapolis. Two of his daughters as well who were virgins reached old age there too, while another daughter of his, filled with the Holy Spirit, remained in Ephesus. And the John who reclined upon the Lord's chest and who was a priest of God wearing the high-priestly plate[84] and a martyr and an outstanding teacher, sleeps in Ephesus."

4. This citation will suffice concerning the places in which they rest in the sleep of peace. Now Gaius, who was mentioned earlier, agrees with this in what he records about Philip's daughters and about his death in the dialogue he writes where he argues with Proculus. He says, "After this there were four prophetesses, the daughters of Philip; his grave is in Hierapolis, a city of Asia, together with his daughters."[85]

5. Luke too mentions them in the Acts of the Apostles while they were still living in Caesarea. He says, "We came to Caesarea and entered the house of Philip the evangelist, who was one of the Seven, and stayed with him. He had four virgin daughters who prophesied."[86]

6. We have, then, set forth in due order what pertains to the times of the apostles and thereafter, as far as we could do so

---

83. "as ... earlier": Rufinus adds; neither Eusebius nor Rufinus in fact quoted Polycrates earlier. They will repeat the following quotation in 5.24.2–3, however; there the Greek text is virtually the same, while the Latin translation differs.

84. The usual translation "plate" for *petalum* (πέταλον) may mislead; the word earlier meant the special ornament on the high priest's headdress, and later came to be the special designation for the high-priestly crown itself. Cf. Richard Bauckham, "Papias and Polycrates on the Origin of the Fourth Gospel," *JTS* NS 44 (1993): 33–41.

85. Gaius: 2.25.6–7; 3.28.1–2; 6.20.3. "After this" = *post haec* = μετὰ τοῦτον ("after him").

86. Acts 21.8–9.

from the writings collected from those of old, and also what pertains to the canon of scripture: the books considered authoritative, and those rejected completely, as well as those in some way in between which have been accepted by the churches simply because they are informative, and not because their authority is unquestioned.[87] Let us now proceed to other matters.

3.32.1. We are told that after Nero and Domitian, the arrogance of the populace in each of the cities broke out into persecution of ours during the time of the one whose period we are now recording. It was during this time that Symeon, son of Cleopas, who, as we said earlier, had been ordained as the second bishop for Jerusalem, was released by martyrdom from the bonds of the flesh. 2. We are assured of this by the same Hegesippus whom we have already summoned as witness several times.[88] What he says is that the man was accused of being a Christian by some sectarians and was subject to many tortures for many days, so that the judge himself together with his friends was astonished at his endurance, until finally he ordered that his life be brought to an end by the same kind of execution that was inflicted on the Lord. 3. I think, though, that it would be more satisfying to hear the very words with which he affirms this. What he says in speaking of the sectarians is as follows: "Some of these same ones accused Symeon, son of Cleopas, of being of the stock of David and a Christian. And thus he became a martyr at the age of 120 under Trajan Caesar before the consular Atticus."[89]

4. He adds that since a search was under way at the time for those descended from David's stock and from the royal tribe, his accusers were among those arrested. That Symeon, now, was among those who heard the Lord, is indicated by the length of his life and the witness of the gospels, where his mother is said to be Mary, the wife of Cleopas.[90] 5. The same writer also says that in addition to those we mentioned earlier, some other grandsons of Jude, one of the Lord's brothers, were found still

87. Compare 3.25.
88. Cf. 3.11 (Eusebius has "Clopas" there as well). Trajan reigned, 98–117. Hegesippus is cited at 2.23.3–18.
89. On Atticus (c. 99–103) see Schürer, 1.516.
90. Jn 19.25.

alive at this time and were made martyrs in Domitian's time.[91] He writes as follows:

6. "They arrived, then, and became the heads of each of the churches as martyrs and relatives of the Lord, and when peace was restored to the church, they remained until the time of Trajan Caesar, until the time when the Lord's cousin Symeon, son of Cleopas, of whom we spoke earlier, was slandered by the sectarians and denounced to the consular as a Christian. And after he had been tortured for a long time, he ended his life in martyrdom, with everyone who was present, including the judge himself, in amazement at how the old man of 120 years bore crucifixion."

7. After this the same writer goes on to say that the church up to then remained a pure, undefiled virgin, since the perverters of the truth and the violators of the divine word were either nowhere to be found, or if by chance there were any, they lay concealed in hidden and secret crevices of the earth. 8. But when the choir of apostles and that whole generation which had heard the Lord with their own ears departed from this life, then the impious error of false doctrine plunged into the empty house, as it were, and since there was no longer anyone to defend the divine property, threw off its disguise, snatched up the weapons of falsehood, and launched an attack upon the apostolic truth.

3.33.1. But while that war was being waged within, the church was being buffeted by persecutions from outside, and such huge crowds of martyrs were being executed each day that Pliny the Younger, who was then governor of a province, was so disturbed at the great number of those who were being killed that he reported to the emperor that countless thousands of people were being slain each day[92] who had been found guilty of committing no crime or doing anything against the Roman laws; they sim-

91. The grandsons of Jude were mentioned at 3.20.1. *Martyres* = μάρτυρες ("witnesses").

92. *quod innumera hominum milia cottidie obtruncarentur.* Eusebius says simply that he "reported to the emperor the number of those being put to death." It sounds as if Rufinus consulted Pliny's *Ep.* 10.96.9 directly: *Multi enim omnis aetatis, omnis ordinis, utriusque sexus etiam vocantur in periculum et vocabuntur. Neque civitates tantum, sed vicos etiam atque agros superstitionis istius contagio pervagata est ...*

ply had been singing hymns before dawn to some god named Christ. As for adultery and other crimes of the sort, they were considered unlawful by them and were completely avoided; in other matters they followed the public laws. 2. Trajan replied to this that Christians should not be searched for, but should be punished if met with.[93] The flames of persecution were thereby partly quenched, it was thought, but opportunities to harm us were, it seems, not unavailable to those who longed to exercise their malice against us. For the populace was at times incited against us, while at other times a magistrate would seize the opportunities offered and deny that he had searched out those whom he had wanted to punish when they were delivered over. 3. Tertullian speaks of this in his *Apology*,[94] which those who wish to know more may consult.

3.34. In Rome, then, Clement, who was the third after the apostles, handed on the ministry of the divine word to Evaristus, after nine years in the priesthood.[95]

3.35. When Symeon, whom we mentioned earlier,[96] passed away in Jerusalem, Justus, who was of those who had come to faith in Christ from the circumcision, received the episcopacy.

3.36.1. During this time one of the apostles' disciples, Polycarp, bishop of the church of Smyrna, was still alive and flourishing in Asia, as was Papias, who exercised the priesthood in Hierapolis. 2. And even in our own time Ignatius is still well known; he received the episcopacy in Antioch, the second in succession after Peter.[97] 3. It is said that he was sent from Syria to Rome and was given to the beasts as a martyr for Christ. 4. As he was traveling through Asia under guard and passing through the several cities, he instructed the people of the churches through evangelical exhortation to persevere in the faith, to keep themselves from the contagion of the sectarians, who were beginning

93. Cf. Pliny, *Epp.* 10.96 and 10.97.
94. *Apol.* 2.6–7.
95. What Eusebius says here is that Clement handed on the office to Evaristus in the third year of the aforesaid emperor; Eusebius had mentioned in 3.4.9 that Clement was the third bishop of Rome, although Rufinus did not translate that part of the section there.
96. 3.32.1–6.
97. 3.22 says that Evodius was the first bishop of Antioch.

for the first time to sprout more abundantly, and to cleave more carefully and tenaciously to the traditions of the apostles; he even asserted that he had left these traditions in writing as a precautionary measure, lest there be any uncertainty among those who came later. 5. When at length he came to Smyrna, where Polycarp was, he wrote from there one letter to the Ephesians and their pastor, in which he also mentions Onesimus, and another letter to the city of Magnesia, which is on the Meander; in it he mentions the bishop, Damaeus. He wrote also to the church in Tralles, which was then, he indicates, governed by Polybius.[98] 6. And in the one he wrote to the Roman church he begged them not to deprive him of the hope of martyrdom out of a desire to spare him torment, and a little later he writes as follows:[99]

7. "From Syria all the way to Rome I am fighting with beasts on land and sea, fastened and bound as I am day and night to ten leopards, the soldiers, that is, set to guard me, who become more savage the better we treat them. But my education is being furthered by their villainy; not that I am thereby justified![100] O salutary beasts, which are being made ready for me! 8. When will they come? When will they be released? When will they be able to enjoy my flesh? I hope they are made even fiercer, and I will invite them to devour me, and will beg them to do so, lest, as at times has happened, they fear to touch my body. I will even go so far as to force them if they hesitate; I will thrust myself upon them! 9. Do me this favor, please; I know what is expedient for me. I am now beginning to be Christ's disciple. Let the envy belonging to human attachment or spiritual depravity begone, that I may deserve to attain Jesus Christ. Fires, crosses, beasts, the scattering of bones, the rending of limbs, the punishment of the whole body, and all of the tortures devised by the devil's skill: let them be heaped upon me alone, if only I may deserve to attain Jesus Christ."

10. This and much else like it he wrote to various churches.

---

98. Cf. Ignatius, *Ep. ad Magn.* 15 and *Ep. ad Eph.* 21.1. Onesimus is mentioned in his *Ep. ad Eph.* 2.1 and 6.2. "Damaeus" is "Damas" in Eusebius and Ignatius, *Ep. ad Magn.* 2.1. Polybius is in *Ep. ad Trall.* 1.1.

99. *Ep. ad Rom.* 5.

100. Cf. 1 Cor 4.4.

He also sent letters to Polycarp as to an apostolic man, commending the church in Antioch to him especially. 11. In writing indeed to the Smyrnaeans he uses the following words, wherever he found them, in speaking of the Savior: "I know and believe that even after the Resurrection he was in the flesh. For when he came to Peter and others, he said to them, 'Come here and see that I am not a bodiless demon.' And they touched him and believed."[101]

12. Irenaeus too knows of his martyrdom and mentions his writings in the following words: "As one of ours said when condemned to the beasts for his witness to Christ, 'I am God's grain; I am ground and kneaded by the teeth of beasts, that I may be made into pure bread.'"[102]

13. Polycarp as well mentions these things in the letter he writes to the Philippians; he says, "I beg you all to devote yourselves to obedience and to practice the patience which you saw in those blessed men Ignatius, Rufus, and Zosimus, and above all in Paul and the other apostles who were among you, knowing that none of these ran in vain, but through faith and justice made their way even to the place prepared for them by the Lord, since they were indeed rendered sharers in his sufferings and did not love the present world, but him alone who for them and for us died and rose."[103]

And shortly after he adds, 14. "Ignatius and you have written to me asking that anyone going to Syria deliver the letters to you;[104] I will do so when I have the time. 15. I will send you Ignatius's letters and any others which have been sent over to us; they will be of the greatest benefit to you, containing as they do an unsurpassable teaching about faith and perseverance according to the Lord's precept."

Such is what is said about Ignatius. After him the church in Antioch was governed by Heros.

3.37.1. Among these same men there flourished in fact the

101. *Ep. ad Smyr.* 3.1–2.
102. Irenaeus, *adv. Haer.* 5.28.4; Ignatius, *Ep. ad Rom.* 4.1.
103. Polycarp, *Ep. ad Philipp.* 9.
104. … *deferat litteras ad vos.* Eusebius/Polycarp: "deliver the letter(s) from you." Cf. Polycarp, *ad Philipp.* 13.

equally famous Quadratus, who together with Philip's daughters is said to have been highly renowned for the grace of
prophecy.[105] There were in addition a great many other disciples of the apostles who were still alive at this time, and who
built the most worthy edifices of faith upon the foundations of
the church which they had laid, amplifying in every way the
preaching of the divine word and sowing widely through every
land the salutary seeds of the kingdom of heaven. 2. There were
a number of them, finally, who were inflamed by a more ardent
desire for the divine way of life and who consecrated their souls
to God's word, fulfilling the salutary precept of perfection: they
first divided their possessions among the needy and thus freed
themselves for preaching the gospel, so that if there were any
provinces where the name of faith was unknown, they might
preach there. 3. They established the first foundations of the
gospel among them and entrusted the office of governing the
church which they had founded to whoever was chosen from
among them, while they themselves would hurry off to other
nations and other provinces, and fulfill the office of evangelist.
Like the apostles in the beginning, they too were accompanied
by the working of divine signs and the grace of the Holy Spirit,
so that you could see entire populations together brought to
the worship belonging to the divine religion as the result of
one address, the faith of the listeners not lagging behind the
words of the preachers. 4. Now since it is impossible for us to list
each of those who first succeeded the apostles in the churches
throughout the earth as leaders, evangelists, and pastors, it will
suffice to mention only those whose writings, connected with
faith and preaching, have been included in the books which
have come down to us, 3.38.1. as for instance Clement and Ignatius and the others whom we mentioned earlier.

   Clement, by the way, in the letter which he wrote to the Corinthians, mentions the letter of Paul to the Hebrews and uses
its testimonies.[106] 2. Thus it is clear that the apostle wrote it in

   105. On Quadratus, cf. 5.17.3–4; Robert M. Grant, *Greek Apologists of the
Second Century* (Philadelphia: Westminster Press, 1988), 35–36, 184.
   106. 1 Clement 17.1, 5; 36. Clement borrows from it without mentioning
its title or Paul's name; Eusebius does not in fact say that Clement mentioned
it by name.

his native language since it was to be sent to the Hebrews, and, as some say, Luke the evangelist translated it, while others say it was Clement himself who did so.[107] 3. The latter is more likely, since the very style of Clement's letter is in harmony with it, and the thought in both writings is strikingly similar. 4. It is said, by the way, that there is another letter of Clement also; we are not familiar with it.[108] 5. And other minor writings of his as well, of some length, are said to be in the possession of a number of people, such as the disputation of Peter and Apion;[109] those of old made no use of them at all, since the pure and integral rule of the apostolic faith is not to be found preserved in them.

3.39.1. Five books of Papias are also in circulation; they have the title *Exposition of the Lord's Words*.[110] Irenaeus says of them, "This is affirmed as well by Papias in his first book, for he wrote five volumes; one of the men of old, he heard John and was Polycarp's fellow disciple and associate."

2. So says Irenaeus about Papias. He himself,[111] however, explains concerning himself that he received the faith not from the apostles but from their disciples. He says,

3. "You will not mind if we explain to you everything which we remember once learning from the presbyters and which we have fully retained, together with their expositions and according to the truth of the matters. For those we listened to did not say much, but handed on the truth, nor did they utter human precepts but the Lord's commandments received from the truth itself. 4. If, that is, someone of those who had followed the apostles would come, I would earnestly question him about what Andrew or Peter had said, or what he had heard from

---

107. Luke and Hebrews: 6.14.2; 6.25.14.

108. Clement's Second Letter to the Corinthians is regarded as spurious.

109. Not preserved. Apion is an occasional figure in the *Clementine Recognitions* and *Homilies*.

110. *Verborum dominicorum explanatio* = λογίων κυριακῶν ἐξηγήσεις, extant in fragments. Papias (c. 60–130) was bishop of Hierapolis in Asia Minor. Cf. Josef Kürzinger, *Papias von Hierapolis und die Evangelien des Neuen Testaments* (Regensburg: Verlag Friedrich Pustet, 1983), and Richard Bauckham, "Papias and Polycrates on the Origin of the Fourth Gospel," *JTS* NS 44 (1993): 44–63. The following citation from Irenaeus is in *Haer.* 5.33.4.

111. "He himself": Eusebius makes it clear that this means Papias: αὐτός γε μὴν ὁ Παπίας …

Philip or Thomas, or from James, or John or Matthew or some other of the Lord's disciples, or what Aristion or the presbyter John or the other disciples would say. For I did not think that the reading of books would be of as much benefit to me as would the teaching coming from a living and immediate voice."

5. Now I think it worthwhile to notice that he mentions the name of John twice, and the one whom he first mentions he associates with Peter, James, Matthew, and the other apostles; that is clearly the one who is the evangelist and apostle. But the other John he distinguishes from him in a way, setting him outside the list of apostles, putting one Aristion before him, and clearly calling him a presbyter; 6. thus one can see that what some people from Asia write about there being two tombs in Ephesus, both of them called John's, is in fact true.[112] If we consider the matter more carefully, perhaps this second John, if he is not identified with the first one, will be the one under whose name the Revelation passes which is known as John's.

7. Now this Papias of whom we are speaking claims that he received the apostles' words from those who had followed them: Aristion and the presbyter John. Hence in his expositions he often mentions explicitly that it was from John and Aristion that he received what he says about each person. 8. He in fact is the one who even records certain marvels in his work which I do not think should be omitted. 9. He indicates for instance that he was told by Philip the evangelist's daughters, the prophetesses, that a dead man rose in his own time. He also reports a great miracle about Justus, surnamed Barsabbas: that he drank poison and took no harm from it because of his faith in the Lord. 10. This is the Justus who after the Savior's Ascension was appointed by the holy apostles with Matthias for the allotment of the apostleship, as is related in the Acts of the Apostles.[113]

11. He speaks as well of a great many other miracles passed on to him by those of earlier times,[114] and of some new para-

112. The notice about the two tombs is repeated in 7.25.16, but omitted there by Rufinus.

113. Acts 1.23.

114. Eusebius speaks of "other things" (he does not say "miracles") "as from an unwritten tradition."

bles of the Savior, and of an unheard-of teaching which smacks
rather of fable: 12. that after the resurrection there will be a
thousand years in which Christ's kingdom will be physically
present on this earth.[115] But what I think is that he took the
spiritual and mystical tradition of the apostles in a physical and
literal sense, and was unable to distinguish what they were saying figuratively as though to nurslings and children. 13. From
the minor works themselves which he wrote, it can be seen that
he is a man of the most limited intelligence and gifts. But he
was the reason why this error spread to many of those belonging to the church after him, since he based the authority of
the dogma solely on its antiquity and not also on the sense of
what it said,[116] as did Irenaeus and anyone else who is seen to
follow him in this matter. 14. He also relates a great many other
things from the Aristion mentioned above, presenting them as
being from the words of the Lord and of the presbyter John
that were passed on to him; those who wish to know more may
read his writings themselves. Let us for our part extract the following passage from what he says about the evangelist Mark:

15. "The presbyter also used to say that Mark was Peter's interpreter and wrote whatever he remembered he had said.[117]
He did not, however, set out in order what the Lord said and
did, since he was not himself a hearer or follower of the Lord; it
was only much later, as I said, that he joined Peter to be of use
in the ministry of preaching, and not in order to write down
the Lord's words. Mark, then, did nothing wrong when he
wrote certain things in such a way as to make it seem as though
he were recollecting things he had heard from time to time.
His only concern was not to omit anything he had heard and
not to write anything that was false."

16. So writes Papias about Mark. About Matthew he says,

115. Cf. Rv 20.4–6.
116. *auctoritatem dogmatis tantum ex vetustate tribuens, non etiam ex ratione dic-
torum.* What Eusebius says is that many of those after him who belonged to the
church (*ekklēsiastikoi*) adopted his view because they relied on his antiquity (τὴν
ἀρχαιότητα τ'ανδρὸς προβεβλημένοις). Cf. Irenaeus, *Haer.* 5.32.1; 34; 35; 36.3.
117. "Interpreter" translates *interpres* = *hermēneutēs.* Armin Daniel Baum,
"Der Presbyter des Papias über einen 'Hermeneuten' des Petrus: zu Eusebius,
Hist. eccl. 3,39,15," *Theologische Zeitschrift* 56 (2000): 21–35, shows that the word

"Matthew wrote in Hebrew,[118] and each person interpreted what he had written as best he could." 17. Such is what he says about Matthew. This same Papias does indeed use proof-texts from the first letter of John and the first of Peter likewise. He includes at the same time some story about the adulterous woman accused by the Jews in the Lord's presence. That passage is also found in the gospel which is called "according to the Hebrews."[119] And let this suffice concerning these matters.

---

here probably means "translator" (from Peter's Aramaic to Greek). On Peter and Mark: 2.15; 6.14.5–7.

118. 3.24.6; 5.8.2; 5.10.3; 6.25.4.
119. Cf. 3.35.5; Jn 8.1–11.

BOOK FOUR

141

22. On Hegesippus and the things he records
23. On Dionysius, bishop of Corinth, and his letters
24. On Theophilus, bishop of Antioch
25. On Modestus
26. On Melito and those he mentions
27. On Apollinarius
28. On Musanus
29. On Tatian's sect
30. On Bardesanes the Syrian and his writing

4.1. In the twelfth year of the reign of Trajan Caesar, Cerdo, who, as we mentioned a little earlier, governed the people of Alexandria,[1] passed away, and after him Primus received the office of priesthood there, the fourth from the apostles. At the same time Alexander was assigned to direct the people in Rome, the fifth in succession after Peter and Paul, when Evaristus had completed the eighth year of his priestly administration.

4.2.1. Now our Savior's teaching and his churches were advancing more and more each day. The Jews, on the other hand, were racked by the closest possible sequence of ruinous calamities. What happened is that when the emperor just mentioned entered upon the eighteenth year of his reign, once again the Jews rose up in a revolt in which a large number of their people perished.[2] 2. For in Alexandria and throughout Egypt and Cyrene they first attacked together the gentiles dwelling among them and near them as though they had been roused by some savage and rebellious spirit, and then in the year following, with the rebellion growing little by little, they mounted a major open offensive against a Roman commander, Lupus, in Egypt.[3] 3. And in fact the Jews were victorious in the opening battle. But the gentiles who fled from the battle burst into Alexandria and killed any Jews they happened upon there. Deprived of their help, the rest who had revolted in Cyrene turned as though in

1. *Alexandrinorum gubernare plebem* = τῆς ἐν Ἀλεξανδρείᾳ παροικίας δηλωθεὶς ἐπίσκοπος ("was the bishop of the see of Alexandria"). The twelfth year was 109. Evaristus is referred to below in 3.34.
2. The occasion for the uprising was Trajan's absence during his conquest of Mesopotamia in 115. On the rebellion, cf. Schürer, 1.529–34.
3. M. Rutilius Lupus was prefect of Egypt 113–117.

desperation to laying waste the farms and strongholds of Egypt
under the leadership of Lucas.[4] The emperor sent against them
Marcius Turbo with infantry and cavalry and a naval force. 4. He
struck down many thousands of Jews, not only those in Cyrene
but also those in Egypt who were aiding Lucas, winning his way
in many battles indeed which lasted some considerable time.

5. And the Roman sovereign, thinking that those Jews too who
dwelt in Mesopotamia would make bold to behave in the same
way, ordered Lucius Quietus to destroy the province completely
and annihilate the whole people.[5] He mustered his troops and
struck down a great multitude of them. In return for this crime
he received from the emperor the governance of the province of
Judea. The Greek gentile historians have recorded these things
too, each in the same chronological order.

4.3.1. After Trajan had reigned for twenty years less six
months, Aelius Hadrianus succeeded to the scepter. Quadratus
addressed to him a book couched in magnificent language defending our religion with the weightiest arguments, since some
evil folk were trying to attack our people under this sovereign.[6]
This book is still retained by us and by many of our brothers.
One can tell from it the greatness of its author and of his mind
and apostolic faith. 2. And one can gather how early he is in
the following words he uses: "Our Savior's works were always
present, living and true, in those who had been healed and in
those who were raised from the dead. For they were not only
seen to rise or to be healed, but they were seen by people constantly, not only when the Savior was there, but even after his
departure, for a long time, so that some who had been healed
or raised by him survived even to our own time."

4. "Lucuas" in Eusebius. Dio Cassius 68.32 says that the Jews were led by
Andreas in Cyrene and Artemion on Cyprus.

5. *praecepit delere provinciam funditus ac totam gentem penitus excidere* = προσέ-
ταξεν ἐκκαθᾶραι τῆς ἐπαρχίας αὐτούς [scl. τοὺς Ἰουδαίους]: "he ordered him to
clear the province of them." Rufinus's translation reflects the savagery with
which the Moorish prince and Roman general Lusius Quietus executed the
order. Cf. Jerome, *Chron.* 115, and Dio Cassius 68.32.1–3.

6. On the identity of this Quadratus, see Antonio Cacciari, "L'archetipo
latente: la notizia eusebiana su Quadrato (*HE* IV.3)," *Adamantius* 14 (2008):
199–206, esp. 199–200.

3. This should suffice concerning him. Aristides as well, a faithful man steeped in the piety belonging to our religion, wrote for Hadrian a book like Quadratus's about the principles of our faith. His writings are still preserved.

4.4. In the third year of this emperor, Alexander, the bishop of Rome, came to the end of both his priesthood and his life when he finished the tenth year. He was succeeded by Xystus. At the same time Primus died in Alexandria in the twelfth year of his priesthood, and Justus received the episcopacy.

4.5.1. Of the dates and successions of the bishops in Jerusalem we have indeed found no record completely preserved in documents,[7] since each of them is represented as having been snatched away by death after exercising the priesthood for such a short time that, as far as I can find from reading the writers of old, 2. there were, it is said, fifteen successions of bishops down to the time of the emperor Hadrian, under whom the Jews were destroyed.[8] All of them are said to have been Hebrews of ancient stock and to have accepted the knowledge of Christ faithfully, and for this reason to have been judged without hesitation as most worthy of the priesthood too by those able to decide concerning the merit of one's faith. It was because the whole church of that time was evidently a compact mass of the Hebrew faithful, beginning with the apostles and lasting obviously until the time of that destruction, when the Jews again rebelled against the Romans and were once more subjugated in mighty battles. 3. Since, then, it was at that time that bishops from the circumcision were no longer appointed, it seems necessary to list together all of the priests, from the first down to that time. The first therefore is James, who was held to be the Lord's brother; after him Symeon was chosen; the third was Justus, the fourth Zacchaeus, the fifth then Tobias, the sixth Benjamin, the seventh John, then Matthias, whom Philip succeeded, who in turn was succeeded by Seneca as the tenth, and thereafter Justus, and in twelfth place Levi, after whom was Ephraem, with Joseph in fourteenth place, and last

7. Eusebius says he found the dates nowhere preserved in writing (γραφῇ).
8. Rufinus twice in this section speaks of the "destruction" (*excidium*) of the Jews, whereas Eusebius speaks of "siege" (*poliorkia*).

of all Judas.[9] 4. These were about all of those who as bishops in Jerusalem had charge of that people from the circumcision, from the apostles until the time we indicated above.

5. In Rome, in the twelfth year of the emperor mentioned above, Xystus, when he had finished twelve years at the helm of the church, was succeeded by Telesphorus, the seventh from the apostles. A year and a month later Eumenes succeeded to the government of the church in Alexandria, the sixth to do so, after his predecessor had governed the people for eleven years.

4.6.1. Now when the disturbances and seditious movements among the Jews began once again to increase, Rufus, the governor of Judea, used the armed forces assigned him by the emperor to suppress the people's violence with extreme violence, slaying many thousands of men, women, and children indiscriminately, claiming their lands for the Roman empire by the law of war.[10] 2. At the time when this happened, the leader of the Jewish army was one Bar Kochba, whose name means "star," a cruel and wicked man in every respect.[11] But he was able to persuade them by his name, as though they were common slaves, that he was a great star fallen from heaven for their salvation, to bring the assistance of light to distressed mortals condemned to lengthy darkness. 3. In the eighteenth year of the emperor, then, when the flames of this war had spread most widely, it was at Beththera, a strongly fortified town near Jerusalem, that the Roman blockade stretched to the point where

9. The list is also in Epiphanius, *Pan.* 66.20.1 (with some variation). In the next sentence, Rufinus adds "about" (*fere*) and modifies Eusebius, who says, "Such was the number of the bishops in Jerusalem ... who were all from the circumcision." The years Rufinus spent in Jerusalem may lend weight to his qualification.

10. The governor in 132 was Q. Tineius Rufus. On this revolt from 132–135, see Schürer, 1.534–557. The impetus seems to have been two unrelated decisions by the emperor Hadrian: to found the city of Aelia Capitolina on the site of Jerusalem (with a temple to Jupiter on the site of the former temple), and to prohibit circumcision generally. Cf. Dio Cassius 69.12–14 and *SHA* Hadrian 14.2.

11. On his name, see Schürer, 1.543–44. His wickedness alleged here and in the next section refers to his punishment of Christians for refusing to support his rebellion, which had been given a Messianic interpretation by some; cf. Justin, *Apol.* 1.31.6, and Jerome, *Chron.* 133.

the combatants within were reduced by hunger and thirst to utter extermination. And after their leader in particular had paid the just penalty for his crime, this whole nation was from then on completely forbidden the whole region round about Jerusalem, not only by divine law but above all by Hadrian's enactments and decrees, so that not even from some high point might it gaze with profane eyes upon its native soil, not even from a distance.[12] The historian Aristo of Pella tells the story.[13]

4. And thus it came about that soon after the Jewish people perished, settlers of foreign nationality came flocking to the city, which with different citizens was itself called Aelia after the emperor Aelius Hadrianus, and having gone over to Roman law changed its customs as well as its name. When the church there began to be gathered from the gentiles, then, Mark was the first to receive the priesthood of the city after the bishops from the circumcision.

4.7.1. With the churches everywhere on earth now shining like the brightest stars, and the faith by which everyone alike had come to believe flawlessly and steadfastly in our Savior and Lord Jesus Christ flourishing in every segment of humanity, the demon who is envious of everything that is good, being the enemy of truth and the constant foe of human salvation, bent his every effort against God's church. 2. While previously he had attacked it through external persecutions and enemies, he now recruited some evil, deceitful men and sought to shake it through an internal war, namely by having these imposters and charlatans merely pretend to belong to our religion and bring to their ruin any of the faithful whom they could fool by their glibness, while those who were ignorant of the mystery of our faith they could remove far from any desire for the true faith and salvation once they were hindered by their perverse

12. Rufinus adds "divine law" (*sanctione divinae legis*). He might have found the double prohibition in Eusebius's *Chronicle;* cf. Jerome, *Chron.* 134–35: *primum dei nutu ... deinde Romanis interdictionibus.*

13. *Aristo Pellaeus historiografus ista persequitur* = Ἀρίστων ὁ Πελλαῖος ἱστορεῖ ("Aristo ... recounts this"). Rufinus thus completes the improbable transformation of the second-century apologist Aristo of Pella into an historian. He may have referred to Hadrian's edict in a dialogue, but that is all that can be inferred with any certainty. Cf. Schürer, 1.37–39.

and lethal acts and assertions. 3. After Menander, then, who, as we said earlier, succeeded Simon, this ancient deceiver of the human race, like some beast hissing through twin mouths and from twin tongues shooting out diabolical venom, brought forth Saturninus, who was born in Antioch, and Basilides, who came from Alexandria. Each of them in his own place established schools of training in a doctrine both impious and hateful to God. 4. Irenaeus indeed indicates that Saturninus's fabrications are in almost every respect the same as Menander's, while Basilides made a show of mystical teaching when he stretched the ideas of his irreligious mind to an immeasurable extent, fond as he was of the marvels of fantasy fiction.[14]

5. Opposing them, though, were a great many of those belonging to the church who stood up courageously for the truth, and by their writings and arguments supported by sound reasoning fought for the apostolic and ecclesiastical tradition, in order that their books might provide for later generations as well a defense and protection against the poison of the heretics. 6. Of these there has come down to us a book by Agrippa Castor, a most famous writer of the time, which offers a quite cogent refutation of Basilides and exposes the cunning and craftiness of the man, which were all too suited to deceive.[15] 7. In expounding his secrets, in sum, he says that he composed twenty-four

14. Menander and Simon: 3.26. Menander, Saturninus (or Saturnilus), and Basilides are in Epiphanius, *Pan.* 23 and 24. The three are mentioned in Irenaeus, *Haer.* 1.24. For Eusebius's dependence on Justin and Irenaeus for his heresiological family tree, see Lorenzo Perrone, "Note per un commento a Eusebio di Cesarea, *Storia ecclesiastica* IV, 7, in *Studi offerti ad Alessandro Perutelli*, ed. P. Arduini et al. (Rome: Aracne, 2008), 2.341–57.

15. On Agrippa Castor, see Jerome, *Vir. illustr.* 21; Theodoret, *Compendium haereticarum fabularum* 1.4. On Basilides: Winrich A. Löhr, *Basilides und seine Schule: eine Studie zur Theologie- und Kirchengeschichte des zweiten Jahrhunderts* (Tübingen: Mohr Siebeck, 1996). The writings of the early second-century Alexandrian Christian exegete Basilides survive in too fragmentary a state to permit a comprehensive view of his doctrine, but its attempted integration of elements of popular Platonism with the gospel message seems to have been regarded by Clement as incompatible with monotheistic Christianity. His scriptural canon was also unorthodox, as the names of his prophets suggest (cf. Löhr, 13n37). On the present passage (Eusebius, 4.7.5–8), see Löhr, 5–14 (including the possible relationship between Agrippa Castor and Irenaeus). For a summary picture of Basilides: Löhr, 324–37.

commentaries on the gospel, while naming for himself prophets called Bar Kabbas, Bar Kof, and others, who never existed but whom he established for himself and called by outlandish names, that their very nomenclature might seem fearsome. He also says that he taught that sacrificial offerings were to be tasted with no regard for conscience nor any scruples, and that the faith might be denied in times of persecution without concern; he also taught his followers to keep silence for five years, like the Pythagoreans. 8. He adds many other things which show how completely he had uncovered and refuted the error of this sect.

9. Irenaeus too writes that one Carpocrates[16] was coeval in time and manners with those mentioned and the originator of another superstition: that of those called "gnostics," from a word meaning "knowledge." He would perform Simon the magician's tricks not secretly, as the other did, but openly in public, and would seek from his deluded audiences open and manifest praise for his wicked arts as though they represented the best and highest of occupations; the darkness of sorcery he brought into open light simply by speaking of love-charms, of the sending of dreams, of familiar spirits, and of other like deceits. He declared accordingly that every human being who wished to enter fully into his mystery, or rather his wickedness, should learn these things, asserting that the only way anyone could escape the rulers of this world was if his foul debts owed to each were paid by way of these misdeeds.

10. It was these servants of his wickedness, then, whom he who is envious of all that is good employed not only to snatch away to eternal darkness those who were deceived by them after they had believed, but also to alienate from the faith those who had not yet believed, as though this disgrace were something that belonged to our religion, since on account of the execrable life of these people, the name itself of Christianity would be shunned by anyone who heard it. 11. This was precisely the origin at that time of the suspicion that we were really irreligious, incestuous folk: that our people were defiled by unlawful sexual intercourse and promiscuous relations with our

16. Irenaeus, *Haer.* 1.25. Cf. G. Bardy, "Carpocratiens," *DHGE* 11.1118–19.

mothers and sisters and polluted with horrid banquets at which the victims of infanticide were served.[17]

12. But the disgrace did not last long once the truth began to be known; the darkness of this superstitious fiction was in fact dispelled at once when the life of ours shone forth more brightly and clearly. 13. And with each of the several sects, which had arisen in opposition to the truth, disappearing or flowing asunder into manifold and variegated kinds, the brightness of the true Catholic Church increased and advanced alone day by day, unadorned by the fashions of the times, its continence and purity and the glory of its divine conduct shining forth through every human nation in its wisdom, teaching, faith, and acts. 14.[18] The flames of this disgrace, then, were quenched as soon as they had been kindled. What remained in everyone's mind was the truth, which always wins its way through its own strength, refutes falsehood, and does not suffer the chastity and decency of the church to be damaged by the meretricious cosmetics of the slanderous. So true is this that from then on until our own time there has been no one so depraved that the reproaches he has concocted have besmirched the morality and decency of our people when they have issued from his sacrilegious mouth. Not only that, but to such an extent did the sweet fragrance from the deeds of the church reach the Romans, the Greeks, the Scythians, the barbarians, and one might almost say those very nations hidden in the furthest parts of the earth, along with the aroma of holy conduct breathing something of the divine; to such an extent was the happy reputation of the Christians brought to the ears and minds of everyone, that every human nation abandoned its ancestral laws and superstitions, and turned to faith in Christ, and every barbarian people put off its native savagery and hastened to Jesus to learn from him, since he is meek and humble of heart.[19]

15. There were also at that time, by God's grace, some most

17. *infanticidii dapibus.* Eusebius just speaks of "unholy food" (ἀνοσίαις ... τροφαῖς). Cf. Epiphanius, *Pan.* 26.5.4–6.

18. Rufinus expands Eusebius's summation in 4.7.14, dwelling especially upon the vast success of the gospel proclamation.

19. Mt 11.29.

learned men who refuted the obscene fabrications of the sectarians convincingly and satisfactorily, and showed how close the connection was between the true faith in the Catholic Church and chastity. 4.8.1. Among them Hegesippus was the most renowned; he 2. handed on fully and faithfully, in simple language, the tradition of the apostolic preaching written out in five books. When he says something about his own time and about those who put up images, he writes as follows:

"They made temples to them which were really tombs, as we can see even now. One of them is Antinous, a slave of Hadrian Caesar, in whose honor the yearly contests are held which are called the 'Antinoian' and were established right in our own time. He also founded a city named after Antinous, and a temple in his honor, and appointed priests and prophets."[20]

3. Justin too, a most faithful follower of our way of life and one most learned in the teachings of the Greeks, writes as follows in his book to Antoninus in defense of our religion: "It does not seem to me irrelevant to mention at this point what recently happened concerning Antinous, whom everyone began to worship as a god out of fear of the sovereign, when they knew who and what sort of person he was a little earlier, and of what ancestry."[21]

4. The same author also mentions as follows the Jewish war which was then being waged: "And indeed in this Jewish war which is now being waged, Bar Kochba, the leader of the Jewish side, has been ordering that the Christians alone, unless they deny Christ, be taken off for torture as blasphemers."[22]

5. He writes in these books as well about his own conversion from the pagan way of life to the faith belonging to the true religion, and that the conversion was not without sound reason and a considered judgment. He says,

"For I myself, trained as I was in the Platonic schools, when I heard the Christians being defamed and saw that they were fearless in the face of death and of every torment, reflected that

---

20. Hegesippus: 2.23.3–19; 3.32. Cf. also *SHA* Hadrian 14.4–7; Dio Cassius 69.11.2–4; Aurelius Victor 14.7–9. The city mentioned here is Antinoöpolis in the Thebaid.

21. *Apol.* 1.29.4.   22. *Apol.* 1.31.6.

it was impossible that they should consort with wickedness and wantonness. Does anyone, once given over to a life of pleasure and ease, who delights to feast on human flesh, gladly embrace death, by which he will at once be deprived of the pleasure for the sake of which he chose to be defamed? On the contrary, he will do all he can to keep living if he can and escape judgment, and not offer himself to a death decreed and promised."[23]

6. The same author also writes that the emperor Hadrian, when he received a letter from the most illustrious governor Serennius Granianus in which he asked about the Christians, replied that it was not right to punish Christians without a trial and recourse to the laws, if they had committed no crime.[24]

7. He inserts a copy of the letter, which runs as follows:

Letter of the Emperor Hadrian to Minucius Fundanus, Proconsul of Asia

4.9.1. "I have received the letter written to me by your predecessor, the most illustrious Serennius Granianus, and I do not

23. *Apol.* 2.12.1–2.

24. *non esset iustum Christianos nullius criminis reos absque iudicio legisbusque puniri* = οὐ δίκαιον εἴη ἐπὶ μηδενὶ ἐγκλήματι ... ἀκρίτως κτείνειν αὐτούς ("it would be unjust to execute them without a trial if they had been charged with nothing"). Rufinus thus strengthens the impression given by the original that Hadrian had in effect declared that the profession of Christianity was not in itself criminal, and had thereby reversed Trajan's ruling in the matter (Pliny, *Ep.* 10.97). The rescript itself does not seem to say this; it simply forbids the authorities to condemn Christians without a trial, on whatever charge. Cf. Eberhard Heck, "Zu Hadrians Christenrescript an Minucius Fundanus (Euseb. *HE* 4.9.1–3)," in *Prinzipat und Kultur in 1. und 2. Jahrhundert: wissenschaftliche Tagung der Friedrich-Schiller-Universität Jena und der Iwane Dshawachischwili Universität Tbilisi, 27. –30. Oktober 1992 in Jena*, ed. Barbara Kühnert et al. (Bonn: Habelt, 1995), 103–17.

Rufinus omits 4.8.8, where Eusebius says that Justin appended the original Latin rescript which he has translated into Greek (Justin, *Apol.* 1.68.4–9). Scholarly opinion about the authenticity of the rescript has been divided, with most nowadays accepting it as genuine. Rufinus's Latin, however, has been judged a translation of Eusebius's Greek rather than a copy of the original. The rescript is addressed to Minucius Fundanus, proconsul of Asia, in answer to a letter sent by his predecessor, Q. Licinius Silvanus Granianus ("Serennius" is a later miscopy).

wish to pass over his report in silence, lest the innocent be disturbed and slanderers given a chance to prey upon them. 2. If
therefore it is clear that the provincials are able to back up this
their petition against the Christians, so that they can charge
them with something in court, I do not forbid them to pursue
the matter. But I will not allow them in this matter to have recourse to entreaties and outcries alone. It is in fact much fairer
for you to examine the allegations at trial, if someone should
want to bring an accusation. If therefore anyone charges the
people mentioned with doing something against the laws, and
proves it, then you too will sentence them to the punishment
that fits their misdeed. 3. But you will, by Hercules, make very
sure that if someone seeks to have any of them prosecuted simply in order to slander them, you will sentence the accuser to
the heavier punishment that suits his villainy."

4.10. Now Hadrian passed away after this in the twenty-first
year of his reign,[25] and Antoninus, surnamed Pius, received the
government of Rome. In his first year Telesphorus passed away
after eleven years in the priesthood in Rome, and Hyginus was
allotted the bishopric of Rome. Irenaeus, however, reports that
Telesphorus ended his life by martyrdom, stating at the same
time that Valentinus, the founder of the Valentinian sect, lived
in the time of Bishop Hyginus, as did Cerdo, a leader of that
error which Marcion later followed, and that they both were
feverishly engaged at the same time in Rome, but in different
impieties. This is what he writes:[26]

4.11.1. "Valentinus came to Rome under Hyginus, but flourished in Pius's time and lasted until Anicetus. As for Cerdo,
who was before Marcion, he too came under Hyginus, who was
the ninth bishop in Rome since the apostle. At times he would
admit his error and seek pardon as though penitent, and at

25. From August 8, 117, to July 10, 138.
26. *Haer.* 3.4.3. On Marcion, see Barbara Aland, *Was ist Gnosis? Studien zum
frühen Christentum, zu Marcion und zur kaiserzeitlichen Philosophie* (Tübingen:
Mohr Siebeck, 2009), 292–352, and Dieter T. Roth, "Marcion's Gospel and
Luke: The History of Research in Current Debate," *Journal of Biblical Literature*
127 (2008): 169–80.

other times he would again teach impiety secretly, but sometimes also openly. He was convicted of this and banned from the assembly of the brethren."

2. So says Irenaeus in the third book *Against Heresies*. In the first book, moreover, he says of Cerdo:[27]

"Cerdo used the opportunity afforded by the followers of Simon for his impiety, came to Rome under Hyginus, and there taught that the god preached by the law and the prophets was not himself the father of Our Lord Jesus Christ, since the former was known, the latter unknown, and the former just, the latter good. Marcion from Pontus, who succeeded him, increased his teacher's madness by discarding all sense of respect in his blasphemies."

3. The same Irenaeus also refutes quite cogently Valentinus's vast and deep error concerning matter and other things, draws him forth like a snake hiding in concealed lairs, and exposes him.[28] 4. He adds to this something about one Marcus, who he says was outstanding in his training in the art of magic.[29] He writes as follows of his profane superstitions, of his secrets which were not so much sacred as sacrilegious, and of his mystical miseries:[30]

5. "Some of them construct a bridal chamber and hold an evil initiation ceremony consecrating him who is brought in with secret chants, as it were, and words which are execrable rather than sacred. They say that what they do is a spiritual wedding, in the likeness of the pairings which take place on high. They bring them to water, moreover, and baptize them, pronouncing over them the words, 'In the name of the unknown father of all, and in truth, the mother of all, and in him who came down into Jesus.' Others moreover utter Hebrew names in dreadful tones over those whom they initiate in order to frighten those listening."

6. So writes Irenaeus about Marcus's followers. When Hyginus, though, passed away in the fourth year of his episcopacy, Pius received the priesthood of the Roman church, with Mark doing likewise in Alexandria when Eumenes died in the thir-

27. 1.27.1–2.
29. *Haer.* 1.31.1.
28. *Haer.* 1.1–9.
30. *Haer.* 1.21.3.

teenth year of his episcopacy. Mark left the helm of the church to Celadion when he passed away after ten years in the priesthood. 7. As for Pius, when he had completed fifteen years in the priesthood in Rome, he handed over the see to Anicetus after him. It was in his time that Hegesippus relates that he himself came to Rome and stayed there until the episcopacy of Eleutherus, who replaced Anicetus. 8. Justin in his philosopher's garb also flourished at this time, preaching God's word and defending the grounds of our faith in both the books he wrote and his verbal arguments. When writing against Marcion, he mentions of him that he was still alive at the time he was writing. Then he says,

9. "Marcion from Pontus, who is still alive today, teaches people to believe that there is another god greater than the creator god. He dins this into people and, using demons as his assistants, has persuaded many to blaspheme and to deny that the god who is the creator of all is the same as Christ's father; it is another one who is greater than he. All of his followers are nonetheless called Christians, just as all philosophers are of course called such by the same word, even though their sects differ."[31]

10. Shortly thereafter he adds, "We also have a book written against all the sects, which we will give you if you want to peruse it."[32] 11. This same Justin wrote also a distinguished work against the pagans, as well as other books on behalf of our religion, which he addressed to the emperor Antoninus, surnamed Pius; he also wrote to the senate, for he lived mostly in Rome. In one of these books, finally, he writes as follows about himself as well, wanting to show who he was and from where:[33]

4.12. "To the emperor Aelius Hadrianus Antoninus Pius Caesar Augustus, and to Verissimus the philosopher, his son, and to Lucius, own son of the philosopher Caesar and adopted son of Pius, to the lover of wisdom and to the sacred senate and the entire Roman people, I, Justin, son of Priscus, son of Bac-

31. *Apol.* 1.26.5–6.

32. *Apol.* 1.26.8. The work to which he refers has not survived. On his works, cf. 4.18.

33. *Apol.* 1.1. In Justin/Eusebius the emperor's name runs "Titus Aelius Hadrianus," etc.

chius, from Neapolis in Palestine, submit this petition as the
one spokesman for all of the men gathered from every part of
the human race who are suffering from being hated unjustly
and subjected to mistreatment."

This emperor was also entreated in Asia by those who were
afflicted by various injustices, and he published the following
response to all the peoples of Asia:[34]

4.13.1. "The emperor Caesar Marcus Aurelius Antoninus Augustus Armenius, pontifex maximus, tribune for the fifteenth
time, consul for the third time, to all the peoples of Asia together, greetings. 2. I do indeed have no doubt that the gods themselves are concerned to see that no criminal escapes notice.
For it is far more fitting that they themselves punish those who
refuse to sacrifice to them, than that you do. 3. But you confirm the opinion which those whom you persecute have of you
when they say that you are impious, godless folk.[35] Hence they
consider it preferable to lay down their lives for their god and
embrace death willingly, than to yield to people like you and
transfer themselves to your religion. 4. Concerning the earthquakes, though, which have occurred and are still occurring,
it will not be unfitting to ease your grief with a timely admonition. For I have discovered that in matters of this sort you apply
the calamities you suffer together to the arousal of hatred for
those others.[36] 5. It is a case in which they experience greater
trust in god, while you, at any time when you know nothing of
such things, neglect the other gods while you banish and expel the religion of the immortal god whom the Christians wor-

34. Eusebius does not say that the emperor was "entreated in Asia" (*inter-
pellatus ... in Asia*) but that he was "also petitioned by other brothers [i.e.,
Christians] in Asia" (Ἐντευχθεὶς ... ὑφ᾽ ἑτέρων ... ἐπὶ τῆς Ἀσίας ἀδελφῶν). The
decree he issued was to the Council of Asia (τὸ κοινὸν τῆς Ἀσίας). The inaccu-
racy of the title that follows is only one of the indications of the spuriousness
of the decree. Cf. G. Bardy, *Eusèbe de Césarée: Histoire ecclésiastique* (Paris: Cerf,
1952–60), 1.177–79.

35. The Greek is ambiguous: βεβαιοῦντες τὴν γνώμην αὐτῶν ἥνπερ ἔχουσιν,
ὡς ἀθέων κατηγοροῦντες: "confirming the opinion they have in leveling the
accusation of godlessness." Who is accusing whom?

36. Eusebius's text here is a long-standing conundrum, apart from the
question of which earthquakes may be meant. Cf. Bardy, *Eusèbe*, 1.178n2.

ship, persecuting even to death those who are his worshipers.
6. It was on behalf of these people that many officials from the
provinces had written to our venerable father as well. His reply
to them was that they should not bother this sort of people in
any way, unless it happened that they were convicted of plotting something against the Roman state. A great many people
have sent reports about them to me as well; in replying to them
I have followed my father's judgment with like restraint. 7. If
therefore anyone persists in bringing lawsuits against this sort
of people where no crime has been committed, let him who
has been denounced on this charge be acquitted, even if it is
proved that he is what he is charged with being, a Christian.
Let him, however, who urged that he was guilty be liable to the
punishment to which he was exposing the other. Published in
Ephesus in the Assembly of Asia."

8. That this took place in this way is also confirmed by Melito, bishop of the church of Sardis, in the book he wrote to the
emperor Verus on behalf of our faith and religion.[37]

4.14.1. This is also the time during which, Irenaeus says,
Polycarp came to Rome when Anicetus was governing the Roman church and conferred with Anicetus about the day of the
Paschal feast. 2. He says some other things about Polycarp as
well which I think it worth including in our narrative. In the
third book *Against Heresies* this is what he records of him:[38]

3. "Not only was Polycarp educated by the apostles, and not
only did he consort with those who had seen the Lord; he was
ordained by the apostles themselves bishop of the church of
Smyrna, and we saw him when we were quite young. 4. For his
life lasted a long time; he lived nobly to a great old age, and
died even more nobly, ending his life by martyrdom. But he
always taught what he himself had learned from the apostles,
and passed on to the church that which alone is to be considered true. 5. The witnesses to this are all the churches established in Asia, as well as those men who in due course became
and remain Polycarp's successors. He is a far truer and more
trustworthy authority in the church, and witness to the truth,

37. On Melito, cf. 4.26.
38. *Haer.* 3.3.4.

than are Valentinus, Marcion, and the other people of perverted mind. He also came to Rome under Anicetus and converted many of the above-mentioned sectarians to the church of God, preaching that the only truth to be held was that which he knew he had received from the apostles and was passing on to the church. 6. There are also those who heard him say that when John, the Lord's disciple who was in Ephesus, had gone into the baths to bathe and there saw Cerinthus, he went out at once and left without bathing, saying, 'Let us flee from here before the very baths collapse in which that enemy of the truth Cerinthus is bathing.'[39] 7. Polycarp once happened upon Marcion, who said to him, 'Acknowledge us!' He answered, 'I acknowledge, I do acknowledge the first-born of Satan!' The apostles and their disciples were then so careful in the practice of their religion that they refused to share even a word with those who had turned aside from the truth. It is as Paul says: 'Avoid a sectarian after a first and second rebuke, realizing that he is perverted and sins, since he has been condemned by himself.'[40] 8. There is also extant Polycarp's quite powerful letter to the Philippians, in which those who perchance are concerned for their salvation can find the character of his faith and preaching."

9. Thus far Irenaeus. Polycarp in that letter he wrote to the Philippians used proof-texts from the first letter of Peter. 10. Now when Antoninus, surnamed Pius, had completed the twenty-second year of his reign, he was succeeded by Marcus Aurelius Verus and Antoninus his son[41] with his brother Lucius.

4.15.1. It was at this time that Polycarp ended his life by martyrdom while Asia was being buffeted by the severest persecutions. I consider it clearly necessary to record it, especially since 2. there is extant a letter written in the name of the church of Smyrna to the churches of Pontus which describes the blessed outcome of his martyrdom. It runs as follows:[42]

39. Cerinthus: 3.28.
40. Ti 3.10–11.
41. *Marcus Aurelius Verus et Antoninus filius eius* = Μάρκος Αὐρήλιος Οὐῆρος, ὁ καὶ Ἀντωνίνος, υἱὸς αὐτοῦ ("Marcus Aurelius Verus, surnamed Antoninus, his son").
42. *Martyrium Polycarpi* 1. Eusebius's text is edited together with the ancient

3. "The church of God which is in Smyrna to the church of God established in Philomelium and to all the holy Catholic churches everywhere: may mercy and peace and the love of God the Father and of Our Lord Jesus Christ be multiplied. We write to you, brothers, about the martyrs and about blessed Polycarp, whose martyrdom was the seal upon the end of the persecutions."

4. And shortly after that, in describing the contests undergone by the other martyrs too, they write as follows:[43]

"In their desire to frighten the onlookers they would lacerate the martyrs with whips right to their innards, so that the hidden parts of the body, those which nature has placed in concealment, were exposed, and sometimes they would spread seashells, which they call *conchylia,* and sharp fragments under the backs of the martyrs, upon whom they expended every kind of torture and variety of punishment, and finally exposed them to the beasts to be devoured. 5. Outstanding among them is said to have been a man of immense courage named Germanicus, who by the grace of divine virtue rebuffed the fear of bodily harm. For when the proconsul tried to influence the man by persuasion and to suggest to him that he should have mercy on himself in the prime of his youth, he did not hesitate at all, we are told, but incited the beast that had been made ready for him as though upbraiding his punishment for its delay, and of his own accord sought a speedy departure from this wicked life.

6. "Now when the crowd of onlookers was struck with amazement at his so wondrous death and began to praise the virtue of the whole Christian people in despising death, everyone shouted aloud, 'Away with the irreligious! Get Polycarp!' 7. From their cries there arose a great uproar, but then a Phrygian named Quintus, who had recently arrived from his part of the world,

---

martyrdom in parallel columns by Gerd Buschmann, *Das Martyrium des Polykarp* (Göttingen: Vandenhoeck & Ruprecht, 1998), 13–34, an arrangement that reveals the freedom with which Eusebius treats the original; "Eusebius not only quotes but 'rewrites' the text …" (Buschmann, 14). On the issues connected with the dating of the martyrdom, see Paul Hartog, *Polycarp's Epistle to the Philippians and the Martyrdom of Polycarp* (Oxford: Clarendon, 2013), 171–86.

43. Rufinus presents Eusebius, 4.15.4–14, as a direct quotation from *Mart. Polyc.* 2–7; Eusebius himself indicates that he is paraphrasing here.

took it upon himself to challenge the beasts and the other tortures; or so he did at first, but then his courage wavered and
in the end his reluctance cost him his salvation. 8. This shows
that it was his rashness and forwardness that had pushed him
to martyrdom, and not his devotion, for he had thrust himself
upon the attention of the tribunal. In his defeat, then, he is
an example to everyone to proceed with caution and circum-
spection in such matters, since it is faith and modesty that are
crowned, and not rashness. Such, then, is the account of what
happened to them.

9. "That marvelous man Polycarp, however, when he first
heard the crowd roused against him by outcries, was in no way
moved, but remained un-frightened, for he was calm in his
manners and serene in the way he looked. He meant to stay in
the same city without fear, but yielded to the entreaties of his
friends and withdrew to a farm near the city where he gave himself up to prayer day and night with a few others; he implored
God to grant peace to the churches in every place, that being
his constant habit throughout his life. 10. Now when he was engaged in prayer three days before his arrest, he saw a vision by
night in which the pillow under his head was consumed by fire.
When he awoke after the vision, he interpreted his dream to
those present, saying that it was certain that he was destined
to meet his death by fire for Christ. 11. With the search party
now pressing close, therefore, he was again forced by his brothers' affection to move to another place. The searchers entered
there not long after and seized two boys, one of whom when
beaten revealed where Polycarp was. They reached him when
the day was now ending. 12. Upon entering there they came
across him resting in an upper room, from which he could easily have moved to another house; 13. but he refused, saying,
'The Lord's will be done.' What is more, when he learned that
those who were to arrest him were there, he went to meet them
and began to address them with a most cheerful and peaceful
face and exceedingly gracious speech, so that they were astonished and wondered why there had been such urgency to issue
the order that a man of such dignity and respectability, of such
great age and eminence of life, should be tracked down and ar-

rested. 14. He, though, without any delay ordered a table to be set for his foes as though they were guests[44] and a sumptuous banquet served them, having been allowed by them one hour for prayer. He prayed then so filled with God's grace, that all of those present were amazed, and even those who had come to arrest him regretted that they had been ordered to take away for execution a man so upright, worthy of God, and venerable in his very age."

15. And further on, the same writing continues verbatim as follows:[45]

"After he had finished his prayer, commemorating all of those, whoever they were, that he had met, the great and the small, the nobles, the commoners, and the whole Catholic Church which is on earth, the time had now arrived and he went forth, and sitting on an ass was led to the city, it being the day of the great Sabbath. He was met on the way by the captain of police, Herod, and his father Nicetas, who took him into their conveyance and tried earnestly to prevail upon him with the words, 'What is wrong with saying that Caesar is lord and sacrificing, and living thereafter in peace?' 16. He at first listened to this in silence, but when they persisted, said to them, 'There is no need to go on. I am not going to do as you say.' And they, when they realized that they were getting nowhere, grew angry and shoved him from the conveyance with hard words, so that he fell headlong and hurt his foot. But just as though no injury had been done him he proceeded quite briskly and eagerly to the stadium to which he had been ordered to be taken.

17. "A huge roar went up when he entered the stadium, and a voice fell from heaven, saying, 'Be brave, Polycarp, and act with courage.' No one could see the source of the voice, but many could hear the sound. The people meanwhile were roused to a perfect frenzy when Polycarp was brought in. 18. When asked from a distance by the proconsul if he was Polycarp, he said he was. 'Show respect for your years, then,' he said, 'and spare

44. *hostibus quasi hospitibus:* Rufinus adds.

45. *Mart. Polyc.* 8–19. The description of Polycarp's martyrdom is patterned after the gospel passion narratives, e.g., the animal on which he rides, the "great Sabbath" (cf. Jn 19.31), Herod, etc. Cf. Buschmann, 166–69.

your extreme old age: swear by Caesar's Fortune, repent of the past, and shout with the others, "Away with the sacrilegious!"' 19. Polycarp looked grimly at the people sitting in the stadium, raised his right hand toward the sky, and with a groan spoke out, 'Away with the sacrilegious!' 20. But the proconsul insisted, 'Swear by Caesar's Fortune, and revile Christ, and I will let you go.' Polycarp replied, 'For eighty-six years I have served him and he has never done me wrong; how can I curse and blaspheme my king who has given me salvation?' And when he was pressed more urgently to swear by Caesar's Fortune, he said, 21. 'If you desire to boast[46] that I swear by Caesar's Fortune, and you feign to ignore who I am, then hear me say with full frankness that I am a Christian. And if you wish to receive an account of the Christian religion, then set a day and listen.' 22. The proconsul said, 'Persuade the people.' Polycarp said, 'You I will answer, for we are taught to show honor to those rulers and authorities who are of God; that honor, namely, which is not opposed to religion; but I owe no satisfaction to a people who have gone insane.'

23. "The proconsul said, 'I have beasts ready who will be set upon you unless you repent at once.' He replied, 'Bring them on; our decision is irrevocable, nor can we change from good to evil by repentance. But it would be better if those who persist in evil changed to what is good.' 24. The proconsul then said, 'I will have you devoured by fire, if the beasts seem to you worthy of contempt and you do not repent of your decision.' He said, 'You threaten me with that fire which burns for a moment and shortly after is extinguished because you know nothing of the everlasting fire of the judgment to come which has been prepared for the irreligious as an unending punishment. But why are you delaying? Bring on whichever you want.' 25. While saying this and many other things like it, Polycarp was filled with confidence together with joy, so that the proconsul was quite astonished at the enthusiasm on his face and the courage of his replies. He sent a crier therefore to the people and ordered him to announce as loudly as possible that Polycarp had

---

46. *si hanc iactantiam quaeris* = εἰ κενοδοξεῖς ("if you fondly imagine").

thrice acknowledged that he was a Christian. 26. When this was heard, the whole crowd of both gentiles and Jews living in Smyrna shouted aloud in a perfect frenzy, 'This is the teacher of all of Asia and the father of Christians, but also a destroyer of our gods! He is the one who teaches so many neither to sacrifice nor to adore the gods!' 27. And after that they shouted to Philip the showman to loose a lion at Polycarp. He answered that he might not, because he had already finished his show. Then they all cried together that Polycarp should be burned alive, 28. for the vision he had seen of the burning pillow had to be fulfilled. 29. This was done more quickly than may be said, the people themselves gathering wood from the baths and from public places, with twigs, and the Jews especially pitching in even more enthusiastically in their usual frenzy; and so the pyre was built with all speed.[47]

30. "Then when the elder had taken off his clothes and unfastened his girdle, he tried to take off his shoes as well, which previously had only been removed by certain religious people who vied with each other to do so out of faith and devotion. Such was the veneration in which he was held by everyone during his whole life. 31. When therefore everything was ready for the fire, and when he was placed on the pyre and they wanted even to fasten him to it with nails, he said, 'Let me be, for he who has given me the strength to endure the pain of the fire will also see to it that I will bear the flames unyieldingly without being fastened by nails. So they used fetters, leaving aside the nails. 32. With his hands tied behind his back, and like a choice ram taken from a great flock, he was offered to almighty God as an acceptable holocaust while he poured out these prayers in the very midst of his suffering:

33. "'God the Father of your beloved and blessed Son Jesus Christ, through whom we have come to recognize you, God of angels and powers and all creation and the whole race of the just who all live in your presence, I bless you who have deigned to bring me to this day and to this hour, that I might share in

47. The portrayal of Jewish hostility here may represent both historical tensions between the Jews and Christians in Smyrna, and the pattern of the gospel passion narrative: Buschmann, 208–13; Hartog (note 42), 226–31.

the martyrs and the cup of your Christ unto the resurrection to eternal life of my soul and spirit[48] through the imperishability of the Holy Spirit. 34. May I be received among them in your sight this day as a rich and acceptable sacrifice; as you have made it ready and marked it out in advance, so you have done. You are God who are true and without deceit, 35. and therefore in everything I praise you and bless you and glorify you through the eternal God and high priest Jesus Christ[49] your beloved Son, through whom and with whom be glory to you in the Holy Spirit, now and for ages to come. Amen.'

36. "When he had intoned 'Amen,' and finished his prayer, the fire was lit by the men who belong to fire everlasting, and when a great flame blazed forth, all of us to whom God granted it saw a miracle. A great many of us have been preserved by the Lord, that we might tell others what we saw. 37. The fire stood above the martyr's body curved in the form of a vaulted chamber, like the sails of a ship billowed out by the wind; his body in the midst was not like burning flesh, but as though it were gold or silver glowing in a furnace. And with that there came to our nostrils an odor as of incense or of the costliest fragrant ointment. 38. In the end, when the ministers of villainy saw that the body could not be consumed by fire, they ordered the executioner to go up and transfix with a sword the body which had defeated the fire. 39. When he did so, so much blood poured out that it quenched the pyre. The people, however, were so struck by the miracle that they departed in amazement at the sight of God's so remarkable favor shown to his chosen ones. This, then, is the admirable apostolic teacher chosen for our times, and the prophetic priest of the church of Smyrna, every word spoken by whom was fulfilled and will be fulfilled in the future.

40. "But he who is jealous of all that is good, the enemy of all the just, when he saw that he had been crowned for the glory of his martyrdom and for the virtues of his outstanding life, and that he had attained the rewards of immortality by his death,

48. The original has "soul and body."
49. Rufinus adds "God"; the original martyrdom reads "the eternal and heavenly high priest," from which Eusebius drops the "heavenly."

bent every effort to see to it that no one yielded his remains for burial to ours who desired this. 41. Nicetas, Herod's father and Dalca's brother,[50] was therefore incited to approach the authorities and request that the body not be released for burial, 'lest,' he said, 'the Christians abandon him who was crucified and begin to worship this man.' The Jews especially were behind this; they kept ours under close observation lest they snatch him from the fire that was still burning. The wretched fools did not realize that we could never abandon Christ who underwent death to save the whole world, 42. nor could we worship anyone else, knowing that he is the true God[51] and is alone to be worshiped. The martyrs, by contrast, we love and venerate as disciples of the Lord, because they kept faith wholly with their Master and Lord, and we hope to share with them as well in faith and perseverance in charity.

43. "Now when the centurion saw how stubbornly contentious the Jews were, he had the body brought forward and burned it up, and thus we gathered the charred bones, made dearer than the costliest gems and finer than any gold by the fire, and gave them the customary burial, as was fitting. 44. This is where we still hold the customary festive gatherings which the Lord makes possible,[52] especially on the day of his passion, and we also celebrate with this the memories of those who suffered previously, so that the spirits of those who follow may be roused to the journey of their predecessors by these outstanding examples. 45. Such is the account of blessed Polycarp, with whom another twelve coming from Philadelphia also achieved martyrdom in Smyrna."

46. Woven into the same letter is the narrative too about a great many other martyrs of that time. Among them, it is said, was one Metrodorus, a presbyter from Marcion's sect, who was handed over to be burned after Polycarp. 47. And included in the martyrs of that time, the most famous there is said to have been one Pionius.[53] Those who wish to know more about him

---

50. *frater autem Dalcae* = ἀδελφὸν [δὲ] δ' Ἄλκης; her name was therefore Alce.

51. *Martyrdom*/Eusebius: "Son of God."

52. There is no equivalent in the original for Rufinus's "still" (*etiam nunc*); there the verb is in the future: "the Lord will make it possible" (παρέξει).

53. The Acts of Pionius place his martyrdom in 250; they mention Metro-

may find it in our writing concerning the martyrs of old: the courage of his replies during each of the interrogations, his addresses to the people on behalf of our faith, how fearless he always was before the judges, teaching and arguing even in the very tribunals, how with his exhortations he lifted up those who had faltered during persecution, and how when in prison he strengthened the spirits of the brothers who came to him to endure martyrdom, what tortures he himself endured in martyrdom, and how he was nailed to the pyre upon which he was placed, in this way bringing his life to its blessed end. 48. After these matters there come the reports of other martyrs as well in Pergamum, the city in Asia: of Carpus and Papirius and of the excellent woman Agathonica, and of many other women,[54] who were crowned with martyrdom for their blessed confessions.

4.16.1. With them that wonderful man Justin, whom we mentioned a little earlier,[55] received the gift of martyrdom in recompense for his faithful and learned tongue after he had offered to the authorities of that time the second book in defense of our religion. It was some philosopher named Crescens, a dog by profession as well as in his manners,[56] who plotted treachery against him, because in disputing with him in the presence of an audience he had not only defeated him but even embarrassed him thoroughly with truth on his side, the result of which was that he obtained martyrdom from the Lord as the palm of his victory. 2. That blessed true philosopher of the truth had the prophetic ability to foretell what would thus happen in that defense which we just said he wrote, speaking openly of it just as it was to take place. His words:[57]

3. "For I expect that I too will be plotted against by one of those whom I oppose for the sake of the truth; I expect to be beaten with rod or club[58] at least by Crescens, who is not a phi-

---

dorus as a Marcionite. Eusebius's narrative of the martyrs which he mentions just below has perished.

54. *aliarumque multarum:* added by Rufinus. Eusebius has "Papylus" instead of Rufinus's "Papirius" above.

55. 4.11.8–11. Irenaeus mentions his martyrdom in *Haer.* 1.28.1.

56. He was a cynic (literally "canine" in Greek).

57. Justin, *Apol.* 2.3 (what precedes this is in 4.17).

58. *spero baculo aut clava feriendum* = προσδοκῶ ... ξύλῳ ἐντιναγῆναι, which

losopher [*philosophos*] but a *philokompos,* not a lover of wisdom but a lover of boasting. Nor is it fitting to call him a philosopher who testifies in public about matters of which he is ignorant, and says that Christians are without God and are irreligious, doing so to gratify and please those who are in error and whom he has entangled in even greater coils of error. 4. For if he is ignorant of Christ's teaching and confutes what he does not know, he is completely worthless, and more worthless by far than the uninstructed, since those who are uninstructed or uneducated take care not to debate matters they do not know, nor to give testimony about things of which they are ignorant. And if he has read the writings which circulate among us, and either does not understand their gist or does understand but pretends otherwise lest suspicion fall upon him too in this regard, then he must be considered far more worthless and detestable: he courts the favor of the unlettered crowd while acting as enemy and betrayer of the truth and piety he approves. 5. For I want you to know that I propounded to him certain questions, his replies to which showed that he knew nothing. 6. So true is what I say that I think that the debates held between us on the topic proposed have been reported to you as well, from which it will be seen all too plainly that he lacks all knowledge of anything having to do with us. But if this matter has not yet come to your attention, I am prepared to debate once again in your presence."[59]

Such are blessed Justin's words, in which, according to what he had foretold, he reached his life's completion by martyrdom through Crescens's treachery. 7. Tatian was someone else who left books worth remembering which were written against the pagans; he was a most learned man who in early life taught rhetoric with great distinction, gaining no small renown from it. After he came over to our cause,[60] he wrote the books in

---

probably means "to be thrust into the stocks." Crescens, also mentioned in 4.16.8–9 (= Tatian, *Oratio* 19.1), is otherwise unknown. Tatian there mentions that he also conspired against him.

59. Rufinus omits the concluding reference to Socrates in Justin/Eusebius.

60. More on Tatian in 4.29.3. Eusebius says nothing about his "conversion." The following quotation is from his *Oratio ad Graecos* 18.2 (where it is the demons who are compared to brigands).

which he mentions Justin as follows: "And that admirable man Justin was quite right in proceeding to say that those people are like brigands."

8. And further on, after he has said something about the philosophers, he adds:

"Crescens, finally, who frequented the great city, outdid everyone else in ravishing children and was no one's inferior in greed for money. 9. And while he persuaded others to despise death, he himself was in such a dreadful mind about it that he handed Justin over to death as to the worst of evils because in preaching the truth he used to show that philosophers were pleasure-loving imposters."[61]

4.17.1. Justin, before he underwent his own martyrdom, described those of the martyrs before him, writing as follows in the first book of his defense:[62]

2. "There was a woman who was united to a vile man and who also at first lived a disgraceful life. After she learned Christ's precepts, she became chaste and tried to persuade her husband to behave otherwise, pointing out to him that among Christian precepts there is the doctrine that eternal punishment looms over those who contemn chastity and justice during their lives. 3. But he persisted in the same indecent behavior, and thus alienated his wife from him by his acts. For since the woman considered it immoral to continue living with her husband, who despised the law of nature and sought new ways to get pleasure, she decided to divorce him. 4. Her relatives intervened, however, and since they promised that her husband would improve, she was forced to resume living with him. 5. When afterwards he went to Alexandria, however, and it was heard that he was behaving even more vilely and seeking occasions for even more serious acts of impurity, the woman gave him a bill of divorce and left, lest by continuing to remain together with him she be considered his accomplice in unchastity. 6. And what did that marvelous husband do who should have been glad that his wife had made such progress in chastity that not only did she do nothing indecent herself, but could not even bear patiently the

61. *Oratio* 19.1.
62. *Apol.* 2.2.

indecency of her husband, whom she had left from the love of chastity when he refused to reform? He accused his wife of a new kind of crime for her chastity: 'She is a Christian,' he said. 7. She for her part presented a petition to you, your majesty, that she might be allowed first to put her affairs in order, and then respond to the charges, which you granted her. 8. Her husband, though, when he was unable to prosecute her,[63] turned his efforts in the following way to seeking the death of one Ptolemy, who had been the woman's teacher in the Christian religion. 9. He had a friend who was a centurion and whom he persuaded to ask Ptolemy if he was a Christian. Ptolemy, a lover of truth, was so far from concealing this, the glory of his profession, that he confessed that he was a Christian to the one who asked. The centurion put him in fetters at once and, after he had been worn down by a long time in the filth of prison, delivered him at last to Urbicius, a magistrate.[64] 10. He asked Ptolemy in the same way only one question: if he was a Christian. Ptolemy, once again aware of the great benefit it meant to him, put the divine religion before himself and testified openly about Christ's teaching power and the practices that belong to all that is good. 11. For one who refuses to admit something that exists certainly judges blameworthy what one denies. 12. No sooner had he confessed, therefore, than he was ordered executed by Urbicius.

63. *cum mulierem non posset arguere* = πρὸς ἐκείνην μὲν μὴ δυνάμενος τὰ νῦν ἔτι λέγειν: "unable now to speak against her any longer": because of the imperial indult (Eunapius, *Hist.* 25.1., complains about the frequent judicial deferrals resulting from such indults). We are not told exactly how she framed her petition, but the general explanation of "putting her affairs in order" (*rem familiarem ordinare* = δοικήσασθαι τὰ ἑαυτῆς), together with Justin's transcription of the Latin word for "bill of divorce" (*repudium*), suggests legal proceedings, and probably a suit for recovery of the dowry (*actio rei uxoriae*). The former husband might be liable to full restitution if he were convicted of gross indecency, as would be the case here; cf. Susan Treggiari, *Roman Marriage: Iusti Coniuges from the Time of Cicero to the Time of Ulpian* (Oxford: Clarendon Press, 1991), 351–52. Since we do not read that she was ever tried for Christianity, and since the following account makes the urban prefect's willingness to send Christians to summary execution quite clear, we can guess that a settlement out of court was reached, each party yielding something. The woman perhaps saved her life at the cost of part or all of her dowry.

64. Q. Lollius Urbicus was *praefectus urbi* probably 146–160; cf. *Prosopographia Imperii Romani Saec. I, II, III*, 5.327.

But a Christian man named Lucius, seeing how rashly the sentence had been pronounced, said to Urbicius, 'May I ask why it is that you have ordered the execution of someone who is not an adulterer, nor a seducer, nor a murderer, nor a robber, nor an abductor, nor someone guilty of any other crime, your only reason being the name of Christian which he acknowledged he bore? What you are doing, Urbicius, is not worthy of the pious emperor, nor of his son, the wisest of boys, nor of the sacred senate.' 13. The other, however, without asking anything further, said to Lucius, 'You, it seems, are a Christian too.' And when Lucius replied, 'You may be sure I am,' Urbicius ordered him to be executed likewise. To which he said, 'I thank you for releasing me from lords most vicious and sending me on to God, the good and best father, and the king of all.' And there was a third man as well who spoke out with like frankness and was punished with a like sentence."

After these words Justin immediately added the matter which we cited a little earlier, namely, "And I expect that I too will be plotted against by one of those whom I have opposed for the sake of the truth," etc.[65]

4.18.1. This man[66] has left us a great many works resulting from his labors, from which we may gather the depth of his learning and his devotion to the divine teachings, and those moved by the love of doctrine and knowledge may derive great benefit. 2. There is extant, that is, the book we mentioned earlier, written on behalf of our religion to Antoninus, surnamed Pius, and to his son[67] and the senate. There is a second book as well containing a defense of our faith which he wrote to Antoninus Verus, the successor of the emperor mentioned above, of whose times we have now begun to tell. 3. There is another book too against the pagans in which he discusses each of our philosophers and those of the Greeks in a most extensive ar-

65. In 4.16.3.
66. On Justin: 2.13.2–4; 4.11.11–4.12.
67. Eusebius: "and to his children." On the second apology mentioned below, see Schwartz, *Eusebius Werke* 2.3.CLIV–CLVII, and Denis Minis and Paul Parvis, *Justin, Philosopher and Martyr: Apologies* (Oxford: Clarendon, 2009), 21–31. Whether there were really two originally is debated. The second one is mentioned in 4.16.1.

gument. He also treats there of some aspects of the nature of demons, but the matter is too long to include here. 4. Another book against the pagans is entitled *Refutation*. Still another of his is about sovereignty,[68] the material for which he drew not only from our books, but from those of the Greeks as well. 5. And there is another entitled *Psaltes*,[69] and still another in the form of notes about the soul in which he includes various questions which occupy the Greek philosophers, promising to contest them and to offer his own views about them in the book containing his answers. 6. He also composed a dialogue as though with the Jews, which he held at Ephesus, with Trypho, the most renowned teacher of the Hebrews; in it he explains how he was himself led by divine grace to belief in the true faith, whereas he had previously studied the teachings of the philosophers with the deepest application, possessed as he was by the desire to find the truth.[70] 7. He also says concerning the Jews that they hatched deadly plots against Christ's church.[71] And he charges Trypho with this, saying,

"Not only did you not repent of what you did wrong; you even chose from Jerusalem men suited for this and sent them through every land, that they might go around and say that an impious sect had arisen, that of the Christians, at the same time defaming us with slanderous charges, so that because of them anyone unfamiliar with us might be afraid to associate with us. You are hereby the cause of death,[72] through the scandals you fabricate, not only for yourselves but for others too."

8. He also writes that the grace of prophecy flourished in the churches even down to his own times. He says too that the Apocalypse of John is from the apostle. He also uses some prophetic proof-texts against Trypho, establishing against him con-

68. *De monarchia* = Περὶ θεοῦ μοναρχίας ("God's sovereignty").

69. Ψάλτης: "cantor."

70. *Dialogus cum Tryphone* 2–8. Text, translation, and commentary: Philippe Bobichon, *Justin Martyr: Dialogue avec Tryphon* (Fribourg: Academic Press, 2003).

71. Eusebius: "they plotted against Christ's teaching."

72. *causa mortis* = ἀδικίας αἴτιοι: "guilty of injustice." In the foregoing sentence, "so that ... associate with us" has no equivalent in the original. Cf. *Dialog.* 17.1.

cerning them that the Jews had removed them from the scriptures and discarded them.[73] And there are many other works of his which are in circulation among a great number of the brothers, and which were judged by those of old to be so worthy and commendable, 9. that Irenaeus is seen borrowing from them and writing as follows in the fourth book *Against Heresies:* "Justin speaks very good sense in the book he wrote against Marcion when he goes on to write that he would never agree with the Lord himself if he said that there was another god besides the creator of all."[74]

And again in the fifth book of the same work he says, "Justin is quite right to affirm that before the advent of the Lord, Satan never dared to blaspheme God, because he did not yet realize that he had been condemned."[75]

10. The foregoing remarks about Justin's works will serve to encourage the more zealous among the faithful to study his books.

4.19. In the eighth year, then, of the emperor mentioned above,[76] Anicetus died in the eleventh year of his episcopacy, and was succeeded by Soter. In Alexandria, Celadion left Agrippinus as his successor after fourteen years in the priesthood. 4.20. In Antioch at this time Theophilus held the high priesthood as the sixth from the apostles. Cornelius had been in fourth place after Hero, and he was succeeded in fifth place by Heros.[77]

4.21. Then Hegesippus too, whom we mentioned earlier, was held in renown, and Dionysius, the bishop of Corinth. Pinytus also, in Crete, was most illustrious among bishops, and Philip, Apollinarius, Melito, Musanus, Modestus,[78] and especially Irenaeus, all of whose outstanding works on the apostolic faith and sound doctrine have come down to us.

4.22.1. Hegesippus in the fifth book of his treatises,[79] where

73. *Dialog.* 82.1; 81.4; 71.1–73.4.   74. *Haer.* 4.6.2.
75. *Haer.* 5.26.2.
76. Eusebius: "as the eighth year [168] … was approaching."
77. Heros: "Eros" in Eusebius.
78. Hegesippus: 4.8.1–2; Modestus: 4.25; Musanus: 4.28.
79. Eusebius: "in the five treatises which have come down to us."

he presents his ideas about his faith with the fullest possible argument, says as well that when he was on his way to Rome, he met in word and charity with a great many bishops in each place, and found them all preachers and teachers of the same faith. He also mentions something about Clement's letter to the Corinthians, which I think I must include in this work. He says,

2. "And the Corinthian church remained sound in doctrine down to Bishop Primus, whom I saw during my voyage to Rome; I stayed with him in Corinth for many days, enjoying the purity of his faith. 3. When I arrived in Rome, I stayed there[80] until Soter succeeded Anicetus and Eleutherus Soter. And in all of these ordinations and in everything else which I saw in the other cities, all was conducted as the law handed down of old and the prophets showed and the Lord decreed."

4. This writer also writes as follows about the sectarians who arose in his time:

"And after James, surnamed 'the Just,' was martyred, testifying to the truth in his own turn just as the Lord had done, Symeon, son of Cleopas, was ordained bishop by divine choice,[81] chosen by all because he was the Lord's cousin. It was for this reason that the church was then called a virgin, since it had not yet been corrupted by the insinuation of spurious doctrines. 5. But one Theobutes, because he had deservedly failed to be elected bishop, began first of all to upset and pervert everything, having achieved his position from [the?] seven sects among the people.[82] Produced by them as well was Simon, whence the Simonians; Cleobius, whence the Cleobians; Dositheus, whence the Dositheans; Gorthaeus, whence the Gorthaeni; and Masbutheus, whence the Masbutheni; as well as the Menandrians,

---

80. *permansi ibi* = διαδοχὴν ἐποιησάμην (whatever that means); did Rufinus read διατριβήν?

81. *electione divina* = ὁ ἐκ θείου αὐτοῦ Συμεών ("Simeon, his uncle's [son]"). See 3.11.

82. *Theobutes quidam ... coepit initio perturbare omnia et conrumpere, qui erat ex septem haeresibus in populo constitutus* = ἄρχεται δὲ ὁ Θέβουθις ... ὑποφθείρειν ἀπὸ τῶν ἑπτὰ αἱρέσεων, ὧν καὶ αὐτὸς ἦν, ἐν τῷ λαῷ: translation? On the listing of the seven sects in the various sources, cf. Bardy, *Eusèbe*, 1.201. Rufinus adds "Masbutheus" as the putative founder of the Masbutheni ("Masbothei" in Eusebius).

who derive from them; and the Marcionists, Carpocratians, Valentinians, Basilidians, and Saturnians. Each of them, in forming a separate schism by various corruptions of the faith, had his own sect and his own sectarians. 6. Out of them have come forth false Christs, false prophets, and false apostles, who in rending the unity of the brothers into different parts, have stained the chaste bed of the church with corrupt doctrine, uttering impiety against the Lord and against his Christ."[83]

7. Our author also lists as follows the sects that existed among the Jews of old: which they were and how many: "There were different sentiments among the circumcision, among the children of Israel that is, which were especially hostile to the tribe of Judah, from which Christ came. They were the Essenes, Galileans, Hemerobaptists, Masbuthaeans, Samaritans, Sadducees, and Pharisees."

8. He writes much else as well, some of which we have already mentioned earlier as was opportune.[84] He also treated of the gospel according to the Hebrews and Syrians, discussed some matters concerning the Hebrew language, and mentioned Jewish traditions, by which he shows that he came to faith in Christ from the Hebrews. 9. In addition, he himself and Irenaeus and the whole choir of those of old said that the book which is called Wisdom was Solomon's, just as are Proverbs and the others.[85] When he dealt with apocryphal writings in opposition to certain heretics, however, he declared that some things in them were perverted and fabricated.

4.23.1. But now we must say something about the blessed Dionysius, bishop of the Corinthian church, whose learning and grace in God's word were a blessing not only for the people whom he governed, but for those who were living far off as well and to whom his letters made him present. 2. There is for

83. Acts 4.26. Rufinus adds the phrase about "the chaste bed of the church" above.

84. 2.23.3–18; 3.12; 3.20.1–7; 3.32; 4.8.1–2.

85. *librum, qui adtitulatur Sapientia, Salomonis dixerunt, sicut et Proverbia et cetera* = πανάρετον Σοφίαν τὰς Σολομῶνος Παροιμίας ἐκάλουν ("they referred to Solomon's Proverbs as 'all-virtuous Wisdom'"). On this confusing title, see Robert M. Grant, *Eusebius as Church Historian* (Oxford: Clarendon, 1980), 138–40. Compare 4.26.14.

instance the one he wrote to the Lacedaemonians about the Catholic faith, in which he speaks most vividly of peace and unanimity. Another is the one to the Athenians, in which he invites them to believe in the gospel and exhorts the more indolent among them, while at the same time accusing some of them of having almost lapsed from the faith when their bishop, Publius, was martyred. 3. He also mentions Quadratus, who succeeded the martyr Publius to the priesthood, and says that due to his labor and diligence some warmth of faith had been revived and restored among them. The same letter indicates that Dionysius the Areopagite, who, as we are told by the Acts of the Apostles, came to believe in Christ when taught by the apostle Paul,[86] was the first bishop to be ordained in Athens by that apostle. 4. There is also in circulation another letter of his to the Nicomedians in which he attacks the heresy of Marcion and presents the rule of the church's faith with marvelous balance. 5. Another of his letters was written to the church of Gortyna along with the other churches on Crete as well; in it he declares that their bishop, Philip, was endowed with great virtues and wonderful zeal. He also says that the feasts of the heretics are to be avoided. 6. He wrote too to the church in Amastris and the other churches with it in Pontus; in the letter he mentioned Bacchylides and Elpistus, saying that they had urged him to write, and he explained in it many of the things in divine scripture, while mentioning as well their bishop, Palmas. He also says a good deal about marriage and chastity, and orders that those who have risen from any fall and turned away from sin be received, even if they are withdrawing from the perversion of heresy. 7. Along with this there is another letter of his to the Cnossians, in which he admonishes and entreats their bishop Pinytus not to place heavy burdens on the necks of the disciples, nor to impose on the brothers the necessity of compulsory chastity, which is a danger to the weakness of numbers of people. 8. In his reply to Dionysius Pinytus writes that he does appreciate the advice offered by a sounder judgment, beseeching him at the same time to send in the future, following upon what he had already written, some writings which will rep-

---

86. Acts 17.34. Cf. 3.4.10.

resent a more substantial and nutritional diet, by which the people of his church may be nurtured unto better progress, lest by always imbibing milk as their food they lead the life of children in a body already growing old. Pinytus has also left us in this letter the tokens of his orthodoxy, the care with which he watched over the people, and a living image of himself, of his learning and wisdom in God's word, reflected in a sort of mirror.

9. There is extant another letter of Dionysius to the Romans, addressed to Bishop Soter, in which he shows how glad he is that the customs handed down of old are maintained in the Roman church. His words:

10. "It has been your custom from the beginning to help all of the brothers with various acts of kindness, to send to many churches in different lands everything they lack, to assuage the poverty of each person in every respect, and even to furnish to the brothers banished to the mines the usual things. Such was the custom of the Roman church from the outset, a practice with which the fathers charged it and which has always been preserved intact. And your blessed bishop Soter has not only maintained what the fathers handed down, but improved it. Not only does he furnish the saints with their physical requirements; he also consoles the visiting brothers by speaking to them in a most kindly and gentle manner, and treating each of them as a pious and religious father."

11. The same writing mentions also Clement's letter to the Corinthians, indicating that by ancient custom and practice that letter had always been read in the church. Then he says, "Today we observed the blessed Day of the Lord, on which we read your letter, which we always read for our admonition, as we do the earlier one written to us by Clement." 12. He also writes about letters of his that had been falsified by certain people:

"I wrote some letters at the request of the brothers which Satan's apostles have filled with tares, removing some things and adding others; woe awaits them in God's judgment! But there is nothing surprising about their attempt to falsify the Lord's words in sacred scripture, when they have tampered with our humble writings."

13. There is extant another letter of Dionysius to the most

faithful sister Chrysophorus,[87] in which he sets before her a feast of reason of the divine word suited to her gender and capacity. Such is our account of Dionysius.

4.24. There are extant three books of instruction written to Autolycus by Theophilus, who, as we said earlier,[88] was bishop of Antioch. Another of his books is against the heresy of Hermogenes; in it he uses proof-texts from the Revelation of John as well. There are also extant other shorter works of his containing various instructional materials. At this time, then, when the heretics were spoiling the pure seed of God's word in every place as though with tares, and defiling the seed-beds of apostolic teaching with spurious admixtures, the priests of God strove everywhere to expel and clear away their bad seed, like vigilant farmers, and, like anxious shepherds, to chase off the wolves stalking Christ's flocks by pursuing them with shouts; they admonished and instructed the brothers, writing even to those at a distance, while if at times they discovered them to be anywhere present with them, they would press them closely and lay them low in disputations, arguments, and debates. Still others, taking thought for later generations, refuted their speculations and perverse objections in the treatises they published. One of them was Theophilus, about whom we are speaking; what we have read shows him contending with distinction in disputation against them—against Marcion, that is. He was succeeded in the priesthood of the Antiochene church by Maximus, the seventh from the apostles.

4.25. Philip too, who as we said earlier was bishop of the church in Gortyna, has himself left us a distinguished work against Marcion. So has Irenaeus, but Modestus[89] acquitted himself even more brilliantly than the others, exposing all of his deceits and tricks when he uncovered the wrappings of the malice beneath which he was hidden.

4.26.1. Melito too, the bishop of the church of Sardis, and

---

87. "Chrysophora" in Eusebius.

88. 4.20. Cf. G. Bardy and J. Sender, *Théophile d'Antioche: Trois livres à Autolycus* (Paris: Cerf, 1948). On Hermogenes below, cf. 2 Tm 1.15.

89. Philip: 4.23.5; cf. Jerome, *Vir. illustr.* 30. Modestus: 4.21; Jerome, *Vir. illustr.* 32.

Apollinarius, who governed the church in Hierapolis, were considered the most famous among them. They likewise presented to the Roman emperor works in defense of our faith which are simply outstanding. 2. The following is an account of their works which have come to our notice.[90] From Melito there are two books on the Passover, one book on the best way of life, and also on the prophets, on the church, on the Lord's Day, on human faith, on the senses, on soul, body, and mind, on the bath, on truth, another on faith, on Christ's birth and on his prophecy, another on soul and body, on hospitality; another book entitled *The Key;* on the devil, on the Revelation of John, on God clothed in a body, and last of all a book addressed to Antoninus Verus.[91] 3. In his work on the Passover he also refers in the following words to the time in which he was writing: "It was under Sergius Paulus,[92] proconsul of Asia, at the time when Sagaris was martyred, that a great debate arose in Laodicea about the Passover, and we have written this during those days."

4. His treatise is also mentioned by Clement of Alexandria in the work where he explains the Passover,[93] saying that he

90. On Melito and Apollinarius, cf. Jerome, *Chron.* 170. The list of Melito's works given by Eusebius himself "is unintelligible in places because of textual corruption, and the other versions of the list ... are all secondary attempts to clear up the difficulties" (Stuart G. Hall, *Melito of Sardis: On Pascha* [Oxford: Clarendon, 1979], xiii). An account of what may or may not be salvaged from the ancient lists of his writings is in Hall, xiii–xvii. For the state of Eusebius's text here, see Bardy, *Eusèbe,* 1.208. Those who wish for a closer look at the additional confusion which Rufinus introduced into the matter may be referred to Schwartz and Mommsen, *Eusebius Werke,* 2.1.380–83.

Eusebius refers here to Melito's two books on the Passover, while in the next section to one such work, which suggests that "book" here means a section of a work: see Hall, xix.

91. Rufinus adds "Verus" (from 4.13.8), which only worsens Eusebius's confusion about the emperor's name. Cf. Schwarz and Mommsen, *Eusebius Werke,* 2.3.87.

92. Eusebius has "Servillius Paulus," a name otherwise unattested. Rufinus may be remembering the Sergius Paulus of Acts 13.7, but his "correction" may still be valid, since one L. Sergius Paulus might in fact have been proconsul of Asia at the time. Or Eusebius might be emended to "Servillius Pudens" = Q. Servilius Pudens, proconsul perhaps after 166; see Hall (note 90 above), xxi. On Sagaris, cf. 5.24.5. The citation here is *Fragment 4.*

93. Cf. 6.13.9. *De Pascha* 26 in *Clemens Alexandrinus* III (GCS, 1970).

was prompted to write by this same treatise which Melito had published previously. 5. Now in the book that he[94] addressed to the emperor, he writes as follows of what was done against us in that time: "What never before has happened is taking place now: the race of the devout is suffering persecution, harried from every side throughout Asia by the new decrees published. For shameless slanderers who desire to seize the property of others have taken advantage of the imperial commands to prowl about day and night like robbers and plunder the innocent." 6. And further on he continues:

"And if in fact they are doing these things at your orders, we must believe that whatever is committed at the behest of a just emperor is good. We even suffer death willingly when we know that it is inflicted by you. The only thing we beg of you is that you yourself first seek out the agents in charge of this impudence, and if the deaths they are inflicting have been ordered by you, that you yourself put an end to them. If, however, this decree, so monstrous and barbaric as it is, is something of which you yourself were unaware, then we beseech you not to disdain us nor to allow your devoted citizens to be slain in such official brigandage."

7. And further on again he adds:

"For the way of life we follow flourished first among the barbarians, but was introduced as well to your Roman culture in the time of Augustus; it was from then on that your empire reached new heights, lifted up under the omens of this religion. You are the happy successor to this empire so happily extended, and together with your son you happily preserve what has been handed on to you. Protect, therefore, what was handed on to you together with your empire, the religion belonging to our way of life,[95] since it brought prosperity to your fathers when it came in. 8. And preserve the faith which grew up along with the prosperity of Augustus himself, since nothing unfortunate happened

94. "He" being Melito. The emperor is Marcus Aurelius. The excerpts that follow are *Fragment* 1 in Hall (pp. 62–65). On the "new decrees" below, cf. Hall, 63n2.

95. Rufinus omits what follows in Eusebius: "which [way of life] your ancestors honored along with the other religions."

to Augustus either when he began or as he advanced; on the contrary, everything flourished and enjoyed great success, with the members of this religion interceding with the highest God for his empire.[96] 9. Nor did any of the emperors, except Nero alone and Domitian, turn against our doctrine at the prompting of scoundrels. It is since their time that we have been slandered by calumnies. 10. But your fathers corrected this error, which had proceeded from ignorance: they afterwards issued frequent punitive decrees against those who dared to cause any trouble to the members of this religion. One of them was your grandfather Hadrian, who sent letters in this regard to many officials, especially to Fundanus, the proconsul of Asia.[97] And your father, the sovereign ruler of the Roman empire together with yourself, sends[98] edicts on their behalf to all the cities in general, and above all to Larisa, Thessalonica, and Athens. 11. But we are much more confident that you are of the same mind, or rather that you will show yourself, we trust, even kindlier by far, since you are a lover of the true way of life and of pure religion."

12. This and much else of exceptional worth may be found in the tract which he wrote and of which we have spoken. Now when he writes in exposition of the scriptures, he lists as an introduction those books of the Old Testament which should be regarded as belonging to the canon. I think it necessary to include this passage.[99]

13. "Melito to his brother Onesimus, greetings. Since your zeal for God's word has prompted you to ask me again and again to cull for you proof-texts from the law and the prophets concerning the Savior and our faith, and at the same time to show the order and number of the books of the Old Testament, I am glad to fulfill your request, aware as I am that you are so eager to learn and so devoted to the faith, that nothing means more to you than eternal life. 14. I want you to know, then, that I have traveled to that place in the east where our preaching began and where all those things were done which

---

96. Rufinus substitutes the intercession of Christians for Eusebius's "the prayers of all."

97. Cf. 4.9.   98. "sent" in Eusebius.

99. Hall, *Fragment* 3 (pp. 64–67).

have been written down and are read,[100] and there I carefully
inquired into all of the writings which are books of the Old
Testament. I therefore found there, after the most exhaustive
investigation, that they are as follows: the five books of Moses:
Genesis, Exodus, Leviticus, Numbers, Deuteronomy; then Joshua, son of Nun, Judges, Ruth, four books of Kings, two books of
Paralipomena, the Psalms of David, the Proverbs of Solomon,
also called Wisdom,[101] Ecclesiastes, the Song of Songs, Job; also
the prophets Isaiah, Jeremiah, one book of the twelve prophets,
Daniel, Ezekiel, Esdras. From them, then, I have sent you *eglo-
gae*, proof-texts extracted and arranged in six books."

This, then, is what we have found out about Melito's works.

4.27. Apollinarius's many works have circulated widely; the
following are those which have reached us: a book in our defense
to the emperor mentioned above; five books against the pagans;
two books on truth;[102] and those he produced later against the
Cataphrygians, Montanus, that is, and his false prophetesses,
who had then first begun to turn aside from the right path.

4.28. There is also extant a tract by Musanus, whom we mentioned earlier; it is written with great elegance of style to certain brothers who had deviated to the heresy of the Encratites,
as it is called, which had recently arisen. It is said that Tatian
was its founder, 4.29.1. the same man we mentioned previously
bearing witness to blessed Justin, whose disciple he was, it is
said.[103] Irenaeus, however, reports the following of him in the
first book against heresies:

100. *ubi gesta sunt illa omnia, quae leguntur scripta.* Melito/Eusebius just have:
"where [the things which interest Onesimus] were proclaimed and done." Rufinus could be read: "which have been written down and are being collected."
Does he want to protect Melito's orthodoxy (and his own) by suggesting that
the canon was still being assembled in Melito's time (if, that is, Melito's canon
would not have been regarded as complete by those of his own time)?

101. In 4.22.9 Rufinus distinguishes Proverbs and Wisdom. On the canon,
see also 3.10.1–3.

102. Rufinus does not have Apollinarius's two books against the Jews in
Eusebius. On the Cataphrygians, see 5.14–19.

103. Musanus is in 4.21; Tatian in 4.16.7–9. Tatian was born c. 120 in As-
syria and became a disciple of Justin in Rome. After Justin was martyred c.
165, Tatian returned to the East. For his writings, see Molly Whittaker, *Tatian:
Oratio ad Graecos and Fragments* (Oxford: Clarendon, 1982).

2. "From Saturninus and Marcion are descended those called Encratites; they reject marriage, which God established of old, implicitly condemning him who from the beginning made male and female for the renewal of the human race. They also preach abstinence from animals, ungrateful as they are to God, who produced them for human use. And they deny that the first human being is saved. 3. This has now been invented by those founded by one Tatian, who introduced blasphemies of this sort. He was one of Justin's students, but as long as he was with him, he did not reveal that he thought anything of the sort. After the other was martyred, though, he broke off from the churches, swollen with a teacher's arrogance and puffed up with boundless conceit, as though he considered himself better than others. He preferred to establish his own mode of teaching rather than following the one passed down by those of old: he introduced certain invisible aeons, according to Valentinus's fables, considered marriage, fornication, and seduction morally equal, and asserted doctrines like those of Marcion and Saturninus. He also devised new arguments to call into question Adam's salvation."[104]

4. And a bit later Irenaeus adds the following as well:[105]

"Not long afterwards one Severus bolstered the heresy just mentioned, providing its adherents with formidable ammunition. Hence they should rather be called 'Severians.' 5. While

104. The reliability of this report in Irenaeus, *Haer.* 1.28.1, has been doubted by Martin Elze, *Tatian und seine Theologie* (Göttingen: Vandenhoeck and Ruprecht, 1960), 106–13, and Emily J. Hunt, *Christianity in the Second Century: The Case of Tatian* (London: Routledge, 2003), 20–51. Tatian represented the ideal of "spiritual marriage" within Syriac Christianity, but was not its originator (Hunt, 145–55). Irenaeus says in 3.28.8 that Tatian based his denial of Adam's salvation on 1 Cor 15.22 ("In Adam all die"). He also says that Marcion taught that none of those portrayed as just in the Old Testament are saved, but only those who are notorious sinners (1.27.3.; Adam is not mentioned either way). On Saturninus and the perdition of man, see Epiphanius, *Pan.* 23.1 ("Saturnilus"). Irenaeus's attempt to link Tatian to these heresiarchs has not been thought persuasive.

105. Eusebius does not say that this next bit is from Irenaeus. On the Severians, see Epiphanius, *Pan.* 45. Hunt, 179–80, refutes what Clement says in *Stromateis* 3.82.2 about Tatian rejecting the Old Testament as inspired by another god. On the Diatessaron, see Hunt, 145–50, and *The Anchor Bible Dictionary*, 2.189–90.

they use the law, the prophets, and the gospels, they distort the meaning of the scriptures with their own interpretation. They belittle the apostle Paul and reject his letters. Nor do they accept the Acts of the Apostles. 6. Their earlier founder, Tatian, however, combined the gospels somehow or other and put together one gospel from the four, which he called the Diatessaron and which is still in wide circulation. He is also said to have changed completely a considerable number of the apostle's words, as though he wanted to correct the order and arrangement of his language. 7. He too has left a countless number of books. But of all his writings, the book he wrote against the gentiles has proved outstanding and most useful."

Such is the account of those matters.

4.30.1. It was at this time, with countless heresies sprouting up everywhere, especially in Mesopotamia, that a man named Bardesanes,[106] who was highly skilled in Syriac and a forceful debater, wrote dialogues against Marcion and a number of others, which he published in his own language. There are many other books of his as well which his disciples translated into Greek. For he was so able in word and doctrine, and effective in disputation, that he had a great number of distinguished men as his followers. 2. He has an extremely cogent dialogue about fate directed to Antoninus. And he wrote much else which was quite useful and urgently needed during the persecutions then. Now they say that he was himself of Valentinus's school at first. 3. But once he had censured his teacher for his error and confuted his foolish fables, he regarded himself as having gone over to a better and correct view of the faith. He did not, however, divest himself completely of the filth and stain of his old errors. Now it was at this time also that Soter, the bishop of the Roman church, reached the end of his life.

106. On Bardesanes (154–222), cf. Epiphanius, *Pan.* 56, and Jerome, *Vir. illustr.* 33. For his book on fate, cf. Ilaria Ramelli (ed.), *Contro it Fato = Kata Heimarmenes (detto anche "Liber Legum Regionum")* (Rome: San Clemente; Bologna: ESD, 2009), and Torsten Krannich and Peter Stein, "Das *Buch der Gesetze der Länder* des Bardesanes von Edessa," *Zeitschrift für Antikes Christentum* 8.2 (2004): 203–29. Also I. Ramelli, "Bardesane e la sua scuola, L'*Apologia* siriaca ascritta a Melitone e la *Doctrina Addai*," *Aevum* 83.1 (2009): 141–68.

BOOK FIVE

1. "Verus" in Eusebius.

Preface.1. Bishop Soter, then, when he had exercised the priesthood in Rome for eight years, was succeeded by Eleutherus, the twelfth from the apostles, in the seventeenth year of the reign of Antoninus Verus.[2] It was at this time that the most savage persecutions broke out against ours in many provinces of the Roman world, kindled by the outcries and turmoil of the public, so that there were many thousands of martyrs in each place. Thus we can easily gather from them the written accounts we found as a memorial of their deeds. 2. And although the fuller narrative of this, one which treats the martyrdoms individually, has been set out by us under its own title and includes extended instruction indispensable to doctrine and knowledge,[3] we will nevertheless select a few matters from the quantity available for insertion in this work when we judge them suitable. 3. Other historians may tell of wars, triumphs, and victories; they may celebrate the mighty deeds of officers and generals; they may relate the deaths of citizens and enemies; they may describe the destruction of homeland, spouses, children, and everything else in various massacres; 4. this our story, which contains the narrative of the things which concern God, will not be unsuitable if it describes the wars experienced by the flesh for the salvation of the soul and the battles sustained by the soul in order to regain its heavenly homeland; if it tells of the conflicts in which it has engaged out of a conviction of the truth and in which it has fought not against mortal forc-

2. 177. This is actually Marcus Aurelius. On the confusion see Arthur C. McGiffert, *The Church History of Eusebius,* in *The Nicene and Post-Nicene Fathers,* Second Series, 1.390–91.

3. See 4.15.47.

es but against spiritual demons, and not for carnal offspring but for spiritual freedom; if, that is, we write of the battles fought not for the acquisition of lands or provinces, but for the kingdom of heaven and the inheritance of paradise, and the purpose of which is not a realm for a mortal king but the glory of triumphs from the God who is the immortal king of all.

5.1.1. Lyons and Vienne are considered the most distinguished cities of Gaul; past them in headlong course rushes the Rhône, most renowned of rivers. 2. The great things done in them in respect to God's martyrs in the time of the Antoninus Verus mentioned above have been described in due course by them in a reliable report and sent to the churches of Asia and Phrygia. 3. Firmer evidence of this may be obtained from this writing, which I cite:

"The servants of Christ living in Vienne and Lyons, cities of Gaul, to the brothers in Asia and Phrygia who cherish the same faith and hope in Christ's redemption as we do, peace to you and grace and glory from God the Father and Christ Jesus Our Lord."

4. And after some introductory remarks, they begin the account of the events as follows:

"The enormity of our affliction and the rage directed by the gentiles at the holy martyrs is beyond the ability of even ourselves who were there to recount accurately, let alone encompass in writing. 5. For the enemy came against us in full strength, as though already signaling its arrival by the harshness of the persecution, and thereby instructing and training its agents to discharge upon God's servants every form of wickedness and cruelty. Thus we were at first forbidden residence in houses, then the use of the baths, then afterwards appearance in public as well, and then finally appearance in any place at all, indoors or out, in public or in private. 6. But God's grace was present, which rescued the weaker among us from their hands and brought forward men firmer than pillars who by their endurance could not only weather the assaults unleashed by the enemy, but go further and seek out and expose themselves of their own accord to all of the agonies whether of taunts or tor-

tures; when the torturers were almost worn out, they thought
they had not yet had enough, since they believed that this was
somehow a delay for them in their haste to get to Christ; they
could all but be heard crying out in what was taking place and
in the power of their endurance that 'the sufferings of this
time are not worthy to be compared to the future glory which
will be revealed in us.'[4]

7. "They bore bravely, therefore, the shouts against them and
the reproaches and mistreatment of the people, and considered
their slander to be high praise. They even put up patiently with
being beaten by them, stoned, and locked up, accepting calmly whatever the fury of the raging populace devised. 8. There
finally came the time when in the presence of the tribune and
the leading men of the city, the brothers were seized and thrust
into prison solely on account of the outcries of the populace,
and reserved until the arrival of the governor, for whom they
were kept. 9. So great was the cruelty he practiced on them that
no one could describe the full exhibition of his savagery. Vettius Epagathus, therefore, one of the brothers, who practiced
a charity which was perfect toward God and faultless toward
others, whose life as a youth had been so scrutinized and commended by all that he was esteemed above even the most respectable elders—for he walked in all the commandments and
ordinances of the Lord without blame,[5] and showed the greatest deference to God's servants as well—was so filled with divine zeal and spiritual fervor that when he saw such cruel punishments being inflicted upon God's servants and their organs
being racked with so many agonies against all law and right, he
could not bear the indignity any more and asked to be heard
in the presence of the noblest citizens, those whose religious
character was unimpeachable. For he was most distinguished
among his own people and most learned. 10. But the judge ob-
durately refused to accept his intercession, and simply asked
him if he was a Christian too. When he affirmed freely and in
ringing tones that he certainly was a Christian, the other said,

4. Rom 8.18.
5. Lk 1.6.

'As advocate for the Christians, he may join the prisoners.' But here they did not know what they were saying; having in himself Jesus, the advocate for us, he was deservedly honored with this name, since he had followed the example of the holy presbyter Zechariah,[6] who had shown the fullness of charity toward the saints. He himself, while he was present among his brothers and undertook the defense of the liberty which is established in our religion, followed the Lord's example and laid down his life for his sheep and his friends. And therefore in this way likewise the disciples, faithful to Christ, will follow the Lamb in the kingdom to come wherever he goes.[7]

11. "With these most noble and faithful leaders, all the remaining choir of saints promptly and eagerly laid down their lives for the freedom of the faith. Some, however, were found to be weaker and unequal to the suffering of persecution, unable to endure it; they were about ten in number, and their lapse left us in mourning and great sadness and dashed the spirits of those many who had been kindled by the faith of the former ones. 12. Thus we were all utterly terrified, not because of the tortures so cruelly inflicted but because we were unsure about whether we would succeed in making our profession, since we were suffering far more keenly from the lapse of ours than from the tortures inflicted. 13. Those, however, whom the Lord judged worthy to replace the lapsed were arrested daily, so that all of those from both churches who appeared zealous and eminent, and by whose efforts and diligence the churches were guided, were likewise detained. 14. It happened also that the pagan slaves of some of ours were arrested, since the order had been publicly given that everyone should be searched for and detained, and at the demon's prompting and the urging of the soldiers who had been so bidden, they invented against us, out of fear of the tortures they saw being inflicted on the saints, something like Thyestean feasts[8] and Oedipodean incest, and other things which we may neither speak nor think of, and

6. The original says that Vettius had in himself the Advocate, "the spirit of Zechariah" (cf. Lk 1.67).

7. Rv 14.4.

8. cannibalism.

which we cannot even believe were ever done among human beings. 15. When this had been published about us among the populace, we began to be looked upon with the greatest horror and loathing by everyone, even by those who formerly thought that we should be regarded with some leniency. And everyone began to clamor together against the Christians and to rage with hatred unquenchable. Then we saw fulfilled what was said by the Lord, 'The time will come when everyone who kills you will think that he is giving obedience to God.'[9]

16. "After that the tortures and agonies inflicted on the saints at Satan's urging pass all description, the purpose being to elicit from their profession as well that we had committed that sort of thing. 17. The fury with which everyone strove for this continued unabated: the populace, the judge, the officials, and the soldiers pressed especially Sanctus, a deacon of Vienne; Maturus, newly baptized but supremely strong in faith and endurance; Attalus, a Pergamene who was a pillar and bulwark of our church in all ways; and a woman, Blandina, through whom Christ showed that what people consider insignificant and contemptible is reckoned as of great glory with God, and that what is by nature fragile his charity renders most sturdy by grace. 18. For when we were all fearful on her account, and even her earthly mistress, who was one of the martyrs, was afraid that Blandina might yield under torture, and from bodily weakness might scarcely endure the tortures connected with her initial profession, she was strengthened with such power of endurance that what first weakened and then failed were the arms of the torturers, who, in accordance with the unremitting hostility of the judge, were relieving each other in turns. Finally, after repeatedly devising new tortures from first light until evening, they confessed themselves beaten, amazed that there was still breath in her when nothing remained of her body but injuries. 19. But as the truly blessed woman afterwards told us, whenever she uttered her profession and declared, 'I am a Christian,' new strength would return to her body and she would renew the contest refreshed, as though her pain had been taken away by her profession. And the more she realized that her devout words quenched the feeling of pain, the more often and

9. Jn 16.2.

eagerly she declared, 'I am a Christian,' and 'Nothing evil is done among us.'

20. "The deacon Sanctus also endured new kinds of punishment, beyond what can be described, beyond what it is right for human nature to bear, and far in excess of the capability of the human frame, the agents of the demons being vehemently intent upon extracting from him some admission of wrongdoing. But the God-filled man thought their cruelty and beastly savagery in interrogation so laughable that he never deigned to tell them from which family home or native place he came, not even his name, but when asked about each of these things, his only answer in all of the tortures was that he was a Christian: 'This is my name, my family, my native place; I am nothing else at all than a Christian.' 21. This filled them with a fury that passes belief, because having exhausted so many different modes of punishment, they had been unable to wring from him so much as the admission of his own name. They finally got up the fires again and applied red-hot strips of brass and iron to his genitals and the more sensitive members. 22. As a result his flesh was charred and fell into the fire, but he himself remained unmoved, unshaken, and unafraid, moderating the human flames in himself from the heavenly and eternal springs which come forth from Jesus's innards.[10] 23. He, though, was a martyr in all his members, and his whole body was one ghastly wound. All resemblance to anything human had vanished in him, the cruelty of his torturers having taken away any possibility of recognizing not only who he was, but what. Christ alone, though, was being recognized in him through the glory of martyrdom, Christ who through his suffering was destroying the forces of the enemy and strengthening his soldiers by the example of endurance, showing everyone that there is nothing terrible where the Father is loved, and nothing painful where faith in Christ is found.

24. "But the workers of wickedness felt no shame whatever at the martyr's virtue. After a few days' thought it occurred to them that if they once again inflicted torture on the still-swollen wounds, which shrank from even the lightest touch, and injured

10. Jn 4.14; 7.38; 19.34.

afresh the now-festering members, one of two things must result: either he would go over to their irreligion, or, if he died under torture, the terror and fear of the cruelty would impress itself upon the others. But the outcome was far different from what these impious folk had thought. It can hardly be credited by the unbelievers, but what happened was that his body was returned to its original condition by the second round of tortures, the second round restoring to his members their proper functioning, which had been taken from them by the original cruel treatment, so that the repeated torments brought him no longer pain, but healing.

25. "Blandina too, whom we mentioned a little earlier,[11] was likewise summoned back to a second round of torments. 26. When, only half-alive and almost on the threshold of death, she had been beaten again and again by the torturers, she woke suddenly as though from sleep, remembered the blessedness to come, and in a steady voice, as though addressing the people from somewhere high and lofty, said, 'You are greatly mistaken, men, in thinking that those people eat the vitals of infants who do not make use even of the flesh of dumb animals.' And thus, persisting in her profession, she was thrust back to rejoin the company of the martyrs.

27. "But after the tyrant's torments had been undone by the perseverance of the blessed martyrs, the devil made ready to attack God's servants with still other devices, in order that, worn out by the suffering of prison and the filth of their confinement, their feet stretched apart to the seventh hole in the stocks, as they say, incredible as that sounds, they might perish in the inmost darkness from all of the different kinds of tor-

---

11. *Sed et Blandina, quam paulo ante memoravimus* = καὶ Βιβλίδα δέ, μίαν τῶν ἠρνημένων ("Biblis too, one of those who had denied ..."). Rufinus thus eliminates Biblis's name, joining her suffering to Blandina's. He may simply have misread the name (not unusual with him) and the participle ἠρνημένων as εἰρημένων ("one of those spoken of"), and then "corrected" the original at the end of 5.1.26 by having her "thrust back" (*retruditur*) into prison rather than simply being joined to the ranks of the martyrs, as in the original, thus preserving her for more suffering in 5.1.41. Or perhaps he simply did not consider the name of the legendary Biblis (Byblis), whose tale of incestuous passion and despair was told at length by the ever-popular Ovid, fit for a Christian.

ture which infuriated savagery might think up. A great many therefore died in the prisons in this way, the Lord accepting this death of theirs, to which the assistance of the divine majesty was not lacking. 28. For some of those who had endured the most savage tortures, and were not allowed to seek any human treatment, began to recover marvelously through the Lord's strength, and suddenly to regain cheerfulness of mind and unhoped-for vigor of body, so that by their exhortation they encouraged the others to persevere. And the ones who did not endure the punishments were rather those who had been recently arrested and whose bodies had not yet been toughened by torture. They then were the ones who were killed by the horror of the filth and the darkness of confinement.

29. "It is not right, though, to pass over in silence the glorious profession of the martyrdom of the blessed Pothinus, bishop of Lyons. He was more than ninety, and infirm of body as one of that age, in every respect almost dead; only the desire for martyrdom kept him alive. 30. He was led to the tribunal, or rather carried there, limp from old age and weakness. His life was being preserved for one thing only, that through it Christ might triumph more magnificently in his frail body. The old man was meanwhile placed before the tribunal. From every side arose the cries of the impious crowd that he was himself Christ. 31. When he was asked by the governor who the God of the Christians was, he replied, 'If you are worthy, you will know.' This unleashed a boundless, uncontrollable rage which seized everyone, so that those standing nearby rained blows and kicks on the old man, showing no respect either for his age or his dignity, while those further off hurled from a distance whatever missiles came to hand in their fury, so that each of them considered the gravest offense to be the failure to commit some crime against the old man. They thought that they were thereby avenging their gods when he rendered his undefiled spirit shortly after they had thrown him half-dead into prison.

32. "It was just at this time that an immense favor was received from God, and mercy was obtained unexpectedly through the ingenuity of Christ the Lord. 33. Something happened which we can scarcely remember ever being done by the persecutors

before: all of those who when first arrested had denied the faith were seized and thrust into prison. And so that no solace might attend these unhappy folk in their disastrous punishment, they were detained no longer as Christians but as murderers and incestuous people. 34. The wretches suffered a double punishment, because while the torments of the others were lightened by the hope and crown of martyrdom, and Christ's charity and the grace of the Holy Spirit alleviated them in their affliction, they by contrast were tortured more severely by their conscience than by the chains to which they were sentenced and the filth of prison, so that they could be distinguished from the others by the very expression on their faces. 35. The others would be brought from their tortures joyful, displaying something divine on their very faces; they considered their fetters precious ornaments, since they had become the good odor of Christ throughout the filth of the prison, so that they seemed to themselves to be confined not in a prison but in a perfumery. The former, however, were sunken in grief, dreadful in their very appearance and more hideous than any kind of ugliness. They were exposed to continuous taunts from the pagans themselves as degenerate cowards who had lost the faith and found themselves indicted; who were deprived of the name of Christians but had not escaped the punishment of murderers. When the others saw what was happening, they were unbelievably strengthened, so that when arrested they resolutely professed themselves Christians and nothing else, without any wavering of mind."

36. And after some extended remarks at this place, they continue somewhat later as follows:

"Afterwards Christ the Lord, by means of the different kinds of martyrdom they suffered, now wove a sort of crown made up of various flowers which he offered to the Father, so that as victors in the great contest they might receive from him the rewards of the eternal prizes. 37. For Maturus, Sanctus, Blandina, and Attalus were placed in the middle of the arena on the days of the public shows, when countless thousands of different peoples were gathered for the exhibition. 38. And once again Maturus and Sanctus, as though nothing had been done previously, were subjected anew to all the various kinds of tortures and flogging, their enemies striving in every way to shatter their endurance and, egged on by the maddened cries of the people, to snatch their crowns from their very heads, so to speak. But the hope in the glory now at hand strengthened their spirits all the more, so that it seemed to them that they were all but touching it and feeling it with their right hands. 39. And when the various tortures had been exhausted and the time for the shows was almost over, and they could not be moved at all from their resolve, and when the fire kindled beneath the iron chair on which they were placed had even burned up their flesh, which had been worn away by flogging, 40. the martyrs' tireless spirits escaped at last when they were beheaded with a sword.

41. "As for Blandina, she was again tied to a post and, stretched out as though on a cross, made ready as food for the beasts. Hanging from the wood, however, her face unafraid and quite joyful, she poured out her prayer to God, beseeching him to grant her fortitude and her other companions in the contest perseverance.[12] And she expected that her requests would be readily fulfilled, her own example being helpful while at the same time teaching that to those who share in Christ's sufferings the sharing in his glory will also certainly be granted. 42. But when none of the beasts dared touch her body, she was taken down from the wood again and returned to prison to be made ready for still other contests, so that through her many victories she might grind down the head of the twisted serpent and rouse the spirits of the brothers to endurance, inasmuch as she herself in her small and frail body had remained undefeated in so

12. Rufinus's determination to downplay the status of women (if not their holiness) is exemplified here where he omits what the original says about the others seeing in Blandina him who was crucified for them (βλεπόντων αὐτῶν ... διὰ τῆς ἀδελφῆς τὸν ὑπὲρ αὐτῶν ἐσταυρωμένον). Likewise below in 5.1.42, Rufinus's "had remained undefeated" replaces the original "had put on Christ" (Χριστὸν ἐνδεδυμένη). The remarkable portrayal of Blandina in the original as a representation of Christ has been studied by Elizabeth A. Goodine and Matthew W. Mitchell, "The Persuasiveness of a Woman: The Mistranslation and Misinterpretation of Eusebius' *Historia Ecclesiastica* 5.1.41," *JECS* 13 (2005): 1–19, esp. 18: "It is precisely Blandina's low social status as a woman and a slave that makes her the perfect Christ figure for Eusebius." Not for Rufinus.

many battles, and had come away crowned from each of the contests.

43. "The people with their cries demanded Attalus too; he was a man quite noble and, what was most noble of all, was of the highest rectitude, and in his faith in Christ always a martyr through all of his trials. 44. When he had been led around in the amphitheater with a placard going before him on which was written 'Attalus the Christian,' the maddened crowd exploded in fury against him. But when the governor was informed that he was a Roman citizen, he ordered him to be put back in prison with the others, reported his case to Caesar, and waited to see what he would decide about him.

45. "Placed in prison, meanwhile, they did not allow the time to pass without profit, but with their vigor of heart and enthusiasm for the faith revived those who seemed weaker; not yet martyrs themselves, they made martyrs of many by their exhortations. Great joy was born from this for mother church,[13] who saw her children, who almost seemed already to have fallen into death, 46. restored to life by them; by their admonitions many of those who by their denials had been rendered like something stillborn were once again, as it were, brought to birth, and Christ was again formed in them.[14] For they were taught by them that God does not want the death of the sinner, but that he be converted and live.[15] 47. When therefore Caesar wrote back that those who persisted should be punished and those who denied released, the judge, on one of the busiest days, when those from all the provinces come together to hold a market-day with us, ascended the tribunal in that most densely packed assembly and ordered the Christians to make themselves ready and to be brought in to furnish a spectacle of tortures to the rest who were there. So there were once again crosses, once again punishments, once again torments. If any Roman citizens were discovered, he sentenced them to be beheaded, and the rest turned over to the beasts. 48. Fervent praise, though, was offered to Christ by everyone for those who

13. "the virgin mother" in the original.
14. Gal 4.19.
15. Ezek 33.11.

earlier had denied but could not be released even though they had denied, and now, when pardon was being offered to those who denied, remained resolute in making their profession, and were recalled from the flock of perdition and joined to the number of the martyrs.

49. "When therefore those just mentioned were being examined, one Alexander, a Phrygian and a physician by profession, a man religious, sensible, dear to all, and popular because of the uprightness of his conduct and life, was standing by the tribunal and, roused by the love of God, was nodding to exhort those under examination to make their profession, so that it was plain to all of the bystanders how he felt. 50. And when the people noticed this and resented it especially on account of those who were now recanting their earlier denials with fresh professions, they shouted against Alexander that he was responsible for this. Ordered by the governor to be brought forward, and asked who he was, he testified openly that he was a Christian, and was condemned at once to be made ready for the beasts. And the next day he was brought out together with Attalus, whom against Caesar's order he [the governor] commanded to be handed over to the beasts as well in his desire to gratify the populace. 51. But when none of the beasts would touch the bodies of the saints, he ordered them, after inflicting every kind of flogging and mode of torture on them, to be executed at last in the sight of the people in the middle of the arena. In all of the punishment he suffered, the blessed Alexander uttered not a single word, but from beginning to end spoke with God within himself continually and persisted in his praises and prayers. 52. As for Attalus, when he was scorched in the iron chair by the live coals thrown underneath, and the smell of charred flesh was borne to the nostrils and mouths of the onlookers, he shouted at the people, 'See now, eating human flesh is what *you* are doing! Why do you investigate us about a hidden crime which is one you commit openly? For we neither eat people nor do anything else wrong!' And when he was asked, 'What name does God have?' he answered, 'Those who are several are distinguished by their names; he who is one needs no name.'[16]

16. Original: "God has no name as humans do."

53. "After them, on the last day of the shows, Blandina was once again brought in with Ponticus, a boy of about fifteen. They had been ordered always to stand by while those earlier were tortured, that they might be even more terrified by seeing the agonies of the others. They were therefore placed in the middle and ordered to swear by the gods. But they on the contrary declared that those by whom they were being pressed to swear were nothing at all. And when they continued to say a great deal more in reproaching the gods of the nations, the mob began to grow even more furious with them, pitying neither the tender age of the boy nor the woman's sex; 54. they made them go the round of all the varieties of tortures in a kind of circle, allowing none of the punishments to be omitted which cruelty had devised. Then Ponticus was strengthened immeasurably in his endurance by the motherly encouragement he received, and persevering in his profession of faith rendered up his spirit undefiled. 55. As for the blessed Blandina, who was the last of all: like the noble mother of them all, she hastened now in peace of mind to follow the children sent ahead to the crown of martyrdom, exulting and rejoicing as though invited to a bridal chamber or a wedding banquet. So it came about that she danced while being flogged and rejoiced while being charred on the grid-irons, and seemed as happy and glad as if she were reclining at a royal feast. After this she was given over to the beasts, but remained unharmed by them. 56. Hence another kind of cruelty was devised: she was tied up in a net and thrown in front of a bull which had been goaded to a fury. When she had been gored by it countless times and tossed around the entire arena, she was not hurt at all, but remained as always happy, as her face showed, and steadfast in spirit, already now in converse with Christ in the very expectation and anticipation of her heart. She was finally ordered to be executed by the sword, the irreligious folk themselves remarking in amazement that there had never been a woman who could endure all that she had.

57. "But their cruelty was not satisfied even so. 58. Incited by the venom of the ancient serpent, their savage, barbaric manners could not be tamed. The very endurance of the saints

roused them to an even greater frenzy, and they were assailed
by a sort of feeling of shame that those being tortured had
proved stronger than their torturers. This goaded both the
judge and the populace to a wicked hatred, that the scripture
might be fulfilled which says, 59 'Let the unrighteous act un-
righteously still, and the unjust behave unjustly still.'[17] In an act
of unheard-of barbarity, the bodies of those who were being
killed in the prison were ordered put out for the dogs, and a
guard was posted day and night lest anyone gather their remains out of consideration of their humanity, and give them
over for burial. The soldier guards kept unburied anything
from the bodies of the martyrs left over from the beasts and
the fire, and the heads with the torsos of those executed, 60.
and one wondered if human cruelty could inflict anything further even on those who had already passed beyond this life. But
the gentiles exulted and glorified their idols, by whose power,
they said, the others had been requited. Those of them, however, who were, it seems, slightly more lenient and sympathetic
would say, 'Where now is their god? And of what use to them
was that religion for which they gave up their lives?' 61. Such
were the various jeers they aimed at us, while we were gripped
by the deepest mourning, chiefly because we could not bury
the bodies, since not even the night afforded us any chance
of doing so, nor did we have the opportunity to win over the
guards with gifts or entreaties or anything else, [because] they
were so alert and careful to make sure that the bones which
finally remained should be given no burial.[18]

62. "And after a few days, when they had not granted the
favor of burial, they burned the martyrs' bones, reduced them
to ashes, and scattered them with other dust of the earth upon
the Rhône River, lest there be any remains of them anywhere;
63. it was as though they were conquering God in this way and,
as they said, removing from them the hope of resurrection
thereby. 'For they hoped,' they said, 'that they would rise again
from their graves some time, and for that reason, under the

17. Rv 22.11.
18. Rufinus omits Eusebius's note here that he has passed over some material before 62.

persuasion of some new superstition or other, they happily subjected themselves to torture and death. Now we shall see if they
rise again, and if their god can assist them and snatch them
from our hands.'"

5.2.1. This is what happened at that time, as is stated in the
letter from the brothers at Lyons. From it one may guess what
might have been happening in the other provinces as well. The
same letter also relates something about the kindness and gentleness of the blessed martyrs, which I think deserves to be added to the foregoing in its own words.

2. "Those who achieved such glory and became martyrs over
and over again after the beasts, the fires, and the plates, in imitation of Christ, who, 'when he was in the form of God, did
not think it plunder that he was equal to God,'[19] neither called
themselves martyrs nor allowed others to do so; but if any of
ours chanced to name them martyrs in letters or in speech,
they rebuked them sternly, saying that the title belonged to
Christ alone, 3. who alone was the faithful martyr to the truth
and who is the firstborn from the dead and the author of eternal life.[20] Or at least the word suited only those who after a
good profession deserved to leave this life and make their way
to God. 'We, however,' they would say, 'lowly and needy as we
are, hope that at least our profession itself may remain safe in
us.' To this end they would also beg the other brothers with
tears to pray for them to the Lord, that they might deserve to
receive martyrdom, the seal of the perfect profession. 4. Their
humility was so great that even when they were in reality martyrs, they avoided boasting of the name. They stood firm before
the gentiles with utter confidence, showing their nobility of
soul by their contempt for injustice and endurance of torment.
They were, then, humble to their brothers, pert to their persecutors, meek to their own, terrible to their foes, submissive
to Christ, dismissive to the devil. 5. They humbled themselves
under God's most powerful hand, by which they have now been
lifted up on high.[21] They were conciliatory toward all, and ac-

19. Phil 2.6.
20. Rv 1.5; Acts 3.15.
21. 1 Pt 5.6. Rufinus omits Eusebius's note at the beginning of 5: "A little
further on they say ..."

cused no one; they loosed everyone and bound no one.[22] They even prayed for their persecutors, using the words of St. Stephen, the first martyr, and saying, 'Lord, do not charge them with this sin.'[23] 6. The battles which the devil unleashed against them were all the more violent because through the abundant charity which they had in Christ Jesus, they called back to life even those who had lapsed and whom that savage beast thought he had already gulped down, bringing them back from his very innards, clinging to them like mothers to their children, and lavishing upon them unstintingly their feelings of compassion. Pouring out to almighty God fountains and rivers of tears for them, they begged God to give them life, 7. and it was granted them. They did not consider that the road leading to the Lord would be pleasant for them, nor did they think that the martyrs' crown would be a happy one, if they had allowed a part of their members to be snatched from the churches and retained by the devil like plunder. Above everything else, however, they loved peace themselves and bade us preserve it, nor did they build any other road to martyrdom than that which lies through peace. They were careful not to leave behind them any dissension among the brothers or any grief for mother church, but they admonished the brothers to have peace always, to guard peace, and especially to preserve charity, the bond of unity and concord."

8. Such is the account preserved by us for the edification of our readers, and not, I hope, in vain; it carries with it the authority of such great men, and is presented on account of those who behave with overweening pomp against their brothers and think that any of them who perhaps waver are to be shut out completely from Christ's compassionate mercy.

5.3.1. The same document contains another narrative which I thought it worthwhile to include because of its instructiveness. 2. One Alcibiades was among those detained in fetters for Christ. He led a life quite demanding and austere, refusing anything in the way of food and partaking only of salt[24] and bread with water. Now when he wanted to continue this severity

22. Mt 18.18.   23. Acts 7.60.
24. Rufinus adds "salt."

of life even when he was put in prison, it was revealed to Attalus after his first profession which he made in the amphitheater, that Alcibiades was not doing well in not using God's creatures and in leaving to the others an example of scandal. 3. Alcibiades, when he realized this, began to accept everything with gratitude, because what the Spirit revealed to the former that he should teach, the same Spirit persuaded the latter to follow. This should suffice concerning this.

4. In Phrygia, therefore, Montanus, Alcibiades, and Theodotus gained for the first time then the reputation of being prophets among a great many people.[25] And since many other powers and graces were still being provided in various churches through the Holy Spirit's gift at that period, it was easy to believe that the grace of prophecy could have been given to them too. And when a serious disagreement arose among the brothers, once again the churches of Gaul declared their judgment and verdict about these people as well, with all respect and explanation of the right faith. They produced the letters of the martyrs who had reached their end among them, letters they had written while in prison to the brothers residing in Asia and Phrygia, and to Eleutherus, bishop of Rome, admonishing him concerning the peace of the church.

5.4.1. They also commended Irenaeus, then still a presbyter of the church of Lyons, to this bishop of Rome, bearing witness to his life, as their words show which follow:

2. "We wish you well in God again and always, Father Eleutherus. We have asked our brother and companion Irenaeus to present this letter to you, and we beg you to consider him recommended. For he is an imitator of the testament of Christ. We know, that is, that it is not one's rank that makes one just; while he does exercise his presbyteral office rightly, we commend him even more for the merit of his life."

3. They list after this the glories of the various martyrs: how

25. *apud quam plurimos in prophetarum opinionem venerunt* = τὴν περὶ τοῦ προφητεύειν ὑπόληψιν παρὰ πολλοῖς ἐκφερομένων [scl. τῶν δ' ἀμφὶ τὸν Μοντανὸν καὶ Ἀλκιβιάδην καὶ Θεόδοτον ...] ("they spread their opinion about prophecy among many"). Rufinus's interpretation seems possible, but the other seems more likely. More on the Montanists in 5.16–19.

many were beheaded, and how many consumed by beasts, by fire, and even by the filth of prison. Those who wish to know more may consult the full account in the letters.

5.5.1. In the time of Antoninus, then, which is when these events are related, the histories report that his brother, the Caesar Marcus Aurelius, was waging war on the Germans and Sarmatians when his army was endangered by thirst. While he was fretting and wondering what relief there might be for the situation, he discovered Christian soldiers in a certain legion whose entreaties, when they knelt down in prayer, as is our custom, were heard by God; 2. and suddenly, against all expectation, there came the heaviest downpour of rain, which quenched the thirst of the army in peril, for which the Christians had prayed, while driving off the enemy, now poised for a lethal onslaught, with repeated lightning flashes and thunderbolts from heaven. 3. The event is in fact reported by the pagan histories,[26] but they do not say that it resulted from the prayers of ours, since they do not believe the other miracles either which ours work. 4. Among ours, though, it is mentioned both by Tertullian and by Apollinarius, one of the Greeks, who also says that that same legion had its name changed by the emperor on account of the remarkable miracle, and was called the "Thundering Legion."[27] 5. Tertullian says that the letters of the emperor Marcus are still extant which state these things more fully.[28]

8. Let us now return to the course of our history. Pothinus, then, was crowned with the other martyrs of Gaul in his ninetieth year, and Irenaeus received the priesthood of the church of Lyons. We have learned that Irenaeus had been a disciple of Polycarp when a boy. He shows by the following words in the third book *Against Heresies* that he wrote this work in the time of Bishop Eleutherus, the time with which we are now dealing:[29]

5.6.1. "When the church had been founded and built, the blessed apostles bestowed the office of bishop upon Linus. Paul

26. Dio Cassius, 72.8–10; *SHA* Marcus Aurelius 24.2.
27. On Claudius Apollinarius, bishop of Hierapolis in Phrygia, cf. 4.27.
28. Rufinus omits the rest of 5.5.5–7, which summarizes and quotes from Tertullian, *Apol.* 5.
29. *Haer.* 3.3.3.

mentions this Linus in his letter to Timothy.[30] 2. He was succeeded by Anencletus, after whom Clement received the priesthood in third place. Now he was with the blessed apostles and
passed his life with them always, and, having been instructed
by them, carried the memory of their tradition as something
fresh, and had the pattern of their preaching always before his
eyes. 3. In Clement's time a serious discord arose among the
brothers in Corinth, so that Clement himself wrote to the Corinthians a compelling letter in the name of the Roman church[31]
in order to recall them to peace and restore their faith, which
had been shaken, expressing in it the tradition of the apostles
which he himself had received from them."

4. And a little further on he says, "This Clement was succeeded by Evaristus, and Evaristus by Alexander. After him Xystus was ordained as the sixth since the apostles, after whom
was Telesphorus, whose martyrdom was glorious. After him
was Hyginus, and then Pius, after whom was Anicetus. He was
succeeded by Soter,[32] who has now 5. obtained the episcopal
office in twelfth place since the apostles, and preserves unimpaired and intact the same teachings of the divine faith which
the apostles handed on."

5.7.1. This is what Irenaeus includes in the books mentioned
above. And in the second book of the same work as well he says
that even in his own time some remnants of the divine power
were found in the churches. He writes,[33]

2. "But they are very far from raising the dead, as did the
Lord, and as the apostles did through prayer. Even the brothers
have done this often in many churches, so that, with the whole
church gathered together to pour out to God an abundance
of fasts and supplications, the spirit of a dead person would

30. 2 Tm 4.21.

31. Irenaeus does not mention that Clement wrote the letter to the Corinthians; he simply says that the church in Rome did so.

32. Irenaeus: Soter was succeeded by Eleutherus. Either Rufinus or the
copy he was using omitted Eleutherus; see apparatus, *ad loc., Eusebius Werke,*
GCS Bd. 2, Teil 1, p. 439.

33. *Haer.* 2.31.2. Eusebius starts the citation awkwardly; in the original,
"they" refers to Simon and Carpocrates and their disbelief in such miracles of
resurrection as are mentioned here.

return, and the person would be restored to life through the prayers of the saints."

And he continues further on:[34]

3. "If they say the Lord did these things only seemingly, let us turn to the prophets, who foretold that he was to do these things and confirmed that he is God's Son, because of which his disciples too do these things in his name, receiving grace from him, to provide salvation to people according to what each deserves.[35] 4. Some of them drive away demons and thus purge those who were under attack, so that sometimes those who have been cured believe and stay in the church. Others receive foreknowledge of the future and see prophetic visions. Others put their hands on the sick and restore them to health. Even the dead have at times been raised by them and have remained with us for many years. 5. Why go on? There is no numbering the individual miracles worked throughout the world in God's churches through the grace and name of Jesus Christ, who was crucified under Pontius Pilate. And those that happen daily are not performed to make money or turn a profit, but, just as grace is received from God freely, so the same grace is provided freely."[36]

6. In another place again the same Irenaeus writes of this as follows: "Just as we have heard that many of the brothers in the church have the grace of the prophets and speak all languages through the Holy Spirit's gift, they also bring to light the mysteries and secrets of God when that is useful."

We included this matter to show that the various gifts of the Holy Spirit remained in the churches down to that time among those worthy, because we promised in fact at the beginning that we would prove this in due course.[37]

5.8.1. Now concerning the order of the canon of divine scrip-

---

34. *Haer.* 2.32.4.

35. *prout unusquisque meruerit* = καθὼς εἷς ἕκαστος τὴν δωρεὰν εἴληφεν παρ' αὐτοῦ ("according to the gift which each [disciple] has received from him").

36. Mt 10.8. The quotation from Irenaeus that follows is from *Haer.* 5.6.1.

37. Rufinus abridges Eusebius carelessly here; what Eusebius says (in 5.8.1) is that he promised to quote earlier sources regarding the canon of scripture. He actually made this promise at 3.3.3, not at the beginning of his history.

ture, let us also give Irenaeus's views by citing his own words once again:

2. "First let us turn to the holy gospels.[38] Matthew for his part published a gospel in writing for the Hebrews in their own language, while Paul and Peter were preaching the gospel in Rome and strengthening the foundations of the church there. 3. After their deaths, Mark, Peter's disciple and translator, set out in writing the gospel which the other had preached. 4. After this, John, the disciple of the Lord, the one who had reclined upon his chest, published a gospel while he was in Ephesus, a city in Asia."

5. This is what he says in the third book of the work mentioned. Now in the fifth book, in writing about the Revelation of John and the number of the name of Antichrist, he speaks as follows:[39]

"Since, then, these things are so, and that number is found in all the true and ancient copies, and these same matters are also confirmed by those who saw John when he was in the body and preaching the word of the Lord, because the number of the beast, according to the sum of the Greek letters written in it ..."[40]

6. Shortly thereafter he adds the following:

"We do not want to hazard a confident statement about the name of the Antichrist. For if it behooved these things to be clearly and openly preached in this present time, his name would certainly have been stated clearly through him at least who wrote the Apocalypse,[41] since that very revelation took place not long ago, but almost in our own time, towards the end of Domitian Caesar."

7. This is what our author explains concerning the Apocalypse. He mentions also the first letter of John and the first of Peter, and cites numerous extracts from them, and accepts as

38. "First ... gospels" translates Eusebius's own introduction to Irenaeus's words, which begin: "Matthew ..." (*Haer.* 3.1.1). "Paul and Peter" below are "Peter and Paul" in Irenaeus. For the Hebrew gospel, cf. 3.24.6; 3.39.16; 5.10.3; 6.25.4. On Mark: 2.15 and 3.39.15. On John: 3.24.7–14.

39. *Haer.* 5.30.1; cf. Rv 13.18.

40. The sentence is incomplete in both Rufinus and the original.

41. Eusebius: "by him who saw the revelation" (τὴν ἀποκάλυψιν).

well the writing entitled the Shepherd's, saying, "It is well written in scripture that 'the first thing to be believed is that there
is one God who created and constructed everything.'"[42] 8. He
also uses proof-texts from the Wisdom of Solomon.[43] He mentions as well, as though from memory, the words of a certain
apostolic man about whose name he is silent.[44] 9. He makes
mention too of Justin the martyr and Ignatius,[45] displays what
they wrote, and promises also to reply in refutation to Marcion's writings.[46] 10. Listen as well to what he says about the
seventy translators of the holy scriptures:

"God became man and the Lord himself saved us. He gave
the sign which is written about the virgin, and not as some of
them say who have just recently dared to translate the scriptures differently and say, 'Behold a young woman will conceive
in her womb and bear a son,' as Theodotion of Ephesus and
Aquila from Pontus, both of them Jewish proselytes, have translated it. They have been followed by the Ebionites, who say that
Christ was born of Joseph."

11. Shortly after he continues,[47]

"Before the Romans established their domain and the Macedonians still possessed Asia, Ptolemy, son of Lagus, wanting to
increase the renown of his library, which he was accumulating
in Alexandria from the books of all the ancient Greeks, asked
those in Jerusalem as well to let him have their Hebrew scriptures translated into Greek.[48] 12. Now since they were subject
to the Macedonians, they sent Ptolemy seventy select elders,
men most learned in the holy scriptures and thoroughly acquainted with both languages; and in this nonetheless it was
God's will and plan that was carried out. 13. [Ptolemy] then
wanted to make trial of each of them and feared they might

42. *Shepherd of Hermas* 26.1. Cf. also 4.20.2.
43. *Haer.* 4.38.3.
44. *Haer.* 4.27.1.
45. Justin: *Haer.* 4.6.2 and 5.26.2. Irenaeus does not mention Ignatius by
name, but cites him at 5.28.4.
46. The promise is in 1.27.4 and 3.12.12. The passage about the seventy
translators is in 3.21.1.
47. 3.21.2.
48. Cf. Josephus, *C. Apion.* 2.45–47.

conceal the truth contained in the divine books by their translation, so he separated them from each other and bade them
translate the same matter separately and keep to the same sequence in translation in each of the several books, 14. until he
had them all once more recalled to his presence together and
compared the translations of each with the others. And then
God was truly glorified, and sacred scripture was recognized
as truly divine. For all of them had written the same things,
with the same verbs, nouns, and sentences, from beginning to
end, so that even the gentiles who were there acknowledged
that it was by God's will[49] that the scriptures had been translated then. 15. And it is not to be wondered at that divine providence thus brought this about, when, even during the captivity
which befell the people under King Nebuchadnezzar, when the
scriptures perished, and the Jews after seventy years returned
to their homeland in the time of Artaxerxes, the Persian king,
God inspired the priest Ezra from the tribe of Levi to restore
all the books and words of the former prophets and give back
to the people the law which had been given through Moses."[50]

Thus far Irenaeus. 5.9. Antoninus, then, after reigning for
nineteen years, left his realm to Commodus upon his death.[51] In
the first year of his reign, Julian received the priesthood in Alexandria when Agrippinus passed away after twelve years as bishop.

5.10.1. It was at that time that Pantaenus, a man most distinguished for his scholarship in every field, was in charge of
instruction in the church school. It was from him[52] that the custom arose of old among them, one which still exists, of having
as teachers of the sacred scriptures in the church school there
only those men who have the highest reputation in knowledge

49. *dei nutu* = κατ' ἐπίπνοιαν τοῦ θεοῦ ("by God's inspiration"). Did Rufinus
read κατ' ἐπίνοιαν?

50. The story of Ezra rewriting the scriptures, which had been destroyed,
is in 2 Esdras 14.19–48.

51. March 17, 180.

52. *ex quo:* there is no equivalent in Eusebius, who says simply that Pantaenus was one of the distinguished principals of the school. Rufinus also
adds the words below about the "founder and originator" (*huius ... officii velut
auctor quidam et dux*). Rufinus's years in Egypt suggest that his additions carry
some weight.

and scholarship. As the sort of founder and originator of this office, then, the man of whom we were speaking was considered quite illustrious, since he had formerly become highly esteemed among the philosophers known as the Stoics. 2. His zeal for God's word was so great, and his love so great, it is said, that in the ardor of his faith and devotion he even traveled to all the nations which are hidden away in the remotest corners of the East, in order to preach the gospel to them, and got as far as Nearer India[53] preaching God's word. For there were still in those times a number of evangelists who in imitation of the holy apostles would roam through various parts of the world and through God's grace and the power of their spirit would bring the word of God and the faith of Christ to whichever peoples knew nothing of it. 3. Pantaenus was considered outstanding and illustrious among them. They say that when he reached the Indians, he found that the apostle Bartholomew had planted the first seeds of the faith among them, and had left Matthew's gospel written in Hebrew, and that Pantaenus brought it back when he found it there at that time.[54] 4. And it was while he was engaged in many other activities in the field of church doctrine in Alexandria that he brought his noble and celebrated life to its wonderful and admirable conclusion, both in teaching his students directly and in leaving to posterity the treasures of his knowledge in his written works.

5.11.1. In his schools of divine instruction the most brilliant star in Alexandria was Clement,[55] the namesake of the successor and disciple of the apostles in Rome. 2. This Clement in fact mentions Pantaenus as his teacher and instructor in the seventh book of the *Dispositions*. He refers to him as well in the first book of the *Stromateis,* in the place where he recounts how he discovered a number of men belonging to the apostolic preaching. He says,[56]

53. *India citerior* (Eusebius just has "India").

54. On the Hebrew gospel, see note 38. Eusebius mentions that Bartholomew brought the gospel there, but not that Pantaenus brought it back. But Jerome agrees with Rufinus (*Vir. illustr.* 36), adding that it was Demetrius of Alexandria who sent Pantaenus to India.

55. On Clement, see 6.13.

56. *Stromateis* 1.11.

3. "The essays in this work are not written for show but as a notebook for old age and a help to memory, so that I may have in them a sort of outline of the wonderful things and of the divine words 4. which it was granted me to hear from holy and blessed men. One of them by whom I was taught was in Achaia, another in Syria, and yet another in the East, in Palestine to be precise; he was of Hebrew stock.[57] Last of all, though, I had as a teacher in Egypt a man to be esteemed above all others for his virtue and knowledge, after whom, as though I had found a hidden treasure, I stopped looking further for anything else. 5. They entrusted to me, as fathers to a son, the truth of the divine teaching which had been passed on to them directly by its primary authorities, the holy apostles Peter, James, John, and Paul. But seldom are sons like their fathers! By God's favor, though, the seeds of the apostolic germination have been planted in us through them."

5.12.1. Narcissus was at this time in charge of the church in Jerusalem; his reputation was such that he is still celebrated in our time. He was fifteenth in succession after those who had been from the circumcision until the time of Hadrian's siege. 2. For as we explained, Mark was the first bishop from the gentiles, and after him was Cassian, then Publius, after whom came Maximus and then Julian, after whom was Gaius and then another Julian, Capito, and Valens, and then Dolichian, after whom came Narcissus, the thirtieth after the apostles.[58]

5.13.1. At this time one Rhodo, who was, as he himself writes, born in the province of Asia, and was educated in Rome, reports that Tatian, whom we mentioned earlier among the oth-

---

57. Eusebius: "One was an Ionian from Greece, one was from Greater Greece, one from Coele Syria, one from Egypt, and still others were in the East: one of them was an Assyrian and another was someone in Palestine who was Hebrew."

58. For the succession of the Jerusalem bishops from the circumcision, see 4.5. For Hadrian's siege, the expulsion of the Jews from Jerusalem, and Mark as the first gentile bishop of Jerusalem, 4.6. There are here only eleven names from Mark to Narcissus. Rufinus omits "Symmachus and another Gaius" after "Gaius," but that still makes only thirteen names. Jerome, *Chron.* 160 and 185, gives fifteen names, putting Maximus and Antoninus after Capito. See also Epiphanius, *Pan.* 66.20.1–2.

er writers, wrote a great many books,[59] especially against Marcion's heresy, which Tatian asserts was divided into different doctrines. He explains as follows who were sundered from that heresy, and why:

2. "It is for that reason that they disagree even among themselves, since they want to affirm what cannot stand. For one of their bunch is Apelles,[60] who used the advantage of his austerity and age to claim that there is one origin of everything, but to assert that the prophets were inspired by an opposing spirit; he had been persuaded to this by some virgin named Philumene who was under the sway of a demonic spirit. 3. Others, though, like the mariner[61] himself, Marcion, introduce two principles; among them are Potitus and Basilicus. 4. They themselves followed the Pontic Wolf, but when they did not find a way out of the difficulties,[62] just as he had not, they turned to what they thought was easier and introduced two principles without offering any proof for their assertion. Still others of them sank into something even worse, affirming not only two but three principles and three natures. Their leader and authority is Syneros, as the representatives of this doctrine themselves say."

59. *Rhodo ... in urbe Roma eruditus refert a Tatiano ... libros quam plurimos ... scriptos* = Ῥόδων ... μαθητευθεὶς ἐπὶ Ῥώμης ... Τατιανῷ ... διάφορα συντάξας βιβλία ... Rufinus thus mistranslates the original, which says that it was Rhodo, who had become Tatian's disciple in Rome, who composed the books against Marcion and who is quoted in the following section. The mistranslation is deliberate, as a comparison with 5.13.8 will show. Rufinus seems to want to shield Rhodo from association with the heretic (cf. 4.28–29), and perhaps also to stress Tatian's inconsistency by portraying him as attacking the doctrines he later supposedly maintained.

60. On the Marcionite Apelles, cf. P. de Labriolle, "Apelle," *DHGE* 3.928–29.

61. There is no need to take this figuratively (unlike the reference to "the Pontic Wolf" in 5.13.4); Tertullian refers to Marcion repeatedly as a "shipmaster" (*nauclerus*): *Adv. Marcionem* 1.18.4; 3.6.3; 4.9.2; 5.1.2; *De praescript. haer.* 30.1–2.

62. *non invenientes exitum rerum* = μὴ εὑρίσκοντες τὴν διαίρεσιν τῶν πραγμάτων ("not discovering the division of things"). Rufinus seems to take *diairesis* in the sense of "explanation" (cf. Lampe, *Patristic Greek Lexicon*, 349). But Elze's reference (75–76 and 114) to Eudemus of Rhodes, *Fr.* 37a (cf. Book 4, note 104), is suggestive in this context: here *diairesis* means the distinction between act and potency as the solution to the problem of speaking of unity and multiplicity in the realm of being.

5. Now he writes about himself that he met with Apelles; his words are as follows:

"For even the aged Apelles spoke with us, and was shown to have taught wrongly about many things. Hence he also asserted that the reason for belief should not be investigated at all, but that each person should persevere in what he believed. For salvation [he said] belonged to those who hoped in the Crucified One, if only they were found in good works. He clearly, though, taught concerning God that, as we said, there is one principle, just as we say."

6. And then, while explaining his entire outlook, he expresses his own feeling too:

"I said to him, 'How can we give an account of the one principle? Explain how it can be maintained.' He replied, 'The prophecies refute themselves, because they contain no truth at all, since they contradict each other and are certainly false, given that they tell against themselves.' How it is that there is one principle, however, he denied that he knew, but said that such was his opinion. 7. And when I adjured him to tell the truth, he affirmed with an oath that he did not know how there is one unbegotten God; he just believed it. From then on he had my scorn and disapproval, since he professed to be a teacher of things of which he said he was ignorant."

8. One Callistion is said in this same work to have been a disciple of Tatian's in Rome;[63] he writes that Tatian composed a book of propositions or questions in which he resolves everything that is obscure or difficult in holy scripture. And Rhodo, already mentioned, promises in his treatises that he will present and refute his propositions.[64] The same author has also a

---

63. *In eodem quoque opere refertur Callistion quidam discipulus extitisse Tatiani* = Ἐν τῷ αὐτῷ δὲ συγγράμματι Καλλιστίωνι προσφωνῶν ὁ αὐτὸς μεμαθητεῦσθαι ἐπὶ Ῥώμης Τατιανῷ ἑαυτὸν ὁμολογεῖ ("he [Rhodo] addresses Callistion and acknowledges that he [Rhodo] was a disciple of Tatian's in Rome"). There is nothing in the original equivalent to Rufinus's *quidam*, which suggests that Callistion's fame had dwindled in the meantime.

64. What Eusebius says is that Tatian promised to "present" (παραστήσειν) the obscurities of scripture in his book of *Problems*. Rhodo announces that he will provide the solutions to the problems in his own work (ἐν ἰδίῳ συγγράμματι τὰς τῶν ἐκείνου προβλημάτων ἐπιλύσεις ἐκθήσεσθαι). Rufinus, as we have seen,

treatise on the Hexaemeron, in which he reports that Apelles wrote a great many irreligious things against the law of Moses and published blasphemous statements against the whole law, disproving, so he thought, and demolishing what is written there. We learned this and much else from the books of the writer just mentioned.

5.14. The enemy of the human race, though, allows himself no respite in his battle against the salvation of humankind, but raises up various and different heresies in each place; among them he brought forth in Asia and Phrygia that greatest serpent of his kind, Montanus, who called himself the paraclete,[65] and with him the women Prisca and Maximilla, whom he boasted of as prophetesses as though resulting from his own inspiration. 5.15. In Rome as well one Florinus fell from the rank of presbyter in the church, together with Blastus, the companion of his wrongdoing and his madness, and they brought many in the church down into their pit with the new inventions they devised against the truth.

5.16.1. Now against the Cataphrygian heresy[66] Apollinarius of Hierapolis, whom we mentioned earlier, furnished the stoutest of shields, and many other highly learned men in that place fought against them in defense of the truth; they have also left us some most impressive documents for use in our history. 2–5.[67] Meanwhile, as we said, Apollinarius wrote against this

---

is anxious to suppress any notice that Rhodo was Tatian's disciple (see note 59 above).

65. On Montanus and the movement he inspired, cf. 5.3.4 and William Tabbernee, *Fake Prophecy and Polluted Sacraments: Ecclesiastical and Imperial Reactions to Montanism* (Leiden: Brill, 2007). He and his followers believed that "the ultimate revelation of the Holy Spirit [was] given to the church via its prophets and prophetesses" (Tabbernee, xxxi). The author suggests that "paraclete" here might have had originally the meaning of "advocate" (on behalf of others, perhaps his prophetesses: 120–21). In addition to the evidence given by Eusebius, see also Epiphanius, *Pan.* 48.

"Prisca" immediately following is "Priscilla" in Eusebius (here and in 5.18.3).

66. Eusebius: τὴν λεγομένην κατὰ Φρύγας αἵρεσιν ("the so-called Phrygian sect"). Apollinarius is in 4.21; 4.26.1; 4.27; 5.5.4.

67. Rufinus abridges 5.16.2–5 in such a way that he gives the impression that the citation which begins in 5.16.6 is from Apollinarius. It is in fact from

heresy and indicated in his opening remarks that while he was passing aside through the churches of Galatia and of the neighboring provinces and saw quite a few people caught in their snares, he admonished many of them, going so far as to hold debates in their presence, and at the brethren's request he also sent them these writings. 6. In them he shows who the author of the heresy is, and then he continues further on as follows:

"The origin of this heresy which has recently arisen against the church is the following. 7. There is said to be a village in Phrygian Moesia which is called Ardabau and in which they say that someone named Montanus, who had recently come to belief in Christ while Gratus was proconsul of Asia,[68] became inflamed with an overwhelming desire for pre-eminence. He thus yielded himself to inimical spirits, and suddenly, in a sort of frenzy, as though swayed by a spirit, began to give utterance to some new things, different from those 8. which had been passed down to the church in succession from those of former times, speaking in a kind of prophetic mode. When those who were then present and listening to him saw this happening, some of them decided that he was like someone filled with a demon, a spirit of error blowing through him to deceive the peoples, and they rebuked him and forbade him to speak out at all, remembering as they did the precept of the Lord and his warning to watch out for false prophets.[69] Others, though, thought that he was like someone filled with the Holy Spirit and granted the grace of prophecy, and, forgetful of the Lord's precept, indulged the spirit of error and seduction to the point where 9. they even took pleasure in urging it to say something. The devil's cunning was behind this to work ruin for the undisciplined. Montanus, when they showed him a degree of veneration beyond what was fitting, proceeded to become so arrogant that he even made two women sharers in the same mad spirit

---

an anonymous source, as the original makes clear in 5.16.2. On this important source cf. Tabbernee (note 65 above), 3–7.

68. Moesia = Mysia. On Ardabau, see Tabbernee, 5n8. The movement began probably c. 165; Montanus died c. 175, Maximilla c. 178/79, Priscilla c. 175: Tabbernee, xxix. On Gratus, see *Prosopographia Imperii Romani Saec. I. II. III.*, 4.224.

69. Mt 7.15.

that filled him, and taught them to rave with him as he did, in order that both sexes might more easily be led astray through both of them.[70] He now blessed those who clung to him more closely, made them conceited by the greatness of his promises, and sometimes also rebuked certain people, warning them not to be caught in unrestrained adulation. There were very few Phrygians, though, who were taken in by their madness. Them he persuaded to blaspheme the church at large throughout the earth, and not only not to show it any respect but not even to cross its threshold. 10. The brethren from Asia arrived on the scene again and again, though, and those madmen raving against the faith of Christ were convicted as heretics and corrupters of the truth, and were expelled from the assembly and fellowship of the church."[71]

11. So he writes in the first book, and throughout his work he refutes the deceptions of the heresy in each of them; in the second volume as well he writes the following of these same folk also:

12. "How remarkable it is that they call us murderers of the prophets because we do not accept their mad fancies! For they say that these are the prophets whom the Lord promised to send to his people.[72] Let them answer us: if Montanus and his women have been sent by God as prophets, which of them has been persecuted by the Jews? Which has been killed by evildoers? Which of them has been detained for the name of the Lord and stood before kings and governors? Who has been flogged in the Jewish synagogues? Who has been stoned?[73] 13. Quite the contrary is what we hear: that their lives have ended in the manner of Judas the traitor. It was the very demon by which they were in-

---

70. Vera-Elisabeth Hirschmann, *Horrenda Secta: Untersuchungen zum frühchristlichen Montanismus und seinen Verbindungen zur paganen Religion Phrygiens* (Stuttgart: Franz Steiner Verlag, 2005), notes the recent conversion of Montanus in 5.16.7, and sees in the ecstatic prophecy of both sexes a continuation of the cult practices of Cybele and Apollo in Phrygia.

71. The original speaks of repeated meetings of the faithful of Asia in many different places to examine the doctrine; it does not necessarily suggest episcopal councils: Tabbernee, 19–20.

72. Mt 23.34.

73. Mt 10.18.

214 RUFINUS OF AQUILEIA

spired, so it is said, that drove each of them at different times
to make an end of life with the noose. 14. And as for that marvelous man, Theodotus by name, who was a sort of first-born of
their prophecy: they say that he once thought he was being tak-
en up into the heavens, and believed the spirit of error, by which
he was lifted up on high and from there brought down to earth,
where his life came to a most wretched end. 15. But these people deny that this happened to Montanus and Theodotus and
the women, although there are many who say it did. So then?
We leave the matter undecided between those who deny it and
those who assert it."

16. Our writer adds somewhat later: "And those most respected men, the holy bishops who lived at that time, 17. Zoticus from Cumane and Julian from Apamea, attempted to restrain the spirit who used to speak in Maximilla, and so they
ordered Themiso to close their mouth and shut up the voice of
the spirit of falsehood and error. And so it was done."[74]

18. And further in proving the falsehood of Maximilla's
prophecy, which had foretold a great number of wars, he says,
19. "That she was lying is clearly to be seen. Thirteen years have
now passed from the time the woman died to the present day,
and nowhere has any war, local or general, broken out at all.
On the contrary, Christians have enjoyed continuous and lasting peace which is secure."

20. In the third book as well he says the following of those
who boast of the many martyrs produced by their heresy:

"Since they have no answer to any of the points which we
mentioned and on which they are proven wrong, they have recourse to the martyrs, saying that they have many martyrs and
that this shows that the prophetic spirit among them is true.
21. So what? Many other heretics have a great many martyrs;
is that a reason for agreeing with them that they too have the

---

74. Rufinus directly contradicts the original, which says that it was Themiso and company who stopped the mouths of Zoticus and Julian. This is
confirmed in 5.18.13. There is more at 5.18.5 on Themiso, who Tabbernee
suggests was the main interpreter of the prophetess, translating her ecstatic
utterances. He might then have stopped the bishops from speaking with the
spirit simply by refusing to translate what it said: Tabbernee, 95–96.

truth? The first ones, for instance, those called Marcionites, have a number of martyrs. But what truth of martyrdom can they have, when they do not have Christ's truth?"

And somewhat later he goes on:

22. "If the holy martyrs, accordingly, who undergo martyrdom for the true faith, find themselves by chance together with those of the Phrygian heresy when they set out from the church to be led to their suffering, they separate from them and reject their company; when they finally hold the palm of martyrdom they in no way regard themselves as in accordance with the spirit of Montanus and Maximilla. We know this was done in our own time as well by Gaius and Alexander in Apamea on the Meander, when they became martyrs from Eumeneia."

5.17.1. In the same work he also mentions the writer Miltiades as someone who had himself written a book against the heresy just mentioned. He includes in his work, accordingly, the following words taken from what he said:[75]

"It is not to be thought that prophesying happens when one is out of one's mind or mad. 2. That is peculiar to false prophets, for when one is mad, one cannot retain the sense of what is just and right. While they undoubtedly begin from ignorance, they end in madness, as we said earlier. 3. And they cannot show that any prophet arose through God's spirit in this way, either in the Old Testament or in the New, since neither Agabus nor Judas nor Silas, nor the four daughters of Philip, nor Ammia, who prophesied in the church in Philadelphia, nor Quadratus, nor any other of their company, is known to have prophesied in this way."[76]

4. A little further on he continues: "If, as they say, those women of Montanus succeeded to the grace of prophecy after Quadratus and Ammia of Philadelphia, and, as they affirm, have

75. Rufinus's abridgement again suggests that the following extract is from Miltiades; the original makes it clear that Eusebius in fact continues to cite the anonymous source here after skipping some passages where the latter has quoted some Montanist sayings. On Miltiades, see Tabbernee, 12–15.

76. Agabus: Acts 11.28; 21.10. Judas and Silas: Acts 15.32. Philip's daughters: Acts 21.9. Quadratus: 3.37.1. Ammia is known only from this chapter. Cf. Tabbernee, 138–40.

been given to the universal church in order to prophesy until the coming of the Lord, their affirmation fails. For it is now almost fourteen years since Maximilla died."

5. Such is what we find in the treatises of the author mentioned above. But Miltiades himself, from what he shows, has left us other works as well from his own pen which are worthy of regard. He wrote a book against the pagans and another against the Jews, and a defense of our faith addressed to the Roman emperors. He also wrote against the Cataphrygian heretics.

5.18.1. Then too a certain Apollonius,[77] an orthodox writer likewise, published a short work against them in which he showed admirable vigilance in proving that their prophecies were false and in refuting the individual words in them; at the same time he exposes in the following words the life and manners of the authors of the heresy:

2. "Let us then see who this new teacher may be. First of all, let his deeds and his works recommend his teaching to us, as the Lord has enjoined. He is the one who taught the dissolution of marriage, who first imposed laws about fasting, who gave the name 'Jerusalem' to the Phrygian towns of Pepuza and Tymion[78] and decreed that everyone should be gathered together in them, who appointed revenue collectors, who receives gifts under the fictitious title of 'offerings,' and who provides salaries to those who preach his word, that they may be induced thereby to devote themselves more assiduously to his teaching."[79]

3. Such are his remarks about Montanus. About his women he writes as follows further on: "We show first of all, though, that these prophetesses left their husbands as soon as they were filled with the spirit. How is it, then, that they lie about Prisca having been a virgin?"

4. And further on he says again, "Do you not think that all of

---

77. Jerome, *Vir. illustr.* 40; Tabbernee, 45–49.

78. On the two places, see William Tabbernee and Peter Lampe, *Pepuza and Tymion: The Discovery and Archaeological Exploration of a Lost Ancient City and an Imperial Estate* (Berlin and New York: Walter Gruyter, 2008), 7–10, 15–30, 39–44, 85–107.

79. On the Montanist offices, cf. Hirschmann (note 70 above), 123–38.

scripture forbids a prophet to accept a gift or money? If then I see that the prophetess has received gold and silver and costly clothing, how can I regard her as a prophetess?"[80]

5. And further on he adds:

"Themisus,[81] though, who is so proud of his reputation among them of being a confessor, lacks the fruits of true confession, because his release from prison was obtained in exchange for a large sum of money. He should of course have conducted himself with humility, but with excessive arrogance he has adopted some measure of apostolic authority and written a letter to all the churches in which he tries to instruct those whose faith is far sounder than his own, and exhorts everyone to accustom their ears to novelties of language. He also blasphemes the Lord, his apostles, and holy church."

6. He also writes as follows of certain others who are honored as martyrs[82] among them:

"But lest we delay overlong, tell us about Alexander, who calls himself a martyr and whom this prophetess has as a dinner companion and whom she adores as a god: has it not turned out that he is guilty of robberies and other criminal acts? It is not we who say so: the public records hold them. Which of them, then, pardons the other's sins? 7. Does the prophetess forgive the martyr his robberies? Or does the martyr forgive the prophetess her crimes of rapacity and greed? The Lord said, 'Have neither gold nor money nor two tunics,'[83] but they do the opposite in everything, acquiring and gathering the things which the Lord ordered even those who have them to discard. For we show that those whom they call prophets and martyrs collect money not only from the wealthy, but from the poor and from orphans and widows too. 8. But if they are confident enough, let them present themselves and hold a debate with us on their behalf, so that, if they are defeated, they may stop engaging in such dealing from then on at least. For it is

---

80. Cf. Tabbernee, *Fake Prophecy*, 103–4.

81. "Themiso" in Eusebius; cf. 5.16.17. On this passage, cf. Tabbernee, 217.

82. Eusebius: "of someone else included in those honored as martyrs …" On Alexander below, cf. Tabbernee, 217–19.

83. Mt 10.9–10.

from his fruits that a prophet is to be recognized or for that matter tested, as even the Lord said, since a tree is known from its fruits,[84] and a prophet proved true from his fruits.

9. "To gain a clearer picture of Alexander, one should know that he was tried by Aemilius Frontinus, proconsul of Ephesus,[85] not for being a Christian, but for robbery; he had already apostasized from Christianity. Afterwards, though, he pretended that he was suffering for the Lord's name so that certain faithful brethren who at that time had some influence with the authorities might intercede for him, and thus he was released. Nor was he welcomed in the church of his native place, where everyone knew he was a robber. If anyone is disinclined to believe what we say, the records are kept in the public archives in Ephesus; 10. these marvelous prophets who serve him, however, do not realize that they are kept there. Since he clearly stands convicted by them, there is no doubt that the prophets[86] are proven ignorant together with him. We can demonstrate these and many other like matters concerning him. But if they feel confident, let them meet us, hear the statement of our charges, and get out of them, if they think they can escape the responsibility for them."

11. Again a little later he adds the following about these prophets:

"If the prophets of these people deny that they have accepted gifts, let them resolve that if they are confuted, they will no longer pretend to be prophets, and I will offer a thousand proofs. I think it is also necessary, however, to examine the other fruits of these prophets as well. Tell me, you prophetesses: is the face of one who prophesies beautified with cosmetics? Does a prophetess apply eye-shadow? Does a prophetess use ornaments and delight in jewelry? Then: does the prophet enjoy games of dice? Does the prophet lend his money at interest? Let them say if prophets may do so; I for my part will prove all of this against them."

84. Mt 7.16–18.
85. *Prosopographia Imperii Romani Saec. I. II. III.*, 1.348.
86. Rufinus speaks twice of "prophets"; the original has "the prophet" in the singular.

12. These and many other persuasive and consistent arguments Apollonius urged against them, indicating as well that he was writing in the fortieth year since Montanus initiated this false prophesying. 13. He tells also of one Zoticus that when Maximilla pretended to prophesy in Pepuza he entered suddenly and began to command the spirit which was speaking in her, in order to restrain it completely, but he was stopped by those who admired them.[87] 14. He also mentions one Thraseas, a martyr, who claimed[88] to have received as from the tradition of those of earlier times that the Savior bade his apostles not to leave Jerusalem until twelve years had passed. He says too that the dead were revived by John in Ephesus, and many other things, all of which firmly confute the heresy referred to above.

5.19.1. Serapion, moreover, who was bishop in Antioch after Maximinus, says the following about this heresy in the letter he wrote to Caricus and Ponticus.[89] After some introductory material he continues:

2. "But so that you may know that this new prophecy or rather new abomination which has emerged is rejected and refuted by the entire brotherhood in the whole world, I have sent you the letter of Claudius Apollinarius, bishop of Hierapolis in the province of Asia, which will give you fuller information about these matters."

3. This letter of Serapion contains the subscriptions too of some bishops and martyrs,[90] of which one runs as follows: "I Aurelius Quirinus, martyr, wish you well." Another is as follows: "Aurelius Publius Julius, bishop from Debeltum,[91] a colony of Thrace: as God in heaven lives, the blessed Sotas in Anchialus

87. Compare 5.16.17 and note 74.
88. Eusebius: "and claimed." Thraseas is in 5.24.4. On the saying about the twelve years below, cf. Clement, *Strom.* 6.5.43.3.
89. "Pontius" in Eusebius. On Serapion's writings, cf. 6.12. On 5.19.1–2, see Tabbernee, 53–55.
90. Rufinus adds "and martyrs." Claudius Apollinarius is in 4.27. The subscriptions below are those subjoined to his letter which Serapion is forwarding; it is hard to say if it is a synodical or episcopal letter. Cf. Tabbernee, 53–54.
91. Eusebius: Aelius Publius Julius. "Debeltum" is Deultum, a Thracian see like Anchialus. Compare this subscription to 5.16.17 and note 74, and 5.18.13.

wanted to expel Priscilla's demon, but her admirers would not allow it."

4. The subscriptions of many other bishops asserting the same thing together are contained in the letter just mentioned. But enough concerning this.

5.20.1. In Rome at this time the rule of church tradition was likewise being ravaged by a number of people through various innovations, on account of which Irenaeus sent writings to different people. One of his short works for instance is extant, which is addressed to Blastus, *On Schism*, and there is another to Florinus,[92] *On Monarchy* or *That God Is Not the Creator of Evil*, since he seemed to be asserting this, although later he fell into the errors of Valentinus. Irenaeus also wrote a book on the Ogdoad in which he indicates that he has followed certain of the successors of the apostles. 2. The conclusion of the book is so nicely worded that I must cite it:

"I adjure you who copy this book, through Our Lord Jesus Christ and his coming in glory, when he will come to judge the living and the dead, that you check what you write and correct it carefully against the copies from which you are copying, as you have undertaken, and that you likewise copy the formula of this oath and include it in what you have copied."

3. I have thought it necessary to include in our work what he so aptly said, so that everyone who may think it worthwhile to read or transcribe this matter may thereby proceed with care, having seen the example of attentive care passed down by men both holy and renowned. 4. Now Irenaeus, in what he writes to Florinus, as we mentioned above, mentions Polycarp, with whom he also says he consorted, writing as follows:

"I can state with confidence,[93] Florinus, that these doctrines you maintain are not sound. These doctrines are not in harmony with the faith of the church. These are doctrines which not even the heretics who were driven from the church could ever have dreamed up. These doctrines teach impiety. These are doctrines which those holy presbyters who preceded us never taught, those

---

92. Blastus and Florinus: see 5.15.

93. *confidenter dico* = ἵνα πεφεισμένως εἴπω ("if I may advance a cautious opinion"). Rufinus must have read πεπεισμένως.

who even saw the apostles and whom you yourself know. 5. For I saw you when I was still a boy in Asia in Polycarp's house and you were so conspicuously successful while still engaged in the government house and eager to please Polycarp. 6. For I remember the events of that time much better than those of the present, because the things we learn as children grow together with the soul itself and cling to it. So I can even tell you the very place where the blessed Polycarp used to sit and engage in discussions, and his gait, his face, his whole way of life, and even his very physical appearance, as well as the discourses which he used to deliver to the people, and the way he used to describe how he had consorted with John and with the others who had seen the Lord himself, and how he remembered everything and recounted the words spoken by the Lord which he had heard from them, and about his powers and teaching. All these things, however, he uttered in harmony with the scriptures, and I then, by God's mercy, which he granted me, wrote them down as I heard them, attentively and zealously, not on paper but in my heart, and by God's grace I guard them faithfully and, so to speak, chew them over uninterruptedly. 7. I take God as my witness, therefore, and in his sight I assure you that if the blessed and apostolic man Polycarp had heard anything of the like, he would have cried out at once and stopped up his ears and, as was his way, would have said, 'My good God, what times these are for which you have preserved me, that I am hearing this!' Would he not also have fled at once from the place in which he was sitting or standing when he heard such words? 8. His attitude moreover can clearly be seen in his letters which he wrote both to the churches nearby and to some of the brethren, admonishing and strengthening them and exhorting them to fidelity."

Thus far Irenaeus.

5.21.1. Now at this time, when Commodus was ruling the Roman empire, peace spread over the churches through every land, and the word of the Lord gathered together souls from every part of the human race to recognize and revere the supreme God.[94] In Rome as well, accordingly, it joined to the

94. Dio Cassius, 73.4.7, says that Commodus's mistress Marcia had great influence with him and favored the Christians.

faith many distinguished and quite wealthy men with their children, wives, and relatives, and their whole families likewise. 2.
But this was not something which the ancient enemy of the salvation of humankind viewed favorably. He immediately therefore set about attacking ours with various devices. He began in
Rome with one Apollonius, a man distinguished in our faith
and in every discipline pertaining to philosophy, and dragged
him off to court, having raised up as his accuser some wretched
person without hope of salvation.[95] 3. And the latter was the
first to be sentenced by Perennius, the judge, to have his legs
smashed, since the law that ordered Christians to be punished
when they were denounced specified that the accuser should
be proceeded against first.[96] 4. After that the blessed martyr
Apollonius was begged to publish in writing the defense of his
faith which he had delivered splendidly and impressively before
the senate and all the people.[97] 5. And then he was beheaded,
in accordance with what the senate had voted. For thus the law
passed by an earlier generation had most evilly decreed.[98]

5.22. During Commodus's reign[99] Eleutherus in Rome was

95. Eusebius specifies that the accuser was a servant (*diakonos*), and Jerome
correctly infers from what befell him that he was a slave (*Vir. illustr.* 42); cf.
Reiner Wiegels, "Die Rolle des Senats im Prozess gegen den Christen Apollonius," in *Ad Fontes! Festschrift für Gerhard Dobesch zum fünfundsechzigsten Geburt-
stag am 15. September 2004,* ed. Herbert Helftner and Kurt Tomaschitz (Vienna: Phoibos, 2004), 539n38 and 39.

96. Tigidius Perennis was praetorian prefect 180–85, which fits the time-
frame here (Wiegels, 537). But such trials would usually be held before the
praefectus urbi, and the senate would never have been involved (Wiegels,
540–41). By omitting the detail about the accuser being a servant, Rufinus
strengthens the impression given by Eusebius that he was punished simply for
having denounced someone as a Christian. Eusebius in 5.5.6 (omitted by Rufinus) says that Marcus Aurelius threatened death to those who accused Christians after their prayers had saved his army from drought (Tertullian says the
same in *Apol.* 5.6).

97. Jerome, *Vir. illustr.* 42, agrees with the detail about the martyr publishing
his defense; Eusebius says that he himself has published his acts and defense.

98. This simply means that Trajan's edict against the profession of Christianity (Pliny, *Ep.* 10.97) still stood. This is just the crowning inconsistency in a
most improbable account, and one cannot be sure what Eusebius's sources were.

99. Eusebius: in the tenth year of Commodus's reign (189). Serapion below
was mentioned in 5.19.

succeeded by Victor after he had been in the priesthood for thirteen years. Demetrius also replaced Julian in Alexandria when he died after ten years. In Antioch too, Serapion, whom we mentioned earlier, was appointed the eighth bishop since the apostles. Then Theophilus in Caesarea in Palestine and Narcissus in Jerusalem had charge of the churches, while Bacchyllus in Corinth and Polycrates in Ephesus were considered notable figures among the bishops. And there are reports of many outstanding priests at the time in other places. We mention those, however, whose faith and knowledge we have been able to discover from their own works.

5.23.1. At the time when these men were governing the churches in the provinces of Asia, a serious issue arose which sprang from an ancient practice, as it were: they thought that the paschal feast should at all events be held on the fourteenth of the moon, when the Jews, that is, are bidden to sacrifice the lamb, and they maintained that the fast should be broken on whatever day of the week the fourteenth of the moon fell, when that custom had never been observed in any other churches at all. As a result, assemblies of bishops 2. and councils were summoned in each province, and when letters had been sent from each place to the others, they all confirmed the one doctrine of the church: that it was never permitted to celebrate the mystery of the Lord's Passover except on Sunday, when the Lord rose from the dead, and that on this day only should the paschal fast be broken. 3. There is still extant the decree of the council held in Caesarea in Palestine, at which the leading figure is Theophilus, bishop of Caesarea, along with Narcissus, priest of Jerusalem. There is also another like decree of a council of Rome over which Bishop Victor is declared to have presided, as did Palmeas[100] of the province of Pontus. The priestly assembly of the Gauls is extant[101] which lists Irenaeus as its head, 4. as [is the case] in Achaia[102] with Bacchyllus, bishop of the Corinthian

---

100. Eusebius: Palmas presided over the bishops of Pontus at their council as the oldest.

101. Or "[The decree of] ... is extant" if *conventus* is in the genitive.

102. Rufinus adds "in Achaia" but omits Eusebius's mention of a council in Osrhoene just before; Sebastian Brock, "Eusebius and Syriac Christianity,"

church, all of whom from their different places reached exactly the same judgment.

5.24.1. The bishops of the region of Asia, though, insisted that the custom passed down to them from those of earlier times should be kept. One of them, Polycrates, who seemingly held first place among them, wrote to Victor, the bishop of the church of Rome, and explained as follows the custom of the ancient tradition which had come down to them:[103]

2. "We, then, keep inviolate the day of the paschal feast, neither adding nor removing anything. For there are great luminaries who have slept in Asia, chosen men of the highest quality, whom the Lord will raise up at his advent, when he will come from the heavens in glory and seek out all of his holy ones, among whom is the evangelist Philip,[104] who fell asleep in Hierapolis, as well as his two daughters, who reached old age as virgins, and another of his daughters who was filled with the Holy Spirit and who fell asleep in Ephesus. 3. There is also John, who reclined upon the Lord's chest, was high priest and wore the high-priestly plate, was a martyr[105] and teacher of the church, and himself fell asleep in Ephesus. There is also Polycarp in Smyrna, bishop and martyr, 4. and Thraseas likewise, bishop in Eumeneia, who completed his life, however, with martyrdom in Smyrna. 5. And what need is there to speak of Sagaris as well, who was likewise a priest and martyr and who rests in peace in Laodicea, to say nothing of Papyrus, Macarius, and Melito,[106] the last of whom was a eunuch for the sake of the kingdom of God and filled with the Holy Spirit; he lies in the city of Sardis awaiting the advent of the Lord from heaven, that he may rise from

---

in *Eusebius, Christianity, and Judaism,* ed. H. W. Attridge and G. Hata (Detroit, MI: Wayne State University Press, 1992), 222, suggests that the Osrhoene reference is a later interpolation.

103. Polycrates of Ephesus is in 3.31.2–3. Part of the citation in 5.24.2–8 is in 3.31.3; the original is the same, but Rufinus's translation is different.

104. Rufinus silently "corrects" Polycrates here, who has "Philip of the twelve apostles."

105. *martyr* = μάρτυς ("witness"). On the high-priestly "plate," cf. Book 3, note 82.

106. Thraseas: 5.18.4. Sagaris: 4.26.3. Eusebius has "Papirius" instead of "Papyrus," and Rufinus adds "Macarius." Melito: 4.26.

the dead. 6. All of them kept the day of the paschal feast on the fourteenth day of the month, according to the gospel, introducing nothing extraneous at all, but preserving the rule of faith throughout. And I, Polycrates, the least among all of you, keep the tradition of my ancestors, those at least whom I have followed from the beginning. For seven of my ancestors were bishops in succession,[107] and I am the eighth; all of them observed the day so that it coincided with the one in which the Jewish[108] people removed the leaven. 7. Hence, beloved brothers, having lived for sixty-five years in the name of the Lord, having the closest acquaintance with many of the world's bishops as well, and having in view the sacred scriptures, I will not be disturbed by what is intended to frighten me, because even my forebears have said, 'One must obey God rather than human beings.'"[109]

8. And shortly afterwards he adds the following about the bishops who were there with him:

"I could also have mentioned the bishops who are present and whom you requested me to summon, as I did. Their names are too many for me to write; all of them, conscious of my insignificance, confirm what we write, certain that it is not in vain that my hair is gray, but that the teaching of Christ has always been my consort."

9.[110] To this, however, Victor, the bishop of Rome, responded quite unyieldingly, trying to sever from communion the churches of all of Asia and of the neighboring provinces indiscriminately, on the grounds that they were declining into heresy, and he sent letters in which he separated everyone at once without distinction from the bond of the church. 10. But this did not please all of the bishops; on the contrary, they wrote to him and ordered him[111] to act rather in the interests of peace and to

107. Rufinus adds "in succession" (*per ordinem*).
108. Rufinus adds "Jewish."
109. Acts 5.29.
110. On 5.24.9–18 see Karl Gerlach, *The Antenicene Pascha: A Rhetorical History* (Leuven: Peeters, 1998), 330–58.
111. *ei iubebant* = ἀντιπαρακελεύονται … αὐτῷ ("they exhorted him by contrast"). This together with Rufinus's addition below: "acting against the best interests of the church" (*velut inutiliter ecclesiae commodis consulentem*) sharpens the tone of opposition to Victor.

concern himself with concord and unanimity. Their letters accordingly are extant as well in which they sharply rebuke Victor for acting against the best interests of the church. 11. Irenaeus, for instance, with the other bishops of Gaul, of whom he was the leader, wrote and confirmed that the mystery of the Lord's Resurrection should be celebrated on Sunday, but he accused[112] Victor of behaving wrongly in severing from the unity of the body so many churches of God of such stature which held to the custom passed down to them from of old. And he admonished him about many other things in the following words:

12. "The controversy is not only about the date of the paschal feast, but also about the very character of the fast. Some think that the fast should be kept for only one day, others two days, others more, and many even think forty, establishing the day by counting up the daytime and nighttime hours.[113] 13. This difference in observance has not begun now for the first time, nor in our time; it started long before us with those, I suspect, who did not hold simply to what was passed down from the beginning, but fell into another custom later from negligence or ignorance. All of them nonetheless, even if they differed in their observance, were and are at peace among themselves and with us, nor did the variance in the fast spoil the harmony in the faith."

14. After this he inserts a story which is so much to the point that we cannot omit it:

112. *arguit* = παραινεῖ ("exhorts").

113. οἱ μὲν γὰρ οἴονται μίαν ἡμέραν δεῖν αὐτοὺς νηστεύειν, οἱ δὲ δύο, οἱ δὲ καὶ πλείονας· οἱ δὲ τεσσαράκοντα ὥρας ἡμερινάς τε καὶ νυκτερινὰς συμμετροῦσιν τὴν ἡμέραν αὐτῶν. Rufinus's translation thus omits the semicolon after πλείονας. If retained, then translate: "Some think they should fast for one day, some two, and some even more; still others measure out their day as forty daytime and nighttime hours." Their "fast-day," in other words, was the forty hours which was traditionally the interval between Jesus's death and resurrection.

The controversy, that is, was for Irenaeus both about the date of Easter and the fast preceding it. Cf. H. F. von Campenhausen, "Ostertermin oder Osterfasten? Zum Verständnis des Irenäusbriefes an Viktor (Euseb. *Hist. Eccl.* 5.24.12–17)," *Vigiliae Christianae* 28 (1974): 114–38. On the Paschal fast, cf. Gerlach (note 110 above), 185–245. The controversy seems to have arisen at this time because of the growing number of Christian immigrants from Asia in Rome, and their descendants, "who [continued] to follow the practice of their homeland for several generations in the imperial city—with the blessings of the Asian bishops.... this one difference was seen as more and more divisive ..." (Gerlach, 249).

"All of those, then, who were presbyters before Soter—Anicetus, Pius, Hyginus, Telesphorus, and Xystus—and who held the priesthood of the church which you now govern, neither kept to this themselves, nor did those who were with them, and yet, even though they did not observe [the custom] in this way, they always kept the peace with those churches who did hold to this observance, however opposed to themselves it may have seemed that the others did not keep to a like observance. 15. But never was anyone rejected from the fellowship of the church for this reason or not accepted when they came from those parts; on the contrary, all of the presbyters who were before you would always send the Eucharist with all due ceremony to all of the churches' presbyters who did not keep the observance in the same way.[114] 16. Blessed Polycarp, now, when he came to Rome under Anicetus, had a number of matters in which they differed slightly, but they met at once in peace. This question they treated in such a way that neither of them defended his own view in stubborn contention. Anicetus was unable to persuade Polycarp not to observe what he knew had been observed by John, the disciple of our Lord, and the other apostles with whom he had always been; nor on the other hand could Polycarp persuade Anicetus to abandon the custom he said he observed in the manner of his predecessors. 17. And even while they differed between them in this way, they communicated with each other in such a way that Anicetus even deferred to Polycarp in the celebration of the priestly ministry, at least as far as showing honor went, and thus they parted from each other in full trust, complete peace, and steadfast charity, so that all the churches, whether or not they kept the paschal feast in this way or not, preserved concord among themselves."

18. In writing in this way Irenaeus achieved what his name

---

114. Cf. Nicholas Paxton, "The Eucharistic Bread: Breaking and Commingling in Early Christian Rome," *The Downside Review* 122, #427 (2004): 79–93, esp. 84–87. The reference seems to be to the practice of sending particles of the Eucharist from the Pope's Mass to the other churches in Rome, including, it seems, congregations presided over by emigrant presbyters from elsewhere, Asia Minor included. The reader will recall that bishops (*episkopoi*) were not infrequently referred to as "presbyters."

means,[115] procuring peace for God's churches, and in his letters not only to Victor but to various governors of churches he likewise asserted that this issue should produce no disagreement in God's churches.

5.25. When in Palestine as well the priests of God Narcissus of Jerusalem and Theophilus, whom we mentioned earlier,[116] met together, and with them Cassius of Tyre, Clarus of Ptolemais, and a great many others likewise, and the question was treated concerning the apostolic tradition on this point among them too, they show as follows, toward the end of their decree, what was decided in their council:

"Let copies of our letter be sent throughout all the churches, that we not be held responsible for the souls plunging into various errors. We declare to you therefore that in Alexandria too the paschal solemnity is celebrated on the same day as it is with us, because their letters are sent to us and they receive what we write, that we may celebrate the feast day at the same time and in concord."

Such is what we have found in the writings of those of old concerning this question.

5.26. In addition to Irenaeus's treatises which we listed above, there is extant another excellent book against the gentiles entitled *On Instruction*[117] and written for one Marcian, as well as dialogues on various subjects in which he includes a great many proof-texts concerning the Letter to the Hebrews and the so-called Wisdom of Solomon. Such is the information about Irenaeus's shorter works as well which has come to our attention.

Commodus, now, after he had reigned for thirteen years, left the realm to Pertinax after him. Pertinax kept it for only six months before he died; Severus received the sovereignty after him.[118]

---

115. Eirēnaios from *eirēnē* ("peace").

116. Theophilus of Caesarea: 5.23.3.

117. *De disciplina* = Περὶ ἐπιστήμης ("On Knowledge"). Eusebius distinguishes this work from the one addressed to Marcian and entitled *Demonstration of the Apostolic Preaching*. Then comes a volume of various discourses in which he mentions and cites Hebrews and Wisdom and quotes some words from them. See also Jerome, *Vir. illustr.* 35.

118. Commodus was strangled to death on December 31, 192. Pertinax suc-

5.27. In his time there were a great many men of renown belonging to the church who were distinguished writers, as may be seen from their works. Among them was Heracletus, who commented on the apostle, and Maximus, who dealt with the question that is the favorite of all the heretics and the subject of endless inquiry: whence comes evil or whence wickedness, and about matter being made and not unmade. There was also Candidus, who wrote on the Hexaemeron, on the beginning of Genesis, that is; Appius,[119] who treated the same topics likewise; Sextus too, who treated the resurrection and a number of other topics; and Arabian and countless others whom it would take too long to list or even to designate by indicating what each was famous for saying. Many of them, though, in confuting the falsehoods which arose in their times from the heretics, have set out the correct and apostolic faith in their books, 5.28.1. as was done with Artemon,[120] the author of that heresy which Paul of Samosata tried later to establish almost now in our own time. It is worth giving an account of what sort of heresy it is. 2. It maintains that the Savior was a mere human being, without God,[121] and it states falsely that this was passed down from of old even by the apostles themselves. One of the church writers we mentioned above replies in opposition to them as follows:

3. "They say that what they themselves now assert is what the apostles themselves received and passed on to others, and that the truth of this teaching was preserved until Victor's time.[122] 4. And how is it then that their successors, Justin, Miltiades, Tatian, Clement, and a host of others, when they wrote against the pagans or against heretics, treated the divinity of Christ with complete frankness? 5. And is there anyone who is unaware of the books of Irenaeus and Melito and the others who lived at the same time, in which Christ is proclaimed as both God and

---

ceeded him on January 1, 193, but was killed on March 28 of that year. Both Didius Iulianus and Severus were proclaimed his successors, but the former was beheaded 66 days later.

119. "Apion" in Eusebius.

120. "Artemas" in the synodical against Paul of Samosata (7.30.16–17).

121. *absque deo:* added by Rufinus.

122. Rufinus omits what the original says about the truth having been corrupted since the time of Victor's successor Zephyrinus.

man? Not only that, but the psalms and canticles which have been written by the faithful brethren from the beginning celebrate Christ as God's Word and God with every form of praise in their hymns. 6. How then can these people now assert that the faith preached for so many generations had its beginning in Victor's time? How can they slander Victor in this way when they know that he expelled from the communion of the church Theodotus the tanner, who was the chief and the father of their irreligion, and who was the first to dare to say in Rome that Christ was a mere human being? If Victor's faith was as they say it was, how is it that he ejected from the church Theodotus, the originator of this blasphemy?"

7. This, then, should suffice concerning Victor. When he had completed ten years as bishop, he was succeeded in the priesthood by Zephyrinus in the ninth year of the reign of Severus.[123] The same writing which we cited above relates the following of Zephyrinus:

8. "I will therefore remind you, brothers, of the things which have taken place among us and which, had they perchance occurred among the Sodomites, might have remedied and converted even them. There was a certain confessor among us called Natalis[124] who made his profession within living memory. 9. He was once duped by one Asclepiodotus and by Theodotus, money-changers, both of them disciples of that Theodotus the tanner who was the first to be expelled from the fellowship of the church for this stupid teaching by Victor, the bishop of Rome then. 10. He agreed to accept a salary from them and to be named bishop of their heresy on settled terms, one hundred and fifty denarii a month. 11. Natalis, when he had gotten himself into this situation by being duped, was often admonished in dreams by the Lord, since our merciful God and Lord Jesus Christ did not want the church to lose his martyr, who amid much suffering had become a witness to him. 12. But when he paid little heed to the visions, swayed as he was by the love of rank and the desire for filthy lucre, he finally passed an entire night being beaten by the holy angels and tortured by se-

123. 201.
124. "Natalius" in Eusebius.

vere punishments. Rising in the morning, he put on sackcloth, strewed ashes on himself, and, mourning his error with copious tears, prostrated himself before Bishop Zephyrinus, and, throwing himself with loud lamentation at the feet of everyone, not only the clergy but even the laity, he stirred the whole church to tears of pity, imploring it to beg forgiveness from Christ for him with continual and unremitting prayers offered on his behalf, while at the same time he showed in the sight of the Lord the bruises and scars on his body which he had received when professing his name; and so he was at last only just readmitted to the communion of the body of the church."

13. The same writer adds the following as well somewhat later:

"They have corrupted the divine scriptures with no regard for the fear of God, while they shamelessly and impiously reject the rule of the ancient faith, ignorant as they are of Christ, whom they have not found because they have not sought him rightly. They have fallen to such a depth of stupidity and irreligion that if one shows them a passage from the scriptures, they counter by inquiring whether the text in question forms a conditional or a disjunctive syllogistic figure, 14. and, abandoning God's holy scriptures, busy themselves with geometry. As those of the earth, they speak of the earth, and therefore they do not know him who is from above and from heaven. Euclid indeed is most popular among them in the study of geometry, and Aristotle and Theophrastus are held in high regard by them, while Galen is worshiped by a number of them.[125] 15. It is by their arts and teachings that they strive to maintain the impiety of their heresy, and they subvert the simplicity of the divine scriptures and the soundness of faith with the deceits of people who do not know God. They do this because they have not

---

125. *Geōmetria* means literally "earth-measurement," but the tendency of the later Platonists to synthesize arithmetic and geometry with philosophy was already well under way at this time (even Aristotle's physics would be "geometricized" in the end). Euclid's *Elements* was much admired for its method of exposition. Cf. Dominic O'Meara, *Pythagoras Revived: Mathematics and Philosophy in Late Antiquity* (Oxford: Clarendon, 1989), esp. 1–23 and 210–13, and, on this passage in particular, Jonathan Barnes, "Galen, Christians, Logic," in *Classics in Progress: Essays on Ancient Greece and Rome,* ed. T. P. Wiseman (Oxford: Clarendon, 2002), 407–11.

been brought near to the faith. And thus they violate the divine scriptures without any fear, and in corrupting them they say they are correcting them. 16. If anyone thinks that what I am saying against them is wrong, the facts are clear to anyone who wants to take their copies and compare them with other copies which are likewise theirs: one will find that they disagree with each other on many points, since each of them corrects them as he sees fit. Those of Asclepiodotus[126] in fact do not agree at all with those of Theodotus. 17. Not only that, but those who perchance copy them for their disciples may add or remove whatever they please, and they declare to everyone that they have copies which have been corrected, or rather corrupted. And again the copies of Hermophilus do not agree with those of Apollonis.[127] Nor for that matter do they even agree with themselves, if you compare the earlier ones with those later. For they are always correcting who are always displeased with their corrections, and they seek out whatever is new, when it will be seen to be contrary to what is in use.

18. "How very offensive this is I cannot imagine they themselves do not know. Either they do not believe that the scriptures have been composed by the divine Spirit, and they are unbelievers, or they think that they themselves are wiser than the Holy Spirit. And what do they show by this if not that they are under a demon's sway? Nor can they deny what they have done, since their own handwriting may be found in the very copies, and they themselves know that it is from their teachers and instructors that I have come to understand as well this perverse method of expounding the scriptures. 19. Some of them, though, no longer deign even to corrupt the scriptures, but deny them outright, the law and the prophets that is, and under cover of this irreligious teaching have fallen into the final abyss of perdition."

This will suffice concerning these matters.

126. "Asclepiades" in Eusebius (but see 5.28.9).
127. "Apolloniades" in Eusebius.

BOOK SIX

The sixth book of the church history of Eusebius of Caesarea translated from Greek into Latin contains the following, the chapter headings being:

26. Beryllus
27. Philip
28. Bishop Dionysius
29. The separation of the Arabians
30. The heresy of the Helcesaites
31. Decius
32. The sufferings of Dionysius
33. The martyrs who suffered in Alexandria
34. What Dionysius wrote
35. Serapion
36. What Dionysius wrote to Novatus

6.1. But when Severus too shook the churches with his persecution, then were magnificent battles of martyrdom waged by Christ's soldiers for the sake of piety, especially in Alexandria, to which the athletes were drawn as though to some stadium of piety from all of Egypt and the Thebaid; and for their endurance of suffering and death they won from God the crowns of immortality. Among them was Origen's father, Leonides, who, when he was martyred for Christ by decapitation, left the other as still a young boy. It will not be out of place to indicate briefly how fully his heart was set on the divine law from then on, especially since he has become so very famous among so very many people. 6.2.1. If in fact one wanted to write the complete life of the man, one may be sure that the relevant material would be so extensive as to require its own work. For now, though, we will include in this work, as briefly as possible, what pertains to him as well: a few things from the many which we have learned either from his letters which have come down to us or from the accounts of others.[1]

2. His life, if I may say so, seems to me worth recording for

1. The bibliography on Origen is vast; there are sections devoted to him and to his general background and influence in the successive volumes of *Adamantius*. On Eusebius's biography of him, see John Dillon, "Holy and Not So Holy: On the Interpretation of Late Antique Biography," in *The Limits of Ancient Biography,* ed. Brian McGing and Judith Mossman (Swansea: The Classical Press of Wales, 2006), 155–67, esp. 155–58.

The tenth year of Severus below was 203. Quintus Maecius Laetus was prefect of Egypt.

posterity even from his infancy. Severus, that is, was in the tenth year of his reign, while Laetus was governing Alexandria and all of Egypt at the time, and Demetrius had received the episcopate there after Julian, 3. when, with the persecution blazing forth in unbounded intensity and many being crowned with martyrdom at this time, Origen, then still a young boy, was kindled with such a desire to achieve martyrdom that he exposed himself to the dangers of his own accord and rushed headlong into the midst of those engaged in the battle, so that he seemed to want to pursue and to seize death itself. 4. And this he could by all means have achieved, if he had not been saved by the Lord's dispensation, so it is thought, for the benefit of the many in the building up of the whole church; saved, that is, through his mother's solicitude, which impeded his desire for a glorious death. 5. When she first besought him with her motherly entreaties to think of himself and to spare his mother, her prayers inflamed his desire for martyrdom all the more, especially because he knew his father was already in prison, and he was making all haste to join him in his imprisonment and martyrdom; but he was prevented by his mother's wiles.[2] For when she sensed that he intended to get up early and rush forth before dawn to the contests, she entered her son's bedroom at night while he was asleep and stole all the clothes in which he could go out of doors, thus forcing him to stay at home. 6. Baffled by his mother's guile and unable either to do anything else or to bear the matter peacefully, he dared to do something beyond his years. He wrote his father that even if he was held back by his mother's wiles, he [the father] should hold to the course upon which he had entered. And he added, "Take care, father, not to decide otherwise on our account."

These were Origen's first childhood lessons, this his infants' school, these the marks of his devotion and piety from his early years, so deeply did his attachment to God take root. 7. As a result he now began to devote himself to the reading of the divine books and to study the divine faith diligently, since his father had already in fact introduced him to them; among the

2. The three references here and below to Origen's mother's "wiles" and "guile" are added by Rufinus.

secular books which he would study at his earliest age he [the
father] began to set before him from time to time a number of
items to be read from our scriptures as well. 8. Then afterwards
he advised him gradually to set more store by them than by
his school studies. And he thenceforth 9. compelled the boy
to spend time each day in reading them and committing them
to memory, not that he was unwilling; on the contrary, he was
quite disposed to learn the matter, since when he read, it was
apparent that he was not satisfied with an elementary understanding of it, but would ply his father with questions about
how to understand and investigate scripture. He would ask him
what he thought it meant to say that scripture was inspired by
the Holy Spirit, and what God intended beneath the simplicity
of the language. 10. His father pretended to chide him and to
forbid him to ask about matters beyond his age, while inwardly
he rejoiced beyond measure, thanking almighty God who had
granted him to be the father of such a scion. 11. He was such
a devoted and attentive father that he is said, accordingly, to
have bent over the boy often while he was sleeping, pulled the
blanket from his chest, and, because God's Spirit was enclosed
within, venerated his chest as a kind of temple and covered it
with kisses before withdrawing, congratulating himself on having been blessed by God with such offspring. These and many
like stories are told about Origen's youth.

12. But when his father finished his life in martyrdom, the
boy, then seventeen, was left with his widowed mother and six
other young brothers in the direst straits, 13. since his father's
property, which was indeed most extensive,[3] was confiscated.
Yet the providence of almighty God did not abandon him; because of his conspicuous interest in scholarship and religion he
was befriended with great warmth by a woman of high station
and vast wealth. At the time, however, she had in her home as
her adopted son one Paul, who was of Antiochene stock and a
most famous follower of an ancient heresy. 14. The young Origen, since he had to stay with him at the time in the woman's
home, gave evidence of his most loyal and Catholic mind which

3. *qui vel maximus erat* [scl. *census paternus*]: Rufinus adds.

he had had since boyhood. For when huge crowds not only of heretics but of many of ours as well converged upon the young man each day as to a teacher and master of the highest renown, because everyone considered him supremely learned, Origen would not yield an inch in his unwillingness even to join with him in prayer, whether for the sake of the honor or even because of their necessary association. For thus had the observance of the ecclesiastical rule been held in honor by him from early age and the company of heretics considered loathsome, as he himself in one of his works says: the teaching of heretics is to be loathed.

15. Not that he lacked interest in secular literature, in which his father had had him educated; he studied it in fact far more diligently even after his father completed his life. He was indeed so well trained in grammar that he was fully qualified even to teach it, and this supplied him with his household necessities.

6.3.1. Now when Origen had charge of a lecture-hall and was teaching grammar, as he himself relates in some of his writings, and the church in Alexandria lacked a teaching post, and everyone had been so upset at the threats and savagery of the persecutors that they had fled, some of the pagans would meet together with him when he was still teaching grammar, in order to hear from him an explanation of our faith and religion. He would not only convert them from faithlessness to the faith, but would form them by his instructions about the perfect life.[4]

2. The first of them was Plutarch, who, when converted by him to our faith, not only kept the precepts of the perfect life, but even reached the totality of beatitude, attaining the palm of martyrdom. The second with him was Heraclas, Plutarch's brother by blood and merit, who, when he had been fully instructed by him in our faith and doctrine and in the practices of the purer life as well, was chosen to govern the church of Alexandria after Demetrius.

3. Now at the time when the persecution was growing more furious while Aquila was governing Alexandria and Egypt,

---

4. "He would not ... perfect life" added by Rufinus. On Plutarch below, see 6.4.1–2.

Origen was in his eighteenth year.[5] He was by this time highly
renowned among everyone, at home and abroad, unbelievers[6]
and believers alike. 4. The main reason for this is that he would
not only strengthen for martyrdom all of the saints in prison
for their profession by his words and exhortation based on a
perfect and spiritual teaching; he would also relieve the punishment of the fetters and the filth of the prison by his many
kindnesses and services. He was also, finally, often present before the judges' tribunals and during the tortures themselves,
sharing in their sufferings with his feelings and thoughts in the
face of the impious interrogations of the judges, eager to render their replies even firmer by the way he looked and nodded,
if one may so say. And when they received their sentences, he
showed the same confidence, placing himself amid all the dangers and, fearless of the persecutors who were watching, bidding the martyrs farewell with a final kiss as well, so that the
pagans more than once made a rush at him for this, but he
would escape, protected by God's right hand and the general
admiration [in which he was held].

5. It is indeed not easy to reckon, and impossible to relate,
how often and how frequently it was—nearly every day in fact—
that that same divine right hand saved him from dangers so
many and so great, while he was tireless and prompt in preaching God's word, nor how often he escaped those lying in wait to
kill him secretly. 6. And to such a pitch did he rouse the fury of
unbelievers while he was so zealous about God's work that units
of soldiers were posted to beset the house in which he was seen
to stay, but they could neither capture nor detain him, since he
was saved by God's protection. The frenzy against him which
had seized upon people's minds had reached such a pitch simply because they saw so many folk being converted through him
from unbelief to our faith. The persecution against him grew
daily to such an extent that not even the entire city of Alexandria in its immensity could hide him, but he passed from house
to house, and yet was everywhere pursued, since they saw in
each place great multitudes being joined through him to God's

5. Claudius Subatianus Aquila became prefect of Egypt in 206.
6. Rufinus adds "unbelievers."

faith. He was successful nonetheless, because perfect teaching was for him not only a matter of language; in what he did as well, he offered examples of a consummate discipline, and it was said of him, 7. so it is told, that here was someone who as he spoke, so he lived, and as he lived, so he spoke, because he acted as he taught and he taught as he acted. It was clear and obvious that divine grace was with him, through which he challenged countless people to imitate him in coming to faith in God. 8. Hence Bishop Demetrius, seeing that great crowds were flocking to him thanks to his outstanding teaching and preaching of God's word, bestowed on him the office of catechizing, that is of teaching, in the church.

6.6.[7] The first after the apostles to hold this post in Alexandria was Pantaenus, the second in succession Clement, and the third Origen, Clement's disciple. Clement in his *Stromateis,* where he indicates in the prefaces the times as well when he wrote the books, brings them down to the end of Commodus's reign. We may thus be sure that it included this very time of Severus with which we are now dealing.

6.7. It was also during this time that another writer, one Judas, discussed the weeks recorded in Daniel;[8] he too mentions the tenth year of the emperor Severus. He also upset many of our faithful by reckoning from the severity of the persecutions that the arrival of the Antichrist, so often talked about, was now already at hand.

Origen, then, with Bishop Demetrius having entrusted the teaching office to him, began to neglect his classes in grammar,[9] and devoted himself to God's word instead. And in fact he adopted a course which showed his maturity: 6.3.9 he handed over the library of pagan books to a certain faithful friend, agreeing with him to pay for it at the rate of four obols a day. This was so that he would not be a burden upon someone's daily expenses or be viewed as keeping a pile of money at home. Spending therefore a great part of his time in such practices, he was con-

---

7. Rufinus transfers 6.6–7 to here. On Pantaenus, see 5.10–11. The reference below is to *Stromateis* 1.21.144.

8. Dn 9.24–27.

9. Eusebius says that he broke them off at once.

sidered a Christian philosopher through and through in his life, his customs, and his exercises, since in order to check his youthful desires and to advance in wisdom, he placed himself under tighter restraints of abstinence day and night. He was unceasingly absorbed in meditations on the divine books in the greatest abstinence, in unceasing fasts, and in almost constant vigils, so that if at any time nature demanded that he snatch a moment of sleep, he did so not on a bed, which he never used, but on the bare ground. 10. Above all, though, he thought that the gospel precepts and the Savior's words should be carried out with the most ardent love and zeal; they bid one not to have two tunics nor to wear shoes nor to give thought to the next day,[10] each of which he strove to fulfill with the greatest diligence and faith, 11. exerting himself beyond his age and strength in the contests of perseverance in cold and nakedness, according to the apostle's admonitions.[11] Thus he offered all who heard him examples of the renunciation of all they possessed and of blessed poverty. He was thereby dear to all and popular, in one matter alone saddening an enormous number of people and offending not a few:[12] those whom he refused out of his strict observance of continence when they wanted to offer him from their resources something at least for the necessaries of life, since he was considered by everyone to be worthy not only of double honor, as the apostle says,[13] but of many times as much honor for his labors in God's word. But he regarded continence as the highest honor he could have. 12. He is also said accordingly to have walked barefoot for many years with no footwear, and to have made no use of wine or other similar things at all, except for those things only which are necessary for life, until he was finally checked by discomfort or rather sickness in his stomach.

13. In molding therefore by such examples of his life and practice those whom he converted from a pagan life and inane philosophy to the true philosophy and wisdom of Christ, he not only taught them to have a faith which resided in the inmost

10. Mt 10.10 and 6.34.

11. 2 Cor 11.27.

12. *nonnullos offendens* added in Rufinus; the editor suggests it may originally have been a gloss on the preceding clause.

13. 1 Tm 5.17.

secret places of the soul by letting them see that he practiced what he taught; he even roused them to the love of martyrdom through the things the daily practice of which strengthened them. Many of them were arrested during the persecution and achieved the palm of martyrdom.

6.4.1. The first of them was Plutarch, whom we mentioned a little earlier.[14] When the people saw him being led to his death and Origen standing by him to rouse his spirit to generosity, the crowd made a rush at him, bent on nearly tearing him to pieces and killing him as the one responsible for his death, except that then too he was snatched from their furious hands by the aid of divine providence. 2. After Plutarch's martyrdom, the second of Origen's disciples to become a martyr was Serenus. 3. The third of his students to be crowned with martyrdom likewise was Heraclides, the fourth a neophyte, Heros. The former, Serenus, was still a catechumen when he achieved his consummation. The fifth from the same school to become a martyr was another Serenus, who after many torments for Christ was even beheaded, it is said. There were also a great many women, among whom was Hera,[15] a catechumen, about whom he says somewhere that she achieved baptism by fire.

6.5.1. There were in addition Potamiaena, the most renowned of women and martyrs, and her executioner himself, Basilides. To this very day the enduring fame of Potamiaena's virtues is celebrated by the inhabitants of the place, because she first underwent enormous countless struggles for her virginity and chastity, and then endured elaborate and unheard-of tortures in being martyred, until finally she finished her life by being burned to death with her venerable mother, Marcella. 2. It is said, then, that Aquila, this being the name of the tyrannical judge,[16] after he had wounded her with cruel tortures, finally threatened Potamiaena's nobility and chastity by telling her that he would hand her over either to the cruelest gladiators or the most shameless pimps. She, when asked what she preferred or chose, uttered against the tyrant a frank answer which in the superstition of the Roman religion was regarded as sacrilegious, 3. and sentence

14. 6.3.2.
16. Aquila: 6.3.3.

15. "Herais" in Eusebius.

was therefore pronounced against her at once. And when Basilides, one of those who customarily perform the duty of executioner, took her off to be tortured and a crowd of both shameless and irreligious people tried to deride her with their words and insults, he undertook to rebuff and drive away those who were assaulting her shamelessly, thus displaying his humanity and pity. She in turn welcomed his religious act on her behalf and his intended kindness, and said, "You may be sure that when I have gone off to my Lord, I will repay you without delay for this good deed." 4. And after these words she courageously accepted the punishment appointed, hot pitch being poured little by little over her members and limbs, and in this way the blessed virgin left earth and went to heaven. 5. Not many days thereafter, however, when Basilides was asked to take an oath for some reason by his fellows, he said that there was no way that he could swear, because he was a Christian,[17] and he affirmed this openly. At first it was thought that he was joking, but then, when he maintained it steadily, he was dragged before the tribunal, and when he persevered there in his profession, he was imprisoned.

6. When our people visited him there and asked him the reason for this sudden and praiseworthy change, he is said to have replied that three days after her martyrdom Potamiaena appeared by his side during the night and placed a crown on his head, saying that she had interceded with the Lord for him and had obtained her request, that, as it is written, the one who welcomed a martyr might receive a martyr's reward.[18] When they heard this the brethren imparted the Lord's seal to him at once, and the next day he was beheaded for his testimony to the Lord. 7. And it is said that Potamiaena bestowed the same favor upon many others of her fellow students in Alexandria at that time, those with whom she had devoted herself to God's word in Origen's school, appearing to them in visions and bestowing on them the crowns of martyrdom obtained from the Lord.[19] But this will do concerning this.

17. On Christian resistance to swearing oaths see 4.15.18–21.

18. Cf. Mt 10.41.

19. Eusebius: "Many others in Alexandria came over suddenly to Christ's word at this time when Potamiaena appeared to them in dreams and summoned them."

6.8.1.[20] During this time, then, when Origen was in charge of instruction in Alexandria, he is said to have done something[21] which appears to have come perhaps from a youthful and immature judgment, but which gave evidence of a mature faith and extraordinary chastity. 2. The words in the gospel, "There are eunuchs who have castrated themselves for the sake of God's kingdom,"[22] he thought were to be carried out literally, and not just figuratively through chastity. And since he was in fact preaching God's word during the persecution both openly and secretly, in concealment, and to both men and women, he proceeded to carry out the Lord's words on his own self in fact and in reality, in order that it would appear that he was affording the unbelievers no chance for malicious gossip. He wanted to keep it secret, since he was not seeking praise from others but reward from God, 3. but he could not hide it; the notice of what he had done came to the attention of Bishop Demetrius. He was at first quite shocked at the audacity of his virtue, and then he praised the intensity and ardor of his faith and his great determination in doing God's work, and exhorted him to "concentrate now on the work of teaching and preaching, now above all when our enemies have no more grounds to disparage us."

4. Such was then Demetrius's attitude when nothing had happened that influenced his feelings and altered his sound judgment. Later, though, when he saw how famous the young man was becoming and how he was lauded to the skies at home and abroad, he was affected by human weakness and began to criticize the deed upon which he had formerly heaped boundless praise. What happened is that Alexander of Jerusalem and Theoctistus of Caesarea,[23] outstanding and eminent men among the bishops of Palestine, when they saw his godly work for God's word, ordained him presbyter and commended him as someone all but worthy of the high priesthood.[24] 5. Everyone praised this as most worthily done and said that not even

20. Rufinus moved 6.6–7 to after 6.3.8.
21. *gestum quid ab eo traditur;* Eusebius says simply that he did it.
22. Mt 19.12.
23. Rufinus adds the two names from 6.19.17.
24. Eusebius: "deemed him worthy of the highest honor."

the honor conferred on him suited his wisdom and virtues, and
Demetrius was deeply stung, and, not finding anything else of
which to accuse him, charged him with this thing which he had
done while still a boy and which he as bishop had praised, and
he now tried to find fault with those who had ordained him. 6.
But this happened later. At that previous time Origen was regarded in Alexandria as a church teacher of great renown who
preached God's word to all whom his fame induced to meet
and hear him, whether seasonably or unseasonably, by day and
by night, in public and in private, as the apostle says;[25] with all
obstacles removed, he carried on with complete freedom and
full confidence.

7. Now when Severus had reigned for eighteen years, he was
succeeded by Antoninus, his son.[26] It was during this time that
there were a great many who sought glory in making their professions but whom God's providence preserved. Among them
was Alexander, whom we mentioned a little earlier[27] and who
was quite renowned for his profession; he was appointed bishop of the church in Jerusalem while Narcissus, who had held
the office of high priest there earlier, was still alive.

6.9.1. Now since our story has reached Narcissus, it seems
right to me to say something about the remarkable deeds of
him about whom a great many things are told indeed by the
inhabitants of the place. We will, however, mention one of his
deeds, from which the other things told of him may acquire
credibility. 2. It happened once that on the solemn day of the
Easter vigil the oil for the lamps ran out, and when the ministers made this known, an immense grief seized the people.
Narcissus, though, relying on faith, ordered the ministers to
draw water and bring it to him. 3. And when they had brought
it, he prayed, blessed the water, and commanded that it be
poured into the lamps. Then there occurred suddenly a wonderful miracle, unheard of in any age: the nature of the water
was changed into the greasy consistency of oil and cast a radiance brighter than usual.[28] As evidence of which, some of the

25. 2 Tm 4.2; Acts 20.20, 31; 28.31.   26. 211.
27. 6.8.4.
28. "and cast ... than usual": Rufinus adds.

oil which had been changed from water was saved by a great many of the religious brethren, so that the proof of this miracle has come down even to us.

4. If this will serve as an indication of his faith and merits, there is another of his deeds which will show likewise how great his virtue was. Since among his other virtues, that is, he possessed great courage and held inflexibly to what was just and right, some worthless scoundrels, who knew they had done wrong and feared they would not escape punishment if convicted of their misdeeds, forestalled this and conspired to circumvent the one whose judgment they feared. They thus concocted against him a notably infamous and injurious crime. They assembled an audience 5. and brought forward witnesses from among themselves to confirm under oath their accusations; one witness placed himself under penalty of being burned to death if he had not told the truth, another of succumbing to jaundice, and a third of losing his eyesight. Now even though none of the faithful or of those who feared God believed the oath, since Narcissus's life, conduct, and chastity were known to all, 6. he himself could not bear the indignity and annoyance of what had been claimed; and besides, he had always wanted to lead a hidden and philosophical life, so he slipped away from the church and its people and spent a great many years in concealment in deserted places and hidden parts of the country.

7. The great eye of divine providence did not remain idle for long, however, but brought down upon those impious men the very retribution which they themselves had determined in the curses contained in their perjury. A tiny spark set on fire the house of the first witness at night, and he was burned to death in the avenging flames with his whole family and household. Another was struck down by the jaundice which suddenly filled him from the bottom of his feet to the top of his head and which he had invoked upon himself. 8. As for the third, he saw how the others had died and recognized that he could not escape the divine eye, and so, presenting himself suddenly before the others with belated remorse, he unfolded in their hearing the whole story of the wicked plot. So many tears did he shed over the enormity that had been committed, though, and so

long did he continue weeping day and night, that in the end he lost his sight. This, then, is the way in which they were punished for their falsehood.

6.10. Since, then, Narcissus had sought out the wilderness and hidden himself in secret places, so that no one might know where he was staying, the bishops of the neighboring churches decided that it was necessary to ordain another in his place; his name was Dius. He had been succeeded by Germanio after governing the church for a short while, and Germanio by Gordius, when suddenly, as though come back to life and given back from heaven, Narcissus unexpectedly appeared and was asked by the brethren to govern the church again. For everyone's love for him had been kindled far more fiercely, whether because he had yielded to malefactors even though innocent or because he valued the hidden philosophical life, and also because the Lord had fulfilled in him the words: "Vengeance is mine; I will repay, says the Lord."[29]

6.11.1. Since Narcissus was now weary with old age, though, and no longer equal to the service of the high priesthood, the divine dispensation summoned Alexander to the old man's assistance through the clearest possible revelation; we earlier mentioned Alexander,[30] who was already bishop of another place. 2. His forebears were from Cappadocia, where he was bishop of a splendid city, and he had hastened to Jerusalem to worship and to see the holy places. The inhabitants of the place were roused by God to welcome him with every mark of love and attention, and they bound him with the power of charity and the knots of affection and did not let him return home. For it was clearly shown by the Lord not only to the blessed man Narcissus but to many others as well, through revelations in public, that they were to keep him in the holy place as bishop. What was above all else the most awe-inspiring was that on the day when it was announced that Alexander was to enter the city and a great multitude of the brethren went out of the gates to meet him, everyone heard a voice from heaven[31] saying

29. Rom 12.19.
30. 6.8.7.
31. Rufinus adds the voice from heaven.

with the greatest clarity, "Welcome the bishop whom God has destined for you!" And since from all of this God's dispensation had been clearly announced to everyone, the bishops of the neighboring cities, when they learned of everything that showed that what was happening concerning him resulted from what God had decided, forced him to remain there. 3. Alexander himself in his letters to the Antinoites, letters which we still have, mentions Narcissus as his companion and partner in the episcopacy, writing as follows of him: "Narcissus greets you, who began to govern this church as bishop before me, and who, placed with me by your prayers, is now in the 116th year of his life; he beseeches you with me to live in harmony."

4. Such is the account of these matters. Now in Antioch Bishop Serapion died and Asclepiades received that see; he was himself one of the confessors of outstanding merit. 5. The Alexander just mentioned makes note of his ordination, writing to the Antiochenes as follows: "Alexander, a slave and prisoner of Jesus Christ, to the blessed church which is in Antioch, greetings in the Lord. The Lord lightened my fetters and widened the narrow confines of my prison as soon as I learned that that most worthy man Asclepiades had received the priesthood of your holy church."

He also shows that he sent this letter to the church of Antioch by the hand of the presbyter Clement; he writes as follows at the end of the letter: "I have sent what I have written to you, lords my brothers, by the hand of the blessed presbyter Clement, a man of the highest excellence in every virtue and one of whom you know and will come to know even better. His presence among us, which God's providence arranged, has both strengthened and increased the Lord's church."

6.12.1. I believe, then, that others are in possession of other minor works of that learned man, Bishop Serapion, but the only ones that have come to us are those which he wrote to one Domnus, who in time of persecution left the faith of Christ and deviated to the superstition of the Jews, and those he wrote to Pontius and Caricus, members of the church.[32] There are other

32. On Serapion, Pontius, and Caricus: 5.19.

letters of his addressed to others as well. 2. We have also received the book which he wrote about the Gospel of Peter and in which he proves that some of the things it says are wrong; he wanted to correct the brethren in Rhosus who had deviated into heresy because of that writing. I think it would be good to include a short passage from his work which will show his opinion of that writing. This is what he writes in a certain place:

3. "As for us, brothers, we receive Peter and the other apostles as we do Christ. But the things which have been written by others and falsely ascribed to them we avoid, since we are acquainted with their thoughts and views and know that such is not what has been passed down to us. 4. What I mean is that when I was with you I thought that everyone among you was sound in faith, and, without running through the book which was offered me and which contained the gospel composed in Peter's name, I said, 'If this is the only thing which seems to be the cause of quarrels among you, let the book be read.' Now, however, I have learned that those who maintained that that book should be read were insisting on this because their outlook represented some concealed heresy, or so I have been told, and thus I shall make haste to come back to you; you may expect me soon! 5. For we know, brothers, to which heresy Marcian belonged, who used to contradict himself, since he did not understand what he was saying. You too will learn what he said from what has been written to you; 6. we found it out from those who learned this same gospel according to what he passed on and succeeded to his knowledge. We call them *dokētai*,[33] because in their very teaching there are a great many ideas borrowed from these same folk. For it is certain that most of their ideas about the savior accord with right reason, but others are different, and those we subjoin."

So wrote Serapion.

6.13.1. As for Clement, there are many books of his extant; those which we have been able to verify that we have are: eight books of the *Stromata*, to which he gave the title: "Titus Flavius Clement's notebooks or *Strōmateis* concerning knowledge according to the true philosophy." 2. By *Strōmateis* we may under-

33. From *dokein*, "seem," because it was held that they thought that Christ only seemed to be human.

stand a work variously composed.[34] His are also the eight books of the *Hypotypōseis,* which we may call "outlines" or "dispositions" and in which he mentions Pantaenus by name as his own teacher, writes of much of what he expounded, and includes his teachings in his work. 3. There is also his book which is an exhortation to the pagans, another which is called *Paedagogus,* and another titled *Who Among the Wealthy Can Be Saved?* Still another shorter work concerns the paschal feast, another is a treatise on fasting, another is about detraction, and there is another exhortation to endurance and still another to those recently baptized,[35] and in addition that which is titled *The Ecclesiastical Canon.* Another concerns those who follow the Jewish interpretation of scripture; it is addressed to the Bishop Alexander mentioned above.

4. Now in the *Strōmateis* he has spread out not only the things which he took from the divine scriptures, but those as well which are found in the pagan authors. For it seemed to him useful in this work to collect and compare with each other those doctrines which are divinely authorized, and those invented by the wise among the Greeks, and even those in currency among the other barbarians. 5. He also refutes the errors of the heretics and includes a great deal of narrative therein, and from all of this he has composed for us a work of enormous learning. His chapters thus deserve the title which he has given them of *Strōmateis,* which means that they are amply and variously clad. 6. He does use examples from those books too which many people do not accept: the Wisdom which is ascribed to Solomon, and the Wisdom of Sirach, which the Latins call Ecclesiasticus.[36] He also includes examples from Barnabas and Clement, and uses too the Letter of Jude.

7. He mentions in addition the writers of old, one Tatian and Cassian as authors of chronicles,[37] along with the Jewish writ-

34. Clement is in 5.11, as is Pantaenus below. *Strōmateis* means "patchwork." Cf. 6.14.1 on the *Hypotypōseis* below.

35. "another exhortation ... recently baptized": Rufinus makes two works out of the one in the original, and does the same with the following title.

36. "which the Latins ...": Rufinus adds. Eusebius includes among the disputed works the Letter to the Hebrews, Barnabas, Clement, and Jude.

37. *Tatiani cuiusdam:* there is nothing equivalent to *cuiusdam* in Eusebius,

ers Philo, Aristobulus, Josephus, Demetrius, and Eupolemus; in comparing to even the oldest of the Greeks our Moses and the Jewish race, he proves that the latter is yet older. 8. He also includes many other tools for an excellent education in this work. And among other things, he includes in the first short book that he himself lived not long after the apostles, and promises to write a commentary on Genesis. 9. Now in the short work he wrote on the paschal festival he acknowledges that he was being pressed by the brethren to write down in books and hand on to posterity what the presbyters, the successors of the apostles that is, had handed on only orally. In it he mentions Melito, Irenaeus, and others, some narratives from whom he includes too.

6.14.1. In the books of the *Hypotypōseis* or "outlines," he expounds together all of divine scripture in succinct discourses, to put the matter briefly. In them he has not omitted even those writings which some consider apocryphal, such as the Apocalypse of Peter.[38] 2. About the Letter to the Hebrews, though, he says that it is clearly the apostle Paul's, but that it was written in Hebrew as being for the Hebrews, and translated into Greek by Luke, who was Paul's disciple. That is why, he says, the style is quite similar to the short work which Luke wrote about the acts of the apostles. 3. The reason why it does not have the usual superscription of the apostle Paul is, as he shows, that it had been decided in advance concerning Paul's name by the Hebrews that they would not accept what he said, and therefore it prudently avoided it, lest they should refuse to read it when they found Paul's name right at the beginning. 4. And shortly thereafter he adds the following:

---

who has already mentioned Tatian in 4.16.7–9 and 4.29.3, and who mentions here his work against the pagans; he speaks only of the encratite Cassian (Julius Cassianus) as having composed a chronicle. On the latter, see Clement, *Strom.* 1.21.101.2; 3.13.91.1; 3.14.95.2.

On Aristobulus, see Schürer, 3.579–87; Demetrius: 3.513–17; Eupolemus: 3.517–21.

On the antiquity of the Jews, see *Strom.* 1.15.72; 1.21.141, 147; 1.23.153–56. Clement promises to write on Genesis in *Strom.* 3.14.95.2; 4.1.3; 6.18.168.4.

38. Rufinus omits the other disputed writings Eusebius lists here: the Letter of Jude and the other Catholic Letters, and the Letter of Barnabas. On Luke and Hebrews cf. 3.38.2 below; 6.25.14.

"And since, as the blessed presbyter used to say, the Lord is said to be the apostle of the Almighty sent to the Hebrews, Paul, who had been assigned to the gentiles, did not, out of humility, style himself apostle of the Hebrews, from deference to the Lord, who had said of himself that he was sent to the sheep of Israel,[39] and also because he was seen to be the apostle of the gentiles."

5. Clement also explains in these books the tradition handed down to him by the older presbyters concerning the order of the gospels, and says that those gospels were set down earlier which contain the genealogies, that is to say those of Matthew and Luke. 6. But the reason for the gospel according to Mark was the following: when Peter had preached God's word in public in Rome and had expounded the gospel in spirit, his listeners asked Mark, who by then had long been his follower, to write down what he knew the apostle had preached. 7. And when Peter found out later that he had done so, he did not forbid what had been done, even though he had not ordered it.[40] And as for John, he says that when he saw afterwards that the gospels contained what was rather according to the flesh, he too wrote what pertains to the spirit at the disciples' behest. Hence he composed a spiritual gospel, filled with the spirit as he was.[41] Such is Clement's account.

8. Now Alexander, of whom we spoke earlier,[42] mentions Clement together with Pantaenus in writing to Origen, speaking of them as men known to him while still on earth. He writes as follows:

"For this is God's will as well, as you yourself know, that the friendship shown me by the fathers should remain intact, or rather should grow even stronger and warmer. 9. And those that we know as fathers are those blessed ones who have gone before us and to join whom we too will soon depart: my truly blessed lord Pantaenus and my holy lord Clement, both of whom taught me much, and any others like them through whom I came to

39. Mt 15.24; Clement, *Hypotypōseis, Fr.* 22.
40. Peter and Mark: 2.15; 3.39.15. Clement, *Hypotypōseis, Fr.* 8.
41. John's gospel: 3.24.7–14.
42. 6.8.4; 6.11.

know you too, a man outstanding in every way and lord and
brother to me."

10. And so do these matters stand. As for Adamantius, another name for Origen, when Zephyrinus was governing the
Roman church, at that time he came to Rome, as he himself
writes somewhere, saying that it had been his desire to see the
most ancient church of the Romans. After spending a short
time there he made haste to return to Alexandria, to the teaching duties with which he had been charged, 11. and there he
carried out the work he had accepted with all solicitude and
religious zeal; Demetrius, then bishop, not only exhorted and
looked after him, but even did so quite openly, so that the
brethren should not lack instruction in religious subjects.

6.15. Origen meanwhile saw that he could not do everything:
carry out research in the deeper and more religious subjects,
and expound sacred scripture, and also take care of the instruction and training of those who were daily being added to
the faith, all of which left him not even an hour free to draw
breath. He was always being called from one thing to another,
so that from first light until late in the evening his lecture-room
was always full, with some people arriving and others not leaving, held fast as they were by the sweetness of God's word. He
thought it better therefore to separate off the crowds of the beginners, hand them over to one of his students, Heraclas, a man
fully and excellently instructed and proven to him in all of the
virtues, and to take him on as a sharer in his office and his work.
For he was highly skilled in speech and wonderfully well educated in all of the subjects of philosophy. He therefore delegated to
him the duty of teaching the elementary subjects to beginners,
keeping to himself the teaching of those mature.

6.16.1. Among his other scholarly endeavors Origen did not
even neglect to study closely and to learn Hebrew, in order to
discover both the kinds of things read by the Jews in Hebrew,
and also the extent of the different publications of the other
translators who had produced translations besides the Seventy. His purpose was to find, besides those in common use by
Aquila, Symmachus, and Theodotion, others hidden away in
obscure places, the names of whose translators he could not

even find written. 2. The only thing he says about them is that he found one in Nicopolis on the coast of Actium, another in Jericho, and others in other places.[43] 4. Hence he was the first to compose one of those famous books in which he wrote out each translation divided into individual columns, putting the Hebrew words themselves in Hebrew letters first of all, followed in second place by the Hebrew words written in Greek letters alongside [the Hebrew]; to this he added as a third version that of Aquila, with Symmachus's in fourth place; that of the Seventy, which is ours, in fifth place; and Theodotion's in sixth. And because of this composition he called these editions a *Hexapla,* meaning something written in a six-fold arrangement. 3. In the Book of Psalms, though, and in a number of other books,[44] he inserted some passages from those other versions, which, since he had found them without the names of their authors, he called the sixth and seventh versions.

6.17. Now it should be realized that one of these translators, Symmachus, was an Ebionite, a member of a heresy that claims that Christ was born of Joseph and Mary as a mere human being and that the law is to be observed according to Jewish custom, as we have already mentioned earlier.[45] Symmachus also wrote some treatises in which he tries to confirm the validity of his heresy from the gospel according to Matthew. Origen writes that he found these things, with Symmachus's translation, in the possession of one Juliana, who said that she had received these books from Symmachus himself.[46]

6.18.1. At this time too a man named Ambrose,[47] who was quite renowned for his family and scholarship and an adherent of Valentinus's doctrine, was confuted by Origen using the truth of the Catholic faith and, bathed in the brightness of the

43. Rufinus rewrites 6.16.3–4 to clarify how the Hexapla was arranged and how extensive it was (Eusebius might be understood to say that it included only the Psalms). He omits the detail that the copy found in Jericho was in a jar in the time of Antoninus, son of Severus, and that Origen made a separate edition of Aquila, Symmachus, Theodotion, and the Septuagint: the Tetrapla.

44. "and in ... books" added by Rufinus.

45. 3.72.2.

46. On Origen, Juliana, and Symmachus, cf. *Historia Lausiaca* 64.

47. On Ambrose see 6.23.

true light, abandoned the darkness of his errors and betook himself to the light and brightness of the Catholic Church. 2. There were many other learned men as well, quite renowned for their scholarship, who responded to Origen's enormous popularity, which had spread everywhere, by flocking to him eagerly, either to strike up arguments with him, or, among those with a better attitude, to hear and to retain the truth. Countless too were those who came from the heretics, were confuted by him, and ceased from their errors in remorse. And all the philosophers of the highest repute, those held in the greatest honor, acknowledged him to be unequaled as a teacher both among ours and among those of their own circles. 3. For it was his custom to introduce those of our lads who he saw were talented and studious to those subjects as well which philosophers usually study as the first elements of their education: the branches of geometry and arithmetic and whatever else concerns training in the art of reasoning. If then it ever became necessary for him to explain some matters from philosophical works, he was listened to even by those men most learned in that subject with such admiration that he was considered to be supreme among them, and as a philosopher to be ranked with those first authors of old. 4. He also encouraged the illiterate and uneducated to study, telling them that it would be of no small advantage to them for their understanding of scripture to acquaint themselves with the liberal arts or even philosophy. For he used to say that this our philosophy was the true one, whose fields of study had been occupied beforehand by that pagan philosophy which is false. He would add that truth should not give up its fields just because falsehood had already arrogated them.[48]

6.19.1. There are accordingly a great many witnesses to his studies among the philosophers too, a number of whom would dedicate their books to him, while others submitted them to him for appraisal. 2. Even that Porphyry, accordingly, who wrote books against us in Sicily in which he denounces the sacred writings, could find nothing to criticize in Origen's trea-

48. "For he used to say ... arrogated them": inserted by Rufinus in place of Eusebius's remark that Origen considered secular philosophy something he needed to study.

tises when he proceeded against the scriptural commentators, and so he turned to insults and slander 3. and found the kind of faults with him which for us are quite deserving of the highest praise, in some cases speaking the truth and in others inventing falsehoods as was his wont.[49] Sometimes he admires him for being a philosopher, and sometimes he stigmatizes him for being a Christian. 4. Listen then to what he says when he goes on concerning him:

"They cleave," he says in speaking of the Christians, "to the follies of the Jewish scriptures, and since there is no coherence or elucidation to be found in them, they betake themselves to certain inconsistent and discordant narratives which do not so much explain what is obscure as gain praise and admiration for those who expound them. For what Moses wrote in simple and unpolished language they insist was divinely authorized and overspread with figures and riddles; and with swollen and conceited minds, their faculty of judgment beset by confusion, they maintain that it is of sacred import, filled with enormous mysteries, among which the inexperienced and uneducated writer cannot make himself clear."

5. And further on he says,

"Now this ridiculous interpretation began with a man whom I too saw, when I was still quite a young child, as occupying the summit of learning overall, as is shown as well by the books which he bequeathed to posterity. It is Origen, whose great glory has spread among their teachers. 6. For he was a hearer of Ammonius, who held the highest place among the philos-

---

49. The classic "collection" of the remnants of Porphyry's work against the Christians was edited by Adolf von Harnack, "Porphyrius, 'Gegen die Christen,' 15 Bücher: Zeugnisse, Fragmente und Referate," *Abhandlungen der königlich Preussischen Akademie der Wissenschaften,* 1916 (1). On this edition, see Jonathan Barnes, *Proof, Knowledge, and Scepticism* (Oxford: Clarendon, 2014), 36n5. The work was composed c. 270, the year of the death of Porphyry's master, Plotinus, whose interpretation of Platonism he wanted to encourage. His acute intelligence, which made him a most formidable critic of Christianity and its scriptural foundations, was thus turned squarely against the use of Plato that he considered so deplorable in Origen. Cf. Jeremy M. Schott, "'Living Like a Christian, but Playing the Greek': Accounts of Apostasy and Conversion in Porphyry and Eusebius," *Journal of Late Antiquity* 1(2) (2008): 258–77.

ophers who were before us. Now Origen, as far as his scholarship went, almost imbibed the whole of his teacher, but when it
came to making a sound decision about how to lead a good life,
he took a path opposite to his teacher's. 7. Ammonius, that is,
who had been a Christian from childhood and born of Christian parents, immediately betook himself to a proper way of life
after he reached the age of reason and arrived at philosophy's
portal. Origen by contrast, who had been a pagan and educated in gentile disciplines, those of the Greeks that is, deviated
into barbarian religious practices, in betaking himself to which
he spoiled and ruined all of that brilliant talent polished by
a philosophical education, and appropriated the bright light
of the teaching and education of the Greeks for foolish stories
and fables. 8. He had grasped, that is, all of Plato's secrets, he
had been instructed in the books of Numenius, Cronius, Apol-
lophanes, and Longinus, as well as those of Moderatus and
Nicomachus, and the treatises of those men supreme among
the Pythagoreans had not escaped his attention. He was even
familiar with the books of Chaeremon the Stoic and Cornutus.
From all of whom he took over and adapted to a barbarian religion and Jewish superstition certain secret and mystical matters current among the Greeks, converting the glory of philosophy to foreign and alien dogmas."[50]

9. So writes Porphyry in the third book against the Christians, in one point speaking truly and in another falsely. What
he reports of the man's scholarship and talent is certainly true.
But he quite obviously speaks falsely when he says that he was
brought over from pagan superstition to Christianity, and that
Ammonius fell from Christianity into pagan errors. 10. Origen,
that is, received the faith and teaching of Christ from his grand-
parents and even remoter ancestors, for we told of his martyred
father a little earlier.[51] And as for Ammonius, the proof that
even amidst his philosophical studies he kept the faith of Christ

50. The original says that Origen learned figurative interpretation from
Chaeremon and Cornutus.
51. 6.1. On Ammonius, and Eusebius's confusion of him with his neopla-
tonist namesake (who wrote nothing), see S. Salaville, "Ammonius," *DHGE*
2.1314–17.

whole and entire, until he breathed his last, may be found in his books, which are still available and which expound our religion quite brilliantly, especially the volume he wrote about the harmony of Moses and Jesus. There are also many other magnificent shorter works of his which are considered outstanding by all scholars. 11. We have spoken thus out of a desire to use the testimony even of our opponents to show how marvelous even they consider Origen's learning and teaching to be. He himself writes as follows about himself in replying to some people who used to criticize him for engaging in studies of this sort:

12. "When I had turned to the study of God's word, however, and our reputation began to spread, and a number of philosophers began for that reason to approach and to meet with us to question or to oppose us, and a great number of heretics were roused as well to assail us, I decided to examine carefully the dogmas of both the philosophers and the heretics, lest I be found unprepared to refute them if I did not know what was contained in their writings. 13. We followed here the example of our predecessor, that apostolic man Pantaenus, who excelled in Greek studies and philosophical learning, and also of Heraclas, who now adorns the chair of the presbytery in Alexandria and whom I found with the teacher of the philosophers engaged already for some years in those studies before I had even made any beginning.[52] 14. So free was this man of any criticism arising from this, however, that he even laid aside the usual clothing which he had previously worn, and adopted the philosophers' garb, which he has continued to wear ever since. The books of the philosophers he has likewise never stopped reading and giving all his energy to pondering them."

15. Such are his words on his own behalf in response to certain complaints. Now while he was occupied at this time in Alexandria with God's word, there suddenly arrived a man in the military service bearing letters for him and Bishop Demetrius and the prefect of Egypt then in office from the Duke of Arabia, begging that Origen be sent out all the way to where he himself was with all speed and the greatest urgency, in order

52. Pantaenus: 5.10–11; Heraclas: 6.3.2.

to expound to him the faith of Christ, which his widespread reputation was declaring that he preached with the utmost brilliance. In response to their plea he went and taught, and they believed, and he returned. 16. Shortly afterwards, though, when civil war broke out in Alexandria,[53] and people dispersed to different places, he left for Palestine and stayed in Caesarea, where the bishops appointed him to lecture in church and expound the divine scriptures, even though he had not yet been ordained presbyter, 17. as we find in the letter of Alexander replying to Demetrius,[54] who had accused him of this long after. This is what he writes:

"As to what you added in your letter, that it was never heard of nor happened that the laity should lecture in the presence of bishops, 18. I do not know why you should wish to assert such an evident falsehood, since it is the custom that wherever people are found who can instruct the brethren in church and console the people, they are always invited by the holy bishops to give a lecture, as were Euelpius[55] by our brother Neon in Laranda, Paulinus by Celsus in Iconium, and Theodore by Atticus in Synnada. Nor is there any doubt that many others in other places are invited by the holy bishops to do the same, wherever there are people who can suitably execute God's work in word and teaching."

19. But this took place later. At this time, though, Demetrius sent a letter to him by select men who were deacons of the church, requiring him with all affection to return to Alexandria and to apply himself to his usual work.

6.20.1. Now there flourished in the churches at that time a great many men of the highest culture, whose letters which they sent to each other we found still preserved in the library

---

53. Caracalla massacred the Alexandrians in 215 in revenge for their mockery of him: Herodian, 5.9; Dio Cassius, 78.22–23; *SHA* Antoninus Caracalla 6.2–3.

54. Rufinus alters the original (or replaces it with another letter which he found in Origen's file); the original says that Alexander of Jerusalem and Theoctistus of Caesarea wrote about Demetrius, not to him. He continues the alteration in the citation below, changing the third person singular in the original to the second person.

55. "Euelpis" in the original.

in Jerusalem. The library had been built by that most learned man Alexander, whom we mentioned earlier,[56] the bishop of the place, and, to be truthful, it is from it that we have taken the material to compose this entire work of our history. 2. One of those men was Beryllus, foremost among the writers, who himself left various short works. He was bishop in Bostra, the chief city of Arabia. There was also Hippolytus, a bishop who himself left a number of writings. 3. There has also come down to us the debate held by one Gaius, a most learned man, against Proculus the Cataphrygian; it took place in Rome in the presence of Bishop Zephyrinus. When he charged the Cataphrygian with having adopted some new scriptures, he himself, among other things, maintained that there were thirteen letters of the apostle Paul, and did not mention the one written to the Hebrews, which even now is not regarded among the Latins as being the apostle Paul's.[57]

6.21.1. Now when Antoninus had completed a reign of seven years and six months, he was succeeded by Macrinus. And when he died a year later, another Antoninus received the government of the Roman empire.[58] In the first year of his reign the bishop of Rome, Zephyrinus, passed away after eighteen years in the priestly office. 2. Callistus received the priesthood after him. After serving for five years he left the see to Urban upon his death. And after Antoninus, the Roman empire, which he had held for only four years, came into the hands of Alexander. That was also the time when Asclepiades died in Antioch and Philetus succeeded to the bishopric.

3. Now the emperor Alexander's mother Mamaea, an extremely religious woman, heard of Origen's reputation, since his glorious fame had spread so widely everywhere that it had reached even the sovereigns' ears. She began then to bend every effort to bring him to her, that she might herself have proof of what she could tell that everyone else admired about his

56. 6.11; 6.13.3.
57. Gaius and Proculus (Proclus): 2.25.6. Hebrews and the Latins: 3.3.5.
58. Marcus Aurelius Antoninus (Caracalla) was killed on April 8, 217. Fourteen months after his successor's death another Antoninus, nicknamed Elagabalus, came to power and reigned 218–222.

writing, speech, faith, prudence, and teaching of every sort.[59]
4. She therefore sent men in the military service to employ every mark of respect and supplication to beg him, as a true expositor of the divine word and as a servant of God, to come to her at Antioch, where [she] was staying at the time. When he had gone there and devoted the amount of effort and time required to get everything done properly which concerns the word of God and the glory of the Lord, and had left those he had instructed firm and steadfast in the faith,[60] he returned to his own school in Alexandria, his presence having made him far more renowned than had his reputation.

6.22. In those days Hippolytus, whom we mentioned a little earlier, produced a short work about Easter among his other writings. In it he draws up some chronological table of the sixteen-year cycle which is usually followed in reckoning the date of Easter, terminating the entire table with the first year of the emperor Alexander by using some or other method of calculation.[61] Other short works of his have reached us as well: one on the Hexaemeron, and on the writings after the Hexaemeron, and against Marcion, and on the Song of Songs, and on some part of the prophet Ezekiel, and against all the heresies. And we may be sure that other minor works of his are in the possession of others as well.

6.23.1. It was at this time as well that Origen began writing commentaries on the sacred scriptures, Ambrose pressing him to do so and urging him with all the force of his prayers and supplications. 2. Ambrose also bent every effort to make sure

59. Severus Alexander's mother, Iulia Avita Mamaea, was a powerful figure in his government from the time of his succession when he was thirteen; cf. Herodian, 5.8.10; 6.1.1–2. Alexander is said to have kept statues of holy souls in his shrine, among them of Apollonius, Christ, Abraham, and Orpheus (*SHA* Severus Alexander 29.2). Thus there is nothing inherently improbable about the following story, although Rufinus emphasizes the empress's respect ("to employ ... to beg him" is his addition). On the possible date, see Bardy, *Eusèbe*, 2.121n7.

60. Eusebius says nothing about confirming anyone's faith, or indeed about converting anyone.

61. *nescio quam supputationem secutus:* Rufinus adds. Hippolytus was mentioned in 6.20.2. On his Easter table, see August Strobel, *Ursprung und Geschichte des frühchristlichen Osterkalenders, TU* 121 (1977): 121–33.

that he was supplied amply and abundantly with everything needed for the task. He brought in seven stenographers to offer him constant assistance and to relieve each other as he dictated almost without stopping;[62] he also employed as many copyists in this same task, as well as the same number of girls highly skilled in penmanship. Having supplied from outside in addition everything needed in full abundance, he demanded of him, as a forceful and religious taskmaster, daily work on this project for God's word, and he himself devoted enormous effort to learning God's word. Hence he [Origen] was viewed as someone above all deserving of that service, one to whom whatever lay secret and concealed in the sacred writings might be introduced.

Meanwhile Bishop Urban in Rome left the see to Pontian after eight years in the priestly ministry. In Antioch Zebennus received the church after Philetus. At this time Origen was asked by the churches in Achaia to come all the way there to refute the heretics who were thriving there openly.[63] As he was on his way there and was necessarily passing through Palestine, he was ordained presbyter in Caesarea by the bishop of that province. But the outrageous resentment which this roused against him, the measures taken to defend him by those who were governing the churches, and the rest of the turmoil stirred up by the resounding success he had enjoyed in preaching God's word—each of these matters really needs its own history. We have touched upon some of them in part in the second book of the *Apologia,* where those who wish to know of them may find them.[64]

6.24.1. He persisted meanwhile in continuous and unremitting labor in expounding the divine books, whether he was residing in Alexandria or Caesarea, as his treatises themselves show.[65]

62. Ambrose: 6.18.1. Stenographers: 6.36.1.

63. Eusebius just says that Origen was called there on urgent church business.

64. Only the first of the six books of the *Apologia* has survived, in Rufinus's translation. Cf. René Amacker and Éric Junod, *Pamphile et Eusèbe de Césarée: Apologie pour Origène* (Paris: Cerf, 2002), and Georg Röwekamp, *Pamphilus von Caesarea: Apologia pro Origene/Apologie für Origenes* (Turnholt: Brepols, 2005). Eusebius collaborated with Pamphilus on this work: 6.33.4.

65. Rufinus omits the rest of 6.24, which gives further details of Origen's lucubrations at this time.

6.25.1. Now while explaining the first psalm he indicates what the canon of the Old Testament is in the following words: "It should be realized that there are twenty-two books in the Old Testament, according to the Hebrews' tradition, according, that is, to the number of the letters in use among them." 2. And a little later he adds,

"There are twenty-two books: Genesis, Exodus, Leviticus, Numbers, Deuteronomy, Jesus, son of Nave, Judges, and the first and second books of the Reigns, which for them is one book, which they call Samuel. The third and fourth books are also one for them; they call it David's Reign. And the first and second books of Paralipomena are considered one; they call it the Words of the Days. First and second Esdras are one book. Then there are the Book of Psalms; the Proverbs of Solomon; another book, Ecclesiastes; and a third book of his,[66] the Song of Songs. There is also one book of the twelve prophets, and the prophets Isaiah, Jeremiah, Ezekiel, Daniel, Job, and Esther. With this they close the canon of the divine books.[67] The Books of Maccabees they consider outside of it."

3. About the New Testament canon too he writes as follows in the first book of his commentaries on the Gospel according to Matthew:

4. "I have learned from tradition about the four gospels that they alone are to be accepted without question in all the churches of God under heaven. For thus have the fathers handed down: that first of all Matthew, who had been a tax-collector, wrote a gospel in Hebrew script which was handed on to those from the circumcision who had believed;[68] 5. that the second was written by Mark in accordance with what Peter had handed on to him; he mentions him in his letter when he says, 'My son Mark greets you.'[69] 6. The third is according to Luke, and is

66. *tertius eiusdem* added by Rufinus.

67. "With this ... books": not in Eusbius's text. Rufinus omits Origen's transliteration of the Hebrew titles of the books. He also omits Ruth after Judges (Origen says they are one book in the Hebrew tradition). On the Old Testament canon cf. also 3.10.1–5 and 4.26.14.

68. Matthew and the Hebrew gospel: 3.24.6; 3.39.16; 5.8.2; 5.10.3.

69. 1 Pt 5.13. On Peter and Mark: 2.15.

commended by the apostle Paul as written for those from the gentiles who had believed.[70] And over and above all of them is the gospel of John."

7. About the apostles' letters he says the following as well:

"But he who was made a suitable minister of a new testament not of the letter but of the spirit,[71] Paul that is, fully preached the gospel round about from Jerusalem even to Illyricum,[72] but he did not write to all the churches he had taught; he wrote only fourteen letters, most of them quite short. 11. A number of people, though, are uncertain about the one written to the Hebrews, inasmuch as it does not seem to verify what he says about himself, namely that he is unskilled in speech.[73] 13. What I say, though, is what my elders have handed down to me, that it is quite clearly Paul's,[74] and all of our elders accepted it as Paul's letter. 14. But if you ask me from whom its wording comes, God knows for sure; the opinion which we have heard, though, is as follows: some used to say that it was from Clement, the disciple of the apostles and bishop of Rome, that the letter received the elegance of its Greek, but not its thought; others attributed this to Luke, who wrote the gospel and the Acts of the Apostles.[75] 8. As for Peter, upon whom Christ's church is being established, he wrote only two letters, about the second of which a number of people are uncertain as well. 9. John too, who reclined upon the Lord's chest,[76] wrote the Apocalypse too after the gospel; in the former, though, he was ordered to keep silent about what the seven thunders had said.[77] 10. He also wrote three letters, two of which are quite short; some people consider these two doubtful."

Such are his remarks.

70. 2 Cor 8.18; cf. also 3.4.7.

71. 2 Cor 3.6.

72. Rom 15.19. Rufinus rearranges the following parts of this section for a smoother presentation.

73. 2 Cor 11.6.

74. *manifestissime Pauli est.* Origen's original is more reserved: the thought (τὰ νοήματα) is Paul's, but the wording and composition are of a disciple recalling what Paul said.

75. Luke and Hebrews: 3.38.2 and 6.14.2.

76. Jn 13.25.

77. Rv 10.4.

6.26. It was meanwhile the tenth year of the above-mentioned Roman sovereign in which Origen had fled from Alexandria and come to Caesarea, leaving the catechetical school to Heraclas, one of his finest students, about whom I spoke earlier.[78] Not long after, though, Bishop Demetrius died too, after serving for forty-three years as bishop of that church, and Heraclas succeeded him.

6.27. Among the bishops of the time Firmilian of Caesarea in Cappadocia was an impressive figure. He had such respect for Origen on account of his knowledge and teaching that he was always urging him to stay with him. And he used to leave the church and hasten to be with him, and would effect a sort of holy exchange: he would summon him there to instruct his church, while at other times he would travel to where he was, with a view to his own progress, and attend his teaching day and night. Alexander too, who as we said earlier[79] governed the church in Jerusalem, and Theoctistus, who had charge of the church in Caesarea, used to spend almost their entire life-time listening to him, and would allow him alone to look after the whole business of teaching the sacred scriptures and church doctrine.

6.28. Now when the emperor Alexander died after reigning for thirteen years, he was succeeded by Maximinus Caesar, who from hatred of the house of his predecessor Alexander[80] stirred up persecutions against the churches. He ordered only those to be punished, however, who had charge of the people and the teaching, since they were the reason why the rest were believers. It was then that Origen wrote his book on martyrdom to Ambrose. It circulated among a great many people, who of their own accord came forward to profess Christ's name, their nerves rock-steady. The result was an enormous number of confessors produced over a three-year period starting with Maximinus's persecution, a period which brought with it the end both of his persecution and his life.

78. 6.15. The year was 231.
79. 6.19.17 (in Eusebius).
80. Rufinus omits what Eusebius says about Alexander's household having a great number of believers (cf. 6.21.3–4). Alexander was killed in 235.

6.29.1. Gordian received the sovereignty after him. Pontian after six years as bishop of Rome was succeeded by Anterus, who after serving no more than a month left the priesthood to Fabian. 2. They say that after Anterus had passed away Fabian returned from the country with his friends, 3. all the people of the church being gathered together to choose a bishop, and different voices shouting different names, as usually happens on such occasions,[81] with the crowd settling on no definite decision. Fabian himself was standing among the others wanting to know what the outcome would be when suddenly, through God's providence, a dove dropped from the sky resembling the one which had descended upon Jesus at the Jordan, bearing the likeness of the Holy Spirit, and rested upon his head. 4. At the sight of which, they say, the mouths and eyes of everyone turned around, and, as though moved by one spirit, they declared him worthy of the episcopacy by God's judgment, and he was placed upon the chair at once and confirmed as the legitimate priest. Some say this happened to him, and others to Zephyrinus.[82] At this time also Babylas received the governance of the church in Antioch when Zebennus died. And in Alexandria when Heraclas succeeded Demetrius, he gave over the catechetical school, which he had received from Origen, to Dionysius, since he too was one of Origen's disciples.

6.30. While Origen himself was staying in Caesarea, countless men flocked to him not only from that region but from far-off provinces, and leaving their native places, followed him as he taught God's way. Among them was none other than that highly renowned man Theodore, who not long ago was most distinguished among the bishops in Pontus, a thoroughly apostolic person in faith, virtues, and knowledge, and also his brother Athenodore. When they were youths, Origen withdrew them from their classes in rhetoric and persuaded them to exchange the usual course of studies in literature for divine philosophy. They devoted themselves to God's word with him for five years

81. *alius de alio, ut fieri solet in talibus,* [*conclamabat*]: Rufinus inserts this in place of Eusebius's "many men of renown and distinction were being considered by the crowd."
82. "Some … Zephyrinus": Rufinus adds.

and made such progress in divine learning and knowledge, and excelled to such a degree in the character of their lives and morals, that both were snatched from their studies while still young in order to be made bishops in the province of Pontus.[83]

6.31.1. Africanus was also distinguished among the church authors of this time. His letter to Origen is preserved in which he objects or suggests to him that the story of Susanna, which is found in Daniel, appears to be made up, and foreign to the prophetic writing. Origen wrote a most splendid reply to him in which he asserts that no attention whatever should be paid to Jewish deceits and trickery, and that only what the seventy translators translated is to be considered authentic in the divine scriptures, since that is what has been confirmed by apostolic authority.[84] 2. Other minor works of this author Africanus have also reached us, above all the chronicle, so carefully and painstakingly composed; in them he mentions that he is hastening to Alexandria, to which he was enticed by Heraclas's widespread reputation: rumor spoke of his immense erudition in the divine and philosophical fields of study, and, as we mentioned earlier, he had received the episcopacy there.[85] 3. Africanus also wrote to one Aristides about the apparent discrepancy in the gospels and why the description of Christ's genealogy is given differently in Matthew and Luke; he shows how obvious is their agreement, as we have related in the first book of this work.[86]

6.32.1. During this time Origen, having published thirty books of commentary on one part of the prophet Isaiah, mentions that he is finishing twenty-five on Ezekiel as he is setting out for Athens.[87] 2. There he also wrote the first five books on

83. Theodore/Gregory and Athenodore: 7.14 and 7.28.

84. The original correspondence is edited in Marguerite Harl, *Origène: Philocalie, 1–20: Sur les écritures, et Nicholas de Lange, La lettre à Africanus sur l'histoire de Suzanne* (Paris: Cerf, 1983), 469–578. The words "asserts ... authority" are Rufinus's addition, a misrepresentation of the original letter, which does affirm the canonicity of the Septuagint and warns against trying to gratify the Jews by accepting only their scriptures (8–9), but says nothing about Jewish tricks or apostolic authority.

85. 6.3.2.

86. 1.7.

87. Eusebius says that he mentioned that he finished those on Ezekiel after reaching Athens.

the Song of Songs. He finished another five after he returned to Caesarea. 3. But there is no need now to list his works, which are almost beyond count, since we have done so in the work where we told of the life of the blessed Pamphilus; there we related how many books of the writers of old, and especially of Origen, he dedicated to the library in Caesarea, which he himself put together with admirable and noble diligence. Those then who wish to know how many of Origen's books have reached us may find them listed there. But now back to our history.

6.33.1. Beryllus, the bishop of Bostra in Arabia, whom we mentioned a little earlier, tried to violate the standard of church teaching and began to teach foreign doctrines alien to the truth, asserting that our Lord and Savior neither existed before his birth in the flesh, nor did he have the substance of divinity on his own,[88] but only the Father's divinity dwelling in him. 2. A great many bishops met together on this account and held extended debates with him. Origen among others was earnestly besought to have it out with the man. His first step was a leisurely discussion with him to investigate carefully what he thought. When he had found it out, he proceeded immediately to show him the nonsense such ideas implied and the impiety attaching to one who asserted them, and thus persuaded him to renounce and reject the notion he had erroneously held, and to return to the true faith and sound doctrine. This is something almost unheard of in such cases: to drive error from the church in such a way that the author of the error is corrected and not lost.[89] 3. The written record of that discussion between Origen and Beryllus is still around, and is itself a proof of his outstanding work. 4. And many other similarly famous and wonderful deeds and words of his have come down to us; we have learned of them from his own letters and from the reports of those before us, but we pass over them for now in accordance with the scope of this history. They can be found in the *Apology* which the martyr St. Pamphilus wrote on his behalf together with me; we afforded

88. ... *neque extitisse ante carnis nativitatem neque propriam deitatis habere substantiam* = μὴ προϋφεστάναι κατ' ἰδίαν οὐσίας περιγραφὴν πρὸ τῆς εἰς ἀνθρώπους ἐπιδημίας μηδὲ μὴν θεότητα ἰδίαν ἔχειν.

89. "This ... lost" added by Rufinus.

each other mutual assistance in sharing our determination and labor when we wrote it with a view to silencing the critical.[90]

6.34. Now Gordian, when he had ruled the Roman empire for six years, was succeeded by Philip together with his son Philip. The tradition concerning him is that he was a Christian and that on the day of the Paschal feast, on the very vigil that is, he wanted to take part and share in the mysteries. But the bishop of the place would not allow him unless he first confessed his sins and stood among the penitents, nor would he be granted any future access to the mysteries at all, unless he first washed away by penance his faults, which, it was said, were great in number. They say therefore that he willingly accepted what the priest had ordered, that the fear of God was in him, and that he showed the most profound religious faith in deed and work.[91]

6.35. In the third year of his reign Heraclas passed away in Alexandria in the sixth year of his episcopacy, and Dionysius received the priestly office.

6.36.1. It was at this time, when Origen had reached his sixtieth year and had acquired the fullest confidence in God's word from his experience, trials, and labors, that he is said to have allowed the discourses he had given in the churches *ex tempore* to be taken down by stenographers,[92] nor (it is said) had he ever before allowed this, but only when the dignity of his life, the length of his years, and the authority conferred by long experience permitted him to do so. 2. Then he replied in eight volumes to one Celsus, an Epicurean philosopher, who had written books against us. He then published twenty-five books of commentary on the Gospel according to Matthew, and wrote a great many commentaries on the twelve prophets, of which only twenty-five volumes have reached us. 3. There are also letters of his to the emperor Philip and to his wife Severa which contain not the least hint of flattery. 4. He wrote as well to Fabian, the bishop of Rome, and to a great many others in charge

---

90. Cf. 2.23.2. Jerome, *Vir. illustr.* 75, says that Pamphilus published his *Defense of Origen* before Eusebius published his.

91. Philip succeeded in 244. The bishop in question is identified as Babylas of Antioch by John Chrysostom, *De S. Bab. c. Gentes* 1.

92. 6.23.2 on the stenographers.

of the churches concerning his Catholic faith. We have dealt with this more clearly in the sixth book of our *Defense* of him. And there are other letters of his written to various people; we have found a hundred of them so far and arranged them in books to preserve them.

6.37. There arose certain people in Arabia at this time who expounded perverted doctrines, asserting that the souls of human beings perish along with their bodies and are undone, and at the time of the resurrection are once again raised anew with their bodies. To drive this disease from the church a vast council of bishops met, and once again Origen was asked by everyone to take part and to speak. And when he had held forth before the entire council of priests, his speech was so impressive that it recalled all of those engulfed in the error of the new doctrine to a right faith and a Catholic outlook.

6.38. There arose another heresy at this time which is called that of the Helcesaites and which he quenched as soon as it appeared. He spoke of it as follows when he was discoursing in church about the eighty-second Psalm:

"Someone has appeared in these days who supposes that he knows something great and beyond what others do, and who makes some impious and ridiculous assertions in defense of some heresy of the Helcesaites which has lately arisen. I will tell you what the heresy maintains lest any of you fall prey to it unawares. They reject some of sacred scripture and then turn around and use whatever proof-texts from the New and Old Testaments that they want. But they reject the apostle Paul completely and maintain that there is nothing wrong with denying during persecution, since those who are unwavering in their hearts remain in faith in their hearts even if they are forced to deny with their mouths. That is what they maintain, and they carry around some book which they say fell from heaven; anyone who hears its words (they say) receives a remission of sins other than the one which Christ gave."[93]

6.39.1. Philip meanwhile was succeeded by Decius after a

---

93. On the Elkesaites, who appeared c. 116, see also Hippolytus, *Refutatio omnium haeresium* 9.13–17; 10.29; and Epiphanius, *Pan.* 19; 30.17; 53.

Decius's succession below was in 249.

reign of seven years. Out of hostility to Philip he unleashed a persecution against the churches in which Fabian was crowned with martyrdom in Rome and left his episcopal see to Cornelius. 2. In Jerusalem Bishop Alexander was once again hauled into court for professing Christ and locked up in prison. With the venerable gray hairs of old age he shone forth pre-eminently, and after he had glorified the Lord with his repeated sufferings and agonies, 3. while he was summoned back and forth from prison to tribunal and tribunal to prison, he died as the tortures were following one upon the other. 4. Mazabanes succeeded him in the priesthood. In Antioch Babylas ended his glorious life in prison after a profession similar in every way to Alexander's. Fabian[94] received the episcopal office after him. 5. But as for the number of things done against Origen in this persecution; the devices and the intensity with which that wickedest of demons fought against him with his whole army; how he endured new crosses, new kinds of punishment, and tortures unheard of in any age, beyond anyone else who was then detained for Christ's name; how the demon in his rage brought to bear all of his weapons against him, even threatening him with fire, and all because of his immense fame for teaching the faith and the truth, so that he was beset by a thousand deaths without even one of them befalling him, despite his yearning; how it all ended for him, his persecutor bending every effort to ensure that neither would death be granted him nor his torment cease; and the letters brimming with tears and every form of compassion which he afterwards wrote concerning these things: those who wish to know of these matters more fully may find a complete account of them in these writings of his.

6.40.1. Now it was at this time that Dionysius, the bishop of Alexandria, was rendered quite famous by the profession he so often made, and magnificent through the variety of his sufferings and tortures, as we are informed with complete reliability from his own letters. 8. He is in fact reported to have replied to some people who were pursuing him, "Why spend yourselves in chasing me around? Tear my head from my neck, since you

94. "Fabius" in Eusebius.

are wearing yourselves out for it so utterly, and present it to the tyrant as a splendid gift."[95]

6.41.1. He writes also to Fabian, the bishop of Antioch, about those who had undergone the contest of martyrdom under Decius in Alexandria, in the following terms:

"It was not when the emperor's decree was issued that the persecution began among us; the demon's agent, who in our city was titled 'divine,'[96] anticipated the sovereign's edicts by an entire year and stirred up the superstitious crowd against us. 2. Inflamed by him, the multitude thirsted for nothing else than the blood of the pious. 3. First of all, then, they seized a devout old man named Metranus[97] and ordered him to utter impious words. When he refused to do so, they battered his whole body limb by limb with cudgels, drilled his face and eyes with sharp rods, drove him out of the city while torturing him, and there drove out the spirit that remained in him with stones. 4. After this they brought out a distinguished woman, Quinta,[98] to the idols and pressed her to worship them; at her refusal, or rather curses, they bound her feet in fetters, dragged her through all the streets of the city, and tore her apart in a shocking and horrible act of torture. 5. Thereupon everyone together burst into the homes of God's servants, snatching, overturning, and defiling everything with savage hatred, seizing whatever was of value and heaping up in the streets whatever was valueless and burning it. 6. But ours accepted with joy this plundering of their goods, as the apostle said of those of old.[99] 7. And when they seized that wonderful old virgin Apollonia, they first gouged out all her teeth, and then, heaping together wood to build a pyre, they threatened to burn her alive unless she uttered their

95. Rufinus omits most of 6.40, where Eusebius cites Dionysius's letter to one Germanus, in which he defends his conduct during the persecution. In the original, Dionysius addresses the words "Why spend yourselves ..." to those rescuing him, against his will, from the soldiers who had arrested him.

"Fabian" just below is once again "Fabius" in Eusebius.

96. *qui dicebatur in civitate nostra divinus:* Rufinus adds; who is being referred to is unknown. See Bardy, *Eusèbe,* 2.145n3. The persecution under Decius began perhaps even before January of 250: see *Cambridge Ancient History*[2] 12.625–35.

97. "Metras" in Eusebius.   98. "Cointha" in Rufinus = Κοῖντα.

99. Hebrews 10.34.

impious words with them. But she, when she saw the pyre kindled, gathered herself briefly and then suddenly sprang from the hands of the impious and jumped of her own accord into the fire with which they had threatened her, so that the very authors of the savagery were terrified at finding that the woman was readier to accept death than her persecutor to inflict it.[100] 8. They also found Serapion at home and tortured him most cruelly, first smashing all the joints in his body and then throwing him down from the upper story. Ours could go nowhere; we might pass through no street; we were free to make our way to no place either by day or by night. As soon as one of ours appeared outside, a shout went up from the crowd and violence broke out, which ended with the one who had been seen being dragged off by the feet or burned to death.

9. "Now when these evils had been growing day by day, suddenly a madness erupting in urban warfare broke out among the persecutors themselves, and while violent strife was raging among them, we were to enjoy a short respite. 10. But the respite was not for long. For edicts of the cruellest sort were immediately issued by the sovereigns through which such savagery was loosed upon us as would 'scandalize even the elect, were that possible,' as the Lord foretold.[101] 11. Everyone being quite terrified by this, some of those people of distinction at once flung themselves willingly into the performance of the impious acts. Others betook themselves in haste to the accursed sacrifices and the impure victims simply when summoned, while a number did so when betrayed by members of their households. Some of them were pale and trembling, so that it looked as though they were the ones being sacrificed and not the ones offering sacrifice to the idols, so much so that they were laughed at by the crowd looking on because they seemed equally afraid of dying and of sacrificing. 12. Others would spring toward the altars so shamelessly that they were striving to affirm that they had never been Christians. These are the ones about whom the Lord foretold that 'those with wealth will be saved with difficulty.'[102]

100. "so that ... inflict it": Rufinus adds.
101. Cf. Mt 24.24.
102. Cf. Mt 19.23; Mk 10.23; Lk 18.24.

The others either followed them headlong or at any rate took to flight. 13. A number of these were arrested and put in prison; some of them denied the faith as soon as they came before the judge, while others endured the tortures for a short time before falling at last. 14. Those, however, who were rendered blessed provided a marvelous sight for God and the angels by their martyrdom, as by the Lord's own spirit they stood like mighty pillars in the strength received from the Lord, as their faith deserved.

15. "The first of them was the venerable Julian, who was so hobbled by gout that he could neither walk nor stand; he was brought up with those who used to carry him in a chair. One of them denied at once, while the other, called Eunus, persevered in professing the Lord Jesus Christ with the aged Julian. They were ordered to be placed on camels, led around through the whole city, and flogged to the bone on either side while the people looked on, until they died in the midst of their beating. 16. But a man in the military service who was at hand held back those who wanted to mock the dead bodies as well, and a cry was suddenly raised against him by the whole crowd. This mighty soldier, now Christ's, was brought before the magistrate and, persevering in his profession in a manner in no wise inferior, was sentenced to execution for his piety. 17. Another man named Macarius,[103] a Libyan, was addressed at length by the magistrate who was pressing him to deny, and when he proved even more resolute than he in professing his faith, he was finally ordered to be burned alive. Epimachus and Alexander as well spent a long time in fetters and under torture in prison, subjected repeatedly to torments and various punishments, and when they persevered in the faith, they were in the end consigned to the flames. 18. There were also four women with them, among whom was the holy virgin Ammonaria,[104] against whom the magistrate strove with the greatest determination, inflicting upon her the severest and most inventive tortures, and that especially because he wished to conquer the resolution she had voiced, with the greatest determination, that she would never do any of the things she was being commanded to

103. "Macar" in Eusebius.
104. "Ammonarion" in Eusebius.

do unlawfully; when she held to her decision she was executed in the end. The second was a venerable old woman, a virgin named Mercuria, and Dionysia, who had borne many children whom she did not prefer to Christ, and another Ammonaria.[105] Since they showed the greatest courage before the judge and he was ashamed to be bested by women, they were put to the sword after sustaining unheard-of methods of torture.

19. "The Egyptians Heron, Arsinus,[106] and Isidore were brought before the magistrate with a boy of fifteen named Dioscorus. He tried the boy Dioscorus first with words and then with blows, as being of an age which might easily be swayed. Finding that he in no wise yielded to him, he tried to torture him more savagely. 20. Then he tore the others apart with various tortures, but when he saw that they were armed with the courage of faith in equal measure, he ordered them delivered to the flames. The boy Dioscorus, though, he reprieved out of admiration for the courage and wisdom with which he replied to him in everything, hoping that he would change his mind because of his youth. This was due not to the tyrant's pity but to the Lord's providence.[107] For now Dioscorus has been granted to us by God for the consolation and support of his people.

21. "Nemesius,[108] another Egyptian, was also falsely denounced as a robber, and when cleared of this charge, was later denounced as a Christian. This time the magistrate extended no leniency, but after inflicting double the number of tortures on him ordered him to be burned with the robbers, unaware that his cruelty was bestowing on this excellent martyr a likeness to the Savior, who bore the cross along with the robbers for the salvation of the human race. 22. Now a band of soldiers had gathered, among whom were Ammon, Zeno, Ptolemy, Ingenuus,[109] and the aged Theophilus. They were standing by the tribunal, and when a certain Christian was being tortured by the magistrate and had come near to the point of denying, they

---

105. Rufinus adds *et alia Ammonaria* to bring the number up to four.
106. "Ater" in Eusebius.
107. "This … providence" added by Rufinus.
108. "Nemesion" in Eusebius.
109. "Ingenes" in Eusebius.

felt their hearts breaking, and with their facial expressions they tried, as it were, to raise up the one who was wavering in his torments. They also at times gestured with outstretched hands, and with the various motions and postures of their whole bodies lifted the spirits of the one who was falling. 23. Everyone turned their way and could tell from their gestures what they themselves professed, but almost before the crowd could raise a cry against them, they sprang forward and declared that they were Christians. Then indeed were the tables turned: their confidence inspired terror in the persecutors and courage in ours, while those who were thought to have been overcome by the torments volunteered to be tortured, and begged to experience the pleasures of what the others had inflicted as terrors, God thus triumphing through his holy ones.

6.42.1. "Nor must we pass over in silence Ischyrion's memorable deed. He had been hired as steward for someone important, and was ordered by him to sacrifice to idols. When he refused, he subjected him to mistreatment, and when he remained steadfast, he coaxed him with flattery. But when he showed his disdain for both approaches, he was, it is said, killed by being stabbed right through his middle with a sharpened, immensely stout staff. 2. But why should I record the vast multitudes wandering about in the deserts and mountains who perished because of hunger, thirst, cold, exhaustion, robbers, and beasts? All of them in imitation of God's chosen prophets were crowned with the glory of martyrdom. 3. Then there was the venerable old Chaeremon, bishop of the Egyptian city of Nilopolis, who departed with his aged wife for Mount Arabian and was seen no more by anyone. Many of the brethren went out repeatedly to look for him, but though they searched everywhere, no one ever found either them or their bodies. 4. Now it is not to no purpose that I have related these matters to you, dearest brother; it was so that you might know how many deeds have been done among us for God's glory by the holy martyrs."

5. And a little further on he continues as follows:

"These divine martyrs, then, who sit with Christ in the heavenly places, share in his reign and his judgment, and with him judge the cases of the brethren who have fallen: they received the fallen[110] and did not reject their repentance and conversion, because they knew that our God, whose martyrs they were, by no means desires the death of those who are dying, but their conversion and repentance.[111] If, then, they accepted certain people and placed them in church, 6. and shared with them as well in prayer and in food,[112] what do you want us to do, brothers? How do you think we ought to act? Does it not behoove us to follow their decision and judgment and not behave harshly and cruelly toward those to whom they showed mercy? I do not think that it is proper for us to rescind their decision, to nullify their act of compassion, to upset what was well done, and to violate such a just and religious practice."

6.43.1. This is what Dionysius says about the lapsed. It was at this time that a presbyter of the Roman church, Novatus,[113] swollen with self-importance, denied any hope of salvation to them, even if they repented worthily. He thus became the leader of the heresy of the Novatianists, who upon separating from the church gave themselves the presumptuous name of "cathari," meaning "pure." 2. A very large priestly council met in Rome[114] on this account, consisting of sixty bishops and as many presbyters and a great many deacons. In each of the provinces besides there were extensive deliberations about this matter, from which decisions were announced concerning what was to be done about the situation. It was decreed therefore that Novatus and those who followed him in his attitude

110. *susceperunt lapsos.* Dionysius says they received *some* of the fallen: τῶν παραπεπτωκότων τινας ... προσελάβοντο. On the martyrs' judgment, cf. Mt 19.28; 1 Cor 6.2–3; Rv 20.4.

111. Ezek 33.11; 2 Pt 3.9.

112. *receperunt quosdam et in ecclesia statuerunt, in oratione quoque et in cibo communicaverunt* = εἰσεδέξαντο καὶ συνήγαγον καὶ συνέστησαν καὶ προσευχῶν αὐτοῖς καὶ ἑστιάσεων ἐκοινώνησαν. What seems to be referred to is the gradual but complete reintegration of the lapsed into full communion; *statuerunt* (= συνέστησαν) is admission among the *consistentes,* the last step before admission to the Eucharist, the ἑστίασις ("banquet").

113. "Novatianus" in other Latin writers.

114. In 251. Novatus (Novatian) belonged to the party that denied that the church had the authority to receive the lapsed back into communion, and when Cornelius, who belonged to the party that favored readmission, was elected to succeed Fabian in 251, he was chosen as rival bishop by his party.

of self-importance and together with him deviated into his in-human frame of mind, preserving nothing of brotherly love, were alien to the church, while those who had fallen during the battle were to be tended with brotherly compassion and healed with the medicines of repentance.

3. Cornelius, bishop of Rome, wrote about this to the church of Antioch, explaining to its bishop Fabian what the council gathered in Rome had decided, and what had been decreed by the Italians, the Africans, and the other Westerners as well. Cyprian for his part published a wonderful book about these matters,[115] in which he states that the lapsed are to be urged to repent, and that those who disagree are strangers to Christ's compassion. 4. There is also another letter of Cornelius to Fabian, the bishop of Antioch, 5. which gives all the particulars about Novatus, who he was and what sort of man in his life and conduct, and how he had departed from the church. In it he says that it was due to a desire to be bishop, which he had secretly harbored, that he had fallen into all of these evils, but that his presumptuousness had been fostered above all by his success in associating with himself some of the best of the confessors at the very outset. 6. Among them was Maximus, a presbyter of the Roman church, and Urban, who had become confessors, as well as Sidonius and Celerinus, who were quite famous among the confessors because they had proved superior to every kind of torture.

"But when they considered more closely," he says, "how in all matters he proceeded with trickery and deceit, lies and perjury, and that he pretended to be good only to deceive the ignorant, they left him with their curses and returned to the church with handsome amends, and in the presence of the bishops and presbyters, and the laymen as well, they first confessed their error and then his tricks and deceptions too."

7. He goes on in the letter to say that "after swearing repeat-

115. *librum ... edidit.* Rufinus is referring to Cyprian's *De lapsis.* What Eusebius says is that Cyprian wrote letters in Latin to Fabius (whom Rufinus persists in calling "Fabian") stating his agreement with Cornelius's views; to them were subjoined another letter of Cornelius on the decisions of the council and yet another about what Novatus had done.

edly to the brethren that he had no desire at all to be bishop, he suddenly and unexpectedly appeared a bishop like a newly fashioned thing, 8. so that he who had always stood up for discipline and established church practice took upon himself the episcopate which he had not received from God. What he did was to get hold of three bishops of the simplest sort from a distant part of Italy, who were unaware of what was going on, or rather who were taken in by his clever trickery, 9. and he wrung from them an imposition of hands that was a travesty of anything lawful.[116] 10. One of them, though, returned to the church immediately, and after confessing his sin was received into communion among the laity, the people too urging that this be done. And in place of the other two who had imposed hands on Novatus 11. other bishops were ordained and sent out. This defender of the gospel, then, did not know that in a Catholic church there is to be one bishop, where he could see that there were forty-six presbyters, 12. seven deacons, seven subdeacons, forty-two acolytes, fifty-two exorcists with lectors and porters, and fifteen hundred widows together with needy folk, all of whom God nourishes in his church."

13. He adds 14. that Novatus was harried by an impure spirit when he was young, that when he had spent some time with the exorcists he fell so gravely ill that he was despaired of, 15. that while lying in bed he was of necessity affused, and that none of the other things which customarily follow baptism were performed upon him in due course, not even the completion by the seal of chrism, so that he could never lay claim to the Holy Spirit.[117]

17. "Then," he says, "when the bishop had acquired a personal attachment to him and wanted to ordain him presbyter, all of the clergy and a great many laity forbade him, saying that it was not right to make someone a cleric who had won the conferral of grace while forced to lie in bed, but the bishop requested

116. Rufinus omits what the original says about the ordainers being drunk and befuddled.

117. Rufinus inverts sections 16 and 17 for a smoother narrative. He then omits 19–21 and the first part of 22, which give details of those who condemned Novatus.

from everyone as a particular favor that he might be allowed this for this one person."

16. He also writes of him that when he was hiding in a cell somewhere during the persecution and was asked by the deacons to assist the catechumens who were facing death, as was customary, he was so afraid to emerge that he denied that he was a presbyter; 18. [he writes too] that when he was distributing the sacrament among the people he would hold the hands of those receiving it and would not allow them to consume it before they swore by what they held in their hands that they would never leave him and return to Cornelius.

22. This and much else of the same sort is what Cornelius wrote concerning his life and conduct and irreligious acts.

6.44.1. Dionysius in writing back to Fabian about him includes a story worth recording. It goes as follows:

2. "Someone in Alexandria named Serapion was one of those who had lapsed, and he had often begged to be taken back, but had never been granted his request. He then became so ill that he lay for three days no longer able to speak, 3. but on the fourth day he recovered a little, called his daughter[118] to him, and said, 'How long are you going to hold me back? Let someone hurry to ask for the presbyter, that I may be released at last.' And when he had said this, he lapsed into silence again. 4. The boy ran to the presbyter at night, but the presbyter was sick and could not come. Since, however, I had ordered that no one should deny the solace of reconciliation to the lapsed who were facing death, especially those who, it was clear, had requested this previously, he gave a little of the Eucharist to the boy who had come to him, bidding him offer it to the old man after soaking it.[119] 5. As the boy was returning, but before he had entered the house, Serapion opened his eyes again and said, 'Have you returned, son? Even though the presbyter could not come, do as you have been ordered, that I may depart.' 6. And when the ceremony was finished, he surrendered his now happier spirit as though chains and fetter of a sort had been broken. Which goes

118. *filiam suam* = τὸν θυγατριδοῦν ("his grandson").
119. *infusum iussit seni praeberi* = ἀποβρέξαι κελεύσας καὶ τῷ πρεσβύτῃ κατὰ τοῦ στόματος ἐπιστάξαι ("soak it and drip it into the old man's mouth").

to show beyond a doubt," he said, "that no one should be cheated of the help which comes from this good thing."

6.45. Dionysius also wrote a letter to Novatus himself; it runs as follows:[120]

"Greetings from Dionysius to his brother Novatus. If, as you say, you have arrived at this point unwillingly, you will show this by leaving off willingly. It would in fact have behooved you to suffer anything rather than see the church divided, nor would it have been less glorious to suffer martyrdom to keep the church from being divided than to keep from sacrificing to idols; the former would in fact have been a higher martyrdom, in my view. For in the latter, each suffers martyrdom for his own soul alone, while in the former it is for the whole church. But now if you can either persuade or even compel the brethren to return to unanimity, the merit attaching to your amendment will outweigh the fault you committed, because the latter will no longer be taken into account, while the former will even be held praiseworthy. But if the others persist in their disbelief, then save your own soul at any rate. I bid you farewell, hoping for the peace I beg of you."

6.46.1. He also wrote the same to Novatian.[121] He sent to the Egyptians as well a letter about the repentance of the lapsed in which he sets out the rules for their penance. And there are in circulation many other excellent writings of Dionysius. 2. He wrote on repentance and a short work of exhortation to martyrdom addressed to Origen, as well as something on repentance to the Laodiceans and Armenians. 3. He also wrote a number of things to Cornelius, bishop of Rome, in which he states too that he had been invited by many bishops, namely by Helenus in Tarsus in Cilicia, Firmilian of Cappadocia, and Theoctistus of Palestine, to come to Antioch to a synod, because there were some there who were trying to sow Novatus's doctrines. 4. He added that when Bishop Fabian[122] of Antioch had died, he

120. Rufinus omits Eusebius's introduction to the letter, which mentions that "Novatus" had excused his behavior on the grounds that some of the brethren had forced him to it. The letter itself is addressed to "Novatian."

121. Eusebius: "Such were his words to Novatus."

122. "Fabius" in Eusebius. Alexander below was mentioned in 6.8.7.

had been succeeded in the episcopacy by Demetrian. He also wrote of the bishop of Jerusalem as follows: "That marvelous man Alexander has ended his life happily in prison and gone on ahead to the Lord."

5. There is another letter of Dionysius to the Romans about ministries,[123] and yet another to them about peace and penance, and then one to some confessors who were still following Novatus in Rome. He wrote two more letters to these same men after they had returned to the church. And in writing on various topics to many other people he has left a most abundant supply of material of instruction and teaching to anyone of scholarly interests.

---

123. *epistula ... de ministeriis* = ἐπιστολὴ διακονική (whatever that means). Rufinus omits the note that the letter was drafted or delivered by one Hippolytus.

BOOK SEVEN

28. The Manichaean heresy which arose then

29. The church members of prominence, some of whom lived to our own time

The seventh book of the church history will be forged for us by Dionysius, most renowned of fathers, famous among bishops, from the material contained in his writings.[1]

7.1. After Decius had reigned over the Roman empire less than two years in all and had been slain together with his sons, and Gallus had become sovereign at the same time that Origen had also died before reaching his seventieth year, he wrote as follows about Gallus to one Hermammon:

"Not even Gallus could see or avoid the evil of Decius, but collided with the same obstacle-stone. When his reign was flourishing at the outset and all was going as he wished, he persecuted the holy men who were beseeching the highest God to grant peace to his realm, and with them he banished both his prosperity and his peace."

7.3. Now while Cornelius was governing as bishop in Rome and Cyprian in Carthage, both of them outstanding in faith, virtue, and piety, the question began to be voiced especially in Africa about whether heretics should be rebaptized. Cyprian and almost all the other priests in Africa decreed that this should be done, but Cornelius and all the other priests in Italy rejected their decrees, even while their priestly concord remained intact;[2] they decided that the rule about this handed down of old by the fathers should be retained, namely that [heretics], after they had renounced doctrine which was erroneous and professed that which was correct, should be purified by the laying-on of hands alone.

1. Cf. Paul Allan Legutko, "The Letters of Dionysius: Alexandrian and Christian Identity in the Mid-Third Century AD," *The Ancient World* 34.1 (2003): 27–41.

Decius's reign mentioned below was 249–251.

2. Rufinus rewrites 7.2–3 to enhance the prestige of Cornelius and Cyprian by additional remarks about their probity and the wide support they enjoyed among their colleagues. He muffles the tone of controversy among them in the original (*manente sacerdotali concordia*) and suppresses Eusebius's remark that Stephen was "highly indignant" (διηγανάτει) at Cyprian. Cf. Cyprian, *Epp.* 74 and 75 on this controversy.

7.2. But after Cornelius finished his life, having held the priesthood for about three years, Lucius received the episcopal chair, and after he had held the priesthood for only eight months he was succeeded by Stephen, who issued a verdict like Cornelius's about not rebaptizing. 7.4. Dionysius addressed a great many writings to him[3] about many church issues. In them he says among other things that all the churches had rejected Novatus's presumptuousness and remained at peace with each other. This is what he says:

7.5.1. "You should realize, though, brother, that all the churches in the East which were formerly disturbed have now returned to a state of harmony,[4] everyone rejoicing to be bound together in unanimity and exulting in the peace which beyond hope has been restored to the church: Demetrian in Antioch, Theoctistus in Caesarea, Mazabanes in Jerusalem, Marinus in Tyre, with Alexander having fallen asleep,[5] Heliodorus in Laodicea, Helenus in Tarsus, and Firmilian in Cappadocia. But to avoid lengthening the letter I have listed for you only the bishops of the leading cities, 2. that it may be clear to you that the rest of them throughout Syria and Arabia are of the same mind as they. And the bishops of Mesopotamia as well to whom you have now written, and Pontus and Bithynia too, are all likewise of one mind and in agreement, and bound together in ardent and mutual charity, they glorify our God."

3. So writes Dionysius. When Stephen had completed two years in the priesthood of Rome, he was succeeded by Xystus. Dionysius wrote likewise to him about baptism, 4. mentioning that his predecessor Stephen, in writing to Firmilian and Helenus and the other bishops of those parts, had ruled that there

---

3. *multa et saepe scripta direxit* = πλεῖστα … αὐτῷ περὶ τούτου (rebaptism) διὰ γραμμάτων … ὁμιλήσας (he wrote what was apparently a long letter on this to him).

4. The original justifies Eusebius's summary of it above, where he speaks of a resumption of concord rather than Rufinus's continuation of it. Dionysius writes of the churches "in the East and beyond," and says that they had been "divided" rather than merely "disturbed," as Rufinus would have it.

5. *Mazabanes in Hierosolymis, dormiente in pace Alexandro Marinus apud Tyrum:* if this is punctuated so that a comma follows *Alexandro,* then Alexander of Jerusalem is referred to; but the Greek does not have this meaning.

should not even be any communion with those who rebaptized, 5. but that the magnitude of the issue should be taken into account, since this was the view taken of it not just by anyone, but by bishops of high standing and prominence.[6] 6. He also said that he had written more fully about this to Dionysius and Philemon, presbyters of Rome.

7.6. He also says something about the heresy of Sabellius, which had appeared in his time, writing as follows:

"And what shall I say about that doctrine which has recently appeared in Ptolemais, a city of the Pentapolis, and which is replete with blasphemies against God the Father and Our Lord Jesus Christ, denying that he is truly the Father's Son and the first-born of all creation, while removing all understanding of the Holy Spirit? In view of this, when both parties had come to me and in the presence of the brethren I had scrutinized the issues in dispute, I also followed the matter up by writing letters, as far as God granted this to my insignificance, in which I explained each thing carefully; I am sending copies to you."

7.7.1. He also mentions the following in the third book[7] on baptism which he wrote to Philemon, presbyter of Rome:

"I for my part both read the treatises of the heretics and examine their traditions, even if I should seem at the time to be defiled by their words. But it is a great advantage to me to be able to refute them from their own words. 2. When finally one of the brethren, a fellow presbyter, restrained me, lest the reading of the heretics should defile me with its filthy stench, I was given a vision from God which confirmed me, 3. and words were communicated to me which clearly said, 'Read whatever comes into your hands, because you have the ability to test and distinguish each thing, this being from the outset the reason for your belief.' I embraced the vision because it agreed

---

6. Rufinus once again mutes the controversy in 7.5.3–5. What Eusebius says is that Dionysius wrote to Xystus that Stephen had written not to, but about, Helenus, Firmilian, and their neighboring bishops, declaring that he would not hold communion with them because they rebaptized heretics (Firmilian's angry reply is in Cyprian, *Ep.* 75). And it is Dionysius who asks Xystus to reflect on the magnitude of the issue, not Stephen the others; he adds that the rebaptism of heretics is in fact the rule in his parts.

7. *in tertio libro* = ἐν τῇ τρίτῃ [scl. "letter"].

with the apostolic pronouncement, 'Read everything and retain what is good.'"[8]

5. In the same work he also mentions that it was not then in Africa for the first time that a ruling had been made by bishops about rebaptizing heretics, but that this matter had been dealt with even before then in a number of churches and councils of bishops, in Iconium for instance and in other places. 6. He writes further in the fourth book[9] on baptism to Dionysius, presbyter of Rome, saying a good deal about Novatus's impiety.

7.9.1. In the fifth book, written to Xystus, bishop of Rome, he mentions the following occurrence as part of his criticisms of the heresy mentioned above. His words:

"I truly need your advice, brother, and request your opinion about a matter that has arisen in our church. For I fear I may go wrong here. 2. There was a brother among us whose fidelity was long-standing, going back even before I was ordained bishop, and even before my predecessor Heraclas was ordained. He was with those who were being baptized, and when he heard what they were asked and how they replied, he came in tears to me, fell at my feet, and began to confess that he had received baptism from heretics in a different way than that in which he now saw it being administered by us, and he did not consider it baptism because that entire profession was full of blasphemies. 3. He added at the same time that he was so stung by this error that he did not even dare raise his eyes to God. He begged therefore to be cleansed and purified by the church's baptism, that he might attain as well the grace of the Holy Spirit. 4. This I did not dare to do, but I said that the communion which he had enjoyed in the church for so long a time would suffice for him, since in receiving the gift of the Eucharist from us he would respond 'amen,' as a result of which he would have been purified

8. *Omnia legite, quae bona sunt tenete,* an echo of 1 Thes 5.21 which Rufinus puts in place of Dionysius's γίνεσθε δόκιμοι τραπεζίται ("be reliable money-changers"). Rufinus omits 7.7.4, which says that Heraclas readmitted heretics without rebaptizing them.

9. "the fourth book" here and "the fifth book" below in 7.9.1 are "letters" in the original. Rufinus omits 7.8, which contains further criticism of Novatian. Perhaps he wants to avoid confusing the issues of the rebaptism of the lapsed on the one hand and of heretics and schismatics on the other.

by the very power of the mysteries, instance by instance. I exhorted him therefore to trust in his faith and in his conscience, by now purified, and, above all, in the fact that he had already been a sharer with us in the mysteries for so long. 5. But he does not cease from his grieving or his tears, nor does he dare to approach the Lord's table any more, so that even when encouraged and urged by us he hardly even dares to attend the prayer."

6. Dionysius wrote this and much else on questions of this sort in his sundry books.

7.10.1. Now Gallus was taken from this life after retaining the sovereignty for less than two years.[10] Valerian with his son Gallienus received the government after him. 2. Dionysius writing again to Hermammon about him speaks as follows:

"A revelation was likewise given to John, so that he said, 'A mouth was given to it speaking boastfully and arrogantly, and power was given to it for forty-two months.'[11] 3. Both of these are fulfilled in Valerian. It is really strange to consider how humane and kind he proved toward God's servants, more so than the others who were before him, so that at the outset he seemed far kindlier even than those who were at least supposedly Christians.[12] That was how greatly he respected the Lord's servants, and his whole house was a church of God. 4. But he was corrupted and expelled from the truth by a certain teacher, the worst sort of instructor, chief of the Egyptian magicians, so that he ordered the men who were just and holy to be persecuted and slain because they opposed the magical arts to which he had subjected himself. For there really were people, and still are, who could repress the deceits of the demons by virtue of their merits. For in order to carry out his impure rituals, accursed mysteries, and unholy ceremonies, he would order prepubescent boys to be killed, parents to be bereft of their children, and human entrails in their tender organs to be sinfully scrutinized, searching for a voice in the place from which he had banished life.[13]

10. 251–253. Hermammon just below was mentioned in 7.1.

11. Rv 13.5.

12. Alexander Severus was favorable to Christians (6.28), and Philip is said to have been Christian himself (6.34).

13. Dionysius identifies this man as Macrianus in the section of 7.10 which

He says a great deal else of this sort about Valerian's sins, adding that he was captured by the barbarians and blinded, and left his sons as successors to his wickedness and impurity.[14]

7.11.1. The same Dionysius related to a certain bishop Germanus how much he had suffered in that persecution and to what tortures he had been subjected on account of God's name, writing to him because of his apparent slander of him.[15] He includes a record of his profession before the governor Aemilian, 6–13. in which, when Dionysius said that only the one God who had made heaven and earth was to be adored, while the others were neither gods nor ought to be adored, he was banished to a settlement in the desert called Cephro.[16] It was especially chosen because the inhabitants there were pagans and quite devoted to idolatrous superstitions. They at first received the exiled Dionysius in a hostile and quite unfriendly manner, but later, when he had begun with the Lord's grace to sow God's word in

Rufinus omits (he is referred to again in 7.23). Fulvius Macrianus was Valerian's chief finance minister (and thus closely associated with the confiscations that accompanied the persecution). The emperor's toleration of Christians at the beginning of his reign (in 253) was doubtless a matter of sheer expediency, but by 257 he had the affairs of state sufficiently in hand to issue the edicts for the suppression of Christianity. At least one motive for the persecution seems to have been the Christian refusal to engage in official public worship; cf. *The Cambridge Ancient History*, 12.637–46.

The last clause in the quotation, "searching ... life" (*vocem illic quaerebat, ubi fugaverat vitam*) is Rufinus's addition. Stories of the sacrifice of children for extispicy by emperors and high officials recur throughout this period; cf. Book 11, note 46.

14. Rufinus omits 7.10.5–9, which points out the moral of Valerian and Macrianus's course with apt scriptural quotations. Valerian's capture and mistreatment by the Persians (in 260) is hinted at in the original (7.10.7) and stated more explicitly in 7.13 (not translated there by Rufinus). But the original says nothing about his being blinded (*luminibus orbatus*); Rufinus alone among the ancient sources has this notice.

"Left his sons" is a careless summary of 7.10.8, which refers to Macrianus, not Valerian. Macrianus's two sons succeeded to the purple after Valerian's capture, but both lost their lives with their father when Valerian's son Gallienus managed to establish himself in 261.

15. Eusebius had cited Dionysius's letter to Germanus in 6.40.1–7 (omitted by Rufinus). Rufinus now heavily abridges the rest of 7.11 with Dionysius's account of his trial and banishment.

16. Rufinus omits the passage indicating that Cephro was in Libya.

them little by little, the greatest part of the savage and barbarous people abandoned their idols, turned to the true God, and
became subject to Christ. 14–17. When this was discovered, they
moved him to another place[17] which was near Alexandria but
void of settlers and nearly empty of inhabitants. But because it
was near the city our people frequented it, and the flock, when
it caught the shepherd's scent, became more cheerful and brav-
er in the contests, 22–23. and so once again they sent a centurion with soldiers, bound Dionysius in chains, and with him Gaius and Peter, inflicted various tortures on them, dragged them
off to the wastes of Libya, and left them in fetters in an utterly
barren place, devoid of all human interest, three days' journey
into the desert from Paraetonium. 24. [Dionysius] speaks of this
in different letters of his. In them he also mentions the presbyter Maximus,[18] and Dioscorus, Demetrius, Lucius, Faustinus,
and Aquila as persons who were quite renowned and who were
outstanding for their profession of faith. He adds that some of
the deacons died on the island[19] after the sufferings entailed
by their profession, but that of their number Faustus and Eusebius survived. He also relates that through God's grace they
were given such confidence and magnanimity that when no one
was allowed access to the brethren held in prison in order to assist them, they nonetheless visited them time and again and saw
to their needs. 25. With the governor growing more frenzied
each day as he slew some people, tortured others, snuffed out
lives with the prison filth and weight of the chains, and above all
ordered that no one should have access to them at all, that he
might add starvation to the other tortures, God still showed favor to his confessors in granting to these deacons that entry was
not denied them even when no one else was welcome.

26. Now it should be noted that this Eusebius, who we said
earlier was a deacon, was later ordained bishop in Laodicea in
Syria,[20] while Maximus, who as we mentioned was a presbyter,

---

17. Colluthion, says 7.11.15.

18. In the original all of the first four are given as presbyters.

19. *in insula* = ἐν τῇ νήσῳ . A variant reading in the manuscripts is νόσῳ ("in
the pestilence"). Rufinus omits Chaeremon among the survivors named below.

20. 7.32.5.

succeeded Dionysius himself as bishop in Alexandria. As for Faustus, who distinguished himself with them as a confessor then, he survived until the persecution which broke out in our time, when at a great old age and full of days, he consummated his life in full martyrdom when he was beheaded. Such is Dionysius's report, and it is quite reliable.

7.12. In Valerian's persecutions, then, many martyrdoms were achieved in Caesarea in Palestine by various people. Among them were three wonderful youths[21] called Priscus, Malchus, and Alexander, who lived on a small property near the city just mentioned. Inflamed by the divine ardor of faith, they began to reproach themselves for laziness and cowardice, because, although the heavenly crowns of martyrdom were being exhibited in the city, they neither desired nor seized them, and although the Lord and Savior had testified that the kingdom of heaven was being snatched away with violence,[22] they themselves were behaving in a sluggish and dispirited manner. Rousing each other, then, with such words, they headed into the city, and when the cruel magistrate made his appearance, rebuked him for his savagery in shedding the blood of the pious. He immediately repaid the noble spirits of the youths with a most worthy sentence: "Let those displeased with the shedding of pious blood be given to the beasts to be devoured."[23] It is also said that some woman who followed the example of the youths' boldness and magnanimity was subjected to a like capital punishment; but she reportedly belonged to Marcion's school.[24]

7.15.1. There was also a man in the military service, Marinus, a resident of Jerusalem[25] renowned for his high office and wealth, 2. upon whom a military distinction was being bestowed among his fellows in accordance with his rank, as is customary, when one of his fellows, smitten by envy, came in pursuit and cried that Marinus could not be advanced to higher rank be-

21. *adulescentes:* Rufinus adds.

22. Mt 11.12.

23. Rufinus adds the details of their remarks to the magistrate, and his sentence.

24. Rufinus shifts 7.13–14 to after 7.19.

25. Eusebius says of Caesarea in Palestine.

cause he was Christian. 3. Marinus was asked by the magistrate if this was so. He testified in ringing tones that it was true, and that he really was Christian. Three hours for deliberation were decreed him by the magistrate to choose whether he wished to sacrifice to the gods and the emperor, or to be put to death as a Christian. 4. When he left the court, Theotecnus, the bishop there, took him by the hand, led him to the church, and there strengthened him in the faith with a long speech, and finally led him inside the altar [area], where he showed him his sword with which he was girt and then offered him the gospel, asking him which of the two he preferred. Marinus with the readiest possible faith stretched out his hand to the gospel, and Theotecnus said, "Hold to what you have chosen, my son, and in despising the present life, hope for that which is eternal. Go forth in confidence and receive the crown which the Lord has prepared for you." He returned to court at once and was summoned by the herald; the time set had come. 5. He brooked no delay, nor did he wait to be asked, but at once declared that he had weighed the matter and that his decision was confirmed by ancestral law: that God was to be obeyed rather than men.[26] The magistrate sentenced him on the spot to be beheaded for his answer.

7.16. The one among them, though, who is mentioned as more renowned than the others and distinguished above the rest on account of his faith is Astyrius, a senator of the city of Rome, a patrician in his nobility and endowments, and renowned as well for his closeness to the emperor and the widespread reputation of his wealth. When he attended the funeral of the martyr just mentioned and received the corpse severed from its head by lifting it on his shoulders and spreading beneath it the garment which he had been wearing, he himself immediately attained as a martyr the honor which he had offered the martyr.[27] And those who saw him while he was still in the body have related to us how his outstanding faith in Christ was seen in many other deeds of renown.

---

26. Acts 5.29.
27. Eusebius does not say that Astyrius was martyred.

7.17. Among them is recorded the following deed of his. In Caesarea Philippi, which the Phoenicians call Paneas, they say that at the foot of the mountain which is called Panius[28] and from which the first streams of the River Jordan spring forth, it was the custom of pagan error to sacrifice a victim on a certain traditional day, the victim suddenly disappearing from sight by some demonic trick. Such was the nature of the most famous wonder by which, apparently, the onlookers were persuaded that the victim had been lifted up to heaven invisibly. It happened, then, that Astyrius was there when this was going on. When he saw how everyone was astonished at this miracle, he lifted up his eyes and hands to heaven with groans and sighs in sorrow over the errors of humankind, and from the depths of his faith, with a flood of tears, he called upon Christ, who is the God over all,[29] to confute the tricks of the deceitful demon and to expose for wretched mortals the secret behind the error. While he was begging and weeping for this, suddenly the victim, which had been believed to have been taken up invisibly, appeared floating on the waters, restored to everyone's sight. Nor could an error of this sort ever be repeated in these places. Thus it was that through the prayer of one Christian the deception practiced for so many centuries was undone along with the demons who were behind it.

7.18.1. Now that we have mentioned this city, it seems right to record too the following event which took place in it and which we consider worth narrating. It is known that the woman who was cured by the Savior when she suffered from a flow of blood, as the gospels relate, was a resident of this city, and her house there is still shown today.[30] 2. In front of the doors of the house there is a pedestal on a higher place which is pointed out; on it is seen an image executed in bronze of the woman represented

28. "Paneion" in Eusebius (the name of the Pan-shrine).

29. *Christum, qui est super omnia deus ... invocat* = ἱκετεῦσαι διὰ Χριστοῦ τὸν ἐπὶ πάντων θεόν ("he besought through Christ the God who is over all").

30. Cf. Mt 9.20–22; Mk 5.25–34; Lk 8.43–48. On the statue see John F. Wilson, "The 'Statue of Christ' at Banias: A Saga of Pagan-Christian Confrontation in 4th-Century Syro-Palestine," *Aram* 18–19 (2006–2007): 1–11. It may actually have been of the emperor Hadrian.

as fallen to her knees and holding out her hands in supplication. Near it stands another statue likewise cast in bronze in the form of a man elegantly clad in a robe and extending his right hand to the woman. By the foot of this statue some new kind of plant sprouts from the pedestal, which, once it appears, usually grows as far as the bronze fringe of the robe; when in its growth the top of the plant touches this, it acquires from it the power to expel all disease and sickness, so that any bodily illness is expelled by a mere sip of this wholesome herb once it has been steeped. If it is picked before it touches the edge of the bronze fringe in its growth, it has none of this power at all.[31] 3. They used to say that this statue bore a likeness to Jesus's features; it has lasted until our own time, as we have viewed it with our own eyes. 4. And it is in no way strange that those of the gentiles who came to believe wanted to offer this sort of gift for the benefits they had received from the Savior, since even now we see images of the apostles Peter and Paul, and of the Savior himself, being drawn and painted. We have also seen old images of them which have been kept by certain people; this appears to me to be a gentile custom observed without distinction, since they usually honor in this way those whom they consider worthy of honor. For the preservation of the tokens of those of old for the memory of those who come after is a display of honor for the former and of love for the latter.

7.19. The chair of James, finally, who as the first bishop on earth was chosen in Jerusalem by the Savior himself and by the apostles, and whom the divine books show to have been Christ's brother,[32] is preserved even today, and on it sit all those to whom the priesthood of that see falls, even to the present time. It is guarded therefore with the greatest solicitude as a memorial of holiness passed down by our ancestors, and is held in great veneration on account of its age and of the sanctity of the first priesthood. But let this suffice concerning this.

31. Rufinus adds details that make it clear that it is a real plant, and not part of the statuary, and how it is to be prepared and taken.

32. Cf. 2.1.3. On James as Christ's brother, cf. Gal 1.19. On his ordination as bishop of Jerusalem by Christ: *Clementine Recognitions* 1.43; on his ordination by Christ and the apostles: *Apostolic Constitutions* 8.35.

7.13.[33] Valerian's son Gallienus, once he had become sole ruler, began to act more leniently and moderately toward ours, even issuing decrees to check the punishment and stop the persecution, and he allowed individuals to supplicate the deity in the way each thought fitting.

7.14. At this same time, when Xystus was still head of the Roman priesthood, Demetrian was in Antioch, and Firmilian was still in charge of Caesarea in Cappadocia, Gregory, who was earlier called Theodore and was one of Origen's disciples, received the governance of the churches of Pontus with his brother Athenodore.[34] At Caesarea in Palestine the episcopate fell to Domnus after Theoctistus, and when he died shortly thereafter he handed on the see to Theotecnus, who was alive in our own time and was himself said to have been a student of Origen's. In Jerusalem Hymenaeus received the priesthood after Mazabanes. All of them governed the churches in peace.

7.21.[35] In Alexandria, though, when there is no external threat of harm, the very fact that the human race is savage, rebellious, and restless would give rise to civil disturbances and wars not for any justifiable reason or for the purpose of defense, but for the purpose of killing and murdering the citizens. Dionysius when he mentions this in his letters reports that the city was so devastated and destroyed by its own residents that where once it had offered barely enough room to make one's way because of the crowds, it was now reduced to a state where it was quite rare to see anyone in the streets, all of which were soaked in the blood of its residents, while the roads were choked with corpses and those who had survived were not enough to bury them. Hence after the fury of the war and the devastation of the sword, the pestilence spread which hung in the foul air from the stench of the corpses, so that whatever had survived the sword was carried off by disease.

33. See note 24 on Rufinus's transferal of 7.13–14 to this point. He heavily abridges this section, in which Eusebius has copied out the imperial rescript referred to below. The unprecedented disaster of Valerian's capture might have persuaded Gallienus that enforcement of the official cult would not after all guarantee the security of the realm; cf. *The Cambridge Ancient History* 12.645–47.

34. Theodore/Gregory and Athenodore: 6.30 and 7.28.

35. Rufinus omits 7.20 (on Dionysius's letters).

7.22.1. Dionysius writes about this in the Easter letter which is customarily written regularly each year[36] as follows:

2. "Others may not think that this is a time of festival, since grief and bitter lamentation do echo through all the streets, while moaning and wailing are heard within the houses because of the many who are dying. 3. As was once told of the first-born of the Egyptians, so now also an immense cry is being raised. 'There is not a house,' as is written, 'without its dead.'[37] 4. For they first of all slew with their own hands the greatest and best portion of the people when they persecuted the holy ones; another part was snatched away by civil war; and the part which remained is now being consumed by the pestilence. But as for us, we have not suspended our festivity even when we were being killed in the persecutions, nor can our celebration ever be hindered when we are ordered to rejoice in tribulation.[38] No place, therefore, which was chosen by the tyrants for our punishment, whether it was a field, a desert, islands, or prison, could hinder our celebration. And the happiest celebration of all was had by the blessed martyrs, who held the Paschal feast in heaven with the holy angels. 5. After this our persecutors turned their hands and weapons against themselves, but not even with this was our feast disturbed. 6. There followed this pestilential disease and fearsome plague, but its terror weighed far more heavily upon those whose expectations about the future offered no relief. We took all this as a kind of training in virtue and as proofs of faith. For even though the illness struck the pagans more frequently and heavily than it did ours, it still did not spare ours completely."

7. And shortly afterwards he adds:

"For many of our brothers perished due to their exceeding charity, when they never left off visiting the sick, and doing so with no hesitation, not only visiting them but ministering to them and carrying out the services which the Lord commanded;

36. "which ... each year": Rufinus adds. After Valerian's capture by the Persians, Alexandria, which housed an imperial mint, was violently divided between the supporters of Gallienus and those of Macrianus and his sons, the prefect himself supporting the latter. More on this at 7.32.7–11.

37. Ex 12.30.

38. 2 Cor 7.4; 8.2; 1 Thes 1.6.

and so, as the contagion spread, they died along with those to whom they had wanted to minister; drawn by the sentiment of love and desirous of sharing the sufferings of those who suffered, they were not slow to transfer the deaths of others to themselves, and became their *peripsēma*,[39] as the Apostle says. 8. A great number, finally, of outstanding and chosen men among ours, among whom were not a few presbyters and deacons and many others of the people, joined themselves to the deaths of this sort out of compassion for the sick with a most courageous and ardent faith, as though the time of martyrdom were at hand, presuming that they would achieve a martyrdom of compassion thereby. 9. And while they devoted themselves to caring for the sick, carrying out the dead, and burying the bodies, they came close to following those whom they had borne to their graves on their own shoulders. 10. The pagans, by contrast, abandoned their own as soon as they fell ill, parents their dear children, husbands their wives, children their parents likewise: as soon as they saw them begin to shake and their faces grow pale with sickness, they drove them from the house, pitched them into the streets half-dead, and left their corpses there unburied, doubling their risk of catching the disease which they had thought to escape thereby, since the stench of the unburied corpses was added to the ferocity of the pestilence."

12.[40] Dionysius says of Gallienus's time that while he was in power God's churches enjoyed lasting peace 7.23.2. and that during the middle of that time Macrianus suddenly dimmed the light of his reign like a thick black cloud. When that was once again dispelled, like a cloud in summer, Gallienus, as he says, shed new light from the past upon the whole world, for he ended both the reign and the life of the cruel tyrant. 4. He also says that he was writing this in the ninth year of Gallienus's reign.

7.24.1. There are also a great many other short works of Dionysius which are quite indispensable and admirable and which

39. "offscouring" (1 Cor 4.13).

40. Rufinus omits 7.22.11 (on Dionysius's letters), 7.23.1 (on Macrianus's betrayal of Valerian), and 7.23.3 (a rhetorical flourish). On Macrianus's fate, cf. note 14 above. In 7.23.4, the year is 261.

are of the greatest benefit to their readers. Among them is his *Future Promises,* the occasion for which was as follows. There was a bishop in Egypt called Nepos. He took a Jewish view of the future promises and taught that they would be fulfilled physically and that the saints would reign with Christ on this earth for a thousand years amid bodily enjoyments, 2. and he tried to prove this doctrine of his from texts from the Revelation of John, concerning which he also published works offering interpretations of this sort.[41] 3. Dionysius therefore wrote to Nepos about the promises, confuting his statement of his position, and right in the first book he explains his view about the divine promises. In the second volume, where he treats of the Revelation of John, he mentions Nepos in these words:

4. "And they produce certain treatises of Nepos upon which they rely heavily and through which they think it can be shown by some indescribable mystery[42] in what manner Christ's kingdom will be upon earth. Now there are many other reasons why I too love and embrace Nepos, whether for his faith or for his learning and enthusiasm for the scriptures, and especially for his skill in psalmody, since many of the brothers are glad to associate with him on this account. I too therefore have a deep respect for him, and all the more so since he has already gone ahead to the Lord. But in fact the truth is to be loved and preferred above all else. If something is rightly said, it should be praised and embraced ungrudgingly, while if something is written that is not so sound, it should be scrutinized and evaluated. 5. And if the person under discussion is present, an oral scrutiny of what seems not so well expressed will suffice, since the questions followed by the answers will bring into agreement what seemed opposed and incompatible. But when writings have been published which are, as some think, rather persuasive, and where teachers have appeared who consider the law and the prophets worthless, who do not follow the gospels, who

41. Cf. Rv 20.4–6. On the controversy see Gerhard Maier, *Die Johannesoffenbarung und die Kirche* (Tübingen: Mohr Siebeck, 1981), 86–104. He places Nepos's death c. 250, and Dionysius's intervention between 253 and 256.

42. *ineffabili quodam sacramento* = ἀναντιρρήτως ("indisputably"). Rufinus must have read ἀρρήτως.

disdain the apostles' writings, who venerate only these books
and that doctrine as something great and as an arcane mystery, and who teach the simpler of our brethren to suppose that
there is nothing sublime or magnificent about the advent and
presence of our God and Savior Jesus Christ or about the glory
of the Resurrection and of our gathering unto him and being
made like him, as promised, but who persuade them to look for
some petty things in God's kingdom, always that which is mortal and not other than what we now see: it then seems necessary
to reply to our brother Nepos about all of this."

6. And further on he continues:

"When we were in the Arsinoite district, then, where that doctrine had by then wound its way about for a long time, so that divisions and discord had sprung up among the brethren, I called
together the presbyters and teachers who were in the churches,
and I initiated a deliberation in public, while at the same time
exhorting the brethren to bring forward without fear whatever might concern them. 7. They then presented to me Nepos's
book as the stoutest of shields and an unassailable wall. I accepted it patiently, sat with them for three continuous days from
first light until evening, and began to scrutinize each of his writings and to show whatever it was in them that was incoherent.
8. And I must say I greatly admired the patience, steadfastness,
and understanding of the brethren, because they set out what
concerned each of the issues in a logical and orderly manner,
and, after they had countered with the utmost vigor our replies
and what was true about the matter had come to light, they then
expressed their agreement nonetheless, without further argument,[43] judging that convictions once formed are not to be held
onto ever after with utter zeal and obstinacy, but that it is better
to change one's views when others have appeared which are better and more correct. Opening their hearts to God, that is, they
heard the word the proof of which came not from human per-

43. Rufinus's translation makes it seem as though all the concessions came
from Nepos's followers; the original suggests that the give-and-take was on
both sides, the section in question being controlled by a verb in the first person plural (ἐποιούμεθα), which leads a train of participles summarizing the
negotiation.

suasion or the power of eloquence but from the affirmation of the divine scriptures. 9. And the proof offered for our position was so clear that Coracion, the one among them who was considered their greatest teacher, leading a life of surpassing merit, stood up in their midst, and in the hearing of everyone announced and declared that no one should mention his teaching any more;[44] the mistake that had been made was enough. Furthermore [he said], not only should none of those [doctrines] be held or followed, but there should not even be any mention of such things, since what the divine scriptures had asserted was so clearly and evidently opposed to them. And all of the other brothers,[45] their hearts filled with joy and happiness at his amendment, could not thank the Lord enough."

7.25.1. And further on, when he comes to the Apocalypse of John, he writes as follows about it:[46]

"Some of those before us thought that this book should be denied any place whatever in the canon of scripture and be rejected; they criticized it chapter by chapter and said that the title of the book was not the true one, 2. but that John's name had simply been put upon a writing not his. Hence [they said] the book could be viewed neither as John's nor as a revelation, being covered as it was by a thick veil of ignorance. They added that there was nothing in it that could be considered worthy of apostolic authority, and they said that the writing was not even by any of the men belonging to the church; it was Cerinthus, the founder of the Cerinthian heresy, who had affixed John's title to a book he himself had written from a desire to establish the authority of his doctrine by giving it the reputation of the apostle's name. 3. 'For this is what Cerinthus's doctrine affirms,' they said, 'that Christ's future kingdom will be earthly, and since he was said to be himself a great lover of the flesh and its lusts, he thought that what should be provided to the

44. What Dionysius says in the original is that Coracion said that he would no longer adhere to or mention the doctrine.

45. Dionysius: "some of the brethren."

46. On Eusebius's presentation of Dionysius's views on Revelation, cf. Maier (note 41 above), 96–104. On the interpretation of Revelation in the early church, see Maier, 1–171.

saints in the promises of the future kingdom was what his own
spirit craved: that the activities of the belly and of sensual pleasure would continue, and there would be plenty of food and
abundance of drink, weddings, and all the other things that go
with them. He also expected a revival of the festivals and Jewish
sacrifices and the victims prescribed by the law.'⁴⁷

4. "As far as I am concerned, though, I would not even dare
to disdain or reject the text of this book, especially since many
of the brethren feel as I do. My judgment about it is rather that
what is written in it exceeds and surpasses the range of human
hearing, and that there is a meaning in it which is secret and
concealed and to be admired by everyone, one which I myself
admire and revere, even if I do not understand it. 5. And I
think this because some divine mysteries are veiled in human
speech, ones which I rather believe in faith than perceive by
judgment, and therefore I do not reject what I do not understand; I admire them the more the less I can grasp them."

6. After this he discusses the text of the work as a whole,
examines each of its sections, and shows clearly that it is quite
impossible that an interpretation of it can be derived if it is tak-
en literally, and then adds:

"When the prophecy as a whole is finished, the prophet calls
blessed those who keep these things. And he also calls himself
blessed, for he says, 'Blessed are those who keep the word of
prophecy of this book, and I, John, who see and hear these
things.'⁴⁸ 7. I do not therefore deny that he is called John and
that this writing is John's. For it is from some saint and without
any doubt written through God's spirit, even if he is not the
apostle John, the son of Zebedee and brother of James, the one
from whom comes the gospel which is inscribed 'According to
John' and the Catholic Epistle."

8. Dionysius therefore repeatedly asserts that it cannot be
doubted that the Revelation is divinely inspired and is John's,
but that it is not apparent to him that this is the John who wrote
the gospel, because this latter nowhere mentions his name or
indicates specifically who he is, 9–11. while the one who wrote

47. Compare 3.28.2–5.
48. Rv 22.7–8.

the Apocalypse mentions his name about three times. 14, 16. He also, after distinguishing between the very styles of writing, says that it was possible that in those times there was another John, one of the saints, to whom God revealed these things.[49]

7.26. There are many other works dealing with ecclesiastical topics which the blessed Dionysius left us in the form of books; anyone of scholarly interests would benefit greatly from reading them. But let us now return to our narrative.

7.27.1. Xystus, after he had administered the priesthood of the Roman church for eleven years,[50] was succeeded by Dionysius, and when Demetrian passed away in Antioch, Paul of Samosata received the priesthood. 2. Paul's view of Christ was so low and unworthy that he perverted the tradition of church teaching, saying that he was merely a human being of ordinary nature. Then Dionysius of Alexandria, when asked to come to a council and prevented from doing so by bodily frailty, represented himself by a letter in which he explained the kind of faith he had in Christ and the veneration in which he held him. But the other shepherds of the churches assembled in Antioch from various places and cities as though against a robber lying in wait for Christ's flocks.

7.28.1. Outstanding among them and surpassing the others were Firmilian from Caesarea in Cappadocia, the brothers Gregory and Athenodore, priests from the province of Pontus, Helenus, bishop of the church of Sardis,[51] Nicomas from Iconium, the outstanding priest Hymenaeus from Jerusalem, and Theotecnus of the neighboring city of Caesarea. Maximus, bishop of Bostra, joined them as well, a worthy associate, and many others too numerous to list individually. There were also a great many presbyters and deacons who came together in the city just mentioned in order to check or rather to destroy this new doctrine. 2. All of these then met together quite often, placed Paul of Samosata before them, and in exposing his

49. The sections omitted by Rufinus in 7.25.9–11 and 7.25.15–27 compare the wording of the Gospel and First Letter of John with that of Revelation.

50. Xystus (Sixtus II) was in office eleven months, not years (August or September of 257 to August of 258).

51. "Tarsus" in Eusebius. Gregory and Athenodore: 6.30 and 7.14.

heresy in repeated discussions and unremitting debates, a heresy he tried sometimes to conceal and sometimes to disguise, strove to prove and publicize its blasphemy. Nor were they able to achieve this in only one or two sessions; they met often and as often broke up without having gotten anywhere.[52]

Now since our history has mentioned the blessed Gregory, I think it most fitting to insert in our narrative as a record for posterity the deeds of this great man, which are spoken of by everyone in the lands of the northeast but which for some reason were passed over. There was a lake in Pontus abounding in fish, the capture of which provided its owners an exceedingly rich income.[53] This property had been inherited by two broth-

52. "Nor were ... anywhere": Rufinus adds. And then, before resuming his translation of Eusebius's account of Paul of Samosata, he inserts some stories about the most famous member of the first council that met to oppose him (in 264), Gregory Thaumaturgus. The stories (in Schwartz/Mommsen 953–956) are not a casual aside, but an important part (he thinks) of his account of the council. Councils, in his view (and in that of his contemporaries), reach sound decisions if they are guided by the Spirit, whose gifts he by no means regards as bestowed in equal measure upon all people, contrary perhaps to what is assumed by those of more democratic sympathies. Rufinus and his contemporaries would have been astonished at the assumption that all Christians are endowed equally with the gift of holiness; they had fresh in their minds the stories in the martyrdoms of the very different responses given by their core-ligionists to the demands of the pagan persecutors that they renounce Christ. It is his view, then, that a council may be certified as orthodox if its leading members are manifestly holy. The holiness need not always be shown through miracles (none are told of Athanasius), but holiness and orthodoxy will always go hand in hand, he assumes. The assumption will be richly illustrated in his account of the Council of Nicaea.

Gregory Thaumaturgus was born 210–215 and died 270–275. On the ancient stories told of him, cf. Stephen Mitchell, "The Life and *Lives* of Gregory Thaumaturgus," in *Portraits of Spiritual Authority: Religious Power in Early Christianity, Byzantium, and the Christian Orient*, ed. Jan Willem Drijvers and John W. Watt (Leiden: Brill, 1999), 99–138, and Benedetto Clausi, "L'altro Gregorio: Intorno alla tradizione agiografica latina sul Taumaturgo," in *Il giusto che fiorisce come palma: Gregorio il Taumaturgo fra storia e agiografia: Atti del Convegno di Staletti (CZ) 9–10 novembre 2002*, ed. Benedetto Clausi e Vincenza Milazzo (Rome: Institutum Patristicum Augustinianum, 2007), 185–223, esp. 195–208.

53. This story is also told by Gregory of Nyssa, although Rufinus's version of it seems independent; cf. Gunther Heil, "De vita Gregorii Thaumaturgi," in *Gregorii Nysseni Sermones, Pars II*, ed. Friedhelm Mann, *Gregorii Nysseni Opera* 10.1 (Leiden: Brill, 1990), 3–57.

ers. But the desire for money, which almost always conquers the hearts of mortals, spoiled their fraternal kinship as well. When the time came to take possession, the brothers met not so much to get fish as to get the better of others, and there followed battles and slaughter and a profusion of human blood rather than of fish. But by God's providence Gregory eventually arrived to offer his assistance. He saw the men fighting and dying and the brothers in a rage, and when he asked the reason for the brothers' deadly fury against each other and their own people, he found that it had simply to do with the catching of fish. Then when the two sides had quieted down a little out of respect for his arrival, he said, "My sons, do not do violence to your rational souls for the sake of irrational animals, nor destroy your brotherly peace from the desire for gain, nor flout God's laws and the rights of nature to boot, but come along with me to the shore of this deadly lake. I will now release you through the Lord's power from all the conflict of this bloody contention." And when he had said this he fixed the staff he held in his hand by the edge of the water on the shore, while everyone was looking on, and he himself knelt down, raised his hands to heaven, and implored God on high as follows: "Lord God of our fathers, when the first man Adam sinned against you and transgressed your command, you moderated the penalty for his fault and diverted to the earth the sentence bearing the curse when you said, 'Cursed [be] the earth in your works.'[54] Take pity now on the blood of these young brothers which is in peril, and order that these waters be accursed in their production of those things for whose sake they forgot their brotherly ties in their rage, so that fish may never appear in this place nor water be left, but it may be a field arable and fertile in crops, and continue forever as a guardian of brotherly concord." No sooner had he finished the prayer than the water, ordered to depart, receded, withdrew rapidly from the sight of those above, returned to its abysses, and left a dry field for the brothers, who were now at peace with each other. And it is said that the land even today teems with crops where once it teemed with ships.

54. Gn 3.17.

There is another deed told of him which is even more famous and more divinely done. There was a narrow plot of land
in the country where a church needed to be built, but a cliff jut-
ting from the nearby mountain to the east and a river flowing
by on the other side did not leave enough room for the church.
And when there was no other place at all, and everyone was
unhappy that they did not have any land on which to build a
church, he is said to have spent the night in prayer, full of faith,
and to have reminded the Lord Jesus persistently of his promise, which was, "If you have faith like a mustard seed and you
say to this mountain, 'Pick yourself up and put yourself into the
sea,' it will certainly happen."[55] He said this with complete faith
and devotion, and when the people came together at first light,
the troublesome cliff was found to have drawn back far enough
to leave room to build the church.

A great many other things are told of him as well, but so as
not to lengthen the narrative excessively, I will pass over the rest
and add just one more of his deeds.[56] He is said to have been
traveling once through the mountain heights during the winter, and when he reached the summit of the pass everything was
covered in snow and there was no inn anywhere, only a temple
of Apollo, to which he made his way, spent the night, and left.
Now that temple had a priest whose custom it was to consult
Apollo's idol and to deliver the replies to those requesting them,
from which, it seems, he made a living for himself. After Gregory left, then, the priest went as usual to present requests for
answers and ask for replies, but no answers came. He repeated
the sacrifices, but the silence persisted. He multiplied his acts
of propitiation, but his words fell upon deaf ears. And while the
priest was dumbfounded at this unfamiliar silence, the demon
came to him in the night and said to him in a dream, "Why do
you call me there where I can no longer come?" And when he
asked why, he said that he had been driven out by Gregory's arrival. When he asked what now could be done about it, he said
he could only be allowed to enter that place if Gregory permit-

55. Mt 17.20; 21.21. The story of Gregory moving a boulder is in Heil (note
53 above), 23.
56. Cf. Heil, 20–23.

ted. When he heard this, the priest took to the road, thinking long and hard and debating reluctantly with himself. Having reached Gregory, he addressed him, explained the matter from the beginning, reminded him of his kindness and hospitality, presented the banished deity's complaint, lamented the loss of his livelihood, and asked that everything be restored to him as it had been initially. The other without delay wrote the following letter: "Gregory to Apollo. I permit you to return to your place and to do as you have been accustomed." The priest took the letter and brought it to the temple, and when it had been placed by the idol, the demon came and gave replies when requested. Then he thought to himself, "If Gregory commanded and that god departed and was unable to return unless ordered, and was again restored at Gregory's command, Gregory is obviously far superior to the one who obeys his orders." Closing the temple doors, then, he went down to Gregory, bringing back with him the letter he had received, explained all that had happened at his place, and at the same time fell at his feet, asking that he might offer himself to the God by whose power Gregory could command the gods of the pagans. And when he showed himself assiduous and persistent, he was made a catechumen by him. He gave himself over to a most chaste and abstinent life, abandoning not only all the errors of the demons but worldly activities as well, and so was also granted baptism. And he made such progress in his manner of life and virtue of faith that he himself succeeded Gregory as bishop.

[Gregory] also left us magnificent testimonies to his abilities in short form. He wrote a most excellent paraphrase of Ecclesiastes, and left an explanation of the Catholic faith in summary form which I think it convenient to add here for the edification of the churches:[57]

"The creed of Gregory, martyr and bishop of Neocaesarea.

57. The Greek form of this creed is in Heil, 17–19 (the apparatus compares it to Rufinus's version). Luise Abramowski, "Das Bekenntnis des Gregor Thaumaturgus bei Gregor von Nyssa und das Problem seiner Echtheit," *ZKG* 87 (1976): 145–66, holds that it was composed by Gregory of Nyssa to update the Christians of his region theologically after the Council of Constantinople of 381.

One God, the Father of the living word, of the subsistent wisdom and of his power and likeness, the perfect parent of the perfect, the Father of the only-begotten Son. One sole God from sole God, likeness and image of the godhead, word achieving and wisdom embracing everything, and power by which all creation could come to be, true Son of the true One, invisible from the invisible, incorruptible from the incorruptible, immortal from the immortal, and eternal from the eternal. One Holy Spirit who has substance from God and who appeared through the Son, image of the perfect Son, perfect cause of the living, holiness providing sanctification, through whom God is known as above all and in all, and the Son as through everyone. The Trinity perfect in majesty, eternity, and dominion is in no way divided or separated. There is therefore in the Trinity nothing made or subordinate or introduced later, as though not subsisting beforehand and entering later. Neither therefore was the Son ever lacking to the Father nor the Holy Spirit to the Son, but the same Trinity is always unalterable and unchangeable."

That should suffice for Gregory. Now let us return to our story. Dionysius rested in peace in Alexandria meanwhile, in the twelfth year of the reign of Gallienus, having served in the priesthood for seventeen years. He was succeeded by Maximus. Gallienus therefore, when he had ruled the Roman empire for fifteen years, died and was succeeded by Claudius. He in turn left the sovereignty to Aurelian after only two years in power.[58]

7.29.1. During this time the final council of bishops met in Antioch at which Paul was accused and clearly convicted of heresy and condemned by all the churches of Christ on earth. 2. It was Malchion, presbyter of the church of Antioch, who pressed the issue the hardest and pursued it with the most powerful arguments. A man of the deepest faith and adorned with every virtue, he was also most eloquent, powerful in speech, and deeply learned in every field; he had even taught rhetoric in that very city. To him, therefore, the whole council of bishops entrusted the debate with Paul, with stenographers taking it down. It was conducted by him so magnificently and meticulously that it was published in writing and is even now held in

---

58. Gallienus died in August of 268. Aurelian succeeded, 270–275.

admiration by everyone.[59] For he alone was able to expose Paul by his own admissions when he was disguising and concealing himself.

7.30.1. When this had thus been done, all the priests together agreed to write a letter addressed to Dionysius of Rome and to Maximus, the bishop of Alexandria, which was sent through all the churches and through which they proved how diligent they had been and announced to everyone that Paul's heresy had been confuted and rejected. At the same time they indicated the issues which had been treated with him and also described his dissolute life as well as his conduct. We have thought it right to include here a few passages.

2. "To Dionysius and Maximus and all the priests and bishops throughout the earth, together with the presbyters and deacons and the whole Catholic Church which is under heaven, Helenus and Hymenaeus, Theophilus, Theotecnus, Maximus, Proculus, Nicomas, Aelian, Paul, Bolasus,[60] Protogenes, Hierax, Eutychius, Theodore, Malchion, Lucius presbyters,[61] and

59. The surviving remnants of the debate were published by Henri de Riedmatten, *Les actes du procès de Paul de Samosate: Étude sur la christologie du IIIe au IVe siècle* (Fribourg en Suisse: Éditions St-Paul, 1952). Their authenticity has been debated since then by some of the most renowned students of the period, with the tide of opinion now flowing toward acceptance. A comprehensive review is offered by Lorenzo Perrone, "L'enigma di Paolo di Samosata. Dogma, chiesa e società nella Siria del III secolo: prospettive di un ventennio di studi," *Cristianesimo nella storia* 13.2 (1992): 253–327. Even with the vindication of de Riedmatten's edition, the assessment of Paul's theology, which appears to include a form of Adoptionist Christology, remains a challenge. Two recent studies are that of U. M. Lang, "The Christological Controversy at the Synod of Antioch in 268/9," *JTS* NS 51 (2000): 54–80, and the magistral survey by Patricio de Navascués, *Pablo de Samosata y sus adversarios: Estudio histórico-teológico del cristianismo antioqueno en el s.III* (Rome: Institutum Patristicum Augustinianum, 2004).

60. "Bolanus" in Eusebius.

61. Rufinus adds "presbyters." The council met in the winter of 268/69, while Antioch was under the control of Palmyra, whose rulers acted first as defenders of, and then rivals to, Roman sovereignty in the east after Valerian's capture and the death of Macrianus and his sons (see note 14). After the death of the emperor Claudius in 270, the Palmyrene queen Zenobia expanded her rule into Egypt and Asia Minor, but was defeated and captured by Aurelian in 272; Antioch fell to him early that year.

all the other bishops, presbyters, and deacons gathered with us from the neighboring cities and provinces, greetings in the Lord to our dearest brethren."

3. And shortly after they add:

"In sending this letter all of us beseech you to care for anyone who may have been infected by this sort of doctrine, just as the men of happy memory Dionysius of Alexandria and Firmilian from Cappadocia wrote previously to the people of Antioch, disdaining to, or rather refraining from, addressing a letter to him who was the author of error. 4. Firmilian himself of happy memory, however, while he was still alive, came twice and criticized and censured him in person, as all of us know and attest who came with him. But when he promised to correct his error, he believed him, hoping that the situation might improve without our religion being tainted by scandal or the disgrace of dissension, and therefore he took no action, Paul meanwhile putting him off guilefully and deceiving man while denying God and violating the faith in which he had been reborn. 5. And when the blessed Firmilian was now finally on his way to Antioch, and had gotten as far as Tarsus, and all of us in Antioch were awaiting his arrival, we were told that he had departed from the world."

6. And further on in describing his life and conduct they add:

"After he has turned from the rule of doctrine to foreign and spurious teachings, it is not necessary to list his prior activities, 7. how it is that while he was formerly needy and extremely poor, and had nothing from his parental estate or any opportunity for a respectable livelihood, he has now become supremely wealthy, and from no other source than his sacrilegious acts and the thefts he has achieved through fraud: he has intimidated the brethren, sold his patronage, and then even after accepting payment failed to carry out his obligations in the affairs he had assumed, reckoning that piety is gain, as it is written.[62] 8. And who could put up with his pride, seeing that

---

62. 1 Tm 6.5. *Ducenarius* just below was properly a salary-grade title applied to procurators, although by this time it could be used honorifically. Fergus Millar, "Paul of Samosata, Zenobia and Aurelian: The Church, Local Culture and Political Allegiance in Third-Century Syria," *JRS* 61 (1971): 13, interprets

he has preferred to appear as a *ducenarius* rather than a bishop. For that is the sort of ostentation with which he has paced through the street, reading over letters openly and dictating them in the sight and hearing of everyone while stenographers attended him in the street. The number of those in file ahead of him and of the mass following him has been so great that everyone who has seen it has shuddered and loathed the divine religion on account of his haughtiness. Such has been his behavior in public. 9. In church he has ordered a dais to be built for him much higher than it had been, the throne to be put in a loftier place, and an audience-chamber to be prepared and furnished, in the manner of the civil magistrates. In speaking to the people he has gestured extravagantly with his right hand, beat his thigh with his palm, bounced up and down on his feet, and struck his footstool noisily. From his listeners he has expected not only approval and applause, but the waving of handkerchiefs to him as in a theater and shouts as though from spectators. This has been expected not only from the men, but even unbecomingly from the women. Any of the listeners who have behaved more respectably and respectfully and kept from making excessive noise have been mocked as though they themselves had behaved insultingly. He has mocked the expositors, both those aged and those already dead, and while detracting from them has boasted of himself shamelessly and impudently, and longed to be praised as an orator rather than as a church teacher. 10. He has put an end to the psalms addressed to Our Lord Jesus Christ as recent innovations, while

the passage as a criticism of Paul's imitation of the manners of high officials. Frederick W. Norris, "Paul of Samosata: *Procurator Ducenarius*," *JTS* NS 35 (1984): 50–70, by contrast, thinks that Paul's ability to enrich himself, as the letter notes, suggests that he actually occupied a high financial office in the civil government.

The reliability of the letter's description of Paul's manners, however, has been called into question by Virginia Burrus, "Rhetorical Stereotypes in the Portrait of Paul of Samosata," *Vigiliae Christianae* 43 (1989): 215–25. She shows how closely it resembles in its many details the lampoon of the charlatan rhetorician by Lucian of Samosata (*Rhetorum Praeceptor*). The suspicion must arise therefore that the portrait of Paul offered by the letter (including its remarks on his relationship with women) is rather a verbal cartoon than a true-to-life picture.

having women sing those composed to himself on the days of
the Paschal feast in the middle of the church, especially those
whom he himself had formerly trained to sing as usual, so that
one shuddered to hear it. 11. For while he himself has denied
that God's Son had come down from heaven, but [maintained
that] he had begun from Mary and had been from the earth at
his outset,[63] the psalms which have been recited to him and by
which he was praised among the people, have spoken of him
as an angel come down from the heavens. And when he has
been present and heard them, not only has he not forbidden
them to be said, but enjoyed listening to them with pompous
demeanor. 12. And what need be said about the women who
have stayed together with him and whom the Antiochenes call
synisactae?[64] So that no question might be raised about him
from their company and cohabitation, he has given his presbyters and deacons as well, those at least who have gratified his
wishes, similar permission to have women living with them. He
even allows them to accumulate wealth, that they may be in
no position to fasten upon their teacher a crime of which they
themselves are chargeable.

"The reason we write these things, beloved brethren, 13. is
that we know how sacred the episcopal priesthood should be,
which is supposed to be a model for the clergy and the people.
For neither are we unaware that some men have fallen when
they have been careless in bringing in young women to live
with them. And even if this does not happen, it is still quite
serious for a priest to be suspected of the like. 14. But how can
he forbid the company of women to those who are weaker when
his own behavior countenances it? 15. He has become so great
and merciless in his power, however, and such a tyrant in his
arrogance, that no one dares even to come forward to charge
or accuse him. 16. But what we have spoken of might be condemned even in someone who keeps to the Catholic faith and

63. *a Maria coepisse et initium habuisse de terra* = Ἰησοῦν Χριστὸν κάτωθεν ("Jesus Christ is from below").

64. Lampe, *Patristic Greek Lexicon*, 1317, defines συνείσακτοι as "virgin companions of a celibate man," and notes that this is the first extant mention of
the word.

perseveres in the truth of church doctrine. This man, though, who has repudiated the mystery of faith and gone over to that most defiled heresy of Artemas[65] (for we had to name the father of his error too): what view is one to take of him or how is he to be cursed?"

17. And much later[66] at the end of the letter they add:

"It has therefore been decided that it is necessary to reject and repudiate this man who resists God and does not acquiesce in the true faith, and to appoint another provided by God's grace to take his place as bishop of the Catholic Church: Domnus, a man adorned with every good thing, the son of Demetrian of happy memory who presided over this very church. We have told you about him that you may realize that you must write to him and accept letters of communion from him. But as for this other man who has been judged unworthy to be in the Catholic Church, he may write to Artemas, and the followers of his heresy may communicate with him."

18. Paul, then, was sundered from the priesthood and communion, Domnus having replaced him as bishop, 19. but he refused to leave the church building, so the emperor Aurelian was appealed to. He issued a quite religious and holy ruling, ordering the church building to be turned over to those to whom the priests of Italy and the Roman bishop[67] should write. And thus Paul added to his other ills the shame of being driven from the

65. "Artemon" in 5.28.1.

66. *post multa* added by Rufinus.

67. *Italiae sacerdotes et Romanus episcopus* = οἱ κατὰ τὴν Ἰταλίαν καὶ τὴν Ῥωμαίων πόλιν ἐπίσκοποι τοῦ δόγματος ("the bishops of the religion in Italy and in the city of Rome"). Millar (note 62 above), p. 15, compares the appeal to Aurelian to the request made to Gallienus by the Egyptian bishops for the recovery of Christian cemeteries (in Eusebius, 7.13, omitted by Rufinus). Gallienus's granting of the request (in the cessation of persecution of the Christians: see note 33 above) would have encouraged the council to proceed to this step.

The request may have been sent in 269, addressed to Claudius, and answered by Aurelian after the other's death in 270. His rescript probably copied the wording of the request, as was customary. It may also reflect the support given to the council's delegation from Antioch by the Italian bishops. And there remains the possibility that it was meant as a sign of support for the pro-Roman sector within the Antiochene church during the Palmyrene ascendancy (cf. Millar, 15).

church by the civil authorities. 20. This in fact was the way Aurelian behaved toward us then, but with the passage of time he began to change his good intentions and, corrupted by bad advice, to plan a persecution against God's churches. 21. He had proceeded so far that, it is said, the letters and documents had already been dictated and only wanted the subscription when God's right hand intervened, thrusting aside that wicked right hand and its subscription.[68] For he was condemned to a sudden death, he who was decreeing the death of the pious, so that God might show that it is not when a tyrant wishes it that we are tortured; it is when he himself approves that we are corrected. 22. Aurelian, then, when he had reigned for six years, was succeeded by Probus, who in turn, after he had been in power for the same length of time, was succeeded by Carus together with his sons Carinus and Numerian. And after they in turn had governed the Roman empire for not more than three years,[69] Diocletian received the sovereignty. He for his part set in motion the severest persecution of our people and destruction of the churches.[70] 23. But shortly before he came to power, Dionysius passed away in Rome after nine years in the priesthood, and Felix received the see.

7.31.1. It was at this time that one Mani, who, as his name suggests, was a maniac driven by demonic impulse, was teaching an odious heresy detestable to everyone. Mani was of Persian stock, in life and manners a barbarian, and so potent in character that he seemed insane or filled with a demon; and that in fact was made evident by the way things turned out. Sometimes he tried to show that he was behaving like Christ, at other times he announced that he was the Paraclete, and, quite beside himself in his madness, he chose twelve disciples after Christ's example and sent them to preach, disseminating idiotic and impious doctrines borrowed from various heretics who had already passed away 2. and offering our world Persian poi-

68. Cf. Lactantius, *DMP* 6.1–2; Constantine, *Oratio ad sanctos* 24.
69. Eusebius: "not even three years in all." Probus: 276–282. Carus, Carinus, and Numerian: 282–285.
70. After "Diocletian" Rufinus omits "and those brought in after him." "Under them," says Eusebius, the persecution took place "in our time."

son to drink.[71] Such is the basis of the Manichean heresy which has spread up to the present day, having begun in the time that Felix presided over the church in Rome. 7.32.1. He served in the priesthood for five years and left the see to Eutychian, who in turn handed on the episcopacy to Gaius after only ten months. Gaius, our contemporary, exercised the priesthood for fifteen years and was succeeded by Marcellinus, who lived to the time of persecution.

2. It was at this time that Timaeus had received the priesthood at Antioch after Domnus, and Cyril after Timaeus. Cyril in turn was succeeded by Dorotheus,[72] who lived on into our own time: a deeply learned man quite interested in the sacred scriptures who was so assiduous that he even learned Hebrew. He had also received a Greek liberal education from the time he was a child. 3. He was a eunuch from birth. Even the emperor held him in high regard as a result and conferred on him the honor of supervising the purple dye-works. 4. We were among his listeners in our boyhood[73] when he expounded the scriptures in church. Tyrannus received the priesthood in Antioch after him; in Tyrannus's time the persecution of the churches increased. 5. In Laodicea Eusebius, who was from Alexandria, became bishop after Socrates. When Eusebius had come to Syria in the affair of Paul of Samosata, he was not allowed to leave again for anywhere else, as Dionysius writes in his letters,[74] because he was so learned in the divine scriptures that the scholarly brethren found him to be a veritable treasure-trove. 6. He in turn was succeeded, one good man after another, as they say, by Anatolius, who was himself from Alexandria and had

71. "Poison" (from the Persians) is the very word Diocletian uses in his order for the extirpation of Manicheanism in 302; cf. *Fontes iuris Romani anteiustiniani* ii.581 (XV.III.4).

Mani (216–275) founded a radically dualistic system of the opposition of light and darkness which spread rapidly inside and outside the Roman empire with a missionary zeal that upset other religions besides Christianity.

72. Eusebius says that Cyril was succeeded by Tyrannus (see 7.32.4). Dorotheus, he says, was a presbyter of Antioch in Cyril's time. Rufinus may have misread Κύριλλος· καθ' ὃν Δωρόθεον ... ἔγνωμεν as μεθ' ὅν.

73. *in pueritia* added by Rufinus.

74. 7.11.24, 26.

been marvelously well educated from boyhood in the liberal arts and philosophy, so much so that he was pressed by all the educated men and philosophers to teach logic[75] in Alexandria. 7. He also gave great assistance to the citizens with his advice and material supplies, they say, at the time of the battle which took place among the citizens of Alexandria. I will mention just one example for the sake of brevity. 8. When the besieged lacked grain, they say, and hunger was pressing more heavily than the enemy, there was a third part of the people which was separate from the two parties attacking each other, since it was loyal to the Romans. It was in this group that Anatolius was then, apart from the fighting. He reported to the commander, informed him of the dire hunger in which the besieged found themselves, 9. obtained a concession from him for the citizens, and arranged its presentation in the following way.[76] He first addressed the two parties at odds with each other and urged them to come to terms with the Romans. But when he saw their unwillingness, he said, "There is at least one thing I believe you will willingly agree to: that any of your company unfit for combat, that has no share with you in the combat but only, of necessity, in the food, you allow to leave through the gates." 11. The proposal was gladly accepted by both parties. They decreed that the noncombatants should leave the camp. Almost all of

75. Eusebius: "to establish the school of Aristotelian philosophy."

76. Eusebius has returned to the situation in Alexandria after Valerian's capture and the hostilities between the supporters of the emperor Gallienus and those of the rebellious prefect, L. Mussius Aemilianus (cf. 7.21–22 and note 36). In Eusebius the two future bishops mentioned in 7.32.5–6 are in opposing camps; his namesake being in the one supporting Gallienus, it is he who petitions the Roman commander (Aurelius Theodotus, sent by Gallienus to put down the prefect) and then tends to the refugees.

Rufinus rewrites the original to eliminate any suspicion of conflict between the two future bishops of repute. He simply excises Eusebius from the story, transfers his activities to Anatolius, and creates for the latter the position of mediator between the two sides by setting the Christians apart from the combatants as a third party aloof from the warfare. In the original, Anatolius addresses the assembly of the anti-Gallienus camp rather than "the two parties at odds" as in the next sentence in Rufinus, and persuades it to let those unfit for combat leave; that he himself belongs to that camp is shown by his participation in the voting for his own proposal in 7.32.10. Rufinus simply omits that section.

those who were famished took advantage of this to break out along with the noncombatants, especially our people, who had been opposed to the war. Anatolius welcomed them all, tending them with both a parent's and a physician's care. And thus he hastened to save the multitude by providing them with food while inculcating in the rest of them, because few remained, a fear of war and a desire for peace. And so he freed that greatest of cities at once from hunger and war with his wise and merciful counsel. 12. Laodicea therefore received him by God's gift as the second bishop from Alexandria after the war we have just mentioned. 13. There are also many excellent short works of Anatolius which have reached us. I think it worthwhile to quote from them what he thought about the Paschal feast:[77]

14. "The beginning of the first month is, then, in the first year, that [beginning] being the start of the nineteen-year cycle; it falls on the twenty-sixth day of the month of Phamenoth according to the Egyptians, on the twenty-second day of the month of Dystros according to the Macedonians, and on the eleventh before the kalends of April according to the Romans. 15. On this day the sun is found not only to have mounted the first section; it already has the fourth day in it,[78] in the first of the twelve sections, that is. Now the first section of the twelve is the vernal equinox, and is itself the beginning of the months, the starting-point of the cycle, the completion of the course of the stars which are called *planetae,* that is "wanderers," and also the end of the twelfth section and the termination of the whole cycle. And therefore we say that those who think that the Paschal feast is to be celebrated before this start of the new year commit no slight error. 16. Nor are we the first to reckon it so; it is shown to have been accepted by the Jews of old and

77. Rufinus omits (just before the citation) "From the Easter Canons of Anatolius." On his computation cf. August Strobel, *Ursprung und Geschichte des frühchristlichen Osterkalenders* (*TU* 121, 1977), 133–35, and Karl Gerlach, *The Antenicene Pascha: A Rhetorical History* (Leuven: Peeters, 1998), 292–95.

78. *quartam iam in ea diem habere:* on heavenly bodies "possessing" certain days, cf. Firmicus Maternus, *Mathesis* 2.28. The "sections" are sections of the zodiac, elsewhere often called *signa.* In 7.32.15 Rufinus refers to a section as *pars* and *particula;* in the *Mathesis, pars* means a third or a thirtieth part of a sign (2.4.1 and 2.5).

to have been observed even before the advent of Christ, as Philo and Josephus clearly demonstrate. And even older than they
are Agathobulus and his student Aristobulus from Paneas,[79]
of whom the latter was one of the seventy elders sent by the
high priests to King Ptolemy[80] to translate the books of the Hebrews into Greek. The king had many questions for them about
Moses's tradition, to which they replied, 17. and so when they
explained the questions concerning the Exodus, they said that
the Passover was not to be sacrificed before the vernal equinox
had passed. Aristobulus in fact adds that on the day of Passover
one should take care not only that the sun is crossing over the
vernal equinox, but the moon as well. 18. For since, he says,
there are two equinoxes, of spring and of autumn, separated
by equal intervals, and the feast day has been set as the fourteenth of the first month once evening begins, when the moon
is observed to be directly opposite the sun, as can be verified
even by the eyes, it is obvious that the sun occupies the vernal
equinox, and the moon, by contrast, the autumnal. 19. I have
also read much else in their books which was set out with the
soundest possible arguments and which show clearly that the
Paschal feast is to be calculated at all events after the equinox."

20. Anatolius has left many other writings as well which must
be admired not only by religious men but by philosophers too;
his wholesome learning may be seen in them by those who wish
to know of it. 21. Theotecnus, who held the priesthood in Caesarea, was the first to lay hands on him for the episcopacy, ap-

79. *Aristobulus ex Paneada* = Ἀριστοβούλου τοῦ πάνυ ("Aristobulus the Great").
Rufinus omits "Musaeus" after Philo and Josephus, and one of the two Agathob-
uli, the teachers of Aristobulus. On this passage see Sabrina Inowlocki, "Trois
auteurs juifs de langue grecque oubliés: Mousaios et les deux Agathobule dans
le témoignage d'Anatole de Laodicée sur la Pâque," *Revue des études juives* 165,
3–4 (2006): 383–96.
80. "sent by the high priests" added by Rufinus. Anatolius gives the king
as "Ptolemy Philadelphus and his father," but the king to whom Aristobulus
dedicated the work referred to in 7.32.17–18 has been identified as Ptolemy
VI Philometor. On Aristobulus (180–145 BCE) see Schürer, 3.579–87. On the
Passover date in this extract from Anatolius, see Schürer, 1.593–94 (note 18
in Schürer for the reference in Philo and Josephus above), and Gerlach (note
77 above), 292–95. On the equinox and the Paschal computation: Gerlach,
275–317.

pointing him successor to his own chair while he himself was still alive. Hence he governed the church of Caesarea together with Theotecnus himself for a time. But when the council was summoned to Antioch against Paul of Samosata, the church of Laodicea claimed Anatolius as its bishop by force as he was passing by, Eusebius having died. 22. After him the last to govern the church in Laodicea before the persecution was Stephen, who was not inferior to those before him in learning and eloquence, but was quite unlike them in faith and virtue, as the fire of persecution proved. He showed no mettle when in the toils of temptation. 23. But his weakness did not immediately show that God was at a loss. For after his fall God provided that church with a bishop named Theodotus, a man endowed not only with words, but with deeds and virtues as well. He was a physician by training, but was transferred by the Lord to the cure of souls. He really had no equal in how clearly he excelled almost all other people in faith, compassion, zeal, watchfulness, and indeed in all the very best practices. He also expended a great deal of labor on the holy scriptures.

24. In Caesarea in Palestine, meanwhile, Theotecnus, who had exercised the episcopacy most skillfully, was succeeded by Agapius. He himself expended much labor and exercised great diligence in governing the people, concerned as he was to show his fatherly care for the needy in particular. 25. It was also he who appointed Pamphilus, a man of the deepest sagacity, whose life, learning, and morals did him the greatest credit, to succeed him as presbyter of that church.[81] But who and how great Pamphilus was, and from where he came, are matters it would not be right to pass over briefly: his life as a whole, his education from childhood, the degree to which he suffered in the persecutions through his various professions, the contests he endured, and the manner in which he achieved the crown of martyrdom besides all else—we have treated this in a special work.[82] 26. It will show how wonderful he was. And there are a great many other wonderful men among the pres-

81. "It was ... church": added by Rufinus.
82. Eusebius's *Life of Pamphilus* has almost completely perished except for one extract in Jerome, *Contra Rufinum* 1.9.

byters of that time who are still remembered among us, such as Hierius[83] in Alexandria and Meletius in Pontus, who later became a bishop. 27. As for Hierius, he was of keen intelligence, exceptionally well educated in holy scripture, exceedingly pure in his life, completely and undisguisedly committed to Christian manners, an unequaled teacher of the church, and a wonderful debater in private and in public, while Meletius was of such kindness and gentleness in his habits that his companions called him "Attic honey."[84] While he was fully trained in every field of study, his ability in oratory was such that he might have been thought to have studied nothing else. 28. But his grasp of the other branches of philosophy, which they divide into five disciplines,[85] was so complete that anyone who tried him in any one of them would think that he had been trained in that one alone from childhood. However magnificent he was as a scholar, though, the virtue of his mind and the integrity of his life were considered far more magnificent in him. We came to know him more fully and completely when he fled to Palestine during the persecution.

29. In Jerusalem Zabdas received the priesthood after Hymenaeus, whom we mentioned a bit earlier,[86] and a short time later he handed on the office to Hermon, who came after him. He in turn retained the apostolic chair which he had received there until the persecution in our own time. 30. In Alexandria Theonas succeeded Maximus, who had succeeded Dionysius, after he completed eighteen years in the priesthood. In his time Achillas, a presbyter of that church noted for his learning, faith, manners, and morals, had charge of the church school. 31. Theonas, after serving in the priesthood blamelessly for nineteen years, handed over the see to Peter, a man pre-eminent among those of outstanding character. He was bishop of that city for twelve entire years. Three of them were before the persecution,

83. Eusebius: "And there are those rarest of men in our own time that we have known, Pierius …" On Pierius cf. Jerome, *Vir. illustr.* 76; Photius, Cod. 118.

84. *mel* = μέλι ("honey").

85. "which … disciplines" added by Rufinus. He probably means ethics, logic, physics, mathematics, and theology. See P. Hadot, "Les divisions des parties de la philosophie dans l'Antiquité," *Museum Helveticum* 36 (1979): 201–23.

86. In 7.14.

while during the remaining nine he underwent various trials. When he found himself continually subjected to every sort of contest in the persecutions, he bound himself with the tighter fetters of continence, concentrated admirably on God's word for the benefit and instruction of the church, labored day and night with unremitting vigilance in exercising his full responsibility as a priest, and so merited the crown of martyrdom by decapitation in the ninth year of the persecution, the twelfth of his episcopacy.[87]

32. Thus far we have been recording the successions of the bishops and the various events from the birth of Our Lord and Savior until the time of the persecution in which the churches too were destroyed. Let us henceforth describe the contests of the martyrs which we saw for ourselves in order to bequeath this to posterity.

87. On Peter see 8.13.7 and 9.6.2.

BOOK EIGHT

1. The persecution of our time, the one that is of Diocletian, Maximian, and Maximinus
2. The destruction of the churches
3. The nature of the persecution
4. The martyrs
5. Those who suffered in Nicomedia
6. Those who were in the sovereign's houses
7. The Egyptians who suffered in Phoenicia
8. Egypt itself
9. The Thebaid
10. The martyr Phileas
11. What took place in Alexandria
12. What some of them taught
13. What took place in Phrygia
14. The sufferings of various other men and women as well
15. The heads of the churches who shed their blood from devotion
16. The manners of the persecutors
17. What happened outside
18. The change for the better
19. The return to the way things were

Having finished the successions of the apostles in seven books, I think it worthwhile in this eighth book to bequeath to posterity what happened in our own times as well, and this is where we shall begin.[1]

1. On the firmer editorial hand which Rufinus used in Books 8–9, cf. Torben Christensen, *Rufinus of Aquileia and the* Historia Ecclesiastica, *Lib. VIII–IX, of Eusebius* (Copenhagen: The Royal Danish Academy of Sciences and Letters, 1989). As the author remarks on p. 9, "Eusebius really worked according to 'a

8.1.1. It is, then, beyond our powers to relate how wonderfully and how magnificently the word of Christ and the teaching of piety made its way through the whole world before the persecution of our own time, and the loftiness which it attained. 2. One indication of this, however, is that some of the Roman sovereigns even bestowed on ours the power to govern provinces and administer justice, 3. and allowed their wives, servants, and their whole households not only to believe in Our Lord Jesus Christ, but to express their faith with full confidence and freedom, so that they took as their trusted and close associates those of whom they could be sure, from their faith in Christ, that they were entirely innocent of falsehood. 4. Such was that most highly renowned man Dorotheus on the imperial chamberlain's staff,[2] who for his faith in the Lord was accounted most trustworthy, so that he was deservedly given more honor and love than the rest. With him were Gorgonius and the others with them who were faithful in the Lord and who were accorded the highest honors within the palace or were deservedly preferred to the others for the governance of provinces in consideration of their fidelity. 5. But who now could worthily describe the multitudes of peoples gathering within the churches and the countless throngs flocking together in each place, especially on the feast days? Not even the old accommodations sufficed for them, but the houses of prayer spread daily, so that their extensiveness seemed to resemble that of cities. 6. So it was that the situation of most of the churches was enhanced by their successful growth, and their glory rose above the earth and, surpassing all else, seemed to be hastening to heaven. For it met with no envy; it was not countered by that evilest demon's spite, because the people was indeed supported by the right hand of heaven, something it still then deserved from God for its practice of piety and devotion to justice.

---

scissors and paste method.' Particularly in the case of lib. VIII–IX, his method produced an untidy account full of repetitions, contradictions, and material of widely different kinds. It is a mess ..." Christensen suggests that Rufinus's alterations and additions were prompted both by his desire to clarify the narrative and by a different assessment of its drift (335).

2. *in cubiculo regum:* nothing similar in Eusebius. See also 8.6.1 and 8.6.5 (8.6.5 also for Gorgonius below).

7. But when morals were corrupted and discipline ruined by the abundance of freedom and leniency, while we envied one another and detracted from one another, while we carped at and criticized each other and conducted internal warfare against each other, while our verbal shafts wounded our neighbors' hearts, while we engaged in discord and contention, leaders against leaders and people against people, while faces dissembled, hearts meditated mischief, speech concealed deceit, and the mass of evils swelled degree by degree, divine providence, contemplating the loss of discipline tolerated by its people from its abundant peace and the excessive license allowed it, proceeded gradually at first to restrain those who were lapsing, and for the time being allowed only those in the service[3] to be assailed by the persecution of the pagans; the situation of the church and the congregations remained still unimpaired. 8. But no understanding of his clemency was restored to the people from this; they rather considered that the course of events took place without divine providence, as though they were ignorant of God, and they thereby persisted in their wrongdoing, and the very ones who were seen as the leaders and rulers of the people blazed against each other in conflicts, jealousy, envy, pride, hostility, and hatred, so that they thought of themselves as despots rather than priests, forgetful as they were of Christian humility as they celebrated the sacred mysteries with profane minds. Then finally, according to the words of the prophet Jeremiah, "the Lord darkened in anger at the daughter of Zion and flung down from heaven the glory of Israel, and did not remember his footstool in the day of his wrath," and as he again says, "the Lord has sunk all the beauty of Israel and torn down all his walls,"[4] 9. and again, as he says in the Psalms, "he has destroyed the testament of his servant, fouled to the earth his sanctification" through the destruction of the churches, "destroyed all his walls, and made his strongholds into fear; all who passed by the way have plundered his people, for all of which we have become a reproach to our neighbors. For he has raised up the right hand of our enemies

3. *in militia*. It was divided into the *militia armata* (army) and *militia officialis* (civil service).
4. Lam 2.1–2.

and turned aside the help of his sword, and has not helped us in battle, but has even destroyed him from purification and dashed his throne to the ground. He has made our days few and above all has poured shame over us."[5]

8.2.1. For the culmination of all the evils reached us when the houses of prayer and the churches of the living God were razed to the ground and destroyed to their very foundations, while the holy scriptures were burned in the middle of the streets. Oh, the horror! We saw with our own eyes the priests of the Lord and shepherds of churches stripped naked in public[6] and dragged here and there shamelessly and impudently by the impious, so that the prophetic words might be fulfilled which run, "Contempt has been poured upon the princes, and he has led them off into an impasse and not on the right way."[7] 2. But it is not our business to describe the many kinds of wrongs done to the priests of God, just as we did not consider it our business to explain in detail how great the fury was which blazed among ours earlier. The only thing which we may record is that we felt the divine hand in God's just judgment and requisite censure. 3. Nor is it of importance to indicate on whose account the storm of persecution broke out, or whom the tempest of infidelity overwhelmed, or how many they were; the only things I shall record are those which will edify ourselves who say them or others who hear them. We shall for this reason tell briefly from now on of the divine contests of the most blessed martyrs to the best of our ability.

4. It was the nineteenth year of Diocletian's reign, the month of March, and the solemn day of the Paschal feast was near,[8] when the sovereign's edicts were posted up through every land ordering that all the churches everywhere were to be razed to the ground, that the sacred scriptures were to be burned, that those of us protected by the privilege of rank were to lose it and be reduced to infamy, and that any slave who remained Chris-

5. Cf. Ps 88.40–46.

6. *publice denudatos:* no exact equivalent in Eusebius.

7. Ps 106.40.

8. February 23, 303; cf. Lactantius, *DMP* 12.1. On the edict and its consequences, *DMP* 12–15.

tian would be unable to attain freedom.[9] 5. All this was said in the edicts first issued against us. Others were added not long after. The order was given that all those in charge of churches in each place were first to be thrust into fetters and then forced by every kind of torture to sacrifice to idols.

8.3.1. Now indeed the priests of God became an enormous spectacle to this world and to angels and human beings[10] when the persecutors in their cruelty rushed them off to torture and they underwent contests which were a wonder to all. Those, however, and they were by far the majority, whom fear subjected and terror sufficed to crush even before the first engagement, I think it better to pass over. The others, of readier mind and stouter faith, suffered the torments. Some were torn apart by flogging, others had their nails torn out, and still others were scorched with red-hot plates. A number of them yielded when exhausted while others persevered to the end. 2. Some of the persecutors, as though moved by pity, brought a number of ours to the unholy sacrifices and raised a shout as though they had sacrificed when they had not sacrificed. Others had not even approached the unclean victims, but these people would cry out that they had already performed the sacrifice, and they would depart, guilty only of suffering in silence the accusation leveled against them. 3. Others, half-dead after their suffering, were thrown out as though dead. Others were dragged off by the feet to be classified among those who had sacrificed. Some did shout out and testify that they had not sacrificed but were Christians, happy to be honored by that confession. A number of them showed even greater confidence in testifying that they had neither sacrificed nor would ever do so. 4. But the soldiers in attendance immediately pounded them on the face and eyes to silence them, and thrust them out violently as though they had consented. That was how eager they were to seem to have fulfilled their objective.

---

9. *si qui ... libertatem consequi non posset* = τοὺς δ᾽ ἐν οἰκετίαις ... ἐλευθερίας στερεῖσθαι ... The interpretation is much debated: are οἱ ἐν οἰκετίαις "household servants"? "private persons"? Rufinus seems to have read οἱ ἐν οἰκέταις and understood the threat to be that of the loss of any chance for a grant of freedom.

10. 1 Cor 4.9.

But they were not permitted to get away with doing these things against the blessed martyrs. Their virtue of patience and magnanimity we will tell as best we can, in accordance with our modest abilities, even though no tongue could do it justice. 8.4.2–4. First of all, therefore, since, as we said, this fire was started from a tiny spark among the servicemen alone,[11] when those in the service who were Christians were singled out and informed that they must either perform the sacrifices or give up the service and life itself, most of them gave up the service for their faith in Christ, and a few even gave up their lives as well.

5. But when the fire which thus started erupted into a conflagration which engulfed peoples and priests, it became impossible to count the number of those martyred daily in almost every city and province. 8.5. In Nicomedia, for instance, one of the men of prominence, distinguished for his worldly honor and rank, no sooner saw the cruel edicts against God's worshipers hanging in the square when he was kindled with the exceeding ardor of his faith, and, with the people looking on, openly seized the document with the unjust law, pulled it down, and tore it to bits while an Augustus was resident in that city together with a Caesar.[12] When they were told what the devout and distinguished man had done, they unleashed upon him every sort of savagery, but could not even manage to make him appear sorrowful to anyone in his torments; his face remained happy and joyful even while his innards were succumbing in his agonies, and the joy of his spirit showed in his face. His torturers as a result suffered more painfully, since they expended every form of torment on one whom they could not even sadden in consequence.

8.6.1. After this the frenzy shifted its attention to one of Dorotheus's[13] associates, those who were on the imperial chamberlain's staff and who had always been regarded as dearly as children. 2. What happened was that when he openly objected to the severe tortures inflicted on the martyr just mentioned, he

11. Cf. 8.1.7. Rufinus abridges 8.4.1–4; the original makes it plain that "the service" here means the military service.

12. Diocletian and Galerius. On the incident, see Lactantius, *DMP* 13.2–3.

13. Dorotheus: 8.1.4.

was himself commanded to come forward and pressed to sacrifice, and when he refused, he was ordered to be hung up and
his whole body torn by whips, that the pain might force him to
do what he was unwilling to do when bidden. 3. But when he remained unmoved, vinegar and salt were ordered to be poured
over his innards, now stripped of the skin. And when he bore
even this torment bravely and courageously, a gridiron spread
with live coals was ordered to be placed in the middle, and
what was left of his body, after it had been worn away by the
flogging, to be put on it, but not all at once; slowly and gradually, that the agony might be prolonged. 4. The ministers of
evil turned his body this way and that, inducing the pain in his
several members one by one and renewing the torment, hoping
to force him to yield, but he remained firm in faith and exultant in hope, and rejoicing in his faith he breathed out his last
breath, his flesh now consumed, and perished in the fire. Such
was the martyrdom with which Peter was adorned, for such was
his name: a true heir to Peter's faith and name. 5. His instructor in doctrine and director in the services performed within
the palace was Dorotheus, the imperial chamberlain,[14] whose
equal in service, faith, and magnanimity was his associate Gorgonius. It was due to their excellent guidance that almost all
the chamberlain's officers persevered intently and freely in
their faith in God. When therefore Dorotheus and Gorgonius
saw Peter bearing up so bravely and freely under the cruel and
savage tortures inflicted on him, they said, "Your majesty, why
are you punishing Peter for a conviction which all of us share?
Why is he charged with what all of us profess? This is our faith,
this our religion and the one conviction common to us." He
summoned them forward nonetheless and ordered them to be
executed by hanging after subjecting them to almost the same
tortures as those before.

6. It was also then that Anthimus, the bishop of that city, received the glory of martyrdom by decapitation when he perse-

14. *cubiculi regii praepositus*. Rufinus goes his own way in 8.6.5, and is slightly anachronistic here, since the title is first attested under Constantius II. *Cubiculo praepositus* is, however, found already in Suetonius (*Domitian* 16.2). Gorgonius below is in 8.1.4. See also Lactantius, *DMP* 14.

vered in professing the Lord Jesus Christ. And almost his whole
flock followed him as a truly good shepherd when he led the way
to martyrdom. What happened is that part of the palace in Nicomedia caught fire at that time. The emperor wrongly suspected
that ours had done it, and, aflame with a boundless rage, he ordered all of ours rounded up indiscriminately and some to be
beheaded with the sword and others to be burned to death. But a
greater fire of faith was burning in them by divine grace. So that
when the officials in attendance asked them one by one if perhaps they chose to be released after sacrificing, neither the men
nor the women would even wait to be asked, but of their own
accord rushed to the flames or vied with each other to bare their
necks to the executioners' swords. And when the excessive cruelty horrified the onlookers themselves, the agents of evil thrust
part of the people into boats, drew them out onto the open sea,
and, when they persevered in their conviction about the faith,
threw them into the depths. 7. Their cruel savagery reached such
a pitch in fact that they dug up again the imperial pages who had
been martyred, and had been buried in the usual civilized way,
and threw their bodies into the sea, saying, "They must not become the gods of the Christians, lest those who refuse to worship
the gods should begin to worship our slaves." For they think that
we pay divine honor to the martyrs. While this was going on in
Nicomedia, where the savage, bloodthirsty author of the cruelty
was himself drooling over the flesh of the pious, 8. no less haste
was shown in the province of Melitene and in Syria to thrust all
the heads of the churches into prison and bind them in fetters,
in accordance with the imperial edicts, while at the same time
men and women of the laity, of both high and low condition,
were snatched up with them, 9. a miserable and repellent spectacle presenting itself in every place. For in the city there was
a sudden silence, in the prisons a crowded throng, in the city
streets not a soul, in the prisons not a vacant place, so that the
sight was not so much of that of convicts being taken to a pen-
itentiary as of the whole city transferred to prison. The chains
forged for murderers, adulterers, poisoners, and tomb-robbers[15]

15. Eusebius: "murderers and tomb-robbers." "All religious folk" below is
Rufinus's replacement for "exorcists."

were now constricting the necks of bishops, presbyters, deacons, lectors, and all religious folk, so that for the criminals there were left neither fetters nor places in the penitentiaries. 10. Now when it came to the attention of the sovereign that the prisons were seething and that there was no room for the criminals because of the punishment imposed on the innocent, fresh decrees were issued that those incarcerated who wished to sacrifice might go free, while those who refused were to be put to death in various ways. And then the multitudes of those martyred in each of the provinces, especially in Africa and Mauretania, the Thebaid and Egypt, are quite beyond anyone's ability to count.

8.7.1. Nor is it in our power to give an adequate account even of those whose contests we ourselves saw in Palestine and Tyre, the largest city in Phoenicia. For so great was the virtue of perseverance which they showed in resisting the tortures inflicted on them in their battle for piety, that one would be disinclined to believe what took place unless one had first believed Our Lord and Savior when he said, "Behold, I am with you all days until the end of the age,"[16] and knew that his power was present to the martyrs. 2. We, however, as I said, tell not of what we heard but of what we saw with our own eyes. Different kinds of tortures were devised, one following upon the other. The bodies of God's martyrs were first torn by whips from top to bottom. After this they were handed on to the beasts, and lions, bears, and leopards were brought on, and every kind of wild animal, boars too and even bulls, their ferocity increased by iron and fire. They were all made ready against God's worshipers, and every cruelty of men, beasts, and the very elements was mustered against them. Facing them were God's worshipers placed naked in the middle of the arena; and thus, rendered even more savage than they were, they burst from the enclosures, filled the stadium in a trice, surrounded the church of the martyrs situated in the middle, paced around and around them repeatedly, and, sensing that the protection of the divine power was present with them, withdrew far from them. At that, however, the frenzy which was checked in the beasts passed over into the men. No one sensed the presence of God's

16. Mt 28.20.

power; no one detected the divine assistance standing by the pious, but those skilled in goading beasts were sent against those defended by God's right hand. The beasts, however, as a demonstration to everyone that they did not lack ferocity, but that God's protection was shielding his worshipers, tore apart in the blink of an eye the very people sent to goad them. And when none of these specialists dared any longer to approach them, the holy martyrs were themselves ordered to stir up the wild animals against them by waving their arms as though in challenge. But not even so did they suffer any harm; if any of the beasts was perchance roused and came near, it immediately turned tail and leaped back.

3, 4. Then indeed did great amazement and fear seize all the spectators as they saw naked persons, most of them still in their youth, placed in the midst of beasts so many and so large, their hands and eyes raised calmly and fearlessly to heaven and their minds fixed wholly upon God, while they not only paid no heed to earthly things but thought little even of their own flesh, the very magistrates trembling in fear as those they had sentenced stood in the midst of the beasts with happy and cheerful faces. But the minds of mortals are so stubborn and ir- religious! The ferocity of the beasts was tamed by God's power, but the fury of the humans was not abated by the example of the wild animals; God continued to be tested by human beings. 5. Others who were real criminals were presented to the beasts. And no sooner did they appear than one was devoured by a lion, another by a leopard, and a third by bears, while yet an- other was tossed to pieces by a bull, and so all of them perished in a trice. But not even when thus incited did the beasts bother God's worshipers in any way, since the divine spirit surround- ed them like the stoutest wall. Truthful indeed is the one who said, "Where there will be two or three of you, I will be there in their midst."[17]

Since, then, human savagery had accomplished nothing in this way, the beasts were ordered to be changed, the first ones being removed and others released in their place. And when these, like the first, did no harm to God's worshipers, they too

17. Mt 18.20.

were removed, and more savage beasts, human ones, were set upon the martyrs; they alone could outdo monsters in their inhumanity, wild animals in their cruelty, and beasts in their atrociousness. 6. They therefore accomplished with their swords what they could not with their beasts. And in order to show that they were in every way worse than monsters, they even forbade the corpses to be buried, but ordered them to be given to the waters. 8.8. Such were the marvelous contests in Tyre in which the venerable martyrs engaged who had come to that city from Egypt.

Now in their own province of Egypt countless others equally glorious, men as well as women, and children along with elderly folk, made little of this present life in seeking the blessedness of future glory in accordance with their faith in Our Lord Jesus Christ. Some of them were delivered to the flames after being beaten, torn with claws, scourged, and tortured horribly in various other ways; others were thrown into the sea; a number were also beheaded, so that they presented their necks to the axes of their own accord; a number starved to death; others were fastened to gibbets, among them some topsy-turvy, with their heads downwards and their feet raised on high.

8.9.1. But in the Thebaid the cruelty enacted defies all description. Instead of claws the torturers used earthenware shards by which the whole body was torn up to the point where all the skin was removed from the flesh. They also allowed women who were so completely naked that not even their private parts were covered to hang for an entire day from machines cunningly constructed so that one of their feet hung aloft while their heads sunk down, a shocking sight. 2. At other times whenever two trees were found next to each other, they would bend the branches of each toward the other by force, tie each of the feet of each martyr to them, and then suddenly release the branches they had bent by force. And when by a natural impulse they returned to their positions, they ripped apart the bodies with them, dismembering them contemptuously. 3. And this did not take place over a few days or a short time; for some years it happened daily that at least ten and sometimes a hundred men and women, and children as well, were being butchered in a single day in the kinds of punishments just mentioned. 4. We ourselves in fact, while we were traveling at that time in Egypt, saw with our own eyes countless numbers of the faithful being offered to a governor of the most savage sort sitting on the front of the tribunal; as they professed themselves Christians, he ordered each of them beheaded, one by one. And when they vied with each other to submit to the sword on their own when they had made their profession, his inhumanity and cruelty remained unmoved either by the sight of how many they were or by the greatness of their virtue; he ordered them all notwithstanding to be taken away and beheaded. They all went out together to a field adjoining the walls,[18] not pulled along by the executioners' fetters but linked by the bonds of faith. No one was missing because no one kept them; they all of their own accord strove each to be ahead of the others in offering their necks to those performing the decapitations. The hands of the executioners failed, and they tired themselves out relieving each other; the edge of the sword was dulled. I would see executioners sitting tired, recovering their strength, reviving their spirits, and changing their swords, while the day itself was not sufficient for carrying out the sentences. 5. None of them, though, not even little children, could be deterred from death; the only thing each of them feared was that, when the setting sun closed the hastening day, they might remain separated from the martyrs' company. So it was that, confident in their faith, they bravely and courageously, with joy and exultation, seized upon the death that was present as the beginning of eternal life. When finally those who had been earlier were slain, the rest did not give themselves over to idleness and inactivity, but each awaited the place of his martyrdom while singing psalms and hymns to God, that by so doing they might breathe their very last in praising God.

6.[19] Truly marvelous was that flock of the blessed, a troop

18. "They … walls": Rufinus adds.

19. Rufinus rewrites 8.9.6–8, drawing, it seems, on the ancient record of the two martyrs below; cf. F. Halkin, "L'Apologie du martyr Philéas de Thmuis (Papyrus Bodmer XX) et les Actes latins de Philéas et Philoromus," *Analecta Bollandiana* 81 (1963): 5–27, esp. p. 7.

of hardy men, a crown of the splendor of Christ's glory! This crown was indeed adorned by a stone more precious than all others and a jewel more renowned, 7. this troop was led by a captain more famous, this flock adorned by a shepherd more renowned. Phileas was his name, the bishop of the city called Thmuis. The distinction which is of the first order, that of the virtue of the spirit, he derived from heaven, while that which is earthly and belongs to the world he derived from his previous occupation of the highest posts in the Roman state; superbly educated as well in the liberal arts and in all of the practices which concern the virtue of the spirit, he also so mastered as last of all that divine philosophy which is before all else, that he outdid all who had gone before. 8. And since most of the men of prominence who were his relatives and kindred lived in the same city, he was brought again and again to the governor, with his relatives, who were numerous persons of great consequence, beseeching him to yield to his admonitions; he was urged to consider his wife and take thought for his children, and not to persist in his obstinacy. He rejected their babbling, however, as though it were a wave dashing against an unyielding rock, pressed on in spirit toward heaven, kept God in view, and regarded the holy martyrs and apostles as his parents and kindred. There was present at that time a man commanding a troop of Roman soldiers whose name was Philoromus. When he saw Phileas surrounded by his tearful relatives and harassed by the cunning governor, who were yet unable to bend or weaken him even slightly, he cried, "Why are you vainly and uselessly trying the man's courage? Why do you want to render unfaithful one who is faithful to God? Why are you forcing him to deny God that he may yield to men? Do you not see that his ears do not hear your words? That his eyes do not see your tears? How can he be swayed by earthly tears whose eyes behold the glory which is heavenly?" When he had said this, the anger of the others was directed toward Philoromus, and they demanded that he receive one and the same sentence as Phileas. The judge gladly agreed and ordered both to be beheaded.

8.10.1. Now since we have mentioned Phileas and spoken of the way he applied his talent and learning, it does not seem out of place to include in this history some extracts from his short works in which he records the martyrs' sufferings, since they belong to our topic. In writing to the people of Thmuis, Phileas after some other things speaks as follows:

2. "Examples of these good things have been offered us by the blessed martyrs, who in persevering along with us in the contests, as they were trained to do from the sacred scriptures, and in keeping the eye of their minds fixed on God, suffered death fearlessly for the sake of piety. For they bore in mind unceasingly that Our Lord Jesus Christ, who became man for our sakes, taught us that we should struggle unto death against sin, since he himself 'did not consider his being equal to God an instance of robbery, but he emptied himself, taking the form of a slave, and being found in the condition of a human being he humbled himself even unto death, death on a cross.'[20]

3. Following his example, the blessed martyrs accepted all the torments and punishments, to avoid violating their conscience concerning their faith, since the perfect charity in them did expel fear.[21] 4. If I wished now to list their virtues of fortitude and to tell of the greatness of their constancy, my command of language would not suffice to render credible what was done, nor would that of others, except those who saw them with their own eyes. For they were exposed to all those who wanted to torment them in any way they liked, and anyone who presented a new kind of torture he had devised at his leisure might inflict it. Some of them were beaten with clubs, some with rods, and some with whips; a number of them were stretched out with straps or hung from ropes. 5. An effort was made to invent new tortures for almost each person. Some were hung with their hands tied behind their backs, stretched apart with pulleys, and torn asunder limb from limb. Being scored by claws now seemed something of the past and hardly serious. And if by chance this kind of torture was inflicted on people, it was not just their sides that were plowed, as is done with robbers and murderers; the claws dug into their stomachs, thighs, shins, and even their nails. Not even their faces and foreheads were exempt from torture. And

20. Phil 2.6–8.
21. Cf. 1 Jn 4.18.

in addition, what went beyond all else, after the human bodies were mutilated most inhumanly, they were exposed in public, stripped not only of clothing but of skin, and were made a cruel spectacle to all who passed by. Some they left splayed on pillars, their arms twisted and bound behind their backs. 6. And now those who were being held up before the governor remained on the 'ponies'²² not only during the time when they were being interrogated or tortured by him, but for almost the whole day, while other business was being transacted, just in case any of them wavered under the pressure of the unremitting punishment. 7. So great was their cruelty and so utterly had they lost all feeling of humanity, that after a body had been completely worn away by tortures and beatings, 8. they ordered it to be dragged back naked to prison by the feet, and there, with their feet confined in stocks and the wounds on their backs still fresh, they were thrown onto a floor strewn with earthenware shards beneath them. 9. Meanwhile the great number who persevered courageously and boldly unto death brought no small shame upon the inventors of wickedness for the cruelty they had practiced in vain. Others when they had recovered their bodily strength would challenge the administrators of punishment to start the contests again. 10. But they were embarrassed to summon them back to be tortured; terrified by their very boldness, they ordered them to be beheaded."

11. Such are the words of the blessed martyr Phileas, a true philosopher in God, which he used to write to the church entrusted to him while he was in fetters and clapped into prison, and by which he made [its members], in union with himself, companions of the martyrs and sharers in the heavenly crowns.

Besides that, who would dare to omit the thing that happened in Phrygia, and during which both the laws common to humanity and those peculiar to the Roman empire were violated? 8.11.1. There was a city there of Christian citizens in which the entire populace, the men of rank, and the curator, as well as the magistrates, professed themselves Christians and refused to sacrifice; the order was given to surround it with soldiers, set fire to it, and burn all of them together, men with

22. "on the 'ponies'" = *in eculeis,* wooden racks for torture.

women, the elderly with the children, the city with its inhabitants, so that not a single person got out of the city, even when the choice was given to those wanting to do so. What was done here to citizens would have been condemned as cruelty if done to an enemy. 2. Now the leader and inspiration of this blessed and extensive martyrdom undertaken by the whole city together was a man renowned for his piety, devotion, and general benevolence, Adauctus, an Italian by birth and homeland, who had held the palatine posts one by one up to that of master of offices, and who was at this time the imperial finance officer in the city just mentioned. It was his courage in professing Christ that the entire populace followed, thereby winning by martyrdom the palm which is truly imperial through the example of their fine leader.[23]

8.12.1. But upon what resources can we draw to list the sufferings undergone by each of the martyrs individually? How for instance could one rehearse even those in which the holy martyrs in Arabia were slain by axes? Or how could one describe what was done in Cappadocia, where the order was given to break the legs of God's worshipers? Who can relate the tortures in Mesopotamia, where they put the Christians to death like pigs, hung from each of their hands and feet to choke upon the fiercely acrid smoke from below—a shocking torture? Others perished in more prolonged torments when placed near a slow fire. And how can I repeat the events in Alexandria which go beyond even the tales of the poets of old? Where they cut off their ears and—a shameful mutilation—their nostrils, chopped off the ends of their hands and of their other limbs, and let their torsos depart amid laughter. 2. How can I recall

23. The impossible career which Rufinus gives to Adauctus is occasioned by his identification of him with the *curator* (= *logistēs*, "financial overseer") in 11.1. Eusebius does not do so, nor in fact does he connect Adauctus with Phrygia at all; what he says is that he advanced through all the imperial posts, including those in the general comptroller's office (ὡς καὶ ... διελθεῖν). This becomes in Rufinus the post of master of offices (*officiorum magisterium*), not attested until 320 and not in any case connected with finances. Rufinus does not explain his curious demotion from one of the highest government posts to that of town curator in Phrygia, but perhaps he tries to soften it by embellishing *curator* with *rationes ... summarum partium administrans*.

the gridirons set upon live coals in Antioch, upon which Christians were placed to be scorched? Among other things, though, I do not think it right to pass over in silence the remarkable deed done by two noble youths. When they were seized and pressed to sacrifice to the idols, they said, "Take us to the altars!" And when they had been taken there, they placed their hands on the blazing fire, saying, "If we pull them back, you may believe that we have sacrificed!" And there they stood, unmoving, until all the flesh had melted off into the fire. Others when they were sought for sacrifice avoided the sacrilegious defilement by ending their lives with a leap from a height, showing less trust in their perseverance but greater care to preserve their faith. 3. Among them was an admirable and venerable woman, attractive both for her beauty and chastity, and of distinguished birth and wealth. She had two virgin daughters who were thoroughly moral and had been reared to the standard of their mother's chastity; they strove to rival in their appearance and character the integrity of their mother, who in her piety had brought them up in the fear of the Lord, according to the divine precept.[24] But the advantages of nature and education of which we have spoken roused evil men to contend fiercely for the virgins and their mother, and they bent every effort to seek them out. But when they withdrew in order to avoid the uproar, the search for them was prosecuted with the utmost zeal. The soldiers who were assigned to this found them and compelled them to proceed to Antioch. But while they were on the way in the conveyance into which the soldiers had forced them, the devout and chaste mother spoke to her daughters: "You know, my sweetest daughters, how I have brought you up in God's discipline; you know that from childhood God has been to you a father, a nurturer, and an instructor, and that together with me you have so loved what is good in modesty and chastity that never have your very eyes been tainted by the sight of impurity, as I know of you. You can see that the whole purpose of this violence is to separate us from God or from chastity. Are these limbs, then, which the common air itself has hardly known, to

24. The mother was Domnina, her daughters Bernice and Prosdoce. Cf. F. O'Briain, "Bernicé," *DHGE* 8.835–37.

be prostituted in the common brothels? No, daughters, I beg you; for our faith in God is not so slight that we are terrified of death, nor do we so despise chastity that we desire to live even in disgrace. I ask you rather that as you follow your mother's example in everything, so you do also in this. Let us forestall the impure hands of these villains, anticipate the assault of these miscreants, and by a death that is pure and chaste condemn this world, which is compelling and dragging us to a life that is impure and unchaste."

4. And when she saw that her daughters were in ardent agreement with her exhortation, they came to a river which was on their way. There they pretended to get down because of a call of nature, and when their guards had withdrawn a short distance out of a natural sense of respect, they drew their garments about them tightly and threw themselves into the swift current of the forbidding river. 5. There were also two other virgins who were sisters and distinguished in every way; of illustrious birth and admirable life, they were still in their youth and quite beautiful in appearance, although more so in spirit, their adornment being their conduct rather than their jewelry; their zeal being altogether commendable, they refused to have their chastity violated by official edicts and laws, and drowned themselves in the sea.[25]

6. This is what took place in Antioch. In Pontus crueler things were done. Sharpened reeds were stuck under the fingernails of some people. Others had melted lead poured down their backs right to their private parts, the usual place for excretion. Women too were treated with utter inhumanity and lack of pity: hot spits and burning charcoal were thrust into their private parts and their inner organs. But what shall I do when I lack the very terms for the crimes committed and cannot find even the words to list the acts of villainy performed? The martyrs, though, bore them all with enormous strength and piety, while the excellent, outstanding magistrates thought that there was only one manner in which their wisdom would be admired by all, and that was if they invented some torture of a novel sort and new-

25. Eusebius says that the demon-worshipers ordered them thrown into the sea.

fangled cruelty. 8. But when they were at last satisfied, not with
how reasonable and considerate they had been, but with how
exceedingly cruel, and they began to contemplate the enormity
of their crime—the cities emptied of their citizens, and citizens
of the highest station; the countryside stripped of husbandmen,
and fathers bereft of their sons and parents of their children—
their mood changed to one of kindness and considerateness,
and they published an imperial edict. 9. It said that it was not
right to put to death so many citizens who stubbornly persisted
in their beliefs, and it decreed that from then on people of this
sort should never be executed; 10. all of those, rather, who held
to this sort of profession were to have their right eyes gouged
out with a knife and cauterized with a branding iron, and their
left hams likewise maimed with a branding iron, and they were
to be sent away to each of the provinces to perform penal labor
in the copper and iron mines. Such was the imperial clemency in the provision it made for citizens of the highest station.
Now they were acting according to their own habits or vices, as
it seems, while crowns of virtue and patience were being made
ready for those just and holy men, Our Lord and Savior testing
thereby the faith of those who believed in him, or rewarding
their merits. 11. But just as it is not only difficult but impossible
to list individually all those who gave glory to God in their sufferings in the flesh, so it likewise seems a distinct mark of ingratitude to omit everyone completely and not to mention explicitly
at least a few. We will therefore record a few of those, especially
the heads of the churches, who were crowned with the glory of
martyrdom, each in his own place.

8.13.1. Let Anthimus, bishop of Nicomedia, be inscribed
by us first as a martyr in Christ's kingdom as he shines forth
in the records of the pious; he was beheaded. 2. After him, as
ever a martyr in his life and zeal, is Lucian, who was a presbyter
of Antioch but was then preaching the kingdom of Christ in
Nicomedia in word and deed.[26] 3. In Tyre the most renowned
among the martyrs were Tyrannion, the bishop of the city, who
had been brought up in Christ's ways from childhood, Zenobi-
us, a presbyter from Sidon, and Silvanus, bishop of Emesa, 4.

26. More on Lucian at 9.6.3. Silvanus of Emesa is at 9.6.1 below.

who was joined to the choirs of martyrs when devoured by the beasts in his own city. 5. In Palestine those beheaded were first Silvanus, bishop in Gaza, with most of the clergy, and also forty together in the mine in Phaeno, while Bishops Peleus and Nilus were burned to death with very many of the clergy. 6. Included among them should also be Pamphilus, the noblest flower of the church of Caesarea and the fruit of a heavenly gift. 7. In Alexandria and throughout Egypt and the Thebaid there was first Peter, the bishop of that city, rising like the morning star among the heavenly bodies, outstanding in his life and conduct, and with him the presbyter Faustus, and Dius and Ammonius, his equals in merit, conduct, and martyrdom. Phileas as well, and Hesychius, Pachomius, and Theodore, bishops from the cities of Egypt, and countless others with them sustained the noblest of martyrdoms. Lest our history exceed its proper length, though, I leave the narrative of their individual contests to their fellow citizens, who can describe them properly and who were present then.[27]

11. Meanwhile the way in which our affairs were being thrown into confusion and brought to ruin by the cruel punishment everywhere enforced did not escape the eternal and ever-wakeful eye. It is true that the Lord had handed over his household to be chastised a little, but the bloodthirsty ministers of brutality vented upon it a great rage, and thus God's avenging right hand made itself felt at once: it led those who had previously ruled the empire in complete prosperity, while they were keeping peace with the church, to introduce such a transformation in things that the Augustus himself reached that degree of senselessness and foolishness that he laid aside the imperial tokens, together with his fellow Augustus, and they lived as private commoners after their reign.[28] And as for the one who had been second in rank

27. Pamphilus: 7.32.25. Peter: 7.32.31. Phileas: 8.9.6–8.10.11. Rufinus omits 8.13.8–10, where Eusebius remarks how peaceful the Roman empire had been before the outbreak of persecution.

28. The two Augusti, Diocletian and Maximian, retired on May 1, 305; succeeding them, in accordance with the constitutional reform effected by Diocletian (with a view to a peaceful succession in power), were their two "Caesars," Constantius I and Galerius Maximianus, who had been second to them in rank. Two new Caesars were chosen to replace them: Severus under

to him and afterwards succeeded him in first place, and who had been the instigator and leader of the persecution against us, he was afflicted with so many different illnesses, bodily decay, and mental sickness, that after prolonged and incurable debility, harassed by the avenging spirits of his crimes, he gave up his wicked life of his own accord.[29]

13. Constantius, though, was behaving with great kindness toward others and with utter devotion towards God. He had neither stained his realm with the blood of the pious out of a passion for partnership, nor destroyed our houses of prayer and places of assembly in a hostile frenzy,[30] like Maximian; on the contrary, he held God's worshipers in veneration and honor. Hence as a religious father he deservedly succeeded in leaving his more religious son Constantine heir to a part of the realm. 14. Now Constantine, from the moment he mounted to the pinnacle of the Roman realm by his father's bequest, was beloved by the citizens, welcomed by the army, and emulated by the powerful, but fearsome to the villainous and the cowardly. And in his observance of religion he strove to outdo by far even his father. Licinius too was by a unanimous decision associated in the government and declared Augustus. 15. This deeply offended Maximinus, because he was still at that time considered only Caesar in the east; being unable to bear it any more, he seized the title of Augustus for himself. As for Maximian, surnamed Herculius, who, as we mentioned a little earlier, had been Diocletian's partner and had laid aside the imperial tokens with him, he was driven forth by his son Maxentius when the latter was usurping power in Rome; he fled to Constantine looking for sympathy, since the latter was his son-in-law, and then hatched plots against him after being welcomed by him loyally. He was caught doing so, to his disgrace, and perished even more dis-

---

Constantius in the west, and Maximinus under Galerius in the east. On this reform of government, see *CAH* 12.68–89.

29. Rufinus adds this note about Galerius, anticipating Eusebius 8.16.3–5. He omits 8.13.12 (the death of Constantius and the divine honors decreed him, and the succession of Constantine). He also in the next sentence, and below in 8.13.13, adds "Maximian" to the original.

30. Contradicted by Lactantius, *DMP* 15.7: Constantius did destroy churches.

gracefully, so that after his death his statues and images were removed, and his name in the public temples was replaced.[31]

8.14.1. His son Maxentius, then, who had usurped power in Rome, pretended at first to venerate our faith in order to conciliate the people to himself, and for this reason he ordered the persecution to cease and Christians to be protected from all harm. 2. But there was nothing even remotely Christian in the rest of his actions or in his life and conduct. For he so wallowed in the dregs of scandals and crimes, and in the slime of impurity, that there was nothing at all of the very worst offenses which he omitted, not only in his life [generally] but even in just one day. Thus he commanded the wives of the senators, especially of the most prominent, to be taken away openly and subjected to his lust, and after defiling them ordered them restored to their husbands, his lust for adultery not having been satisfied so much as altered. 3. But so great was the fear that weighed upon the fathers and people that they dared not show openly even that they were in fear; they bore their unaccustomed servitude with groans and were restrained by fear from

31. On July 25, 306, Constantine was hailed by the soldiers at York as Augustus after the death of his father, Constantius I, but he claimed only the title of Caesar, which Galerius acknowledged, Severus being advanced to the rank of Augustus over him. Rome, however, resentful at subjection to the tax census and the abolition of the praetorian guard, refused to accept Severus and proclaimed Maximian's son Maxentius *princeps* in the same year. The following year he took the title of Augustus and called his restive father out of retirement to support him. Neither Severus nor Galerius succeeded in putting him down, Severus being killed in the attempt, and Maximian formed an alliance with Constantine in Gaul, giving him his daughter Fausta in marriage and bestowing the title of Augustus on him.

In 308 Maximian quarreled with his son, and after an unsuccessful attempt to depose him fled to Constantine. Galerius summoned a conference to Carnuntum on November 11 of the same year to reach a new political settlement. With Diocletian in attendance, Galerius declared his old associate Licinius Augustus, and Maxentius a public enemy. Constantine and Maximinus were given the title *filii Augustorum,* but refused it, and in 309/10 were recognized by Galerius as Augusti in turn. Maximian now plotted against Constantine to usurp the title of Augustus for himself, but was discovered and forced to commit suicide in 310.

Rufinus here adds details about Maxentius and his father; the full tale is in Lactantius, *DMP* 28–30.

planning any stroke for freedom, since he was driven no longer by anger but by the lust for killing. Thus on a certain day he commanded his soldiers to go out through the streets of the whole city and slay with their swords everyone they met, of any age and sex; and countless crowds of the Roman people were cut down not by enemy swords but by those of citizens. 4. As for the senators, especially those among them who were more renowned for their position or wealth, charges were invented against them, and they were sentenced and outlawed as guilty. 5. And he added as the crowning point to his crimes the practice of magic, which he pursued with the greatest zeal and in furtherance of which noble women who were pregnant were sought out and subjected to ghastly rituals in which they were cut in half. Tiny infants were seized and their entrails yanked out of their insides to be examined.[32] Lions were also slain and, by means of certain fabrications and prayers composed by demonic craft, wars, it was said, were averted, and it was believed that the justice of the realm could be upheld through injustice. 6. And to all of these evils was added the following: that everyone in the rest of the cities and farms who had been terrified by the usurper's cruelty thought that they had no way to secure their lives, and leaving their fields betook themselves to secluded places of concealment, so that, with no more plowing or sowing being done, hunger had invaded the city and everywhere else, so that there was no further sustenance for life.

7. In the east and in Egypt, now, Maximinus exercised a tyranny that was in every way similar in its cruelty and madness, so that just as the one was the partner of the other in tyranny,[33] so he also seemed to emulate him in crime, 8. and one could not have told which of them more deserved the palm of wickedness. Maximinus in fact seemed to outdo his partner in evil in this: that he would also decree public honors and the highest offices for the teachers of magic and the evil arts. Then too he

32. Cf. 7.10.4 with note 13. On extispicy, cf. Auguste Bouché-Leclercq, *Histoire de la divination dans l'antiquité* (Paris: Leroux, 1879–82), 1.166–74.

33. *in tyrannide socius.* This loosely represents φιλίαν κρύβδην σπενδόμενος ("he made a secret alliance of friendship" [with Maxentius]). Lactantius reports this more fully in *DMP* 43.3–4.

was quite superstitiously devoted to the worship of images, so that he would not consent to even the slightest move without recourse to auguries, divinations, and portents. 9. He was hence a keener and more vigorous persecutor of us than those before. He also ordered the restoration of all the old shrines long ago abandoned by even zealous worshipers, and appointed as their priests and prelates in each province men of prominence who had already held high posts, granting them in addition salaries and military attendants. Which is not surprising, since he would promote flagrant evildoers to be governors of provinces and military commanders. 10. But this vain activity required enormous supplies of gold and silver. As a result all the provinces everywhere were stripped bare in various ways, and as opportunity afforded; assessments were increased, taxes were multiplied, any of those who were wealthier were condemned on the most abstruse or even fabricated charges, and others were outlawed as well, and thus he separated all people alike from their paternal properties and their ancestral families. It was from this that he enriched his close associates and accomplices with mountains of gold, so to speak. 11. At banquets he was so immoderate and so drunken that he was thought insane, his wits gone in an alcoholic stupor, and what he had ordered to be done while besotted he did not know the next day that he had ordered. In wallowing in luxury, opulence, and dissolution of every sort, he afforded his soldiers the most disgraceful examples. Thus all wanton, impudent, and licentious behavior on the part of those in charge of the soldiers and the provinces went unpunished because of the emperor's example. 12. Among other things he was especially anxious not to pass by any of even the smallest villages, to say nothing of the cities, without violating the noble matrons discovered in each place, and defiling the virgins. 13. It goes without saying that such a man, such a great enemy of chastity, morals, justice, and fairness of every sort, was also an enemy and persecutor of Christians. The degree of cruelty he showed against them matched his eagerness to outdo his predecessors in crime. He longed to inflict fires, plates, crosses, beasts, drowning in the sea, the severing of limbs, the gouging out of eyes, and special tortures to

each of the limbs, while his victims were found to be more courageous and persevering in bearing them than he was clever
and skillful in devising them. 14. For he was often conquered
not only by men but even by women on fire with God's word
and the ardor of faith, who, while they were women when they
were arrested, were crowned like mighty men in the battle; they
preferred to suffer death at once, or rather, conversely, to seek
it out rather than to have their bodies defiled.

15. Now while he was being driven headlong by two demanding masters, lust and cruelty, there was in Alexandria someone named Dorothy,[34] of a quite prominent family, enormous
wealth, and prominent kin. But even more notable about her
than these things were the beauty of her intelligence and application and her determination to master all the other honorable arts. Now her appearance and beauty were so glorious that
one would have thought her a wonderful and special creation
of God. She, however, was eager to be lovelier in her religious
attitude and moral life than in her bodily appearance, and
so she made the fairest of all decisions: to consecrate to God
rather than to human gratification what men thought beautiful and attractive, and so she remained a virgin consecrated to
God. But he who was befouling things divine and human with
his lust and cruelty knew only the loveliness of her appearance
and not of her intelligence and resolution as well, and so he set
himself to violate the virgin and desecrate her chastity. When
he discovered that she was a Christian, though, and according
to his own edicts should be subject to his punishment rather
than his lust, he began to hesitate, unsure of where to take his
course. Lust, however, which enjoyed a wider dominion within
him, prevailed in his hesitating mind, and he sent secret messages to the virgin, who was expecting to be seized and taken
off for torture and martyrdom, proposing fornication. She replied, reasonably enough, that it would be wrong of her to defile the temple of her body, which she had once consecrated to
God, with the worship of idols or the pollution of lust, and that
she was accordingly ready to die; she added that it did not be-

34. Rufinus adds the name "Dorothy" to the original; the rest of his expanded version of the account may simply be rhetorical elaboration.

come the cruel tyrant to resort to flattery or gentleness, nor was it worthy of him to soften his harsh disposition in her regard when it was daily hardened by the blood of Christians poured forth in waves. When his lust, kindled by her reply, blazed more hotly, and he decided that unless she yielded to his words he would proceed by force, that purest of virgins abandoned all her property, home, and family, and departed secretly by night with a few quite trusty servants and with her dearest companion, chastity, leaving the tyrant mocked, foolish, and witless.

16. There were many other women of prominence and virgins whom he assailed in like manner as with her, and whom in like manner he found readier to die than to serve his lust; he subjected them to cruel tortures. They far more willingly and happily suffered death than all the others, since they believed that double crowns were being made ready for them by the Lord, not only for piety but also for chastity. Now among these narratives there is found a wonderful deed which I do not think it right to pass over in silence: that done by a woman in Rome of the highest station, Sophronia, whose husband was prefect of Rome under the usurper Maxentius.[35] 17. When he learned of the woman's beauty, he acted as usual, sent his ministers of fornication, and ordered the woman brought to him. She reported the matter to her husband. When he was told, he pondered at length, and finally said with a deep groan, "What shall we do, when we must either bear these things or die?" Then when she saw that her terrified husband had betrayed her chastity from fear of death, she said to those who had been sent, "Wait a little until I arrange and adorn myself as is fitting, and then I will go." She thereupon entered her bedroom, and after she had knelt and prayed in order to immolate her chastity to God, she snatched up a sword and stabbed through her chest and innards, sending these last words to the usurper by way of her maids-in-waiting: "May Christian women please the

35. Rufinus alone gives the name of the wife of the *praefectus urbis* "Junius Flavianus, who left office on 9 February 312, a mere three and a half months after his appointment, probably ... after his wife committed suicide" (Timothy D. Barnes, *The New Empire of Diocletian and Constantine* [Cambridge, MA: Harvard University Press, 1982], 112).

tyrant better like this!" 18. Thus did the tyrants rage in the east as well as the west, armed as they were by one demonic spirit, and kindled by the same equal vices, while by contrast the virtue of spirit and constancy of faith of the Christians were thereby accorded greater esteem and splendor.[36]

8.16.1. But when for ten continuous years the emperor Maximian in the east had also raged with a like cruelty against the Christians and slaughtered countless thousands of worshipers of the true God, and when his drunkenness had lent unremitting strength to his cruelty and lust, which neither prudence nor repletion halted or stayed, divine providence came to the aid of its worshipers and brought relief to those it had tried by fire. 2. For divine retribution pounced upon the very author of the crime. 4. He who had swaggered about with his corpulent flesh stuffed full suddenly swelled up, his innards distended and festering. A sore then originating more deeply within his chest consumed from within all the insides of his intestines as the corruption spread. Afterwards, when some passages had opened to the surface through festering ulcers, a countless multitude of worms began to swarm out in waves from the veins inside the decayed sore. The stench was so unbearable 5. that no one could approach, not even the physicians, since his corpulent flesh, nourished upon every delicacy, gave off a heavy odor of decay from corruption.

He then ordered most of the physicians put to death, since they could offer no remedy for the illness nor bear its stench. One of them who was there to be killed rather than to heal was inspired by God to say, "Why, your majesty, do you make the mistake of thinking that what God inflicts men can rescind? This disease is not human, nor can it be cured by physicians. But remember how much you have done against God's servants and how impiously and profanely you have behaved toward the divine religion, and you will realize from where you are to seek healing. For I can die with the rest, but you will not be cured by physicians."[37]

36. Rufinus omits 8.15, which summarizes the state of hostility among the sovereigns.
37. Rufinus adds the remarks by the physician. The emperor spoken of in

8.17.1. Then did Maximian first realize that he was a human being, and, mindful of the enormity of his crimes, he acknowledged first of all that he had erred and behaved impiously, and he began to act as though to make amends to God. He then called together those in public office under him and ordered a law to be drafted and issued immediately providing not only that the persecution of Christians should cease and that they should be protected from all injustice, but also that their churches should be allowed to be rebuilt, in order that while they were devoting themselves to their usual rites and supplications they might petition the most high God for his salvation too. 2. The order having been executed more quickly than it was spoken, edicts were sent at once to each of the cities in the following form:[38]

3. "The emperor Caesar Galerius Maximianus Invictus Augustus, Pontifex Maximus, Aegyptiacus, Thebaicus, five times Sarmaticus, twice Persicus, six times Carpicus, Armeniacus, conqueror of the Medes and the Adiabeni, twenty times of the tribunate, nineteen times emperor, eight times consul, father of the homeland, proconsul, 4. and the emperor Caesar Flavius Valerius Constantinus Pius Felix Invictus Augustus, Pontifex Maximus, of the tribunate, five times emperor, consul, father of the homeland, proconsul.

8.16 is Galerius Maximianus (Rufinus having already mentioned the death of the other Maximian in 8.13.5). The story is told more fully in Lactantius, *DMP* 33, and mentioned in *Excerpta Valesiana* 8, Zosimus, 2.11, and Orosius, 7.28.13.

In 8.13.11 Rufinus had remarked (independently of Eusebius) that Galerius took his own life as a result of his illness. Orosius, 7.28.13, agrees (independently of Rufinus?). Lactantius by contrast says that it was the disease that killed him (*DMP* 35.3).

Rufinus omits 8.16.3 (a scriptural quotation pointing the events with a moral).

38. The disparity in tone between the decree itself and the alleged motive for its issuance suggests that while the former is genuine, the story of Galerius's sickness, repentance, and death is shaped by the story of the sickness, repentance, and death of Antiochus Epiphanes in 2 Mc 9; cf. J. L. Creed, *Lactantius: De Mortibus Persecutorum* (Oxford: Clarendon, 1984), xxxviii–xxxix. It was issued on April 30, 311 (Lactantius, *DMP* 35.1), in the name of all the emperors (*DMP* 36.3), so that it must originally have included the name and titles of Maximinus. Some manuscripts of Eusebius also include the name and titles of Licinius (who later fell out with Constantine) in 8.17.5 (omitted by Rufinus).

6. "Among the other measures we take for what is advantageous to the state, we had first of all desired to govern all things according to the ancient laws and the official practices of Roman custom, adding to this the wish that the Christians, who had abandoned the ancestral religion, might return to it. 7. But they have decided somehow within themselves to show such resistance in this matter, that they in no way wish to return to the practice of the ancient religion established by our ancestors; each one prefers to establish a law for himself of his own choice, and a different people comes together in different places. 8. And when an edict was published by us in their regard ordering them to return to the ancestral laws established of old, most of them preferred to expose themselves to the penalties and subject themselves to countless deaths rather than obey such commands, 9. and we have seen that many still persist in this decision, so that they neither pay due honor to the heavenly gods nor appear to give adequate attention to their own religion. We therefore, having regard to the mildness characteristic of our clemency with which we are accustomed to extend mercy to all people, have judged that our leniency should be willingly shown toward them as well, that they may again be Christians and may build and restore the places of assembly in which they used to pray, in such a way, however, that they do nothing against public order. We will explain to officials in other letters the policy they are to follow. 10. Having thus been favored with this mark of clemency, they should supplicate their God for our safety and for the maintenance of the state, so that with the state protected from all harm, they too may remain safe and sound in their own homes."

11. This document, which was translated from Latin into Greek, we have put back into Latin.[39] But let us see what happened thereafter.

39. Eusebius says that he has translated the edict from Latin into Greek. The original Latin is in Lactantius, *DMP* 34; Rufinus has not copied it.

BOOK NINE

9.1.1. When imperial edicts of this sort were published throughout Asia and Pontus, a sudden light shone forth as though from the deepest darkness. But Maximinus, who in the east had turned the post of Caesar into a totalitarian regime, acted as though he could not bear to have the means for his cruelty taken away from him. Since he neither liked the edict nor dared oppose it, he did not let the law be published openly and come to everyone's attention, but ordered the officials orally to grant a temporary respite to the Christians.[1] 2. But Sabinus, who held the office of prefect at that time, wrote to the officials of all the provinces, prefixing the emperor's law[2] and revealing

1. For an assessment of Maximinus's directives in Book 9, see Valerio Neri, "Documenti e narrazione storica nel libro IX dell' *Historia ecclesiastica* di Eusebio di Caesarea," *Adamantius* 14 (2008): 218–28.

2. *praelatam imperatoris inserens legem* = τὴν βασιλέως ἐμφαίνει γνώμην διὰ Ῥωμαϊκῆς ἐπιστολῆς ("he communicated the emperor's decision in a letter in Latin"). A similar wording is found below in 9.1.7: "prefixing the law" (*legem-*

to everyone what Maximinus had tried to conceal. 7. The officials in turn sent the edicts to each of the cities, prefixing the law, and ordered everyone held in prison to be released, and those kept in the mines or in bonds of every kind to be set free. 8. When this had been done, it was as though the sun's brightness had returned to sky and earth after a terrible storm, with the leaders of our people filling the assemblies in each city with throngs, holding councils, restoring the priesthoods, and furnishing each of the churches with whatever it seemed to lack. When this was being done, great amazement seized the unbelievers among the gentiles at the sudden and enormous change of affairs, so that in very wonder they were forced to admit that the great and only true God was the one the Christians worshiped. 9. And those of ours who had persevered in the contests faithfully and bravely went about in complete confidence and joy. Those, however, who had behaved in a spineless and worldly manner hastened with every mark of humility and supplication to beg for healing from those who had remained in good health, and through them entreated almighty God to be reconciled to them. 10. Those furthermore who had been released from the mines made their way through each city in high and exalted spirits and manifested indescribable joy and exultation to God's churches, 11. proceeding through the city streets and the villages with psalms and hymns. Those consequently who not long before had seen them dragged off to the mines in fetters and chains and now watched them returning home joyful and exultant, were astonished and glorified God. As a result, even those who previously had shown themselves hostile and opposed to us now congratulated us on the miracle of this sudden change, and regarded our joy as theirs too.

9.2. Now while this was going on in the countryside, the villages, and the cities, and the Christian population was rejoic-

---

que praeferentes = τὴν βασιλικὴν διὰ γραμμάτων ἐμφανῆ καθιστῶσι γνώμην ("they published the imperial decision through letters").

The text of the praetorian prefect Sabinus's letter in 9.1.3–6 is so depreciative of Christianity that it was suppressed in later editions of Eusebius in order to protect Constantine from contamination by association with it (it is written in the name of all the emperors) and consequently is not found in Rufinus; see Bardy, *Eusèbe*, 44n3.

ing with seemly exultation, the tyrant who is the enemy of all that is good could not bear not to destroy the happiness with his innate wicked fury. Maximinus, that is, who, as we said earlier, governed the east and Egypt like a tyrant, did not allow ours to remain in peace for more than six months, and then he applied himself at once to whatever he could devise to upset us. He first tried to think up some pretexts to prevent ours from meeting in the cemeteries. Then he incited some utterly depraved men of Antioch to send a delegation against us to demand that Christians not be allowed to live in their own native place. He initiated the delegation through the agency of one Theotecnus, the curator of Antioch, a man of depraved character and utterly wicked conduct.[3] He also forced the other terrified citizens in each of the cities to commit a like crime as well, and arranged for a delegation of this sort to be sent from each of the provinces. And there were many other things he devised against us from his singular hatred and obstinate contentiousness, until he had completely reinstated all the evils which had been abated. In his evil mind and evil heart he felt he was suffering from a sort of thirst and hunger unless he saw the flesh of the citizens being torn and their blood pouring out.

9.3. It was in connection with this that he thought he had found an excellent opportunity in the fact that in Antioch an image of the Zeus of Friendship, recently consecrated with certain magical arts and impure rites of dedication, had been so constructed as to deceive the eyes of onlookers and appear to display portents and produce responses. Everyone was assured that this was certain, even the emperors themselves. And after everyone had come to believe it, it was further claimed that this god had given responses to the effect that Christians should not live in the cities nor in places near the cities, but should be driven further away, insofar as that was possible.[4]

3. On Theotecnus see *PLRE* 1.908. His end is related in 9.11.5–6. The rest of 9.2 is added by Rufinus in anticipation of what Eusebius says in 9.4.1–2 about the delegations from the other cities. It agrees with Lactantius, *DMP* 36.3–4.

4. On responsive statues (speaking or otherwise) see Youssef Hajjar, "Divinités oraculaires et rites divinatoires en Syrie et en Phénicie à l'époque grécoromaine," *ANRW* II.18.4.2290–93. On the statue of Zeus here, 2264.

9.4.1. When this became known, everyone who lived anywhere in each of the cities and provinces under the tyrant's rule issued a similar ruling about Christians, knowing that he would be pleased with this, 2. and, sending delegations to him, were granted by the emperor what they had been invited by him to request. And then once again a furious persecution was rekindled against us, Maximinus meanwhile showing the utmost zeal in appointing priests and prelates for the images in each of the cities and provinces;[5] he loaded them with honors and gifts 3. and did everything he possibly could to surpass everyone else in granting favors, that he might make them the readier to hate and kill Christians. And the more appreciative he showed himself of those who he could tell were more cruel and wicked toward ours, the more he succeeded in this.

9.5.1. And although he had the power to do whatever he liked, since he had by now taken to himself even the rank of Augustus, which had not been granted him, he still wished to appear to be doing these things with some justification. Some records were fabricated which pretended to concern Our Savior before Pilate and which contained every sort of blasphemy against Christ.[6] He ordered these records to be sent throughout all the provinces of his realm, prefaced by his edict, and to be posted up in each of the cities, the villages, and even the countryside, and bade them to be given to the teachers of children as well, that they might give them to the children for memorization in place of the material usually dictated to them to practice and to master.

2. Now as this was being carried out in every place with earnest wickedness, the duke of Damascus, having learned of his emperor's pleasure regarding Christians and being anxious to please him in such matters, found some highly disreputable women on the streets, had them brought before him, and subjected them to intense interrogation, by means of which he might force them to confess as a matter of public record that they had once been Christians and that they knew that during their sacred ceremo-

5. Compare Lactantius, *DMP* 36.4–5.
6. Maximinus's seizure of the title of Augustus is found in 8.13.15. The Acts of Pilate, says Eusebius in 9.5.1, were forged by those in 9.4 who wished to please the emperor. Cf. 1.9.3 and note 83.

nies there were some foul and impure acts committed. These and other like outrages, which no upright person could even bear to hear, he made the women set down in the records, which he sent on to the emperor. And he likewise ordered them to be posted up in each of the cities and provinces, although the duke had not long to enjoy his trick. 9.6.1. For after a short bout of despair born of insanity he took his life with his own hands.

Ours, then, were once again banished, persecuted, and tortured. The provincial officials raged against us even more savagely, as though they were showing the emperor something he would welcome. In Tyre, for instance, a city in Phoenicia, three youths[7] were seized when they professed themselves Christians, and exposed to the beasts; with them was Bishop Silvanus, who had exercised the priesthood for forty years and was a man venerable for his kindness of heart and indeed for his advanced age. 2. It was also at this time that Peter,[8] the bishop of Alexandria, whom we mentioned earlier, truly both a priest and a sacrificial victim for God, was suddenly seized and beheaded as though at Maximinus's behest; he was outstanding in every way and adorned with all the virtues; in the sacred scriptures and in God's word he was the equal of all those before him; he was remarkable for his prudence and was in every respect perfect. Together with him were slain many other bishops from Egypt. 3. Lucian too, a presbyter of Antioch and a man outstanding in morals, self-control, and learning, was addressed as follows by the governor when brought before the official's tribunal:[9] "Why do you follow a sect you cannot explain when you are a man of intelligence and prudence? Or if you have an explanation, let us hear it." And having been given permission to speak, he is said to have delivered the following sort of speech concerning our faith:[10]

7. *tres iuvenes:* Eusebius just says *treis,* and makes Silvanus one of them. On Silvanus, cf. 8.13.3 (where he is said to be bishop of Emesa).

8. Peter is in 7.32.31 and 8.13.7.

9. Eusebius says that Lucian was brought to Nicomedia, where the emperor was staying, and made his defense ἐπὶ τοῦ ἄρχοντος ("before the ruler" or "before the official").

10. It is impossible to say where Rufinus may have found this discourse attributed to Lucian (one of his longer insertions), and, given its extensive rem-

"It is no secret that the God we Christians worship is one God proclaimed to us by Christ and breathed into our hearts by the Holy Spirit. Contrary to what you think, that is, we are not controlled by the error of some human persuasion, nor are we deceived by the unexamined tradition of our ancestors, as others are. Our authority concerning God is God. For that sublime majesty could never glide into the perception of the human mind unless it were conveyed by the power of its spirit or disclosed by the explanations of its word and wisdom. I acknowledge that we too once erred and thought that the images which we ourselves constructed were the gods of heaven and creators of the earth, but the frailty of their existence stood exposed by the consecration bestowed by us. The degree of reverence inherent in them was the degree of gracefulness conferred by the hands of their artisans. But the almighty God, whose creation it was fitting that we should be, and not he the work of our hands, took pity on human error and sent into this world, clothed in flesh, his wisdom, which was to teach us that the God who had made heaven and earth was to be sought not in what is made by hand but in what is eternal and invisible. He also established laws of life and precepts of discipline for us: to live frugally, rejoice in poverty, practice kindness, work for peace, embrace purity of heart, and preserve patience. Not only that, but all of these things you are now doing against us he foretold would happen to us: that we would be brought to kings and placed before judges' tribunals[11] and slain as a sacrificial victim. That is why he himself, accordingly, who as God's word and wisdom was immortal, offered himself to death, that when placed in a body he might set us an example of patience. Nor did he by his death deceive us to whom he rose after the third day, not as those records of Pilate have it which are now being written in untruth, but as innocent, blameless, and pure he accepted death for one reason only, that he might conquer it by rising again.

---

iniscences of Tertullian and Lactantius, how freely he may have reworked it if he translated it. The study by G. Bardy, *Recherches sur Saint Lucien d'Antioche et son école* (Paris: Beauchesne, 1936), 134–63, is indispensable.

11. Cf. Mt 10.18, Mk 13.9, and Lk 21.12.

"The things of which I speak were not done in some hidden place, nor do they lack witnesses. Almost the greater part of the world now confirms this truth, entire cities do so, or, if they are for some reason viewed with mistrust, the country folk too, who are ignorant of fabrication, bear witness to these things. If they are still not believed, then I will offer you the testimony as well of the place in which the event took place. The very place in Jerusalem confirms these matters, as does the rock of Golgotha, sundered under the weight of the gibbet,[12] and the cave which, once the gates of hell were wrenched apart, returned the body restored to life again, that it might be borne thence to heaven in a purer state. And if these things which have their existence on earth still seem of less worth to you, then accept from heaven another faithful guarantor. I present to you the sun itself as witness to these things; when he saw them being done by the impious on earth, he hid his light at midday in heaven.[13] Search in your annals; you will find that in Pilate's time when Christ suffered, the sun was driven away and darkness broke in upon the day. Wherefore if you refuse to credit the earth, heaven, and the blood of those from whom you seek the truth by torture, how will you ever believe my words and assertions?"

And when he had almost begun to persuade his listeners by these words, the order was given to hurry him off into prison and to kill him there, where he was away from the turmoil of the people. 4. And in other places likewise this cruelest of tyrants stirred up such evil against us as was far more atrocious and lethal than anything that had gone before.

9.7.1. For when ever was it that we were opposed by delegations from provinces and cities? When ever was it that so many imperial edicts of such importance appeared against us, that the order was even given to engrave on bronze tablets the laws issued against us? When ever was it that the order was given that children's school exercises should concern Pilate and Jesus, in order to slander us, and that the whole day should be spent in reciting texts teeming with fabricated blasphemies? Now in these laws which he had posted up in each of the cities

12. Mt 27.51.
13. Mk 15.33; Lk 23.44–45.

engraved in bronze as though they would last forever,[14] 8, 9. he wrote proudly and boastfully of the ideal temperateness of the air and the increasing fertility of the land since the time when the Christians were being driven from their dwellings and cities, and of the richer abundance of crops, 12. adding that therefore the attempts made to propitiate the immortal gods were perfectly justifiable, since no victims sacrificed to them were as acceptable as the expulsion of the race of humans hateful to them from every place in which their majesty was worshiped. 13. He also said that because they had presented to the emperor this petition, which was so pious and religious, they might in return request whatever they thought would be of benefit to them, no matter how difficult it might seem, and it would be granted, so long as they took greater care to forbid Christians access of any sort to the cities.

15. Certainly, then, as far as human power could make it so, our affairs and resources were so severely reduced that, as is written, "even the elect might have been shocked"[15] at them. 16. But after it seemed to human eyes that we had been left with nothing whatever of our resources, the providence of almighty God did not allow weak human minds to run the risk of sheer despair. Immediately, without delay, while the impious edicts were still being sent to some of the cities further off, it checked the insolence of the tyrant's voice, 9.8.1. which had spoken of luxuriant crops and fertile fields in recompense for the banishment of Christians, by holding back the rain in the clouds and leaving the crops dried out and barren. The grass in the fields also dried up, denying not only produce to people but also fodder to livestock, and a loathsome, monstrous famine spread everywhere. The temperateness of the air as well, which in his impious guile he had spoken of as a servant, was changed to such a foul state that human bodies were covered with the most ghastly sores, which are called *ignis sacer,* along

14. 9.7.3–14 in Eusebius consists of extracts from Maximinus's rescript to the anti-Christian resolutions of the cities that had written to him; it is under the lemma "Translation of Maximinus's rescript to the resolutions against us, taken from the monument in Tyre." It was delivered perhaps in the summer of 312.

15. Mt 24.24.

with those called carbuncles, so that they invaded even people's faces and eyes, with the result that those who chanced to
escape death were deprived of their eyesight. Other pestilential
diseases likewise felled enormous numbers of men and women,
and infants beyond count especially.[16] 2. And as if that were not
bad enough, when he compelled the Armenians, who had once
been most friendly and supportive of the Roman people, to
change from the practice of the Christian religion, to which all
of them were completely devoted, to the worship of idols, and
to venerate demons instead of God, they were made into enemies instead of friends, and adversaries instead of allies, and
made ready to repel his wicked edicts by force, and went to war
of their own accord.[17]

3. All of these things added together demanded satisfaction
of him for his stupid insolence, in requital for his boasting that
through the banishment and persecution of Christians he had
at his service peace and the abundance of all things and the
very temperateness of the air. 4. While therefore he and the
army were heavily and grievously engaged in the Armenian war,
the people in the cities and villages, to whom he had promised,
on the authority of his laws, that all things divine and human
would turn out successfully, were being devastated by a dire
and merciless famine. 5. In the cities so many multitudes were
felled each day that there was not even room to bury them. In
the countryside and villages most of the houses were left completely empty. 6. Wherefore if some people, when they saw
doom approaching, took their children to the city to sell them,[18]
they themselves perished with their children, from the sale of
whom they had hoped to feed themselves, when the buyer tar-
ried or withdrew from the bargain, being himself about to die.
Some people sought out the roots of plants and tried to keep
themselves alive on their juices, but, made reckless by famine,

16. "Other … especially": Rufinus adds.

17. There is no other evidence of such a war, nor is it inherently probable,
whether Eusebius has the Armenian kingdom in view, or some community of
Armenians within the Roman empire. Cf. Karin Mosig-Walburg, "Der Arme-
nienkrieg des Maximinus Daia," *Zeitschrift für alte Geschichte* 55 (2006): 247–55.

18. Eusebius says that people sold their dearest things (τὰ ἑαυτῶν φίλτατα);
he says nothing (directly) about the sale of children.

perished when they imbibed something deadly. 7. Women too
who were mistresses of households and well born were forced
by famine to forget propriety and go out into the streets to seek
alms, and those whom modesty used not to allow to look at the
faces of others were compelled by famine to beg for a bit of food
or even to seize it for themselves. 8. A great many went about so
exhausted that they might have been taken for fleshless statues
rather than humans; repulsive in appearance, their eyes sunk-
en, they staggered around this way and that, all but collapsing,
begging for alms no longer with their voices but with their last
breaths. Thus it often happened that if people saw a bit of bread
of which they were unable to avail themselves, they tried to
stretch out their hands, but their bodily strength was unequal to
their desire, and they collapsed during the ineffectual attempt
in disappointment at this blow. 9. Wherefore if by chance those
among the wealthy were moved by pity and wanted to share
some food with the needy, they were restrained and smothered
by their multitude, in which there was no one it seemed right
to refuse, and so they abandoned their attempt and were unable to carry out their intended act of mercy on account of the
violence of those whom famine had made reckless. Everything
meanwhile through all the streets and alleys was filled with the
corpses of the dead, nor was there anyone at all to bury them,
since those as well who, it appeared, were still alive were weak
from illness and, as it were, about to die immediately. The resulting sight was lamentable, 10. including that of a great many
being devoured by dogs. 11. Thus two mighty plagues, hunger
and pestilence, divided the people between them: famine devastated all of the poor, who earned their daily living by the work
of their hands, as its neighbors near at hand, while pestilence
claimed as its own those who seemed wealthy and abounding
in riches, so that one might see a house belonging to a family
with many members left empty in a short time, everyone dead,
the infection having spread rapidly from one to the other. 12.
Thus famine and pestilence, waging from separate camps a war
with death alone as the outcome, devastated cities and countryside. 13. Such was the recompense for the laws of Maximinus
and his conceit and arrogance and the judgment he passed on

the Christians; such was his piety toward God and the grandeur of the religion given from heaven, as he claimed.

14.[19] Now when the unburied corpses of the dead whom famine had consumed were lying in the streets, and those whom the pestilence had slain, one and all, remained likewise unburied in the houses, as we said above, and when moreover those who had apparently survived were all pressed by hunger to cry aloud spontaneously and implore the Christians for compassion and pity, and now to beg humbly those whom shortly before they had driven from their homes and native places for the assistance they customarily offered in the form of food for those alive and proper burial for the unburied dead, they were acknowledging that they alone were moved by mercy, that they alone preserved what is proper to humanity and piety, that there was no other religion as true, as holy, and as perfect in every respect in its advocacy of the care to be offered to all human beings as neighbors and kin, and that there was no other god beside the Christians'. Then indeed our people, who truly by God's grace had in no way found themselves under the sway of either famine or pestilence, to everyone's enormous surprise, quite forgot any wrong done them and in their usual way, trained as they were by the Lord's precepts to show mercy even to their enemies, would vie with one another to offer food, as each was able, and to support and restore those who were perishing, and to share not only food with them but affection too, with the result that even a little seemed to suffice for the needy, when it was offered with the deep affection of piety. Those too who were suffering from the infection of illness and whom none of the pagans, not even their own kin, would go in to see, they would heal with their frequent and attentive visits, nor did they suffer anything at all from infection, protected as they were by divine grace; they also saw to the burial of those who had died and fulfilled what was due them by nature. Thus the mere entry of the Christians into the cities and villages was enough to alter the sight of the calamities in a short time, and that in turn inscribed in the hearts of everyone, through the events and deeds them-

---

19. Rufinus expands the original of 9.8.14 with rhetorical elaboration.

selves, the message that the religion of the Christians was true
and pious, a message which proved far more tenacious than the
tyrant's claim, engraved in bronze, that it was false.

15. When therefore ours behaved in this way and through
the goodness of their deeds—a sort of silent sermon—the truth
about our God was recognized, the words recorded in Genesis
were seen to be fulfilled: "the Egyptians were in darkness pal-
pable and thick, while the children of Israel had light in all of
their dwellings."[20] Our God nonetheless proceeded to be glorified in his saints and to extend through more successful results
the virtuous work which had been begun, and once again to
kindle the brightness of his light for us who found ourselves in
darkness. That is, he "fed us with the bread of tears and gave us
tears to drink, but in moderation," as the prophet said.[21] Such
is therefore the moderation of his correction and emendation:
he is not indignant with us continually, nor is he angry with us
forever, but he is reconciled with his servants who hope in him.

9.[9].[22] When therefore the most religious emperor Constantine, the son of that excellent and likewise supremely tem-
perate sovereign Constantius, was preparing for war against
Maxentius, the tyrant in Rome, and was leading his army (he
was in fact already a supporter of the Christian religion and a
worshiper of the true God, but had not yet received the sign of
the Lord's passion, our customary initiation), he was making
his way in a state of anxiety, turning over in his mind the many

20. Ex 10.23.
21. Ps 79.6.
22. Rufinus here substitutes his own account for Eusebius's 9.9.1–3. His
story of Constantine's fear of the looming battle is told more circumstantially
in the anonymous *Life of Constantine* in Joseph Bidez, *Philostorgius: Kirchengeschichte* (Berlin: Akademie Verlag, 1981), 379–80 (424.5–425.10). Here Constantine's fear increases after he scouts out the enemy forces; the story is also
told in Nazarius, *Panegyr. Lat.* IV (X).18.2–4, where the theme of the emper-
or's fear is again present (here it is that the enemy will be too terrified to give
battle). Zonaras 13.1.9–10 says that Constantine feared Maxentius's sorcery.
François Heim, "Constantin dans l'*Histoire ecclésiastique* de Rufin: fidelités et
infidelités à Eusèbe," *Euphrosyne* NS 29 (2001): 201–10, suggests that Rufinus
portrays Constantine as reflecting the feelings of the Christians of Aquileia in
the face of the Gothic threat, while God's reassurance and his victory remind
them of Stilico's aversion of the threat at the battle of Pollentia in 402.

difficulties of the looming war and lifting his eyes to heaven again and again, that he might pray for divine assistance for himself from there, when through his drowsiness he saw in the sky in the east the sign of the cross glowing fiery red. And when he was terrified by the daunting sight and confounded by the novel spectacle, he saw angels standing by him who said, "Constantine, *toutōi nika!*" which means, "Herewith be victorious!" Restored then to good cheer and certain now of victory, he marked on his forehead the sign of the cross which he had seen in heaven, and, given that he was invited by heaven to believe, he does not seem to me inferior to him to whom heaven likewise spoke, "Saul, Saul, why do you persecute me? I am Jesus of Nazareth."[23] The difference is that the invitation came when he had never yet been a persecutor, but was already a follower. He thereupon transformed the sign which had been shown him in the sky into the military standard, and what they call the *labarum* he made to look like the Lord's cross, and thus, fitted out with the weapons and standards of religion, he went forth against the weapons of the impious. Not only that, but he is also said to have had likewise in his right hand the sign of the cross wrought from gold.[24]

Now I do not think it will be judged irrelevant if we digress briefly to explain also what the devout leader's intention was in waging this war. When therefore by the help of the divine power he had been made certain of victory, the spirit of the devout prince was nonetheless harried by another anxiety, namely that he had been named Roman emperor and father of the homeland, and that he wanted if possible to outdo in piety and religion all those who had been sovereigns before him, and that he was being forced to wage war not only on the homeland, but on the very city of Rome, the head of the Roman empire, nor could he restore freedom to the homeland without attacking

23. Acts 9.5.

24. On the vision of the cross and the making of the *labarum* standard, cf. Lactantius, *DMP* 44.5; Eusebius, *Vit. Const.* 1.28–31; Philostorgius 1.6; 1.6a; *Life of Constantine* in Bidez (note 22 above), 380 (425.5–10).

On Constantine's invasion of Italy and defeat of Maxentius in 312, see T. D. Barnes, *Constantine and Eusebius* (Cambridge, MA: Harvard University Press, 1981), 41–43.

RUFINUS OF AQUILEIA

the homeland, which the tyrant had occupied. Hence his spirit
was distressed, and day and night he begged God, with whom
he now felt on familiar terms, 9.9.4. that he might not stain
his right hand with Roman blood now that he had furnished
it with the protection of the salvific sign. This he asked for day
and night, and divine providence granted it to him. When he
had pitched camp not far now from the Milvian Bridge, behold, Maxentius suddenly came forth to meet him as though
he had been seized by divine force, and rushing out of the
gates of Rome he ordered the rest of the army to follow him, he
himself being armed and leading the way to the confrontation.
Now he had ordered the river to be spanned by boats arranged
to form a trap and leveled off with planks placed upon them.
When therefore he himself, mounted and in the forefront, forgot what he had done and started across the bridge with a few
others, the boats went down, and he sank into the depths, thus
canceling the future casualties of the entire war with the loss of
his one wicked head and preserving the undefiled right hand
of the devout prince from the taint of the blood of citizens.

5. Then indeed one could see that what was done in this
case was just as worthy as what was done in that of Moses and
the Hebrew people to have said of it, "Pharaoh's chariots and
his force he has flung into the sea. His chosen mounted officers, even his captains, he has sunk into the Red Sea and with
the sea has covered them."[25] For thus Maxentius and his armed
escort with him sank into the depths, and he fell from the very
planks he had made ready for the death of the devout prince.
6. The following words are suited to him as well: "He dug a pit
and excavated it and fell into the hole which he made. His grief
has redounded upon his own head and his wickedness come
down upon his own pate."[26] This may be fittingly applied to
the impious, 8. while over Constantine as God's servant those
words may be worthily recited which Moses after his victory
sang to his fallen enemies: "Let us sing to the Lord, for glori-

25. Ex 15.4–5.
26. Ps 7.16–17 (LXX). Rufinus omits 9.9.7, about the collapse of the bridge,
to which he has already referred. On the trick bridge see also Lactantius, *DMP*
44.9, and Zosimus 2.16.4.

362

ously has he been honored, horse and rider he has flung into the sea. My helper and protector is he, and he has become my salvation. Who is like you among the gods, Lord? Who is like you, glorious among the holy ones, wonderful in renown, working marvels?"[27] 9. This too is what Constantine was singing—in facts and deeds if not in words—to the high God by whom he had won victory, as he entered Rome to celebrate his triumph. Then indeed did everyone, with their wives and children, the senate and people of Rome, joyfully welcome Constantine as the author of salvation and restorer of freedom, liberated as they were from an overwhelming pestilence and rescued from the yoke of tyrannical brutality. 10. But he did not let his spirit yield to the praises of the people and their acclamations or to the applause of that great and renowned city, nor did he ascribe what had been done to his own power but to the divine gift. As soon, then, as the senate erected images of him in honor of his triumph, he ordered the standard of the Lord's cross to be depicted in his right hand and to be inscribed underneath: 11. "In this special sign, which is the token of true valor, I rescued the city of Rome, the senate, and the Roman people from the yoke of tyranny and restored it to its original freedom and nobility."[28]

12. At this same time Licinius, who had not yet fallen to the depth of madness which he later reached, collaborated with him even then in recognizing and professing God as the author of all the good things that were theirs, and so in making common cause to establish a law in which they accorded the fullest praises to the God of the Christians, and stated that he was the author of all of their valor and achievement, and had given them the victory over the tyrant, and that therefore everyone was to offer him veneration and worship.[29] They also

27. Ex 15.1–2, 11.

28. His victory was won on October 28, 312. Rufinus here gives the inscription from memory; it is not a translation of Eusebius; cf. Heim (note 22 above), 208.

29. *ab universis huic venerationem cultumque deferendum.* There is nothing similar in Eusebius, who mentions two documents that Constantine and Licinius indited: "an absolutely perfect law on behalf of Christians expressed in the fullest terms" (νόμον ὑπὲρ Χριστιανῶν τελεώτατον πληρέστατα διατυποῦνται)

sent this law to Maximinus, who was ruling the east at the time
and who appeared to desire to be on good terms with them.

13. But he was terrified at the momentous deeds accomplished
by the emperors, and even though what they had written was evidently opposed to him and foreign to his policy, he still did not
dare to resist it, while on the other hand he was ashamed to appear to have been reduced to yielding unwillingly to the authority of others, and so out of fear and shame, the most wretched of
advisers, he decided to promulgate a law on behalf of Christians,
similar in tenor, as though on his own initiative and authority.

9.9ᵃ 1–9.³⁰ In it he asserts that his ancestors, the previous
Augusti, had decided that the Christian people should be
completely exterminated as hostile to the worship of the gods,
and that he had shared the same view for a time. But since [he
says] it is just when that people is thought to have been most
effectively repressed that it grows and increases the more, he
would rather that anyone be welcomed who might be brought
by gentle persuasion to worship the gods, but that no one be
forced unwillingly, but that it be left up to each person to worship God in the way preferred by each, and that no trouble or
disturbance be caused the provincials on this account. 10. Such

___

and an account of their victory over the tyrant, which they sent to Maximinus
along with the law. The account, says Eusebius, spoke of "the marvelous things
God had done for them" (τῶν πεπραγμένων εἰς αὐτοὺς ἐκ θεοῦ τὰ παράδοξα).

Lactantius refers to this communication in *DMP* 44.11 (cf. N. H. Baynes,
"Two Notes on the Great Persecution," *Classical Quarterly* 18 [1924]: 193–94).
It was of course indited by Constantine, who associated his ally Licinius with
his victory.

Rufinus's abridgement of this anticipates Constantine's later religious policy, as expressed in Eusebius, *Vit. Const.* 2.44–46: "Eusebius records a series of
measures from the autumn of 324 which demoted the traditional religions of
the Roman empire from their central place in public life and declared Christianity to be not merely the personal religion of the emperor, but the preferred,
perhaps even the official, religion of the Roman empire" (T. D. Barnes, "From
Toleration to Repression: The Evolution of Constantine's Religious Policies,"
Scripta Classica Israelica 21 [2002]: 200).

30. Rufinus here summarizes Eusebius, 9.9ᵃ 1–9, the copy of Maximinus's
letter to the praetorian prefect Sabinus. Issued in December of 312, it announces (in reluctant compliance with the communication of his colleagues)
the suspension of the anti-Christian enactments promulgated previously (in
the summer of 312?) and contained in Eusebius, 9.7.3–14 (cf. note 14 above).

was what Maximinus wrote to the prefect Sabinus, while everyone knew that he was not doing so willingly but was issuing his decision from a feigned benevolence. 11. None of ours accordingly dared either to hold councils or to undertake anything in public which had to do with religion—to repair the churches or to discharge any such task as is customary with us 12. and which the law sent him by the emperors had ordered to be done. But that impious and inwardly savage man allowed only what fear wrung from him, nor did he change his attitude in anything until divine retribution fetched him the blows he deserved. 9.10.1. What happened is that when in defiance of his merits and capabilities he took for himself the name and authority of Augustus, he who possessed no measure of prudence, sobriety, or moderation in his presumptuous arrogance and swollen pride, he began to exalt and raise himself up even against his partners in government, whose regal manner shone forth in the integrity of their morals and the grace of their sobriety and religion. He made bold therefore first of all to appoint himself first among them in rank, 2. and soon after broke the treaty with Licinius, attempted war against him, and, having shortly thrown everything into upheaval, tried at one time to disturb the cities and at another to wear out the army.[31] And in the end, relying on the demons and on the divine power of his gods, he went forth to war with an immense multitude of soldiers. 3. But victory fled from him who was odious to God and men and went over to the other side. 4. And when his army had fallen in battle, the few survivors, seeing him bereft of military resources and divine favor, surrendered to those who were more valiant. He for his

31. Maximinus's seizure of the title of Augustus is in 8.13.15. He was actually senior to his colleagues according to the date of his appointment as Caesar. Licinius and he had almost come to blows after Galerius's death in 311 when they raced to occupy his territory. Licinius subsequently formed an alliance with Constantine, and Maximinus with Maxentius, but with the latter's death, the communication from his colleagues announcing toleration for Christianity, and the cementing of their alliance by the marriage of Licinius and Constantine's sister Constantia in Milan in February of 313, Maximinus may have felt that his tenure was under threat. His invasion of Europe forced Licinius to leave Milan in haste and collect what troops he could to meet him near Adrianople, where he soundly defeated him and forced him to retreat. The fullest account is in Lactantius, *DMP* 45–47.

part, as soon as he saw that he had been deceived by his gods
and deserted by his men, took off the imperial tokens, which
he had never fittingly worn anyway, mixed in with the crowd of
attendants who were fleeing, removed himself from the battle in
a shameful and wretched manner, and skulked through fields
and villages until he finally escaped to the places which seemed
to be free of his enemies, keenly aware of how much truer than
his own baseless convictions were the words of sacred scripture
which proclaim, 5. "A king is not saved by the abundance of his
force, nor will a giant be saved in the abundance of his strength.
Delusive is the horse for safety, in the greatness of its power it
will not be saved. Behold, the eyes of the Lord are upon those
who fear him, who hope in his mercy, that he may free their
souls from death."[32]

6. When therefore the tyrant had returned to his own territory attended by the deepest disgrace and ignominy, the first thing
he did was to act as though kindled by some justifiable rage in
ordering the deaths of a great many of the priests of his gods
and soothsayers, those whom he had previously admired and
whose replies he had trusted in going to war, as though they were
deceitful and treacherous and had betrayed his welfare and his
realm. After that he offered glory and praise to the God of the
Christians, and with belated repentance, having meditated an
about-face at the very moment of his life's condemnation, when
he was bringing upon himself a most miserable death, which his
diseases were contending to inflict, he wrote a law on behalf of
the freedom and security of Christians, a copy of which follows:

7. "The emperor Caesar Galerius Maximinus Germanicus
Sarmaticus,[33] pius felix invictus Augustus. Having as we do a
constant solicitude for our provincials and a determination
to attend to their needs and interests, we never cease to take
thought for what concerns the public and common good and
is considered valuable and agreeable to all. 8. Hence I am sure
that it is well known and obvious to everyone that the order
to prohibit Christian assemblies which had been issued by our

32. Ps 32.16–19.
33. Rufinus omits "Gaius" after "Caesar" and alters "Valerius" to "Galerius." The edict was issued at Nicomedia probably in May of 313.

parents, the divine princes Diocletian and Maximian, was the incentive for a great many acts of plundering and pillage committed by officials, and that this went on day after day to the harm of our provincials, whose interests we have especially at heart, so that they were nearly despoiled of their property and possessions. Concerning this matter we issued a law last year that those wishing to join this people and religion should be prohibited by no one whomsoever in following their wish and free choice, but should satisfy their desire and be allowed to do as they liked with no fear or suspicion. 9. It has not escaped us even now, however, that some magistrates have once again tried to upset our provincials and to disturb them as though by our authority, in order to render them less inclined to practice the religion they love. 10. In order therefore that all uncertainty and fear may be removed, we prescribe by the law contained in this our edict, that all should be informed that those who follow the Christian sect and religion are permitted, by this generous indulgence of ours, to devote themselves, as each of them may choose and prefer, to this religion and rite. We also allow them to erect houses of prayer, that is churches, as they may choose. 11. In order indeed that this our generosity may be augmented in every respect, we also prescribe the following by this law: that any houses, farms, or lands of any kind previously belonging to Christians which were transferred by order of our parents to the imperial treasury,[34] no matter which of them may have been acquired by anyone or divided up[35] or conferred on anyone as a gift, are all to revert to their former legal standing among the Christians and to be restored, all of them, to their rightful owners, that in this matter as well everyone may enjoy the bounty of our piety."

12. Such were the laws now at last issued by Maximinus, who less than a year earlier had prescribed against us penalties on bronze tablets, as though they were to last forever, in which he ordered us to be banished from cities and countryside as impious folk, and driven from almost the entire land.[36] But not even

---

34. *ad fisci ius fuerant sociata:* Eusebius adds "or seized by any city."

35. *sed si qua distracta:* Rufinus adds.

36. In Eusebius, 9.7.3–14.

then was his conversion complete and sincere; he was offering
these laws to God as a kind of bribe. And because the hope he
had placed in his gods had deceived him in battle previously,
he attempted to go to war by these means as though he had
changed his patronage, 13. not realizing in his supreme foolishness that God cannot be bought off with favors and gifts by
men who are depraved from the outset.[37] When therefore he
had equipped the army plentifully and prepared to wage an
unjust war, 14. he was seized by pains in his innards and began
to shake vehemently, so that he could not even lie on a bed, but
kept springing forth from his chamber and dashing himself
flat to the ground. He who was once a glutton who was always
full of wine now could not stand the taste of food, even if it just
touched his lips, or the very odor of wine. Thus with his flesh
wasted away from lack of food and from dryness, the unhappy
man achieved only one thing: finding himself at the end of his
life, he acknowledged that God's retribution was just and that
he was paying the penalty for his crimes which he deserved. 15.
Having already lost his eyes to his disease, however, and then
seen more clearly how impiously he had acted against Christ,
he brought his life to an end.[38]

9.11.1. But with the death of him who used to treat the Christians at one time with unheard-of cruelty and at another with
feigned indulgence, the frank generosity of the legitimate rulers, which was now beyond all suspicion, resulted in the beginning of the restoration of the churches to a condition far
brighter even than it had been before, while God's word and
Christ's teaching were disseminated far more gloriously and
freely. Then indeed did the enemies of the faith come at last to
rue their savagery and cruelty, so that they were ashamed even
to show themselves in public, nor did they dare to look others
in the face. 2. For when Maximinus himself was the first to be
declared by imperial edict an impious tyrant, odious to God
and men, and his portraits and bronze images were ordered

37. The comment about bribery is added by Rufinus.
38. *vivendi finem fecit* = τὴν ψυχὴν ἀφίησιν ("he gave up the ghost"). The other sources do not suggest suicide; cf. Lactantius, *DMP* 49.7; Eutropius, 10.4.4;
Epit. Caes. 40.8. He died in Tarsus c. August of 313.

some to be thrown and cast down and others to be effaced by being painted over in dark colors, such a great turnabout in affairs was suddenly effected that the very name of him who once had pronounced eternal punishment against the Christians was now either uprooted from human memory or preserved in an atmosphere of opprobrium and disgrace, 3. and his officials too, whom he had employed as agents of crime in their tyrannical dominions, were ordered by the legitimate rulers to be killed as accomplices of his impiety and cruelty. 4. Among them the chief deputy in his infamous behavior was Peucedius, who was promoted by him to the consulship twice and thrice and headed a government ministry,[39] and also Quintianus,[40] who likewise occupied the highest offices in his realm and who butchered the Christians in Egypt with unexampled savagery and cruelty, along with many others who abetted Maximinus's impiety. 5. One of them was Theotecnus, who discovered that God is in the end the avenger of profane deeds; thanks to an idol consecrated in Antioch he had even been honored by Maximinus with the post of governor.[41] 6. But when Licinius came to Antioch and ordered those devoted to magic to be questioned under torture, those who were priests and diviners of the new idol, and their associates and even their teachers were seized. And when they were asked by what means the idol gave answers or seemed to perform marvels, they at first pretended ignorance, but later, when interrogated more intensely, they revealed how the whole show had been devised and put together, and declared that it was all a sham worked out by Theotecnus. He therefore ordered that Theotecnus himself, as the originator of the great deception, should be the first to be subjected to the tortures he deserved, and after him as well the rest of the ministers of magic whom he had appointed priests and diviners of the newfangled demon.

39. "Peucetius" is the correct form. *praefecturae tenuit culmen* = τῶν καθόλου λόγων ἔπαρχος πρὸς αὐτοῦ καθεσταμένος ("appointed by him chief finance minister"). Cf. *PLRE* 1.692.

40. "Culcianus" in Eusebius (Clodius Culcianus, prefect of Egypt 303–306; cf. *PLRE* 1.233–34).

41. Theotecnus and the idol are in 9.2–3.

7. To them were added Maximinus's sons, whom he had already taken as partners in his government, and he also subjected to the same tortures his relatives, who had proved quite vexing to citizens and provincials on account of their connection with him. Stupid and senseless they were, who did not hear the warning in the divine writings which runs, 8. "Do not trust in princes nor in the children of men, in whom there is no salvation. Their spirit will go forth and return to its earth; in that day all their thoughts will perish."[42] But we whose hope and salvation are founded in almighty God and in the universal king, Christ our savior and the redeemer of our souls, gladly accept correction from him and await peace and mercy from him likewise.[43]

9(10).1.7. Thus there suddenly perished that impious breed of human beings, odious to God and mankind, as we explained above, so that it was clear that what the Holy Spirit had foretold was justly fulfilled in them: "I saw the impious man raised on high and lifted up like the cedars of Lebanon, and I passed by, and behold, he was not there, and I sought out his place, and did not find it."[44] 8. And then when every cloud had vanished and a happy day now beamed more brightly even than usual upon the lands, and the splendor of its sun illumined the churches of Christ, there remained nowhere a spiteful eye that could view these things otherwise, 9(10).2.1. but all mortals, from their experience of the horror of the tyrant's cruelty which had now passed, extended us their good will even when they did not embrace our faith, and everyone without exception declared that it was the true God who aided the pious, and confirmed that the hope of those who trusted in Christ was sound. Everyone was accordingly filled with a joy that was as it were divinely bestowed,

42. Ps 145.3–4.

43. For the different endings in Eusebius, 9.11.8, cf. apparatus *ad loc.* in Schwartz/Mommsen, 2.852. Rufinus now proceeds immediately to his (abridged) translation of Eusebius's Book 10; in his preface he has explained that he omitted much of the original material in this book and joined the rest of it to Book 9. I have indicated this by numbering the remaining sections 9(10). Book 10 in Rufinus's work as a whole is, then, the first book of his own continuation of the history.

44. Ps 36.35–36.

especially when they saw those places which just before had been destroyed by the tyrants' impious machines, rising higher and brighter as they were rebuilt, and lofty temples being raised in place of modest assembly-halls. 2. For assistance came from the good will of the Christian rulers,[45] which through the religious laws issuing from it cheered our spirits all the more in that they wrote quite often to the bishops in person, paid the priests the honor of their deepest respect, and also generously supplied what was needed for the expenses.

9(10).3.1. Our people meanwhile were celebrating festivals with great frequency and with complete joy and exultation as churches were dedicated throughout the cities and each of the places. The priests would gather together, nor did it seem irksome even for those located far away to meet, since no distance seemed long to the eyes of charity. 2. Groups of people would also assemble with other groups, and as true members of the one body of Christ would rejoice to be joined and associated together, so that the prophet's manner of speaking could be seen to be fulfilled in them when he foretold in words of mystery that "bone was gathered to bone and joint to joint";[46] 3. it is rightly said of them as well that one spirit and one soul is instilled into all of the members, since there is one faith in them all and one God is worshiped by all, and from one mouth all sing hymns to God. A splendid grace furthermore shone forth in the priests and ministers and in everything which concerns religious observance. 4. In one place there stood choirs singing psalms with youths and virgins, older people with younger, praising the Lord's name, while in another the sacred services were performed in due and orderly succession. The assembly too of high priests and priests,[47] venerable for their very age, was most resplendent from where it was seated far off.

---

45. *iuvabat enim Christianorum principum favor;* "rulers of the Christians" might suggest itself as an alternate translation, but the expression would be unusual for Rufinus. Neither Constantine nor of course Licinius were members of the church, whatever Rufinus might mean by calling them "Christian." Eusebius just has "the sovereign emperors" (βασιλεῖς οἱ ἀνωτάτω).

46. Ezek 37.7.

47. *pontificum quoque et sacerdotum consessus: pontifex* is a usual term for "bishop" in the Christian Latin of the time, but it occurs in this sense only here

9(10).4.1.[48] If anyone furthermore was inspired by the Lord's grace to deliver some remarks to the people, the mouths and eyes of everyone would turn to him in complete silence and in the expectation that something from heaven would be announced to them through him. Such was the depth of the reverence preserved by the listeners, such the constancy of the order among the priests. First one and then another would speak, accordingly, and not only two or three, as the Apostle says, with the others weighing what was said;[49] utterance was rather given in the opening of their mouths[50] to any number whatever, so that what Moses had said was more fully verified among them: "Who will grant the whole assembly of the Lord to prophesy?"[51] For there was never any jealousy; no one felt any envy; God's gifts were ministered to God's peoples; each person sought to abound in what builds up the church, as is written.[52] And all of this was done in charity, so that each tried to outdo the others in showing them honor, and each considered the others better than himself. For all the simpler folk admired and looked up to those who instructed the peoples by the wisdom of their discourse, while the wise and educated men preferred those who could feel more confident in offering sacrifices to God because of their purity of life and unaffected simplicity; the office of immolating sacrifice was entrusted to those whose purity of heart was preserved by a more genuine simplicity of life. Thus each person was most interested in seeking in others some way of showing them preference.

Since therefore the glory of the churches advanced with such simplicity in the sight of God and men, and was considered a sort of image on earth of heavenly realities, and since the de-

---

in Rufinus's history. A comparison of this passage with 9(10).8.14, where τοὺς ἐπισκόπους is translated *episcopos ceterosque sacerdotes dei,* suggests that Rufinus is using "priest" here in the sense of "presbyter."

48. 9(10).4.1 is Rufinus's own composition, a series of vignettes of church services and assemblies. In the original, 10.4 is Eusebius's panegyric on Paulinus of Tyre, who was later suspected of harboring "Arian" sympathies, and 10.5–7 is a collection of imperial ordinances concerning the church. Rufinus continues his abridged translation at 9(10).8.2–4.

49. 1 Cor 14.29.   50. Cf. Eph 6.19.
51. Nm 11.29.   52. 1 Cor 14.12.

vout sovereign Constantine exulted as well in such things above
all and was filled with inexhaustible joy at the progress of the
churches as he grew each day in faith and piety, he did not think
it enough for God's priests to treat them as his equals; he wanted to place them far above himself and venerate them as a kind
of image of the divine presence. And since in accordance with
all of this everyone cherished him no longer as an emperor but
as a father, 9(10).8.2–4. unhappy envy could not bear to see the
peace of our people grow with its cheerful prosperity or his efforts on our behalf remain unchallenged. What happened is
that Licinius, who earlier, on account of the probity of his character, the integrity of his life, and the merit of his virtues, had
not only been taken by him as partner in government but received into kinship by the bond arising from his marriage to
Constantine's sister,[53] saw that the emperor ruled over everyone
not so much by force and fear as by love and religion and was
held in the highest veneration by everyone, especially the Christians; and assailed by human weakness, or rather overthrown by
inhuman envy, 5. he began to hatch secret plots to deceive the
noble sovereign, striving to accomplish this above all through
his close associates and servants.[54] 6. But he for his part had no
inkling of his treachery and plots, but since he trusted fully in
God, he relied at all points for his protection on the sign which
had been shown him from heaven, and for this reason he could
not fall victim to any snares.

7. Now when neither the memory of his benefits nor the favor of his relationship by marriage could induce Licinius to repress the savagery of his temper that had given rise to the crime

53. Licinius married Constantia in 313. Eusebius here contradicts himself
when he as much as says that Constantine raised Licinius to imperial rank; in
8.13.14 he refers to Licinius's elevation in 308 (at the Conference of Carnuntum) by the other Augusti.

54. *idque quam maxime per familiares ac ministros molitur:* Rufinus adds. He
alludes to the story told in *Excerpta Valesiana* 15 about Licinius refusing Constantine's proposal that Bassianus (Constantine's brother-in-law) should be
created Caesar for Italy. Bassianus was then incited by his brother Senicio,
Licinius's associate, to plot against Constantine, but was discovered and executed, and Licinius's refusal to surrender Senicio resulted in a state of open
hostility between the two sovereigns. Cf. also Eusebius, *Vit. Const.* 1.50.

in contemplation, nor did his plots succeed through his secret machinations, 8. he decided that the emperor was being helped by the prayers of the Christians and for that reason had remained secure. Swayed therefore by senseless anger, he declared war openly on the emperor and broke the faith and partnership of the realm, while he made ready to persecute ours from a personal and particular hatred, the cause of his complaint being that the Christians did not give themselves over on his behalf, as they did on Constantine's, to the official prayers enjoined upon them.[55] 9. He therefore, who a little earlier had inflicted the severest punishment on those who during the time of the tyrants had done anything cruel to the Christians, now reversed himself, turned his shafts around against our people, and consecrated the first sacrileges of his tyranny with our blood. 10. For he first ordered anyone who was Christian to leave his palace and then to leave any branch of the service.[56] 11. The pestilence advanced thereafter, with tyrannical edicts ordering everyone who professed themselves Christian to be clapped in prison. He immediately found a way, though, to outdo in cruelty his predecessors. He issued an edict in which he added that no one should bring food or drink to anyone sent to prison, saying that it was unjust to show mercy or kindness to those whom he himself had condemned with his laws. And thus multitudes of those in prison died of starvation.[57]

14. Now he thought that his tyranny would remain still more secret thereby, while actually even this seems of minor note as his savagery of spirit grew. He lost no time in extending his furious cruelty to the bishops and the other priests of God; he first trumped up ingenious accusations against all of the more prominent ones and those of greater fame or higher repute

55. The remark about the neglect of Christian prayers for Licinius is taken from Eusebius, 10.8.16.

56. On Licinius's anti-Christian enactments, cf. Eusebius, *Vit. Const.* 1.55–56. Eusebius, as we see in 10.8.16, suggests that the reason was his suspicion that Christians favored his enemy.

57. On Licinius's denial of food to prisoners, see Eusebius, *Vit. Const.* 1.54. Rufinus rearranges the following sections of book 9(10) to achieve a smoother narrative, putting 8.12–13 after 8.15, which in turn he puts after 8.17, omitting 8.16 (whose remarks about prayer he has already incorporated in 8.8).

for their wisdom and doctrine, and bidding them to be indicted on charges of injurious behavior or some other pretended crime, he ordered them to be punished simply because they had been denounced, without conducting any investigation of the cases. 17. He furthermore employed thereafter a kind of cruelty unexampled in any age against everyone who had refused to perform his foul sacrifices: he did not order them to be handed over to the torturers, as the tyrants who had preceded him had done, nor to torments and anguish, but to be given to the butchers, that they might hang them contemptuously like swine over chopping blocks, hack them to bits, and throw the pieces into the sea as food for the fish.[58]

15. The churches too, which he had already in his own time caused to be built by the joint edicts,[59] he once again tore down, and in every respect did all that he could to surpass the cruelty of all the tyrants who had preceded him. 12. Not only that, but whatever laws had been wisely and fittingly instituted by those of former times he changed so that they were barbarous in style;[60] his greed knew no bounds; he altered the assessments; fields empty of husbandmen he repopulated with taxes. 13. And when in addition he banished men on false charges, he tore their wives from their lawful marriages and joined them to his slaves and attendants, while he himself, despite his age, took pleasure in adultery and the seduction of virgins.[61] But when, once equipped with weapons and virtues of this sort, he began to play the tyrant more fiercely, Constantine, who was adorned with true virtues and fortified by perfect piety toward God, made ready to counter such enormous and frequently repeated offenses. 9(10).9.1. Nor was the victory in any way difficult, when the cause was more just, the faith purer, and the virtue more eminent. 6. And once Licinius was thrown down and

---

58. Compare Eusebius, *Vit. Const.*1.51 and 2.1–2.

59. *communibus edictis:* cf. Lactantius, *DMP* 48.13 (following the letter issued under Constantine's and his names).

60. Cf. Eusebius, *Vit. Const.* 1.55. *Epit. Caes.* 41.8 mentions his contempt for scholarship, especially jurisprudence (*forensem industriam*).

61. Cf. *Excerpt. Val.* 22; Aurelius Victor 41.5; *Epit. Caes.* 41.8; Julian, *Caesars* 315D. Licinius's benefits to the cities and countryside, by contrast, are noted by Libanius, *Or.* 30.6, and *Epit. Caes.* 41.9.

all memory of his tyranny removed, [Constantine] alone came into possession of the entire Roman empire together with his sons.[62] Then indeed the condition of the state was marked by equable moderation and an oversight most worthy of the Roman name. Great fear held sway among the barbarian nations, while in the provinces the sense of fealty was greater than fear. All was restful and undisturbed by internal wars, and all mortals lived peacefully, happily, and securely. The extent to which the increase in the church's glory was due to the zeal of the devout emperor defies description, as does the care he showed in providing for the needy. His spirit was ardent in faith in God, and his kindly and generous heart, battened upon good works. 8. The prosperity and peacefulness of the current conditions were in fact such as to wipe out the memory of the past evils. For with his frequent edicts published everywhere he had not only annulled the tyrants' enactments against Christians and restored a legitimate system of law; he also bestowed many privileges on the churches and the highest honors on the priests. Dear to God and men thereby, he administered the entire Roman empire with both a religion that was pure and a virtue of spirit and moderation that exceeded all of those before him.

62. Rufinus omits 10.9.2–5, which mentions Constantine's oldest son, Crispus, whom he executed in 326; he thus further abridges Eusebius's already summary account of the hostilities between the two emperors, from the Battle of Cibalae in 316–317 to Licinius's final defeat at Chrysopolis on September 18, 324. He also omits 10.9.7 (rhetorical decoration).

PREFACE OF RUFINUS TO
THE CONTINUATION

HE RECORD OF the affairs of the church with which
Eusebius has provided us extends to this point. We for
our part have briefly added, to the best of our ability, the events which followed in the course of time down to
the present, and which we either found in the writings of those
before us or we remembered, obedient as always to the injunc-
tions of our father in religion.*

* Chromatius of Aquileia. On the written sources from which Rufinus drew,
see the indispensable article by Y.-M. Duval, "Sur quelques sources latines de
l'*Histoire de l'Église* de Rufin d'Aquilée," *Cassiodorus* 3 (1997): 131–51. He identifies Jerome's *Chronicle* both as the most important among them and as the
occasion of many of his errors of chronology. The others are the *Tractatus* of
Gaudentius of Brescia and the writings of Hilary and Athanasius.

BOOK TEN

10.1. When Alexander had received the priesthood at Alexandria after Achillas, who had succeeded Peter Martyr, the favorable state of our affairs was upset by a disagreement among us, because we had peace and respite from persecutions and the glory of the churches was enhanced by the merits of the confessors. What happened is that some presbyter in Alexandria named Arius, a man devout in appearance and aspect rather than in virtue, but wrongfully desirous of glory, praise, and novelty, began to put forward some perverted ideas concerning the faith of Christ, which had never entered into discussion before. He tried to divide and separate the Son from that substance and nature of God the Father which is eternal and ineffable, something which upset many in the church.[1] Bishop Alexander, who was by nature gentle and peaceful, desired to recall Arius from his perverted enterprise and impious assertions by his assiduous admonitions, but did not succeed, because the virus of his pestilential teaching had already infected so many not only in Alexandria, but in other cities and provinces to which it had spread; and since he believed that it would be fatal to ignore such a matter, he brought it to the attention of many of his fellow priests. The issue became more widely known. Word of it reached the ears even of the devout sovereign, since he looked after our concerns with an interest and diligence that was unbounded. He then, in accordance with the decision of the priests, summoned a council of bishops to the city of Nicaea, and there ordered Arius to present himself to the three hundred and eighteen bishops in session and to be judged concerning his assertions and arguments.[2]

10.2. Now I do not think it right to omit the marvelous thing which the sovereign did in the council. For when the bishops had come together from almost everywhere and, as usually happens, were submitting complaints against each other arising from various causes, he was constantly being importuned by each of them, petitions were being offered, wrongdoings were being brought up, and they were giving their attention to these matters rather than to the purpose of their gathering. But he, seeing that these quarrels were hindering the most important business at

1. On the succession of Peter (300–311), Achillas (311–312), and Alexander (313–328) see Theodoret, *HE* 1.2.8. On Arius's religious appearance, cf. Epiphanius, *Pan.* 69.3.1. On Arius's teaching, see Winrich A. Löhr, "Arius Reconsidered," *ZAC* 9 (2005): 524–60, and 10 (2006): 121–57; Rowan Williams, *Arius: Heresy and Tradition*[2] (London: SCM Press, 2001), 95–245 and 247–67; and Lewis Ayres, *Nicaea and its Legacy: An Approach to Fourth-Century Trinitarian Theology* (Oxford: Clarendon, 2004), 1–84.

2. On the break between Alexander and Arius, cf. Epiphanius, *Pan.* 68.4.1–3 and 69.3–9; Theodoret, *HE* 1.2.12; Philostorgius, 1.7a. On the Council of Nicaea: Eusebius, *Vit. Const.* 3.6–21; Athanasius, *De decretis* 19–20; *Ad Afros* 5; Socrates, 1.8; Athan., *Dokument* 22–26, 29–30; Hefele-Leclercq 1.423–49; Manlio Simonetti, *La crisi ariana nel IV secolo* (Rome: Studia Ephemeridis "Augustinianum" 11, 1975), 77–95; Williams, 48–71; Sara Parvis, *Marcellus of Ancyra and the Last Years of the Arian Controversy 325–345* (Oxford: Clarendon, 2006), 38–95.

hand, set a certain day on which any bishop who thought he had a complaint to make might submit it. And when he had taken his seat, he accepted the petitions of each. Holding all the petitions together in his lap, and not disclosing what they contained, he said to the bishops, "God has appointed you priests and given you power to judge even concerning us, and therefore it is right that we are judged by you, while you cannot be judged by human beings. For this reason, wait for God alone to judge among you, and whatever your quarrels may be, let them be saved for that divine scrutiny. For you have been given to us by God as gods, and it is not fitting that a man should judge gods, but only he of whom it is written, 'God has stood in the assembly of the gods, in its midst he has judged between gods.'[3] And therefore put aside these matters and, free from contentiousness, give your attention to making decisions concerning the faith of God." Having spoken thus, he ordered all the petitions containing complaints to be burned up together, lest the dissension between priests become known to anyone.

Now when the issue concerning faith had been discussed in the bishops' council for many days, and quite a few there put forward different views and vigorously supported Arius's initiative, there were still more who abhorred the impious enterprise. And since there were at the council a large number of priest-confessors, they were all opposed to Arius's novelties. But those who supported him were men clever in disputation and therefore opposed to simplicity in faith.

10.3. Now we may learn how much power there is in simplicity in faith from what is reported to have happened there. For when the zeal of the devout emperor had brought together priests of God from all over the earth, philosophers too and logicians of great renown and fame gathered in a state of expectancy. One of them, who was celebrated for his dialectical ability, used to hold ardent debates each day with our bishops, men likewise by no means unskilled in the art of disputation, and the result was a magnificent display for the learned and educated men who gathered to listen. Nor could the philosopher be cornered or trapped in any way by anyone, for he met the

3. Ps 81.1; Socrates, 1.8.18–20; Sozomen, 1.17.3–6.

questions proposed with such rhetorical skill that whenever he seemed most firmly trapped, he escaped like a slippery snake. But that God might show that the kingdom of God is based upon power rather than speech, one of the confessors, a man of the simplest character who knew only Christ Jesus and him crucified,[4] was present with the other bishops in attendance. When he saw the philosopher mocking our people and proudly displaying his skill in dialectic, he asked everyone for a chance to exchange a few words with the philosopher. But our people, who knew only the man's simplicity and lack of skill in speech, feared that they might be put to shame in case his holy simplicity became a source of laughter to the clever. But the elder insisted, and he began his discourse in this way: "In the name of Jesus Christ, O philosopher," he said, "listen to the truth. There is one God who made heaven and earth, who gave breath to man whom he had formed from the mud of the earth, and who created everything, what is seen and what is not seen, with the power of his word and established it with the sanctification of his spirit. This word and wisdom, whom we call 'Son,' took pity on the errors of humankind, was born of a virgin, by suffering death freed us from everlasting death, and by his Resurrection conferred on us eternal life. Him we await as the judge to come of all that we do. Do you believe that this is so, O philosopher?" But he, as though he had nothing whatever that he could say in opposition to this, so astonished was he at the power of what had been said, could only reply to it all that he thought that it was so, and that what had been said was the only truth. Then the elder said, "If you believe that this is so, arise, follow me to the church, and receive the seal of this faith." The philosopher, turning to his disciples and to those who had gathered to listen, said, "Listen, O learned men: so long as it was words with which I had to deal, I set words against words, and what was said I refuted with my rhetoric. But when power rather than words came out of the mouth of the speaker, words could not withstand power, nor could man oppose God. And therefore if any of you was able to feel what I felt in what was said, let him believe in Christ and follow this old man in whom God

4. 1 Cor 2.2.

has spoken." And thus the philosopher became a Christian and rejoiced to have been vanquished at last.[5]

10.4. There was also at the council the man of God Bishop Paphnutius from Egypt, one of the confessors whom Maximian, after gouging out their right eyes and severing their left hams, had condemned to the mines. But there was in him such a grace of miracles that signs were worked through him no less than through the apostles of old. For he put demons to flight by a mere word and cured the sick by prayer alone. He is also said to have returned sight to the blind and given back soundness of body to the crippled. Constantine regarded him with such veneration and love that many times he called him into the palace, embraced him, and bestowed fervent kisses on the eye which had been gouged out in his confession of faith.[6]

10.5. If any of their number could have been even more outstanding, it is said to have been Spyridon as well, a bishop from Cyprus, who was one of the order of prophets, as far as we too learned from what was said by those who had seen him. He remained a shepherd even after he was appointed bishop. Now one night when thieves approached the sheepfold and stretched forth their greedy hands to make an opening to bring out the sheep, they found themselves held fast by invisible bonds and remained so until daybreak as though they had been handed over to torturers. Now when the elder got ready to lead the sheep out to pasture in the morning, he saw the youths stretched out there, hanging from the sheepfold without human fetters. When he learned why they had been so punished, he loosed with a word those whom he had deservedly bound, and lest they should have nothing to show for their nocturnal labors, he said, "Take one of the rams for yourselves, lads, so that you will not

5. Cf. Sozomen, 1.18.1–4. On holy men versus philosophers, cf. Rufinus, *Historia monachorum* 28; Palladius, *Historia Lausiaca* 38.11; Epiphanius, *Pan.* 66.11; Cassian, *Coll.* 15.3; 5.21.

6. Socrates, 1.11, identifies Paphnutius as a bishop from the Upper Thebaid who persuaded his fellows at the council to reject a proposal to impose clerical celibacy (the attribution to him of this intervention is uncertain). Cf. Thelamon, *PC*, 464. Eusebius/Rufinus, 8.14.13 mentions Maximinus Daia as gouging out the eyes of Christians; his uncle Galerius Maximianus was an equally notable persecutor. Rufinus may have confused the two names.

have come for nothing; but you would have done better to get it by request than by theft."[7]

They also relate of him the following miracle. He had a daughter named Irene, who, after she had faithfully served him, died a virgin. After her death someone came who said he had entrusted to her a deposit. The father did not know of the affair. A search of the whole house failed to reveal anywhere what was sought. But the one who had left the deposit pressed his claim with weeping and tears, even avowing that he would take his own life if he could not recover what he had deposited. Moved by his tears, the old man hurried to his daughter's grave and called her by name. She said from the grave, "What do you want, father?" He replied, "Where did you put this man's deposit?" She explained where it was, saying, "You will find it buried there." Returning to the house, he found the thing where his daughter, from the grave, had said it was, and returned it to the one who had asked for it. There are many other miracles of his mentioned which are still talked about by all.[8]

7. On Spyridon of Tremithus, cf. Paul van den Ven, *La légende de S. Spyridon évêque de Trimithonte* (Louvain: Bibliothèque du *Muséon*, 1953), and Gérard Garitte, "L'édition des Vies de saint Spyridon par M. Van den Ven," *Revue d'histoire ecclésiastique* 50 (1955): 125–40. It was not uncommon for bishops to work at various trades to support themselves (in order to remain independent of the rich and able to admonish them): see Epiphanius, *Pan.* 70.2.2, 80.4.7–8, 80.5.5–6.4.

On the theme of malefactors and enemies magically or miraculously immobilized in pagan and Christian (especially monastic) literature, cf. A.-J. Festugière, "Lieux communs littéraires et thèmes de folk-lore dans l'hagiographie primitive," *Wiener Studien* 73 (1960): 123–52, esp. 146–48. It is a commonplace that the holy person gives the thief what he came for: cf. Thelamon, *PC* 409.

8. On the custom of depositing money in temples, see Cicero, *Laws* 2.16.41; Xenophon, *Anabasis* 5.3.6; Plautus, *Bacchides* 306–7. On consulting the dead about missing deposits, cf. Herodotus, 5.92; *Apophthegmata Patrum* 19.12; Augustine, *De cura pro mortuis gerenda* 11.13.

The stories Rufinus tells about the holy men in 10.3–5 are not digressions from his narrative of the Council of Nicaea, but an integral part of it; they are meant to demonstrate the exceptional holiness of at least some of its members and thus to indicate the presence of the Holy Spirit to the council. Modern readers of more egalitarian sympathies may assume that the gifts of the Spirit are more equally bestowed and that the guidance of the Spirit at the council would have emerged more clearly from a circumstantial narrative of its

There were still in those times, then, very many resplendent men of the sort in the Lord's churches, of whom quite a few were present at the council. Athanasius, at that time a deacon of Bishop Alexander of Alexandria, was there too, aiding the old man with his abundant counsel. During that time the council met each day, and it did not dare to proceed carelessly or recklessly to a decision about such a serious matter. Arius was often summoned to the council, his propositions were scrutinized in painstaking detail, and the most careful consideration was given to the question of what position or decision to take against them. Finally after long and detailed discussion it was decided by all, and decreed as though by the mouth and heart of all, that the word "homoousios" should be written, that is, that the Son should be acknowledged to be of the same substance as the Father, and this was most firmly declared by the vote of them all. There were then only seventeen, it is said, who preferred Arius's creed and who affirmed that God's Son had been created externally from nothing existing, and had not been begotten from the Father's very divinity. The decision of the council of priests was conveyed to Constantine, who revered it as though it had been pronounced by God and declared that anyone who should try to oppose it he would banish as contravening what had been divinely decreed. Six only there were who suffered themselves to be expelled with Arius, while the other eleven, after taking counsel together, agreed to subscribe with their hands only, not their hearts. The chief designer of this pretense was Eusebius, bishop of Nicomedia.[9] During that

procedure. But a church which had with it the confessor-bishops displaying the signs of the demoniacally-inspired persecutions and of the heroic sanctity which had overcome them on the one hand, and the memory of the many bishops who had yielded to those persecutions on the other (e.g., 8.3.1), would be likely to think otherwise. We have already seen this narrative procedure at work in Rufinus's account of the council which condemned Paul of Samosata (7.28, note 52), and we will see it again at 10.18, when the council that condemned Athanasius is abandoned by the confessor-bishops before it gets fairly under way.

9. There were actually only two bishops who were exiled with Arius: Secundus of Ptolemais and Theonas of Marmarica; cf. Philostorgius, 1.9; Theodoret, *HE* 1.7.15. For a list of twenty-two "Arianizing" bishops (at Nicaea?) cf. Philostorgius, 1.8a. The tradition of six bishops who supported Arius is

time, then, the subscriptions were written in one way or another, some sincerely and some not, as later events proved, particular regulations were made concerning each of several church customs, and so the council dissolved. There is here inserted the exposition of faith of those who had assembled.

10.6. Creed of Nicaea:

"We believe in one God, the Father almighty, maker of all things visible and invisible, and in one Lord Jesus Christ, Son of God, born as only-begotten of the Father, that is, of the Father's substance, God from God, light from light, true God from true God, born (*natum*), not made, *homoousios* with the Father, that is, of the same substance as the Father, through whom all things were made, those in heaven and those on earth. Who for the sake of us human beings and our salvation came down and was incarnate, and becoming a human being suffered and rose on the third day, and ascended to heaven, from where he is to come to judge the living and the dead. And in the Holy Spirit. But those who say that there was a time when he was not, and before he was born he was not, and that he was made out of nothing existing, or who say that God's Son is from another subsistence or substance[10] or is subject to alteration or change, the catholic and apostolic church anathematizes.

---

echoed in Theodoret, 1.5.5 and 1.7.14. Cf. also Socrates, 1.8.31–33, and Sozomen, 1.21.1–5.

The powerful influence exercised by Eusebius over all the churches of his region as bishop of the imperial residence of Nicomedia (before 318) and later of Constantinople (338) will be seen in the later developments of the "Arian crisis," as for instance in 10.13–14. See Daniel De Decker, "Eusèbe de Nicomédie. Pour une réévaluation historique-critique des avatars du premier Concile de Nicée," *Augustinianum* 45 (2005): 95–170.

10. *ex alia subsistentia vel substantia,* translating ἐξ ἑτέρας ὑποστάσεως ἢ οὐ-σίας. Marius Victorinus seems to have been the first to translate ὑπόστασις as *subsistentia* (hesitantly), Rufinus the first to apply the translation to the Creed of Nicaea. Cf. M. Victorinus, *Adversus Arium* 2.4 and 3.4. On the distinction between ὑπόστασις and οὐσία, see Jürgen Hammerstaedt, "Hypostasis," *RAC* 16.986–1035. Rufinus in translating Gregory Naz., *Or.* 2.36, had rendered ὑπό-στασις as *subsistentia ac persona,* so that the reader would not confuse it with *substantia;* cf. C. Moreschini, "Rufino traduttore di Gregorio Nazianzeno," *AAAd* 31 (1987): 1.236. The earlier Latin translators of the Creed had found this passage difficult; cf. *EOMIA* 1.298–99. Rufinus's solution was generally accepted, and *subsistentia* became part of the technical vocabulary of Latin

I. They decree in addition[11] that it is to be observed in the churches that no one who castrates himself because of unwillingness to endure sexual desire is to be admitted to the clergy.

II. No one recently admitted to baptism from paganism and its way of life is to be made a cleric before being carefully examined.

III. No bishop or other cleric is to live with women who are not relatives, but only with his mother, sister, aunt, or persons related in this way.

IV. A bishop is, if possible, to be ordained by the bishops of the whole province. If this is difficult, then certainly by not fewer than three, but in such a way that either the presence or the authority of the metropolitan bishop in particular is involved. Without him they consider the ordination invalid.

V. A bishop is not to receive anyone, whether a cleric or a layman, whom another bishop has expelled from the church. Lest, however, there be no remedy for something which has been unjustly done because of strife or anger, as sometimes happens, they decree that twice each year councils are to be held in each province by all the provincial bishops and judgment passed on such matters, so that if by chance something was done unjustly by one of them, it may be put right by the others, or if rightly, it may be confirmed by all.

---

theology. See also note 46 below. His version of the Creed is, mysteriously, almost the same as that known as the *Interpretatio Caeciliani* (*EOMIA* 1.106 and 108), which, according to Schwartz (1.204–6), was produced later.

For the original text of the Creed of Nicaea, see *DEC* 1.5.

11. For the original Canons of Nicaea, see *DEC* 1.6–16. For commentary, see Hefele-Leclercq, 1.503–620. For the various Latin versions, see *EOMIA* 1.112–43 and 178–243. For commentary on these versions, see Hefele-Leclercq, 1.1139–76; Schwartz, 4.159–275.

Rufinus's version is independent of the earlier one to which the Canons of Sardica became attached. It abridges and occasionally glosses the original, and the numeration is slightly different. It does not include the final Canon 20 of the original (against kneeling for prayer on Sundays and during Eastertide). Pope Innocent (402–17) had it excerpted, together with the Creed, under the title *Abbreviatio,* and in that form it often appears in the early Latin canonical collections. Cf. F. Maassen, *Geschichte der Quellen und der Literatur des canonischen Rechts* (Gratz: Leuschner & Lubensky, 1870), 33–34; Hefele-Leclercq, 1.1163–65; Schwartz, 4.205; 4.218.

VI. The ancient custom in Alexandria and the city of Rome is to be maintained whereby [the bishop of the former] has charge of Egypt, while [the bishop of the latter] has charge of the suburbicarian churches.[12]

VII. If by chance in ordaining a bishop two or three should disagree for some reason, the authority of the rest of them, and especially that of the metropolitan with the rest, is to be considered more valid.

12. *Et ut apud Alexandriam vel in urbe Roma vetusta consuetudo servetur, quia vel ille Aegypti vel hic suburbicariarum ecclesiarum sollicitudinem gerat.*

This corresponds to the first part of the original Canon 6, which runs: Τὰ ἀρχαῖα ἔθη κρατείτω τὰ ἐν Αἰγύπτῳ καὶ Λιβύῃ καὶ Πενταπόλει, ὥστε τὸν Ἀλεξανδρείας ἐπίσκοπον πάντων ἔχειν τὴν ἐξουσίαν, ἐπειδὴ καὶ τῷ ἐν τῇ Ῥώμῃ ἐπισκόπῳ τὸ τοιοῦτον σύνηθές ἐστιν. Ὁμοίως δὲ καὶ κατὰ τὴν Ἀντιόχειαν καὶ ἐν ταῖς ἄλλαις ἐπαρχίαις τὰ πρεσβεῖα σώζεσθαι ταῖς ἐκκλησίαις ["The ancient customs of Egypt, Libya, and Pentapolis shall be maintained, according to which the bishop of Alexandria has authority over all these places, since a similar custom exists with reference to the bishop of Rome. Similarly in Antioch and the other provinces the prerogatives of the churches are to be preserved" (*DEC* translation)].

Schwartz (4.205) attributes the "suburbicarian gloss" to Rufinus himself; J. Gaudemet thinks it precedes him: cf. *L'église dans l'empire romain* (Paris: Sirey, 1958), 445. The gloss is based on the words "Egypt, Libya, and Pentapolis" in the original canon; these provinces would later (during the prefecture of Modestus, 367–371) be formed into the (civil) diocese of Egypt. Now a diocese was normally governed by a "vicar," but the diocese of Italy was divided into the two regions of *Italia annonaria* to the north, under the *vicarius Italiae,* and the *suburbicariae regiones* of the center and south, which were under the *vicarius urbis.* In a sense, then, the southern half of Italy could be seen as equivalently a diocese, as being under its own vicar, and Rome was located within it (although it was governed by the *praefectus urbis*). Cf. Hefele-Leclercq, 1.1182–1202, esp. 1.1197–98.

Since the original canon grounds itself upon the practice of the church of Rome in acknowledging the ecclesiastical authority of the bishop of Alexandria over what would become an entire (civil) diocese, Rufinus in his gloss defines more precisely which "diocese" the bishop of Rome governs, sharply reducing thereby the extent of papal authority set out in the earlier Latin version of this canon: *Ecclesia Romana semper habuit primatus, teneat autem et Aegyptus ut episcopus Alexandriae omnium habeat potestatem, quoniam et Romano episcopo haec est consuetudo (EOMIA* 1.121). Schwartz (4.205) thinks that Rufinus is deliberately confining papal authority to the region of Italy south of his own homeland, perhaps in reply to the anti-Origenist pressure he had felt from that quarter.

VIII. The precedence in honor given of old to the bishop of Jerusalem is to be preserved, the dignity of the metropolitan of that province being maintained nonetheless.

IX. As for the Cathari, whom we know as Novatianists, if they should repent and return to the church, having confessed the doctrines of the church: the clerics should be received into the clergy, but only after receiving ordination. If one of their bishops comes to one of our bishops, he should sit in the place of the presbyters, to be sure, but the title of bishop should remain with him alone who has ever held the Catholic faith, unless he has freely decided to honor him with that title, or if he has decided to look for a vacant bishopric for him. That is up to him.

X. There are not to be two bishops in one city.

XI. Those who are incautiously advanced to the priesthood and afterward confess some misdeed they have done, or are convicted by others, are to be deposed. Those also who are among the lapsed and who by chance have been ordained through ignorance are to be deposed when recognized.

XII. Those who, although not tortured, have lapsed during the persecutions and do penance sincerely are to spend five years among the catechumens and for two years after that are to be joined to the faithful in prayer alone, and in that way are afterward to be taken back.

XIII. Those who in order to profess the faith have left the service and then have once again sought to enter it are to do penance for thirteen years and afterward to be taken back, provided they do penance sincerely. It is also, however, in the bishop's power to adjust the term if he sees that they are giving careful and fruitful attention to their penance.

XIV. But as for those penitents who are dying, they decree that no time must be spent [doing penance]. If someone who has received communion recovers, however, he is to complete the times set or at least do as the bishop determines.

XV. As for catechumens who have lapsed, they have decreed that for three years they are to be separated from the prayer of the catechumens, and afterward to be taken back.

XVI. No one, whether a bishop or even another cleric, is to attempt to move from a lesser city to a greater church.

XVII. No cleric who for no good reason has left his church and roams about among the other churches is to be received into communion.

XVIII. No one is to steal away someone who belongs to someone else and ordain him a cleric in his own church without the consent of the one to whom he belongs.

XIX. No cleric is to charge interest, or an augmentation on grain or wine, the original amount of which, when let out, customarily yields a return of half again or even twice as much; if he does so, he is to be deposed as guilty of filthy lucre.

XX. Deacons are not to be given precedence over presbyters, nor are they to sit where the presbyters do or distribute the Eucharist when they are present; they are simply to assist while the others do that. But if there is no presbyter present, then only may they distribute as well; those that do otherwise are ordered to be deposed.

XXI. The Paulianists,[13] also called Photinians, are to be rebaptized.

XXII. Deaconesses likewise, because they do not in fact receive the imposition of hands, should be placed among the laity."

So, then, once they had formulated decrees concerning these matters in a way consonant with respect for the divine laws, and also had handed down to the churches the ancient canon regarding the observance of Easter, so that no further inconsistency should arise, everything was duly settled and the peace and faith of the churches was preserved, one and the same, in the East and the West.

10.7. It was at this time that Helena, Constantine's mother, a woman matchless in faith, devotion, and singular generosity, just the sort of mother whom Constantine would have, and whom one would expect him to have, was alerted by divine visions and traveled to Jerusalem, where she asked the inhabitants where the place was where the sacred body of Christ had hung fastened to the gibbet. It was hard to find, because an image of Venus had been fixed there by the persecutors of old,

---

13. "Paulianists" are followers of Paul of Samosata. Rufinus associates with him Photinus, bishop of Sirmium (ca. 344–51), who was likewise accused of denying Christ's divinity.

so that any Christian wishing to worship Christ in that place would seem to be worshiping Venus. For this reason the place was unvisited and almost forgotten. But when, as we said, the pious woman had hastened to the place indicated to her by a sign from heaven, and had pulled away everything profane and defiled, she found deep down, when the rubble had been cleared away, three crosses jumbled together. But her joy at the discovery was darkened by the fact that the crosses were indistinguishable from each other. There was also found the inscription which Pilate had made with Greek, Latin, and Hebrew letters, but not even it showed clearly enough which was the Lord's gibbet. Here, then, human uncertainty demanded divine evidence.

There happened to be in the city a woman of high station who lived there and who was lying near death of a serious illness. Macarius was bishop of the church at the time. When he saw the perplexity of the queen and of all who were also present, he said, "Bring here all the crosses which have been found, and God will now disclose to us which one it was that bore God." And going in with the queen and the people to the woman who was lying there, he knelt down and poured out to God a prayer of this sort:

10.8. "O Lord, who through your only-begotten Son have deigned to bestow salvation on the human race through the suffering of the cross, and now have most recently inspired the heart of your handmaid to seek the blessed wood on which our salvation hung, show clearly which of these three was the cross destined for the Lord's glory, and which of them were made for the punishment of slaves, that this woman who lies here half dead may be called back from the gates of death to life as soon as the wood of healing touches her."

Having said this, he first touched her with one of the three, but it did not help. He touched her with the second, and again nothing happened. But when he touched her with the third, she at once opened her eyes, got up, and with renewed strength and far more liveliness than when she had been healthy before, began to run about the whole house and glorify the Lord's power. The queen then, having been granted her prayer with such a clear token, poured her royal ambition into the construction of a wonderful temple on the site where she had found the cross. The nails too, with which the Lord's body had been fastened, she brought to her son. He made of some of them a bridle to use in battle, and with the others he is said to have equipped himself with a helmet no less useful in battle. As for the wood of healing itself, part of it she presented to her son, and part she put in silver reliquaries and left in the place; it is still kept there as a memorial with unflagging devotion.[14]

The venerable queen also left the following mark of her devout spirit. She is said to have invited to lunch the virgins consecrated to God whom she found there and to have treated them with such devotion that she thought it unfitting for them to perform the duties of servants; rather, she herself, in servant's garb, set out the food with her own hands, offered the cup, and poured water over their hands, and the queen of the world and mother of the empire appointed herself servant of the servants of Christ.

This took place in Jerusalem. In the meantime Constantine,

14. Helena (ca. 249–329) visited Syria and Palestine toward the end of her life in order to see the holy places. The only useful account of this visit is in Eusebius, *Vit. Const.* 3.42–43 (no mention of the cross). Cf. R. Klein, "Helena," *RAC* 14.355–75, esp. 367–69.

Cyril of Jerusalem, in his letter of 351 to the emperor Constantius, speaks in part 3 of the Savior's cross having been found in Jerusalem in Constantine's time, the divine grace having granted the discovery of the holy places to him who sought them rightly; he does not mention Helena. Cf. E. Bihain, "L'Épître de Cyrille de Jérusalem à Constance sur la vision de la croix (*BHG*[3] 413)," *Byzantion* 43 (1973): 264–96.

The tradition of Helena finding the cross is first found in Ambrose, *De obitu Theodosii* 45–47 (composed in 395). Rufinus is the first to tell the story about the sick woman; in Ambrose's account it is the inscription on the true cross which allows Helena to identify it. Both agree that Helena made gifts for her son from the nails; in Ambrose they are a bridle and a diadem. Cf. Socrates, 1.17; Sozomen, 2.1; Theodoret, *HE* 1.18. The luxuriant growth enjoyed by this story is described by G. W. Bowersock, "Helena's Bridle and the Chariot of Ethiopia," in *Antiquity in Antiquity: Jewish and Christian Pasts in the Greco-Roman World,* ed. Gregg Gardner and Kevin L. Osterloh (Tübingen: Mohr Siebeck, 2008), 383–93. The various representations of Helena in Byzantine literature is studied by Andriani Georgiu, "Helena: The Subversive Persona of an Ideal Christian Empress in Early Byzantium," *JECS* 21.4 (2013): 597–624.

trusting in his faith, conquered by force of arms on their own soil the Sarmatians, the Goths, and the other barbarian nations,[15] except for those which had already achieved peace by treaties of friendship or surrender. The more he submitted to God in a spirit of religion and humility, the more widely God subjected everything to him. He also sent letters to Antony, the first desert-dweller, as to one of the prophets, begging him to beseech the Lord for him and his children.[16] Thus he was eager to commend himself to God not only by his own merits and his mother's devotion, but also through the intercession of the saints.

Now because we have mentioned the great man Antony, I would have liked to say something about his virtues, way of life, and soberness of mind, such that living alone he had only the companionship of wild animals, triumphed over the demons, pleased God more than all other mortals, and left glorious examples of his way of life to the monks even of today, but the short work written by Athanasius and published as well in Latin has forestalled me.[17] For this reason we will pass over what has already been said by others and mention those things which, however reliable the record of them may be, have escaped the notice of those far removed from them through not being so well known.

10.9. In the division of the earth which the apostles made by lot for the preaching of God's word, when the different provinces fell to one or the other of them, Parthia, it is said, went by lot to Thomas, to Matthew fell Ethiopia, and Nearer India, which adjoins it, went to Bartholomew. Between this country and Parthia, but far inland, lies Further India. Inhabited by many peo-

---

15. The Goths were beaten in 332 and the Sarmatians in 334.

16. Cf. [Athanasius], *Life of Antony* 81.

17. The ascription to Athanasius of the Greek *Life of Antony* is controversial; see G. J. M. Bartelink, *Athanase d'Alexandrie: Vie d'Antoine* (Paris: Cerf, 2004). The debate over the Athanasian authorship is considered on pp. 27–35. The life was very soon translated into Latin twice: one version was by Evagrius of Antioch ca. 370 (printed in PG 26:837–978); the other translation, anonymous, was perhaps done earlier. The modern edition is again that of Bartelink, *Vita di Antonio* (Milan: Mondadori, 1974). The two Latin translations are noticed in Bartelink (2004), 95–98.

ples with many different languages, it is so distant that the plow of the apostolic preaching had made no furrow in it, but in Constantine's time it received the first seeds of faith in the following way. A philosopher named Metrodorus, they say, penetrated to Further India for the purpose of viewing the places and investigating the continent.[18] Encouraged by his example, one Meropius as well, a philosopher of Tyre, decided to go to India for the same reason; he had with him two small boys whom as his relatives he was instructing in letters. The younger was called Aedesius and the older Frumentius. When therefore the philosopher had viewed and acquainted himself with the things on which his mind was feasting, and he had set out on the return voyage, the ship in which he was sailing put in to some port to obtain water and other necessaries. It is the custom of the barbarians there that whenever the neighboring peoples announce that their treaty relations with the Romans have been disrupted, they kill all the Romans they find among them. The philosopher's ship was attacked and everyone with him put to death together. The boys, who were discovered under a tree going over and preparing their lessons, were saved because the barbarians pitied them and brought them to the king. He made one of them, Aedesius, his cupbearer, while to Frumentius, whose intelligence and prudence he could see, he entrusted his accounts

18. On the mission of Thomas to Parthia, see 3.1.1. On India and Thomas: *Acts of Thomas* 1 and Chromatius of Aquileia, *Sermo* 26.4. On India and Bartholomew, see 5.10.3 and Jerome, *Vir. illustr.* 36.

To understand Rufinus's geographical description, it is helpful to remember that "India" could mean subcontinental India, or Ethiopia/Aksum, or south Arabia/Yemen. Cf. Philip Mayerson, "A Confusion of Indias: Asian India and African India in the Byzantine Sources," *Journal of the American Oriental Society* 113.2 (1993): 169–74. For an exhaustive survey of the geographical muddle (which was growing steadily in the late classical period), see Pierre Schneider, *L'Éthiopie et l'Inde: Interférences et confusions aux extrémités du monde antique (VIIIe siècle avant J.-C.–VIe siècle après J.-C.)* (École française de Rome, 2004). By "Further India" (*India ulterior*) Rufinus clearly meant one of the first two regions mentioned above; cf. Schneider, 437, and Ilaria Ramelli, "Il cristianesimo in India dall'età costantiniana al V secolo," in Cristiano Dognini-Ilaria Ramelli, *Gli apostoli in India nella Patristica e nella letteratura sanscrita* (Milan: Medusa, 2001), 103–20.

On the adventurer Metrodorus, see Ammianus, 25.4.23; also Socrates, 1.19; Sozomen, 2.24; Theodoret, *HE* 1.23; Philostorgius, 2.6.

and correspondence. From that time on they were held in high honor and affection by the king. Now when the king died and left as heir to the kingdom his wife and her young son, he also left it to the free choice of the youths what they would do. But the queen begged them to share with her the responsibility of ruling the kingdom until her son should grow up, as she had no one more trustworthy in the kingdom, especially Frumentius, whose prudence would suffice to rule the kingdom, for the other gave evidence simply of a pure faith and sober mind.

Now while they were doing so and Frumentius had the helm of the kingdom, God put it into his mind and heart to begin making careful inquiries if there were any Christians among the Roman merchants, and to give them extensive rights, which he urged them to use, to build places of assembly in each location, in which they might gather for prayer in the Roman manner. Not only that, but he himself did far more along these lines than anyone else, and in this way encouraged the others, invited them with his support and favors, made available whatever was suitable, furnished sites for buildings and everything else that was necessary, and bent every effort to see that the seed of Christians should grow up there.[19]

10.10. Now when the royal child whose kingdom they had looked after reached maturity, then, having executed their trust completely and handed it back faithfully, they returned to our continent, even though the queen and her son tried very hard to hold them back and asked them to stay. While Aedesius hastened to Tyre to see his parents and relatives again, Frumentius

19. Wherever on the map Rufinus may have imagined it as being, the kingdom evangelized by Frumentius was clearly Aksum: cf. Athanasius, *Apologia ad Constantium* 31. On the legends which surrounded him, cf. B. W. W. Dombrowski u. F. A. Dombrowski, "Frumentius/Abbā Salāmā: Zu den Nachrichten über die Anfänge des Christentums in Äthiopien," *Oriens Christianus* 68 (1984): 114–69.

On trade between Rome and Aksum, cf. Eusebius, *Vit. Const.* 4.7.1 (Indian and Ethiopian envoys bearing gifts for Constantine); *C. Th.* 12.12.2 (dated 356); A. Dihle, "Die entdeckungsgeschichtlichen Voraussetzungen des Indienhandels der römischen Kaiserzeit," *ANRW* 2.9.2.546–80.

The anti-Roman practice described by Rufinus is otherwise unheard-of, and the attack on the ship seems an act of piracy rather than policy: Thelamon, *PC* 66. Jerome mentions the dangers of Red Sea voyages in *Ep.* 125.3.

journeyed to Alexandria, saying that it was not right to conceal what the Lord had done. He therefore explained to the bishop everything that had been done and urged him to provide some worthy man to send as bishop to the already numerous Christians and churches built on barbarian soil. Then Athanasius, for he had recently received the priesthood,[20] after considering attentively and carefully what Frumentius had said and done, spoke as follows in the council of priests: "What other man can we find like you, in whom is God's spirit as in you, and who could achieve such things as these?" And having conferred on him the priesthood, he ordered him to return with the Lord's grace to the place from which he had come. When he had reached India as bishop, it is said that such a grace of miracles was given him by God that the signs of the apostles were worked by him and a countless number of barbarians was converted to the faith. From that time on there came into existence a Christian people and churches in India, and the priesthood began. These events we came to know of not from popular rumor, but from the report of Aedesius himself, who had been Frumentius's companion, and who later became a presbyter in Tyre.

10.11. It was at this time too that the Georgians, who dwell in the region of Pontus, entered into a commitment to the word of God and the faith in the kingdom to come. The cause of this

20. *nuper sacerdotium susceperat.* The chronology does not square with that suggested by Constantius's letter to the rulers of Aksum (Athanasius, *Apologia ad Constantium* 31), which does indeed say that Athanasius ordained Frumentius bishop of their realm but implies that this took place recently: they are to send Frumentius to be examined by George of Alexandria to make sure his teaching is orthodox before he has a chance to corrupt the Christians in their country. Athanasius, it says, is after all a convicted criminal. Now Athanasius became bishop in 328, but the letter is from the year 356. Thelamon therefore conjectures that Rufinus has deliberately falsified the chronology in order to make it appear that the mission to Aksum took place in Constantine's time rather than Constantius's, Constantine being one of the great heroes of his history, while his son was a deluded persecutor (Thelamon, *PC* 62). Richard Klein, *Constantius II und die christliche Kirche* (Darmstadt: Wissenschaftliche Buchgesellschaft, 1977), 240, thinks that the chronology can still be squared if *susceperat* is understood as Athanasius's resumption of episcopal office after one of his exiles—that is, in 338 or 346. But that is stretching the language a bit.

great benefit was a woman captive who lived among them and led such a faithful, sober, and modest life, spending all of her days and nights in sleepless supplications to God, that the very novelty of it began to be wondered at by the barbarians. Their curiosity led them to ask what she was about. She replied with the truth: that this was simply her way of worshiping Christ as God. This answer made the barbarians wonder only at the novelty of the name, although it is true, as often happens, that her very perseverance made the common women wonder if she were deriving some benefit from such great devotion.

Now it is said that they have the custom that, if a child falls sick, it is taken around by its mother to each of the houses to see if anyone knows of a proven remedy to apply to the illness. And when one of the women had brought her child around to everyone, according to custom, and had found no remedy in any of the houses, she went to the woman captive as well to see if she knew of anything. She answered that she knew of no human remedy, but declared that Christ her God, whom she worshiped, could give it the healing despaired of by humans. And after she had put the child on her hair shirt and poured out above it her prayer to the Lord, she gave the infant back to its mother restored to health. Word of this got around to many people, and news of the wonderful deed reached the ears of the queen, who was suffering from a bodily illness of the gravest sort and had been reduced to a state of absolute despair. She asked for the woman captive to be brought to her. She declined to go, lest she should appear to pretend to more than was proper to her sex. The queen ordered that she herself be brought to the captive's hovel. Having placed her likewise on her hair shirt and invoked Christ's name, no sooner was her prayer done than she had brought it about that she rose up healthy and vigorous, and taught her that it was Christ, God and Son of God most high, who had conferred healing upon her, and advised her to invoke him whom she should know to be the author of life and well-being, for it was he who allotted kingdoms to kings and life to mortals. She returned joyfully home and disclosed the affair to her husband, who wanted to know the reason for this sudden return to health. When he in his joy at his wife's cure ordered gifts to be presented to the woman, she said, "O king, the captive deigns to accept none of these things. She despises gold, rejects silver, and battens on fasting as though it were food. This alone may we give her as a gift: if we worship as God the Christ who cured me when she called upon him."

But the king was not then inclined to do so and put it off for the time, although his wife urged him often, until it happened one day, when he was hunting in the woods with his companions, that a thick darkness fell upon the day, and with the light removed there was no longer any way for his blind steps through the grim and awful night. Each of his companions wandered off a different way, while he, left alone in the thick darkness which surrounded him, did not know what to do or where to turn, when suddenly there arose in his heart, which was near to losing hope of being saved, the thought that if the Christ preached to his wife by the woman captive were really God, he might now free him from this darkness so that he could from then on abandon all the others and worship him. No sooner had he vowed to do so, not even verbally but only mentally, than the daylight returned to the world and guided the king safely to the city. He explained immediately to the queen what had happened. He required that the woman captive be summoned at once and hand on to him her manner of worship, insisting that from then on he would venerate no God but Christ. The captive came, instructed him that Christ is God, and explained, as far as it was lawful for a woman to disclose such things, the ways of making petition and offering reverence. She advised that a church be built and described its shape.

The king therefore called together all of his people and explained the matter from the beginning, what had happened to the queen and him, taught them the faith, and before even being initiated into sacred things became the apostle of his nation. The men believed because of the king, the women because of the queen, and, with everyone desiring the same thing, a church was put up without delay. The outer walls having quickly been raised, it was time to put the columns in place. When the first and second had been set up and they came to the third, they used all the machines and the strength of men and oxen to get it raised halfway up to an inclined position, but no machine could lift it the rest of the way, not even with efforts repeated again and again; with everyone exhausted, it would not budge. Everyone was confounded, the king's enthusiasm waned, and no one could think what to do. But when nightfall intervened and everyone went away and all mortal labors ceased, the woman captive remained inside alone, passing the night in prayer. And when the worried king entered in the morning with all his people, he saw the column, which so many machines and people had been unable to move, suspended upright just above its base: not placed upon it, but hanging about one foot in the air. Then indeed all the people looking on glorified God and accepted the witness of the miracle before them that the king's faith and the captive's religion were true. And behold, while everyone was still in the grip of wonder and astonishment, before their very eyes the column, with no one touching it, gradually and with perfect balance settled down upon its base. After that the remaining columns were raised with such ease that all that were left were put in place that day.

Now after the church had been magnificently built and the people were thirsting even more deeply for God's faith, an embassy of the entire people was sent to the emperor Constantine on the advice of the captive, and what had happened was explained to him. They implored him to send priests who could complete God's work begun among them. He dispatched them with all joy and honor, made far happier by this than if he had annexed to the Roman empire unknown peoples and kingdoms.[21] That this happened was related to us by that most faith-

---

21. Rufinus's is the earliest extant account of the conversion of the *Hiberi* or Georgians. Thelamon conjectures that behind the story of the *captiva* who introduced Christianity to their land there lay a typical Georgian narrative of the foundation of a cult or shrine. Such accounts often feature a woman called a *kadag* who is a possessed intermediary between the divine and human realms and who is often referred to as "captive" or "seized." Certain elements in Rufinus's story, such as the taking of sick children around to the neighbors, the strict separation of the sexes (the king evangelizes the men, and queen the women), the distinction between the exterior and interior architecture of the church, and the mysterious hanging column, have a peculiarly Georgian ring. But we cannot say how Christianity was really introduced to the country, since,

ful man Bacurius, the king of that nation who among us was captain of the court garrison [*domesticorum comes*] and whose chief concern was for religion and truth; when he was the frontier commander [*limitis dux*] in Palestine, he spent some time with us in Jerusalem in great concord of spirit.[22] But let us return to our topic.

10.12. After Helena, the mother of the devout sovereign, had passed from this light laden with the highest honors of the Roman empire, Constantia, then Licinius's widow, was consoled by her brother, the Augustus. It happened that she came to be acquainted with a presbyter who covertly supported the Arian party. He at first divulged nothing at all of this to the sovereign's sister, but when long familiarity gave him his opportunity, he began gradually to suggest that Arius had been the target of envy, and that his bishop, stung by jealousy because Arius was so popular with the people, had stirred up the argument out of private

---

however it happened, the story came to be told in the usual Georgian fashion, in which the new cult was authenticated by the miraculous activities of the shaman. Rufinus took and retailed the story at face value, although its setting within Constantine's reign may be his own contribution. Cf. Thelamon, *PC* 93–119; Socrates, 1.20; Sozomen, 2.7; Theodoret, *HE* 1.24.

On Georgia and the history of its Christianization, see Otar Lordkipanidse and Heinzgerd Brakmann, "Iberia II (Georgien)," *RAC* 17.12–206, esp. 34–35 and 40–57. There is archaeological evidence of the spread of Christianity here in the fourth century before the conversion of the king here mentioned (Mirian III); see Christopher Haas, "Mountain Constantines: the Christianization of Aksum and Iberia," *Journal of Late Antiquity* 1.1 (2008): 101–26. Lordkipanidse and Brakmann, 51, remark that Rufinus may have followed here his usual inclination to shift edifying material from Constantius's reign to his father's; it was Constantius who strove to keep the Iberian king loyal to him (Ammianus, 21.6.8).

On the story of the column, see Annegret Plontke-Lüning, *Frühchristliche Architektur in Kaukasien: Die Entwicklung des christlichen Sakralbaus in Lazika, Iberien, Armenien, Albanien und den Grenzregionen vom 4. bis 7. Jh. (Veröffentlichungen zur Byzanzforschung XIII)* (Vienna: Verlag der österreichischen Akademie der Wissenschaften, 2007), 156–61. It appears in other sources, with variations, but always in connection with the legendary woman, Nino, and the conversion of the king.

22. On Bacurius cf. Ammianus, 31.12.16; Zosimus, 4.57.3 and 4.58; Socrates, 1.20.20; Libanius, *Epp.* 1043–1044; 1060; *PLRE* 1.144; D. Hoffmann, "Wadomar, Bacurius, und Hariulf," *Museum Helveticum* 35 (1978): 307–18. Libanius in his letters seems to consider him a fellow pagan.

motives of rivalry. By frequently saying these and like things, he impressed his attitude upon Constantia. It is said that when she was dying and her brother was visiting her and speaking to her in a kindly and religious way, she asked him as a last favor to receive the presbyter into his friendship and to listen to whatever he would propose to him that had to do with his hope of salvation. She herself, she said, had no concerns now that she was departing from the light, but she was worried about her brother's situation, lest his empire fall to ruin on account of the innocent being punished. He accepted his sister's advice, believing that her concern for him was genuine, and lent his ear to the presbyter, in the meantime ordering Arius to be summoned from exile so that he could explain his views about the faith. Arius then composed a creed, which, while it did not have the same meaning as ours, yet seemed to contain our words and profession. The emperor was indeed amazed, and thought that the very same views were set out in his exposition as in that of the council held previously. But in no respect did he slacken his vigilance of mind; he referred him once again to a council's scrutiny, for in fact priests from all over the world were being invited to gather for the dedication of Jerusalem. He wrote to them concerning him that if they approved his exposition of faith and found either that he had previously been convicted out of jealousy, as he maintained, or was now corrected of his error, they should judge him with clemency, if, that is, his bishop, Alexander, would agree; such, after all, had been the moderation of the council that it had passed sentence not against his person but against the falsehood of his doctrines. But those who from the first had supported his endeavors and subscribed insincerely made no difficulty about receiving him. When he reached Alexandria, however, he could get nowhere with his plans, because while tricks work with the ignorant, they just raise a laugh from the knowledgeable.[23]

23. On Constantia, cf. H. A. Pohlsander, "Constantia," *Ancient Society* 24 (1993): 151–67. She and her niece Constantina were sometimes confused (e.g., Philostorgius, 1.9).

Arius had been exiled to Illyricum within a year of the Council of Nicaea, but was invited by Constantine to court in a letter of November 27, 327 (Athan., *Dokument* 33). Arius's creed is Athan., *Dokument* 34 (translated in Rowan Williams, *Arius* [London: Darton, Longman and Todd, 1987], 255–56). He was re-

In the meantime, while this vain commotion was going on in Alexandria, the venerable Augustus Constantine died in a suburban villa of Nicomedia in the thirty-first year of his reign, having left his children written in his will as heirs in succession to the Roman world. Because Constantius, to whom he had bequeathed the eastern empire, was not present at the time, it is said that he summoned in secret the presbyter who we said earlier had been recommended by his sister and had thereafter been held in friendship, entrusted to him the will he had written, and bound him by oath to hand it over to no one but Constantius, when he came. Since it was the latter whom the palace eunuchs also supported, news of the emperor's death was skillfully suppressed until Constantius's arrival, many who tried to seize power were put down, and the state remained safe and undamaged. But when Constantius arrived, the presbyter restored what had been committed to him. The emperor in his desire for the realm was on account of this favor so bound to him that, anxious as he was to govern others, he cheerfully allowed himself to be governed by him. From that time on, having subjugated the emperor to himself, he began to speak about restoring Arius and to urge him to compel the priests who were reluctant to agree.[24]

---

stored to communion by some council of bishops no later than early in 328, but neither Alexander nor later Athanasius would take him back. He probably resided in Libya thereafter until finally in 333 he wrote to Constantine complaining about not being received back into his home church (Athan., *Dokument* 27.5).

The emperor, thinking that he was threatening schism, put his rehabilitation on the agenda of the Council of Jerusalem, which met in 335 to celebrate the dedication of the Church of the Holy Sepulchre. On this large and lavishly conducted council, cf. Eusebius, *Vit. Const.* 4.43–48. The emperor's letter to it, which Rufinus mentions, has not survived but is referred to in the council's own letter, reproduced in Athanasius, *De synodis* 21. The impression Rufinus gives of the freedom Constantine granted the council to judge Arius (*si expositionem fidei eius probarent*) is not to be trusted. The council's letter makes it clear that the emperor had vouched for Arius's orthodoxy in his own letter to it (Athanasius, *De synodis* 21.4) and urged his readmission to communion; it also says that it is appending a copy of the emperor's letter, which makes it likely that its summary of that letter is accurate. Cf. Sozomen, 2.27.

Cf. T. D. Barnes, "The Exile and Recall of Arius," *JTS* NS 60.1 (2009): 109–29.

24. On Constantine's final days, cf. G. Fowden, "The Last Days of Constan-

10.13. At that time the priesthood was being exercised in Alexandria by Alexander, in Jerusalem by Maximus the confessor, and in Constantinople likewise by Alexander, as we learn from the writings of Athanasius. Now Eusebius, who was in Nicomedia and about whose pretense in subscribing we spoke earlier, seized his chance: having become friendly with the sovereign through the offices of the presbyter, he bent his efforts to rolling everything back and rendering invalid the council's actions. He got Arius, who was residing in Alexandria to no purpose, to come, and through imperial edicts had a fresh council summoned to Constantinople. Those who convened were mostly of the party of Arius and Eusebius. Time and again they met with Alexander to try to get him to receive Arius, but they did not defeat him, however much abuse they poured on him. Finally they told him they were setting a day on which he should understand that he would either receive Arius or, if he refused, he would be expelled from the church and driven into exile, and there would be someone else to receive him. Alexander spent the whole night before the day in question lying at the foot of the altar in tears and prayer, commending the church's cause to the Lord. When dawn had broken and Alexander continued in prayer, Eusebius with all his company, like the standard-bearer of an army of heretics, went up in the morning to Arius's house and bade him follow him to the

---

tine: Oppositional Versions and Their Influence," *JRS* 84 (1994): 146–70. He died on May 22, 337, having appointed his three surviving sons—Constantine, Constantius, and Constans—and his nephew Dalmatius "Caesars" over the four parts of the empire. His body was conveyed to Constantinople, and in due course Constantius arrived from Antioch. The course of events immediately following is not altogether clear, but Dalmatius and all other possible rivals to the sons of Constantine I were killed, probably by soldiers determined to maintain the dynasty. On September 9, 337, the three brothers were proclaimed Augusti in Pannonia and reallocated the empire among themselves: Constantius got the east, and the others managed an uneasy division of the rest, with Constans apparently chafing under his older brother's attempts to supervise the administration of his territory (Italy, Africa, and most of the Balkans). See note 30 below. On the sources, see Paschoud, *Zosime*, 1.246–47.

The story about the presbyter and will appears first in Rufinus, but it probably precedes him; see Klein (note 20 above), 2. In Philostorgius, 2.16, the will is entrusted to Eusebius of Nicomedia.

church without delay, declaring that Alexander, unless he were present and consented, should be driven from the place.

10.14. Everyone therefore was waiting with great interest to see where the perseverance of Alexander or the importunity of Eusebius and Arius would lead; the importance of the affair was holding everyone in suspense. Arius, hemmed in by a crowd of bishops and laity, was making his way to the church when he turned aside at a call of nature to a public facility. And when he sat down, his intestines and all his innards slipped down into the privy drain, and thus it was in such a place that he met a death worthy of his foul and blasphemous mind. When news of this was later brought to the church to Eusebius and to those with him who were pressing the holy and innocent Alexander to receive Arius, they departed overcome with shame and covered with confusion. Then was fulfilled to the glory of the Lord the word which Alexander had cried to God in prayer, saying, "Judge, O Lord, between me and the threats of Eusebius and the violence of Arius!"

Now these events caused some slight and short-lived embarrassment; but the heretics met together, fearful that the affair would be reported to the emperor Constantius just as it had happened, and that not only would he disown their perfidy, in which he had been so cleverly ensnared, but would also visit upon the authors of his deception stern treatment through his imperial power. They therefore arranged through the eunuchs, whom they had already won over to their perfidy, that, as far as could be done, the emperor should hear a commonly agreed-upon version of Arius's death, and that he should learn nothing that would hint of God's punishment. Having done this, they continued the efforts they had begun with respect to the faith.[25]

25. Rufinus's chronology is badly and perhaps deliberately muddled. Alexander of Alexandria had died and been succeeded by Athanasius in 328. Athanasius was condemned by the Council of Tyre in 335 and banished by Constantine to Gaul. Despite the urging of the Council of Jerusalem, which was in effect a continuation of that of Tyre, the Alexandrian church did not welcome Arius upon his return, riots broke out, and Constantine called him back to Constantinople (Socrates, 1.37.1–2), where the council to which Rufinus refers met in 336. Constantine, despite what Rufinus says, was very much alive

10.15. Athanasius, then, received the see of Alexandria upon the death of Alexander. Now the heretics were already well aware that he was a man of keen intelligence and altogether tireless in the management of the church, since he had come to the Council of Nicaea with his old bishop Alexander, by whose counsel the tricks and deceits of the heretics had been unremittingly exposed. As soon, then, as they found out that he had been made bishop, they concluded that their concerns would find no easy way past his vigilance, as in fact turned out to be true, and so they cast about everywhere for deceptions to use against him.

Now I do not think it out of place to trace back briefly his early years and to explain how he was educated as a boy, as we have found out from those who lived with him. Once when Bishop Alexander was celebrating the day of Peter Martyr in Alexandria, he was waiting in a place near the sea after the ceremonies were over for his clergy to gather for a banquet. There he saw from a distance some boys on the seashore playing a game in which, as they often do, they were mimicking a bishop and the things customarily done in church. Now when he had gazed intently for a while at the boys, he saw that they were also performing some of the more secret and sacramental things. He was disturbed and immediately ordered the clergy to be called to him and showed them what he was watching from a distance. Then he commanded them to go and get all the boys and bring them to him. When they arrived, he asked them what game they were playing and what they had done and how. At first they were afraid, as is usual at that age, and refused, but then they disclosed in due order what they had done, admitting that some catechumens had been baptized by them at the hands of Athanasius, who had played the part of bishop in their childish game. Then he

during the whole episode, but Rufinus may well have falsified the chronology in order to spare him the shame of having exiled Athanasius and brought Arius back (cf. Thelamon, *PC* 35).

The story of Arius's death was repeated endlessly, beginning with Athanasius, *De morte Arii* 2–4 and *Ad episcopos Aegypti* 19. This sort of death was regarded as a special sign of divine wrath; e.g., 2 Mc 9.5–28; Acts 12.23; Josephus, *Antiq.* 17.168–70; Lactantius, *DMP* 33; Eusebius, *HE* 2.10.7; Ammianus, 14.11.24–25.

carefully inquired of those who were said to have been baptized what they had been asked and what they had answered, and the same of him who had put the questions, and when he saw that everything was according to the manner of our religion, he conferred with a council of clerics and then ruled, so it is reported, that those on whom water had been poured after the questions had been asked and answered fully need not repeat the baptism, but that those things should be completed which are customarily done by priests. As for Athanasius and those who had played the parts of presbyters and ministers in the game, he called together their parents, and having put them under oath, handed them over to be reared for the church. But a short time later, after Athanasius had been thoroughly educated by a clerk and received adequate instruction from a teacher of literature, he was given back at once to the priest by his parents, like a deposit from the Lord kept faithfully, and like another Samuel was brought up in the Lord's temple. And so he was appointed by Alexander, as he was going to his fathers in a good old age, to wear the priestly ephod after him.[26]

But he had such struggles to undergo in the church for the integrity of the faith that the following passage seems to have been written about him too: "I will show him how much he will have to suffer for my name."[27] For the whole world conspired to persecute him, and the princes of the earth were moved,[28] nations, kingdoms, and armies gathered against him. But he kept in view that divine utterance which runs: "If camps are set up against me, my heart will not fear; if battle is waged against me, in him will I hope."[29] But because his deeds are so many and so exceptional that their greatness allows me to omit nothing, while on the other hand their multitude forces me to pass over a great many of them, my mind wavers in uncertainty, unable

26. Alexander died on April 17, 328, and Athanasius succeeded him on June 8. Stories of heroes acting out their future roles while children are common enough; see, for instance, Herodotus, 1.114–15; *SHA,* Severus 1.4 and Albinus 5.2; Photius, *Bibl.* cod. 258; Thelamon, *PC* 337. Cf. Socrates, 1.15; Sozomen, 2.17.6–10.

27. Acts 9.16.   28. Ps 2.1–2.
29. Ps 26.3.

to decide what to keep and what to omit. We shall therefore relate a few of the things which are of consequence; his fame will tell the rest, but it will certainly recount the lesser matters, for it will find nothing that it can add.

10.16. When Constantius, then, had obtained sole control of the eastern empire upon the death of his brother Constantine,[30] who was killed by soldiers not far from Aquileia by the river Alsa, Constans, the brother of them both, was ruling the West with fair diligence. Now while Constantius, regal in nature and spirit, looked pretty favorably upon those who had been the first supporters of his reign, he was cleverly misled into perfidy by depraved priests acting through the eunuchs, and he eagerly supported their wicked designs. But they feared that Athanasius might sometime gain access to the sovereign and instruct him fully, according to the scriptures, in the truth of the faith, which they were distorting. So they proceeded to accuse him to the sovereign in every possible way of every sort of crime and outrage, even to the point of showing the emperor an arm from a human body which they presented in a case, claiming that Athanasius had severed it from the body of one Arsenius in order to use it for magic.[31] They made up as well a great many other crimes and misdeeds.

30. When Constantine II succeeded to power with his brothers in September of 337, he acted as though he were the sole sovereign by releasing, for instance, from exile the bishops who were from the east, Athanasius included. Constantius immediately countered this by establishing contact with his brother Constans and the Illyrian troops, forcing Constantine to choose between accepting a division of territory or civil war with his brothers (see note 24 above). In 340, however, Constantine tried to enforce his claim to monarchy by using Constantius's conflict with Persia as an excuse to bring his army into Constans's territory as though it were on the march to reinforce the eastern front, but he was ambushed and killed by Constans's officers; Constans thereby became the sole ruler of the western empire. Cf. Bruno Bleckmann, "Der Bürgerkrieg zwischen Constantin II und Constans (340 n. Chr.)," *Historia* 52.2 (2003): 225–50. Constantine's claim to monarchy seems in fact to be echoed in the words *Constantius orientis regnum solus obtinuit Constantino fratre . . . interfecto.*

31. *magicae artis gratia:* "for magical purposes" (rather than "by magical means"). The magical use of bodily parts of persons put to death was well enough known (cf. PW 14.332–33), and the charge of sorcery against Athanasius was long remembered (Ammianus, 15.7.8).

10.17. Their purpose was that the emperor might order Athanasius to be condemned at a council he would summon, and he did order one to convene in Tyre, sending as his representative one of the counts. He was assisted by Archelaus, then Count of the East, and by the governor of the province of Phoenicia. There Athanasius was brought, the case with the human arm was shown around, and an indignant horror invaded the souls of all, religious and ordinary folk alike.[32]

10.18. This Arsenius, whose arm had reportedly been cut off, had once been a lector of Athanasius, but fearing rebuke for some fault, he had withdrawn from his company. These outrageous men considered his concealment ideal for their schemes, and kept him hidden, when they began to hatch their plot, with someone they believed they could fully trust with their misdeed. But while in hiding Arsenius heard of the crime they intended to commit in his name against Athanasius. Moved either by human feeling or divine providence, he secretly escaped his confinement in the silence of the night, sailed to Tyre, and on the day before the final day of the trial presented himself to Athanasius and explained the affair from the beginning. Athanasius ordered him to stay in the house and not let anyone know he was there. In the meantime the council was summoned; some of those who gathered were aware of the calumny concocted, and almost everyone was hostile to and prejudiced against Athanasius. The confessor Paphnutius, whom we mentioned earlier, was there at the time and was aware of Athanasius's innocence. Now he saw Bishop Maximus of Jerusalem sitting with the others whom the shameful plot had

32. Cf. note 25 above: despite what Rufinus says, the Council of Tyre was held in 335 during Constantine's reign, and it was Constantine who banished Athanasius at the end of it. Rufinus may simply be trying to shift the responsibility for the act onto his son.

The count mentioned is Flavius Dionysius, former governor of Syria. Archelaus was Count of the East (?) in 340 and governor of Phoenicia in 335; cf. *PLRE* 1.100. On the council, cf. Eusebius, *Vit. Const.* 4.41–42; Athanasius, *Apologia contra Arianos* 71–86; *P. Lond.* 1914, in H. I. Bell, *Jews and Christians in Egypt* (London: British Museum, 1924), 53–71; Epiphanius, *Pan.* 68.8–9; Ammianus, 15.7.7–8; Socrates, 1.28–32; Sozomen, 2.25; Theodoret, *HE* 1.29–31; Philostorgius, 2.11.

united; together with him he had had an eye gouged out and a ham severed and thus had become a confessor, but because of his excessive simplicity he suspected nothing of the monstrous behavior of the priests. He went up to him fearlessly where he was sitting in their midst and said, "Maximus, you bear along with me one and the same mark of confession, and for you as much as for me the gouging out of the eye that is mortal has procured the brighter sight of the divine light. I will not let you sit in the council of evildoers and go in with the workers of malice." And taking hold of him, he lifted him up from their midst, informed him in detail of what was taking place, and joined him thereafter in lasting communion with Athanasius.[33]

In the meantime the case was being presented. The first accusation to be presented was of some woman who said that she had once received Athanasius as a guest and during the night, caught quite unawares, had been forcibly violated by him. Athanasius was ordered to be presented to her. He entered with his presbyter Timothy and told him that after the woman had finished speaking, he himself would keep still and Timothy should respond to what she had said. So when the woman finished the speech she had been taught, Timothy turned to her and said, "Is it true, woman, that I once stayed with you? Or that I forced you, as you claim?" Then she, with the effrontery common to such women, snarled at Timothy, "You, you forced me; you defiled my chastity in that place!" At the same time, turning to the judges, she began to swear to God that she was telling the truth. Then embarrassment at being made ridiculous began to come over everyone, because the plot involving the crime which had been invented had so easily been laid bare without the accused having said anything. But the judges were not allowed to question the woman about where she was from or by whom and how the calumny had been devised, since the prosecutors were able to conduct the trial as they liked. They proceeded from this to the other charge. A crime was revealed never before heard of. "Here," they said, "we have something

33. The indignant departure of the confessor-bishops indicates the unworthiness of the council; see note 8 above. Despite what Rufinus says, Maximus did vote to depose Athanasius (Socrates, 2.24.3).

about which no one can be deceived by artful speech; the matter is something for the eyes, and speech falls silent. This severed arm accuses you, Athanasius. This is Arsenius's right arm; explain how you cut it off or to what purpose." He replied, "Which of you knew Arsenius and may recognize that this is his right arm?" Some of them stood up and said that they knew Arsenius quite well; among them were several who had no knowledge of the plot. Athanasius then asked the judges to order his man brought in whom the matter required. When Arsenius had been brought in, Athanasius lifted his face and said to the council and the judges, "This is Arsenius." And raising his right hand likewise, he said, "This is also his right hand, and this his left. But as for where this hand comes from which they have presented, that is for you to investigate." Then something like night and darkness fell upon the eyes of the accusers, who did not know what to do or where to turn. For the witnesses confirmed that it was Arsenius, whom they had just before said they knew. But because the council was being held not to judge the man but to ruin him, a clamor suddenly arose from all sides that Athanasius was a sorcerer who was deceiving the eyes of the onlookers, and that such a man should by no means be allowed to live any longer. And they rushed at him, ready to tear him apart with their own hands. But Archelaus, who with the others was presiding at the council by the emperor's command, snatched him from the hands of his assailants, led him out by secret ways, and advised him to seek safety by flight, as it was the only way he could reach it. The council, however, met again as though nothing whatever had come to light and condemned Athanasius as having confessed to the crimes with which he had been charged. And having concocted minutes in this form and sent them throughout the world, they forced the other bishops to assent to their crime, the emperor compelling them to this.[34]

34. As Rufinus indicates, the charges against Athanasius were disciplinary, not doctrinal, whatever the ulterior motives of his opponents may have been. But Rufinus passes over in silence the main accusation that he had used violence against clergy who had refused to accept his authority because they considered his ordination invalid.

Athanasius had previously been charged with the murder of Arsenius and

10.19. Hence Athanasius was now a fugitive at large in the whole world, and there remained for him no safe place to hide. Tribunes, governors, counts, and even armies were deployed by imperial orders to hunt him down. Rewards were offered to informers to bring him in alive if possible, or at least his head. Thus the whole power of the empire was directed in vain against the man with whom God was present. During this time he is said to have remained concealed for six successive years in a dry cistern, never seeing the sun. But when his presence was revealed by a servant woman, who seems to have been the only one aware of the good offices of her masters, who had offered him concealment, then as though warned by God's Spirit, he moved to another place on the very night they came with informers to arrest him, six years after having come there. Those therefore who had come in vain, and who found that the owners too had fled, punished the woman as a false informer.

10.20. But lest his concealment cause trouble for someone

---

had cleared himself with Constantine in 334 by producing his alleged victim alive and having his identity confirmed by the bishop of Tyre (Athanasius, *Apologia contra Arianos* 63.4–70). The story is of the sort that easily gets repeated out of context (as in fact happens in Epiphanius, *Pan.* 68.10.1–2), so when it shows up again at the Council of Tyre, one's first inclination is to discount it as an errant tale. But Sozomen also relates it, along with the story about the woman, in his account of the council, and he goes on to remark that the latter story is not included in the acts (2.25.11). That implies that the story about Arsenius was, and this squares with what Athanasius himself says about Arsenius being present at the council in refutation of the murder charge (*Apol. contra Arianos* 72.2). Evidently, then, the old murder charge was raked up again (as Sozomen in fact plainly says in 2.25.7). Small wonder that Constantine was persuaded of the council's unfairness when he heard of it (Athanasius, *Apol. contra Arianos* 9.5). It strengthens the general impression that the Council of Tyre was procedurally untidy, often disorderly, and occasionally chaotic. The unruliness of Athanasius's suffragans made matters worse; the behavior of Paphnutius toward Maximus of Jerusalem is quite in line with what we read elsewhere (Epiphanius, *Pan.* 68.8.2–5).

Athanasius escaped from Tyre secretly by night and sailed to Constantinople, where he accosted the emperor and persuaded him to summon his opponents to court and let him meet them there. Six of the leading bishops arrived shortly and brought a new charge against Athanasius: that he had threatened to interrupt the grain shipments from Egypt to the capital. The hearing turned stormy, and in the end Athanasius lost both his temper and his case; Constantine banished him to Trier on November 7, 335.

and provide an opportunity for calumniating the innocent, the fugitive, presuming that there was no safe place for him any longer in Constantius's realm, withdrew to Constans's region.[35] He was received by him with considerable honor and devotion. And having carefully investigated his case, news of which had reached him, he wrote to his brother that he had learned as something certain that the priest of God most high Athanasius had suffered banishment and exiles wrongly. He would therefore act rightly if he restored him to his place without causing him any trouble; if he did not want to do so, then he would take care of the matter himself by gaining entrance to the inmost part of his realm and subjecting the authors of the crime to the punishment they richly deserved. Constantius, terrified by the letter because he realized that his brother was capable of carrying out his threat, bade Athanasius with pretended kindness to come to him of his own accord, and, having rebuked him lightly, allowed him to proceed to his own church in safety. The emperor, though, at the prompting of his impious counselors, said, "The bishops have a small favor to ask of you, Athanasius: that you concede one of the many churches in Alexandria to the people who do not wish to hold communion with you." But at God's prompting he found a stratagem on the spot. "O emperor," he replied, "is there anything that may be denied you if you request it, seeing that you have the power to command everything? But there is one thing I ask: that you allow me also a small request." He promised to grant anything he wanted, even if it was difficult, if only he would concede this one thing, so

35. The chronology here is completely muddled. Athanasius returned from exile to Alexandria on November 23, 337, after Constantine's death and upon the initiative of his oldest son, who restored all banished bishops to their cities. His life was never in any danger. He was deposed again, however, by the Council of Antioch of 338/39 (on charges of violence and improper resumption of his see). The council appointed Gregory the Cappadocian to replace him, an attempt was made to arrest him, and he escaped and sailed to Italy on April 16, 339.

Rufinus's description of Athanasius's concealment corresponds rather to the period of 356 to 362, when the bishop was being hunted by Constantius and remained in hiding in his city or nearby until the emperor's death. For a different version of how he remained hidden, cf. Palladius, *Historia Lausiaca* 63 (see Athanasius, *Festal Index* 32).

Athanasius said, "What I ask is that since there are some people of ours here as well"—for the interview was taking place in Antioch—"and they do not want to communicate with these folk, one church may be given over to their use." The emperor happily promised this, since it seemed to him quite just and easy to grant. When he presented the matter to his counselors, however, they answered that they wished neither to accept a church there nor to yield one in their city, since each of them was looking to his own interests rather than to those of people not present. The emperor, then, marveling at his prudence, bade him hurry off to receive his church.[36]

But when Magnentius's villainy had robbed the emperor Constans of his life and realm together, then once again those who in past times had incited the sovereign against Athanasius began to revive his hatred, and when he had fled from the church, they sent in his place George, their companion in perfidy and cruelty. For first they had sent someone named Gregory. Once again there were flight and concealment, and imperial edicts against Athanasius were put up everywhere promising rewards and honors to informants. The sovereign too, when he had come into the west to avenge his brother's murder and recover his realm, and had taken sole possession of the empire once the usurper was eliminated, proceeded to wear out the western bishops and by deception to compel them to assent to the Arian heresy; to this the condemnation of Athanasius was prefixed, he being, as it were, the great barrier which had first to be removed.

10.21. For this reason a council of bishops was summoned to Milan. Most of them were deceived, but Dionysius, Eusebi-

36. The emperor Constans was persuaded to take up the cause of Athanasius and other exiled eastern bishops. The Council of Sardica of 342 or 343, which he summoned to review their cases, cleared the exiles and ordered their restoration, but Athanasius did not enter Alexandria again until October of 346, after Constans had written to his brother threatening to invade his realm, if necessary, to restore him. There are different versions of his letter in Socrates, 2.22.5, Theodoret, *HE* 2.8.55–56, and Philostorgius, 3.12. On the Council of Sardica, see Sara Parvis, *Marcellus of Ancyra and the Lost Years of the Arian Controversy 325–345* (Oxford: Clarendon, 2006). On its date: pp. 210–17. On Constans's threat: 200–206.

us, Paulinus, Rhodanius, and Lucifer announced that there
was treachery lurking in the proceedings, asserting that the
subscription against Athanasius had no other end in view than
the destruction of the faith. They were driven into exile. Hilary
joined them too, the others either not knowing of the trick or
not believing that there was one.[37]

37. Widespread dissatisfaction with Constans's rule led to the usurpation
of Magnentius, one of his generals, in January of 350. Constans was killed,
and Magnentius began sounding out possible dissidents in the other half of
the empire, among them Athanasius (Athan., *Apol. ad Constantium* 6–10). He
also appeared to represent himself as a defender of the rights of those loyal to
the Creed of Nicaea; cf. John F. Drinkwater, "The Revolt and Ethnic Origin
of the Usurper Magnentius (350–353), and the Rebellion of Vetranio (350),"
Chiron 30 (2000): 131–59, and Stefano Conti, "Religione e usurpazione: Mag-
nenzio tra cristianesimo e paganesimo," in *Antidoron: Studi in onore di Barbara
Scardigli Forster*, ed. Paolo Desideri, Mauro Moggi, and Mario Pani (Pisa: ETS,
2007), 105–19.
    When Constantius arrived in Sirmium in 351 to prosecute the war against
the usurper, its bishop, Photinus, had long been notorious for his denial of
the preexistence of Christ, a doctrine he was thought to have derived from
Marcellus of Ancyra. A council met in Sirmium that year and condemned
Photinus, Marcellus, and Athanasius. Its synodical letter has not survived,
so we cannot tell directly how the council associated the three, but Sulpicius
Severus suggests that the condemnation of Marcellus (as Photinus's master)
was seen by many as effectively annulling the Council of Sardica, which had
cleared him. If so, then Athanasius's absolution by the same council was void,
and his deposition by the Council of Antioch remained valid, particularly
if, as was rumored, he himself had suspended Marcellus from communion
(*Chronicle* 2.37.1–5).
    Liberius of Rome in 352 or 353 convoked an Italian synod to consider a
reply to the Council of Sirmium based on the opposing dossiers in the case;
it cleared Athanasius but requested a larger council to meet in Aquileia to
review the issue. Athanasius himself sent a delegation to Constantius; it was
unsuccessful. The council requested for Aquileia met instead in Arles, where
the court was, in 353. The letter of the Council of Sirmium was presented to
it, and those present were told to subscribe it under threat of exile. Paulinus
of Trier asked that doctrine be first discussed in order to make sure that all
those present were fit to be judges, but his request was refused and he was banished. Constantius was then asked by Liberius to call another council (Hilary,
Fragmenta Historica A VII 6); it met in Milan in 355, with the same subscription
being demanded of those present.
    Eusebius of Vercelli tried again to put doctrine on the agenda by declaring
himself ready to subscribe what was demanded if everyone would first subscribe the Creed of Nicaea. Dionysius of Milan was just about to do so when

10.22. But subsequent events showed that such had been the plan behind the proceeding. For once they had been gotten out of the way, no time was lost in summoning a synod to Ariminum. There shrewd and cunning men easily tricked the simple and inexperienced western priests, using what the easterners had put together at Seleucia and putting the question to them in this way: Whom do you prefer to adore and worship, the *homoousios* or Christ? But since they did not know what the word "homoousios" meant, such talk aroused disgust and abhorrence in them, and they declared that they believed in Christ, not the *homoousios*. Thus the majority, with the exception of a few who knowingly lapsed, were deceived, and set themselves against what the fathers at Nicaea had written, decreeing that *homoousios* should be removed from the creed as a word unknown and foreign to scripture, and defiling their communion by associating with heretics. This was the time when the face of the church was foul and exceedingly loathsome, for now it was ravaged, not as previously by outsiders, but by its own people. Those banished and those who banished them were all mem-

---

Valens of Mursa, one of Athanasius's enemies, snatched pen and paper away, shouting that he was out of order (Hilary, *Ad Constantium Augustum* 3(8).1). The story was widely circulated and bolstered Athanasius's attempt to identify his cause with that of Nicene orthodoxy.

Eusebius, Dionysius, and Lucifer of Cagliari, who refused to subscribe, were exiled; Eusebius went to Scythopolis in Palestine and Lucifer to Germanicia in Syria, but both seemed to move around a good deal in the east during their time there. Constantius's officials carried the synodical of the Council of Sirmium around to the bishops who had not attended the aforementioned councils and demanded their subscription; see T. D. Barnes, *Athanasius and Constantius* (Cambridge: Harvard University Press, 1993), 115–16. Hilary of Poitiers was banished to Phrygia after the Council of Béziers in 356; see Carl L. Beckwith, "The Condemnation and Exile of Hilary of Poitiers at the Synod of Béziers (356 C.E.)," *Journal of Early Christian Studies* 13.1 (2005): 21–38. We do not know why or when Rhodanius of Toulouse was exiled.

Gregory had died in 345 before Athanasius returned to Alexandria; George the Cappadocian was appointed by the Council of Antioch of 349 to replace Athanasius but could not enter the city until a year after Athanasius had left it in February of 356 to escape arrest. Constantius's letter to the Alexandrians leaves no doubt that he considered Athanasius worthy of death for his crimes (Athan., *Apol. ad Constantium* 30). On measures taken against those loyal to Athanasius, see Athan., *Festal Index* 29–32).

bers of the church. Nowhere was there altar, immolation, or
libation, but transgression, lapse, and the ruin of many. Alike
was the punishment, unequal the victory. Alike was the affliction, unequal the boast, for the church grieved over the fall of
those as well who were forcing the others to lapse.[38]

38. Constantius became convinced that the rifts in the church, including
those caused by the new "anomoean" doctrine (of the dissimilarity of God
the Father and the Son), could be repaired only by a general council, and he
called one to meet in Nicomedia in 358. But the city was destroyed by earthquake that summer, and by the following summer it had been decided to hold
separate councils in Ariminum and Seleucia (in Isauria). The court had decided to press the bishops to accept a new creed which would outlaw the use of
the controversial word *ousia* in statements of faith, thus rescinding the Creed
of Nicaea; see J. N. D. Kelly, *Early Christian Creeds* (London: Longman, 1972[3]),
289–91.
    The Council of Ariminum met in July with over four hundred attending.
Due largely perhaps to Hilary of Poitier's correspondence from exile, the westerners now appreciated the importance of the Creed of Nicaea, and most of
them refused to subscribe the new one. A minority of about eighty seceded,
each side sending a delegation to court, as the councils had been instructed. Constantius refused to receive the majority delegates and wore them
down through tedium and fear until they gave in and subscribed his creed
on October 10. When they returned to Ariminum the majority refused them
communion, but the praetorian prefect Flavius Taurus told the bishops they
could not go home until they subscribed. The opposition gradually dwindled
to twenty, who finally gave in when told they might formulate their subscriptions as they liked. The subscription to an agreement was not then, as now, a
bare name like a signature, but a complete sentence or sentences summarizing the body of the document to which it was attached. It was regarded as an
authentic interpretation of it, as Valens of Mursa, one of the Arian leaders
there, had been sharply reminded by the emperor himself when he had tried
to omit a key phrase in his own subscription to the new creed the previous
May (Epiphanius, *Pan.* 73.22.6). Thus the council fathers were told they might
include in their subscriptions whatever they felt was lacking in the main body
of the new creed. Valens himself wrote in his that the Son of God was not a
creature like other creatures, the ambiguity of which was evidently not noticed by the others until later, when the rumor began spreading that they had
signed an Arian creed. After they had authorized a new delegation to court,
they were allowed to break up. Rufinus's story of how the majority was tricked
is thus quite wide of the mark.
    The Council of Seleucia got under way late in September with 160 in at-
tendance, and as in Ariminum the majority refused to accept the new creed,
taking its stand instead on the Creed of the Dedication Council of Antioch
of 341 (on this creed, see Kelly, 268–71); the minority in favor of the new

10.23. Liberius, then, was exercising the priesthood at the time in the city of Rome following Julius, the successor of Mark, whom Silvester had preceded; he was banished, and his deacon Felix was put in his place by the heretics. Felix was tainted not so much by sectarian difference as by the connivance surrounding his communion and ordination.[39]

10.24. In Jerusalem Cyril now received the priesthood after Maximus in an irregular ordination, and vacillated sometimes in doctrine and often in communion. In Alexandria George exercised the episcopacy seized by force with such lack of moderation that he seemed to think he had been entrusted with a magistracy rather than with a priesthood involving religious responsibilities.[40]

---

creed seceded, and both sides sent a delegation to court. The majority delegates were as stubborn as their Ariminum counterparts had been, but the court could now represent them as recalcitrants hindering the work of church unity, and on the last day of the year they finally yielded and subscribed. Cf. Hilary, *Fragmenta historica* A.V, VI, VIII, IX; B.VIII; Athanasius, *De synodis* 8–12; Jerome, *Altercatio Luciferiani et Orthodoxi* 17–19; Augustine, *Opus imperfectum contra Iulianum* 1.75; Sulpicius Severus, *Chronicle* 2.41.1–2.45.4; Socrates, 2.37; Sozomen, 4.16–19, 4.22–23; Theodoret, *HE* 2.18–21; 2.26.4–11; Philostorgius, 4.10–11; *EOMIA* 1.541; Hefele-Leclercq, 1.929–55; Barnes, 144–48; Simonetti, 313–49.

The Council of Constantinople of 360 promulgated the court-appointed creed, the supporters of which are often called "homoeans," since the creed declared that the Son is simply like (*homoios*) the Father without qualification.

39. Liberius succeeded Julius in 352. He refused to condemn Athanasius and was banished to Beroea in Thrace. There he eventually yielded and subscribed the condemnation together with some creed (which? see R. P. C. Hanson, *The Search for the Christian Doctrine of God* [Edinburgh: T. & T. Clark, 1988], 358–62, and H. C. Brennecke, *Hilarius von Poitiers und die Bischofsopposition gegen Konstantius II* [Berlin: de Gruyter, 1984], 273–97), and was allowed to return to Rome in 357. See also 10.28. His archdeacon Felix was consecrated to replace him by three bishops at court, including the powerful Acacius of Caesarea (Jerome, *Vir. illustr.* 98). The "connivance" Rufinus mentions refers to the oath which had been taken by the Roman clergy not to accept another bishop while Liberius lived and which most of them broke (Jerome, *Chronicle* 349; *Collectio Avellana* 1.2). His judgment about Felix still stands in sharp contrast to that of Athanasius, who tarred him with the Arian brush (*Historia Arianorum* 75.3), but it is supported by Theodoret, *HE* 2.17.3.

40. Maximus of Jerusalem had offended Acacius by receiving Athanasius after condemning him at the Council of Tyre, but he may have died before he

10.25. In Antioch a great many things were certainly done in a decidedly irregular fashion at various times. For after the death of Eudoxius, when many bishops from various cities were doing their utmost to acquire the see, they finally transferred there Meletius of Sebaste, a city in Armenia, contrary to the decrees of the council. But they drove him back into exile, because against their expectation he began to preach in church not Arius's faith, but ours. A large group of people who followed him when he was ejected from the church was sundered from the heretics' fellowship.[41]

10.26. In the meantime, that the luxuriant evil might at last turn its rage upon itself too, the priests and people who under Arius's guidance had been originally sundered from the

---

could be deposed; it was reported, however, that Acacius had driven him from Jerusalem and ordained Cyril in his place (Socrates, 2.38.2). Cyril succeeded Maximus in 348. He was never exiled, although he was deposed more than once by the homoean party, but he continued on as head of at least some of the Christians there, despite the presence of the rival homoean episcopate. He died March 18, 387. See Peter Van Nuffelen, "The Career of Cyril of Jerusalem (c. 348–87): A Reassessment," *JTS* NS 58 (2007): 134–46.

Rufinus's characterization of George is quite accurate: his greed knew no bounds (Ammianus, 22.11.3–10; Epiphanius, *Pan.* 76.1).

41. When Leontius of Antioch died in 357, Eudoxius managed to obtain from Constantius some sort of permission to assist with the pastoral needs in the city, and before the emperor knew it, he had transformed it into imperial approval to succeed to the see (Socrates, 2.37.7–9; Sozomen, 4.12.3–4; Theodoret, *HE* 2.25.1–2; 2.26.1; *Haer. fab.* 4.2). The following year, however, he had to withdraw from the city when Constantius made it clear he did not support him. He was transferred to Constantinople by the council meeting there in 360, and Meletius, from Sebaste in Armenia or Beroea in Syria, was chosen by popular acclaim bishop of Antioch. His preaching so offended the homoeans, though, that he was promptly banished to Armenia and replaced by Arius's old associate Euzoius. The offending homily is in Epiphanius, *Pan.* 73.29–33. On the divisions in Antioch, cf. K. M. Spoerl, "The Schism in Antioch since Cavallera," in *Arianism after Arius*, ed. M. R. Barnes and D. H. Williams (Edinburgh: T & T Clark, 1993), 101–26. The clean bill of doctrinal health that Rufinus gives Meletius testifies to the complete confidence he reposed in Basil's opinion of him, but the simple description of his theology as *nostra fides* hardly does justice to its development. See Spoerl, 110–26. On Meletius in general, see Thomas R. Karmann, *Meletius von Antiochien: Studien zur Geschichte des trinitätstheologischen Streits in den Jahren 360–364 n. Chr.* (Peter Lang: Frankfurt am Main, 2009).

The conciliar decree to which Rufinus refers is Canon 16 of Nicaea (see 10.6).

church were split afresh into three sects and parties. Those who we earlier said had not agreed to the pretenses of Eusebius and the rest, but had suffered exile with Arius, would not even hold communion afterward with Arius himself when he returned from exile, because with his feigned confession he had accepted communion with those who acknowledged that the Son is of the same substance as the Father. With quite unrestrained or rather impudent blasphemy they maintained what Arius had first taught: that the Son had not been born (*natum*), but created and made out of what did not exist. After their death one Aetius propounded this, and after Aetius Eunomius developed the doctrine even more vigorously and extensively. He was a man leprous in body and soul and outwardly afflicted with jaundice, but exceedingly able in debate; he wrote much against our faith and gave rules about debate to the members of his sect. Even today the Eunomian heresy is named after him. There was another named Macedonius, whom, after ejecting or rather killing our people in Constantinople, they had ordained bishop and whom, because he acknowledged the Son as like the Father, they ejected, even though he blasphemed the Holy Spirit just as they did. The reason was that he was teaching concerning the Son things similar to what he said of the Father. But he is not associated with our people, his views about the Holy Spirit being at variance with ours. Thus that fell beast which Arius had first caused to raise its head as though from the underworld suddenly appeared in triple form: the Eunomians, who say that the Son is in all respects different from the Father, because there is no way in which that which is made can be like its maker; the Arians, who say that the Son can indeed be said to be like the Father, but by the gift of grace, not by a natural property, to the extent, that is, that a creature may be compared to the Creator; and the Macedonians, who say that while the Son is in all respects like the Father, the Holy Spirit has nothing in common with the Father and the Son. This is what took place among them, but as is written of such people, "they are rent and not stung."[42] For very many of those who

---

42. Reference uncertain. On the three groups in question, see Hanson, 557–636, 760–72. On Aetius, see T. A. Kopecek, *A History of Neo-Arianism* (Cam-

could be seen to lead a stricter life, and a great number of monastic houses in Constantinople and the neighboring provinces, and prominent bishops, preferred to follow Macedonius's error.

10.27. But the emperor Constantius, while he was preparing to go with an army against Julian, whom he had left as Caesar in Gaul and who had of his own accord presumed to take the rank of Augustus, died at Mopsucrenae, a town in Cilicia, in the twenty-fourth year of his reign after his father's death.[43]

10.28. After him Julian as sole ruler received as a legitimate sovereignty what he had presumed to take. At first, as though critical of what Constantius had done, he bade the bishops be released from exile, but afterward he rose against our people with every hurtful stratagem. At that time the bishops still left there were released from exile. For Liberius, bishop of the city of Rome, had returned while Constantius was still alive; but whether this was because he had yielded to what he wanted and subscribed, or whether it was a favor to the Roman people, who had begged for him as he was going forth, I have not discovered for certain.

---

bridge, MA: Philadelphia Patristic Foundation, 1979), 61–132. On Eunomius: Kopecek, 145–76, 299–543; R. P. Vaggione, *Eunomius of Cyzicus and the Nicene Revolution* (Oxford: Clarendon, 2000). On his leprosy, see Philostorgius, 10.6. On heresy as leprosy, cf. Quodvultdeus, *Liber promissionum* 2.6.10–11 (CCL 60).

On the tangled history of Paul of Constantinople and Macedonius, see Barnes, 212–17. When Alexander of Constantinople died in 337, Paul was consecrated irregularly but expelled by Constantius and replaced by Eusebius of Nicomedia. Eusebius died in 341. Paul's supporters tried to restore him, but the "Arians" installed Macedonius, who battled with Paul's supporters throughout his tenure. That came to an end when he was deposed by the Council of Constantinople of 360 and replaced by Eudoxius, although the official grounds of dismissal were disciplinary, not doctrinal (Socrates, 2.42.3).

43. Constantius, who was without a male heir, proclaimed his cousin Julian Caesar on November 6, 355, and sent him to Gaul under careful supervision. Julian turned out to be an excellent and popular administrator and general, to the alarm of Constantius, who ordered him to send units to the east for the Persian war in the winter of 359/60. The units rebelled and declared Julian Augustus in February of 360. Constantius was on the march to engage him in battle when he died at Mopsucrenae on November 3, 361. Cf. A. H. M. Jones, *The Later Roman Empire* (Oxford: Clarendon, 1964), 1.117, 120; Paschoud, *Zosime*, 2.83–88.

Now Eusebius begged Lucifer, since they had both been exiled to neighboring parts of Egypt, to go with him to Alexandria to see Athanasius and together with the priests still there
to formulate a common policy regarding the situation of the
church. But he refused to attend, sending instead his deacon to
represent him, and with set purpose made his way to Antioch.
There the parties were still at odds, but hopeful of reunion if
the sort of bishop could be chosen for them with whom not just
one people but both could be satisfied; but Lucifer with excessive haste ordained as bishop Paulinus, a man certainly Catholic, holy, and in all respects worthy of the priesthood, but not
someone to whom both peoples could agree.[44]

10.29. Eusebius meanwhile made his way to Alexandria, where
a council of confessors gathered, few in number but pure in faith
and numerous in merits, to discuss with all care and deliberation
in what way tranquility might be restored to the church after the
storms of heresy and whirlwinds of perfidy. Some fervent spirits
thought that no one should be taken back into the priesthood
who had in any way stained himself by communion with the heretics. But others in imitation of the Apostle sought not what was
advantageous to themselves but to the many, and followed the
example of Christ, who, being the life of all, humbled himself
for the salvation of all and went down to his death, that in this
way life might be found even among the dead; they said that it
was better to humble themselves a little for the sake of those cast
down, and bend a little for the sake of those crushed, that they

44. On Julian's edict allowing the bishops to return (issued in 360 before
Constantius's death?), see Barnes, 154.

Lucifer was represented at the Council of Alexandria by two deacons, not
one; cf. *Tomus ad Antiochenos* 9.3.

The factions in Antioch were the following: those loyal to Bishop Eustathius, deposed in 327, who were led by Paulinus; those loyal to Meletius; the
"Arians" under Euzoius. There was also a group led by the presbyter Vitalis,
who represented Apollinarian views, but they may not have worshiped separately. Cf. Epiphanius, *Pan.* 77.20.3–24.2; R. Devreesse, *Le patriarcat d'Antioche*
(Paris: Lecoffre, 1945), 20–21. When Rufinus refers to the parties at variance,
he means the first two.

Lucifer and Eusebius had not been exiled to Egypt but, rather, during
their exile had been able to move around in the east (cf. note 37 above); Eusebius by this time had already visited Antioch (10.31).

might raise them up again and not keep the kingdom of heaven for themselves alone on account of their purity. It would be more glorious if they merited to enter there with many others, and therefore they thought the right thing was to cut off the authors of the perfidy alone, and to give the other priests the power of making a choice, if perchance they should wish to renounce the error of perfidy and return to the faith of the fathers and to the enactments. Nor should they deny admission to those returning, but should rather rejoice at their return, because the younger son in the gospel too, who had wasted his father's property, merited not only to be taken back when he had come to his senses, but was regarded as worthy of his father's embraces and received the ring of faith and had the robe put on him; and what did that signify but the tokens of priesthood? The older son did not win his father's approval by his jealousy of the one who was taken back, nor did the merit he had gained by not misbehaving equal the censure he incurred by not showing leniency to his brother.[45]

45. When news of Constantius's death reached Alexandria, George was put into prison, from which he was later dragged by a mob and lynched on December 24, 361. Athanasius returned to his city on February 21, 362, and lost little time in summoning a council that proved to be a turning point in the history of the doctrinal alliances of the fourth century. On the council, see Karmann (note 41 above), 168–305. The full council met first to decide how to reintegrate into communion the bishops who had subscribed the "homoean" creed appointed by Constantius. Its synodical letter has not survived as such, but Martin Tetz in "Ein enzyklisches Schreiben der Synode von Alexandrien (362)," ZNW 79 (1988): 262–81, claimed that the so-called Epistula Catholica, found among the spurious Athanasian literature, was in fact the first part of its general letter (the text is edited, 271–81). A comparison of the beginning of this letter with the beginning of the account in 10.29 suggests that Rufinus had read it (or some version of it): both compare the recent upheavals caused by the heretics to storms from which the church must steer to the desired calm; cf. quo pacto post haereticorum procellas et perfidiae turbines tranquillitas revocaretur ecclesiae ... discutiunt with Epistula Catholica (1): ὑπεξελθεῖν καθάπερ ἀπὸ κλύδωνός τινος εἰς λιμένα καὶ σώζειν ἑαυτοὺς ὀφείλετε.

This has been contested, however, by Y.-M. Duval, "La place et l'importance du Concile d'Alexandrie ou de 362 dans l'Histoire de l'Église de Rufin d'Aquilée," Revue des études augustiniennes 47.2 (2001): 285n14, and by Karmann, 181–84. Duval argues that the comparison of the doctrinal controversies to stormy weather was commonplace, and that Rufinus's account of the decisions reached by the council comes from material he could have found in Athanasius's Ep. ad Rufinianum (PG 26:1180B–1181A) and in Jerome's Alter-

10.30. When therefore that priestly and apostolic body had approved these counsels brought forth from the gospel, responsibility for the east was by decree of the council committed to Asterius and to the others who were with them, while the west was assigned to Eusebius. There was of course included in the conciliar decree a fuller treatment of the Holy Spirit as well: that the Holy Spirit too should be believed to be of the same substance and divinity as the Father and Son, and there should be no mention at all of anything created or inferior or posterior in the Trinity. There was also a discussion drawn from scripture about the difference between "substances" and "subsistences"; in Greek these terms are *ousiai* and *hypostaseis*. For some said that they thought that "substance" and "subsistence" meant the same thing, and as we do not speak of three substances in God, neither should we speak of three subsistences. Others, however, who thought that "substance" meant something very different from "subsistence," said that "substance" designated the very nature itself of a thing and the principle of its consistence, whereas the "subsistence" of each of the persons indicated the fact that [the person] exists and subsists. And therefore because of the heresy of Sabellius, three subsistences should be confessed, since that would make it clear that three

---

catio Luciferiani et Orthodoxi 17–19. That leaves, however, the exposition of the parable of the robe given to the Prodigal Son (Lk 15.22), which seems to be more than mere rhetorical elaboration by Rufinus. The robe attracted a rich exegetical tradition, well reviewed by A. M. Piredda, "La veste del figliol prodigo nella tradizione patristica," *Sandalion* 8–9 (1985–86): 203–42. It was the "first robe," the robe of holiness given to Adam before he sinned, and restored to redeemed humanity in Christ. In the Jewish tradition this robe of Adam's is a high-priestly vestment handed down through a succession of eldest sons; according to J. D. M. Derrett, this interpretation reappears in Christian literature with Ambrose ("The Parable of the Prodigal Son: Patristic Allegories and Jewish Midrashim," *Studia Patristica* 10.1 [1970]: 219–24). In Ambrose's exposition of the parable, the son is given the robe of wisdom, the priestly garb Rebekah puts on her younger son (*Expos. Luc.* 7.231; *Expos. Ps. CXVIII* 13.15; *De Iac.* 2.2.9). If Rufinus, however, is here reporting the contents of the synodical letter, then the exposition of the Prodigal Son's robe as a priestly garment antedates Ambrose.

It would be useful in any case to distinguish the question of the validity of Tetz's attribution from that of the accessibility to Rufinus of the synodical.

subsistent persons were meant and eliminate any suspicion that we belong to that faith which acknowledges the Trinity only nominally and not in actual reality. There was also included a statement about the incarnation of the Lord, that the body which the Lord assumed lacked neither sensation nor soul. All of which having been stated with restraint and moderation, each went his own way in peace.[46]

10.31. But Eusebius, when he had returned to Antioch and found there a bishop ordained by Lucifer contrary to his promise, left in embarrassment and indignation without granting his communion to either party, because upon his departure from there he had promised to see to it in the council that that person would be ordained from whom neither party would defect. For the people who had remained loyal to Meletius on

46. Asterius was bishop of Petra; Eusebius, of Vercelli. On Sabellius, see 7.6. On the translation of *ousia* and *hypostasis*, see note 10 above.

quod quasi tres subsistentes personas significare videretur: translated as "since that would make it clear that three subsistent persons were meant": *quasi* indicates motive or reason here, not comparison; cf. 10.31, where Meletius is said to have retained the loyalty of his followers *quasi pro recta fide.*

Rufinus in 10.30 describes the decisions taken not by the full council but by a special commission which met afterwards to deal with the divisions among the Christians in Antioch. Its letter has become known by the later title of *Tomus ad Antiochenos* (edited in *Athanasius Werke* 2.340–51). On this document, see Karmann, 193–305. Rufinus has clearly drawn from it here, the doctrinal points being treated there in the same order as he has them. Despite what he says, it does not attempt to distinguish *ousia* and *hypostasis,* nor does it declare itself for those who prefer to speak of three hypostases rather than one; it simply affirms the sufficiency of the Creed of Nicaea. The fact, however, that the document does not use *ousia* and *hypostasis* as equivalent terms paved the way for their eventual distinction, so that Rufinus is reporting not the actual language of the *Tomus,* but the results to which it would contribute. (The formulation that he attributes to the council, *substantia ipsam rei alicuius naturam rationemque, qua constat, [designat], subsistentia autem uniuscuiusque personae hoc ipsum quod extat et subsistit [ostendit],* reflects rather the distinction popularized by the Cappadocian Fathers; for Athanasius himself the terms remained synonymous; cf. J. Hammerstaedt, "Hypostasis," *RAC* 16.1020–23.) The same may be said of his statement about what it taught about the Holy Spirit (cf. Karmann, 246n209, 249n213, and 293n284). As for the Incarnation, Rufinus, followed by Socrates (3.7.2–10) and Sozomen (5.12.3), mentions that it was treated by the council, but we cannot tell from their reports if they mean the full session or the commission (Karmann, 251n217).

account of his orthodoxy after he had been driven from the church had not joined the earlier Catholics, those, that is, who had been with Bishop Eustathius and among whom was Paulinus, but maintained their own autonomy and place of assembly. Eusebius wanted to reunite these people, but since he had been forestalled by Lucifer, he could not, and so he departed. Then when Meletius returned from exile, since the people with him were more numerous, he took over the churches and from then on maintained his own alliance with other eastern bishops,[47] and he was not joined with Athanasius.

Meanwhile Lucifer, taking it hard that Eusebius had not accepted the bishop he had ordained in Antioch, thought that he in turn might not accept the decisions of the Council of Alexandria, but he was constrained by the bond of his representative, who had subscribed at the council with his authority. For he could not reject him who possessed his authority; but if he received him, he had to watch all his plans go for nought. Having thought long and hard about this, since there was no way out, he decided to receive his legate and to maintain a different attitude toward the others, one that was more satisfactory to him. He returned therefore to Sardinia, and I am not sure whether his death arrived too soon for him to change his mind—for rash initiatives are usually corrected by time—or whether he continued in his frame of mind unwaveringly. In any event, it is from here that the Luciferian schism, which still has a few adherents, took its start.[48] Eusebius for his part went around the east and Italy acting as physician and priest alike. He recalled each of the churches to the renunciation of infidelity and soundness of orthodoxy, especially when he discovered that Hilary, who as we

47. *propriam synodum cum ceteris orientalibus episcopis habuit.* For σύνοδος in the sense of an alliance or group of bishops in communion with one another, cf. Basil, *Ep.* 89.1; Epiphanius, *Pan.* 71.1.8; 73.34.5. When Rufinus says that the Meletian group was *numerosior,* he means in relation to those led by Paulinus; the largest Christian group in Antioch were the homoeans (Karmann, 157n27).

48. On Lucifer and the schism named after him, see Sulpicius Severus, *Chronicle* 2.45.8; G. F. Diercks, *Luciferi Calaritani Opera Quae Supersunt* (CCL 8, 1978), vii–xxxvii. Jerome says he died during Valentinian's reign (364–375); *Vir. illustr.* 95.

mentioned earlier had been banished with the other bishops, had already returned and from his place of residence in Italy was making the same efforts to restore the churches and revive the faith of the fathers.

10.32. The only difference was that Hilary, a man naturally gentle and peaceful and at the same time learned and most adept at persuasion, was achieving his purpose more carefully and skillfully. He also published some excellent books about the faith, in which he so carefully expounded both the cunning of the heretics and the way in which our people had been deceived and their unfortunate gullibility, that with his faultless teaching he corrected both those with him and those far off whom he could not address in person. Thus these two men, like two great lights of the world, lit up Illyricum, Italy, and Gaul with their brightness, so that all the darkness of heresy was driven from even the most remote and hidden corners.[49]

10.33. Now Julian, once he had come into the east to drive out the Persians by war and begun to be carried away by the unconcealed craze for idolatry which earlier he had kept secret, showed himself more astute than the others as a persecutor in that he ruined almost more people by rewards, honors, flattery, and persuasion, than if he had proceeded by way of force, cruelty, and torture. Forbidding Christians access to the study of the pagan authors, he decreed that elementary schools should be open only to those who worshiped the gods and goddesses.

49. On Hilary, see J. Doignon, "Hilarius von Poitiers," *RAC* 15.139–67. During his exile he remained in touch with the bishops in Gaul and collected the records of the post-Nicene eastern councils. He was taken to the Council of Seleucia of 359, where he presented his creed and accompanied its delegation to Constantinople. There he protested so vigorously against the course of events in the church that in 360 the emperor told him to return to Gaul. He spent some time in Milan trying unsuccessfully to bring down its homoean bishop Auxentius, until finally the emperor Valentinian ordered him to leave in 365. He died in 367.

For Hilary's theology, see Carl L. Beckwith, *Hilary of Poitiers on the Trinity: From De Fide to De Trinitate* (Oxford: Clarendon, 2008). For his activities after returning from exile, Y.-M. Duval, "Vrais et faux problèmes concernant le retour d'exil d'Hilaire de Poitiers et son action en Italie en 360–363," *Athenaeum* NS 48 (1970): 251–75. The "books about the faith" which Rufinus mentions may well be the first three books of what is now called his *De Trinitate*.

He ordered that posts in the [armed or civil] service should be given only to those who sacrificed. He decreed that the government of provinces and the administration of justice should not be entrusted to Christians, since their own law forbade them to use the sword. And he progressed daily in devising such laws as embodied all sorts of ingenious and cunning policies, while at the same time they did not appear particularly cruel.[50]

10.34. But he could not keep up the pretense of philosophy toward Athanasius. For when, like loathsome serpents swarming from their lairs, his irreligious gang of sorcerers, philosophers, diviners, and soothsayers had made its way to him, they all alike declared that they would accomplish nothing by their arts unless he first got rid of Athanasius, the one who stood in the way of them all.

10.35. Once again an army was sent, once again officers, again the church was assailed. And when the people stood around him in grief and tears, he is said to have spoken to them prophetically. "Do not," he said, "be distressed, my children; this is a small cloud which passes quickly." And when he had left and was making his way by boat on the Nile River, the count who had been sent for this purpose found out which way he had gone and set out after him forthwith. And when by chance Athanasius's boat had put in at a certain place, he learned from the passers-by that his assassin was behind him and that at any moment, if he did not look out, he would be upon him. All those with him were terrified and tried to persuade him to seek refuge in the desert. But he said, "Do not be frightened, my children; let us rather go to meet our assassin, that he may realize that the one protecting us is far greater than the one pursuing us." And turning his boat around, he set his course to meet his pursuer. He in turn, hav-

50. On Julian's concealment of his paganism until he became emperor, see Ammianus, 21.2.4. He did not forbid Christian youths access to schools, and in fact wanted them to attend so that they could learn paganism and be converted to it. But he did rule that teachers had to be pagans; see his *Ep.* 61; Ammianus, 22.10.7 and 25.4.20. On Julian's religious policy in general, see Theresa Nesselrath, *Kaiser Julian und die Repaganisierung des Reiches. Jahrbuch für Antike und Christentum Ergänzungsband. Kleine Reihe* 9 (Münster: Aschendorff, 2013).

Militiae cingulum refers to both the armed and civil services. Julian, *Ep.* 83, says that pagans are to be preferred for public office; cf. also Socrates, 3.13.1.

ing no reason to suspect that the one he was after was coming toward him, ordered the company to be asked, as though they were passers-by, if they had heard where Athanasius was. When they replied that they had seen him on the move not far off, he hurried by with all speed, hastening in vain to capture the man he could not see before his very eyes. But he returned to Alexandria, protected by God's power, and there remained safely in hiding until the persecution ceased.[51]

10.36. Julian also gave another sign of his madness and folly. When he had offered sacrifice to Apollo by the Castalian spring in Daphne, a suburb of Antioch, but had received no answers to his questions and asked the priests of the demon the reasons for the silence, they said, "The burial place of the martyr Babylas is nearby, and for that reason no answers are given." Then he ordered the Galileans, for thus he called our people, to come and remove the martyr's tomb. The whole church therefore came together, mothers and men, virgins and youths, and with immense rejoicing pulled along the martyr's coffin in a long procession singing psalms with loud cries and exultation and saying, "May all those be put to shame who worship carven idols and who trust in their images!" This psalm the whole church sang in the hearing of the sacrilegious sovereign over a distance of six miles with such exultation that the sky rang with the shouts. He became so furious that the next day he ordered Christians to be arrested at random, thrust into prison, and subjected to punishment and torture.[52]

51. Julian's frequent consultation of soothsayers is well attested: cf. Libanius, *Or.* 37.5; Ammianus, 23.5.10–14; John Chrysostom, *De S. Babyla* 77.

It would be difficult to exaggerate the importance of his decision to single out Athanasius from among all the bishops for exile, since it lent credence to the latter's long-standing claim that the real reason for the opposition he had endured almost from the beginning of his episcopate was the desire to destroy the Christian faith. Cf. Julian, *Epp.* 110, 111, 112; Athanasius, *Historia acephala* 11 and *Festal Index* 35; Theodoret, *HE* 3.9; Sozomen, 4.10.4; Barnes, 158–59.

52. Cf. Ps 96.7. The facts about the early third-century Antiochene martyr-bishop Babylas are difficult to sort out, but tradition says that he was put to death because he had expelled the emperor Philip from church for murdering a hostage; see M. A. Schatkin and P. W. Harkins, *Saint John Chrysostom Apologist* (Washington, DC: The Catholic University of America Press, 1985), 47–70.

Julian's own brother Gallus had been responsible for having Babylas's body

10.37. Salutius, his prefect, did not approve of this, although he was a pagan, but he followed his order and tortured a youth named Theodore, the first who chanced to be arrested, from first light until the tenth hour with such cruelty and so many changes of torturers that history cannot recall the like. Raised aloft on the rack and with a torturer busy on either side of him, he did nothing but repeat with a calm and joyous countenance the psalm which the whole church had sung the day before. When Salutius saw that he had exhausted all his cruelty to no purpose, he is said to have returned the youth to prison, gone to the emperor, reported what he had done, and advised him not to try anything else of the sort, or else he would win glory for the others and ignominy for himself. We ourselves later saw Theodore in Antioch, and when we asked him if he had felt the pain fully, he said that while he had felt some slight pain, a youth had stood by him wiping away his perspiration with the purest white cloth while he was sweating and had kept applying cool water to him, and he had enjoyed it so much that he was unhappy when he was ordered off the rack. The emperor, then, threatening to do a better job of subduing the Christians after his victory over the Persians, set out but never returned. Wounded either by his own men or by the enemy—we do not know which—he brought to an end there his reign as Augustus, upon which he had presumed to enter, after a year and eight months.[53]

10.38. Now such were his acuteness and cunning in decep-

---

moved to the shrine in Daphne in order to convert it to Christian use (Sozomen, 5.19.12–14). What infuriated Julian was the destruction by fire of the temple of Apollo there shortly after he had reopened the prophetic Castalian spring and had had the martyr's body removed. He thought the Christians had done it, and he ordered the main church in Antioch closed; see Ammianus, 22.12.8–13.3; Julian, *Misopogon* 361BC; John Chrysostom, *De S. Babyla* 80–95; Socrates, 3.18–19; Sozomen, 5.19–20; Theodoret, *HE* 3.10–12; Philostorgius, 7.8; *De S. Hieromartyre Babyla* (PG 50:532).

53. Julian appointed Saturninus Secundus Salutius praetorian prefect of the east in 361; he accompanied Julian to Antioch in 362. He was a close friend, well educated, and a firm pagan; see Paschoud, *Zosime,* 2.64.

Julian died on June 26, 363. The ancient reports about his death are too numerous to list here, yet even the earliest ones disagreed about whether he had been killed by the enemy or by one of his own men, and with what kind of weapon; see Paschoud, *Zosime,* 2.203–5.

tion that he even deluded the unhappy Jews, enticing them with the sort of vain hopes that he himself entertained. The very first thing he did was to summon them to himself and ask them why they did not offer sacrifice, when their law included commandments for them about sacrifices. Thinking an opportunity had come their way, they answered, "We cannot do so except in the temple in Jerusalem. For thus the law ordains." And having received from him permission to repair the temple, they grew so arrogant that it was as though one of the prophets had been restored to them. Jews came together from every place and province and began to make their way to the site of the temple, long since consumed by fire, a count having been assigned by the emperor to push forward the work, which was pursued with all earnestness and financed with both public and private funds. Meanwhile they insulted our people and, as though the time of the kingdom had returned, threatened them harshly and treated them cruelly; in a word, they behaved with monstrous arrogance and pride. Cyril was the bishop of Jerusalem, following Maximus the confessor. The foundations, then, having been cleared, and quicklime and stone procured, nothing more was needed before new foundations could be laid the next day once the old ones had been dislodged. The bishop, however, having carefully weighed both what was contained in Daniel's prophecy about the times, and what the Lord had foretold in the gospels, insisted that the Jews would never be able to put a stone upon a stone there. Thus the suspense grew.[54]

54. Cf. Dn 9.24–26; Mt 24.2; Mk 13.2; Lk 19.44. On Julian's project to rebuild the temple, cf. his *Ep.* 204; Ammianus, 23.1.2. The count was Alypius; cf. *PLRE* 1.47. On the whole episode see Johannes Hahn, "Kaiser Julian und ein dritter Tempel? Idee, Wirklichkeit, und Wirkung eines gescheiterten Projektes," in *Zerstörungen des Jerusalemer Tempels: Geschehen—Wahrnehmungen—Bewältigung,* ed. J. Hahn (Tübingen: Mohr Siebeck, 2002), 237–62 (the ancient sources are listed on pp. 259–60.) Jerusalem and its temple had been razed by Titus; Hadrian had later built a temple to Jupiter on the site when he refounded the city as Aelia Capitolina. That temple had been abandoned since Constantine's time. Hadrian's law forbidding the Jews access to Jerusalem had never been totally enforced, but it was repeated by Constantine: see Augustine, *Sermo* 5.5; Thelamon, *PC* 298–300. On the prophecy about a stone not being left on a stone, see Cyril, *Catecheses* 15.15. On Jewish women selling their valuables to contribute to the project, see Gregory Naz., *Or.* 5.4.

10.39. And behold, on the night which alone remained before the work was to begin, there was a violent earthquake, and not only were the stones for the foundations tossed far and wide, but almost all the buildings round about were leveled to the ground. The public porticoes too, in which the multitude of Jews was staying who were clearly intent on completing the project, tumbled to the ground, burying all the Jews inside. At daybreak, thinking that it had escaped the misfortune, the remaining multitude hurried together to look for those who had been buried.

10.40. Now there was a chamber sunk in the lower part of the temple which had its entrance between two porticoes that had been leveled to the ground; in it were kept some iron implements and other things necessary for the work. Out of it there suddenly burst a globe of fire which sped through the square, weaving this way and that and burning and killing the Jews who were there. This happened again and again with great frequency throughout the whole day, checking the rashness of the obstinate people with the avenging flames, while meanwhile all who were there were in such great fear and trembling that in their terror they were forced, however unwillingly, to admit that Jesus Christ is the one true God. And so that these things would not be held to have happened by chance, on the following night the sign of the cross appeared on everyone's clothing so clearly that even those who in their unbelief wanted to wash it off could find no way to get rid of it. Thus the Jews and pagans in their fright abandoned both the site and the useless project.[55]

55. The lethal balls of fire are reported by Ammianus, 23.1.3. The chamber mentioned seems to have been an underground portico built in Herod's time. The fire could have resulted from an explosion of underground gas caused by the earthquake; cf. Thalamon, *PC* 306. The cross marked on the spectators' clothing is mentioned in Gregory Naz., *Or.* 5.7.

BOOK ELEVEN

11.1. After Julian's death a legitimate government was restored to us at last with Jovian; for he appeared at once as emperor, confessor, and averter of the error which had been introduced for evil. For with the army on alert and the barbarian pressing close, our leaders, after discussing the crisis, elected Jovian, who, as he was being seized and taken off to receive the tokens of command, is said to have announced to the army, profaned by Julian's sacrilegious acts, that he could not command them because he was a Christian. They all with one voice are said to have answered, "We are Christians too!" Nor would he agree to accept the command before he had heard what they said, according to report. Then God's mercy came to his assistance without delay, and beyond all hope, the enemy having closed in on all sides with no chance of escape, they suddenly saw envoys approaching from the barbarians who sued for peace, who promised as well to sell food and other provisions to the army, which was prostrate from famine, and who with boundless clemency corrected the rashness of our people. After he had secured peace for twenty-nine years and returned to Roman soil,[1] and the brighter light which had arisen in the east shone upon our land, he proceeded with all moderation to restore the state after what had seemed great storms, and the care of the churches was not for him a lesser matter. But he did not act heedlessly like Constantius; warned by his predecessor's fall, he summoned Athanasius with a respectful and most dutiful letter. He received from him an outline of the faith and a plan for setting the churches in order. But an early death ruined these so religious and happy beginnings; eight months after his accession he died in Cilicia.[2]

1. Jovian succeeded Julian on June 27, 363. The words *contraque omnem spem ... subito emissos a barbaris oratores adesse vident pacemque deposcere* remind one of Ammianus, 25.7.5: *Persae praeter sperata priores super fundanda pace oratores ... mittunt,* and may perhaps suggest a common source. For Ammianus, however, the Persians' clemency was only feigned: *Condiciones autem ferebant difficiles et perplexas, fingentes humanorum respectu reliquias exercitus redire sinere clementissimum regem* (i.e., the Persian king; 25.7.6). Jovian was in a hurry to return to Roman soil, though, because Julian was thought to have named his relative Procopius his successor before he opened the campaign (Ammianus, 25.3.2; 25.7.10). He therefore agreed to what was regarded as a disgraceful surrender of territory and alliances in return for a thirty-year peace treaty (25.7.11–14). Cf. Socrates, 3.22.1–8; Sozomen, 6.3.1–2; Theodoret, *HE* 4.1.1–4.2.3; Zosimus, 3.30–34; Eutropius, 10.17.

2. Athanasius sailed from Egypt on September 6, 363, to meet Jovian even before the latter reached Antioch. Cf. Annette von Stockhausen, "Athanasius in Antiochien," *ZAC* 10 (2006): 86–102. Jovian's letter to him in *Athanasius Werke* 2.357 is genuine, but incomplete; see von Stockhausen, 89–90. Athanasius's letter to him (*AW* 2.352–56) contains an exposition of the Creed of Nicaea. Despite what Rufinus says, there is no reason to think that Jovian sent for him, although the emperor's letter compliments him on his courage and respectfully allows him to return to his church.

Athanasius was only one of a crowd of church leaders and other interested parties who hastened to seek Jovian while he was still on the homeward march; those among them who tried to oppose Athanasius were rebuffed (*AW* 2.352–56). Jovian, while he rescinded Julian's orders banishing Athanasius, restoring state support of pagan worship (Athanasius, *Historia acephala* 12), and canceling the grain allowances to the churches (Theodoret, *HE* 4.4), refused to take sides in the controversies among his fellow Christians. He simply

11.2. Valentinian, whom Julian had expelled from the service because of the faith, succeeded him. But the Lord fulfilled in him what he had promised, restoring to him in the present age even more than a hundredfold; for because he had left the service for the sake of Christ, he received the empire. He took as his partner in government his brother Valens, choosing for himself the west while he left the east to him.[3] But Valens went off in his fathers' path by supporting the heretics. He sent bishops into exile and while Tatian was governing Alexandria went so far as to hand over presbyters, deacons, and monks to torture and to the flames, and plotted many wicked and cruel deeds against God's church. But all this took place after Athanasius's death, for while he was still alive he was restrained as though by some divine power; he might rage against the others, but against him he dared do no hostile deed.[4]

---

made it clear that he esteemed Meletius of Antioch no less than Athanasius, and many of their colleagues soon found it convenient to publish a pro-Nicene declaration (Socrates, 3.25). This happy result of Jovian's policy of benign neglect encouraged stories that he had officially established the Creed of Nicaea (Theodoret, *HE* 4.2.3) and may also be behind Rufinus's claim that he received a church policy (*ecclesiarum disponendarum modus*) from Athanasius. Cf. also Philostorgius, 8.5–6.

Jovian died in Dadastana on February 17, 364. Both the exact location of the place (in Bithynia?) and the cause of his death are uncertain; see Ammianus, 25.10.12–13; Paschoud, 2.238.

3. The "hundredfold" refers to Mk 10.30. Valentinian succeeded Jovian on February 26, 364, and a month later named Valens his colleague. Julian had expelled him from the army officer corps and banished him for failure in duty, or so it was alleged; rumor had it that the real reason was Valentinian's repugnance for pagan rites (Sozomen, 6.6.2–6; Theodoret, *HE* 3.16.1–3; Philostorgius, 7.7). Jovian recalled him. On the ancient sources concerning Jovian's and Valentinian's reputations as Christian confessors, see Noel Lenski, "Were Valentinian, Valens, and Jovian Confessors Before Julian the Apostate?" *ZAC* 6 (2002): 253–76.

4. Valens had been baptized by the homoean Eudoxius of Constantinople (Socrates, 4.1.6), and he reinstated his creed, which Constantius had officially established toward the end of his reign. He expelled once again all the bishops originally banished by Constantius who had returned under Julian's amnesty (Athanasius, *Historia acephala* 16). The attempt to eject Athanasius, however, met with such popular protest that the order was rescinded after four months (under the pretext that he had been recalled by Jovian and so was exempt from Valens's general order), and he returned from hiding to remain in tranquil

11.3. During this time, then, in the forty-sixth year of his priesthood, Athanasius, after many struggles and many crowns of suffering, rested in peace. Asked about his successor, he chose Peter to be sharer and partner in his troubles. But Lucius, a bishop of the Arian party, flew at once like a wolf upon the sheep. As for Peter, he immediately boarded a ship and fled to Rome. Lucius, as though the material on which his cruelty could work had been taken from him, became even more savage toward the others and showed himself so bloodthirsty that he did not even try to preserve an appearance of religion. When he first arrived, such enormous and disgraceful deeds were done against the virgins and celibates as are not even recorded in the pagan persecutions. Hence after the banishment and exile of citizens, after the slaughter, torture, and flames with which he brought so many to their deaths, he turned the weapons of his madness against the monastic houses. He laid waste the desert and declared war on the peaceable. He set out likewise to attack simultaneously the three thousand or more men who were scattered throughout the desert in secret and solitary dwellings; he sent an armed force of cavalry and infantry; he chose tribunes, commanders, and officers as though he were going to do battle against the barbarians. When they arrived, they witnessed a new kind of war: their enemies exposed their necks to the swords and said only, "Friend, for what have you come?"[5]

---

possession of his see until his death (*Historia acephala* 17–18). On Valens's religious policy, see Noel Lenski, *Failure of Empire: Valens and the Roman State in the Fourth Century A.D.* (Berkeley: University of California Press, 2002), 242–63.

Flavius Eutolmius Tatianus was prefect of Egypt, 367–70, so *PLRE* 1.876 assumes that the persecution referred to took place in 368–69, and not after Athanasius's death, as Rufinus says. But as Barnes, 298, points out, the so-called *Barbarus Scaligeri,* an originally Alexandrian chronicle, lists Tatian as prefect again after Athanasius's death (*Chronica minora* 1.296).

5. Mt 26.50. Athanasius died on May 2, 373. He designated Peter to succeed him a few days before his death (*Historia acephala* 19). Lucius was a presbyter of George who had led the "Arians" of Alexandria after George's death; it is not known when and where he was ordained bishop. Peter did not get away immediately after his entry into the city; he was arrested and locked up but later escaped and fled to Rome (Socrates, 4.21.4; Sozomen, 6.19.2, 5).

There is no exaggeration in Rufinus's summary of the scenes which accompanied Lucius's arrival in Alexandria, when the (pagan) governor sent his

11.4. At that time those of Antony's disciples who were living in Egypt, and especially in the desert of Nitria, and who on account of their life and advanced age were considered to be the fathers of the monks, were Macarius, Isidore, another Macarius, Heraclides, and Pambo; they were held to be companions in the lives and deeds not of other mortals but of the angels on high. I speak of what I was there to see, and I report the deeds of those whose sufferings I was granted to share. These men led the Lord's army equipped not with mortal weapons but with religious faith, an army which conquered by dying and which, victorious in the shedding of its blood, would follow Christ to heaven. While they were in their tents praying and waiting for their killers, a man was brought to them whose limbs, and especially his feet, had long since shriveled up; but when they anointed him with oil in the Lord's name, the soles of his feet were at once made strong. And when they said, "In the name of Jesus Christ, whom Lucius is persecuting, arise, stand on your feet, and return home," he got up at once and, jumping about, blessed God, thus showing that God was really in them.

Now a short time earlier a blind man had asked to be led to Macarius's cell, which was in the desert three days' journey distant. But when his guides had expended much labor in bringing him there, he did not find Macarius at home. Greatly disappointed, he simply could not assuage his unhappiness at lacking the consolation of being healed. But then, plucking up his faith, he said to those who had brought him, "Please take me up to the part of the wall where the elder usually sleeps." When he had been brought there, he put on the palm of his hand a little of the dry mud with which the wall was seen to have been plastered, and asked also that they draw some water from the well from which he usually drank. With the moisture he softened the clod, plastered the mud over his eyes, and washed them with the water that had been drawn, and at once received his sight, so

---

troops to clear the churches of those loyal to Peter; the grim tale is set out in Peter's own account, quoted copiously by Theodoret (*HE* 4.22) and supported by Epiphanius (*Pan.* 68.11.4–6). The persecution extended to all the clergy and religious in Egypt who refused to accept Lucius, and it was still going on when Epiphanius was writing the later sections of the *Panarion* (376?). Cf. Lenski (note 4 above), 255–57.

that he was able to return home unassisted. But he did not behave like the lepers in the gospel whom the Lord criticized for
their ingratitude after he had healed them; rather, he returned
with his whole household and gave thanks to God, explaining
what had happened.

This same Macarius had a hyena's den near his cell. One day
the beast brought her blind cubs to him and laid them at his
feet. When he realized that the animal was beseeching him
concerning the cubs' blindness, he asked the Lord to grant
them sight. They received it and followed their mother back to
the den. Shortly afterward she emerged with the cubs, carrying
in her mouth a great bunch of woolly sheepskins; she brought
them to the elder as though they were a gift in return for the
favor received, left them on his doorstep, and departed. But
if we were to relate each of the miracles, we would fail of our
planned brevity, especially since these things deserve to be told
of in a book of their own.[6]

But none of them caused Lucius any shame, nor did he show
any respect for the miracles. On the contrary, he ordered those
fathers to be taken from their flock, or, rather, clandestinely

6. A subtle reference to the "Lives of the Monks" composed originally in
Greek (text: A.-J. Festugière, *Historia Monachorum in Aegypto* [Brussels: So-
ciété des Bollandistes, 1961]) and translated by Rufinus into Latin (text: E.
Schulz-Flügel, *Rufinus. Historia Monachorum* [Berlin: de Gruyter, 1990]).

"The lepers in the gospel" is a reference to Lk 17.11–19.

On the monks referred to here by name, cf. C. Butler, *The Lausiac History of Palladius* (Cambridge: *Texts and Studies* VI, 1898 and 1904), 2.185,
190–94. Macarius the Egyptian (Rufinus, *HM* 28), also called "the Elder" or
"the Great," is sometimes confused with Macarius of Alexandria (*HM* 29; cf.
Thelamon, *PC* 380–81). For Isidore, cf. Palladius, *HL* 1; for Pambo, *HL* 10.

Oil was often used by the monks for healing; see Thelamon, *PC* 394. The
pagan Egyptians used to come to the temples for healing, and people would
scratch some plaster from the walls. The scratches can still be seen, even from
times after a temple was Christianized. The water from the temple well, sometimes spoken of as the saliva of the god of the temple, was used for the same
purpose; see Thelamon, *PC* 384–85.

For the story of Macarius and the hyena, cf. Greek *HM* 21.15–16; Palladius,
HL 18.27–28. There are many stories about monks living in peace with wild
beasts, especially lions; the underlying theme is the reestablishment of the
conditions before the Fall. Cf. Cassian, *De institutis coenobiorum* 9.8; Thelamon,
PC 389–90.

seized, and brought to an island in one of the marshes of Egypt, on which he had found out that there was not a single Christian, to live there deprived of any comfort and of their usual activities. The elders were thus taken by night, with only two attendants, to the island, on which there was a temple greatly revered by the inhabitants of the place. And behold, when the elders' boat touched shore there, the virgin daughter of the priest of the temple was suddenly seized by a spirit, and, moving through the midst of the temple, began to give vent to loud shouts and shrieks which echoed to heaven, whirling about repeatedly and with shrill cries jerking her head frenziedly in every direction. And when the people gathered to watch this enormous portent, especially since it was the priest's daughter, whom they held in particular honor, she was snatched into the air, and they followed her to the elders' boat. There, cast down at their feet and lying prostrate, she began to cry, "Why have you come here, O servants of God most high, to drive us from our ancient and long-held habitations? In this place we have been hiding since being driven out from everywhere else. How is it that we have found no way to hide from you? We yield our ancient dwellings; take your people and lands!" When she had spoken thus, the spirit of error fled at their reprimand, and the girl, restored to her senses, lay with her parents at the feet of the apostles of our time. They used this as the starting-point to preach to them the faith of the Lord Jesus Christ, and brought them at once to such a complete conversion that with their own hands they immediately tore down the temple, ancient and greatly revered though it was, and lost no time in building a church; nor did they need any time to consider, since their conviction about the situation had arisen not from speech but from a deed of power. When this was made known in Alexandria, however, Lucius, afraid that even his own people might rightly come to hate him, seeing as he had now openly declared war not on men, but on God, ordered that they be called back secretly and returned to the desert. While this was taking place in Egypt, the flames of persecution did not die down even in other places.[7]

7. Cf. Socrates, 4.24.13–17; Theodoret, *HE* 4.21.7–14; Sozomen, 6.20. For other stories of monks converting pagans, cf. Rufinus, *HM* 7.6.5–7.7.9; 9.7.16–20.

11.5. For Edessa in Mesopotamia, which is adorned with the relics of the apostle Thomas, is a city of the faithful. When the emperor saw there for himself the people who had been ejected from the churches meeting in a field, he is said to have become so angry that he struck his prefect with his fist because they had not been driven from there as well, as he had ordered. The prefect, however, although he was a pagan and had been mistreated by the emperor, was still considerate enough to let the citizens know by surreptitious means that he was due to go forth the next day to slaughter the people, so that they might take care not to be found in the place. And in the morning when he went forth, he made an even more fearful appearance than usual with his retinue, and a great stir, so that as few people as possible, or perhaps even no one at all, might be put in any danger. But he saw more people than usual heading for the place, running at full speed, hurrying as though fearful lest anyone should miss death. At the same time he saw some common woman come bursting out of her house with such haste and speed that she paused neither to close the door nor to cover herself properly as women should; she was pulling with her a small child and hurrying along at such a rate that she even collided with the retinue. At which, unable to restrain himself any longer, he said, "Seize that woman and bring her here!" When she had been brought to him, he said, "Unhappy woman, where are you hastening with such speed?" "To the field," she said, "where the Catholic people meet." "And have you not heard," he said, "that the prefect is making his way there to kill everyone he finds?" "I have heard it and so I am hurrying, that I may be found there." "And where," he asked, "are you taking the child?" "So that it too," she replied, "may deserve to attain martyrdom." When that mildest of men heard that, he ordered his retinue to go back, and his conveyance to turn its course to the palace, and going in he said, "Your majesty, I am ready to suffer death, if you order, but the deed you command I cannot carry out." And when he had reported all that concerned the woman, he checked the emperor's madness.[8]

8. Cf. Socrates, 4.18; Sozomen, 6.18; Theodoret, *HE* 4.17.1–4. The official is Domitius Modestus, praetorian prefect of the east, 369–377. Rufinus's portrait

11.6. During this time the church shone with a light purer than gold in the fire of persecution. For the faith of each person was tested not by words but by exiles and imprisonments, since being Catholic was not an honor but a crime, especially in Alexandria, where the faithful were not even free to bury the bodies of the dead. While Lucius was behaving thus with all arrogance and cruelty, Mavia, the queen of the Saracens, began to rock the towns and cities on the borders of Palestine and Arabia with fierce attacks and to lay waste the neighboring provinces at the same time, and when she had worn down the Roman army in frequent battles, killed many, and put the rest to flight, she was sued for peace. She said she would agree to it only if a certain monk named Moses were ordained bishop for her people. He was leading a solitary life in the desert near her territory and had achieved great fame because of his merits and the miracles and signs God worked through him. Her request, when presented to the Roman sovereign, was ordered to be carried out without delay by our officers who had fought there with such unhappy results. Moses was taken and brought to Alexandria, as was usual, to receive the priesthood. Lucius arrived, to whom the ceremony of ordination was entrusted. Moses, when he saw him, said to the officers who were there and were anxious to make haste, and to the people, "I do not think that I am worthy of so great a priesthood, but if it is judged that some part of the divine dispensation is to be fulfilled in me, unworthy as I am, then I swear by our God, the Lord of heaven and earth, that Lucius shall not lay upon me hands that are defiled and stained by the blood of the saints."

---

of him as a humane pagan is to be taken with the usual grain of salt. He had been a tepid Christian until Julian's accession, when he converted to paganism, but he returned to Christianity around 365, well before he was appointed praetorian prefect and therefore before this episode; cf. PW 15.2323–25. Gregory Nazianzen portrays Rufinus's *vir moderatissimus* as descending upon the churches like a lion to its prey; baptized by the homoeans, he enthusiastically carried out Valens's measures against the Catholics (*Or.* 43.48). Cf. note 21 below.

This episode may have occurred in 375. Valens's use of force to impose homoean Christianity began after Athanasius's death in 373; see Lenski, *Failure of Empire,* 243; 257–58.

Lucius, seeing himself branded by a censure so grave in the eyes of the multitude, said, "Why, Moses, do you so readily condemn someone whose faith you do not know? Or if someone has spoken to you unfavorably of me, listen to my creed, and believe yourself rather than others." "Lucius," he replied, "stop trying to assail me as well with your treacherous illusions. I know well your creed, declared as it is by God's servants condemned to the mines, by the bishops driven into exile, by the presbyters and deacons banished to dwellings beyond the pale of the Christian religion, and by the others handed over, some to the beasts and some even to fire. Can that faith which is perceived by the ears be truer than that which is seen by the eyes? I am sure that those with a correct belief in Christ do not do such things." And thus Lucius, now loaded with even more disgrace, was forced to agree that he might receive the priesthood from the bishops he had driven into exile, since the need to look to the welfare of the state was so pressing. And having received it, he both preserved the peace with the fiercest of peoples and maintained unimpaired the heritage of the Catholic faith.[9]

11.7. Now when in Alexandria the foul darkness of the perfidy of the foggy teacher was covering the people and the city, the Lord kindled Didymus to be like a lamp shining with divine light. Of his life and character we think it necessary to make brief mention, if only in passing, since he is believed to have been given by God for the glory of the church. When he was a child, he was deprived of his eyesight even before he knew the first letters of the alphabet, but he was inflamed with an even greater desire for the sight of the true light; nor did he despair of gaining what he sought, since he had heard what is written in the gospel: "What is impossible for human beings is possible for

9. The most probable account that can be derived from the ancient sources is that Mavia, the wife of a Saracen tribal chieftain, decided to display her martial resolve after her husband's death by a series of border raids to secure her position and to persuade the Romans to renew their treaty with her people. She will have been Christian herself, but the appointment of Moses will hardly have been as essential to the negotiations as Rufinus makes out. For an assessment of the ancient sources and the modern literature, see Oliver Schmitt, "Noch einmal zu 'Mavia, der Königin der Sarazenen,'" *Mediterraneo antico* 7.2 (2004): 859–77.

God."[10] Trusting in this divine promise, he prayed to the Lord unceasingly not that he might receive sight in his physical eyes, but the illumination of the heart. He combined study and labor with his prayers and had recourse to continuous and uninterrupted hours of wakefulness not for reading but for listening, that what sight gave to others hearing might give to him. But when as usual sleep had overtaken the readers after their nocturnal work, Didymus, believing that the silence was not given for repose or idleness, would recall everything that he had received like a clean animal chewing its cud,[11] and would retrace in his mind and memory what he had earlier understood from the reading of the books which the others had run through, so that he seemed not so much to have heard what had been read as to have copied it out on the pages of his mind. Thus in a short time, with God as his teacher, he arrived at such expert knowledge of things divine and human that he became the master of the church school, having won the high esteem of Bishop Athanasius and the other wise men in God's church. Not only that, he was so well trained in the other disciplines, whether of dialectic or geometry, astronomy or arithmetic, that no philosopher could ever defeat or reduce him to silence by proposing any question from these arts; he no sooner heard his answers than he was convinced that he was an expert in the discipline in question. A number of people with the help of stenographers took down what he said, his debates with others, and his replies to the issues raised, all of which is still held in great admiration. We, however, who were both to some extent disciples of his when he spoke in person, and also read what he said as taken down by a good number of people, perceived a far greater grace and something divine and above human speech which sounded rather in those words which came from his mouth. The blessed Antony, too, when he was on his way down to Alexandria from the Thebaid to bear witness against the Arians with the faith of Athanasius, consoled him with these marvelous words: "Do not be troubled, Didymus, because you are deemed deprived of your physical eyes, for what you lack are those eyes which mice,

10. Lk 18.27.
11. Lv 11.3.

flies, and lizards have; rejoice rather that you have the eyes
which angels have, by which God is seen, and through which a
great light of knowledge is being kindled for you."[12]

11.8. Egypt, then, was flourishing at that time not only with
men steeped in Christian learning, but also with those who dwelt
throughout the great desert and worked the signs and wonders
of the apostles in simplicity of life and sincerity of heart. Those
of them whom at that time we ourselves saw and by whose hands
it was granted us to be blessed are the following: Macarius of the
upper desert; another Macarius of the lower; Isidore in Scete;
Pambo in Cellulae; Moses and Benjamin in Nitria; Ischyrion,
Elias, and Paul in Apeliotes; another Paul in Foci(?); and Poe-
men and Joseph in Pispir, which was called Antony's mountain.
We learned as well from reliable report that a great many other
men of this sort dwelt in Egypt, so that the apostle's statement
was truly fulfilled: where sin abounded, grace has abounded far
more.[13] Mesopotamia also at this same time had noble men who
excelled in this same way of life. Some of them we saw with our
own eyes in Edessa and in the region of Carrhae, while we heard
about even more of them.[14]

12. Didymus (ca. 310–398) was Rufinus's master and bequeathed to him
his admiration for Origen. Cf. Richard A. Layton, *Didymus the Blind and His
Circle in Late-Antique Alexandria: Virtue and Narrative in Biblical Scholarship* (Ur-
bana and Chicago: University of Illinois Press, 2004). Rufinus and the other
sources are assessed on pp. 13–23. Didymus's debt to Greek philosophy, especially Aristotle, is revealed by the Tura papyri; see pp. 26–35. Antony visited
Alexandria for three days in July or August of 338; see Athanasius, *Festal Index*
10; *Life of Antony* 69–71.

13. Rom 5.20.

14. On the names of the monks and places, see Butler, *Lausiac History*,
1.199–203 and 2.187–190. *alius Paulus in Focis:* for a possible identification of
the place, see A. Calderini, *Dizionario dei nomi geografici e topografici dell'Egitto
greco-romano* (Milan: Cisalpino-Goliardica, 1987), 5.104.

For Apeliotes, Nitria, Cellulae (or Cellia), and Scete, see H. G. Evelyn
White, *The Monasteries of the Wâdi 'n Natrûn* (New York: Metropolitan Museum of Art, 1932), 2.17–39. Cellulae is described in Rufinus, *HM* 22. Nitria is
mentioned in *HM* 21, and Pispir and Antony's mountain in Palladius, *HL* 21.1.

On the two Macarii, Isidore, and Pambo, cf. 11.4. *HL* has two Moseses at 19
and 39.4. Benjamin is in *HL* 12, and Elias in the Greek *HM* 7.

On the Mesopotamian monks, see Theodoret, *Histoire des moines de Syrie*,
ed. P. Canivet and A. Leroy-Molinghen (Paris: Cerf, 1977–79).

11.9. But Cappadocia was no less fertile than either of these; if anything, it gave us an even richer crop in Gregory and Basil. It therefore bore a generous harvest of many saints, produced a luxurious vineyard of religious folk, and brought forth the Lord's fresh olive shoot. But it was especially they who, like two sons of plenty standing on the right and left of the lamp-stand,[15] shone forth like two luminaries in the sky, so that I think it would be good to recall a little of their earlier lives. Both were of high station, both studied in Athens where they were fellow students, and both upon leaving the lecture hall were sought after as rhetoricians. But as wonderfully as Basil practiced this art, Gregory still more wonderfully disdained it. And since he had given himself wholly to God's service, he presumed upon his companion's love to such an extent that he removed Basil from the professor's chair which he was occupying and forced him to accompany him to a monastic house, where for thirteen years, they say, having put aside all the writings of the worldly pagans, they gave their attention solely to the books of holy scripture, the understanding of which they did not presume to derive from themselves, but from the writings and authority of those of old who were themselves known to have received the rule of understanding from apostolic tradition. They sought the treasures of wisdom and knowledge hidden in these vessels of clay by examining their commentaries on the prophets in particular.[16]

15. Zec 4.11–14.
16. Cf. 2 Cor 4.7. The errors in Rufinus's biographical sketch of Basil and Gregory are so egregious as to seem almost deliberate, and in fact Thelamon conjectures that he has fictionalized the account to make it more edifying (*PC* 441–42). But the words *per annos, ut aiunt, tredecim* do not support this theory; *ut aiunt* suggests that Rufinus was drawing on some source, and the specific figure of thirteen years serves no obvious purpose and is found in no known source. C. Moreschini conjectures that he used some life of Gregory now lost ("Rufino traduttore di Gregorio Nazianzeno," *AAAd* 31 [1987]: 229).
What is true in Rufinus's account is that both were from noble families and studied together in Athens; Basil was there, 349/50–355, and Gregory, perhaps 345–356. Basil taught rhetoric in Caesarea (Cappadocia), 355–356, then spent 356 touring the monasteries in Coele Syria, Mesopotamia, Palestine, and Egypt, returned in 357, was baptized in 357/58, and retired to the family estate to lead the ascetic life. He persuaded Gregory, but only after

Now when they had learned as much as they needed, divine providence called them to instruct the people; each was drawn by a different route to the same task. Basil went round the cities and countryside of Pontus and began by his words to rouse that province from its torpor and lack of concern for our hope for the future, kindling it by his preaching, and to banish the callousness resulting from long negligence; he compelled it to put away its concern for vain and worldly things and to give its attention to him. He taught the people to assemble, to build monastic houses, to give time to psalms, hymns, and prayers, to take care of the poor and furnish them with proper housing and the necessities of life, to train virgins, and to make the life of modesty and chastity desirable to almost everyone. In a short time the appearance of the whole province was so transformed that a generous crop and a luxuriant vineyard had sprung into view in what had been a dry and barren field.[17]

Gregory for his part would not allow good seed to lie on top of thorns or be scattered among rocks,[18] but he cultivated the

---

much effort, to join him there in 358; Gregory had been teaching rhetoric in Nazianzus since finishing studies (quite contrary to what Rufinus says). But they were together there for only two years; Gregory's father, the bishop of Nazianzus, brought him back to assist him in his church. Cf. Basil, *Epp.* 2 and 14; Gregory Naz., *Epp.* 1, 2, 4, 5, 6; *Carmen de sua vita* 300–311 and 350–56; Gregory of Nyssa, *Vita S. Macrinae* 6; P. J. Fedwick, "A Chronology of the Life and Works of Basil of Caesarea," and J. Gribomont, "Notes biographiques sur s. Basile le Grand," in *Basil of Caesarea: Christian, Humanist, Ascetic*, ed. P. J. Fedwick (Toronto: Pontifical Institute of Mediaeval Studies, 1981), 3–19 and 21–48; P. Gallay, *La vie de Saint Grégoire de Nazianze* (Paris: E. Vitte, 1943); Raymond Van Dam, *Families and Friends in Late Roman Cappadocia* (Philadelphia: University of Pennsylvania Press, 2003), 155–84; Andrew Radde-Gallwitz, *Basil of Caesarea: A Guide to His Life and Doctrine* (Eugene, OR: Cascade, 2012), 22–42, 90–107, 133–50.

17. Gregory's father compelled him to accept ordination as presbyter in 361/62. Basil was ordained presbyter probably in 362 by Eusebius of (Cappadocian) Caesarea, whom he succeeded upon his death in 370. Rufinus's summary of Basil's social and ascetical work is quite accurate; he demanded a high degree of asceticism in those he baptized and expected that generosity to the needy would be an essential part of it. Cf. Susan R. Holman, *The Hungry Are Dying: Beggars and Bishops in Roman Cappadocia* (New York: Oxford University Press, 2001).

18. Lk 8.6–7.

good earth of his heart with unremitting diligence and continuous discipline, achieving much greater results in himself than Basil did in others. While Basil had charge of receiving what those who renounced the world laid at his feet and of dividing it according to the needs of each, Gregory, content with the mystery of having nothing and possessing everything,[19] longed only for the riches of wisdom and clung to them with great desire. While Basil taught the multitude to assemble together and to have concern for one another's needs, Gregory by his own example, because he was unencumbered and free, preached to everyone with the apostolic message, "I wish you to be without concern," and "The Lord is near; have no concern," but as servants of Christ be concerned with one thing only: the time of the Lord's return for the wedding.[20] Basil showed his compassion in commiserating with those who misbehaved and calling them back from their misdeeds; Gregory by the gift of his divine eloquence removed the temptations to misbehavior and did not allow those to fall who, once shattered, could only with difficulty be restored. Basil was pure in faith, Gregory freer in preaching. Basil was humble before God, Gregory before others as well. Basil conquered the arrogant by disdain, Gregory by reason. Thus a different grace in each of them achieved one work of perfection.

When therefore Basil, who not long after was bishop of Caesarea in Cappadocia, was about to be banished by Valens for the faith, he was hailed into the prefect's court and subjected to the terrors and grievous threats customary to that power, and told that unless he obeyed the sovereign's orders he might expect to be put to death at once. He is said to have replied with calm fearlessness to the prefect who was threatening him, "And I wish I had some worthy gift to offer to him who would give Basil earlier release from this knotted bag." And when he was given the intervening night to consider, he is reported to have replied once more, "I will be tomorrow who I am now, and you will certainly be no different." And behold, that night the emperor's wife was racked with pain as though under tor-

19. 2 Cor 6.10.
20. 1 Cor 7.32; Phil 4.5–6; Lk 12.36.

ture, while their son died, their only son: in retribution, it is believed, for his father's impiety. Thus there came messengers before daybreak to ask Basil to intercede for them in prayer, lest they too should die, and indeed with far more justice. That is how it came about that when Valens drove out all the Catholics, Basil stayed in the church for the rest of his life without compromising the bond of communion.[21]

Now Gregory, who had succeeded his father as bishop in the town of Nazianzus, bore steadfastly the disturbances of the heretics. But when peace was restored, he did not refuse the plea to come to Constantinople to instruct the church. There in a short time he did so much to cure the people of the chronic poisons of the heretics that it seemed to them that they were

21. Later historians, Rufinus included, conflated the several occasions between 370 and 372 when Valens and various of his officials met or confronted Basil. See Raymond Van Dam, "Emperors, Bishops, and Friends in Late Antique Cappadocia," *JTS* NS 37 (1986): 53–76.

The prefect in the story is none other than Modestus, encountered earlier in 11.5 doing his best to protect the Catholics from Valens's wrath; cf. note 8 above. Gregory of Nyssa relates two attempts he made, mixing threats and promises, to get Basil to accept the emperor's faith (*Contra Eunomium* 1.127–38 and 139–43). In neither case is the order of exile or the emperor's son mentioned. Gregory of Nazianzus likewise reports two such attempts, although the prefect is mentioned explicitly only in the first of them (*Or.* 43.48–51, 54). In the second, Basil is just about to be sent off into exile at night when the emperor's son falls ill; Valens revokes the order of exile and asks Basil to come and pray for him. Basil does so, and the son rallies temporarily but later dies. The incident may have occurred early in 372.

Given Valens's inclination to replace pro-Nicene bishops with others of homoean sympathies, his attitude toward Basil remains something of a mystery. "More than simply *allowing* Basil to govern the churches of Cappadocia, Valens actively supported him. He set him in charge, together with another bishop, of appointing new bishops for the Roman province of Armenia Minor and the client kingdom of Armenia.... Furthermore, Valens patronized Basil's massive charitable efforts in Caesarea ..." (Radde-Gallwitz, *Basil of Caesarea*, 3n16). Part of the explanation will be found in the powerful pro-Nicene friends Basil had at court; cf. Umberto Roberto, "Il *magister* Victor e l'opposizione ortodossa all'imperatore Valente nella storiografia ecclesiastica e nell'agiografia," *Mediterraneo antico* 6.1 (2003): 61–93, and "Opposizione e consenso nell'impero di Valente. Considerazioni a proposito di un recente libro," *MA* 8.1 (2005): 1–16.

Rufinus of course will have had no interest in reducing the hostility between his hero and the heterodox emperor.

becoming Christians and seeing the new light of truth for the first time, now that the teacher of religion was instructing them; much as he did this by his words, yet he taught them still more by his example, and it seemed that he told his disciples nothing which he had not done first. But envy followed upon glory, and there were some who began to resist him and to advance objections of little merit so that another bishop might be ordained, he himself returning to his own place. This he heard being whispered and murmured only, but he brought out into the open what nobody had dared tell him: "Let there not be any dissension among God's priests on my account," he said. "If this storm has arisen because of me, take me away and throw me into the sea, and let your agitation cease." He then returned to his church and spent the rest of his life there. Because he was advanced in age and physically weak, he designated his own successor, who could take charge of the church and allow him the leisure of his infirmity and old age.[22]

22. Gregory was ordained bishop, much against his will, by Basil and his father in 372. The occasion was Valens's division of the province of Cappadocia into two, leaving Caesarea the capital of only Cappadocia Prima. The bishop of the *metropolis* or provincial capital, the "metropolitan," had certain powers over the other bishops of the province, and when Tyana was made the capital of the new province of Cappadocia Secunda, its bishop claimed this authority as well as independence from Basil. The division of Cappadocia, which probably took place in 372, has often been viewed as a move against Basil, but it may have been done for simple administrative reasons; see Van Dam, "Emperors, Bishops, and Friends," 55.

Basil in turn backed his claim to continuing authority over the whole of Cappadocia with the erection of new bishoprics with suffragans loyal to him; he made Gregory bishop of Sasima, a tiny but strategic town. But the bishop of Tyana kept him from taking possession of his see, so he stayed in Nazianzus and assisted his father. At the latter's death in 374, he agreed to take charge of the church in Nazianzus only temporarily, until a successor could be chosen. When this did not happen, he fled to Seleucia in Isauria in 375(?) and stayed there until 379. In this year the Catholics of Constantinople asked him to come to be their bishop, a request he accepted reluctantly. He lodged there in a house he called "Anastasia," which became the church of the Nicene loyalists. He was attacked by other Christian groups, but he drew growing crowds to hear him, among them Jerome.

Theodosius entered Constantinople on November 24, 380; two days later he turned the homoeans out of the churches, which he handed over to Gregory (see 11.19). The Council of Constantinople, which began in May of 381,

We still have as well some wonderful testimonials to the genius of both men in the form of sermons which they delivered *ex tempore* in the churches. Of these we have translated into Latin about ten of the short discourses of each of them, as well as the monastic rules of Basil, hoping if possible and with God's help to translate more of their works. Basil also had two brothers, Gregory and Peter, of whom the first so rivaled his brother in doctrinal exposition and the second in works of faith, that either was simply another Basil or Gregory. We also still have some short, excellent works of the younger Gregory. But enough about them.[23]

---

elected him bishop of Constantinople, but the bishops of Egypt and Macedonia, when they arrived the following month, protested that the election had been irregular. They probably cited Canon 15 of Nicaea, which prohibits the transfer of bishops from one see to another. Gregory offered his resignation to the council and to the emperor, and it was accepted (after some hesitation) by Theodosius. His farewell address to the council (*Or.* 42) contains no allusion to Jonah. Rufinus gives a parallel account of Gregory's resignation, with the same allusion, in the preface to his translation of Gregory's discourses.

Gregory left the city before the end of the council (July 9, 381) and retired to his home in the village of Arianzus. But Nazianzus still had no permanent bishop since his father had died in 374, and he was pressed to fill the vacancy. He entrusted the church instead to the presbyter Cledonius, but it was troubled by Apollinarian sectarians, and toward the end of 382 Gregory resumed charge of it. The controversies proved too much for him, however, and after requesting his metropolitan in vain for a successor, he simply left Nazianzus for good in 383, retiring once again to Arianzus. His departure forced the issue, and Eulalius was chosen to succeed him. He died ca. 390. See Gallay, *La vie de S. Grégoire* (note 16 above), 105–243.

23. In the preface to his translation of Basil's sermons, Rufinus gives the number as eight; see M. Simonetti, *Tyrannii Rufini Opera* (CCL 20, 1961), 237. There is some question about just which of Basil's discourses Rufinus meant here; see P. J. Fedwick, "The Translations of the Works of Basil Before 1400," in his *Basil of Caesarea* (note 16 above), 466–68; H. Marti, "Rufinus' Translation of St. Basil's Sermon on Fasting," *Studia Patristica* 16.2 (1985): 419.

For his translation of Gregory of Nazianzus's discourses, cf. A. Engelbrecht, *Tyrannii Rufini orationum Gregorii Nazianzeni novem interpretatio* (CSEL 46, 1910); Moreschini, "Rufino traduttore di Gregorio Nazianzeno" (note 16 above), 1.227–85.

For his translation of Basil's monastic rules, see K. Zelzer, *Basili Regula* (CSEL 86, 1986). The rules seem to have gone through three editions, of which Rufinus translated the second. The Greek original of this has vanished, leaving only the Latin and Syriac translations. A comparison of them shows that Rufi-

In the west, meanwhile, Valentinian, his religious faith untarnished, was ruling the state with the vigilance traditional to Roman government.

11.10. Damasus succeeded Liberius in the priesthood in the city of Rome. Ursinus, a deacon of this church, unable to accept his being preferred to himself, became so unhinged that with the aid of some naïve, inexperienced bishop, whom he persuaded, and a riotous and unruly gang which he got together, he forced through his ordination as bishop in the Basilica of Sicininus, overturning in his path law, order, and tradition. This caused such a riot, or rather such battles between the people siding with the two men, that the places of prayer ran with human blood. The affair resulted in such ill will toward a good and innocent priest, due to the conduct of that misguided man, the prefect Maximinus, that the case led even to the torture of clerics. But God, the protector of the innocent, came to the rescue, and punishment reverted upon the heads of those who had plotted treachery.[24]

nus's is a true translation and not his own invention. The second edition, then, known as the *Asceticum Parvum,* was the basis on which Basil himself elaborated his so-called *Asceticum Magnum.* Anna M. Silvas has studied Rufinus's translation in *The Asketikon of St Basil the Great* (Oxford: Clarendon, 2005), 102–29.

optantes … eorum plura transferre: there is no evidence that he fulfilled his plan; see A. Di Berardino, ed., *Patrology* 4, trans. Rev. Placid Solari, OSB (Westminster, MD: Christian Classics, Inc., 1986), 252.

24. Damasus succeeded Liberius on October 1, 366. He had accompanied Liberius into exile in 355, but then returned to Rome and entered into communion with Felix, who had been ordained at court to replace Liberius. After the latter returned from exile, however, he was reconciled with him. But when Liberius died (September 24, 366), the faction loyal to Felix elected Damasus his successor, while the faction that had remained loyal to Liberius chose the deacon Ursinus. The election was embittered by what was regarded as Liberius's betrayal of Athanasius and of orthodoxy, and by the memory of the Roman clergy's perjury in accepting Felix (cf. Book 10, note 39). Battles raged before and after the election, and Damasus requested help from the city prefect. His partisans attacked the Liberian basilica on October 26, leaving 137 dead. See Ammianus, 27.3.12–13; Jerome, *Chronicle* 366; *Collectio Avellana* 1.5–14; Socrates, 4.29; Sozomen, 6.23.1–2; J. N. D. Kelly, *The Oxford Dictionary of Popes* (Oxford: Clarendon, 1986), 32–33.

The bishop who ordained Ursinus was Paul of Tibur (Tivoli); the Basilica of Sicininus is Santa Maria Maggiore.

Flavius Maximinus after various governorships was *praefectus annonae,*

11.11. In Milan meanwhile Auxentius, the bishop of the heretics, died, and the people were divided into two parties with different loyalties. The disagreement and strife were so serious and dangerous that they threatened the very city with speedy disaster, should either side not get what it wanted, since each desired something different. Ambrose was then governor of the province. When he saw the city on the brink of destruction, he immediately entered the church, as his office and the place required, in order to calm the riotous crowd. While engaged there in a lengthy speech about law and public order for the sake of peace and tranquility, there suddenly arose from the people fighting and quarreling with each other a single voice which shouted that it would have Ambrose as bishop; they cried that he should be baptized forthwith, for he was a catechumen, and given to them as bishop, nor could there be one people and faith otherwise, unless Ambrose was given to them as priest. While he struggled and resisted strongly against this, the people's wish was reported to the emperor, who ordered it to be fulfilled with all speed. For it was thanks to God, he said, that this sudden conversion had recalled the diverse religious attitudes and discordant views of the people to a single viewpoint and attitude. Yielding to God's grace, Ambrose received the sacred initiation and the priesthood without delay.[25]

368–370; *vicarius Urbis,* 370–371; and *praefectus praetorio Galliarum,* 371–376. He became steadily more brutal and arrogant as his career advanced. His role as judge in sorcery trials made him greatly feared among the nobility during his terms in Rome. See Jones, 1.141; *PLRE* 1.577; *RE* suppl. 5 (1933), 663. Rufinus's remark about him remains obscure, however, and as chronologically careless as usual. The emperor banished Ursinus and his partisans (in 368?) to northern Italy, where they continued to disturb the church by slandering Damasus and eventually allying themselves with the Milanese "Arians"; cf. Ambrose, *Ep.* 5(11). On the whole history of the disputed election and its aftermath, see A. Van Roey, "Damase," *DHGE* 14 (1960): 48–50.

25. The homoean Auxentius had replaced the deposed Dionysius in 355 (cf. 10.21) and had remained in office until his death in 373 or 374, despite the best efforts of Hilary of Poitiers to bring him down. Ambrose was born in Trier in 337 or 339, became a rhetor, and ca. 370 was appointed governor of Liguria and Aemilia, with his residence in Milan. He was consecrated bishop on either December 1, 373, or December 7, 374.

Ambrose mentions his election in *Ep.* 14(63).65, where he says, "How I re-

11.12. During this time Valentinian, who had made his way from Gaul to Illyricum to fight the Sarmatians, was struck down by sudden illness there when the war had just begun; he left as heirs to the empire his sons the Augustus Gratian and Valentinian, who was quite young and had not yet received the imperial tokens. But pressure from those who were trying to usurp power as though the government were vacant forced him to assume the purple even though his brother was absent; Probus, then prefect, faithfully carried the matter out.[26]

11.13. In the eastern empire meanwhile the Goths, driven

---

sisted being ordained! And at last, when forced to it, [how I sought] at least to have the ordination delayed! But the rule was overruled by the pressure [*Sed non valuit praescriptio, praevaluit impressio*]. My ordination, though, was approved by the judgment of the western bishops and by the example of the easterners." "The rule" [*praescriptio*] refers to canon 2 of Nicaea (against rapid advancement from baptism to ordination). The reference to the eastern bishops is an allusion to Nectarius of Constantinople, who was elected bishop while still a catechumen (cf. 11.21). It should be noted that Ambrose's biographer Paulinus, normally cited as the standard source for this episode, draws on Rufinus here; see M. Pellegrino, *Paolino. Vita di S. Ambrogio* (Rome: Studium, 1961), 16–19. In *De paenitentia* 2.8.67 and *De officiis* 1.14 Ambrose talks about how he was "snatched" from life as a civil official to the episcopacy and had to teach others before he himself had learned.

Rufinus's is the first formal account of Ambrose's election; was he influenced by Eusebius's report of the election of Fabian (6.29.3–4)? Cf. Thelamon, *PC* 339. Paulinus adds details such as the child's voice nominating Ambrose and his efforts to dissuade the people (*Vita Ambrosii* 6–9). The emperor, he says, "was delighted to hear that the officials appointed by him were being sought for the priesthood" (8.2).

26. Valentinian died in Illyricum of a stroke on November 17, 375. He had already had his eight-year-old son Gratian proclaimed Augustus in 367 in order to help secure the dynasty. Gratian, now sixteen, succeeded him in Trier. On November 22 government ministers proclaimed Gratian's young half-brother Valentinian Augustus in order to secure the loyalty of the Illyrian army. Valentinian, then four, and his mother Justina were staying near Sirmium at the time. Valens and Gratian accepted the move, perhaps after some initial irritation. See Ammianus, 30.10; Zosimus, 4.19; Ps. Aurelius Victor, *Epit.* 45.10; Philostorgius, 9.16; Klaus M. Girardet, "Die Erhebung Kaiser Valentinians II. Politische Umstände und Folgen (375/76)," *Chiron* 34 (2004): 109–44.

Probo tunc praefecto fideliter rem gerente: Petronius Probus was praetorian prefect of Italy, Africa, and Illyricum, 368–375 (see *PLRE* 1.736–40). Rufinus is the only ancient source to mention him explicitly as the one behind the plan.

from their homes, spread throughout the provinces of Thrace
and began a savage destruction of cities and countryside with
their weapons. Then Valens did begin to turn his weapons away
from the churches and toward the enemy, and with belated
regret ordered bishops and presbyters to be recalled from exile and monks to be released from the mines. But he was surrounded by the enemy on an estate to which he had fled in fear
from battle, and paid the price for his impiety by being burned
to ashes, having reigned his first year with his brother and afterward for fourteen years with his brother's sons as well. This
battle was the beginning of evil times for the Roman empire
from then on.[27] Gratian, then, with his very young brother, succeeded to the eastern empire as well after his uncle's death. In
piety and religious fervor he excelled almost all of the previous
rulers. He was vigorous in armed combat, physically quick, and
intelligent, but his mirth found expression in youthful boister-
ousness that was almost excessive, and his modesty was greater
than was expedient for the state.

11.14. Seeing that it would be good to have a man of mature age to share the many cares of government, and since, as
holy scripture teaches, two are better than one, he associated
Theodosius with himself, giving him charge of the east and retaining the west for his brother and himself. After many religious and courageous deeds, however, he was killed in Lyons
by Maximus, the usurper from Britain, who acted through the

27. In 376 the Goths of southern Russia asked to be received into the Roman empire in order to escape the Huns. Valens agreed to accept them and
to give them land in Thrace if they would serve in the army. In the autumn of
376 they were ferried across the Danube, and a start was made in settling and
enrolling them, but as winter came on, many of them were still in the transit
camp. When provisions ran short, greedy officials began selling them into slavery in return for food. The remaining Ostrogoths, who had not yet received
permission to cross into Roman territory, took advantage of the ensuing disturbances to cross the river. The last straw was the massacre of a Visigothic
escort by a Roman officer; all the Goths rose in revolt and plundered Thrace.
Valens met them at Adrianople on August 9, 378, and was routed in a battle
that was indeed the *initium mali* for the empire; two-thirds of the Roman army
perished there together with the emperor. See Ammianus, 31.12–13; Zosimus,
4.29.1–2; Jerome, *Chronicle* 378; *Consularia Constantinopolitana* 378; Socrates,
4.38; Sozomen, 6.39–40; Lenski, *Failure of Empire* (note 4 above), 320–67.

duke Andragathius: an act of treachery by his own people rather than an enemy stroke.[28]

11.15. In Italy Valentinian, terrified by his brother's murder and in dread of the enemy, gladly pretended to embrace the peace which Maximus pretended to offer. Meanwhile Justina, a disciple of the Arian sect, boldly uncorked for her gullible son the poisons of her impiety, which she had kept hidden while her husband was alive. Thus while residing in Milan she upset the churches and threatened the priests with deposition and exile unless they reinstated the decrees of the Council of Ariminum by which the faith of the fathers had been violated. In this war she assailed Ambrose, the wall of the church and its stoutest tower, harassing him with threats, terrors, and every kind of attack as she sought a first opening into the church she wanted to conquer. But while she fought armed with the spirit of Jezebel, Ambrose stood firm, filled with the power and grace of Elijah. She went about the churches chattering noisily and

28. "Two are better than one": Eccl 4.9. Theodosius was born in 347 in Gallaecia. His father distinguished himself as a general under Valentinian I in Britain, Moesia, and Africa, but was executed in Carthage in 375/76 by Valentinian or Gratian for reasons unknown. Theodosius had fought with distinction against the Sarmatians in 374, but retired to his estate in Spain upon his father's death. Gratian, needing an experienced general as colleague in the wake of the disaster at Adrianople, recalled him and on January 19, 379, proclaimed him Augustus in Sirmium.

eique orientis procuratione permissa partes sibi ac fratri occiduas reservavit: most of the sources say that the territory given to Theodosius corresponds exactly to Valens's old domain, although Sozomen reports that he was given Illyricum as well (7.4.1). See Paschoud, *Zosime*, 2.386.

Rufinus refers obliquely to Gratian's unpopularity. He had many admirable qualities, but he lacked both interest in administration and advisers who could supply for his inexperience. He alienated the regular army by consorting with his barbarian auxiliaries and adopting their fashions. His fiscal policies, including the withdrawal of financial support for the pagan cults, disaffected the nobility. Magnus Maximus seems to have been *comes Britanniarum* at the time of his revolt in the spring or summer of 383. When Gratian marched against him, his troops abandoned him, and he fled with his retinue to Lyons, pursued by Andragathius, *magister equitum* of Maximus, who in the end tricked him into attending a banquet apart from his bodyguard and assassinated him there; the date was August 25. See Zosimus, 4.35; Ambrose, *In psalm.* 61.24–26; Paschoud, 2.412–15.

trying to rouse and kindle discord among the people, but when she failed, she regarded herself as having been wronged, and complained to her son. The youth, indignant at the tale of outrage concocted by his mother, sent a band of armed men to the church with orders to smash the doors, attack the sanctuary, drag out the priest, and send him into exile forthwith. But the steadfastness of the faithful was such that they would rather have lost their lives than their bishop.[29]

29. Maximus sent an embassy to Theodosius to offer peace on terms of coexistence and alliance. Theodosius pretended to agree but secretly made preparations to attack him. See Zosimus, 4.37; Paschoud, 2.422–23.

Justina was the widow of the usurper Magnentius. She married Valentinian ca. 370 and bore him the son who became co-emperor with Gratian at Valentinian's death. When the Goths overran Thrace after the Battle of Adrianople, she was forced to move with her son from Sirmium to Milan. Once there they requested a church where their homoean court could worship, and Gratian gave them one. He returned it to the Catholics following the promulgation of *C.Th.* 16.5.6 (January 381), which declared Nicene Catholicism to be the only legal religion and outlawed assemblies within cities of Photinians, Arians, and Eunomians. See D. Williams, "Ambrose, Emperors, and Homoians in Milan: The First Conflict over a Basilica," in *Arianism after Arius,* ed. M. Barnes and D. Williams (Edinburgh: T & T Clark, 1993), 127–46.

There is much that remains unclear about where, when, and why the "basilica conflict" took place, and certainly Rufinus is no help. With Gratian dead and Valentinian II only fourteen years old, the empress evidently thought the time was ripe to recover the church she had lost in 381. Around Lent of 385 the consistory ordered Ambrose to yield a basilica, probably the Portiana, so that it could be used by the homoeans. He refused. The demand was then made, as Easter drew near, to give up the New Basilica. Ambrose again refused. Rumors flew, messengers hurried to and from court, troops and police moved about, and the people were gripped by a fever of excitement, but finally on Holy Thursday (April 10) the court gave up.

Some time later the same year the homoean bishop Mercurinus Auxentius, who had been deposed from his see of Durostorum by Theodosius, sought refuge with Justina, and together they drafted a law that would permit them to assemble (the project in which Benivolus in 11.16 refused to cooperate). The law, *C.Th.* 16.1.4, of January 23, 386, permits the assemblies of those who hold to the decrees of the Councils of Ariminum (359) and Constantinople (360). On its basis the court on March 27 required Ambrose to hand over the New Basilica. He refused. On the next day the request was made for the Portian Basilica, and the same answer was given. On the following day (Palm Sunday) imperial hangings were put up in the Portian Basilica, but the people flocked to it and remained there until the court gave up its attempt to seize it.

The government apparently made one further try at expropriating a

11.16. Meanwhile imperial decrees contrary to the faith of the fathers were sent for drafting to Benivolus, who then had charge of the records office. But this faith had been held in holy awe by him since infancy, and he said that he could not make impious statements and speak against God. Then, lest the queen's plans be foiled, he was promised advancement if he did as he had been told. But he desired to advance in faith rather than in honors, and so he said, "Why do you promise me higher rank in return for impiety? Take away the one I have; only let my conscience remain clear about the faith." Saying this, he threw down his belt at the feet of those who were ordering the impious deed.[30]

Ambrose for his part did not ward off the queen's fury with hand or weapon, but with fasts and unceasing vigils at the foot of the altar set himself to win God by his prayers for his and the church's cause. And when Justina had spent a good while contriving these schemes and methods of attack, to no avail, Maximus, eager to rid himself of the stigma of usurpation and to show himself a legitimate ruler, declared in a letter he sent that what she was attempting was impious and that the faith of God

---

church, probably the Portian Basilica; this is the occasion described by Augustine in *Confessions* 9.7.15, when Ambrose, shut up inside with his flock, taught them the antiphonal singing of psalms to keep up their spirits. See Ambrose, *Epp.* 75–77; 75a; F. H. Dudden, *The Life and Times of St. Ambrose* (Oxford: Clarendon, 1935), 270–97; A. D. Lenox-Conyngham, "A Topography of the Basilica Conflict of A.D. 385/86 in Milan," *Historia* 31 (1982): 353–63, and "Juristic and Religious Aspects of the Basilica Conflict of A.D. 386," *Studia Patristica* 18.1 (1985): 55–58; G. Gottlieb, "Der Mailänder Kirchenstreit von 385/86," *Museum Helveticum* 42 (1985): 37–55; G. Nauroy, "Le fouet et le miel. Le combat d'Ambroise en 386 contre l'arianisme milanais," *Recherches augustiniennes* 23 (1988): 3–86; H. Maier, "Private Space as the Social Context of Arianism in Ambrose's Milan," *JTS* NS 45 (1994): 72–93; T. D. Barnes, "Ambrose and the Basilicas of Milan in 385 and 386: The Primary Documents and their Implications," *ZAC* 4 (2000): 282–99; Marcia L. Colish, "Why the Portiana? Reflections on the Milanese Basilica Crisis of 386," *JECS* 10.3 (2002): 361–72.

30. On Benivolus's part in the drama, see note 29, paragraph 4, above. The *magister memoriae* was a chancery official responsible for drafting official documents and speeches. Little is known otherwise about Benivolus (see *Prosopographie chrétienne du Bas-Empire* 2.298–99 [*magister memoriae*]), but Rufinus draws here from Gaudentius of Brescia's report of him (*Tractatus* Praef. 5). He retired to private life. The *cingulum* or belt bore the insignia of rank in the civil and military services.

was being attacked and the laws of the Catholic Church destroyed; at the same time he began to move toward Italy. Justina, under pressure from both her enemy and her awareness of her impiety, fled with her son upon learning this and was the first to undergo the exile she had planned for God's priests.[31]

11.17. Theodosius, however, kept faith both with the realm and with the memory of Gratian's good character and deeds; coming with all the forces of the east, he avenged his just blood and, once the usurpation had been put down, restored to Valentinian both the Catholic faith violated by his irreligious mother, who died at this time, and the realm. And after he had ridden into Rome in a glorious triumph, he returned to his own territory.[32]

31. Maximus's letter is preserved (*Collectio Avellana* 39); it alludes clearly to Ambrose's recent plight: *Audio ... novis clementiae tuae edictis ecclesiis catholicis vim illatam fuisse, obsideri in basilicis sacerdotes, multam esse propositam, poenam capitis adiectam et legem sanctissimam sub nomine nescio cuius legis everti* (*CA* 39.3). He made his move toward Italy in the first half of 387, whereupon Valentinian fled by ship to Thessalonica with his mother and sister Galla (see Zosimus, 4.42–43; Paschoud, 2.434).

Claudio Antognazzi, "'Ad imperatorem palatia pertinent, ad sacerdotem ecclesia': La teologia politica di Ambrogio nei primi dodici anni del suo episcopato (374–386)," *Annali di scienze religiose* 9 (2004): 271–97, claims that Rufinus is wrong in saying that Justina fled with her son, and that she must have died previously, as suggested by Ambrose, *De obitu Valentiniani* 28 (see 274n9). But Rufinus is supported by Zosimus, 4.43.1; 4.44; 4.53.3; 4.46.1.

32. Once arrived in Thessalonica, Justina appealed to Theodosius to restore her son to his realm and promised him the hand of her daughter Galla in exchange. The emperor, recently widowed, was captivated by Galla's beauty and promised to do so on the condition that she and her family renounce the homoean faith and embrace Catholicism. The deal was struck, and Theodosius in the summer of 388 began moving in strength through Upper Pannonia toward Aquileia, where Maximus was staying. Andragathius, Maximus's general, had fortified the Alpine passes, but then, persuaded that an attack by sea was imminent, he left the army in order to direct naval operations on the Adriatic. When Theodosius's forces came upon the leaderless army of the usurper, they brushed aside the Alpine defenses and fell upon the main body at Aquileia. The victory was not bloodless (despite what Rufinus pretends in 11.32), but it was quick (Pacatus, *Panegyr.* 34.1–2), and Maximus was taken and executed on August 28. See Zosimus, 4.44–46; Paschoud, 2.436–44; *Panegyr. Lat.* (Mynors) 2(12).32.2–44.2; Orosius, 7.35.1–5; Theodoret, *HE* 5.15.

Justina evidently lived to see her son restored to his throne but died shortly thereafter (Zosimus, 4.47.2; Theodoret, *HE* 7.14.7).

11.18. During this time the devout sovereign was branded with an ugly blemish through the demon's cunning. It happened when a military officer was attacked during a riot in Thessalonica and killed by the angry people. Furious at the atrocity when the unexpected news was announced, he ordered the people to be invited to a circus, to be surrounded suddenly by soldiers, and to be cut down by the sword indiscriminately, anyone who was there, and thus to satisfy not justice but rage. When he was reproved for this by the priests of Italy, he admitted the crime, acknowledged his sin with tears, did public penance in the sight of the whole church, and, putting aside the imperial pomp, patiently completed the time prescribed him for it. To all of this he added something wonderful: he made it a law from then on that the punitive decrees of sovereigns should not be executed until thirty days had elapsed, in order not to lose the opportunity for leniency, or even, should circumstances suggest, for reconsideration.[33]

11.19. He returned therefore to the east, and there showed the greatest care and eagerness, as he had since the beginning of his reign, in driving out the heretics and handing over the churches to the Catholics. He exercised such restraint in doing so that, spurning all motives of revenge, he took measures to restore the churches to the Catholics only insofar as the true faith could make progress once the obstacle to its being preached

33. The incident took place in the summer of 390 when Butheric, *magister militum per Illyricum,* was lynched by a mob for refusing to release a popular charioteer imprisoned for immorality. Theodosius ordered a massacre of the citizens in reprisal, and then thought better of it and countermanded the order, but it was too late. At least seven thousand were killed in the circus after being treacherously invited there.

News of this reached Ambrose while he was presiding at the Council of Milan of 390, a gathering of Italian and Gallican bishops met to reach a decision about communion with Felix of Trier. The bishops agreed that some reprimand was called for, and Ambrose finally decided to suspend the emperor from communion. His letter to him, a masterpiece of tact, is *Ep.* 11(51). What exactly happened next is not known, but eventually Theodosius did do public penance in church and was readmitted to communion at Christmas. See Sozomen, 7.25.1–7; Theodoret, *HE* 5.17–18.19. The law in question is *C.Th.* 9.40.13; it is dated August 18, 390, so Theodosius had already enacted it before he began his penance.

had been removed. He behaved unpretentiously toward the priests of God, while to all others he showed his kingly spirit in his faith, piety, and generosity. He was easy to approach, showing no imperial haughtiness in speaking to commoners. Through his exhortation and generosity churches in many places were amply furnished and magnificently built. He gave much to those who asked, but frequently offered yet more. The worship of idols, which, following upon Constantine's initiative, had begun to be neglected and demolished, collapsed during his reign. For these reasons he was so dear to God that divine Providence granted him a special favor: it filled with the prophetic spirit a monk in the Thebaid named John, so that by his counsel and replies he could learn whether it would be better to remain at peace or go to war.[34]

11.20. Before this, meanwhile, Bishop Apollinaris of Laodicea in Syria, a man who was otherwise quite well educated but who had too great a weakness for disputation and enjoyed going against whatever anyone else said—such was his unfortunate talent for flaunting his intelligence—produced from his contentiousness a heresy according to which the Lord assumed only a body, but not a soul as well, in the Incarnation. Pressed on this point by clear passages in the gospel where the Lord and Savior himself states that he has a soul and lays it down when he wants and takes it up again, and where he says that it is troubled and saddened even unto death,[35] he later changed his

34. "Theodosius was implacable against heretics: no less than eighteen constitutions directed by him against them are preserved in the Code. In general he went no further than to bar their meetings and confiscate their churches or the private houses in which they held their conventicles" (Jones, 1.166).

Sacrifices for divination were forbidden, and the pagans in fact stopped offering sacrifice at all in the temples, which were not, however, officially closed. "But petitions for the demolition of temples or their conversion into churches were favourably received, and a blind eye was turned on unauthorized attacks upon them. The result was that a large number of temples was destroyed, with or without official sanction" (Jones, 1.167).

The monk was John of Lycopolis; cf. Greek *HM* 1.1; Rufinus, *HM* 1.1; Palladius, *HL* 35.2; Thelamon, *PC* 342. Eutropius was used as an intermediary; cf. Claudian, *In Eutrop.* 1.312–13.

35. Mt 26.38; Mk 14.34.

position, and, lest he should appear quite defeated, said that while he did have a soul, it was not inclusive of that by which it is rational, but only of that by which it vivifies the body. The Word of God himself, he states, supplied for the rational part. This teaching was first rejected by Damasus and Bishop Peter of Alexandria, in a council assembled in the city of Rome, in the following terms: they ruled that whoever said that the Son of God, who, just as he was truly God so also was truly a human being, lacked anything human or divine, should be considered alien to the church. This judgment was ratified in Alexandria and Constantinople by conciliar decree, and from then on the Apollinarians, turning aside from the church, have maintained an episcopate for their sect together with their own doctrines and churches.[36]

11.21. In the city of Rome, then, Siricius received the priesthood of the church after Damasus. Those who obtained the apostolic sees in Alexandria and Jerusalem were Timothy in the

36. Apollinaris (ca. 310–ca. 390) became bishop of Laodicea ca. 360 and was a close friend of Athanasius. His doctrine, which sprang from his strong opposition to Arianism, was designed to ensure the immutable sinlessness of Christ. It was condemned by synods in Rome ca. 374 and 377 and by the Council of Constantinople of 381. Apollinaris seceded from the church ca. 375. See Epiphanius, *Pan.* 77; Socrates, 2.46.9–11; H. Lietzmann, *Apollinaris von Laodicea und seine Schule* (Tübingen: Mohr, 1904); E. Mühlenberg, *Apollinaris von Laodicea* (Göttingen: Vandenhoeck u. Ruprecht, 1969); bibliography in Joseph T. Lienhard, "Two Friends of Athanasius: Marcellus of Ancyra and Apollinaris of Laodicea," *ZAC* 10 (2006): 56–66.

Lietzmann, 47–48, points out that Rufinus's report on Apollinaris comes from the same well-informed source used by Julian of Eclanum (in Augustine, *Opus imperfectum contra Iulianum* 4.47); it may have been Theodore of Mopsuestia's *De incarnatione*.

The Roman synod attended by Damasus and Peter of Alexandria that rejected Apollinaris's teaching (it was not the first to do so, whatever Rufinus says) took place in 377, before Peter's return to Alexandria the following year. Damasus refers to it in his letter to the eastern bishops in Theodoret, *HE* 5.10. Rufinus's formulation of its condemnation of the teaching that Christ "lacked anything human or divine" (*vel humanitatis vel deitatis minus ... habuisse*) corresponds perfectly to the Greek version of Damasus's: ἤτοι ἀνθρωπότητος ἢ θεότητος ἔλαττον ἐσχηκέναι (Theodoret, *HE* 5.10.5).

Nothing more is known of the Alexandrian synod that confirmed the Roman sentence. The synodal document of the Council of Constantinople (381) that condemned Apollinaris has not survived; see Lietzmann, 30.

former city, when Peter died, and after him Theophilus, and in the latter city John after Cyril. When Meletius died, Flavian took his place in Antioch. Paulinus, however, who had always remained in communion with the Catholics, was still alive, and this caused a good many quarrels and disputes there on many occasions, nor did the fiercest struggles between the different parties, thrust parried by counter-thrust, with the very elements of earth and sea worn out in the struggle, ever succeed in producing any measure of peace, since there no longer seemed to be any disagreement about doctrine. The same was true in Tyre, where Diodore, one of the long-standing Catholics proven by perseverance in trial, was made bishop by the confessors with Athanasius's approval; but his mildness was looked down upon, and someone else was ordained by Meletius's party. In many other eastern cities as well, the priests' quarrels resulted in confusion of this sort. In Constantinople, in fact, Nectarius went from urban praetor to catechumen, and, following upon his recent baptism, received the priesthood.[37]

11.22. In Alexandria meanwhile fresh disturbances broke out against the church contrary to the faith of the times; the occasion was as follows. There was a basilica built for official use which was age-worn and quite untended, and which the emperor Constantius was said to have donated to the bishops who preached his perfidy; long neglect had so reduced it that only the walls were still sound. The bishop who had charge of the church at that time decided to ask the emperor for it so that the growth of the houses of prayer might keep pace with

37. The terms of office of the bishops mentioned are as follows: Siricius, 384–399; Peter II of Alexandria, 373–381; Timothy I, 381–385; Theophilus, 385–412; John of Jerusalem, 386–417; Flavian I of Antioch, 381–404; Nectarius of Constantinople, 381–397.

On the schism in Antioch, cf. Book 10, note 41. *ipsisque in hoc elementis terrae marisque fatigatis* refers to the innumerable journeys by land and sea undertaken by various parties in the effort to achieve reconciliation.

Nothing further is known of this Diodore of Tyre; he is mentioned in Athanasius, *Ep.* 64 (PG 26:1261).

The courtly Nectarius succeeded Gregory of Nazianzus (cf. 11.9 and note 22). Sozomen, 7.8, in what is by far the fullest account of his election, makes him the emperor's choice; Socrates, 5.8.12, the people's. The two accounts are not of course irreconcilable.

the growing number of the faithful. He received it and was setting about restoring it when some hidden grottoes and underground chambers were discovered on the site, which smacked more of lawlessness and crimes than of religious services. The pagans, therefore, when they saw the dens of their iniquity and caverns of their offenses being uncovered, could not bear to have these evils exposed, which long ages had covered and darkness had concealed, but began, all of them, as though they had drunk the serpents' cup,[38] to rave and rage openly. Nor was it just their usual noisy demonstrations; they wielded weapons, battling up and down the streets so that the two peoples were at open war. Our side far outweighed the other in numbers and strength, but was rendered less violent by religious restraint. As a result, when many of ours had been wounded repeatedly, and some even killed, [the pagans] took refuge in a temple as a sort of stronghold,[39] taking with them many Christians whom they had captured. These they forced to offer sacrifice on the altars which were kindled; those who refused they put to death with new and refined tortures, fastening some to gibbets and breaking the legs of others and pitching them into the caverns which a careworn antiquity had built to receive the blood of sacrifices and the other impurities of the temple.

They carried on in this way day after day, first fearfully and then with boldness and desperation, living shut up within the temple on plunder and booty. Finally, while they were spilling the blood of the city folk, they chose one Olympus, a philosopher in name and raiment only, as leader in their criminal and reckless enterprise, so that with him in the forefront they might defend their stronghold and maintain the usurpation. But when those charged with maintaining the laws of Rome and administering justice learned what had happened, they rushed to the temple in terrified agitation and asked the reasons for this rash behavior and the meaning of the riot in which the blood of citizens had been so wickedly shed before the altars. But [the pagans] barricaded the entrance and with confused and dis-

38. Cf. Dt 32.33; 1 Cor 10.21.
39. *ad templum quasi ad arcem quandam refugiebant:* Sozomen, 7.15.3, says that it was the Serapeum.

cordant voices replied with outcries rather than explanations of what they had done. Messages, however, were sent to them to remind them of the power of the Roman government, of the legal penalties, and of the normal consequences of behavior of the sort, and since the place was so fortified that nothing could be done except by drastic action against those attempting such madness, the matter was reported to the emperor. Being more inclined to correct than to destroy the errant because of his great clemency, he wrote back that satisfaction was not to be sought for those whom their blood shed before the altars had made martyrs and the glory of whose merits had overcome the pain of their death; that being said, however, the cause of the evils and the roots of the discord which had risen up in defense of the idols should be extirpated completely, so that once these were eliminated, the reason for the conflict might also disappear. Now when this letter arrived and both peoples met together at the temple following a sort of short-term truce, no sooner had the first page been read out, the introduction to which censured the vain superstition of the pagans, than a great shout was raised by our people, while shock and fear assailed the pagans, each of whom sought to hide somewhere, to find alleys through which to flee, or to melt unnoticed into our crowds. Thus all who were there realized that God's presence lending boldness to his people had put to flight the demon's fury which had earlier raged among the others.[40]

40. The destruction by the Christians of Alexandria of the great temple of Serapis in 391 had been foreshadowed by the anti-pagan campaign pursued so ardently by the praetorian prefect Cynegius in Egypt and elsewhere during his term of 384–388 (see Paschoud, 2.424–26). Christian monks throughout his territory had pillaged and destroyed rural and even urban shrines, although no law existed justifying such acts (Libanius, *Or.* 30.8–23). Even so, the razing of the most splendid temple of antiquity sent a shock through the empire: the story of the violent end of Serapis and his house, which Rufinus begins here, was repeated endlessly and lost nothing in the telling, symbolizing as it did the replacement of paganism by Christianity as the official religion of the state. It tended in fact to gather and assimilate to itself other stories of other Christian attacks on Egyptian paganism from the time of George of Alexandria onward, a tendency to which Rufinus's habitual carelessness with chronology gladly lent itself. For a study of the ancient sources and their relationship, see Antonio

Baldini, "Problemi della tradizione sulla 'distruzione' del Serapeo di Alessandria," *Rivista storica dell'antichità* 15 (1985): 97–152.

Rufinus gives it more attention than any other event for this reason, and also perhaps because of the close relationship between Egypt and Aquileia, the city through which the Egyptian cults were introduced to the north of Italy and beyond; see M.-C. Budischovsky, "La diffusion des cultes égyptiens d'Aquilée à travers les pays alpins," *AAAd* 9 (1976): 202–27, and "Les cultes orientaux à Aquilée et leur diffusion en Istrie et en Vénétie," *AAAd* 12 (1977): 99–123; F. Cassola, "Aquileia e l'Oriente mediterraneo," *AAAd* 12 (1977): 67–97; C. Dolzani, "Presenze di origine egiziana nell'ambiente aquileiese e nell'alto adriatico," *AAAd* 12 (1977): 125–34.

Even in his account the distinction is still just visible between the events taking place in the episcopates of George (alluded to in the reference to Constantius's "bishops") and of Theophilus (referred to finally at the end of 11.26). George's hostility to pagan temples and his desire to acquire their property is well attested. Julian says that the Alexandrians were provoked to lynch George when he seized the Serapeum with the prefect's help and stripped it of its statues and decorations (*Ep.* 60.379AB). It is evident that he did not destroy the temple, or Julian would have mentioned that as an even better excuse for leniency toward the Alexandrians, and that Julian restored to the shrine of his great patron the objects George had removed. In Ammianus, 22.11.7–8, George is heard to wonder aloud how long the temple of the Genius will stand, a remark that stuns the bystanders and forms in them the resolve to do away with him at the first chance. Whether or not the "temple of the Genius" was the Serapeum is disputed (Baldini, 130n70). Socrates, 3.2 (paralleled by Sozomen, 5.7.5–6), says that Constantius donated a ruined Mithraeum to George, who discovered some grisly cultic relics in its cellars while it was being purified. He paraded them through the streets and thereby incited the pagans to riots and the murder of Christians, who then gave up converting the Mithraeum to their own use. But the pagans harbored their anger and at the first opportunity (when Constantius's death was announced) proceeded to lynch George. The various accounts are not irreconcilable. George was rumored to have cast greedy eyes on all the temples of Alexandria (Ammianus, 22.11.6), and he might well have provoked its citizens by all of the acts reported of him.

As for Theophilus, the relationship between his actions and the policies of Theodosius is not altogether clear. Cynegius's activities in Egypt (see *Consularia Constantinopolitana* 388) would have encouraged the idea that the emperor turned a blind eye toward attacks on idols, but none of Theodosius I's surviving laws authorize them, not even *C. Th.* 16.10.11 of June 16, 391. This edict applied to Egypt the ban on pagan worship contained in *C.Th.* 16.10.10 of February 24, 391, and was issued in response to the riots described by Rufinus here. It was forbidden to visit temples, worship idols, offer incense or libations to them, and perform animal sacrifices; but the destruction of temples is prescribed neither here nor in any other edict. Thus the parallel account in Socrates, 5.16, which begins by saying that the emperor ordered the demoli-

RUFINUS OF AQUILEIA

11.23. I suppose that everyone has heard of the temple of Serapis in Alexandria, and that many are also familiar with it. The site was elevated, not naturally but artificially, to a height of a hundred or more steps, its enormous rectangular premises extending in every direction. All of [the rooms], mounting to the ceilings on the highest level, were vaulted, and with the lamps fitted up above and the concealed sanctuaries divided each from the other, showed how they were used for various services and secret functions. On the upper level, furthermore, the outermost structures in the whole circumference provided space for halls and shrines and for lofty apartments which normally housed either the temple staff or those called *hagneuontes*,

---

tion, under Theophilus's supervision, of the temples in Alexandria, must be treated with caution. No reason is given for the order, and no disturbances occur when the Serapeum is brought down; only when the cultic objects are displayed in public do the riots begin. The account thus sounds confused, despite (or perhaps because of) being based on eyewitness accounts (5.16.9, 13–14). Sozomen, however, does agree that the emperor ordered the demolition of the Alexandrian temples (7.15.7); Rufinus is vaguer, but his words in context suggest the same. The question, therefore, of whether Theodosius did in fact issue such an order must remain undecided, as must that of the reason for his sudden turn against paganism evident in the edicts of 391. On this see A. Lippold, "Theodosius I," PW Suppl. 13.891–92, 956–58, and K. L. Noetlichs, "Heidenverfolgung," *RAC* 13.1160–61.

Sozomen, in contrast to the other two historians, says that it was a temple of Dionysus which Theophilus was purifying and which yielded from its cellars the cultic items the display of which caused the riot. But from then on his account parallels Rufinus's closely. J. Schwartz, "La fin du Sérapéum d'Alexandrie," in *Essays in Honor of C. Bradford Welles* (New Haven: American Society of Papyrologists, 1966), 109, suspects that their reports of the strife preceding the destruction of the statue of Serapis are just reproductions of events that took place in George's time.

On the philosopher Olympus or Olympius, see *Damascii Vitae Isidori Reliquiae,* ed. C. Zintzen (Hildesheim: Olms, 1967), *fr.* 91, 93–94, 97.

The government officials involved in the episode remain anonymous in Rufinus's account, but we learn from Eunapius, *Vit. Philosoph.* 472, and Sozomen, 7.15.5, that Evagrius was prefect of Egypt at the time; Romanus was *comes Aegypti.* It was they to whom *C.Th.* 16.10.11 was addressed.

Sophronius's account of the destruction of the Serapeum (cf. Jerome, *Vir. illustr.* 134) may have been one of Rufinus's sources. On the date of the destruction (early in 392, apparently) see Johannes Hahn, "*Vetustus error extinctus est*—Wann wurde das Sarapeion von Alexandria zerstört?" *Historia* 55.3 (2006): 368–83.

meaning those who purify themselves. Behind these in turn were porticoes divided off from each other in rows to form a quadrangle which ran around the whole circumference on the inside. In the middle of the entire area was the sanctuary, outstanding for its precious columns, the exterior fashioned of marble, spacious and magnificent to behold. In it there was a statue of Serapis so large that its right hand touched one wall and its left the other; this monster is said to have been composed of every kind of metal and wood. The interior walls of the shrine were believed to have been covered with plates of gold overlaid with silver and then bronze, the last as a protection for the more precious metals.[41]

There were also some things cunningly and skillfully devised to excite the amazement and wonder of those who saw them. There was a tiny window so orientated toward the direction of sunrise that on the day appointed for the statue of the sun to be carried in to greet Serapis, careful observation of the seasons had ensured that as the statue was entering, a ray of sunlight coming through this window would light up the mouth and lips of Serapis, so that to the people looking on, it would seem as though the sun were greeting Serapis with a kiss.[42]

41. Another ancient description of the Serapeum is offered by Aphthonius of Antioch; see H. Rabe, *Aphthonii Progymnasmata* (Leipzig: Teubner, 1926), 38–41, with the commentary of John of Sardis, 227–30. See also Ammianus, 22.16.12–13, and *Expositio totius mundi et gentium* 35–36. For a description of the statue and its origin: Clement Alex., *Protrept.* 4.48. We cannot be sure of its provenance: see Thelamon, *PC* 173–75. Livy too describes a temple of gold-plated walls dedicated to Zeus in Antioch by Antiochus Epiphanes (41.20.9). The Serapeum was not elevated artificially, but stood on the hill of Rhacotis. The results of archaeological research on the site are given in Michael Sabottka, *Das Serapeum in Alexandria: Untersuchungen zur Architektur und Baugeschichte des Heiligtums von der frühen ptolemäischen Zeit bis zur Zerstörung 391 n. Chr.* (*Études alexandrines* 15, 2008. Cairo: Institut français d'archéologie orientale, 2008). Aphthonius's and Rufinus's descriptions are given and compared on pp. 313–28.

Hagneuontes is an imprecise term, since it could refer to those dedicated either temporarily or permanently to various forms of abstinence; see Thelamon, *PC* 203–5. The temple ministers are described in *Expositio mundi* 36.

42. The existence of the window is confirmed by Alexandrian coinage, and the same arrangement for sun and window is found in other Egyptian temples. The Egyptians thought of the sun as reviving the statues of gods by

And there was another trick of this kind. Magnets, it is said, have the natural power to pull and draw iron to themselves. The image of the sun had been made by its artisan from the very thinnest iron with this in view: that a magnet, which, as we said, naturally attracts iron, and which was set in the ceiling panels, might by natural force draw the iron to itself when the statue was carefully placed directly beneath it, the statue appearing to the people to rise and hang in the air. And lest it betray what was going on by quickly dropping, the agents of the deception would say, "The sun has arisen so that, bidding Serapis farewell, he may depart to his own place." There were many other things as well built on the site by those of old for the purpose of deception which it would take too long to detail.[43]

Now as we started to say, when the letter had been read our people were ready to overthrow the author of the error, but a rumor had been spread by these very pagans that if a human hand touched the statue, the earth would split open on the spot and crumble into the abyss, while the sky would come crashing down at once. This caused the people some bewilderment for a moment, until one of the soldiers, armed with faith rather than weapons, rose up with a two-edged axe he had seized and smote the old fraud on the jaw with all his might. A roar went up from both sides, but the sky did not fall, nor did the earth collapse. Thus with repeated strokes he felled the smoke-grimed deity of rotted wood, which, upon being thrown down, burned as easily as dry wood when it was kindled. After this the head was wrenched from the neck and from the bushel, which was discarded, and dragged off; then the feet and the other members were chopped off with axes and dragged apart with ropes attached, and piece by piece, each in a different place, the decrepit dotard was burned to ashes before the eyes of the

---

shining on them and thus recharging them with vital force. The image of the sun kissing Serapis is found on coins and lamps of the period; see Thelamon, *PC* 183–84, 195–97.

43. The use of magnets in temple ceilings for the purpose Rufinus describes is well attested; see Claudian, *Magnes* 22–39; Pliny, *Natural History* 34.148 (a magnet in the ceiling of an Alexandrian temple); Ausonius, *Mosella* 315–17; Augustine, *City of God* 21.6; Thelamon, *PC* 182, 184.

Alexandria which worshiped him. Last of all the torso which was left was put to the torch in the amphitheater, and that was the end of the vain superstition and ancient error of Serapis.[44]

The pagans have different views about his origin. Some regard him as Jupiter, the bushel placed upon his head showing either that he governs all things with moderation and restraint or that he bestows life on mortals through the bounty of harvests. Others regard him as the power of the Nile River, by whose richness and fertility Egypt is fed. There are some who think the statue was made in honor of our Joseph because of the distribution of grain by which he aided the Egyptians in the time of famine. Still others claim to have found in Greek histories of old that a certain Apis, a householder or a king residing in Memphis, provided ample food from his own store to the citizens when the grain ran out in Alexandria during a famine. When he died they founded a temple in his honor in Memphis in which a bull, the symbol of the ideal farmer, is cared for; it has certain colored markings and is called "Apis" after him. As for the *soros* or coffin in which his body lay, they brought it down to Alexandria, and by putting together *soros* and *Apis* they at first called him "Sorapis," but this was later corrupted to "Serapis." God knows what truth, if any, there is in all this. But let us return to the subject.[45]

44. The Egyptians feared the world would collapse in chaos if the customary rites were not performed; see Thelamon, *PC* 200n19 (papyrological evidence); *Corpus Hermeticum,* Asclepius 24; Ps. Jamblicus, *De mysteriis* 6.7; Epiphanius, *Pan.* 18.3.1–2.

The description of the soldier with the axe sounds like Valerius Maximus's story of the destruction of the temple of Serapis in Rome, when the consul L. Aemilius Paulus, in execution of a senate resolution, "seized an axe and smashed in the doors of the temple when none of the workmen dared touch it" (1.3.4). Eunapius, *Vit. Philosoph.* 472, attests that the Serapeum was razed to the ground on this occasion. For another version of the story, cf. Theodoret, *HE* 5.22.3–6.

For the bushel (*modius*) with which Serapis was crowned, see note 45 below.

45. Serapis was originally Ousor-Hapi, the Memphite god of the dead, represented as a mummified man with a bull's head bearing the solar disk surmounted by two feathers between the horns. The Greeks at first called him Osorapis. He was assimilated to Jupiter and to the sun; see Thelamon, *PC* 189, 193. For the pagan traditions about him, see Tacitus, *Hist.* 4.84; Plutarch, *De Iside* 61.376A; Clement Alex., *Protrept.* 4.48.6.

Rufinus connects the words *modius* ("bushel"), *modus* ("restraint"), and

11.24. Once the very pinnacle of idolatry had been thrown down, all of the idols, or rather monstrosities, throughout Alexandria were exposed to the same kind of destruction and similar disgrace through the efforts of its most vigilant priest. The mind shudders to speak of the snares laid by the demons for wretched mortals, the corpses and the crimes uncovered in what they call "shrines," the number of decapitated babies' heads found in gilded urns, the number of pictures of the excruciating deaths of poor wretches. The pagans scattered in flight in their very confusion and shame when these were brought to light and displayed to public view, but even so, those who could bear to remain were amazed at how they had been enmeshed for so many centuries in such vile and shameful deceptions. Hence many of them, having condemned their error and realized its wickedness, embraced the faith of Christ and the true religion. To pass, for instance, over the other enormi-

---

moderari ("govern"): cum mensura modoque cuncta ... moderari. The bushel-crown is a reminder of the connection of Serapis with Osiris, the god of grain. It was also a symbolic Nile measure, since the crops depended on the seasonal flooding of the river; see Thelamon, PC 191–92.

One tradition connecting Joseph with Serapis derives from his ancestry: he is Σάρρας παῖς (Firmicus Maternus, De errore profanarum religionum 13.2). See also Tertullian, Ad nationes 2.8.9–18; Paulinus of Nola, Carmen 19.100–106. Maternus, 13.2, says that the Egyptians divinized Joseph, transforming him into Serapis, and crowned him with the bushel to commemorate his feeding of the people.

Apis was connected with Memphis in Greek legend, as Rufinus says; Clement of Alexandria, for instance, says that Apis, king of Argos, founded Memphis, also called Serapis (Strom. 1.106.4–5). Epiphanius, Pan. 4.2.6, equates Apis with Inachus, who built Memphis. Rufinus, however, is the only one who ascribes a donation of food to him; perhaps he is assuming a connection with Joseph.

The Hapi-bull was originally a fertility god, as Rufinus suggests. When he was slain after his allotted lifetime, a diligent search was conducted for his successor, which could be identified by the marks on its hide, especially the image of a crescent moon; the priestly scribes knew how to verify them. After being weaned, the calf was taken to Memphis, raised amid every luxury in a sacred enclosure, and treated as divine. Cf. Ammianus, 22.14.6–8; Aelian, De natura animalium 11.10.

The derivation of "Serapis" from σορός and "Apis" is found also in Plutarch, De Iside 29.362C (along with other derivations) and in Clement Alex., Strom. 1.106.6.

ties committed elsewhere, the children violently killed and the virgins disemboweled for extispicy, I shall record only one of them, which was brought to everyone's notice as having been committed in the temple of Saturn; from it one may get some idea of the others not mentioned.[46]

11.25. They had a priest of Saturn named Tyrannus. He used to tell whichever of the nobles and leading men who worshiped in the temple and whose wives attracted his lust that Saturn had told him (pretending that the deity had spoken in answer) that his wife was to spend the night in the temple. The one so informed, overjoyed that the deity had deigned to summon his wife, would send her to the temple elegantly adorned, and laden with offerings as well, lest she be spurned for coming empty-handed. The wife was locked inside in full view of everyone, and Tyrannus, once the doors were shut and the keys handed over, would depart. Then, when silence had fallen, he would make his way through hidden underground passages and creep right into the very statue of Saturn, entering through wide-open cavities—for the statue had been hollowed out in the back and was fastened snugly to the wall—and while the lamps were burning within the shrine, a voice from the hollow bronze statue would speak suddenly to the woman rapt in prayer, so that the unfortunate woman would tremble for fear and joy,

46. Human sacrifice, especially of virgins and children for the purpose of extispicy, is well enough attested for classical antiquity and afterward, although some of the literary references are hard to evaluate. Didius Iulianus, when he was emperor in 193, is reported frequently to have killed children as part of a magic rite to find out the future (Dio Cassius, 74.16.5). Sextus Empiricus mentions human sacrifice still being practiced ca. 200 (*Pyr.* 3.208, 221). Ammianus reports an officer being convicted in 371/72 of eviscerating a woman in order to perform haruspicy on her fetus (29.2.17). Eusebius cites instances of extispicy performed on children at *HE* 7.10.4 and 8.14.5. Other references are fictional, such as *SHA* Heliogabalus 8.1–2 and the horrifying scene in Achilles Tatius, *Leucippe* 3.15, 19. The emperor Julian and his followers were often accused by the Christians of such things; see Theodoret, *HE* 3.26; Socrates, 3.13.11; John Chrysostom, *De S. Babyla* 79. For Egypt, see J. G. Griffiths, "Human Sacrifices in Egypt: The Classical Evidence," *Annales du service des antiquités de l'Égypte* 48 (1948): 409–23. Archeology has discovered the use of urns to bury the remains of child sacrifices in North Africa; cf. J. B. Rives, "Tertullian on Child Sacrifice," *Museum Helveticum* 51 (1994): 54–63, esp. 60.

thinking that she had been found worthy to be addressed by a deity so great. After the foul deity had spoken to her in whatever terms he chose to increase her fear or arouse her lust, the wicks would be snuffed by some device and suddenly all the lamps would go out. Then, descending upon the poor woman in her amazement and confusion, he would inflict upon her the adultery disguised by his impious speech. When he had carried on in this way for quite some time with all the wives of those wretches, it happened that one of the women of chaste character was horrified at the misdeed and, listening closely, recognized Tyrannus's voice, returned home, and reported the criminal deception to her husband. Furious at the wrong done to his wife, or rather to himself, he had Tyrannus charged and handed over to torture. With his conviction and confession and his secret misdeeds brought to light, shame and disgrace flooded all the houses of the pagans with the discovery of adulterous mothers, uncertain fathers, and illegitimate children. When all this was revealed and publicized, there was a rush to extirpate the crimes, too, along with the idols and shrines.[47]

11.26. As for Canopus, who could list the outrages connected with its superstitions? There was what amounted to a state school of magic there under the guise of the study of the priestly writing, for so they call the ancient writing of the Egyptians. The pagans revered the place as a source and origin of demons to such an extent that its popularity was far greater than that of Alexandria. Now it will not be out of place to explain briefly how the tradition accounts for the error connected with this monster as well. They say that once upon a time the Chaldaeans made a tour carrying with them their god, fire, and held a contest with the gods of all the provinces, the winner of which should be regarded by all as god. The gods of all the other provinces were of bronze or gold or silver or wood or stone or whatever material

47. The story sounds like the one about Paulina and Decius Mundus told by Josephus (*Antiq.* 18.65–80). Saturn/Kronos is identified by Plutarch with Anubis (*De Iside* 44.368E), the god whom Decius Mundus pretended to be. Josephus in turn is influenced by Ps. Callisthenes, *Historia Alexandri Magni* 1.4–6. Many examples have been found of statues hollowed out from behind so that priests could speak through them; see Thelamon, *PC* 241–42.

is of course ruined by fire. And thus fire prevailed everywhere. When the priest of Canopus heard this, he thought of a clever plan. Earthenware water pots are commonly manufactured in Egypt which are densely stippled all over with tiny holes, so that when cloudy water trickles through them, the sediment is strained out and it becomes purer. He took one, stopped up the holes with wax, painted it over in various colors, filled it with water, set it up as a god, and on its top carefully fitted the head cut off an old statue said to have been that of Menelaus's helmsman. Afterwards the Chaldaeans arrived, the contest was held, the fire was kindled around the water pot, the wax stopping the holes melted, the fire was quenched by the perspiring pot, and the priest's craft gave the victory to Canopus over the Chaldaeans. Hence the very statue of Canopus was in the form of a water pot, with tiny feet, a neck drawn in and, as it were, squashed, a bulging stomach, and an equally rounded back, and on account of this tradition he was worshiped as an all-conquering god. But whatever he may once have done to the Chaldaeans, now with the arrival of the priest of God, Theophilus, neither his perspiration nor his wax-covered tricks were of any avail; everything was destroyed and razed to the ground.[48]

48. Contests between magicians were not uncommon in this age. In Chaldaean theurgy fire was the primal and sacred principle; the Egyptians, by contrast, revered water as the source of life. The Nile was assimilated to Osiris, whose enemy was Set, later identified with Typhon. He was the principle of dryness and thus of death, a fiery, serpentine deity whose color, red, was also that of the desert he inhabited.

Canopus was the name of both the city and the god, who was represented as a potbellied jar with the head of Osiris; since Osiris was worshiped at Canopus in this form, the very name "Canopus" had come to be applied to this deity; see Thelamon, *PC* 207–8. Canopus had been Menelaus's helmsman; he died in Egypt of snakebite during the voyage home from the Trojan War and was buried where the city later sprang up. See Strabo, 17.1.17; Ammianus, 22.16.14; Hecataeus of Miletus, *Fr.* 308. What Rufinus offers, then, is some version of an originally etiological myth of the Canopus shrine: the victory of Osiris over the power of fire and of Canopus over the serpentine god that had killed him. Cf. Thelamon, 211–13, 224.

The city was famous as a pleasure resort, as Strabo and Ammianus note. The original Egyptian name Kahi-Noub was still remembered; see Aelius Aristid., *Or.* 36.109. It also had several temples of great renown which as usual were also schools for the teaching of sacred writing; the characters compos-

11.27. But nothing was done which resulted in the place becoming deserted. The dens of iniquity and age-worn burial grounds were demolished, and lofty churches, temples of the true God, were put up. For on the site of Serapis's tomb the unholy sanctuaries were leveled, and on the one side there rose a martyr's shrine, and on the other a church. I think it would be worthwhile to explain why the martyr's shrine was built.[49]

11.28. In Julian's time the ferocity of the pagans sprang forth in all its savagery, as though their reins had gone slack. Thus it happened that in Sebaste, a city of Palestine, they frenziedly attacked the tomb of John the Baptist with murderous hands and set about scattering the bones, gathering them again, burning them, mixing the holy ashes with dust, and scattering them throughout the fields and countryside. But by God's providence it happened that some men from Jerusalem, from the monastic house of Philip, the man of God, arrived there at the same time in order to pray. When they saw the enormity being perpetrated by human hands at the service of bestial spirits, they mixed with those gathering the bones for burning, since they considered dying preferable to being polluted by such a sin, carefully and reverently collected them, as far as they could in the circumstances, then slipped away from the others, to their amazement or fury, and brought the relics to the devout father Philip. He in turn, thinking it beyond him to guard such a treasure by his own vigilance, sent the relics of this spotless victim to Athanasius, then supreme high priest, in the care of his deacon Julian, who later became bishop of Parentium. Athanasius received them and closed them up within a hollowed-out place in the

---

ing it were regarded as holding magical powers. To learn hieroglyphics was to learn the magical formulas contained in them (Thelamon, 226).

Perspiring statues were widely known in antiquity. The waters of the Nile were regarded as the bodily fluids of Osiris, which were believed to be preserved in a jar kept in the Eighteenth Nome. Examples from Egypt of the representation of gods as jars with heads go back to the Pharaonic age (Thelamon, 210, 220).

49. It was usual for Christians to call pagan temples "cemeteries" or "burial grounds." Eunapius in *Vit. Philosoph.* 472 records the settlement of monks in Canopus after the destruction of the temple there and the building of a martyr's shrine. The church to which Rufinus refers was known as the Angelium or Evangelium (Thelamon, *PC* 264).

sacristy wall in the presence of a few witnesses, preserving them in prophetic spirit for the benefit of the next generation, so that, now that the remnants of idolatry had been thrown down flat, golden roofs might rise for them on temples once unholy.[50]

But after the death of Serapis, who had never been alive, which temples of any other demon could remain standing? It would hardly be enough to say that all the untended shrines in Alexandria, of whichever demon, came down almost column by column. In fact, in all the cities of Egypt, the settlements, the villages, the countryside everywhere, the riverbanks, even the desert, wherever shrines, or rather graveyards, could be found, the persistence of the several bishops resulted in their being wrecked and razed to the ground, so that the countryside, which had been wrongly given over to the demons, was restored to agriculture.[51]

11.29. Another thing was done in Alexandria: the busts of Serapis, which had been in every house in the walls, the entrances, the doorposts, and even the windows, were so cut and filed away that not even a trace or mention of him or any other demon remained anywhere. In their place everyone painted the sign of the Lord's cross on doorposts, entrances, windows, walls, and columns. It is said that when the pagans who were left saw this, they were reminded of an important matter which had been

50. Julian himself mentions pagan attacks on Christians: *Misopogon* 357C, 361A; *Ep.* 114.438B. See also Sozomen, 7.21.1; Philostorgius, 7.4; *Chronicon Pasch.* 295CD.

On the belief that the relics of John the Baptist were located in Sebaste, cf. Jerome, *Ep.* 46.13, 108.13. According to another tradition recorded in Sozomen, 7.21, John's head was found by monks of Jerusalem and eventually brought to Constantinople in Theodosius's time. The report does not necessarily contradict Rufinus's, who seems to represent an Alexandrian tradition authenticating and advertising the Baptist's relics and shrine built by Theophilus. Rufinus in fact may have drawn from Theophilus's own writing on the subject; see T. Orlandi, *Storia della chiesa di Alessandria* (Milan: Cisalpino, 1967), 1.94–96, 120–21; Baldini, 124n57, 136n83, 144.

51. On the site of the Alexandrian Serapeum a church was built and named after Theodosius's son Arcadius (Sozomen, 7.15.10). On the conversion of the temple of Isis in Menuthis, near Canopus, into a church of the Evangelists, see P. Athanassiadi, "Persecution and Response in Late Paganism," *Journal of Hellenic Studies* 113 (1993): 15. See also Rufinus, *Historia monachorum* 7.7 (conversion by the monk Apollonius of pagans, who burn their idol).

committed to them from of old. The Egyptians are said to have this our sign of the Lord's cross among the letters which they call "hieratic," or priestly, as one of the letters making up their script. They state that the meaning of this letter or noun is "the life to come." Those, then, who were coming over to the faith out of astonishment at what was happening said that it had been handed down to them from of old that the things now worshiped would remain until they saw that that sign had come in which there was life. Hence it was the former priests and ministers of the temples who came over to the faith rather than those entertained by the tricks of error and devices of deceit.[52]

11.30. Now it was the custom in Egypt to bring the gauge of the rising Nile River to the temple of Serapis, as being the one who caused the increase of water and the flooding; so when his statue was overthrown and burned, everyone of course unanimously declared that Serapis, mindful of this injury, would never again bestow the waters in their usual abundance. But so that God could show that it was he who ordered the waters of the river to rise in season, and not Serapis, who, after all, was much younger than the Nile, there began then such a succession of floods as never before recorded. And thus the practice began of bringing the measuring rod itself, or water gauge, which they call a *pēchys*, to the Lord of waters in the church. When these events were reported to the devout sovereign, he is said to have stretched out his arms to heaven and exclaimed

52. Putting the sign of the cross on pagan temples to exorcise their gods, which the Christians believed to be demons, was normal procedure, as archeology reveals. The *ankh* symbol, to which Rufinus refers, and which with several variations was cruciform, meant "life" in Egyptian; the gods and goddesses are represented holding it, sometimes to the nostrils of dead kings. The ancient Greek texts translate it as "eternal life." The Egyptian Christians were aware of this meaning and consciously adopted it as a sign of the cross that divine Providence had arranged to appear among the hieroglyphics. See Thelamon, *PC* 271–72.

According to another account in Socrates, 5.17, and Sozomen, 7.15.10, the cruciform sign was found in the ruins of the Serapeum and occasioned numerous conversions among the pagans.

On prophecies of the destruction of pagan religion and of the temples of Isis and Serapis, see Clement Alex., *Protrept.* 4.50 (*Or. Sib.* 5.484–85, 487–88); *Corpus Hermeticum*, Asclepius 24; Eunapius, *Vit. Philosoph.* 473.

with great joy, "I thank you, Christ, that this age-old error has been demolished without harm to that great city!"[53]

53. During the civilizing of the Nile valley, Nilometers seem to have been installed within the precincts of various temples scattered along the length of the river in Egypt, thus allowing accurate measurement of the annual flood from the time and place the waters began to rise. Such measurement was essential to irrigation control and harvest forecasts (and thus to tax levies). The Nilometers used for this purpose, unlike the ceremonial instrument to which Rufinus refers, were water scales chiseled on walls where the river would reach or on columns erected in cisterns; the cisterns were connected with the river by pipes and furnished with windows and lamps for illumination. Archeology has discovered on some Nilometers a small rectangular recess to mark the height the water had to reach for proper irrigation; the announcement that it had been reached was the signal for one of the great religious feasts of the year.

The role played in all this by the πῆχυς or *ulna* mentioned by Rufinus is not altogether clear. A portable cubit-rule seems of little use in measuring the rise of a river. But archeology has found indications that the wooden "sacred cubit" was in fact kept within the Nilometer, and perhaps within the recess mentioned above. It was carried in the annual procession celebrating the river rise, together with a golden vase holding the new water, and that is what Rufinus must mean when he talks about bringing the gauge to the temple. The procession began and ended in the Serapeum; otherwise its route is unknown. Thelamon thinks that when Rufinus mentions the temple where the procession ended (*mensura ... ad templum Serapis* [*deferebatur*]), he means the temples of Serapis in each place along the Nile (over a dozen in all), each of which helped measure the flood (*PC* 276–77). The Alexandrian Serapeum itself was hardly suited to accurate river measurement because of its location, although it did have a Nilometer in an underground cistern connected with the subterranean aqueducts of the ancient city; the aqueducts were fed from the "Canal of Alexandria." But it may have been the administrative center of flood control for the whole country.

On the measurement of the Nile and irrigation, see Pliny, *Natural History* 5.10.57–58. On Nilometers, H. Jaritz, "Wasserstandsmessungen am Nil—Nilometer," *Mitteilungen aus dem Leichtweiss-Institut für Wasserbau* 89 (Braunschweig, 1986, no consecutive pagination). On the Alexandrian Nilometer, F. E. Engreen, "The Nilometer in the Serapeum at Alexandria," *Medievalia et humanistica* 1 (1943): 3–13; A. Rowe and B. R. Rees, "A Contribution to the Archeology of the Western Desert: IV," *Bulletin of the John Rylands Library* 39.2 (1957): 492. On the Nile festival and procession, D. Bonneau, *La crue du Nil* (Paris: Klincksiek, 1964), 429–30.

Much remains unclear about the process of transferring this vast system of water control from temple to church. Constantine is reported to have abolished the Nile priesthood and moved the cubit-rule to the church, with no diminishment of the annual flood, predictions to the contrary notwithstanding (Eusebius, *Vit. Const.* 4.25; Socrates, 1.18.2–3). Julian later restored the mea-

11.31. The life of Valentinian, meanwhile, who had been governing the country in the west with all the zeal of one of his age, was brought to an end by a noose for reasons still unknown. There are some who asserted that it was due to a plot by his general, Arbogast, a view commonly held by the people. Others said that the general was innocent of the crime, but had been the reason why the youth had gotten so angry that he was driven to the deed [suicide], namely because he had not allowed him completely free rein in governing since he was not yet of age. Several priests, however, who undertook an embassy of peace from the one created [emperor] afterward, testified in Theodosius's presence that the general was innocent of the crime.[54]

---

suring rod to the Serapeum (Sozomen, 5.3.3), where the traditional rites to ensure the flood were still going on when Libanius wrote *Pro templis* in 386 (cf. *Or.* 30.35). Guardianship of the ceremonial "Nilometer" was obviously important, but did it bring with it effective control of the whole irrigation system, with the considerable political and economic power that would have meant? Athanasius, for instance, was at least reputed to wield great economic influence (*Apol. contra Arianos* 9.3–4, 18.2, 60.2, 87.1); is this part of the reason? The difficulty is that control of the irrigation system implies supervision of the network of Nilometer temples, and it is hard to imagine the bishop of Alexandria, even such a one as Athanasius, achieving this without the conversion of the temple staffs to Christianity, a conversion that evidently took place only in Theophilus's time.

The close connection between the Nile flood-control system and the temples was partly religious. The Nile was held to be divine; the rites in his honor were meant to ensure that he fertilized the land each year (Libanius, *Pro templis;* Tertullian, *Ad nationes* 1.9.3 and *Apologeticum* 40.2; Aelius Aristid., *Or.* 45.32). But it was also partly technical; the temple staffs were trained to use and maintain the Nilometer system, and it may be supposed that they took care to preserve their indispensability. Hence Rufinus's passing mention in 11.29 of the conversion of these staffs (*hi, qui erant ex sacerdotibus vel ministris templorum*) suggests that at least in Theophilus's time, effective control of the Nile did pass to the church, with all that that meant. The pagan Nile feasts were replaced by Christian ones; in each place the cult of the river god was replaced by that of the local saint or St. Michael (Thelamon, 277). Bonneau, *La crue du Nil,* 435–39, describes the Christianization of the liturgy of the Nile rise.

The harm that Theodosius exclaims the city has escaped has been variously interpreted to mean the high flood waters Rufinus mentions or the religious riot described earlier.

54. Arbogast was a barbarian, perhaps of Frankish stock, who had risen to

11.32. Theodosius was aroused all the same and took up arms against Eugenius, who had succeeded the one who had died. But first he sought God's will through John, the monk we mentioned earlier. He was the one who had foretold to him the first bloodless victory over Maximus; this time he promised him another victory, but not without great bloodshed on both sides.[55]

11.33. In making ready then for war, he put his stock not so much in arms and weapons as in fasts and prayers; guarded not so much by the night watch as by nightly vigils in prayer, he would go around to all the places of prayer with the priests and people, lie prostrate in sackcloth before the reliquaries of the martyrs and apostles, and implore assistance through the faithful intercession of the saints. But the pagans, who are always reviving their errors with the help of fresh mistakes, renewed the sacrifices and bloodied Rome with deathly victims, examined the innards of livestock, and from the divination of entrails proclaimed that victory for Eugenius was assured. Flavian, who was then prefect, engaged in this in a spirit of deep superstition and great fervor, and it was owing to his statements that they assumed that Eugenius's victory was assured, since he

the position of *comes rei militaris* or perhaps *vicarius magistri militum* when Gratian sent him in 380 to help Theodosius against the Goths. Theodosius kept him and included him in his staff, perhaps with the rank of *magister militum,* in the campaign against Maximus in 388. Following the usurper's defeat, he was sent to Gaul to deal with his son and stayed in the west as Valentinian's guardian and regent.

The present episode took place in the spring of 392 in Vienne, by which time Arbogast certainly held the rank of *magister militum;* a couple of sources say he assumed the title without permission. Valentinian died on May 15, 392, after a period of fruitlessly trying to assert himself in the government of his territory; he was twenty years old. The sources are divided on whether it was murder or suicide, and the question can no longer be decided. See Zosimus, 4.53–54; Socrates, 5.25.1–5; Sozomen, 7.22.2; Philostorgius, 11.1; John of Antioch, *Excerpta de insidiis, Fr.* 79; B. Croke, "Arbogast and the Death of Valentinian II," *Historia* 25 (1976): 235–44; G. Zecchini, "Barbari e romani in Rufino di Concordia," *AAAd* 31 (1987): 2.43–44.

The embassy was sent in the autumn of 392 in an attempt to avoid civil war; see Zosimus, 4.55.3–4; *Excerpta de insidiis, Fr.* 79; Paschoud, 2.459.

55. On the monk John, cf. 11.19. On Theodosius's victory over Maximus, cf. 11.17 and note 32.

had a great reputation for being wise. But when Theodosius, confident in the assistance provided by the true religion, began to force the Alpine passes, the first to flee were the demons, fearfully aware of how deceitfully they had received the many victims offered to them in vain. Next were those who taught and professed these errors, especially Flavian, who was chargeable with shameful rather than criminal behavior. While he could have gotten clear, being a man so deeply cultured, he considered that he deserved death more justly for having erred than for having committed any misdeed.[56]

The others mustered their forces, and, having set ambushes on the upper slopes of the passes, they themselves waited to give battle on the way down the mountain. But when contact was made with those in front and they surrendered on the spot to the legitimate sovereign, a desperate combat ensued with the others encountered at the bottom of the gorges. For a while the outcome was in doubt; the barbarian auxiliaries were being routed and put to flight before the enemy. But this took place not so that Theodosius might be conquered, but so that he might not appear to have conquered thanks to the barbarians. When he saw his forces in retreat, he took his place on a lofty crag from where he could observe and be observed by both armies, and throwing down his weapons he turned to his

56. The extent to which Rufinus has portrayed this battle as the last conflict between Christianity and paganism has been set out by Alan Cameron, *The Last Pagans of Rome* (New York: Oxford University Press, 2011), 93–131. Flavius Eugenius, the former chancery bureau chief elevated by Arbogast to the imperial throne in succession to Valentinian on August 22, 392, was no pagan, whatever some sources may suggest. The praetorian prefect Virius Nicomachus Flavianus, by contrast, had published a prediction that Christianity was to last only a year of years and thus to end in 394 (Augustine, *City of God* 18.53; see also Sozomen, 7.22.4–5), and his mantic sacrifices on Eugenius's behalf suggested the immensely influential scenario elaborated by Rufinus.

The reference to the flight of the demons is purely figurative; there is no reason to think that Eugenius actually fought under pagan banners or statues, or, for that matter, that there were more pagans in his army than in Theodosius's (Cameron, 99, 102–7).

The battle lasted two days, ending with Eugenius's death on September 6, 394. It took place at Frigidus Fluvius, 36 miles from Aquileia on the route to Emona. The ancient accounts of the battle, in addition to Zosimus, 4.58, are collected in Paschoud, 2.488–500. Commentary: Paschoud, 2.467–68, 474–87.

accustomed source of help, prostrating himself before God. "Almighty God," he prayed, "you know that it was in the name of Christ your Son that I undertook this war in order to exact what I consider just retribution. If this is not so, then punish me, but if I have come here in a just cause and in confidence in you, then stretch out your right hand to those who are yours, lest the gentiles say, 'Where is their God?'"[57]

The officers who were with him, certain that the prayer of the devout sovereign had been accepted by God, drew fresh courage for battle. Most notable was Bacurius, a man outstanding in faith, purity, and valor of spirit and body, and one who had won a position as an ally on Theodosius's staff. He slew whoever was nearest him with spear, arrows, and sword, thrust through the packed and crowded ranks of the enemy, and, with their ranks broken, made his way to the usurper himself through thousands of fleeing men and heaps of corpses.

Now the impious may find this hard to believe, but it has been established that following the prayer which the emperor poured out to God, a wind of such violence arose that it turned the enemy shafts back upon those who had launched them. The wind continued to blow with such force that all the enemy missiles were to no avail, and the adversaries' spirit was broken, or rather rebuffed by heaven, despite the courageous efforts of General Arbogast, who strove in vain against God. And so Eugenius was led to Theodosius's feet with his hands tied behind him, and there ended his life and his battle. Then indeed more glory accrued to the devout sovereign's victory from the failed

57. Cf. Ps 113.10. Other sources say that Theodosius's enemies drew up their lines in the plain. Rufinus's words *in descensu montis* suggest that they were right at the foot of the mountain. On the ambush and the location of the gorge in question, see Paschoud, 2.482–83. Eugenius's troops, hidden in ambush by the top of the pass, allowed Theodosius's forces to march by and then moved in to occupy the position, thus trapping the emperor between the usurper and themselves. Theodosius, meanwhile, engaged the enemy in front of him with his Gothic allies, 10,000 of whom were lost when they were trapped in a gorge; he thus had plenty to pray about when night fell. But during the night or in the morning, the enemy occupying the top of the pass defected to him. His staff advised him to withdraw to Illyricum and regroup, but he believed the defection was an answer to his prayers and decided to push forward; see Paschoud, 2.483–84.

expectations of the pagans than from the death of the usurper, the pagans whose empty hopes and false prophecies meant that the punishment they suffered in dying was less than the shame they felt while they were alive.[58]

11.34. Afterward the emperor, foreseeing what was to come and anxious to put the affairs of the state in order, sent at once to the east, where he had left his children in safe hands when he set out for war. He bade the Augustus Arcadius to keep the realm which had long since been handed over to him there. Honorius he invested with equal rank and ordered him to hasten to the empire of the west. When he had welcomed him with fatherly kisses and embraces and handed over to him the government of the western realm, he himself went on to a better place to receive the reward he deserved with the most devout sovereigns, having guided the Roman empire successfully for seventeen years.[59]

58. On Bacurius, cf. 10.11 and note 22. On the story of the miraculous wind, see Cameron (note 56 above), 115. Ambrose seems to be the first to mention it, in his *Explanatio Psalmi* 36.25 (March, 395); here the wind arises before the battle is joined. It is brought into the middle of the battle by Claudian, *Panegyricus de tertio consulatu Honorii Augusti* 94–95, but he is drawing on Silius, *Punica* 9.491–524; Rufinus, in turn, is drawing on Claudian, it seems.

59. Cf. Zosimus, 4.59. Honorius had already been given the rank of Augustus on January 23, 393, in Constantinople; see Paschoud, 2.468. Theodosius died on January 17, 395, in Milan, having been made Augustus in January of 379. On the division of the empire between Theodosius's sons, see Kaj Sandberg, "The So-Called Division of the Roman Empire in AD 395: Notes on a Persistent Theme in Modern Historiography," *Arctos* 42 (2008): 199–213.

INDICES

INDEX OF NAMES

Entries are identified in terms of book, chapter, and paragraph numbers. The book and chapter numbers can be located in the header at the top of each right-hand page of the book.

Alexander of Jerusalem, 6.8.4–5,
6.8.7, 6.11.1–3, 6.11.5, 6.13.3,
6.14.8–9, 6.19.17–18, 6.20.1, 6.27,
6.39.2–4, 6.46.4
Alexander of Rome, 4.1, 4.4, 5.6.4
Alexander of Tyre, 7.5.1
Alexander the Alabarch, 2.5.4
Alexander 1, martyr, 5.16.22
Alexander 2 martyr, 6.41.17
Alexander 3 martyr, 7.12
Alexandria, 2.4.2, 2.5.2, 2.6.2–3,
2.9.2, 2.16.1, 2.17.7, 2.23.23,
3.14, 3.21, 4.1, 4.2.2–4, 4.4, 4.5.5,
4.11.6, 4.17.5, 4.19, 5.8.11, 5.9–
11, 5.22, 5.25, 6.1, 6.2.2, 6.3.1,
6.3.3, 6.3.6, 6.6, 6.8.6, 6.14.10,
6.19.13, 6.19.16, 6.19.19, 6.24.1,
6.26, 6.31.2, 6.40.1, 6.41, 6.44.2,
7.11.14–17, 7.11.26, 7.21, 7.27.2,
7.28, 7.30.1, 7.30.3, 7.32.5–12,
7.32.26, 7.32.30, 8.12.1, 8.13.7,
8.14.15, 9.6.2; Arius causes dissen-
sions among Christians of, 10.1; its
bishop has authority over Egypt,
10.6(VI); Frumentius visits, 10.10;
Arius returns to, 10.12; Alexander bishop of, 10.13; Athanasius
succeeds Alexander as bishop
of, 10.15; festival of Peter Martyr
kept in, 10.15; one of its churches
requested from Athanasius for
Arians, 10.20; George conducts
himself as tyrant there, 10.24;
Eusebius of Vercelli goes there to
see Athanasius, 10.28; Council of
Alexandria (362), 10.29–30; Tatian prefect of, 11.2; Lucius seizes
see of, 11.3; news of conversion of
pagans by exiled monks reach-
es, 11.4; persecution of Nicene
Christians there, 11.6; Didymus
teaches there, 11.7; Antony comes
there to support Athanasius, 11.7;
Apollinaris condemned in, 11.10;
Timothy succeeds Peter as bishop
of, 11.21; pagan riots, 11.22;

destruction of pagan temples of,
11.23–25, 28–29; religious repu-
tation of among pagans surpassed
by Canopus, 11.26; spared from
destruction despite riots, 11.30
Alexas, Salome's husband, 1.8.13
Alsa River: Constantine II killed near,
10.16
Amastris, 4.23.6
Ambrose, Origen's patron, 6.18.1,
6.23, 6.28
Ambrose of Milan: elected bishop,
11.11; resists Justina's attempt to
appropriate a church, 11.15–16
Ammia, prophet, 5.17.3–4
Ammon, martyr, 6.41.22–23
Ammonaria 1, martyr, 6.41.18
Ammonaria 2, martyr, 6.41.18
Ammonius, martyr, 8.13.7
Ammonius, philosopher, 6.19.6–7,
6.19.9–10
Ananias, courier of Abgar, 1.13.5,
1.13.9
Ananias, father of Jesus, a mystic,
3.8.7
Ananias, high priest, 2.23.21–24
Anatolius of Laodicea, 7.32.6–22
Anchialus, 5.19.3
Andragathius: officer of usurper
Maximus, assassinates Gratian,
11.14
Andrew, apostle, 3.1.1, 3.25.6, 3.39.4
Anencletus of Rome, 3.13, 3.15, 5.
6.2
Anicetus of Rome, 4.11.1, 4.11.7,
4.14.1, 4.14.5, 4.19, 4.22.3, 5.6.4,
5.24.14, 5.24.16–17
Annanias, high priest, 1.10.4
Annas, high priest, 1.10.2, 1.10.4
Annianus of Alexandria, 2.24, 3.14
Anterus of Rome, 6.29.1–2
Anthimus of Nicomedia, 8.6.6, 8.13.1
Antichrist, 3.18.2, 5.8.6, 6.7
Antinoites, 6.11.3
Antinous, favorite of Hadrian,
4.8.2–3

INDEX OF HOLY SCRIPTURE